A COMPLETE MANUAL

OF

ENGLISH LITERATURE.

By THOMAS B. SHAW, M. A.

EDITED, WITH NOTES AND ILLUSTRATIONS,

By WILLIAM SMITH, LL. D.,
AUTHOR OF BIBLE AND CLASSICAL DICTIONARIES,
AND CLASSICAL EXAMINER IN THE UNIVERSITY OF LONDON.

WITH

A SKETCH OF AMERICAN LITERATURE.

By HENRY T. TUCKERMAN.

SHELDON & COMPANY,
NEW YORK & CHICAGO.

C. M.

The present work, which was originally published under the title of "Outlines of English Literature," has been entirely re-written with a special view to the requirements of Students, so as to make it, as far as space would allow, a complete History of English Literature. The Author devoted to its composition the labor of several years, sparing neither time nor pains to render it both instructive and interesting. In consequence of Mr. Shaw's lamented death the MS. was placed in my hands to prepare it for publication as one of Mr. Murray's STUDENT'S MANUALS, for which purpose it seems to me peculiarly well adapted. Through long familiarity with the subject, and great experience as a teacher, the Author knew how to seize the salient points in English literature, and to give prominence to those writers and those subjects which ought to occupy the main attention of the Student. Considering the size of the book, the amount of information which it conveys is really remarkable, while the space devoted to the more important names, such as Bacon, Shakspeare, Milton, Dryden, Addison, Sir Walter Scott, and others, is sufficient to impress upon the Student a vivid idea of their lives and writings. The Author has certainly succeeded in his attempt "to render the work as little dry — as readable, in short — as is consistent with accuracy and comprehensiveness."

As Editor, I have carefully revised the whole work, completed the concluding chapters left unfinished by the Author, and inserted at the end of the first and second chapters a brief account of Anglo-Saxon, Norman, and early English Literature, in order to render the work as useful as possible to Students preparing for the examination of the India Civil Service, the University of London, and the like. Moreover I have, in the other Notes and Illustrations, given an account of the less important persons, which, though not designed for continuous perusal, will be useful for reference, for which purpose a copious Index has been added. All living writers are, for obvious reasons, excluded.

W. S.

LONDON, January, 1864.

SECOND EDITION.

IN this Edition a few errors in names and dates have been corrected, and considerable additions have been made to the later chapters of the work. A brief account of the lives and works of more than two hundred and twenty authors has been added; and it is believed that the work, in its present form, will be found to contain information respecting every writer who deserves a place in the history of our literature

W. S.

LONDON, January, 1865.

A BRIEF MEMOIR OF THE AUTHOR.

Thomas Budd Shaw, born in Gower Street, London, on the 12th of October, 1813, was the seventh son of John Shaw, F. R. S., an eminent architect. From a very early period of his life, though of delicate constitution, he manifested that delight in the acquisition of knowledge which was continued throughout his subsequent career. In the year 1822 he accompanied his maternal uncle, the Rev. Francis Whitfield, to Berbice in the West Indies, where that gentleman was the officiating clergyman, and who was eminently qualified as a scholar and an accomplished gentleman to advance his nephew in his studies and in the formation of his character. On his return from the West Indies, in 1827, he entered the Free School at Shrewsbury, where he became a favorite pupil of Dr. Butler, afterwards Bishop of Lichfield. Here the writer of this brief record recollects that it was remarked of the subject of it that, although inferior to some of his contemporaries in the critical exactness of his scholarship, he was surpassed by none in the intuitive power with which he comprehended the genius and spirit of the great writers of antiquity. At this early period also, apart from school exercises, he rapidly accumulated that general and varied knowledge of books and things which when acquired seemed never to be forgotten.

From Shrewsbury, in 1833, Mr. Shaw proceeded to St. John's College, Cambridge. On taking his degree, in 1836, he became tutor in the family of an eminent merchant; and subsequently, in 1840, he was induced to leave England for Russia, where he commenced his useful and honorable career, finally settling in St. Petersburgh in the year 1841. Here he formed an intimacy with M. Warrand, Professor at the University of St. Petersburgh, through whose influence, in 1842, he obtained the appointment of Professor of English Literature at the Imperial Alexander Lyceum. His lectures were eagerly attended: no professor acquired more thoroughly the love and respect of his pupils, many of whom continued his warmest admirers and friends in after life. In October in the same year he married Miss Annette Warrand, daughter of the Professor.

In 1851 he came to England for the purpose of taking his Master of Arts degree; and on his return to Russia was elected Lector of English Literature at the University of St. Petersburgh. His first pupils were the Princes of Leuchtenburg; and, his reputation being now thoroughly established, he was in 1853 engaged as tutor and Professor of English to the Grand Dukes, an appointment which he retained till his death.

For nine years Mr. Shaw's position was in every respect enviable: happy in his married life, loved by his pupils, respected and honored by all for his high attainments and many virtues, his life passed in peace and prosperity. A few years more, and his means would have enabled him to retire and pass the evening of his life in literary pursuits. But this was not to be. In October, 1862, he complained of pain in the region of the heart; yet he struggled hard against his malady, until nature could bear no more. For a few days before his death he suffered acutely, but bore his sufferings with manly fortitude. On the 14th of November he was relieved from them, dying suddenly of aneurism. His death was regarded as a public loss, and his funeral was attended by their Imperial Highnesses, and a large concourse of present and former students of the Lyceum. A subscription was raised, and a monument is erected to his memory.

The following is a list of such of Mr. Shaw's works as have come to our notice.

In 1836 he wrote several pieces for "The Fellow," and "Fraser's Magazine." In 1837 he translated into verse numerous German and Latin poems, and wrote a few original poems of merit, some of which appeared in "The Individual." Two well-written pieces, "The Song of Hrolfkraken the Sea King," and "The Surgeon's Song," were contributions to "Fraser's Magazine." In 1838 and two following years he contributed several translations from the Italian to "Fraser." In 1842 he started "The St. Petersburgh Literary Review;" he also published in "Blackwood" a translation of "Anmalet Bek," a Russian novel, by Marlinski. In 1844 he published his first work of considerable length, a translation of "The Heretic," a novel in three volumes, by Lajetchnikoff. The work was well received, and an edition was immediately reprinted in New York. In the following year appeared in "Blackwood" his "Life of Poushkin," accompanied by exquisite translations of several of the finest of that poet's productions. In 1846 his leisure time was entirely occupied in writing his "Outlines of English Literature," a work expressly undertaken at the request of the authorities of the Lyceum, and for the use of the pupils of that establishment. The edition was speedily sold, and immediately reprinted in Philadelphia. A second edition was published by Mr. Murray in 1849; and the edition now offered to the public is the fruit of his later years and mature judgment. It may, indeed, be said to be an entirely new work, as the whole has been re-written. In 1850 he published in the "Quarterly" an exceedingly original and curious article, entitled "Forms of Salutation."

CONTENTS

CHAPTER V.

CHAPTER VI.

CHAPTER VII.

CHAPTER VIII.

CHAPTER IX.

CHAPTER X.

CHAPTER XI.

CHAPTER XII.

CHAPTER XIII.

CHAPTER XIV.

CHAPTER XV.

CHAPTER XVI.

CHAPTER XVII.

CHAPTER XVIII.

CHAPTER XIX.

CHAPTER XX.

CHAPTER XXI.

CHAPTER XXII.

CHAPTER XXIII.

CHAPTER XXIV.

sufficient to destroy the prejudice, so common not only among foreigners, but even among Englishmen, of regarding all the inhabitants of Scotland as Celts alike; of representing William Wallace, for instance, in a Highland kilt — a mistake as ludicrous as would be that of painting Washington armed with a tomahawk, or adorned, like a Cherokee chief, with a belt of scalps or a girdle of wampum. It is probable that even the half-Romanized Britons who first invited the Saxon tribes to come to their assistance were speedily involved by their dangerous allies in the same persecution as their savage mountain countrymen: at all events one fact is certain, that the Celt in general, whether friendly or hostile, possessing a less powerful organization and a less vigorous moral constitution than the Teuton, was in the course of time either quietly absorbed into the more energetic race, or gradually disappeared, with that fatal certainty which seems to be an inevitable law regulating the contact of two unequal nationalities, just as the aboriginal Indian has disappeared before the descendants of the very same Anglo-Saxons in the New World. It is only a peculiar combination of geographical conditions that has enabled the primeval Celt to retain a separate existence on the territory of Great Britain, while the predominance — a numerical predominance only — of the Celtic race in the population of Ireland may be traced to other, but no less exceptional causes.

§ 5. The true parentage, therefore, of the English nation, is to be traced to the Teutonic race. The language spoken by the Northern invaders was a Low-Germanic dialect, akin to the modern Dutch, but with many Scandinavian forms and words. Like the people who spoke it, it was possessed of a character at once practical and imaginative; at once real and ideal; and required but the influence of civilization to become a noble vehicle for reasoning, for eloquence, and for the expression of the social and domestic feelings. In the modern English, all ideas which address themselves to the emotions, and all those which bring man into relation with the great objects of nature and with the sentiments of simple existence, will be invariably found to derive their linguistic representatives directly from the Teutonic tongue. The conversion of the Anglo-Saxons to Christianity, which took place in the sixth century, brought them into contact with more intellectual forms of life, and with a higher type of civilization: the transfer of their religious allegiance from Thor, Woden, Tuisk, and Freya to the Saviour, while it softened their manners, exposed their language to the modifying influences of the corrupt but more civilized Latin literature of the Lower Empire, and gave rapid proof how improvable a tongue was that in which they had hitherto produced nothing, probably, but rude war-songs and sagas like that of Beowulf. A very varied and extensive literature soon arose among the Anglo-Saxons, embracing compositions on almost every branch of knowledge, law, historical chronicles, ecclesiastical and theological disquisitions, together with a large body of poetry in which their very peculiar metrical system was adapted to subjects derived either from the Scriptures, or from the mediæval lives of the saints. The curious, but rather tedious, versified paraphrase of the Bible by Cædmon — generally attributed to the middle of the seventh century — was long considered to be one of the most ancient among the more considerable Saxon poems; but the discovery, at Copenhagen, of the *Lay of Beowulf*, to which we have just alluded, has furnished us with a specimen of Anglo-Saxon poetry decidedly more ancient, as well as far more interesting; inasmuch as, having been composed in all probability at a period anterior to the general conversion of the race to Christianity, it is free from any traces of that imitation of the rhetorical style of the lower Latinity which prevents Cædmon from being a good representative of the national literature of his race. This poem, the picturesque vigor of which gives it a right to be placed among the most interesting monuments of early literature, is not inferior in energy and conciseness to the *Nibelungen-Lied*, though undeniably so in extent of plot and development of character. The subject is the expedition of Prince Beowulf, a lineal descendant of Woden, from England to Norway, on the adventure of delivering the king of the latter country from a kind of demon or monster which secretly enters the royal hall at midnight, and destroys some of the warriors who are sleeping there. This monster, called in the poem the Grendel, is probably nothing but the poetical personification of some dangerous exhalations from a marsh, for it is represented as issuing from a neighboring swamp, and as taking a refuge in the same abode, when, after a furious combat, Beowulf succeeds in driving it back, together with another evil spirit, into the gloomy abyss. The description of the voyage of Beowulf in his "foamy-necked" ship along the "swan-path" of the ocean, of his arrival at the Norwegian court, and his narrative of his own exploits, are in a very similar style to the ancient Scandinavian Sagas. The versification of this, as well as of all Saxon poetry in general, is exceedingly peculiar; and the system upon which it is constructed for a long time defied the ingenuity of philologists. The Anglo-Saxons based their verse not upon any regular recurrence of syllables, accented and unaccented, or regarded, as among the Greeks and Romans, as long or short; still less upon the employment of similarly sounding terminations of lines or parts of lines, that is, upon what we call rhyme. With them it was sufficient to constitute verse, that in any two successive lines — which might be of any length — there should be at least three words *beginning* with the same letter. This very peculiar metrical system is called *alliteration*.*

The language in which these works are composed is usually called *Anglo-Saxon;* but in the works themselves it is always styled *English*, and the country *England*, or the land of the Angles. The term *Anglo-Saxon*, is meant to distinguish the Saxons of England from the Saxons of the Continent, and does not signify the Angles and Saxons. But why *English* became the exclusive appellation of the language spoken by the Saxons as well as the Angles, is not altogether clear. It has

* For a fuller account of Anglo-Saxon literature, see Notes and Illustrations (A).

been supposed by some writers that the Saxons were only a section of the Angles, and consequently that the latter name was always recognized among the Angles and Saxons as the proper national appellation. Another hypothesis is, that, as the new inhabitants of the island became first known to the Roman see through the Anglian captives who were carried to Rome in the sixth century, the name of this tribe was given by the Romans to the whole people, and that the Christian missionaries to Britain would naturally continue to employ this name as the appellation both of the people and the country.* Some modern writers have proposed to discard the term *Anglo-Saxon* altogether, and employ *English* as the name of the language, from the earliest date to the present day. But, as has been already observed in a previous work of the present series, "a change of nomenclature like this would expose us to the inconvenience, not merely of embracing within one designation objects which have been conventionally separated, but of confounding things logically distinct: for, though our modern English is built upon and mainly derived from the Anglo-Saxon, the two dialects are now so discrepant, that the fullest knowledge of one would not alone suffice to render the other intelligible to either the eye or the ear." For all practical purposes, they are two separate languages, as different from one another as the Italian from the Latin, or the present English from the German.

For a long period the Saxon colonization of Britain was carried on by detached Teutonic tribes, who established themselves in such portions of territory as they found vacant, or from which they ousted less warlike occupants; and in this way there gradually arose a number of separate and independent states or kingdoms. This epoch of our history is generally denominated the *Heptarchy*, or Seven Kingdoms, the names of the principal of which may still be traced in the appellations of our modern shires, as Essex and Northumberland. As might easily have been foreseen, one of these tribes or kingdoms, growing gradually more powerful, at last absorbed the others. This important event took place in the ninth century, in the reign of Egbert, from which period to the middle of the eleventh century, when there occurred the third great invasion and change of sovereignty to which the country was destined, the history of the Anglo-Saxon monarchy presents a confused and melancholy picture of bloody incursions and fierce resistance to the barbarous and pagan Danes, who endeavored to treat the Saxons as the Saxons had treated the Celts. The only brilliant figure in this period is the almost perfect type of a patriot warrior, king, and philosopher, in the person of the illustrious Alfred; whose virtues

* For further particulars see the "Student's Manual of the English Language" pp. 14, 15. It is there shown that the common account of the imposition of the name of England upon the country by a decree of King Egbert, is unsupported by any contemporaneous or credible testimony; and that the title of *Angliæ* or *Anglorum Rex*, is much more naturally explained by the supposition that *England* and *English* had been already adopted as the *collective* names of the country and its inhabitants.

would appear to posterity almost fabulous, were they not handed down in the minute and accurate records of a biographer who knew and served him well. The two fierce races, so obstinately contending for mastery, were too nearly allied in origin and blood for their amalgamation to have produced any very material change in the language or institutions of the country. In those parts of England, principally in the North and East, as in some of the maritime regions of Scotland, where colonies of Danes established themselves, either by conquest or by settlement, the curious philologist may trace, in the idiom of the peasantry and still more clearly in the names of families and places evident marks of a Scandinavian instead of an Anglo-Saxon population. As examples of this we may cite the now immortal name of *Havelock*, derived from a famous sea-king of the same name, who is said to have founded the ancient town of Whitby, the latter being the Scandinavian *Hvitby*. As to memorials of the Saxons, preserved in the names of men, families, or places, or in the less imperishable monuments of architecture, they are so numerous that there is hardly a locality in the whole extent of England where a majority of the names is not pure and unaltered Saxon; the whole mass of the middle and lower classes of the population bears unmistakable marks of pure Saxon blood: and the sound and sterling vigor of the popular language is so essentially Saxon, that it requires but the re-establishment of the now obsolete inflections of the Anglian grammar, and the substitution of a few Teutonic words for their French equivalents, to recompose an English book into the idiom spoken in the days of Alfred.

§ 6. It would be, however, an error to suppose that *all* the words of Latin origin found even in the earlier period of the English language were introduced after the introduction into England of the Norman-French element; that is to say, after the conquest of the country by William in the eleventh century. For a long time previous to that event the cultivation of the Latin literature in the monasteries and among the learned, as well as the employment of the Latin language in the services of the Church, must have tended to incorporate with the Saxon tongue a considerable number of Latin words. Alfred, we know, visited Rome in his youth, acquired there a considerable portion of the learning which he unquestionably possessed, and exhibited his patriotic care for the enlightenment of his countrymen by translating into Saxon the "Consolations" of Boëthius. The Venerable Bede, and other Saxon ecclesiastics, composed chronicles and legends in Latin, and we may therefore conclude that, though the sturdy Teutonic nationality of the Anglo-Saxon language guarded it from being corrupted by any overwhelming admixture of Latin, yet a considerable influx of Latin words may have become perceptible in it before the appearance of Normans on our shores. It is also to be remarked that the superior civilization of the French race must have exerted an influence on at least the aristocratic classes; and the family connections between the Saxon dynasty and the neighboring dukes of Normandy, of which the reign of Edward the Confessor furnishes examples, must have tended to increase the Gallicizing character perceptible in Anglo-Saxon writings previous to the Conquest. In tracing the influence of that mighty revolution on the language, the institutions, and the national character of the people, it will be advisable to advert separately to its effects as regarded from a political, a social, and a philological point of view.

The most important change consequent upon the subjugation of the country by the Normans was obviously the establishment in England of the great feudal principle of the military tenure of land, of the chivalric spirit and habits which were the natural result of feudal institutions, and lastly, of the broad demarcation which separated society into the two great classes of the Nobles and the Serfs. It is unnecessary to say that the feudal institutions, which lay at the bottom of all these modifications, were totally unknown to the original Saxons who established themselves in England, and were indeed utterly repugnant to that free democratic organization of society which they brought with them from their native Germany, and which Tacitus shows to have universally prevailed among the primitive dwellers of the Teutonic swamps and forests. The Scandinavian pirates, who carried devastation over every coast accessible to their "sea-horses," and who, under the valiant leadership of Hrolf the Ganger, wrested from the feeble and degenerate successors of Charlemagne the magnificent province to which they gave their own North-man appellation, adopted, from the force of circumstances, that strong military organization which could alone enable a warlike minority to hold in subjection a more numerous but less vigorous conquered people. Like the Lombards in Italy, like a multitude of other races in different parts of the world and in different historical epochs, they found feudal institutions an indispensable necessity of their position; and what had been forced upon them at their original occupation of Normandy they naturally practised on their irruption into England. But as the invasion of William was carried on under at least a colorable allegation of a legal right to the inheritance of the English throne, his investiture of the crown was accompanied by a studied adherence to the constitutional forms of the Saxon monarchy; and it was perhaps only the obstinate resistance of the sullen, sturdy Saxon people, that at length wearied him into treating his new acquisition with all the rigor of a conquering invader. The whole territory was by his orders carefully surveyed and registered in that curious monument of antiquity, which still exists, entitled *Domesday Book:* the severest measures of police, as for example the famous institution of the Curfew (which was, however, no new invention of William to tyrannize over the enslaved country, but a very common regulation in feudal states), were introduced to keep down the rising of the people; the territory was divided into 60,000 fiefs; the original Saxon holders of these lands were as a general rule ousted from their estates, which were distributed, on the feudal conditions of *homage* and general defence, to the warriors who had enabled him to subjugate the country; vast tracts of inhabited lands were depopulated and transformed into forests for the chase, and the higher functions of the Church and State were with few exceptions confided to men of Norman blood. The natural consequence of such a state of things, when it continued, as it did in England, through the reigns of the long series of Norman and Plantagenet sovereigns, was to create in the country two distinct and intensely hostile nationalities. The Saxon race gradually descended to the level of an oppressed and servile class; but being far superior in numbers to their oppressors, they ran no risk of being absorbed and lost in the dominant people. The high qualities, too, of the Norman race, qualities which made them greatly superior in valor, wisdom, and intellectual activity, to any other people then existing on the continent of Europe, no less saved them from gradually disappearing in the subjugated population. It required several ages to amalgamate the two nationalities; but, partly in consequence of their high, though very different merits, and partly in consequence of a most peculiar and happy combination of circumstances, they *were* ultimately amalgamated, and formed the most vigorous people which has ever existed upon earth. In the present case the two nationalities were not dissolved in each other, but like some chemical bodies their affinities combined to form a new and powerful substance. But for several centuries the two fierce and obstinate races felt nothing but hatred towards each other, a hatred cherished by the memory of a thousand acts of tyranny and contempt on the one part, and savage revenge and sullen degradation on the other. Macaulay has well observed that, "so strong an association is established in most minds between the greatness of a sovereign and the greatness of the nation which he rules, that almost every historian of England has expatiated with a sentiment of exultation on the power and splendor of her foreign masters, and has lamented the decay of that power and splendor as a calamity to our country. This is, in truth, as absurd as it would be in a Haytian negro of our time to dwell with national pride on the greatness of Lewis XIV., and to speak of Blenheim and Ramillies with patriotic regret and shame. The Conqueror and his descendants to the fourth generation were not Englishmen: most of them were born in France: their ordinary speech was French: almost every high office in their gift was filled by a Frenchman: every acquisition which they made on the continent estranged them more and more from the population of our island." Though every trace of this double and hostile nationality has long passed away, abundant monuments of its having once existed may be still observed in our language. The family names of the higher aristocracy in England are almost universally French, while those of the middle and lower orders are as unmistakably German. Thus our peerage abounds in Russells (Roussel), Mortimers (Mortemar), Courtenays, and Talbots, while the Smiths, Browns, Johnsons, and Hodgkins plainly betray their Teutonic origin. Under the Norman *régime* the Saxon subdivisions of the country were transformed from the democratic *shire* into the feudal *county*, administered by a military governor or count. The ancient Saxon *witanagemote*, or *thing*, was metamorphosed into the feudal *Parlement*, the members of which occupied their seats, not as elective representatives of the people, but in their feudal capacity as vassals in the enjoyment of military fiefs. Thus the great ecclesiastical dignitaries took part of right in the deliberations of the legislative body, in their quality of holders of lands, and as such disposing of a certain contingent of military force.

But it is with the effects of the Norman Conquest upon the language of the country that we are at present concerned: and it is here that the task of tracing the process of admixture between the two races becomes at once more complicated and more interesting. On their arrival in Normandy, the piratical followers of Hrolf the Ganger had found themselves exposed to the civilizing influences which a small minority of rude conquerors, placed in the midst of a subject population superior to them in numbers as well as intellectual cultivation, can never long resist with success. Like the hordes of barbarian invaders who shared among them the territories of the Roman empire, the Northmen, with the Christianity of the conquered nation, imbibed also the language and civilization so intimately connected with that Christianity, and in an incredibly brief space of time exchanged for their native Scandinavian dialect a language entirely similar, in its words and grammatical forms, to the idiom prevalent in the northern division of France. It was a repetition of the introduction of Greek art and culture into republican Rome: —

Græcia capta ferum victorem cepit et artes.

The language thus communicated by the subject to the conquered nation was a dialect of that great Romance speech which extended during the Middle Ages from the northern shore of the Mediterranean to the British Channel, and which may be defined as the decomposition of the classical Latin. It was soon divided into two great sister-idioms, the Langue-d'Oc and the Langue-d'Oil (so called from the different words for *yes*), the general boundary or line of demarcation between them being roughly assignable as coinciding with the Loire. The former of these languages, spoken to the south of this river, was closely allied to the Spanish and Italian, and was subsequently called the Provençal; the latter was the parent of the French. Knowing the circumstances under which such a dialect as the Romance was formed, it is no difficult problem to establish *à priori* the changes which the mother-tongue, or Latin, must have undergone, in its process of transformation into what, though afterwards developed into regular and beautiful dialects, was at first little better than a barbarous jargon. The language of ancient Rome, a highly inflected and complicated tongue, naturally lost all, or nearly all its inflections and grammatical complexity. Thus the Latin substantive and adjective lost all those terminations which in the original language expressed relation, as the various cases of the different declensions; these relations being thenceforward indicated by the simpler expedient of prepositions.

§ 7. The literary models introduced into England by the Norman invasion were no less important than the linguistic changes consequent upon the admixture of their Romance dialect with the Saxon speech. Together with the institutions of feudalism the Normans brought with them the poetry of feudalism, that is, the poetry of chivalry. The *lais* and *romances*, the *fabliaux* and the legends of mediæval chivalry soon began to modify the rude poetical sagas and the tedious narratives of the lives of saints and hermits which had formed the bulk of the literature of Saxon England. Few subjects have excited more lively controversy among the learned than the origin and specific character of the Romance literature. In particular the distinction between the compositions of the Norman Trouvères and of the Provençal Troubadours has given rise to many elaborate dissertations and many contending theories: and yet the fundamental question may be easily, and, we think, not unsatisfactorily, solved by the simple comparison of the two terms. *Trouvère* and *Troubadour* are obviously the two forms of the same word as pronounced respectively by the population who spoke the Langue-d'Oil and the Langue-d'Oc. The natural and picturesque definition of a poet as a *finder* or *inventor* bears some analogy with the term *Skald*, or *polisher* of language, by which the same idea was represented among the Scandinavians, with the Greek ποιητής, a term exactly reproduced in the *Maker* of the Lowland Scots; and the beautiful qualification of the poetic art as *el gay saber* and *la guaye science*, no less faithfully corresponds to the idea contained in the Saxon term *gleeman*, applied to the singer or bard, whose invention furnished the joy of the banquet. Now, if we keep in mind the characteristic differences which are universally found to distinguish a Northern as compared with a Southern people, we shall generally find that in the former the imagination, the sentiments, and the memory are most developed, while the latter will be more remarkable for the vivacity of the passions and the intensity — and consequently also the transitory duration — of the affective emotions. We might therefore predict *à priori*, given respectively a Northern and a Southern population, that among the former an imaginative or poetical literature would have a natural tendency to take a *narrative*, and among the latter a *lyric*, form: for narrative is the necessary type in which the first-mentioned class of intellectual qualities would clothe themselves, while ardent and transitory passion would as inevitably express itself in the lyric form. And this is what we actually find, on comparing the prevailing literary type of the *Trouvère* with that of the *Troubadour* literature. It is evident that the composition of long narrative recitals of real or imaginary events would require a certain degree of literary culture, as well as a considerable amount of leisure; and therefore many of the interminable romances of the Trouvères may be traced to the ecclesiastical profession; while the shorter and more lively lyric and satiric effusions which constitute the bulk of the Troubadour literature were frequently the productions of princes, knights, and ladies, the power of writing verse being considered as one of the necessary accomplishments of a gentleman: —

"He coude songes make, and wel endite."

Concerning the source from which the Romance poets, both of the Northern and Southern dialects, drew the materials for their chivalric fictions, great diversity has prevailed; and the various theories which have been broached on this curious subject may be practically reduced to two hypotheses; the one tracing these inventions to an Oriental, and the other to a Celtic source; while a third class of investigators have endeavored to assign to them a Teutonic paternity, whether in the general German or the exclusively Scandinavian nationality. Each of these theories has been supported with much ingenuity, and defended with an immense display of learning: but they are all equally obnoxious to the reproach of having been made too exclusive: the existence of the well-marked general features of Chivalric Romance long before the European nations acquired, by the Crusades, any familiarity with the imagery and scenery of the East renders the first hypothesis untenable in its full extent; while the second is in a great measure invalidated by the comparatively barbarous state into which the Celtic tribes had generally fallen at the time when the Chivalric literature began to prevail, and the little knowledge which the Romance populations of Europe possessed of the ancient Gaulic language and historical legendary lore. It is true that the Trouvères almost invariably pretend to have found the subjects of their narratives in the traditions, or among the chronicles of the "olde gentil Bretons," just as Marie de France refers her reader to the Celtic or Armorican authorities; but this was in all probability in general a mere literary artifice, like that which induced other poets to place the *venue* of their wondrous adventures in some distant and unknown region: —

"In Sarra, in the lond of Tartarie."

The important part played in these legends by the half-mythical Arthur and his knights might seem to argue in favor of a Celtic origin for these fictions; for if ever such a personage as Arthur really existed he must have been a British prince; but when we remember that Arthur, though mentioned in the authentic traditional poems of the ancaint Britons, is a comparatively insignificant character, and that these same traditions contain no trace whatever of the existence of that chivalric state of society of which Arthur and his *preux* are the ideal, we shall find ourselves as much warranted in accepting the authenticity of a Celtic origin on these grounds, as in attributing the chivalric character with which Alexander, Hector, and Hercules are also invested in the mediæval poets, to an intimate acquaintance with the Homeric and classical poems, from which the Troubadour may indeed have borrowed some striking names and leading incidents, but with the true spirit of which every line shows him to be unacquainted.*

§ 8. For two centuries after the Norman conquest, the Anglo-Saxon

* See Notes and Illustrations (B), *Anglo-Norman Literature.*

and the Norman-French continued to be spoken in the island, as two distinct languages, having little intermixture with one another. The most important change, which converted the Anglo-Saxon into Old English, and which consists chiefly in the substitution of the vowel *e* for the different inflections, was not due in any considerable degree to the Norman conquest, though it was probably hastened by that event. It commenced even before the Norman conquest, and was owing to the same causes which led to similar changes in the kindred German dialects. The large introduction of French words into English dates from the time when the Normans began to speak the language of the conquered race. It is, however, an error to represent the English language as springing from a mixture of Anglo-Saxon and French; since a mixed language, in the strict sense of the term, may be pronounced an impossibility. The English still remained essentially a German tongue, though it received such large accessions of French words as materially to change its character. To fix with precision the date when this change took place is manifestly an impossible task. It was a gradual process, and must have advanced with more or less rapidity in different parts of the country. In remote and less frequented districts the mass of the population long preserved their pure Saxon speech. This is sufficiently proved by the circumstance, that even in the present day, the inhabitants of such remote, or *upland* districts, still show in their patois an evident preponderance of the Saxon element, as exhibited in the use of many old German words which have long ceased to form part of the English vocabulary, and in the evident retention of German peculiarities of pronunciation. "Nothing can be more difficult," says Hallam, "than to determine, except by an arbitrary line, the commencement of the English language; not so much, as in those of the Continent, because we are in want of materials, but rather from an opposite reason — the possibility of tracing a very gradual succession of verbal changes, that ended in a change of denomination. For when we compare the earliest English of the thirteenth century with the Anglo-Saxon of the twelfth, it seems hard to pronounce why it should pass for a separate language, rather than a modification or simplification of the former. We must conform, however, to usage, and say that the Anglo-Saxon was converted into English: 1. by contracting or otherwise modifying the pronunciation and orthography of words; 2. by omitting many inflections, especially of the noun, and consequently making more use of articles and auxiliaries; and 3. by the introduction of French derivatives. Of these the second alone, I think, can be considered as sufficient to describe a new form of language; and this was brought about so gradually, that we are not relieved of much of our difficulty, whether some compositions shall pass for the latest offspring of the mother, or for the earliest proofs of the fertility of the daughter."

The picturesque illustration, so happily employed by Scott in the opening chapter of *Ivanhoe*, has often been quoted as a good popular exemplification of the mode in which the Saxon and French elements were blended: the common animals serving for food to man, while under the charge of Saxon serfs and bondmen, retained their Teutonic appellation; but when served up at the table of the Norman oppressor received a French designation. As examples of this, he cites the parallels *Ox* and *Beef*, *Swine* and *Pork*, *Sheep* and *Mutton*, *Calf* and *Veal*. It is curious to see, on examining the grammar and vocabulary of the early English language, as exhibited in the writings of our old poets and chroniclers, how often the primitive Saxon forms continued very gradually to become effaced, while the French orthography and pronunciation of the newly introduced words have not yet become harmonized, so to speak, with the general character of the new idiom. Thus, in the following lines of Chaucer: —

> "The sleer of himself yet saugh I there,
> His herte-blood hath bathed al his here;
> The nayl y-dryve in the shode a-nyght;
> The colde deth, with mouth gapyng upright.
> Amyddes of the tempul set mischaunce,
> With sory comfort and evel contynaunce."

In these verses we see the Saxon grammatical forms combined with a large importation of Norman-French words, which have not yet lost their original accentuation. The old German is found running into, as it were, and overlapping the lately-introduced Gallicism. Such was the state in which Chaucer found the national idiom at the beginning of the fourteenth century, and the admirable genius of that great poet may be said to have put the last touch to the consolidation of the English language. For a considerable period after his time, however, such writings as were addressed to the sympathies of the lower classes continued to retain much of the Saxon characteristics in orthography, grammatical structure, and versification; for example, traces of the peculiar alliterative system are perceptible for a period long subsequent to the reign of Richard II., while the elaborate compositions addressed to the still purely Norman nobility retain much of the French spirit in their diction and imagery.

§ 9. Though it is impossible to assign any exact date to the change of Anglo-Saxon into English, the chief alterations in the language may be arranged approximately under the following epochs: —

I. *Anglo-Saxon*, from A. D. 450 to 1150.

II. *Semi-Saxon*, from A. D. 1150 to 1250 (from the reign of Stephen to the middle of the reign of Henry III.), so called because it partakes strongly of the characteristics of both Anglo-Saxon and Old English.

III. *Old English*, from A. D. 1250 to 1350 (from the middle of the reign of Henry III. to the middle of the reign of Edward III.).

IV. *Middle English*, from A. D. 1350 to about 1550 (from the middle of the reign of Edward III. to the reign of Edward VI.).

V. *Modern English*, from A. D. 1550 to the present day.*

* The writers who wish to discard the term *Anglo-Saxon* call the Anglo-Saxon *First English*, the Semi-Saxon *Second English*, and give the name of *Third English* to the remaining periods.

The three first periods scarcely belong to a history of English *literature*, and consequently only a brief account of them is given in the Notes and Illustrations appended to the present chapter. The real history of English literature begins with Chaucer, in the brilliant reign of Edward III.

NOTES AND ILLUSTRATIONS.

A.—ANGLO-SAXON LITERATURE.
A. D. 450-1150.

The earliest literature of the Anglo-Saxons bears the impress of the religious culture under which it was formed. Unlike their brethren, who sung their old heroic lays in their primeval forests, the conquerors of the rich provinces of Britain had sunk from action to contemplation, and their literature was artificial. There was but little difference of time in the development of poetry and prose; and the works produced were, with only three exceptions, the elaborate compositions of educated men, rather than the spontaneous products of genius, inspired by a people's ancient legends. The chief subjects were moral, religious, historical, and didactic. Under the tutelage of the Church, the most lasting monuments of Anglo-Saxon prose literature were written in Latin; and the vernacular tongue was chiefly employed in translating the learned works of such men as Bede and Alcuin. What value it possesses is chiefly for its matter; for it almost entirely wants that beauty of form, which alone raises literature to an art.

I. The VERNACULAR POETRY scarcely retains a trace of that wild epic fire which is seen in the Scandinavian *Sagas*. (1.) We have only three specimens of old national songs, written in the spirit of the continental Germans, and probably composed, in part at least, before their migration to England. The first of these is the *Lay of Beowulf*, which is fully described in the text. Its spirit is that of the old heathen Germans. It seems to have been originated at the primitive seat of the Angles, in Schleswig, and to have been brought over to England about the end of the fifth century. The other two are the *Traveller's Song*, and the *Battle of Finnesburg*, the scene of which seems to be on the Continent. It is only in the tenth century that we again meet with compositions of this class, in the patriotic poems on *Athelstane's Victory at Brunanburgh* (A. D. 938), on the *Coronation* (A. D. 958), and the *Death of Edgar* (A. D. 975), and on the *Battle of Maldon* (A. D. 993). (2.) Of *Religious Poetry*, the chief specimen is the so-called *Metrical Paraphrase of the Scriptures*, which Bede ascribes to CÆDMON, a monk of Whitby, in the seventh century. Some modern writers assign the work to a much later date. But whatever be the date, it is a striking poem, and appears to have supplied Milton with some hints. One passage strikingly resembles Milton's soliloquy of Satan in hell. CYNEWULF (in Latin Kenulphus), a monk of Winchester, and abbot of Peterborough in 992, is highly eulogized by a local historian; but we have only two short poems which preserve his name in a sort of acrostic of Runic characters. ALDHELM, the great Latin writer mentioned below, wrote poetry in the vernacular, and is said to have translated the *Book of Psalms* into Anglo-Saxon verse. These poems were preserved orally, not only by the minstrels, but as exercises of memory by the monks. Hence the MSS. exhibit very great diversities.

II. ANGLO-SAXON LITERATURE IN LATIN demands notice before the vernacular prose literature, as the latter was, for the most part, based upon the former. It was the product of foreign ecclesiastical influence. The earliest missionaries were imbued with the learning of the Western Church and great schools were soon founded in Kent and the South, and afterwards in Northumbria. In the latter part of the seventh century, THEODORE OF TARSUS became Archbishop of Canterbury, and, with his friend the ABBOT ADRIAN, taught both Greek and Latin literature. In the eighth century, books were so multiplied, that Alcuin complains to Charlemagne of the literary poverty of France as compared with England. He also gives an account of the great library at York, from which and other lists we can see what writers formed the taste of the seventh, eighth, and ninth centuries. There was a decided preference for the Greek authors above the Latin. The classical poets were read, but with a religious suspicion, and the works most valued were those of the Fathers and the Christian poets, whose faults are closely imitated in the Latin poetry of the Anglo-Saxon churchmen. The ecclesiastical taste was strengthened and the literary treasures increased by the habit of visiting Rome, which became frequent in the eighth century. Many women were celebrated for their learning.

(1) *Anglo-Latin Poetry.*

ALDHELM, of Sherborne, founder of the abbey of Malmesbury (b. about A. D. 656, d. A. D. 709), was the most distinguished pupil of Adrian. His poetry is turgid and full of extravagant conceits. He wrote in hexameters *De Laude Virginitatis* (besides a prose treatise on the same theme), a book of *Ænigmata* in imitation of Symposius, and a poem on the *Seven Cardinal Virtues*. These, with a few letters, are all his extant works. The great prose writer ALCUIN (see below) was also fertile in Latin verse. His style is simpler than Aldhelm's, but less animated. His best poem is an *Elegy on the Destruction of Lindisfarne by the Danes*. The long poem on the *Church of York* has also some good descriptive passages. He also wrote *Epigrams*, *Elegies*, and *Ænigmata*. Columban, Boniface, Bede, and Cuthbert, wrote some Latin verses; and, passing over a few others, the list concludes, in the tenth century, with the *Life of St. Wilfred*, by FRIDEGODE, and the *Life of St. Swithun* by WOLSTAN.

(2) The *Latin Prose Literature* of the Anglo-Saxons consists of religious treatises, works on science and education, and histories in which the ecclesiastical element preponderates; but its most interesting remains are the letters of Alcuin and Boniface, for the light they throw on contemporary history and manners.

(a) The period opens with some writers, who were not Saxons, but of the old Celtic race, which had preserved British Christianity, or had learned it anew from Ireland. Passing over the obscure *Historia* of GILDAS, son of the British King of Alcluyd (Dumbarton), in the sixth century, and NENNIUS, whose work is probably not genuine, in the seventh, we come to ST. COLUMBANUS (lived about A. D. 543-615) of Ireland, who, having joined the lately founded monastery at Bangor, set out thence at the head of a mission to the eastern parts of Gaul, Switzerland, and the south-west of Germany. He wrote in Latin several theological treatises, some poems, and five letters. Nearly two centuries later Ireland sent forth JOHANNES SCOTUS, surnamed from his native land ERIGENA (d. A. D. 877), who settled in France, and became, by his dialectic skill and his acquaintance with the doctrines of Neo-Platonism, one of the founders of the philosophical sect of the *Realists*. The story of his coming to England on Alfred's invitation is more than doubtful.

(b) The earliest Anglo-Saxon prose writer in Latin is WILFRED (lived A. D. 634-709), Archbishop of York and apostle of Sussex, who succeeded, after a troubled life, in uniting the churches of the Anglo-Saxon kingdoms. His works are lost; but he deserves mention as the founder of the school of learning at York, which was fostered by Bishop EGBERT (A. D. 678-766), and produced BEDE and ALCUIN, the two great names of the Anglo-Saxon Latin literature.

The course of BEDE (A. D. 672-735), surnamed the "Venerable," is a perfect type of the outward repose and intellectual activity of the monastic life, in its best aspect. At the age of seven he was placed under the teaching of Benedict Biscop, in the monastery of Wearmouth; became a deacon at nineteen, and a priest at thirty. Whether he visited Rome is uncertain. He only left his monastery on rare visits to other religious houses; and his dying moments were divided between religious exercises and dictating the last sentences of a work which he just lived to finish.

His works embrace the whole compass of the learning of his age. Numbering no less than forty-five, they may be divided into four classes: *Theological*, consisting chiefly of commentaries on the Scriptures, pervaded by the allegorical method; *Scientific Treatises*, exhibiting the imperfect knowledge of science, from Pliny to his own time; *Grammatical Works*, which display much learning; with some correct but lifeless Latin poems; *Historical Compositions*, which place him in the first rank among writers of the middle ages. The History of his own Monastery and the Life of St. Cuthbert deserve mention; but his great work is the *Ecclesiastical History of the Anglo-Saxons* from their first settlement in England. He used the aid of the most learned men of his time in collecting the documents and traditions of the various kingdoms, which he relates with scrupulous fidelity and in a very pleasing style. The *History* was translated into Anglo-Saxon by King Alfred.

Bede was surrounded by a body of literary friends, as Acca and others, among whom the most distinguished was EGBERT, Archbishop of York (about A. D. 678-766), the reformer of his diocese, and founder of the splendid library already mentioned. His writings are chiefly on points of discipline, and two of them, the *Confessionale* and *Pœnitentiale*, were published in Anglo-Saxon as well as in Latin. ST. BONIFACE (*Winfrid*), a native of Crediton in Devonshire (lived about A. D. 680-755) and the apostle of Western Germany, has left a collection of valuable letters, amounting (with those addressed to him) to a hundred and six. The eighth century closes with the great name of ALCUIN (about A. D. 735-804). He was born at York, and, like Bede, was placed in a convent in his infancy. Trained in the school of Archbishop Egbert, he became the favorite pupil of that prelate's kinsman and successor, Albert, on whose appointment to the archbishopric (A. D. 766), the school was intrusted to Alcuin, just ordained a deacon. Eanbald, a pupil of Alcuin, on succeeding to the archbishopric (A. D. 780), sent Alcuin to Rome, and this mission caused his introduction to Charlemagne, at whose court he resided with magnificent appointments till A. D. 790, and again from A. D. 792 to his death. His works were commentaries, dogmatic and practical treatises, lives of saints, and several very interesting letters. His Latin poems have been already noticed. He is chiefly important in the History of English Literature, as another example, like that of Erigena, of what the Continent gained from the learning of these islands. The name of ASSER, Bishop of Sherborne (d. A. D. 910), is connected with a Latin history of King Alfred, of very doubtful authenticity. The renowned DUNSTAN (A. D. 925-988) wrote commentaries on the Benedictine rule, and other works. Of his contemporary ODO (d. 961), we have only a single letter. A few other names might still be mentioned.

III. The VERNACULAR ANGLO-SAXON PROSE LITERATURE contains few but great names Above all shines that of KING ALFRED (A. D. 848-901), the story of whose early training and life-long self-discipline needs not to be recounted here. His early love for the old national poetry, the growing neglect of Latin even by the priests, and the eager desire, of which he himself tells us, that the people might enjoy the treasures of learning collected in the churches for security from the invaders, urged him to the culture of the native tongue for popular instruction. While inviting over learned men to repair the decay of scholarship, the king himself set the example of translating existing works into the vernacular. Having learned Latin only late in life, he did not disdain the help of scholars, such as Bishop Asser, in clearing up grammatical difficulties, while he brought to the work untiring industry, great capacity of comprehending the author's general meaning, and sound judgment upon points needing illustration. His most important translations were those of Bede's *Ecclesiastical History*, the *Ancient History* of Orosius, Boethius *de Consolatione Philosophiæ*, and, for the use of the clergy, the *Pastorale* of St. Gregory. According to William of Malmesbury, Alfred had commenced an Anglo-Saxon version of the Psalms shortly before his death. Among the works falsely attributed to him are *Alfred's Proverbs*, a translation of *Æsop's Fables*, and a metrical version of the *Metres* of Boethius. Many works were translated by the king's order or after his example; for instance, the *Dialogues of St. Gregory*, by Werfred, Bishop of Worcester. The new intellectual impulse, given by Alfred's policy of calling foreign scholars into the realm, which was followed by other kings down to the eve of the Conquest, sustained the revival of Anglo-Saxon literature in full activity for some time.

The great light of the tenth century was ALFRIC, Archbishop of Canterbury, surnamed Grammaticus (d. A. D. 1006), whose opposition to Romish doctrines called attention to his work, and so gave an impulse to Anglo-Saxon studies in modern times. His eighty *Homilies* are his chief work. He also translated the Books of Moses, and wrote other theological treatises. As a grammarian he labored to revive the neglected study of Latin by his *Latin Grammar* (from Donatus and Priscian), his *Glossary* and *Colloquium* (a conversation book). He appears as a scientific writer in the *Manual of Astronomy*, if it is rightly assigned to him. He is often confounded with two other Alfrics, the name being common among the Anglo-Saxons. There was an Alfric, Abbot of Malmesbury (d. A. D. 994), and an Alfric, surnamed Bata, Archbishop of York (d. 1051), a devoted disciple of the great Alfric, whose Grammar and Colloquium he republished, besides writing a life of Bishop Ethelwold (A. D. 925–984). In the eleventh century we need only mention WULFSTAN, Archbishop of York (d. 1023), the author of some homilies.

It remains to notice two great monuments of Anglo-Saxon prose literature, the *Chronicle* and the *Laws*. The *Saxon Chronicle* is a record of the history of the people, compiled at first, as is believed, for Alfred, by Plegmund, Archbishop of Canterbury, who brought it down to A. D. 891. Thence it was continued, as a contemporary record, to the end of the Anglo-Saxon period, in the middle of the twelfth century. It breaks off abruptly in the first year of Henry II. (A. D. 1154). "It is a dry chronological record, noting in the same lifeless tone important and trifling events without the slightest tinge of dramatic color, of criticism in weighing evidence, or of judgment in the selection of the facts narrated" (Marsh, *Origin and History of the English Language*, Lect. iii. p. 103). This want of historical talent, as the same writer observes, prevents our learning from it much of our ancestors' social life, or of the practical working of their institutions.

The fragments of the *Anglo-Saxon Laws* contain some as early as the reign of Ethelbert, King of Kent, reduced, however, to the language of a later age. Alfred, who began the work, says that, with the advice of his *Witan*, he rejected what did not please him, but added little of his own. The work was then submitted to and adopted by the *Witan*. His chief followers in these labors were Athelstane, Ethelred, and Canute. (See Schmid, *Gesetze der Angel-Sachsen*, 2d ed. 1858.)

B.—ANGLO-NORMAN LITERATURE.
A. D. 1066–1350.

The Norman Conquest had both a destructive and a reconstructive influence on the literature of the country. The ordinance, forbidding the Saxon clergy to aspire to any ecclesiastical dignity, confined the literary activity that was left to the monasteries, except in the case of those who were willing to adapt themselves to the new state of things. The Anglo-Saxon learning gradually died out by the middle of the twelfth century; its chief work being the completion of the *Saxon Chronicle* in the monastery of Peterborough. The chief works of learning were composed in Latin; while for lighter compositions the English adopted the language of their conquerors. On the other hand, the Normans introduced a new and most potent element of intellectual activity. The fifty years preceding the Conquest had witnessed a great revival of learning on the Continent, originating from the Arabs, who had themselves become imbued with the Greek learning of the conquered East. Thus the revival of letters in the eleventh century, like the brighter revival in the fifteenth, owed its source to the ancient Greeks; but with this great difference: while, in the latter case, inspiration was drawn from the great poets and orators, the Arabs were chiefly attracted by the physical, logical, and metaphysical works of the school of Aristotle. The Aristotelian logic and spirit of systematizing were eagerly applied to theology, especially in France. The monasteries of Caen and Bec, in Normandy, became distinguished seats of the new science; and in them were trained LANFRANC and ANSELM, the first great lights of Anglo-Norman learning. Indeed Anselm is often regarded as the founder of the *Scholastic Philosophy*, which was the fruit of the new movement. But he is only a connecting link. The old method of treating theology, followed by the Fathers, was based on the foundation of faith in the dogmatic statements of Scripture. The scholastic philosophy aspired to establish a complete system of truth by a chain of irrefragable reasoning. Anselm only applied its methods to the establishment of separate doctrines; while ABELARD, breaking away from the old foundation of faith, which Anselm tacitly assumed, made the same methods the instruments of scepticism. He was met by ST. BERNARD, who took his stand upon the old patristic ground. "Scholasticism," says Mr. Arnold (*Eng. Lit.* p. 15), "made a false start in the school of Bec; its true commencement dates a little later, and from Paris." Its founder was PETER LOMBARD, called the "Master of the Sentences," from his *Four Books of Sentences*, published in A. D. 1151. Thus the same age produced St. Bernard, the last of the Fathers, and Peter Lombard, the first of the schoolmen. In England there is no trace of the new learning before the Conquest, though she had helped to prepare for it by sending forth such men as Erigena and Alcuin. Erigena, indeed, as early as the ninth century, had employed philosophical methods in religious discussion; but he was a Platonist; the schoolmen were Aristotelians. The new learning not only entered in the train of the Conqueror, but was fostered by his personal influence. William, and nearly all his successors, down to Henry III., were themselves well educated, and patronized literature and art. The displacement of the Saxon bishops and abbots seems to have arisen from contempt for their illiteracy, as well as from political motives; and their places were filled by the most learned of the Norman ecclesiastics, as Archbishops Lanfranc and Anselm, HERMAN, Bishop of Salisbury, who founded a great library, GODFREY, Prior of St. Swithin's at Winchester, who wrote Latin epigrams in the style of Martial, and GEOFFREY, an eminent scholar from the University of Paris, who founded a school at Dunstable, and acted, with his scholars, a drama of his own on the Life of St. Catharine. Numerous as were the Saxon monasteries, no less than five hundred and fifty-seven new religious houses were founded, from the Conquest to the reign of John. All of these, as well as the cathedrals, had schools for those destined to the church, and general schools were founded in the towns and villages. The twelfth century witnessed the foundation of our two great Universities; but they were at first regarded rather as portals to the continental Universities, to which English subjects resorted in great numbers, especially to Paris, where they formed one of the four "nations." Classical learning revived at the Universities, and was extended from the Latin poets to Greek and even Hebrew, in the thirteenth century, chiefly by the influence of ROBERT GROSSETESTE, Bishop of Lincoln. About the same time, the invention of the art of making paper from linen rags more than made up for the growing lack of parchment, and gave a new mechanical impulse to literature.

Meanwhile, the tenacity with which the English language held its ground among the common people, caused the ultimate fruit of these movements to be shown in the formation of a truly *English* literature in the thirteenth and fourteenth centuries.

It remains to mention the classes of literature and the chief writers of the period. Literature being cultivated almost entirely by the clergy and the minstrels, nearly all the prose works were in Latin, and the poetry in Norman-French; exclusive, however, of the contemporaneous Semi-Saxon literature (see below, C). An age of violence and oppression permitted but little popular literature, in the proper sense.

1. ANGLO-NORMAN AND ANGLO-SAXON LITERATURE IN LATIN. — 1. *Theologians and Schoolmen.* — LANFRANC (b. A. D. 1005, d. A. D. 1089) was a Lombard of Pavia, where, after studying in other Italian Universities, he practised as a pleader. Removing to Normandy, he opened a school at Avranches (A. D. 1035 or later), which became a centre of elegant Latinity. In A. D. 1042 he suddenly joined the small abbey of Bec; was elected prior, and opened a school, which soon surpassed that of Avranches. He soon found a wider field for his ambition as the counsellor of Duke William; and being sent by him on a mission to Rome, he distinguished himself by defending the doctrine of transubstantiation, against Berengarius of Tours. In A. D. 1066 (the year of the Conquest), William made him abbot of his new monastery of St. Stephen at Caen, and in 1070 he became Archbishop of Canterbury, in place of the deposed Saxon prelate Stigand. His reform of the Anglo-Saxon Church and severity towards its clergy concern us here less than his invitations to learned foreigners whereby he founded a new school of science and literature in England. His great work was the *Treatise against Berengarius* (written A. D. 107[illegible] or 1080); he also wrote Commentaries on Scripture, and Letters. Many of Lanfranc's works are lost. ANSELM (b. A. D. 1033, d. 1109) was also an Italian, of Aosta. His eagerness for learning led him to Bec, where he succeeded Lanfranc as prior and afterwards became abbot in place of Herluin (A. D. 1078). Most of his works were composed here, while he gained the highest reputation for piety, and taught diligently. On his second visit to England, in A. D. 1092, the voice of the bishops and barons forced William Rufus to appoint him as the successor of Lanfranc, who had been dead four years. Anselm's troubles in the primacy belong to history rather than literature; but amidst them all he continued to write and teach. It is unnecessary to enumerate his many works, which are less important than his influence on the learning of his age. They consist of theological and dialectic treatises, homilies, devout meditations, and letters. His claims to a share in the Hymnology of the church are doubtful. Besides many distinguished prelates, only inferior in fame to these two, some of whom are mentioned above, we may name two writers of more general literature, JOHN OF SALISBURY (died Bishop of Chartres in A. D. 1182), an Englishman, who wrote a treatise *De Nugis Curialium et Vestigiis Philosophorum*, besides Latin verses; and PETER OF BLOIS (d. after A. D. 1198), whose letters throw much light on the characters and manners of his time; he wrote many other works, and an interesting poem on Richard's misfortunes in Palestine. The *English Schoolmen* were for the most part of the Anglo-Saxon race, but lived chiefly abroad. ALEXANDER HALES, "the Irrefragable Doctor," a native of Gloucestershire, was the teacher of St. Bonaventure. He lived and taught abroad, and died at Paris, A. D. 1245. JOHANNES DUNS SCOTUS, "the Subtle Doctor," taught at Oxford and Paris, and died at Bologna, A. D. 1308. WILLIAM OF OCCAM (b. A. D. 1300, d. A. D. 1347, at Munich), "the Invincible Doctor," spent most of his life at the court of the German Emperor, whose cause he maintained against the Pope. Though the pupil of the great Realist, Duns Scotus, he was the head of the school of the *Nominalists*, who held that our abstract ideas are merely general expressions of thought, not necessarily corresponding to real existences. At Oxford, the Franciscan friar, ROGER BACON (about A. D. 1214-1292), by his devotion to physical science, gained the reputation of a sorcerer, while dimly anticipating some of the great inventions of later times, among which is thought to have been that of gunpowder. His *Opus Majus* is an inquiry into "the *roots of wisdom;*" namely, language, mathematics, optics, and experimental science. That he had begun to cast off the scholastic trammels, and already to question nature in the spirit of his great namesake, is shown by his saying, on a disputed fact in physics, "I have tried it, and it is not the fact, but the very reverse."

2. *Latin Chronicles* of past and contemporary

history had already been commenced before the Conquest. Their writers were churchmen, and mostly of the Saxon race; and, with a few exceptions, they confined themselves to the history of England. Passing over the more than doubtful work ascribed to INGULPHUS, Abbot of Croyland (A. D. 1075–1109), and its continuation (to A. D. 1118), we have a History of the Norman Conquest by WILLIAM OF POITIERS, a follower of the Conqueror, extending from A. D. 1035 to A. D. 1067; but the beginning and end are lost; we know that it came down to A. D. 1070. FLORENCE OF WORCESTER (d. A. D. 1118) compiled a chronicle from the Creation to the year of his death, chiefly from the Saxon Chronicle, and the Chronology of Marianus Scotus, a German monk. EADMER'S (d. A. D. 1124) history is chiefly a monument to the fame of Anselm. ORDERICUS VITALIS (b. A. D. 1075, near Shrewsbury, d. after A. D. 1143), wrote an Ecclesiastical History in thirteen books, from the Creation to the latter year. The best of all these chroniclers is WILLIAM OF MALMESBURY (about A. D. 1140), who dedicated his history to Robert, Earl of Gloucester, natural son of Henry I. It is in two parts; the *Gesta Regum Anglorum*, in five books, from the landing of Hengist and Horsa to A. D. 1120, and the *Historia Novella*, in three books, down to A. D. 1142. The work is written in the spirit and manner of Bede. He also wrote a Life of Wulfstan, a history of the English Bishops, and other works. His contemporary, HENRY OF HUNTINGDON (d. after A. D. 1154), also a worthy follower of Bede, though inferior to William, wrote a History of England, from the landing of Julius Cæsar to the accession of Henry II. (A. D. 1154). To the eight books of the history he added his other works, forming four more, the last consisting of his Latin poems. GEOFFREY OF MONMOUTH (d. A. D. 1154) also inscribed to Robert, Earl of Gloucester, his *Historia Britonum*, which professes to be a translation of an old British chronicle brought over from Brittany by Walter, Archdeacon of Oxford, in nine books: it relates the legendary story of the British kings, from Brutus, the great-grandson of Æneas, to the death of Cadwallader, son of Cadwallo, in A. D. 688. The lively Welshmam keeps his country's traditions free from those rationalizing attempts, which "spoil a good poem, without making a good history;" and he provided for the romance writers some of their best stories, among the rest, that of Arthur and the Knights of the Round Table. His work was abridged by ALFRED or ALURED OF BEVERLEY, and continued by CARADOC OF LANCARVAN to A. D. 1154. The latter work is only known in a Welsh version, which has been translated into English. Another learned Welshman, GIRALDUS CAMBRENSIS (Gerald Barry, b. about A. D. 1146, d. A. D. 1223), wrote topographical works on Wales and Ireland, an account of his own life, and many other works, including Latin poems. He was about the most vigorous and versatile author of his time.

AILRED OF RIEVAUX, in Yorkshire (b. A. D. 1109, d. A. D. 1166), has left an admirable account of the *Battle of the Standard* (A. D. 1138), and several theological works. ROGER DE HOVEDEN (*i. e.* of Howden, in Yorkshire) continued Bede's History from A. D. 732 to A. D. 1202, transcribing many documents of great historical value. GEOFFREY DE VINSAUF wrote an important work on the Crusade, in which he followed Richard Cœur de Lion. MATTHEW PARIS (a monk of St. Alban's) wrote his celebrated *Historia Major*, from the Norman Conquest to the year of his death, A. D. 1259. Much of it consists of open plagiarisms from the *Chronicle*, or *Flores Historiarum*, of ROGER DE WENDOVER, also a monk of St. Alban's, who died Prior of Belvoir, May 6th A. D. 1237. This work extends from the Creation to the nineteenth year of Henry III. (A. D. 1235), and the latter part is very valuable. It was published by the Rev. Henry O. Coxe, for the English Historical Society, 5 vols. 8vo., London, 1841-1844. Another monk of St. Alban's, WILLIAM RISHANGER, continued the work of Matthew Paris, probably to the fifteenth of Edward II. (A. D. 1322), but the latter part of his book is lost. NICHOLAS TRIVET wrote an excellent history, from Stephen to Edward I. (A. D. 1135-1307), which was edited by Mr. T. Hog, London, 1845. From these two works was compiled the *Chronicle of St. Alban's*, which is plagiarized (like Roger of Wendover by Matthew Paris) in the *Historia Anglicana* of WALSINGHAM, published by Mr. Riley, 1863. Another chronicler of the 14th century is RALPH OR RANULPH HIGDEN, a Benedictine monk of St. Werburgh at Chester, where he died at a great age, about A. D. 1370. His *Polychronicon* was a universal History in seven books. Only the part preceding the Norman Conquest was printed in Gale's *Scriptores XV.* (Oxon. 1691, fol.); but John de Trevisa's English translation of the whole work, completed before the end of the century, was printed by Caxton, who added an eighth book, in A. D. 1482. Some authorities ascribe to Higden the *Chester Mysteries*, performed in A. D. 1328. The *History of Samson, Abbot of Bury St. Edmunds* (A. D. 1173-1202), by JOCELIN OF BRAKELOND, only recently discovered, has furnished the materials for Mr. Carlyle's vivid picture of the old abbot and his age (*Past and Present*, 1843).

Besides the writings of these chroniclers (and several almost as important might be named), we have a mass of public rolls and registers, beginning with *Domesday Book;* but these official documents hardly belong to literature.

3. The frequent resort of Englishmen to the University of Bologna gave an impulse to the study of Civil Law, which excited the emulation of the great masters of the Common Law, and so produced, towards the end of the twelfth century, the first great treatise on the laws of England, the *Tractatus de Legibus et Consuetudinibus Angliæ*, by the chief justiciary, RANULF DE GLANVIL (d. A. D. 1190).

4. The *Letters* of the leading churchmen of the age, besides the value of their matter, afford many good specimens of Latin composition. Beginning with Lanfranc and Anselm the series comes down to THOMAS A BECKET and STEPHEN LANGTON, but by far the most valuable for their matter, and the most interesting for their literary excellence, are those of John of Salisbury and Peter of Blois, which reveal to us much both of the political and the scholastic history of the latter half of the twelfth century. The letters of ROBERT GROSSETESTE have been edited by Mr. Luard, 1861; and the works

of John of Salisbury are thoroughly analyzed in the monograph of Dr. Schaarschmidt, Leipzig, 1862.

5. *Latin Poetry* was cultivated as an elegant accomplishment by the men of learning, as Lawrence of Durham, Henry of Huntingdon, John of Salisbury, John de Hauteville, and others. But a more natural, though irregular school was formed under the influence of the minstrels, the application of whose accentual system of verse to Latin, in defiance of quantity, gave rise to the *Leonine Verse*, which was used for epigrams, satires, and also for the hymns of the Church. The term *Leonine* describes specifically verses rhymed as well as accentual; but both forms are common. Leonine verse was naturalized in Europe by the end of the eleventh century. It was applied to hymnology by St. Bernard, St. Thomas Aquinas, and Pope Innocent III.; and every one is familiar with some of the finest of these hymns, as the *Dies Iræ* and *Stabat Mater*. (See the *Hymni Ecclesiæ*, Oxon. 1838. A curious instance of its use in England is furnished by the epitaph on Bede, the first line of which

"Continet hæc theca Bedæ venerabilis ossa,"

was transformed by later ingenuity into

"Continet hæc fossa Bedæ venerabilis ossa."

A further stage of license is seen in the frivolous *Macaronic Poetry*, which abounds not only in Latin words of the strangest formation, but in mixtures of different languages, as in the following example, in Latin, French, and English, belonging to the early part of Edward II.'s reign (Marsh, p. 247): —

"*Quant honme deit parleir*, videat quæ verba loquatur,
Sen covent aver, ne stultior inveniatur.
Quando quis loquitur, *bote resoun reste therynne*,
Derisum patitur, *ant lutel so shall he wynne*; —

and so on. "This confusion of tongues," adds Mr. Marsh, "led very naturally to the corruption of them all, and consequently none of them were written or spoken as correctly as at the period when they were kept distinct."

But the Leonine, as indeed also the regular verse, was chiefly used for satire, especially by the secular clergy and by laymen against the regular clergy and the vices of the age. Here is one example: —

"Mille annis jam peractis
Nulla fides est in pactis;
Mel in ore, verba lactis,
Fel in corde, fraus in factis."

It was employed also for all manner of light and popular pieces. The earliest known writer in this style was HILARIUS, a disciple of Abelard, and probably an Englishman, who flourished about A. D. 1125. A mass of such poetry, probably by various writers, is ascribed to WALTER MAPES, or MAP, Archdeacon of Oxford under Henry II., under the general title of *Confessio Goliæ*, — Golias being the type of loose livers, especially among the clergy. Map also wrote in regular Latin verse, and in prose *De Nugis Curialium*. He was an author, too, in Anglo-Norman poetry and prose, chiefly on the legends of Arthur. Altogether he seems to have been one of the most active minds of the age.

The regular Latin writers were up in arms against the Leonines. GEOFFREY VINSAUF, already noticed as a chronicler, addressed to Pope Innocent III. a regular poem, *De Nova Poetria*, of great merit, and containing interesting allusions to contemporary history. His overstrained lament for Richard's death is satirized by Chaucer even while addressing him as

"O Gaufride, dear maister soverain."

One of the last and best examples of the regular Latin poetry is the work of JOSEPHUS ISCANUS (Joseph of Exeter, d. about A. D. 1210) *De Bello Trojano*, which was so popular as to be used in schools with the classic poets. He also wrote a Latin poem entitled Antiocheïs, on Richard's expedition to Palestine. But the whole style was doomed to extinction before a more vigorous rival than the Leonines — the vernacular poetry which sprang up in imitation of the French minstrelsy — and it had almost disappeared by the middle of the thirteenth century.

II. The ANGLO-NORMAN FRENCH LITERATURE was, as already observed, chiefly in poetry, and the production of laymen, whether the professional minstrels, or knights and even kings, who deemed it a gentlemanly accomplishment to sing as well as act the deeds of chivalry. RICHARD CŒUR DE LION (d. A. D. 1199) was the type of the latter class; and the style he cultivated and patronized was that of the *Troubadors* (see the text). Every one knows the legend of the discovery of the place of his captivity by his *tenson* with the minstrel Blondel, and his *sirvente* against his barons, composed in prison, has come down to us with a few other fragments.* (See the great work of Raynouard on Provençal Poetry). But the great mass of the poetry which the Normans brought in was that of the *Trouvères*. It may be arranged in four classes: — (1.) *Romances*, relating chiefly to these four cycles of legends: — *Charlemagne and his Paladins*, of whom the Norman minstrel Taillefer is said to have sung at Hastings; † *Arthur and his Knights*, founded on the legends of Wales and Brittany; *Cœur de Lion*, his exploits and sufferings; and *Alexander of Macedon*, the chief poem of this cycle (the *Alexandreïs*, A. D. 1184) giving its name to the *Alexandrine Verse*; — (2.) The *Fabliaux*, or Metrical Tales of Real Life, often derived from the East; — (3.) *Satires*, of which the Esopian fable was a common form, as in that tale common to Europe, *Reynard the Fox*; and (4.) *The Metrical Chronicles*. Of these last a most important example is the *Brut d'Angleterre* of WACE (d. after A. D. 1171), who also wrote, in French, the *Roman de Rou* (*Romance of Rollo*). His Brut, borrowed from Geoffrey of Monmouth, became the source of the *Brut* of Layamon (see below). Though this French poetry is of great importance in our literature, as it furnished both subjects and models for later English poets, there are few of its writers whose names require special mention. We have religious and moral poems in French of a very early date; and the universally accomplished ROBERT GROSSETESTE, Bishop of Lincoln, wrote in this as well as other styles. GEOFFREY DE VINSAUF composed metrical chronicles in French as well as Latin; and he had a rival in BENOIT DE

* The *sirvente* was a piece for one performer, the *tenson* a duet between two.

† There is a question, however, whether his song was of the Paladin Roland, or of Rollo, the founder of the Norman line.

ST. MAUR (fl. A. D. 1180), author of the *Romance of Troy* and *Chronicle of the Dukes of Normandy*. GEOFFREY GAIMAR (about A. D. 1148) wrote a *Chronicle of the Anglo-Saxon Kings*. THOROLD was the author of the *Roman de Roland*, and a *Roman d'Alexandre* is ascribed to THOMAS OF KENT, who is variously placed in the twelfth and fourteenth centuries. The *Roman de la Rose*, imitated by Chaucer, is the earliest French work of the thirteenth century. Other favorite romances were *Havelok the Dane*, the *Gest of King Horn*, *Bevis of Hampton*, and *Guy of Warwick*. Most of the authors of these works were native Englishmen, though they wrote in French, which had become almost the sole vehicle of popular literature.

The *Prose Versions of the Romances in Norman French* were written chiefly by Englishmen. The most important series was formed by those of Arthur, containing the *Roman de St. Graal* (or *Holy Cup*), the *Roman de Merlin*, the *Roman de Lancelot*, the *Quête du St. Graal*, and the *Roman de la Mort Arthus;* with a sequel, in two parts, the *Roman de Tristan* (or Tristrem). The chief writer was WALTER MAPES (already mentioned); but the *St. Graal*, *Merlin*, and second part of *Tristan*, were by ROBERT DE BARRON, and the first part of the *Tristan* by LUCES DE GAST.

A digest of these romances, made by Sir Thos. Malory, who was alive under Edward IV., has been edited by Mr. Wright, from the last black-letter edition of 1634, under the title of "*La Mort d'Arthure*. The History of King Arthur and the Knights of the Round Table," London, 1858.

Excepting some versions of portions of Scripture, these are the only important works in Anglo-Norman prose, till we come to the grand *Chronicle* of SIRE JEAN FROISSART, the liveliest picture which an imaginative historian ever drew of events witnessed for the most part by himself. Froissart was born at Valenciennes about A. D. 1337, but his Chronicle extends over the whole reigns of Edward III. and Richard II. (A. D. 1326-1400). He was also a great poet, and on his last visit to England (1396) he presented his poetical works to King Richard II.

C.—SEMI-SAXON LITERATURE.
A. D. 1150-1250.

The end of the *Saxon Chronicle* marks the close of the old Anglo-Saxon Language, as well as Literature; for the chronicler does not throw down his pen before he has begun to confuse his grammar and to corrupt his vocabulary with French words. The language dies out in literature, to appear again as almost a new creation, the basis of our English, but not at first in a finished form. The state of transition occupies two centuries, from about the accession of Henry II. (1154) to the middle of the reign of Edward III. (1350), when Chaucer rose. The compositions of this age can hardly be divided by any clear line of demarcation; but the first of the two centuries, to the middle of Henry III.'s reign, may be conveniently assigned to the *Semi-Saxon* period, the second to the *Old English*. The writers in both dialects were for the most part translators and imitators of the Norman poets; and their works may be assigned to the same four heads. There are, however, a few more original fragments such as the *Song of Canute*, as he rowed past Ely, recorded by the monk of Ely, who wrote about A. D. 1166; the *Hymn* of ST. GODRIC (d. A. D. 1170), and the *Prophecy*, said by various chroniclers to have been set up at *Here* (A. D. 1189). But three chief works may be chosen as most characteristic of the language of the Semi-Saxon period.

(1.) LAYAMON'S *Brut*, or *Chronicle of Britain*, of which there are two texts, one much earlier than the other. The title of "the English Ennius," formerly applied to Robert of Gloucester, may now fairly be transferred to Layamon. He tells us that he was a priest of Ernley, near Redstone, on the Severn (probably *Lower Arley*), and that he compiled his work partly from a book in *English* by St. Bede, which can only mean the translation of the *Historia Ecclesiastica* ascribed to Alfred, partly from one in *Latin* by St. Albin and Austin, and partly from one made by a *French* clerk, named Wace, and presented to Eleanor, queen of Henry II. He seems, however, to have followed only Bede in the story of Pope Gregory and the English slaves at Rome; his second authority appears to be but a confused reference to the Latin text of the Historia Ecclesiastica; and his work was really founded upon the *Brut* of Wace, already noticed. This he amplified from 15,300 lines to 32,250, partly by paraphrasing, partly by inserting speeches and other compositions, such as the Dream of Arthur, which show much imaginative power, and partly by the addition of many legends, from Welsh and other sources not used by Geoffrey of Monmouth. He makes several allusions to works in English which are now lost. The date of the completion of the work, usually assigned to the latter years of Henry II., should probably be brought below A. D. 1200, after John's accession. The style of the work bears witness to Norman influence, both in the structure of the verse and the manner of the narrative, but not nearly so much as might have been expected from the translator of a French original. The earlier text has not fifty words of French origin, and both texts only about ninety. "We find preserved," says Sir F. Madden, "in many passages of Layamon's poem the spirit and style of the earlier Anglo-Saxon writers. No one can read his description of battles without being reminded of the Ode on Athelstan's victory at Brunanburgh." After noticing resemblances in grammar and languages, he adds, "A foreign scholar and poet (Grundtvig), versed both in Anglo-Saxon and Scandinavian literature, has found Layamon's beyond comparison the most lofty and animated in its style, at every moment reminding the reader of the splendid phraseology of Anglo-Saxon verse. It may also be added, that the colloquial character of much of the work renders it peculiarly valuable as a monument of the language, since it serves to convey to us, in all probability, the current speech of the writer's time." (*Preface*, pp. xxiii., xxiv.) His verse also retains the alliterative structure of the Anglo-Saxon poetry mingled with the rhyming couplets of the French the former predominating. Besides *alliteration*, which consists in the sameness of initial consonants, Layamon uses the kindred device of *assonance*, that is, the concurrence of syllables containing the same vowel. The rhyming couplets are founded (as Dr. Guest has shown, *History of English*

Rhythms, vol. ii., pp. 114 foll.) on the Anglo-Saxon rhythms of four, five, six, or seven accents, those of five and six being the most frequent. The important bearing of Layamon's dialect on the history of the formation of the English language is fully discussed by Sir F. Madden (*Preface*, pp. xxv.-xxviii.), who concludes that "the dialects of the western, southern, and midland counties contributed together to form the language of the twelfth and thirteenth centuries, and consequently to lay the foundation of modern English. To the historical student the work is important as the last and fullest form of the old Celtic traditions concerning early British history. (*Layamon's Brut, &c., with a Literal Translation, Notes, and a Grammatical Glossary.* By Sir Frederick Madden, K. H. Published by the Soc. of Ant., 3 vols., 1847.)

(2.) *The Ancren Riwle* (the Rule of Female Anchorites, *i. e. Nuns*) a code of monastic precepts, drawn up in prose by an unknown author, about the end of the twelfth century or beginning of the thirteenth, and edited for the Camden Society by the Rev. James Morton, 1853, is also most valuable for the history of our language. Its proportion of French words is about four times that of Layamon; the English is rude and the spelling uncouth.

(3.) The *Ormulum* is so called by its author after his own name, ORM or ORMIN. It was a series of homilies in verse on the Lessons from the New Testament in the Church Service, on an immense scale. The extant portion contains nearly 10,000 lines (or rather couplets) of fifteen syllables, only differing from the "common service metre" by ending with an unaccented syllable, and entirely free from the Anglo-Saxon alliteration. Apart from the peculiar system of spelling, to which the author attaches great importance, and which deserves study, its language differs far less than Layamon's from the English of the present day. Written in the east or north-east (perhaps near Peterborough) the Ormulum occupies in the Anglian literature a place answering to that of the *Brut* in the Saxon; and it tends to prove that the former dialect was the first to throw off the old inflections. The work only exists in one MS. (in the Bodleian Library), which is thought to be the autograph; its handwriting, ink, and material, seem to assign it to the earlier part of the thirteenth century. The character of the language, and the regular rhythm of the verse, however, lead some to place it decidedly after the middle of the thirteenth century, and therefore in the *Old English* period.

The versification seems to be modelled on the contemporary Latin poetry. The language has a small admixture of Latin ecclesiastical words, with scarcely a trace of Norman French. "I am much disposed to believe," says Mr. Marsh (*Origin and History, &c.*, p. 179), "that the spelling of the Ormulum constitutes as faithful a representation of the oral English of its time as any one work could be at a period of great confusion of speech." The work has been edited with Notes and a Glossary, by R. M. White, D. D., 2 vols., Oxf. 1852.

Other works in Semi-Saxon that have been printed are the *Homily of St. Edmund*, in Thorpe's *Analecta*, the *Bestiary* and *Proverbs* falsely ascribed to King Alfred, in the *Reliquiæ Antiquæ*, the *Address of the Soul to the Body*, printed by Sir Thomas Phillipps in 1838, and reprinted by Mr. Singer in 1845; and the *Legend of St. Catharine*, edited by Mr. Morton for the Abbotsford Club, in 1841.

D. — OLD ENGLISH LITERATURE.
A. D. 1250-1350.

By the middle of the reign of Henry III. the language finally lost those inflectional and other peculiarities which distinguish the Anglo-Saxon from the English; but it retains archaisms which sufficiently distinguish it from the language of the present day to justify the title of *Old English*.

Some regard the short proclamation of Henry III., in A. D. 1258, as the earliest monument of Old English, while others consider it as Semi-Saxon. It is printed and fully discussed by Marsh (*Origin and History, &c.*, pp. 189, foll.). The *Surtees Psalter* stands also on the line dividing the two periods, being probably not later than A. D. 1250.

Among the chief literary works of this period is the metrical *Chronicle* of ROBERT OF GLOUCESTER, from the legendary age of Brutus to the close of Henry III.'s reign. The latter part, at all events, must have been written after A. D. 1297. The earlier part closely follows Geoffrey of Monmouth, but the old prose chronicler is more truly poetical than his metrical imitator. The verse is the long line (or couplet) of fourteen syllables, divisible into eight and six; its movement is rough and inharmonious. The *Chronicle* was printed from incorrect MSS., by Hearne, 2 vols. 8vo., Oxon., 1724; and this edition was reprinted in London, 1810. Short works by Robert of Gloucester, on the *Martyrdom of Thomas à Becket* and the *Life of St. Brandan*, were printed by the Percy Society in 1845. A collection of Lives of the Saints is also attributed to this author, whose works, though of small literary merit, are valuable for the light they throw on the progress of the English language.

On a still larger scale is the metrical chronicle of ROBERT MANNYNG, or ROBERT OF BRUNNE, the last considerable work of the Old English period. It is in two parts. The first, translated from the *Brut* of Wace, reaches to the death of Cadwallader; the second, from the Anglo-Norman of Peter de Langtoft, comes down to the death of Edward I. (A. D. 1307). The second part only has been published, with the editions of Robert of Gloucester mentioned above. The work is evidently an imitation of Robert's, and of about equal literary merit. The language is a step nearer to modern English, the most important changes being the use of *s* for *th* in the third person singular, and the introduction of nearly the present forms of the feminine personal pronoun. The verse is smoother than that of Robert of Gloucester. The first part is in the eight-syllable line of Wace; the second is partly in the same metre, and partly in the Alexandrine, the heroic measure of the age.

Far more interesting in themselves are the popular poems of this age, translated or imitated for the most part from the French, and belonging to the same classes of *Romances*, *Fabliaux*, and *Satires*. But there are some ballads and songs of genuine native origin, as early as the middle of the thirteenth century. Such are the story of the Norfolk peasant-boy, *Willy Grice;* the song beginning "Sumer is i-cumen in," the oldest to which the notes are added, and many of the pieces (including political ballads) printed by Warton, Percy, Ritson, and Wright.

One of the most pleasing of these poems is the *Owl and Nightingale*, a dispute between the two birds about their powers of song, consisting of about 1800 verses in rhymed octosyllabic metre.

The satirical poem, called the *Land of Cockayne*, which Warton placed before the reign of Henry II., is at least as late as A. D. 1300, and is clearly traced to a French original. It is somewhat doubtfully ascribed, with other poems, to MICHAEL OF KILDARE, the first Irishman who wrote verses in English. It is a satire upon the monks. That the *Metrical Romances* should have been translated from the French, is a natural result of the fact, that French was the language of popular literature for some generations after the Conquest. Many of the legends were, indeed, British and Anglo-Saxon; but this may be accounted for by the affinity of the Britons and Armoricans, and the close connection between the Norman and the later Anglo-Saxon kings. Nor is it probable that the *Trouvères* should have missed many of these legends. Their poetry at first amused the leisure and enlivened the banquets of the conquerors; but, as the two races became one, and as the Anglo-Saxon tongue died out, they began to be translated into the new-formed language of the English people. The most popular of these, such as *Havelok*, *Sir Tristram*, *Sir Gawaine*, *Kyng Horn*, *King Alesaunder*, and *Richard Cœur de Lion*, may be referred to the beginning of Edward I.'s reign. They are followed by a series of poems by unknown authors, far too numerous to mention, down to and considerably below the age of Chaucer, many of which are printed in the collections mentioned below. The change, by which these English Metrical Romances superseded the French originals, may be referred to the fourteenth century. In the fifteenth their popularity, besides being divided with the prose romances, yielded, at least among the educated classes, to the regular poetry of Chaucer and his school; but they only ceased to be generally written after the beginning of the sixteenth. It was not till three hundred years later that Sir Walter Scott revived the taste for a kind of poetry, similar in form, but appealing to very different sentiments. Among the *Minor Poems*, other than Romances, are many imitations of the French *Fabliaux*, or Tales of Common Life. The *Satires*, both political and ecclesiastical, undoubtedly helped the progress of freedom under Henry III. and his successors, and prepared the way for Wickliffe, if they do not rather exhibit a state of popular feeling demanding such a teacher.

The chief authorities for these four periods are Wright, *Biographia Britannica Literaria*. Vol. I. *The Anglo-Saxon Period*, Lond. 1842; Vol. II. *The Anglo-Norman Period*, Lond. 1846; Percy, *Reliques of Ancient English Poetry*, first published in 1765; Warton, *History of English Poetry*, 1774, edited by Price, 3 vols. 8vo., Lond. 1840; Tyrwhitt, *Chaucer's Canterbury Tales*, with Preliminary Essays, 1775; Pinkerton, *Scottish Poems*, 3 vols. 1792; Herbert, *Robert the Devylle*, 1798; Ritson, *Ancient Songs*, and other collections; Ellis, George, *Specimens of Early English Metrical Romances*, 3 vols. 8vo. 1805; Wright, *Political Songs of England* from John to Edward II., 1839; the publications of the Roxburghe Club, the Bannatyne, Maitland, Abbotsford, and Camden Societies, the Society of Antiquaries, &c.; Chambers, *Cyclopædia of English Literature;* Craik, *History of English Literature and the English Language*, 2 vols., 1861; Marsh, *Origin and History of the English Language*, 1862.

CHAPTER II.

THE AGE OF CHAUCER. A. D. 1350—A D. 1400.

§ 1. The fourteenth century a great period of transition — Chaucer, the type of his age. § 2. His literary predecessors, especially GOWER. § 3. Influence of WICLIFFE. § 4. CHAUCER: his personal history, character, and appearance § 5. Two periods in his literary career, corresponding to the *Romantic* and *Renaissance* tendencies. The religious element: his relations to Wicliffe. § 6. Critical survey of his works. Of the Romantic type: — (i.) *Romaunt of the Rose;* (ii.) *Court of Love;* (iii.) *Assembly of Fowls;* (iv.) *Cuckow and Nightingale;* (v.) *The Flower and the Leaf;* (vi.) *Chaucer's Dream;* (vii.) *Boke of the Duchesse;* (viii.) *House of Fame.* Of the Renaissance type: (ix.) The *Legende of Good Women;* (x.) *Troilus and Cresseide.* § 7. The CANTERBURY TALES; the Prologue and Portrait Gallery. § 8. Plan incomplete. The existing Tales; their arrangement, metrical forms, and sources. § 9. Critical examination of the chief Tales, in their two classes, serious and humorous. The two prose Tales. § 10. Chaucer's services to the English language.

§ 1. THE fourteenth century is the most important epoch in the intellectual history of Europe. It is the point of contact between two widely-differing eras in the social, religious, and political annals of our race; the slack water between the ebb of Feudalism and Chivalry, and the "young flood" of the Revival of Letters and the great Protestant Reformation. As in the long bright nights of the Arctic summer, the glow of the setting sun melts imperceptibly into the redness of the dawning, so do the last brilliant splendors of the feudal institutions and the chivalric literature transfuse themselves, at this momentous period, into the glories of that great intellectual movement which has given birth to modern art, letters, and science. Of this great transformation the personal career, no less than the works, of the first great English poet, CHAUCER, will furnish us with the most exact type and expression; for, like all men of the highest order of genius, he at once followed and directed the intellectual tendencies of his age, and is himself the "abstract and brief chronicle" of the spirit of his time. Dante is not more emphatically the representative of the moral, religious, and political ideas of Italy, than Chaucer of English literature. He was, indeed, an epitome of the time in which he lived; a time when chivalry, about to perish forever as a political institution, was giving forth its last and most dazzling rays, "and, like the sun, looked larger at its setting;" when the magnificent court of Edward III. had carried the splendor of that system to the height of its development; and when the victories of Sluys, of Crécy, and Poitiers, by exciting the national pride, tended to consummate the fusion into one vigorous nationality of the two elements which formed the English people and the English language. It was these triumphs that gave to the English character in peculiar *insularity;* and made the Englishman, whether knight or yeoman, regard himself as the member of a separate and superior race, enjoying a higher degree of liberty and a more solid material welfare than existed among the neighboring continental monarchies. The literature, too, abundant in quantity, if not remarkable for much originality of form, was rapidly taking a purely English tone; the rhyming chronicles and legendary romances were either translated into, or originally composed in, the vernacular language.

§ 2. Thus, among the predecessors of Chaucer, the literary stars that heralded the splendid dawning of our national poetry, Richard Rolle, Laurence Minot, and the remarkable satirist Langlande in South Britain, and Barbour, Wyntoun, and Blind Harry in Scotland, all show evident traces of a purely English spirit.* The immediate poetical predecessor of Chaucer, however, was undeniably GOWER, whose interminable productions, half moral, half narrative, and with a considerable infusion of the scholastic theology of the day, though they certainly will terrify a modern reader by their tiresome monotony and the absence of originality, rendered inestimable services to the infant literature, by giving regularity, polish, and harmony to the language. Indeed, the style and diction of Gower is surprisingly free from difficult and obsolete expressions; his versification is extremely regular, and he runs on in a full and flowing, if commonplace and unpoetical, stream of disquisition. It is very curious, as an example of the contemporary existence of the French, the Latin, and the vernacular literature at this period in England, that the three parts of Gower's immense work should have been composed in three different languages: the *Vox Clamantis* in Latin, the *Speculum Meditantis* in Norman-French, and the *Confessio Amantis* in English.†

§ 3. In endeavoring to form an idea of the intellectual situation of England in the fourteenth century, we must by no means leave out of the account the vast influence exerted by the preaching of Wicliffe, and the mortal blow struck by him against the foundations of Catholic supremacy in England. This, together with the general hostility excited by the intolerable corruptions of the monastic orders, which had gradually invaded the rights, the functions, and the possessions of the far more practically-useful working or parochial clergy, still further intensified that inquiring spirit which prompted the people to refuse obedience to the temporal as well as spiritual authority of the Roman See, and paved the way for an ultimate rejection of the Papal yoke. Much influence must also be attributed to Wicliffe's translation of the Bible into the English language, and to the gradual employment of that idiom in the services of the church, towards the perfecting and regulating of the English language; an influence similar in kind to the settlement of the German language by Luther's version of the same holy book, though, perhaps, less powerful in degree; for in the latter case

* For an account of Chaucer's predecessors, see Notes and Illustrations (A)

† For a fuller account of Gower, see Notes and Illustrations (B).

the reading class in Germany must have been more numerous than in the England of the fourteenth century.*

§ 4. Geoffrey Chaucer was born in 1328, and his long and active life extended till the 25th of October, 1400. Consequently the poet's career almost coincides, in its commencement, with the splendid administration of Edward III.; and comprehends also the short and disastrous reign of Richard II., whose assassination preceded the poet's death by only a few months. In the brilliant court of Edward, in the gay and fantastic tourney, as well as in the sterner contests of actual warfare, the poet appears to have played no insignificant part. He is supposed to have been sprung of wealthy, though not illustrious parentage, and must have been of gentle blood; his surname, which is the French *Chaussier*, evidently pointing at a continental — at that period equivalent, in a certain degree, to an aristocratic — origin. Besides this, we have distinct proof, not only in the fact of his having been "armed a knight" (which is shown by his evidence in the disputed cause of the Scrope and Grosvenor arms), but also in the honorable posts which he held, that Chaucer must have belonged to the higher sphere of society His marriage, too, with Philippa de Roet, a lady of Poitevin birth, the daughter of a knight, and one of the maids of honor in attendance upon Queen Philippa, would still further tend to confirm this supposition.

Though but little credit is due to the details set forth in the ordinary biographies of the poet, I will condense into a rapid sketch such as are best established; for every trait is interesting that helps us to realize the individual existence of so illustrious a man.

The inscription upon his tomb in Westminster Abbey, which still exists, though the recumbent Gothic statue of the poet, originally a portrait, has become unhappily so defaced that even the details of the dress are no longer distinguishable, fixes the period of his birth in 1328, and that of his death in 1400. This tomb, however, was not erected till 1556, by Mr. Nicholas Brigham, probably an admirer of his genius. Chaucer calls himself a *Londenois* or *Londener* in the *Testament of Love*. In his *Court of Love* he speaks of himself under the name and character of "Philogenet — *of Cambridge*, Clerk;" but this hardly proves that he was educated at Cambridge. According to an authentic record, he was taken prisoner in 1359 by the French at the siege of Rhétiers, and being ransomed, according to the custom of those times, was enabled to return to England, in 1360.

His marriage with Philippa de Roet, which took place in 1367, may have brought him more under the notice of the court; for in 1367 we find him named one of the "valets of the king's chamber," and writs are addressed to him under the then honorable designation "dilectus valettus noster." His official career appears to have been active and even distinguished: he enjoyed during a long period various profitable offices connected with the customs, having been comptroller of the

* For an account of Wicliffe and his school, see Notes and Illustrations (C).

important revenue arising from the large importation of Bordeaux and Gascon wines into the port of London; and he seems also to have been occasionally employed in diplomatic negotiations. Thus, he was joined with two citizens of Genoa in a commission to Italy in 1373, on which occasion he is supposed to have made the acquaintance of Petrarch, then the most illustrious man of letters in Europe. Partly in consequence of his marriage with Philippa de Roet, whose sister, Catherine Swynford, was first the mistress and afterwards the wife of John of Gaunt, and partly perhaps from sharing in some of the political and religious opinions of that powerful prince, Chaucer was identified to a considerable degree both with the household and party of the duke of Lancaster; and the death of the duchess Blanche in 1369 is believed to have suggested to him the subject of his *Boke of the Duchesse*, and the *Complaynte of the Blacke Knyght*. One of the most interesting particulars of his life was his election as representative for Kent in the parliament of 1386, which was dissolved in December of the same year.

The year 1382 was the signal for a great and unfavorable change in the poet's fortunes. In consequence of the active part taken by him in the struggle between the court and the city of London, on occasion of the re-election of John of Northampton to the mayoralty, Chaucer fell into disgrace and difficulty, and was exposed to serious persecution, and even imprisoned in the Tower, whence he is said to have attained his liberation only on condition of accusing and denouncing his associates. This imprisonment lasted three years; and in addition to heavy fines and the loss of his offices, the poet underwent a severe domestic calamity in the death of his wife, in 1387. The catastrophe in his affairs to which we have alluded was, however, followed by a partial restoration to favor; for in 1390 he was appointed to the office of clerk of the king's works, which he held for only about a year; and there is reason to believe that, though his pecuniary circumstances must have been, during a great part of his life, proportionable to the position he occupied in the state and in society, his last days were more or less clouded by embarrassment. It is with regret that we are obliged to abandon the supposition, founded on insufficient evidence, of his having resided, during the latter part of his life, at Donnington Castle. It is more probable that the close of his career was passed at Woodstock, where a house was long shown as having been the poet's residence. His death took place at Westminster, and the house in which this event occurred was afterwards removed to make room for the chapel of Henry VII.

If we may judge from an ancient and probably authentic portrait of Chaucer, attributed to his contemporary and fellow-poet, Occleve, as well as from a curious and beautiful miniature introduced, according to the fashion of those times, into one of the most valuable manuscript copies of his works, our great poet appears to have been a man of pleasing and acute, though somewhat meditative and abstracted countenance, wearing a long beard; and he seems to have become somewhat corpulent towards the end of his life, at which time the *Canterbury Tales* were written. These peculiarities of personal appearance, as well as some others, giving indications of his manners and character, are also alluded to by the poet himself in the *Tales* themselves. When Chaucer is in his turn called upon by the host of the Tabard, himself represented as a "large man," and a "faire burgess," to contribute his story to the amusement of the pilgrims, he is rallied by honest Harry Bailey on his corpulency, as well as on his studious and abstracted air: —

> "What man art thou?" quod he,
> "Thou lokest as thou woldest fynde an hare:
> For ever on the ground I se the stare.
> Approach nere, and loke merrily.
> Now ware you, sires, and let this man have space.
> He in the wast is shape as wel as I:
> This were a popet in an arm to embrace,
> For any womman, smal and fair of face.
> He semeth elvisch by his countenance,
> For unto no wight doth he dallaunce."

The good-nature with which the poet receives these jokes, and the readiness with which he commences a new story when uncourteously cut short, all seem to point to the gentlemanly and sociable qualities of an accomplished man of the world.

§ 5. The literary and intellectual career of Chaucer seems to divide itself naturally into two periods, closely corresponding with the two great social and political tendencies which meet in the fourteenth century. The earlier productions of Chaucer bear the stamp and character of the Chivalric, his later and more original creations of the Renaissance literature. It is more than probable that the poet's visits to Italy, then the fountain and centre of the great literary revolution, brought him into contact with the works and the men by whose example the change in the taste of Europe was brought about. Dante, it is true, died before the birth of Chaucer; and though his influence as a poet, a theologian, and a metaphysician, may not yet have fully reached England, yet Chaucer must have fallen under it in some degree. There is a third element in the character of Chaucer's writings, besides the imitation of the decaying Romance and the rising Renaissance literature, which must be taken into account by all who would form a true conception of his intellect; and this is the religious element. It is difficult to ascertain how far the poet sympathized with the bold doctrines of Wicliffe, who, like himself, was favored and protected by John of Gaunt, fourth son of Edward III. It is, however, probable, that though he sympathized — as is shown by a thousand satirical passages in his poems — with Wicliffe's hostility to the monastic orders and abhorrence of the corruptions of the clergy, and the haughty claims of papal supremacy, the poet did not share in the theological opinions of the reformer, then regarded as a dangerous heresiarch. Chaucer probably remained faithful to the creed of Catholicism, while attacking with irresistible satire the abuses of the Catholic ecclesiastical administration. How intense that satire is, may be gathered from the contemptible and odious traits which he has lavished on nearly all his portraits of monastic personages in the *Canterbury Tales;* and not less clearly from the strong contrast he has made between the sloth, sensuality, and trickery of these persons, and the almost ideal perfection of Christian virtue which he has associated with his Persoune, the only member of the secular or parochial clergy he has introduced into his inimitable gallery. It is by no means to be understood that the principal works of this great man can be ranged *chronologically* under the two strongly marked categories just specified; or that all those bearing manifest traces of the Provençal spirit and forms were written previously, and those of the Renaissance or Italian type subsequently, to any particular epoch in the poet's life; but only that his earlier productions bear a general stamp of the one, and his later of the other literary tendency; while the greatest and most original of all, the *Canterbury Tales*, may be placed in a class by itself.

§ **6.** A brief critical examination of Chaucer's works may serve to point out, however imperfectly, the boundless stores of imagination and pathos, of wisdom and of wit, which the father of English poetry has embodied in language that has never been surpassed, and seldom equalled, for harmony, variety, and picturesqueness. I shall reserve to the last the more detailed analysis of the *Canterbury Tales.* On a rough general inspection of the longer works which compose the rather voluminous collection of Chaucer's poetry, it will be found that about eight of them are to be ascribed to a direct or indirect imitation of purely Romance models, while three fall naturally under the category of the Italian or Renaissance type. Of the former class the principal are the *Romaunt of the Rose*, the *Court of Love*, the *Assembly of Fowls*, the *Cuckow and the Nightingale*, the *Flower and the Leaf*, *Chaucer's Dream*, the *Boke of the Duchesse*, and the *House of Fame.* Under the latter we must range the *Legend of Good Women*, *Troilus and Creseide*, *Anelyda and Arcyte*, and above all the *Canterbury Tales.*

(i.) The *Romaunt of the Rose* is a translation of the famous French allegory *Le Roman de la Rose*, which forms the earliest monument of French literature in the thirteenth century. The original is of inordinate length, containing, even in the unfinished state in which it was left, 22,000 verses, and it consists of two distinct portions, the work of two very different hands. It was begun by Guillaume de Lorris, who completed about 5000 lines, and was continued after his death by the witty and sarcastic Jean de Méun: the former of these authors died in 1260, and the latter probably about 1318, which will make him nearly the contemporary of Dante. The portion composed by Lorris has great poetical merit, much invention of incident, vivid character-painting, and picturesque description; the allegorical coloring of the whole, though wire-drawn and tedious to our modern taste, was then highly admired, and gave the tale immense popularity. The continuation by Méun, though following up the allegory, diverges into a much more satirical spirit, and abounds in what were then regarded as most audacious attacks on religion, social order, the court, and female reputation. Even at this distance of time it is impossible not to admire the boldness, the vivacity, and the severity of the satire. According to the almost universal practice of the old Romance poets, the story is put into the form of a dream or vision; and the principal allegoric personages introduced, as Hate, Felony, Avarice, Sorrow, Elde, Pope-Holy, Poverty, Idleness, &c., are of the same kind as usually figure in the poetical narratives of the age. Lover, the hero, is alternately aided and obstructed in his undertakings, the principal of which is that of culling the enchanted rose which gives its name to the poem, by a multitude of beneficent or malignant personages, such as Bel-Accueil, Faux-Semblant, Danger, Male-Bouche, and Constrained-Abstinence. Chaucer's translation, which is in the octosyllabic Trouvère measure of the original, and consists of 7699 verses, comprehends the whole of the portion written by Lorris, together with about a sixth part of Méun's continuation; the portions omitted having either never been translated by the English poet in consequence of his dislike of the immoral and anti religious tendency of which they were accused, or left out by the copyist from the early English manuscripts. The translation gives incessant proof of Chaucer's remarkable ear for metrical harmony, and also of his picturesque imagination; for though in many places he has followed his original with scrupulous fidelity, he not unfrequently adds vigorous touches of his own. Thus, for example, in the description of the Palace of Elde, a comparison between the original and the translation will show us a grand image entirely to be ascribed to the English poet: —

> Travail et Douleur la herbergent,
> Mais ils la tient et enfergent,
> Et tant la batent et tormentent,
> Que mort prochaine li présentent.

> With hir Laboùr and Travàile
> Logged ben with Sorwe and Woo,
> That never out of hir court goo.
> Peyne and Distresse, Sykenesse and Ire,
> And Malencoly, that angry sire,
> Ben of hir paleys senatoures;
> Gronyng and Grucchyng hir herbejeours,
> The day and nyght, hir to turment,
> And tellen hir, erliche and late,
> That Deth stondith armed at hir gate.

(ii.) The *Court of Love* is a work bearing, both in its form and spirit, strong traces of that amorous and allegorical mysticism which runs through all the Provençal poetry, and which seems to have been developed into substantive institutions in the Cours d'Amour of Picardy and Languedoc, whose *arrêts* form such a curious example of the refining scholastic subtleties of mediæval theology transferred to the fashions of chivalric society. It is written in stanzas of seven lines, each line being of ten syllables; the first and third rhyming together, as do the second, fourth, and fifth, and again the sixth and seventh. It is written in the name of "Philogenet of Cambridge," clerk (or student), who is directed by Mercury to appear at the Court of Venus. The above designation has induced some critics to suppose that the poet meant under it to indicate himself, and have drawn from it a most unfounded supposition that Chaucer had studied at Cambridge. The poet proceeds to give a description of the Castle of Love, where Admetus and Alcestis preside as king and queen. Philogenet is then conducted by Philobone to the Temple, where he sees Venus and Cupid, and where the oath of allegiance and obedience to the twenty commandments of Love is administered to the faithful. The hero is then presented to the Lady Rosial, with whom, in strict accordance with Provençal poetical custom, he has become enamoured in a dream. We then have a description of the courtiers, two of whom, Golden and Leaden Love, seem to be borrowed from the Eros and Anteros of the Platonic philosophers. The most curious part of the poem is the celebration of the grand festival of Love on May-day, when an exact parody of the Catholic Matin service for Trinity Sunday is chanted by various birds in honor of the God of Love.

(iii.) In the *Assembly of Fowls* we have a poem not very dissimilar in form and versification to the preceding. The subject is a debate carried on before the Parliament of Birds to decide the claims of three eagles for the possession of a beautiful *formel* (female or hen) of the same species, which perches upon the wrist of Nature. The principal incidents of this poem were probably borrowed from a *fabliau* to which Chaucer has alluded in another place, and the popularity of which is proved by the existence of several versions of the same subject, as for instance, *Hueline et Eglantine*, *Le Jugement d'Amour*, and *Florence et Blancheflor*.

(iv.) The *Cuckow and the Nightingale*, though of no great length, is one of the most charming among this class of Chaucer's productions: it describes a controversy between the two birds, the former of which was among the poets and allegorists of the Middle Ages the emblem of profligate celibacy, while the Nightingale is the type of constant and virtuous conjugal love. In this poem we meet with a striking example of that exquisite sensibility to the sweetness of external nature, and in particular to the song of birds, which was possessed by Chaucer in a higher degree, perhaps, than by any other poet in the world; as witness the following inimitable passage: —

"There sat I downe among the faire floures,
And sawe the birdes trippe out of hir boures,
There as they rested hem alle the night;
They were so joyful of the dayes light,
They began of May for to done honoures.

They coude that service al by rote;
There was many a lovely note!
Some songe loud as they had plained,
And some in other manner voice yfained,
And some al oute with the fulle throte,

They proyned hem, and maden hem right gay,
And daunceden and lepten on the spray
And evermore two and two in fere,
Right so as they had chosen hem to-yere
In Feverere upon Saint Valentine's day.

And the rivere that I sat upon,
It made such a noise as it ron,
Accordaunt with the birdes armony,
Me thought it was the beste melody
That mighte ben yheard of any man."

(v.) The *Flower and the Leaf* is, like the preceding poems, an allegory related in the form of a chivalric and pastoral adventure. A lady, unable to sleep, wanders out into a forest on a spring morning — an opening or *mise en scène* which often recurs in poems of this age — and seating herself in a delicious arbor, listens to the alternate song of the goldfinch and the nightingale. Her reverie is suddenly interrupted by the approach of a band of ladies clothed in white, and garlanded with laurel, agnus-castus, and woodbine. These accompany their queen in singing a roundel, and are in their turn interrupted by the sound of trumpets and by the appearance of nine armed knights, followed by a splendid train of cavaliers and ladies. These joust for an hour, and then advance to the first company, and each knight leads a lady to a laurel to which they make an obeisance. Another troop of ladies now approach, habited in green and led by a queen, who do reverence to a tuft of flowers, while the leader sings a "bargaret," or pastoral song, in honor of the daisy, "si douce est la Marguerite." The sports are broken off, first by the heat of the sun which withers all the flowers, and afterwards by a violent storm of thunder and rain, in which the knights and ladies in green are pitifully drenched; while the white company shelter themselves under the laurel. The queen and ladies in white then comfort and refresh the green band, and the whole retire to sup with the party of the white; the nightingale, as they pass along, flying down from the laurel to perch upon the hand of the white queen, while the goldfinch settles upon the wrist of the leader of the green party. Then follows the explanation of the allegory: the white queen and her party represent Chastity; the knights the Nine Worthies; the cavaliers crowned with laurel the Knights of the Round Table, the Peers of Charlemagne, and the Knights of the Garter, to which illustrious order, then recently founded, the poet wished to pay a compliment. The queen and ladies in green represent Flora and the followers of sloth and idleness. In general the flower typifies vain pleasure, the leaf, virtue and industry; the former being "a thing fading with every blast," while the latter "abides with the root, notwithstanding the frosts and winter storms." The poem is written in the seven-lined stanza, and contains many curious and beautiful passages.

(vi., vii.) The two poems entitled *Chaucer's Dream*, and the *Book of the Duchess*, though now found to be separate and distinct works, were long confounded together. This error was caused by the similarity of their style and versification (for they are both written in the octosyllabic Trouvère measure, the same as that employed in the *Romaunt of the Rose*), and in some degree also by the connection of their subject with John of Gaunt, Chaucer's friend and patron, and the marriage of that nobleman with Blanche, heiress of Lancaster. This prince, then bearing the title of Earl of Richmond, was united to his cousin in 1359, and the Duchess dying ten years after, John was married a second time, in 1371, to Constance, daughter of Peter the Cruel, King of Spain. Both poems are allegorical; and allude, though sometime rather obscurely as regards details, to the courtship of John of Gaunt and his grief, under the person of the Black Knight, at the loss of his first wife. There may be traced in the *Dream* allusions to Chaucer's own courtship and marriage, to which we have referred in our biographical remarks, and which took place about 1360.

(viii.) For its extraordinary union of brilliant description with learning and humor, the poem of the *House of Fame* is sufficient of itself to stamp Chaucer's reputation. It is written in the Trouvere measure, and under the fashionable form of a dream or vision, gives us a vivid and striking picture of the Temple of Glory, crowded with aspirants for immortal renown, and adorned with myriad statues of great poets and historians, and the House of Rumor, thronged with pilgrims, pardoners, sailors, and other retailers of wonderful reports. The Temple, though originally borrowed from the *Metamorphoses* of Ovid, exhibits in its architecture and adornment that strange mixture of pagan antiquity with the Gothic details of mediæval cathedrals, that strikes us in the poetry and in the illuminated MSS. of the fourteenth century: and in the description of the statues of the great poets we meet with a curious proof of that mingled influence of alchemical and astrological theories perceptible in the science and literature of Chaucer's age. In richness of fancy it far surpasses Pope's imitation, *The Temple of Fame*.

(ix.) The *Legend of Good Women* is supposed, from many circumstances, to have been one of the latest of Chaucer's compositions, and to have been written as a kind of *amende honorable* or recantation for his unfavorable pictures of female character; and in particular for his having, by translating the *Roman de la Rose*, to a certain degree identified himself with Jean de Méun's bitter sarcasms on the sex. Though the matter is closely translated, for the most part, from the *Heroides* of Ovid, the coloring given to the stories is entirely Catholic and mediæval. The misfortunes of celebrated heroines of ancient story are related in the manner of the Legends of the Saints, and Dido, Cleopatra, and Medea are regarded as the Martyrs of Saint Venus and Saint Cupid. The poet's original intention was to compose the legends of nineteen celebrated victims of the tender passion; but the work having been left incomplete, we possess only those of Cleopatra, Thisbe, Dido, Hypsipyle, Medea, Lucretia, Ariadne, Philomela, and Phillis. The poem is in ten-syllable heroic couplets, the rhymed heroic measure, and exhibits a consummate mastery over the resources of the

English language and prosody, and many striking passages of description interpolated by Chaucer. A few droll anachronisms also may be noted, as the introduction of cannon at the Battle of Actium.

(x.) The poem which the generations contemporary with, or succeeding to, the age of Chaucer placed nearest to the level of the *Canterbury Tales*, was unquestionably the *Troilus and Creseide;* and this judgment will be confirmed by a comparison of the two works; though the wonderful variety and humor of the *Tales* has tended to throw into the shade, for modern readers, the graver beauties of the poem we are now about to examine. The source from which Chaucer drew his materials for this work was indubitably Boccaccio's poem entitled *Filostrato*. The story itself, which was extremely popular in the Middle Ages (and its popularity continued down to the time of Elizabeth, Shakespeare himself having dramatized it), has been traced to Guido di Colonna, and to the mysterious book entitled *Trophe* of the equally mysterious author Lollius, so often quoted in Chaucer's age, and respecting whom all is obscure and enigmatical. Some of the names and personages of the story, as Cryseida (Chryseis), Troilus, Pandarus, Diomede, and Priam, are obviously borrowed from the *Iliad;* but their relative positions and personality have been most strangely altered; and the principal action of the poem, being the passionate love of Troilus for his cousin, her ultimate infidelity, the immoral subserviency of Pandarus, all of which became proverbial in consequence of the popularity of this tale, — all details, in short, bear the stamp of mediæval society, and have no resemblance whatever to the incidents and feelings of the heroic age, a period when the female sex was treated as it is now in Eastern countries, and when consequently that sentiment, which we call chivalric or romantic love, could have had no existence. Chaucer has frequently adhered to the text of the *Filostrato*, and has adopted the musical and flowing Italian stanza of seven lines; but in the conduct of the story he has shown himself far superior to his original, the characters of Troilus, Pandarus, and Creseide in the *Filostrato*, contrasting very unfavorably with the pure, noble, and ideal personages of the English poet, whose morality, indeed, is far higher and more refined than that of his great Florentine contemporary. I may remark in conclusion, that this beautiful poem is of great length, nearly equal in this respect to the Æneid of Virgil, and that it abounds in charming descriptions, in exquisite traits of character, and in incidents which, though simple and natural, are involved and developed with great ingenuity.

§ 7. Chaucer's greatest and most original work is, beyond all comparison, the *Canterbury Tales*. It is in this that he has poured forth in inexhaustible abundance all his stores of wit, humor, pathos, splendor, and knowledge of humanity: it is this which will place him, till the remotest posterity, in the first rank among poets and character-painters.

The exact portraiture of the manners, language, and habits of society in a remote age could not fail, even if executed by an inferior hand, to possess deep interest; as we may judge from the avidity with which we contemplate such traits of real life as are laboriously dug up by the patient curiosity of the antiquary from the dust and rubbish of bygone days. How great then is our delight when the magic force of a great poet evokes a whole series of our ancestors of the fourteenth century, making them pass before us "in their habit as they lived,' acting, speaking, and feeling in a manner invariably true to general nature and stamped with all the individuality of Shakespeare or Molière The plan of the *Canterbury Tales* is singularly happy, enabling the poet to give us, first, a collection of admirable daguerreotypes of the various classes of English society, and then to place in the mouths of these persons a series of separate tales highly beautiful when regarded as compositions and judged on their own independent merits, but deriving an infinitely higher interest and appropriateness from the way in which they harmonize with their respective narrators. The work can be divided into two portions, which are, however, skilfully mixed up and incorporated: the first being the general *prologue*, describing the occasion on which the pilgrims assemble, the portraits of the various members of the troop, the adventures of their journey and their commentaries on the tales as they are successively related: and the second the tales themselves, viewed as separate compositions.

The general plan of the work may be briefly sketched as follows. The poet informs us, after giving a brief but picturesque description of spring, that being about to make a pilgrimage from London to the shrine of St. Thomas à Becket in the Cathedral of Canterbury, he passes the night previous to his departure at the hostelry of the Tabard in Southwark. While at the inn the hostelry is filled by a crowd of pilgrims bound to the same destination:—

"In Southwerk at the Tabard as I lay,
Redy to wenden on my pilgrimage
To Canterbury with ful devout corage,
At night was come into that hostelrie
Wel nyne and twenty in a companye *
Of sondry folk, by aventure i-falle
In felawschipe, and pilgryms were thei alle,
That toward Canterbury wolden ryde."

The goodly company, assembled in a manner so natural in those times of pilgrimages and of difficult and dangerous roads, agree to travel in a body; and at supper the Host of the Tabard, a jolly and sociable personage, proposes to accompany the party and serve as a guide, having, as he says, often travelled the road before; and at the same time suggests that they may much enliven the tedium of their journey by relating stories as they ride. He is to be accepted by the whole society as a kind of judge or moderator, by whose decisions every one is to abide. As the journey to Canterbury occupies one day, and the return another, the plan of the whole work, had Chaucer completed it,

* But in his subsequent enumeration (see next page) Chaucer counts thirty persons.

would have comprised the adventures on the outward journey, the arrival at Canterbury, a description, in all probability, of the splendid religious ceremonies and the visits to the numerous shrines and relics in the Cathedral, the return to London, the farewell supper at the Tabard, and dissolution of the pleasant company, which would separate as naturally as they had assembled. Harry Bailey proposes that each pilgrim should relate two tales on the journey out, and two more on the way home; and that on the return of the party to London, he who should be adjudged to have related the best and most amusing story should sup at the common cost. Such is the *setting* or framework in which the separate tales are inserted; and the circumstances and general *mise en scène* are so natural and unforced, that no reader refuses credence to the ancient tradition of our great poet's having founded his work upon an actual pilgrimage to Canterbury, in which he had himself taken part. The tales themselves are admirably in accordance with the characters of the persons who relate them, and the remarks and criticisms to which they give rise are no less humorous and natural; some of the stories suggesting others, just as would happen in real life under the same circumstances. The pilgrims are persons of all ranks and classes of society; and in the inimitable description of their manners, persons, dress, horses, &c., with which the poet has introduced them, we behold a vast and minute portrait gallery of the social state of England in the fourteen century. They are — (1.) A Knight; (2.) A Squire; (3.) A Yeoman, or military retainer of the class of the free peasants, who in the quality of an archer was bound to accompany his feudal lord to war; (4.) A Prioress, a lady of rank, superior of a nunnery; (5, 6, 7, 8.) A Nun and three Priests, in attendance upon this lady; (9.) A Monk, a person represented as handsomely dressed and equipped, and passionately fond of hunting and good cheer; (10.) A Friar, or Mendicant Monk; (11.) A Merchant; (12.) A Clerk, or Student of the University of Oxford; (13.) A Serjeant of the Law; (14.) A Franklin or rich country-gentleman; (15, 16, 17, 18, 19.) Five wealthy burgesses or tradesmen, described in general but vigorous and characteristic terms; they are A Haberdasher, or dealer in silk and cloth, A Carpenter, A Weaver, A Dyer, and A Tapisser, or maker of carpets and hangings; (20.) A Cook, or rather what in old French is called a *rôtisseur*, i. e. the keeper of a cook's-shop; (21.) A Shipman, the master of a trading vessel; (22.) A Doctor of Physic; (23.) A Wife of Bath, a rich cloth-manufacturer; (24.) A Parson, or secular parish priest; (25.) A Ploughman, the brother of the preceding personage; (26.) A Miller; (27.) A Manciple, or steward of a college or religious house; (28.) A Reeve, bailiff or intendant of the estates of some wealthy landowner; (29.) A Sompnour, or Sumner, an officer in the then formidable ecclesiastical courts, whose duty was to summon or cite before the spiritual jurisdiction those who had offended against the canon laws; (30.) A Pardoner, or vendor of Indulgences from Rome. To these thirty persons must be added Chaucer himself, and the Host of the Tabard, making in all thirty-two.

§ 8. Now, if each of these pilgrims had related four tales, viz., two on the journey to Canterbury, and two on their return, the work would have contained 128 stories, independently of the subordinate incidents and conversations. In reality, however, the pilgrims do not arrive at their destination, and there are many evidences of confusion in the tales which Chaucer has given us, leading to the conclusion that the materials were not only incomplete, but left in an unarranged state by the poet. The stories that we possess are 25 in number, and are distributed as follows: The Knight; The Miller; The Reeve; The Cook, to whom two tales are assigned; * The Man of Law; The Wife of Bath; The Friar; The Sompnour; The Clerk of Oxford; The Merchant; The Squire, whose tale is left unfinished; The Franklin; The Second Nun; The Canon's Yeoman — a personage who does not form a part of the original company, but joins the cavalcade on the journey; The Doctor; The Pardoner; The Shipman; The Prioress; Chaucer himself, to whom two tales are assigned in a manner to which I shall refer presently; The Monk; the Nun's Priest; The Manciple, and the Parson. Thus it will be seen that many of the characters are left silent, while some of them relate more than one story, and two persons altogether extraneous are introduced. These are the Canon and his Yeoman, who unexpectedly join the cavalcade during the journey; but it is uncertain whether this episode, which was probably an afterthought of the poet, takes place on the journey to or from Canterbury. The Canon, who is represented as an Alchemist, half swindler and half dupe, is driven away from the company by shame at his attendant's indiscreet disclosures; and the latter, remaining with the pilgrims, relates a most amusing story of the villanous artifices of the charlatans who pretended to possess the Great Arcanum. The stories narrated by the pilgrims are admirably introduced by what the author calls "prologues," consisting either of remarks and criticisms on the preceding tale, and which naturally suggest what is to follow, of the incidents of the journey itself, an excellent example of which is the drunken uproariousness of the Miller and the Cook, or of the infinitely varied manner in which the Host proposes and the Pilgrims receive the command to perform their part in contributing to the common entertainment. The Tales are all in verse, with the exception of two, that of the Parson, and Chaucer's second narrative, the allegorical story of Melibœus and his wife Patience. Those in verse exhibit an immense variety of metricial forms, ranging from the regular heroic rhymed couplet, in which the largest portion of the work is composed, as well as the general prologue and introductions to each story, through a great variety of stanzas of different lengths and arrangement, down to the short irregular octosyllable verse of the Trouvère Gestours, and — in the case of the Tale of Gamelyn — the

* The first is broken off abruptly almost at the beginning, and the second is by some suspected not to be the work of Chaucer at all, as it is written in a style and versification unlike the rest of his poems, and seems to belong to an older and ruder period of English literature. The Cook's Tale of *Gamelyn*, if really written by Chaucer, was perhaps intended to be related on the journey home.

long tonic, not syllabic, measure of the old English popular legend, which was itself a relic of the ancient Saxon metrical system. All these forms Chaucer handles with consummate ease and dexterity; indeed, it may be boldly affirmed that no English poet whatever is more exquisitely melodious than he: and the nature of the versification will often assist us in tracing the sources from whence Chaucer derived or adapted his materials. Of him it may be truly said, as Molière affirmed of himself, that "il prenait son bien où il le trouvait," for he appears in no single demonstrable instance to have taken the trouble to invent the intrigue or subject-matter of any of his stories, but to have freely borrowed them either for the multitudinous fabliaux of the Provençal poets, the legends of the mediæval chroniclers, or the immense storehouse of the Gesta Romanorum, and the rich treasury of the early Italian writers, Dante, Petrarch, and Boccaccio.

§ 9. The Tales themselves may be roughly divided into the two great classes of serious, tragic, or pathetic, and comic or humorous; in both styles Chaucer has seldom been equalled, and assuredly never surpassed. His wonderful power of object and character-painting, the incomparable conciseness and vividness of his descriptions, the loftiness of his sentiment, and the intensity of his pathos, can only be paralleled by the richness of his humor and the outrageously droll, yet perfectly natural extravagance of his laughable scenes. Both in the one style and in the other, the peculiar *naiveté* and sly infantine simplicity of his language add a charm of the subtlest kind, the reality of which is best proved by the evaporation of this delicate perfume in the process, so often and so unsuccessfully attempted, of modernizing his language. The finest of the elevated and pathetic stories are the *Knight's Tale* — the longest of them all, in which is related the adventure of Palamon and Arcite; — the *Squire's Tale*, a wild half-Oriental story of love, chivalry, and enchantment, the action of which goes on "at Sarray (Bakhtchi-Sarai) in the lond of Tartary;" the *Man of Law's Tale*, the beautiful and pathetic story of Custance; the *Prioress's Tale*, the charming legend of "litel Hew of Lincoln," the Christian child murdered by the Jews for so perseveringly singing his hymn to the Virgin; and above all the *Clerk of Oxford's Tale*, perhaps the most beautiful pathetic narration in the whole range of literature. This, the story of Griselda, the model and heroine of wifely patience and obedience, is the crown and pearl of all the serious and pathetic narratives, as the Knight's Tale is the masterpiece among the descriptions of love and chivalric magnificence.

I will rapidly note the sources from which, as far as can be ascertained at present, Chaucer derived the subjects of the narratives above particularized. The *Knight's Tale* is freely borrowed from the *Theseida* of Boccaccio, many of the incidents of the latter being themselves taken from the *Thebais* of Statius. Though the action and personages of this noble story are assigned to classical antiquity, it is needless to say that the sentiments, manners, and feelings of the persons introduced are those of chivalric Europe; the "Two Noble Kinsmen," Palamon and Arcite, being the purest ideal types of the knightly character, and the decision of their claims to the hand of Emilie by a combat in *champ clos*, an incident completely alien from the habits of the heroic age. The *Squire's Tale* bears evident marks of Oriental origin; but whether it be a legend directly derived from Eastern literature, or received by Chaucer after having filtered through a Romance version, is now uncertain. It is equal to the preceding story in splendor and variety of incident and word-painting, but far inferior in depth of pathos and ideal elevation of sentiment; yet it was by the *Squire's Tale* that Milton characterized Chaucer in that inimitable passage of the *Penseroso* where he evokes the recollections of the great poet: —

"And call up him that left half-told
The story of Cambuscan bold,
Of Cambal, and of Algarsife,
And who had Canace to wife
That owned the virtuous ring and glass;
And of the wondrous horse of brass
On which the Tartar king did ride."

The *Man of Law's Tale* is taken with little variation from Gower's voluminous poem "*Confessio Amantis*," the incidents of Gower's narrative being in their turn traceable to a multitude of romances, as for instance those of *Emare*, the *Chevalier au Cygne*, the *Roman de la Violette*, *Le Bone Florence de Rome*, and the inexhaustible *Gesta Romanorum*. The character of the noble but unhappy Custance, beautiful as it is, is idealized almost beyond nature; and the employment of the Italian stanza harmonizes well with the tender but somewhat enervated graces of the narrative. The legend of the "litel clergion," foully murdered by the Jews at Lincoln, and whose martyrdom is so miraculously attested, was in all probability founded on fact, at least so far as regards cruel punishment having been inflicted on the Jews accused of such a crime. An infinity of ballads were current in England and Scotland on this subject, and one indeed has been preserved in Percy's *Reliques of Ancient English Poetry*, entitled "The Jewes Daughter." Moreover there still exists a record of the trial of some Jews for the assassination of a Christian child at Lincoln in 1256, in the reign of Henry III. Though Chaucer has retained the principal incidents of the English legend, he has laid the scene in Asia; but many allusions to the story of Hugh of Lincoln prove that the fundamental action is identically the same. The tale is exquisitely tender and graceful in sentiment, and exhibits precisely that union of religious sentimentality and refinement which makes it so appropriate in the mouth of Madame Eglantine the Prioress.

The pedigree of the most pathetic of Chaucer's stories, that of Patient Griselda, narrated by the clerk of Oxford, is traceable to Petrarch, who communicated the incidents to his friend Boccaccio. The latter has made them the groundwork of one of the novels of the *Decameron*, viz., the 10th and last of the Tenth Day; and there is evidence that the pathos of this beautiful story was found to transgress the limits of ordinary endurance. The submission of Griselda to the ordeals imposed upon her conjugal and maternal feelings by the diabolical tyranny of the Marquis of Saluzzo, her husband, seems exaggerated beyond all the bounds of reality. Yet we should remember that the very intensity of Griselda's sufferings is intended to convey the highest expression of the inexhaustible goodness of the female heart.

The finest of Chaucer's comic and humorous stories are those of the Miller, the Reeve, the Sompnour, the Canon's Yeoman, and the Nun's Priest. Though all of these are excellent, the three best are the Miller's, the Reeve's, and the Sompnour's; and among these last it is difficult to give the palm of drollery, acute painting of human nature, and exquisite ingenuity of incident. It is much to be regretted that the comic stories turn upon events of a kind which the refinement of modern manners renders it impossible to analyze; but it should be remembered that society in Chaucer's day, though perhaps not less moral in reality, was far more outspoken and simple, and permitted and enjoyed allusions which have been proscribed by the more precise delicacy of later ages. The first of these irresistible drolleries is probably the adaptation to English life — for the scene is laid at Oxford — of some old fabliau; the *Reeve's Tale* may be found in substance in the 6th novel of the Ninth Day of the *Decameron:* the *Sompnour's Tale*, though probably from a mediæval source, has not hitherto been traced. The admirable wit, humor, and learning, with which in the *Canon's Yeoman's Tale* Chaucer exposes the rascalities of the pretenders to alchemical knowledge, may have been derived from his own experience of the arts of these swindlers. The tale may be compared with Ben Jonson's comedy of the *Alchemist*. The tale assigned to the Nun's Priest is an exceedingly humorous apologue of the Cock and the Fox, in which, though the *dramatis personæ* are animals, they are endowed with such a droll similitude to the human character, that the reader enjoys at the same time the apparently incompatible pleasures of sympathizing with them as human beings, and laughing at their fantastic assumption of reason as lower creatures.

I have remarked, some pages back, on the circumstance of two of the stories being written in prose. It may be not uninteresting to investigate this exception. When Chaucer is applied to by the Host, he commences a rambling puerile romance of chivalry, entitled the *Rhyme of Sir Thopas*, which promises to be an interminable story of knight-errant adventures, combats with giants, dragons, and enchanters, and is written in the exact style and metre of the Trouvère narrative poems — the only instance of this versification being employed in the *Canterbury Tales*. He goes on gallantly "in the style his books of chivalry had taught him," and, like Don Quixote, "imitating, as near as he could, their very phrase;" but he is suddenly interrupted, with many expressions of comic disgust, by the merry host: —

> "'No mor of this, for Goddes dignite!'
> Quod our Hoste, 'for thou makest me
> So wery of thy verray lewednesse,
> That, al so wisly God my soule blesse,

Myn eeres aken for thy drafty speche.
Now such a rym the devel I byteche!
This may wel be rym dogerel,' quod he."

There can be no doubt that the poet took this ingenious method of ridiculing and caricaturing the Romance poetry, which had at this time reached the lowest point of effeteness and commonplace. Chaucer then, with great good-nature and a readiness which marks the man of the world, offers to tell "a litel thing in prose;" and commences the long allegorical tale of *Melibœus and his wife Patience*, in which, though the matter is often tiresome enough, he shows himself as great a master of prose as of poetry. Indeed it would be difficult to find, anterior to Hooker, any English prose so vigorous, so harmonious, and so free from pedantry and affectation, as that of the great Father of our Literature: —

"The morning-star of song, who made
His music heard below;
Dan Chaucer, the first warbler, whose sweet breath
Preluded those melodious bursts, that fill
The spacious times of great Elizabeth
With sounds that echo still."

The other prose tale is narrated by the Parson, who, being represented as a somewhat simple and narrow-minded though pious and large-hearted pastor, characteristically refuses to indulge the company with what can only minister to vain pleasure, and proposes something that may tend to edification, "moralité and vertuous matiere;" and commences a long and very curious sermon on the Seven Deadly Sins, their causes and remedies — a most interesting specimen of the theological literature of the day. It is divided and subdivided with all the painful minuteness of scholastic divinity; but it breathes throughout a noble spirit of evangelical piety, and in many passages attains great dignity of expression.

Besides these two Canterbury Tales, Chaucer wrote in prose a translation of Boëthius' *De Consolatione*, and an imitation of that work, under the title of *The Testament of Love*, and an incomplete astrological work, *On the Astrolabe*, addressed to his son Lewis in 1391.

The general plan of the *Canterbury Tales*, a number of detached stories connected together by their being narrated by a troop of imaginary pilgrims, is similar to the method so frequently employed in the thirteenth and fourteenth centuries, and of which we find examples in the *Decameron* of Boccaccio, the *Cent Nouvelles Nouvelles*, and a multitude of similar collections of stories. The idea may have come originally from the East, the very inartificial plan of the *Thousand and One Nights* being not altogether dissimilar, in which the stories of the inexhaustible princess Dinarzadeh are inserted one within the other, like a set of Chinese boxes. Chaucer's plan, however, must be allowed to be infinitely superior to that of Boccaccio, whose ten accomplished young gentlemen and ladies assemble in their luxurious villa to escape from the terrible plague, the magnificent description of which forms the

Introduction, and which was then, in sad reality, devastating Florence. Boccaccio's interlocutors being all nearly of the same age and social condition, — for they are little else but repetitions of the graceful types of Dioneo and Fiammetta, — it was impossible to make their tales correspond to their characters as Chaucer's do; independently of the shock to the reader's sense of propriety in finding these elegant voluptuaries whiling away, with stories generally of very doubtful morality, the hours of seclusion in which they find a cowardly and selfish asylum during a most frightful national calamity.

§ **10.** Chaucer rendered to the language of his country a service in some respects analogous to that which Dante rendered to that of Italy. He harmonized, regulated, and made popular the still discordant elements of the national speech. The difficulty of reading and understanding him has been much exaggerated: the principal rule that the student should keep in mind is that the French words, so abundant in his writings, had not yet been so modified, by changes in their orthography and pronunciation, as to become anglicized, and are therefore to be read with their French accent; and secondly, that the final *e* which terminates so many English words was not yet become an *e mute*, and is to be pronounced as a separate syllable, as *love, hope, lovë, hopë*; and finally, the past termination of the verb *ed* is almost invariably to be made a separate syllable. Some curious traces of the old Anglo-Saxon grammar, as the inflections of the personal and possessive pronouns, are still retained; as well as of the Teutonic past participle, in the prefix *i* or *y* (*ifalle, yron*, German *gefallen, geronnen*), and a few other details of the Teutonic formation of the verb.

NOTES AND ILLUSTRATIONS.

A. — THE PREDECESSORS OF GOWER AND CHAUCER.

By the middle of the fourteenth century the spirit of patriotism evoked by Edward III., and the influence of the continental Renaissance, were united to call forth a vigorous national literature. Its chief product, as in most similar cases, was poetry, but the earliest works in prose that can be properly called English belong to the same age. In A. D. 1356, Mandeville dedicated his *Travels* to Edward III.: in 1362 Parliament was first opened by a speech in English; Chaucer had begun to write; and Gower had exchanged the French and Latin of his earlier works for his mother tongue. That meeting of different influences, referred to in the text, may be illustrated by the fact that the last great hero of chivalry, the Black Prince, and Occam (see p. 22, *b*), the last and greatest of the English schoolmen, lived in the same century with Chaucer, the father of English poetry, and Wicliffe, the herald of the Reformation. The new literature may be distinguished from that of the two preceding centuries of transition (though it is difficult to draw the precise line of demarcation) by its substance as well as its form. While the language has become so like modern English, that it can be read with tolerable ease, by pronouncing syllables which are now mute, allowing for the retention of some inflectional forms, especially in the pronouns and verbs, and taking the trouble to learn the meaning of a few words now obsolete, the subjects are no longer borrowed entirely from the monkish chroniclers or the Norman minstrels, and those so borrowed are treated with the independence of native genius. These characteristics are first fully seen in Chaucer, and in a less degree in Gower in proportion to his far less commanding genius; but these two had several precursors in England, while a vigorous native literature grew up in the Anglo-Saxon parts of Scotland. ADAM DAVIE and RICHARD ROLLE (d. 1349), or Richard of Hampole, near Doncaster, writers of metrical paraphrases of Scripture, and other religious pieces, belong properly to the Old English period, the former being the only English poet named in the reign of Edward II. Richard Rolle also wrote, in the Northumbrian dialect, a poem called *The Pricke of Conscience*, in seven books, and nearly 10.000 lines. It has been published by Mr. Morris, 1863. The first poet of any merit, known to us by name, is LAWRENCE MINOT (about A. D. 1352). His poems were discovered by Tyrwhitt, in 1775, and printed by Ritson in 1796 (reprinted in 1825), with an Introduction on the reign and wars of Edward III. They celebrate ten victories of that king in his wars with France and Scotland, except that the first gives an account of the battle of Bannockburn (A. D. 1314), as an introduction to that of Halidon Hill (A. D. 1333) and others by which it was avenged. The last, the taking of Guisnes (A. D. 1352), gives an approximate date for the author, who may, however, of course have written the other poems nearer the events. Equal in spirit to the best of our heroic ballads, they have more sustained power and more finished composition. Their language is a border dialect, near akin to the Scotch. It is quite intelligible, when a few obsolete words and constructions are mastered. Among their varied measures, we meet with the animated double triplet, familiar in the poems of Scott. In Minot's poems rhyme is regularly employed; while the frequent alliterations not only remind us of the principle of Anglo-Saxon composition, but prove how much the popular ear still required that artifice.

There is another famous poem of the same age, constructed by a mixture of alliteration and rhythmical accent, without rhyme; the alliteration being stricter than that of the Anglo-Saxons themselves. This is the *Vision of Piers Ploughman*, or rather the *Vision of William concerning Piers* (*or Peter*) *Ploughman*, an allegory of the difficulties in the course of human life, kindred in conception to Bunyan's great work, and in its day scarcely less popular. Its prevalent spirit is that of satire, aimed against abuses and vices in general, but in particular against the corruptions of the church, from a moral (though not doctrinal) point of view closely resembling that of the later Puritans, with whom it was a great favorite. It consists of nearly 8000 double verses (or couplets), arranged in twenty "*passus*," or sections, so little connected with each other as to appear almost separate poems. Each couplet has two principal accents, with a considerable license as to the number of syllables. The alliteration falls on three accented syllables in each couplet, namely, on both those of the first line and on the first in the second line (and sometimes on the second). As these peculiarities can only be understood by an example, we give the opening of the poem, which also shows where the scene of the vision is laid, among the Malvern Hills (the passage is quoted with the modernized spelling and explanations of Professor Craik): —

"In a *s*ummer *s*eason,
When *s*oft was the *s*un,
I *sh*oop me into *sh*rouds*
As I a *sh*eep† were;
In *h*abit as a *h*ermit
Un*h*oly of werkes,‡
Went *W*ide in this *W*orld
*W*onders to hear;
Ac* on a *M*ay *m*orwening,
On *M*alvern hills,
Me be*f*el a *f*erly,†
Of *f*airy me thought."

This opening marks the probable residence of the poet. The third couplet, with other internal evidence, points to his having been a priest. The date seems to be tolerably well fixed by his allusions to the treaty of Bretigny, in 1360, and to the great tempest of January 15, 1362, of which he speaks as of a recent event. Tradition ascribes the work to a certain ROBERT LANGLANDE; but in the Latin title the author is called William. Nothing whatever is known of his personal history. His acquaintance with ecclesiastical literature agrees with the supposition that he was a churchman; and he was evidently familiar with the Latin poems ascribed to Walter de Mapes. The great interest of his work is its unquestionable reflection of the popular sentiment of the age. Langlande is as intensely national as Chaucer; but, while the latter freely avails himself of the forms introduced by the Anglo-Norman literature, the former makes a last attempt to revive those of the Anglo-Saxon. This effort, combined with his rich humor and unsparing satire, gained him unbounded popularity with the common people. The *Vision of Piers Ploughman* was first printed in 1550; the last reprint in black letter is that of Dr. Whitaker, 1813; a far better edition was published by Mr. Wright, with Introduction, Notes, and Glossary, in 2 vols. 12mo. Lond. 1842; but the numerous MSS. of the work would still repay a careful collation. Langlande had numerous imitators. The *Creed of Piers Ploughman*, a work of the same school, and often ascribed to the same author, is supposed to have been written about twenty or thirty years later than the *Vision*. It is more serious in its tone, and more in harmony with the religious views of Wicliffe. The *Complaint of Piers Ploughman* is found in a volume of political and satirical songs, which also contains a poem on the misgovernment of Rich. II., hinting at his deposition. These political poems concur with Gower's *Vox Clamantis* to give us a vivid impression of the evils which provoked the Lancastrian revolution.

English Prose Literature begins with SIR JOHN DE MANDEVILLE, who was born at St. Alban's about A. D. 1300, and left England for the East in 1322. His travels and his service under Oriental sovereigns gave him an extensive knowledge of Palestine, Egypt, Persia, and parts of India, Tartary, and China. He resided three years at Pekin. On his return he wrote an account of what he professed to have seen, and dedicated the book to Edward III. in A. D. 1356. He died at Liege, A. D. 1371. Mandeville's work is neither wholly nor even chiefly, original. He borrows freely from the chroniclers and other old writers, preferring what is most wonderful; and his own observations have so much of the marvellous as to discredit his testimony. The work is now chiefly interesting as the earliest example, on a large scale, of English prose. Mandeville himself tells us that he wrote it first in Latin, then translated it into French, and afterwards into English, 'that every man of my nation may understand it." Such is not the process

* Put myself into clothes. † Shepherd.
‡ Probably a vagabond friar.

* And. † Wonder.

of creating a work of literary art; and accordingly the English of Mandeville is straightforward and unadorned, and probably a fair example of the spoken language of the day. As compared with Robert of Gloucester, it shows a great increase of French words. No work of the age was more popular. It exists in a large number of MSS. The earliest printed edition, in English, is that of Wynkyn de Worde, Westminster, 1499, 8vo.; but an Italian translation, by Pietro de Cornero, had been previously printed at Milan, 1480, 4to. The standard English edition is that printed at London, 1725, 8vo., and reprinted, with an Introduction, Notes, and Glossary, by Mr. Halliwell, London, 1839, 8vo. The translation of the Latin *Polychronicon* of Ralph Higden (see p. 30), by JOHN DE TREVISA, Vicar of Berkeley, completed in the year 1385, is chiefly interesting as having been printed by Caxton, 1482, with an additional book bringing down the narrative from 1357 to 1460. It was also printed by Wynkyn de Worde in 1485. It is a curious proof of the change which a single century made in the language, that Caxton thought it necessary "somewhat to change *the rude and old English*, that is to wit, certain words which in these days be neither used ne understood." Several other translations, made by Trevisa from the Latin, exist only in MS.

The great *Scottish Poet* of this age, JOHN BARBOUR, Archdeacon of Aberdeen (b. about A. D. 1316, d. A. D. 1396), was rather a contemporary than a precursor of Chaucer, like whom he deserves to rank as the father of a national literature. His *Bruce*, in 13,000 rhymed octosyllabic lines, is a chronicle of the adventures of King Robert I., of very high merit. The lowland Scottish dialect was formed under exactly the same influences as the English, from which it differed rather less than in the present day. To confound it with the language of the aboriginal Celts is an error akin to painting Wallace in tartans and a kilt. Barbour also paid several visits to England, and studied at Oxford in his mature age. Before this time there are hardly any names in Scottish literature, except the schoolman MICHAEL SCOT, who resided abroad, and was scarcely known at home except by his fabulous reputation as a wizard; THOMAS LERMONT, the Rhymer, of Ercildoune, erroneously called the author of the romance of *Sir Tristram;* and the Latin chronicler, JOHN OF FORDUN, a canon of Aberdeen, whose *Scoti-chronicon* contains the legendary and historical annals of his country to the death of David I. The later and less celebrated contemporary of Barbour, ANDREW WYNTOUN (b. about A. D. 1350, d. after 1420), Prior of Lochleven, wrote a metrical chronicle in nine books, of Scottish and general history. BLIND HARRY, the Minstrel, belongs to the following century.

B.—JOHN GOWER.

The transition made in our language and literature about the middle of the fourteenth century cannot be better illustrated than by the writings of John Gower, the contemporary and friend of Chaucer, and the author of three great poetical works, the first in French, the second in Latin, and the third in English. Gower is assumed to have been somewhat older than Chaucer, as the old writers generally name him first; he survived him by eight years, Chaucer having died in A. D. 1400, and Gower in A. D. 1408. But the precedence must be awarded to Chaucer, not only for the vast superiority of his genius, but as the earlier writer *in English*. It may be questioned whether Gower would have written in English at all, except in conformity to the taste created by Chaucer. Their early friendship is evinced by Chaucer's dedication of *Troilus and Creseyde* to Gower, by a title which became a fixed epithet of the latter poet:—

> "O MORAL GOWER! this booke I direct
> To thee, and to the philosophicall Strode,
> To vouchsafe there need is to correct
> Of your benignities and zeales good."

And the continuance of their friendship (in spite of conjectures founded on insufficient evidence) is attested by the compliment paid to Chaucer in Gower's *Confessio Amantis* (finished in 1393), where Venus greets Chaucer

> "As my disciple and my poete,"

and after speaking of "the dittees and songes glad," composed "in the floures of his youth" for her sake, and of which

> "The land fulfilled is ouer all,"

exhorts him to employ his old age in writing his "*Testament of Love.*"

Two of the *Canterbury Tales*, those of the Man of Law and the Wife of Bath, are borrowed from Gower, unless both poets derived them from a common source.

Caxton made Gower a native of Gowerland in South Wales, and Leland claimed him as a member of the family of Gower of Stittenham, in Yorkshire, from which are sprung the noble houses of Sutherland and Ellesmere. But Sir Harris Nicolas and others have proved, from existing deeds, and from the comparison of seals with the arms on Gower's tomb, that the poet was *an esquire of Kent*, and probably of the same family as Sir Robert Gower of Multon (Moulton) and Kentwell, in Suffolk, who died in or before A. D. 1349, and whose daughter and coheiress Joan conveyed the manor of Kentwell to John Gower (the poet) on June 28, 1368. From this and similar evidence it appears that Gower was sprung from a family of knightly rank, and that he possessed estates in Kent, Norfolk, Suffolk, and probably in Essex; though he lived much in London, and apparently in close connection with the court. There is no ground for the common statement that he followed the legal profession. About the year 1400, he speaks of himself as both old and blind. His will still exists, made on the 15th of August, 1408, and proved by his widow, Agnes, on the 24th of October following, so that he must have died between those two dates. There can be little doubt that his wife was the same as the Agnes Groundalf whose marriage to John Gower, at St. Mary Magdalen's, Southwark, on the 28th of January, 1397, is recorded in the register of William of Wykeham, preserved at Winchester. If so, the poet married in his old age. His will leaves it doubtful whether he had issue. He lies buried, according to his own directions, in St. Mary Overy's (now St. Saviour's), Southwark, of which church he is said to have been a benefactor, beneath a splendid canopied tomb, bearing his arms and effigy, the head resting on his three volumes; the wall within the three arches being painted with figures of Charity, Mercy, and Pity. The story of his having been a fellow-student with Chaucer, either at Oxford or Cambridge, is as unfounded as most of Leland's other statements about him, but his works furnish proof of his having received the best education his age could bestow, and of his command of the languages then in use.

Gower's three great works were the *Speculum Meditantis*, in French; the *Vox Clamantis*, in Latin; and the *Confessio Amantis*, in English.

(1.) The *Speculum Meditantis* is now entirely lost; the short French poem which Warton describes under the title being an entirely different work. It was a collection of precepts on chastity, enforced by examples. But there are still extant *Fifty French Ballads* by Gower, in a MS. belonging to the Duke of Sutherland, and edited by the late duke for the Roxburghe Club, in 1818. "They are," says Pauli (*Introd. Essay*, p. xxvi.), "tender in sentiment, and not unrefined with regard to language and form, especially if we consider that they are the work of a foreigner. They treat of Love in the manner introduced by the Provençal poets, which was afterwards generally adopted by those in the north of France. A few specimens cannot fail to give a favorable idea of Gower's skill and expression." These were about the last works of any importance written in the Anglo-Norman French, which was now so fully regarded as a foreign language, that Gower apologizes for his French, saying, "I am English," while he gives as a reason for using the language, that he was addressing his ballads

"Al Universite de tout le monde."

Some verses addressed to Henry IV., after his accession, prove that Gower continued to write in French to the end of his life.

(2.) Of Gower's great Latin poem, the *Vox Clamantis*, Dr. Pauli gives the following account: —

"Soon after the rebellion of the commons in 1381 [under Richard II.], an event which made a great impression on his mind, he wrote that singular work in Latin distichs, called *Vox Clamantis*, of which we possess an excellent edition by the Rev. H. O. Coxe, printed for the Roxburghe Club, in 1850. The name, with an allusion to St. John the Baptist, seems to have been adopted from the general clamor and cry then abroad in the country. The greater bulk of the work, the date of which its editor is inclined to fix between 1382 and 1384, is rather a moral than an historical essay; but the *first book* describes the insurrection of Wat Tyler in an allegorical disguise; the poet having a dream, on the 11th of June, 1381, in which men assume the shape of animals. The *second book* contains a long sermon on fatalism, in which the poet shows himself no friend to Wicliffe's tenets, but a zealous advocate for the reformation of the clergy. The *third book* points out how all orders of society must suffer for their own vices and demerits; in illustration of which he cites the example of the secular clergy. The *fourth book* is dedicated to the cloistered clergy and the friars; the *fifth* to the military; the *sixth* contains a violent attack on the lawyers; and the *seventh* subjoins the moral of the whole, represented in Nebuchadnezzar's dream, as interpreted by Daniel." (*Introd. Essay*, p. xxix.) There are also some smaller Latin poems, in leonine hexameters; among them one addressed to Henry IV., in which the poet laments his blindness.

(3.) Gower's latest poem, the *Confessio Amantis*, was written in English, with a running marginal commentary in Latin, something like that to the *Ancient Mariner* of Coleridge. Its composition seems to be due to the success of Chaucer. We again quote from Dr. Pauli: "The exact date of the poem has not been ascertained, but there is internal evidence, in certain copies, that it existed in the year 1392-3. As this point involves a question of grave importance with respect to the author's behavior and position in the political events of the day, it will be necessary to enter more fully into the subject. He unquestionably issued two editions of the work, which, however, as will be distinctly seen in the present edition, vary from each other only at the commencement and at the end; the one being dedicated to King Richard II., the other to his cousin, Henry of Lancaster, Earl of Derby. In the king's copy the poet describes at length how he came rowing down the Thames at London one day, and how he met King Richard, who, having invited him to step into the royal barge, commanded him to write a book upon some new matter. In that addressed to Henry he says, that the book was finished, *the yere sixteenth of King Richard* (A. D. 1392-3), an important fact, which has been hitherto overlooked by all writers on the subject, including even Sir H. Nicolas (*Life of Chaucer*, p. 39), who states that Gower did not dedicate his work to Henry until he had ascended the throne." Having shown that the dedication was made when Henry was not yet King, or even Duke of Lancaster, but Earl of Derby, — a title which he bore in 1392-3, — Pauli proceeds: "The one version abounds in expressions of the deepest loyalty towards his sovereign, for whose sake he intends to write *some newe thing* in English; the other mentions the year of the reign of King Richard II., is full of attachment to Henry of Lancaster,

'*with whom my herte is of accorde*,'

and purports to appear in English for England's sake." The inference from all this is, that Gower, seeing the fatal tendency of Richard's course, early attached himself to Henry of Lancaster, from whom there is still extant a record of his receiving a collar in 1394 (probably in acknowledgment of the dedication of his poem), and whom he more than once addresses with affection and respect in his minor pieces. Hence the commencement of the *Confessio Amantis* would fall before 1386, when Richard came of age, and began his arbitrary government. Hence, also, the omission of the compliment to Chaucer at the end of the poem, in the edition inscribed to Henry, may be explained by motives of policy, without inferring any personal alienation.

The Prologue is in the same strain of dissatisfaction with the existing order of things, which pervades the *Vox Clamantis*; and the poet comforts himself with the same resource, the divine government of the world, as revealed in the vision of Nebuchadnezzar. Yet how little he shares the opinions of Wicliffe is proved by his reference to

"This new secte of lollardie."

Pauli gives the following outline of the work: "The poem opens by introducing the author himself, in the character of an unhappy lover in despair, smitten by Cupid's arrow. Venus appears to him, and after having heard his prayer, appoints her priest called Genius, like the mystagogue in the Picture of Cebes, to hear the lover's confession. This is the frame of the whole work, which is a singular mixture of classical notions, principally borrowed from Ovid's *Ars Amandi*, and of the purely medieval idea, that as a good Catholic the unfortunate lover must state his distress to a father confessor. This is done, in the course of the confession, with great regularity and even pedantry; all the passions of the human heart, which generally stand in the way of love, being systematically arranged in the various books and subdivisions of the work. After Genius has fully explained the evil affection, passion, or vice under consideration, the lover confesses on that particular point, and frequently urges his boundless love for an unknown beauty, who treats him cruelly, in a tone of affectation which would appear highly ridiculous in a man of more than sixty years of age, were it not a common characteristic of the poetry of the period. After this profession, the confessor opposes him, and exemplifies the fatal effects of each passion by a variety of apposite stories, gathered from many sources. At length, after a frequent and tedious recurrence of the same process, the confession is terminated by some final injunctions of the priest — the lover's petition in a strophic poem addressed to Venus — the bitter judgment of the goddess, that he should remember his old age, and leave off such fooleries;

> "For loves lust and lockes hore
> In chambre accorden neuer more" —

his cure from the wound caused by the dart of love, and his absolution, received as if by a pious Roman Catholic.

"The materials for this extensive work [more than 30,000 lines], and the stories inserted as examples for and against the lover's passion, are drawn from various sources. Some have been taken from the Bible; a great number from Ovid's *Metamorphoses*, which must have been a particular favorite with the author; others from the medieval histories of the siege of Troy, of the feats of Alexander the Great — from the oldest collection of novels, known under the name of the *Gesta Romanorum*, chiefly in its form as used in England — from the *Pantheon* and *Speculum Regum* of Godfrey of Viterbo, from the romance of *Sir Lancelot* and the *Chronicles* of Cassiodorus and Isidorus." (*Introd. Essay*, pp. xxxiii. xxxiv.) There is also a vast amount of alchemical learning from the *Almagest*, and an exposition of the pseudo-Aristotelian philosophy of the middle ages. The author's fancy lies almost buried under the mass of his learning, and his laborious composition shows none of Chaucer's humor, or passion, or love of nature. In the language of the new school of poetry, to which Chaucer's genius had given birth, Gower embodies most of the faults of the romance writers. Still he has his merits. "The vivacity and variety of his short verses evince a correct ear and a happy power, by the assistance of which he enhances the interest in a tale, and frequently terminates it with satisfaction to the reader." (W. W. Lloyd in Singer's Shakspeare, vol. iv. p. 261.) The Saxon element is as conspicuous in his language as in Chaucer's; but he uses a larger number of French words, as might have been expected from his early habits of composition. The frequent want of skill in the construction of his sentences shows that it was no easy task for him to write so long a work in English. There are some forms peculiar to him, as ***I sigh*** for ***I saw***, and ***nought*** for ***not***. He seldom uses alliteration. We have a long chain of testimony to Gower's popularity, from his own age to that of Shakspeare, who speaks of him thus: —

> "To sing a song that old was sung,
> From ashes ancient Gower is come,
> Assuming man's infirmities,
> To glad our ear and please our eyes."
> (*Pericles.*)

The *Confessio Amantis* was first printed by Caxton, Lond. 1483, fol. (the British Museum has two copies of this rare work), and by F. Berthelette, Lond. 1532, fol., reprinted 1554, fol. (both in black letter). None of the modern editions deserve mention in comparison of that by Dr. Reinhold Pauli, Lond. 1857, 3 vols., 8vo., whose *Introductory Essay* contains all that is known of the poet and his works.

C. — WICLIFFE AND HIS SCHOOL.

The revolution effected by Chaucer in poetry was accompanied and aided by an entirely new development of religious literature, which, besides its higher fruits, rendered a similar service to our prose literature. The new liberty of thought, which found expression in popular literature, showed itself also in a sifting of ecclesiastical pretensions, which led to a direct appeal to Scripture; and the reforming teachers satisfied this demand by translating the Bible into the mother tongue. In the other Protestant countries of Europe, the revival of national literature has been connected with a similar work, and, if the German Bible of Luther, and the Danish version of 1550, exerted a more powerful influence over the respective languages than the Wicliffite translations, one chief reason is, that they appeared after the invention of printing, by which art they were immediately and indefinitely multiplied. In England this great work is ascribed to JOHN DE WICLIF, WICLIFFE, or WYCLIFFE (b. about A. D. 1324, d. A. D. 1384). He was born at Wicliffe, near Richmond, in Yorkshire; studied at Oxford; became the priest of Fylingham, in Lincoln; and successively Master and Warden of Balliol College and Canterbury Hall, Oxford. He began early to attack the corruptions of the Church; and after his deposition from the latter post by Archbishop Langham, and the Pope's rejection of his appeal, he gave all his energies to the work of reform, both by his writings and by theological lectures at Oxford. For a long time he was not only unmolested, but was regarded as a champion of the Anglican Church. In 1374 he was a member of a commission sent to Avignon, which obtained concessions from the Pope on the question of induction into benefices. He was rewarded by the crown with a prebend at Worcester, and the vicarage of Lutterworth, in Leicestershire, which he held till his death, being secured from the storm of persecution, which soon arose, by the protection of the king's son, John of Gaunt. It was in the retirement of Lutterworth, after he had been driven from his chair at Oxford,* that Wicliffe, aided by his friends and disciples, undertook the work of Bible translation. Their version was the basis of that of Tyndale, as the latter was of the Authorized Versions of 1535 (Coverdale's) and 1611 (King James's, which is still in use); but three centuries and a half elapsed before the original translation of the New Testament, and nearly five centuries before the whole, appeared in print. The New Testament was edited by the Rev. John Lewis, 1731, fol.; by the Rev. H. H. Baker, 1810, 4to.; and in Bagster's *English Hexapla*, 1841 and 1846, 4to. The Old Testament has only lately been published, in the splendid edition of the Rev. J. Forshall and Sir Frederick Madden, Oxf. 1850, 4 vols. 4to. The authorship of the several parts has long been the subject of discussion. According to the latest editors, the Old Testament and Apocrypha, from *Genesis* to *Baruch* (in the order of the LXX.), was translated by a priest named HEREFORD, and the rest of the Old Testament and Apocrypha, as well as the whole of the New Testament, by Wicliffe. The whole work was revised, in a second edition, by PURVEY, who has left us a very interesting essay on the principles of translation. The first version seems to have been completed about A. D. 1380, and the edition of Purvey before 1390; so that this English Bible was generally circulated, so far as the jealousy of the church would permit, by the end of the fourteenth century. Its excellence is to be ascribed to two chief causes, the religious sensibility of the translators, whose spirit was absorbed in their work, and the simple vocabulary and structure of the language, which presented itself newly formed to their hand. Translated as it was from the Vulgate, it naturalized, chiefly in a Latin form, a large stock of religious terms, almost confined before to theologians, and at the same time enlarged and modified them. Above all, by preserving the uniformity of diction and grammar, suited to the sacred dignity of the work, and which is not found in nearly so high a degree in Wicliffe's own treatises, it laid the foundation of that religious or sacred dialect, which has contributed to secure dignity and earnestness as prevailing characters of our common speech. While satires of the type of *Piers Ploughman* gratified the popular disgust at the corruptions in high places, the newly-opened well-spring of truth taught them the cure for these evils; and their eager reception of both classes of works enriched their language as well as influenced their thoughts. Chaucer, imbued with popular sympathies, and connected with the political party that protected Wicliffe, could not but be subject to these influences.

* Regular professorships not being yet established, Wicliffe taught at Oxford by that right which, though now dormant, is still inherent, as their names imply, in the Degrees of *Doctor* and *Magister*.

CHAPTER III.

FROM THE DEATH OF CHAUCER TO THE AGE OF ELIZABETH. A. D. 1400–1558.

1. Slow progress of English literature from Chaucer to the age of Elizabeth Introduction of printing by CAXTON. Improvement of prose. § 2. Scottish literature in the fifteenth century: KING JAMES I.; DUNBAR; GAWIN DOUGLAS; HENRYSON; BLIND HARRY. § 3. Reign of Henry VII., sterile in literature. HENRY VIII.; SIR THOMAS MORE. § 4. Religious Literature: Translations of the Bible; Book of Common Prayer; LATIMER; FOXE. § 5. Chroniclers and Historians: LORD BERNERS' Froissart; FABYAN; HALL. § 6. Philosophy and Education: WILSON'S *Logic;* SIR JOHN CHEKE; ROGER ASCHAM'S *Schoolmaster* and *Toxophilus.* § 7. Poets: SKELTON; BARKLAY and HAWES; WYATT and SURREY. § 8. Ballads of the fifteenth and sixteenth centuries: their sources, metre, and modes of circulation. Modern collections by Percy, Scott, &c. Influence on the revival of romantic literature. Ballads of the Scottish borders and of Robin Hood.

§ 1. THE progress of English Literature, inaugurated in so splendid a manner by the genius of Chaucer, though uninterrupted, was for a long time comparatively slow. Many social and political causes contributed to retard it for a time, or rather to accumulate the nation's energies for that glorious intellectual burst which distinguishes the Age of Elizabeth, making that period the most magnificent in the history of the English people, if not in the annals of the human race. The causes just alluded to were the intestine commotions of the Wars of the Roses, the struggle between the dying energies of Feudalism and the nascent liberties of our municipal institutions, and the mighty transformation resulting from the Reformation.

In point of splendor, fecundity, intense originality, and national spirit, none of the most brilliant epochs in the history of mankind can be considered as superior to the Elizabethan. In universality of scope and in the influence it was destined to exert upon the thoughts and knowledge of future generations, no other epoch can be brought into comparison with it. Neither the age of Pericles nor that of Augustus in the ancient world, nor those of the Medici and of Louis XIV. in modern history, can be regarded as approaching in importance to that period which, independently of a multitude of brilliant but inferior luminaries, produced the Prince of Poets and the Prince of Philosophers — William Shakespeare and Francis Bacon. But the interval between the end of the fourteenth century and the latter part of the sixteenth, though destitute of any names comparable for creative energy to that of Chaucer, was a period of great literary activity. The importation into England of the art of printing, first exercised among us by CAXTON, who was himself a useful and laborious author, and who died in 1491, unquestionably tended to give a more regular and literary form to the productions of that age; the increase in the number of printed books seems in particular to have been peculiarly efficacious in generating a good prose style, as well as in enlarging the circle of readers and extending the influence of popular intellectual activity, as for example by disseminating the habit of religious and political discussion. Thus Mandeville, regarded as one of the founders of prose writing in England, and who, at the period of Chaucer, gave to the world the curious description of his travels and adventures in many lands,* was followed by CHIEF JUSTICE FORTESCUE (fl. 1430–1470), who, besides his celebrated Latin work "De Laudibus Legum Angliæ," also wrote one in English on "The Difference between an Absolute and Limited Monarchy." †

§ **2.** But the most brilliant names which occupy the beginning of this interval are those of Scotsmen. JAMES I. (1394–1437), who was taken prisoner when a child (1405) and carefully educated at Windsor, must be regarded as a poet who does equal honor to his own country and to that of his captivity. This accomplished prince was the author of a collection of love-verses under the title of the *King's Quhair* (i. e. *Quire* or *Book*), written in the purest English and breathing the romantic and elegant grace which the immense popularity of Petrarch had at that time made the universal pattern throughout Europe. His own national dialect, too, was that of the Lowland Scots, then and long after the language of literature, of courtly society, and of theology, and by no means to be regarded as the mere *patois* or provincial dialect which it has become since the union of the two crowns has destroyed the political independence of Scotland. In it James composed a number of songs and ballads of extraordinary merit, recounting with much humor his own amorous adventures; some, unfortunately, of a character rather too warm for the delicacy of modern times. This intellectual and patriotic prince was assassinated in 1437 at Perth, by the nobles, among whom his own uncle was a chief conspirator, to revenge the king's concessions to the people. Besides King James, Scotland produced about this time several poets of great merit, the chief of whom are WILLIAM DUNBAR (about 1465–1520), and GAWIN or GAVIN DOUGLAS, Bishop of Dunkeld (1474–1522), the former a truly powerful and original genius, and the second a voluminous and miscellaneous poet, whose example tended much to regularize and improve the national dialect, and to enrich the national literature. Among Dunbar's numerous poetical compositions we must in particular specify his wild allegorical conception of "*The Dance of the Seven Deadly Sins*," a fantastic and terrible impersonation, with the intense reality of Dante and the picturesque inventiveness of Callot. Gawin

* For an account of Mandeville see p. 54.

† Sir John Fortescue was originally a Lancastrian. He accompanied Henry VI. into exile; was afterwards taken prisoner at the battle of Tewkesbury in 1471, and was attainted. He obtained his pardon by acknowledging the title of Edward IV.

Douglas is now chiefly remembered as the translator of Virgil into Scottish verse, and in both this and his original compositions the reader will be struck by the much greater preponderance of French and Latin words in the dialect of Scotland than in contemporary English writings. This is partly to be attributed to the close political connection maintained by Scotland with France, with which country she generally sided out of hostility to England; and partly, no doubt, to a kind of pedantic affectation, a sort of Scottish *estilo culto*, like the Gongorism of the Spaniards. ROBERT HENRYSON (d. about 1500), a monk or schoolmaster of Dunfermline, wrote, in imitation of Chaucer, the *Testament of Faire Creseide*, and the beautiful pastoral of *Robin and Makyne* (in Percy's *Reliques*). Another Scottish poet, known under the appellation of BLIND HARRY or HARRY THE MINSTREL, but concerning the details of whose life nothing accurate has been discovered, wrote, in long rhymed couplets, a narrative of the exploits of the second great national hero, *William Wallace*. This work is not destitute of vigorous and picturesque passages. BARBOUR and the other writers of the fourteenth century have been already mentioned (p. 55).

§ 3. The reign of Henry VII., as might have been expected from the sombre character of that politic prince, was by no means favorable to literary activity; but Henry VIII. was possessed of much of the learning of his age, and even distinguished himself by his controversial writings against Luther. The title of "Defender of the Faith," by which the Pope recompensed this sceptred polemic, has been ever since retained in the style of English sovereigns — a singular example of the vicissitudes of names. The great and good chancellor Sir Thomas More, the poets Skelton, Wyatt, and Surrey, belong to this memorable reign. Of the three last we shall speak among the poets. Sir THOMAS MORE (1480–1535) is unquestionably one of the most prominent intellectual figures of this reign, whether as statesman, polemic, or man of letters. The ardent attachment which More felt to the Catholic religion, and which he so often testified by acts of persecution, contrary to his gentle and genial character, he firmly maintained when himself persecuted and in the presence of a cruel and ignominious death. His philosophical romance of the *Utopia*, written in Latin, is a striking example of the extreme freedom of speculative and political discussion, exercised not only with impunity, but even with approbation, under the sternest tyranny. The fundamental idea of this work was borrowed from the *Atlantis* of Plato. It is one of the earliest of many attempts to give, under the form of a voyage to an imaginary island, the theory of an ideal republic, where the laws, the institutions, the social and political usages, are in strict accordance with a philosophical perfection. England has been peculiarly fertile in these sports of political fancy. Bacon also left an unfinished sketch of an imaginary republic; and the *Oceana* of Harrington is a similar attempt to realize the theory of a perfectly happy and philosophic government.*

* Of Sir Thomas More's English works, the most remarkable, on account of its style, is his *Life of Edward V.*, which Mr. Hallam pronounces to be "the

§ 4. Parallel with the improvement of general literature, and indeed in no small measure connected with it, must be noted the very general diffusion of religious controversy connected with the doctrines of the Reformation, and the dissemination of English translations of the Scriptures. TYNDALE and COVERDALE, the former of whom was burned near Antwerp, in 1536, and the latter made Bishop of Exeter about the middle of the same century, gave to the world the first portions, and the two together the whole, of the sacred writings in an English version; and the compilation of the English *Book of Common Prayer* in the reign of Edward VI. combined with the diffusion of the Scriptures in the English language to furnish the people with models of the finest possible style — grave and dignified without ostentation, vigorous and intelligible without vulgarity. The Liturgy itself was little else but a translation, with some few omissions and alterations, from the Latin Mass-book of the Catholic Church; but the simple and majestic style of the version, as well as that preserved in the English translation of the Bible, has endowed the Anglican Church with the noblest religious diction possessed by any nation in the world. It was formed at the critical period in the history of our native tongue when the simplicity of the ancient speech was still fresh and living, and yet when the progress of civilization was sufficiently advanced to adorn that ancient element with the richness and expressiveness of a more polished epoch. The singular felicity of these circumstances has had an incalculable effect on the whole character of our language and literature, and has preserved to the English tongue the force and picturesqueness of the fifteenth century, while not excluding the refinements of the nineteenth. Nor is it possible that the majestic style of our older writers can ever become obsolete, while the noble and massive language of our Bible and Prayer-Book continues to exert — as it probably ever will — so immense an influence on the modes of thinking and speaking of all classes of the population. Many of our ancient preachers and controversialists too, like good old HUGH LATIMER, burned as a heretic by Mary in 1555, and the chronicler of the Protestant Martyrs, JOHN FOXE, who died in 1587, contributed, in writings which, though sometimes rude and unadorned, are always fervent, simple, and idiomatic, to disseminate among the great mass of the people not only an ardent attachment to Protestant doctrines, but a habit of religious discussion and consequently a tendency to intellectual activity.

§ 5. Independently of purely religious disquisition the period anterior to the reign of Elizabeth was not barren of literary productions of more general interest. LORD BERNERS, governor of Calais under Henry VIII., translated into the picturesque and vigorous English of that day the *Chronicle of Froissart*, that inexhaustible storehouse of chivalrous incident and mediæval detail. The translation is not only remarkable for fidelity and vivacity, but the archaism of Berners' language, by preserving to the modern English reader the quaintness of

first example of good English language pure and perspicuous, well-chosen, without vulgarisms or pedantry."

the original, produces precisely the same impression as the picturesque old French.

It is curious to trace the gradual transformation of historical literature. Its first and earliest type, in the ancient as well as the modern world, is invariably mythical or legendary, and the form in which it then appears is universally poetical. The legend, by a natural transition, gives way to the chronicle or regular compilation of legends; and the chronicle becomes, after many ages of civilization, the mine from whence the philosophical historian extracts the rude materials for his work. As the detached legendary or ballad episodes of Homer verge into the *chronicle history*, so fresh in its infantine simplicity, of Herodotus, or the old rude Latin ballads into the chronicle history of Livy, and as these in their turn generate the profound philosophical reflections of Thucydides or Tacitus, so in the parallel department of modern literature in England, we find the fabulous British legends combining themselves in the Monastic and Trouvère chronicles, and these again generating the prosaic but useful narratives from which the modern historian draws the materials for his pictures and reflections. In the minute and gossiping pages of such writers as old FABYAN (d. 1512), who was an alderman and sheriff of London, and EDWARD HALL (d. 1547), who was a judge in the Sheriff's Court of the same city, we find the transition from the poetical, ballad, or legendary form of history. Their writings, though totally devoid of philosophical system or general knowledge, and though exhibiting a complete want of critical discrimination between trifling and important events, are extremely valuable, not only as vast storehouses of facts which the modern historian has to sift and classify, but as monuments of language and examples of the popular feeling of their time. In England these chronicles wear a peculiar *bourgeois* air, and were indeed generally, as in the case of the former of these writers, the production of worthy but not very highly-cultivated citizens. Mixed with much childish and insignificant detail, which, however, is not without its value as giving us an insight into the life and opinions of the age, we find an abundant store of facts and pictures, invaluable to the modern and more scientific historian.*

§ 6. Among numerous works on philosophy and education (which now takes its place as a branch of literature) THOMAS WILSON'S *Treatise of Logic and Rhetoric*, published in 1553, must be regarded as a work far superior in originality of view and correctness of literary prin-

* The earliest English Chronicle is John de Trevisa's translation of Higden' 'Polychronicon,' with a continuation by Caxton down to 1460, which is noticed on p. 55. Next comes the metrical chronicle of John Harding, coming down to the reign of Edward IV. (See p. 69.) Then follow the Chronicles of Fabyan and Hall, mentioned in the text. Fabyan's Chronicle, which he called the *Concordance of Histories*, begins with the fabulous stories of Brute the Trojan, and comes down to his own time. Hall's Chronicle, first printed by Grafton in 1548, under the title of *The Union of the Two Noble and Illustrious Families of York and Lancaster*, gives a history of England under the houses of York and Lancaster, and of the reigns of Henry VII. and Henry VIII.

ciple to anything that had at that time appeared in England or elsewhere, relative to a subject of the highest importance; and the writings of SIR JOHN CHEKE (1514–1557) not only rendered an inestimable service to philology by laying the foundation of Greek studies in the University of Cambridge, where he was professor, but tended powerfully to regulate and improve the tone of English prose. The excellent precepts given by Wilson and Cheke concerning the avoidance of pedantic and affected expressions in prose, and in particular their ridicule of the then prevailing vice of alliteration and exaggerated subtlety of antithesis, were exemplified by the grave and simple propriety of their own writings. To the same category as the preceding writers mentioned will belong ROGER ASCHAM (1515-1568), the learned and affectionate preceptor of Elizabeth and the unfortunate Jane Grey. His treatise entitled the ***Schoolmaster***, and the book called ***Toxophilus***, devoted to the encouragement of the national use of the bow, are works remarkable for the good sense and reasonableness of the ideas, which are expressed in a plain and vigorous dignity of style that would do honor to any epoch of literature. The plans of teaching laid down in Ascham's ***Schoolmaster*** have been revived in our own day as an antidote to shallow novelties, and his advocacy of the bow has been more than carried out by the modern rifle.

§ **7.** But though the popular literature of England in the reign of Henry VIII. naturally took, from the force of contemporary circumstances, a polemical, controversial, or philosophical tone, and writers busied themselves chiefly about those great religious questions which were then exciting universal interest, there were poets who cannot be passed over by one desirous of forming an idea of the intellectual character of that momentous period of transformation. JOHN SKELTON, the date of whose birth is unknown, but who died in 1529, was undoubtedly a man of considerable classical learning. He is spoken of by Erasmus, who passed some time in England, where he was received with warm hospitality by More, and even read lectures before the University of Cambridge, as "litterarum Anglicarum decus et lumen." He belonged to the ecclesiastical profession, was rector of Diss in Norfolk, and incessantly alludes in his writings to the honor of the laurel which he had received from Oxford; but whether this indicates a specific personal distinction, conferred upon him alone, or merely an academical degree, is not quite clearly established. He appears also to have enjoyed the privilege of wearing the king's colors or livery, and to have been to a certain degree the object of court favor: but there is reason to believe that he was not remarkable for prudence or regularity of conduct. His poetical productions, which are tolerably voluminous, may be divided into two very marked and distinct categories, his serious and comic or satiric writings. The former, which are either eulogistic poems addressed to patrons or allegorical disquisitions in a grave, lofty, and pretentious strain of moral declamation, will be found by the modern reader, who may be bold enough to examine them, insupportably stiff, tiresome, and pedantic, exhibiting, it is true, considerable learning, an elevated tone of ethical disquisition, and a pure and sometimes vigorous English style, when the poet can free himself from the trammels of Latinizing pedantry: but they are destitute of invention and grace. These poems, however, were in all probability much admired at a time when, English literature being as yet in its infancy, readers as well as writers thought more of borrowed than original conceptions, and placed learning — which was of course admired in proportion to its rarity — higher than invention. But it is in his comic and satirical writings that Skelton is truly original; he struck out a path in literature, not very high it is true, but one in which he had no predecessors and has found no equals. He engaged, with an audacity and an apparent impunity which now appear equally inexplicable, in a series of the most furious attacks upon the then all-powerful favorite and minister Wolsey: and in the whole literature of libels and pasquinades there is nothing bolder and more sweeping than these invectives. They are written in a peculiar short doggerel measure, the rhymes of which, recurring incessantly, and sometimes repeated with a rapidity that almost takes away the reader's breath, form an admirable vehicle for violent abuse, invariably couched in the most familiar language of the people. He has at once perfectly described and exemplified the character of his "breathlesse rhymes" in the following passage:-

"For though my rime be ragged,
Tattered and jagged,
Rudely raine-beaten,
Rusty and mooth-eaten,
If ye take wel therewith
It hath in it som pith."

All that is coarse, quaint, odd, familiar, in the speech of the commonest of the people, combined with a command of learned and pedantic imagery almost equal to the exhaustless vocabulary of Rabelais, is to be found in Skelton; and his writings deserve to be studied, were it only as an abundant source of popular English. In one strange extravaganza, entitled "*The Tunning of Elinour Rummyng*," he has described the attractions of the browst of a certain alewife, and the furious eagerness of the women of the neighborhood to taste the barley-bree of Dame Rummyng, who is said to have been a real person and to have kept an alehouse at Leatherhead, in Surrey. Elinour and her establishment, and her thirsty customers, are painted with extraordinary humor and with a vast fecundity of images, some of which are so coarse as to exceed all bounds of moderation and even of decency. Of the humor, knowledge of low life, and force of imagination displayed, there can be but one opinion. Another very strange pleasantry of this humorist is the *Boke of the Sparrow*, a sort of dirge or lamentation on the death of a tame sparrow, the favorite of a young lady who belonged to a Convent. The bird was unfortunately killed by a cat, and after devoting this cat in particular and the whole race of cats in general to eternal punishment in a sort of humorous excommunication, the poet proceeds to describe a funeral service performed, for the repose of Philip

Sparrow's soul, by all the birds; in which we have a parody of the various parts of the Catholic funeral ritual. In this work, as well as in most of Skelton's writings, we find Latin and French freely intermingled with his nervous and popular English; and this singularly heightens the comic effect. Skelton's purely satiric productions are principally directed against Wolsey, and against the Scottish king and nation, over whose fatal defeat at Flodden the railing satirist exults in a manner unworthy of a generous spirit. His principal attacks upon Wolsey are to be found in the poems entitled the *Booke of Colin Clout*, *Why Come Ye not to Court*, and the *Bouge of Court.*

Two poets, who flourished nearly at the same time, Stephen Hawes and Alexander Barklay, deserve mention for the influence they exerted on the intellectual character of their age, though their writings have fallen into neglect. STEPHEN HAWES (fl. 1509), the elder of the two, whom Warton describes as the "only writer deserving the name of a poet in the reign of Henry VII.," was a favorite of that monarch, and the author of the *Pastime of Pleasure*, a long and in many passages a striking allegorical poem in the versification of old Lydgate. ALEXANDER BARKLAY, who lived a little later under Henry VIII. and died at an advanced age, at Croydon, in Surrey, in 1552, translated into English verse Sebastian Brandt's once-celebrated satire of the *Ship of Fools*, an epitome of the various forms of pedantry and affectation.* In the writings of both we see the rapid development of flexibility and harmony of English versification, the approach to that consummate perfection which was at no long period to be attained by Spenser and Shakspeare, under the influence, particularly in the former case, of the enlightened imitation of Italian metrical melody. How rapid this progress in taste and refinement really was, may be deduced from an examination of the poems of Sir THOMAS WYATT (the elder) and the EARL OF SURREY, who were nearly contemporaries in their lives and early deaths. The former was born in 1503, and died in 1541; the second, one of the most illustrious members of the splendid house of Howard, was born in 1517, and beheaded, under a false and absurd charge of high treason, by Henry VIII., in 1547. Both these nobles were men of rare virtues and accomplishments, Wyatt the type of the wit and statesman, and Surrey of the gallant cavalier; and both enjoyed a high popularity as poets. In their works we plainly trace the Italian spirit, and the style of their poems, though not free from that amorous and metaphysical casuistry which the example of Petrarch long rendered so universal throughout Europe, is singularly free from harshness of expression and that uncouthness of form which is perceptible in the earlier attempts of English poetry.

Surrey may justly be regarded as the first English classical poet. He was the first who introduced blank verse into our English poetry, which he employed in translating the second and fourth books of Virgil's Æneid. "Surrey," says Mr. Hallam, "did much for his own country

* Brandt was a learned civilian of Basel, and published in 1494 a satire in German with the above title.

and his native language. His versification differs very considerably from that of his predecessors. He introduced a sort of involution into his style, which gives an air of dignity and remoteness from common life. It was, in fact, borrowed from the license of Italian poetry, which our own idiom has rejected. He avoids pedantic words, forcibly obtruded from the Latin, of which our earlier poets, both English and Scots, had been ridiculously fond. The absurd epithets of Hoccleve, Lydgate, Dunbar, and Douglas are applied equally to the most different things, so as to show that they annexed no meaning to them. Surrey rarely lays an unnatural stress on final syllables, merely as such, which they would not receive in ordinary pronunciation — another usual trick of the school of Chaucer. His words are well chosen and well arranged." Wyatt is inferior to Surrey in harmony of numbers and elegance of sentiment. Their "Songs and Sonnettes" were first collected and printed at London by Tottel, in 1557, in his *Miscellany*, which was the first printed poetical miscellany in the English language.

§ 8. I cannot better conclude this transitional or intercalary chapter than by making a few remarks on a peculiar class of compositions in which England is unusually rich, which are marked with an intense impress of nationality, and which have exerted, on modern literature in particular, an influence whose extent it is impossible to overrate. These are our national *Ballads*, produced, it is probable, in great abundance during the fifteenth and sixteenth centuries, and in many instances traceable to the "North Countrée," or the Border region between England and Scotland. This country, as the scene of incessant forays from both sides of the frontier during the uninterrupted warfare between the two countries, was naturally the theatre of a multitude of wild and romantic episodes, consigned to memory in the rude strains of indigenous minstrels. No country indeed (excepting Spain, in the admirable *romances* which commemorate the long struggle between the Christians and the Moors, and the collection containing the cycle of the Cid) possesses anything similar in kind or comparable in merit to the old ballads of England. They bear the marks of having been composed, somewhat like the Rhapsodies of the old Ionian bards from which the mysterious personality whom we call Homer derived at once his materials and his inspiration, by rude wandering minstrels. Such men — probably often blind or otherwise incapacitated from taking part in active life — gained their bread by singing or repeating them. These poets and narrators were a very different class from the wandering troubadours or jongleurs of Southern Europe and of France; and living in a country much ruder and less chivalric, though certainly not less warlike than Languedoc or Provence, their compositions are inimitable for simple pathos, fiery intensity of feeling, and picturesqueness of description. In every country there must exist some typical or national form of versification, adapted to the genius of the language and to the mode of declamation or musical accompaniment generally employed for assisting the effect. Thus the legendary poetry of the Greeks naturally took the form of the Homeric hexameter, and that of the Spaniards the loose *asonante* versification, as in the ballads of the Cid, so well adapted to the accompaniment of the guitar. The English ballads, almost without exception, affect the iambic measure of twelve or fourteen syllables, rhyming in couplets, which, however, naturally divide themselves, by means of the *cæsura* or pause, into stanzas of four lines, the rhymes generally occurring at the end of the second and fourth verses. This form of metre is found predominating throughout all these interesting relics; and was itself, in all probability, a relic of the old long unrhymed alliterative measure, examples of which may be seen in the *Lay of Gamelyn*, or in the more recent *Vision of Piers Plowman*. The breaking up of the long lines into short hemistichs, to which I have just alluded, may have been originally nothing but a means for facilitating the copying of the lines into a page too narrow to admit them at full length: and the readiness with which these lines divide themselves into such hemistichs may be observed by a comparison with the long metre of the old German *Nibelungen Lied*, each two lines of which can be easily broken up into a stanza of four, the rhymes being then confined, as in the English ballads, to the second and fourth lines.

Written or composed by obscure and often illiterate poets, these productions were frequently handed down only by tradition from generation to generation: it is to the taste and curiosity, perhaps only to the family pride, of collectors, that we owe the accident by which some of them were copied and preserved; the few that were ever printed, being destined for circulation only among the poorest class, were confided to the meanest typography and to flying sheets, or *broadsides*, as they are termed by collectors. Vast numbers of them — perhaps not inferior to the finest that have been preserved — have perished forever. The first considerable collection of these ballads was published, with most agreeable and valuable notes, by Bishop THOMAS PERCY, in 1765, and it is to his example that we owe, not only the preservation of these invaluble relics, but the immense revolution produced, by their study and imitation, in the literature of the present century. It is no exaggeration to say that the old English ballads had the greatest share in bringing about that immense change in taste and feeling which characterizes the revival of romantic poetry; and that the relics of the rude old moss-trooping rhapsodists of the Border, in a great measure, generated the admirable inspirations of Walter Scott. Constructed, like the Homeric rhapsodies or the Romances of Spain, upon a certain regular model, these ballads, like the productions just mentioned, abound in certain regularly recurring passages, turns of expression and epithets: these must be regarded as the mechanical or received aids to the composer in his task; but these commonplaces are incessantly enlivened by some stroke of picturesque description, some vivid painting of natural objects, some burst of simple heroism, or some touch of pathos. Among the oldest and finest of these works I may cite "the grand old ballad" of *Sir Patrick Spens*, the *Battle of Otterburne*, *Chevy Chase*, the *Death of Douglas*, all commemorating some battle, foray, or military exploit of the Border. The class of which the above are striking specimens, bear evident marks, in their subjects and the dialect in which they are composed, of a Northern, Scottish, or at least Border origin: it would be unjust not to mention that there exist large numbers, and those often of no inferior merit, which are distinctly traceable to an English — meaning a South British — source. To this class will belong the immense cycle or collection of ballads describing the adventures of the famous outlaw Robin Hood, and his "merry men." This legendary personage is described in such a multitude of episodes, that he must be considered a sort of national type of English character. Whether Robin Hood ever actually existed, or whether, like William Tell, he be merely a popular myth, is a question that perhaps no research will ever succeed in deciding: but the numerous ballads recounting his exploits form a most beautiful and valuable repertory of national tradition and national traits of character. In the last-mentioned class of ballads, viz. those of purely English origin, the curious investigator will trace the resistance opposed by the oppressed class of *yeomen* to the tyranny of Norman feudalism; and this point has been turned to admirable account by Walter Scott in his romance of *Ivanhoe*, in those exquisitely delineated scenes of which Robin Hood, under the name of the outlaw Locksley, is the hero. In these compositions we see manifest traces of the rough, vigorous spirit of popular, as contradistinguished from aristocratic, feeling. They commemorate the hostility of the English people against their Norman tyrants: and the bold and joyous sentiment which prevails in them is strongly contrasted with the lofty and exclusive tone pervading the Trouvère legends.

NOTES AND ILLUSTRATIONS.

A.—MINOR POETS.

From the death of Chaucer there is a dreary blank in the history of English poetry. The first writer who deserves mention is

THOMAS OCCLEVE (fl. 1420), a lawyer in the reign of Henry V. But he hardly deserves the name of a poet, as his verses are feeble and stupid. Very few of his poems have been printed.

JOHN LYDGATE (fl. 1430) is a writer of greater merit. He was a monk of Bury, in Suffolk; he travelled into France and Italy, and was well acquainted with the literature of both countries. He wrote a large number of poems, of which one of the most celebrated is a translation of Boccaccio's *Fall of Princes*, which he describes as a series of *Tragedies*. His two other larger works are, the *Story of Thebes* translated from Statius, and the *History of the Siege of Troy*. Gray formed a high opinion of his poetical powers. "I pretend not," he says, "to set him on a level with Chaucer, but he certainly comes the nearest to him of any contemporary writer I am acquainted with. His choice of expression, and the smoothness of his verse, far surpass both Gower and Occleve. He wanted not art in raising the more tender emotions of the mind."

JOHN HARDING (fl. 1470) wrote in verse a Chronicle of England, coming down to the reign of Edward IV., to whom he dedicated the work. The poetry is wretched, and deserves only the attention of the antiquary.

THE SCOTTISH POETRY occupies a higher place than the English in the fifteenth and the first half of the sixteenth centuries. BARBOUR and WYNTON belong to the fourteenth century, and are spoken of in the Notes and Illustrations to the preceding chapter (p. 55). They are followed by JAMES I., DUNBAR, GAWIN DOUGLAS, HENRYSON, and BLIND HARRY, mentioned in the text (pp. 60, 61). To these should be added SIR DAVID LYNDSAY (1490-1557), the Lyon King at Arms, and the friend and companion of James V. His poems are said to have contributed to the Reformation in Scotland. In his satires he attacked the clergy with great severity. "But in the ordinary style of his versification he seems not to rise much above the prosaic and tedious rhymers of the fifteenth century. His descriptions are as circumstantial without selection as theirs; and his language, partaking of a ruder dialect, is still more removed from our own." (Hallam.)

It has been remarked above (see p. 67) that Surrey and Wyatt's poems were published in Tottel's *Miscellany*, which was the first printed poetical miscellany in the English language. Among the other contributors to this collection, though their names are not mentioned, were SIR FRANCIS BRYAN, the nephew of Lord Berners, the translator of Froissart, and one of the brilliant ornaments of the court of Henry VIII.; GEORGE BOLEYN, VISCOUNT ROCHFORD, the brother of Anne Boleyn, beheaded in 1536; THOMAS, LORD VAUX, Captain of the Island of Jersey under Henry VIII., some of whose poems are also printed in the collection called the "Paradise of Dainty Devices" (see p. 85), and who is described by Puttenham in his Art of Poesie as "a man of much facilitie in vulgar makings;" and NICHOLAS GRIMOALD (about 1520-1563), a lecturer at Oxford, whose initials, N. G., are attached to his "Songes" in Tottel's Miscellany. He was a learned scholar, and translated into English some of the Latin and Greek classics.

To this period, rather than to that of Elizabeth, belongs THOMAS TUSSER (1527-1580), one of the earliest of our didactic poets, who was born at Rivenhall in Essex, was educated at Cambridge, and passed two years at court under the patronage of William, Lord Paget. He afterwards settled as a farmer at Cattiwade in Suffolk, where he wrote his work on Husbandry, of which the first edition appeared in 1557 under the title of "A Hundreth Good Pointes of Husbandrie." He practised farming in other parts of the country, was a singing man in Norwich cathedral, and died poor in London. His work, after going through four editions, was published in an enlarged form in 1577, under the title of "Five Hundred Points of Good Husbandrie, united to as many of Good Huswiferie." It is written in familiar verse, and "is valuable as a genuine picture of the agriculture, the rural arts, and the domestic economy and customs of our industrious ancestors." (Warton.)

B.—MINOR PROSE WRITERS.

One of the chief prose writers of the fifteenth century was PECOCK (fl. 1450), Bishop of Asaph, and afterwards of Chichester. Though he wrote against the Lollards, his own theological views were regarded with suspicion, and he was, in 1457, obliged to recant, was deprived of his bishopric, and passed the rest of his life in a conventual prison. His principal work, entitled the *Repressor of overmuch blaming of the Clergy*, appeared in 1449. There is an excellent edition of this work by C. Babington, 1863. With respect to its language, Mr. Marsh observes that, "although, in diction and arrangement of sentences, the *Repressor* is much in advance of the chroniclers of Pecock's age, the grammar, both in accidence and syntax, is in many points nearly where Wicliffe had left it; and it is of course in these respects considerably behind that of the contemporary poetical writers. Thus, while these latter authors, as well as some of earlier date, employ the objective plural pronoun *them*, and the plural possessive pronoun *their*, Pecock writes always *hem* for the personal and *her* for the possessive pronoun. These pronominal forms soon fell into disuse, and they are hardly to be met with in any English writer of later date than Pecock. With respect to one of them, however,—the objective *hem* for *them*,—it may be remarked that it has not become obsolete in colloquial speech to the present day; for in such phrases as *I saw 'em*, *I told 'em*, and the like, the pronoun *em* (or *'em*) is not as is popularly supposed, a vulgar corruption of the full pronoun *them*, which alone is found in modern books, but it is the true Anglo-Saxon and old English objective plural, which, in our spoken dialect, has remained unchanged for a thousand years."

SIR THOMAS MALORY (fl. 1470), the compiler and translator of the *Morte Arthur*, or History of King Arthur, printed by Caxton in 1485. Caxton, in his preface, says that Sir Thomas Malory took the work out of certain books in French, and reduced it into English. It is a compilation from some of the most popular romances of the Round Table. The style deserves great praise. See also p. 32, B.

JOHN FISHER (1459-1535), Bishop of Rochester, put to death by Henry VIII., along with Sir Thomas More. Besides his Latin works he wrote some sermons in English.

SIR THOMAS ELYOT (d. 1546), an eminent scholar in the reign of Henry VIII., by whom he was employed in several embassies. He shares with Sir Thomas More the praise of being one of the earliest English prose writers of value. His principal work is *The Governor*, published in 1531, a treatise upon education, in which he deprecates the ill-treatment to which boys were exposed at school at this period.

JOHN LELAND (1506-1552), the eminent antiquary, was educated at St. Paul's School, London, and at Oxford and Cambridge. He received several ecclesiastical preferments from Henry VIII., who also gave him the title of the King's Antiquary. Besides his Latin works he wrote in English his *Itinerary*, giving an account of his travels, a work still of great value for English topography.

GEORGE CAVENDISH (d. 1557), not Sir William, as frequently stated, was gentleman-usher to Cardinal Wolsey, and wrote the life of the Cardinal, from which Shakspeare has taken many passages in his Henry VIII.

JOHN BELLENDEN (d. 1550), Archdean of Moray, in the reign of James V., deserves mention as one of the earliest prose writers in Scotland. His translation of the Scottish History of Boethius, or Boecius (Boece), was published in 1537.

JOHN BALE (1495-1563), Bishop of Ossory in Ireland, was the author of several theological works and of some dramatic interludes on sacred subjects (see p. 114). But the work by which he is best known is in Latin, containing an account of illustrious writers in Great Britain from Japhet to the year 1559.

CHAPTER IV.

THE ELIZABETHAN POETS (INCLUDING THE REIGN OF JAMES I.). A. D. 1558-1625.

§ 1. Characteristics of the Elizabethan age of Literature. § 2. The less known writers of this period: GASCOIGNE; TURBERVILLE; THOMAS SACKVILLE, Lord Buckhurst. § 3. EDMUND SPENSER: his personal history; the *Shepherd's Calendar;* his friendship with Harvey and Sidney; favored by Leicester and Elizabeth; disappointments at court; residence in Ireland; misfortunes, and death. § 4. Analysis and criticism of the *Faery Queen:* brilliancy of imagination; defects of plan; allusions to persons and events. § 5. Detailed analysis of the Second Book, or the *Legend of Temperance.* § 6. Versification of the poem; adaptation of the language in the metre; Spenser's boldness in dealing with English. § 7. Character of Spenser's genius: his minor works. § 8. SIR PHILIP SIDNEY: his accomplishments and heroic death: his *Sonnets, Arcadia,* and *Defence of Poesy.* § 9. Other leading Poets of the age: — (i.) DANIEL; (ii.) DRAYTON; (iii.) SIR JOHN DAVIES; (iv.) JOHN DONNE; (v.) BISHOP HALL; English Satire. § 10. Minor Poets: PHINEAS and GILES FLETCHER; CHURCHYARD; the Jesuit SOUTHWELL; FAIRFAX, the translator of Tasso.

§ **1.** THE Age of Elizabeth is characterized by features which cause it to stand alone in the literary history of the world. It was a period of sudden emancipation of thought, of immense fertility and originality, and of high and generally diffused intellectual cultivation. The language, thanks to the various causes indicated in the preceding chapters, had reached its highest perfection; the study and the imitation of ancient or foreign models had furnished a vast store of materials, images and literary forms, which had not yet had time to become commonplace and overworn. The poets and prose writers of this age, therefore, united the freshness and vigor of youth with the regularity and majesty of manhood; and nothing can better demonstrate the intellectual activity of the epoch than the number of excellent works which have become obsolete in the present day, solely from their merits having been eclipsed by the glories of a few incomparable names, as those of Spenser in romantic and of Shakspeare in dramatic poetry. It will be my task to give a rapid sketch of some of the great works thus "darkened with the excess of light."

§ **2.** The first name is that of GEORGE GASCOIGNE (1530-1577), who, as one of the founders of the great English school of the drama, as a satirist, as a narrative and as a lyric poet, enjoyed a high popularity for art and genius. His most important production, in point of length, is a species of moral or satiric declamation entitled the *Steel Glass*, in which he inveighs against the vices and follies of his time. It is written in blank verse, and is one of the earliest examples of that kind of metre, so well adapted to the genius of the English language, and in which, independently of the drama, so many important compositions were afterwards to be written. The versification of Gascoigne in this work, though somewhat harsh and monotonous, is dignified and regular; and the poem evinces close observation of life and a lofty tone of morality. His career was a very active one; he figured on the brilliant stage of the court, took part in a campaign in Holland against the Spaniards, and has commemorated some of the unfortunate incidents of this expedition in a poem in seven-lined stanzas, entitled *The Fruits of War;* and many of his minor compositions are well deserving of perusal. He was an example of a type of literary men which abounded in England at that period, in which the active and contemplative life were harmoniously combined, and which brought the acquisitions of the study to bear upon the interests of real life.

Nearly contemporary with this poet was GEORGE TURBERVILE (1530–1594), whose writings exhibit a less vigorous invention than those of Gascoigne. He very frequently employed a peculiar modification of the old English ballad stanza which was extremely fashionable at this period. The modification consists in the third line, instead of being of equal length to the first, viz. of six syllables, containing eight. It must not, however, be understood from this that Turbervile did not employ a great variety of other metrical arrangements. The majority of his writings consist of love epistles, epitaphs, and complimentary verses.

A poet whose writings, of a lofty, melancholy, and moral tone, undoubtedly exerted a great influence at a critical period in the formation of the English literature, was THOMAS SACKVILLE, Lord Buckhurst (1536–1608), a person of high political distinction, having filled the office of Lord High Treasurer. It was for his children that Ascham wrote the *Schoolmaster.* He projected, and himself commenced, a work entitled *A Mirrour for Magistrates*, which was intended to contain a series of tragic examples of the vicissitudes of fortune, drawn from the annals of his own country, serving as lessons of virtue to future kings and statesmen, and as warnings of the fragility of earthly greatness and success. Sackville composed the *Induction* (Introduction) of this grave and dignified work, and also the first legend or complaint, in which are commemorated the power and the fall of the Duke of Buckingham, favorite and victim of the tyrannical Richard III. The poem was afterwards continued by other writers in the same style, though generally with a perceptible diminution of grandeur and effect. Such collections of legends or short poetical biographies, in which celebrated and unfortunate sufferers were introduced, bewailing their destiny, or warning mankind against crime and ambition, were frequent in literature at an earlier period. Chaucer's *Monk's Tale*, and the same poet's *Legend of Good Women*, are in plan and character not dissimilar: nay, the origin of such a form of composition may be traced even to the vast ethical collection of the *Gesta Romanorum*, if not to a still higher antiquity; for the *Heroides* of Ovid, though confined to the sufferings of unhappy love, form a somewhat similar gallery of examples. The *Mirrour for Magistrates* is written in stanzas of seven lines, and exhibits great occasional power of expression, and a remarkable force and compression of language, though the general tone is gloomy and somewhat monotonous. Some of the lines reach a high elevation of sombre picturesqueness, as these, of old age: —

> "His scalp all pilled, and he with eld forlore,
> His withered fist still knocking at death's door,"

which is strikingly like what Chaucer himself would have written.*

§ 3. A period combining a scholar-like imitation of antiquity and of foreign contemporary literature, principally that of Italy, with the force, freshness, and originality of the dawn of letters in England, might have been fairly expected, even *à priori*, to produce a great imaginative and descriptive work of poetry. The illustrious name of EDMUND SPENSER (1553–1599) occupies a place among the writers of England similar to that of Ariosto among those of Italy; and the union in his works — and particularly in his greatest work, the *Faëry Queen* — of original invention and happy use of existing materials, fully warrants the unquestioned verdict which names him as the greatest English poet intervening between Chaucer and Shakspeare. His career was brilliant, but unhappy. Born in 1553, a cadet of the illustrious family whose name he bore, though not endowed with fortune, he was educated at the University of Cambridge, where he undoubtedly acquired an amount of learning remarkable even in that age of solid and substantial studies. He is supposed, after leaving the University, to have been compelled to perform the functions of domestic tutor in the North of England; and to have gained his first fame by the publication of the *Shepherd's Calendar*, a series of pastorals divided into twelve parts or months, in which, as in Virgil's *Bucolics*, under the guise of idyllic dialogues, his imaginary interlocutors discuss high questions of morality and state, and pay refined compliments to illustrious personages. In these eclogues Spenser endeavored to give a national air to his work, by painting English scenery and the English climate, by selecting English names for his rustic persons, and by infusing into their language many provincial and obsolete expressions. The extraordinary superiority, in power of thought and harmony of language, exhibited by the *Shepherd's Calendar*, immediately placed Spenser among the highest poetical names of his day, and attracted the favor and patronage of the great. The young poet had been closely connected, by friendship and the community of tastes and studies, with the learned Gabriel Harvey — a man of unquestionable genius, but rendered ridiculous by certain literary *hobbies*, as, for example, by a mania for employing the ancient classical metres, founded on quantity, in English verse; and he for some time infected Spenser with his own freaks. Through Harvey, Spenser acquired the notice and favor of the accomplished Sidney; and it was

* For a further account of the *Mirrour for Magistrates*, see Notes and Illustrations (A).

at Penshurst, the fine mansion of the latter, that he is supposed to have revised the *Shepherd's Calendar*, which he dedicated, under the title of the *Poet's Year*, to "Maister Philip Sidney, worthy of all titles, both of Chivalry and Poesy." Sidney, in his turn, recommended Spenser to Dudley Earl of Leicester, and the powerful favorite brought the poet under the personal notice of Elizabeth herself. The great queen, surfeited as she was with all the refinements of literary homage, certainly had not, among the throng of poets that filled her court, a worshipper whose incense arose before her altar in richer or more fragrant clouds; but the poet, in his court career, naturally exposed himself to the hostility of those who were the enemies of his protectors; and there are several traditions which relate the disappointments experienced by Spenser at the hands of the great minister Burleigh, whose influence on the mind of his mistress was too firmly established to be seriously shaken by the Queen's attachment to her favorites. Spenser has left us a gloomy picture of the miseries of courtly dependence. The poet appears to have been occasionally employed in unimportant diplomatic services; but on the nomination of Lord Grey de Wilton as Deputy or Lieutenant of Ireland, Spenser accompanied him to that country as secretary, and received a grant of land not far from Cork, which he was to occupy and cultivate. This estate had formed part of the domains of the Earls of Desmond, and had been forfeited or confiscated by the English Government. Spenser resided several years at Kilcolman Castle, during which time he exercised various important administrative functions in the government of the then newly-subjugated country. It was during his residence in Ireland that he composed the most important of his works, among which the first place is occupied by his great poem of the *Faëry Queen*. About twelve years after his first establishment in the province of Munster, the flame of revolt, communicated from the great rebellion called Tyrone's Insurrection, which had been raging in the neighboring province of Ulster, spread to the region which surrounded Spenser's retreat. He had probably rendered himself hateful to the half-savage Celtic population whom the English colonists had ejected and oppressed: indeed the very curious little work entitled *A View of the State of Ireland*, in which he has described the curious manners and customs of the indigenous race, indicates plainly enough that the poet shared the prejudices of his race and position. Kilcolman Castle was attacked and burned by the insurgents. Spenser and his family escaped with difficulty, and with the loss not only of all they possessed, but with the still more cruel bereavement of a young child, which was left behind and perished in the house. Completely ruined, and overwhelmed by so tragic an affliction, the poet returned to London, where he is reported to have died in the greatest poverty, forgotten by the court and neglected by his patrons, in 1599. He was, however, followed to the grave with the unanimous admiration of his countrymen, who bewailed in his death the loss of the greatest poet of his age. He was buried with great pomp in Westminster Abbey, near the tomb of Chaucer.

§ 4. Spenser's greatest work, *The Faëry Queen*, is a poem the subject of which is chivalric, allegorical, narrative, and descriptive, while the execution is in a great measure derived from the manner of Ariosto and Tasso. It was originally planned to consist of twelve books of moral adventures, each typifying the triumph of a Virtue, and couched under the form of an exploit of knight-errantry. The hero of the whole action was to be the mythical Prince Arthur, the type of perfect virtue in Spenser, as he is the ideal hero in the vast collection of mediæval legends in which he figures. This fabulous personage is supposed to become enamoured of the Faëry Queen, who appears to him in a dream; and arriving at her court in Fairy-Land he finds her holding a solemn feudal festival during twelve days. At her court there is a beautiful lady for whose hand the twelve most distinguished knights are rivals; and in order to settle their pretensions these twelve heroes undertake twelve separate adventures, which furnish the materials for the action. The First Book relates the expedition of the Red-Cross Knight, who is the allegorical representative of *Holiness*, while his mistress Una represents true *Religion;* and the action of the knight's exploit shadows forth the triumph of Holiness over the enchantments and deceptions of Heresy. The Second Book recounts the adventures of Sir Guyon, or *Temperance;* the Third those of Britomartis — a female champion — or *Chastity*. It must be remarked that each of these books is subdivided into twelve cantos, consequently that the poem, even in the imperfect form under which we possess it, is extremely voluminous. The three first books were published separately in 1590, and dedicated to Elizabeth, who rewarded the delicate flattery which pervades innumerable allusions in the work with a pension of 50*l.* a year. After returning to Ireland Spenser prosecuted his work, and in 1596 he gave to the world three more books, namely, the Fourth, containing the Legend of Cambell and Triamond, allegorizing *Friendship;* the Fifth, the Legend of Artegall, or of *Justice;* and the Sixth, that of Sir Calidore, or *Courtesy*. Thus half of the poet's original design was executed. What progress he made in the six remaining books it is now impossible to ascertain. There are traditions which assert that this latter portion was completed, but that the manuscript was lost at sea; while the more probable theory is, that Spenser had not time to terminate his extensive plan, but that the dreadful misfortunes amid which his life was closed prevented him from completing his design. The fragment consisting of two cantos of *Mutability* was intended to be inserted in the legend of *Constancy*, one of the books projected. The vigor, invention, and splendor of expression that glow so brightly in the first three books, manifestly decline in the fourth, fifth, and sixth; and it is perhaps no matter of regret that the poet never completed so vast a design, in which the very nature of the plan necessitated a monotony that not all his fertility of genius could have obviated. We may apply to the *Faëry Queen* the paradox of Hesiod — "the half is more than the whole." In this poem are united and harmonized three different elements which at first sight would appear irreconcilable; for the skeleton or framework of the action is derived from the feudal or chivalric legends; the ethical or moral sentiment from the lofty philosophy of Plato, combined with the most elevated Christian purity; and the form and coloring of the language and versification are saturated with the flowing grace and sensuous elegance of the great Italian poets of the Renaissance. The principal defects of the *Faëry Queen*, viewed as a whole, arise from two causes apparently opposed, yet resulting in a similar impression on the reader. The first is a want of unity, involving a loss of interest in the story; for we altogether forget Arthur, the nominal hero of the whole, and follow each separate adventure of the subordinate knights. Each book is therefore, intrinsically, a separate poem, and excites a separate interest. The other defect is the monotony of character inseparable from a series of adventures which, though varied with inexhaustible fertility, are all, from their chivalric nature, fundamentally similar, being either combats between one knight and another, or between the hero of the moment and some supernatural being — a monster, a dragon, or a wicked enchanter. In these contests, however brilliantly painted, we feel little or no suspense, for we are beforehand nearly certain of the victory of the hero; and even if this were otherwise, the knowledge that the valiant champion is himself nothing but the impersonation of some abstract quality or virtue, would be fatal to that interest with which we follow the vicissitudes of human fortunes. Hardly any degree of genius or invention can long sustain the interest of an allegory; and where the intense realism of Bunyan has only partially succeeded, the unreal phantasmagoria of Spenser's imagination, brilliant as it was, could not do other than fail. The strongest proof of the justice of these remarks will be found in the fact that those who read Spenser with the intensest delight are precisely those who entirely neglect the moral lessons typified in his allegory, and endeavor to follow his recital of adventures as those of human beings, giving themselves voluntarily up to the mighty magic of his unequalled imagination. Another result flowing from the above considerations is, that Spenser, though extremely monotonous and tiresome to an ordinary reader, who determines to plod doggedly through two or three successive books of the *Faëry Queen*, is the most enchanting of poets to him who, endowed with a lively fancy, confines his attention to one or two at a time of his delicious episodes, descriptions, or impersonations. Independently of the general allegorical meaning of the persons and adventures, it must be remembered that many of these were also intended to contain allusions to facts and individuals of Spenser's own time, and particularly to convey compliments to his friends and patrons. Thus Gloriana, the Faëry Queen herself, and the beautiful huntress Belphœbe, were intended to allude to Elizabeth; Sir Artegall, the Knight of Justice, to Lord Grey; and the adventures of the Red-Cross Knight shadow forth the history of the Anglican Church. In all probability a multitude of such allusions, now become obscure, were clear enough, when the poem first appeared, to those who were familiar with the courtly and political life of the time; but the modern reader, I think, will little regret the dimness in which time has plunged these allusions, for they only still further complicate an allegory which of itself often detracts from the charm and interest of the narrative.

§ **5.** As a specimen of Spenser's mode of conducting his allegory, I will give here a rapid analysis of the Second Book, or the *Legend of Temperance*. In Canto I. the wicked enchanter, Archimage, meeting Sir Guyon, informs him that a fair lady, whom the latter supposes to be Una, but who is really Duessa, has been foully outraged by the Red Cross Knight. Guyon, led by Archimage, meets the Red-Cross Knight, and is on the point of attacking him, when the two champions recognize each other, and, after courteous conference, part. Sir Guyon then hears the despairing cry of a lady, and finds Amaria, newly stabbed, lying beside a knight (Sir Mordant), and holding in her lap a babe with his hands stained by its mother's blood. After relating her story, the lady dies. Canto II. describes Sir Guyon's unsuccessful attempts to wash the babe's bloody hands. He then finds his steed gone, and proceeds on foot to the Castle of Golden Mean, where dwell also her two sisters, Elissa and Perissa — Too Little and Too Much — with their knights. Canto III. describes the adventures of the Boaster, Bragadocchio, who has stolen Guyon's steed, but who is ignominiously compelled to give it up, and is abandoned by Belphœbe, of whom this canto contains a description, of consummate beauty. In Canto IV Guyon delivers Phaon from the violence of Furor and the malignity of the hag Occasion. Canto V. describes the combat of Guyon with Pyrochles, who unbinds Fury, and is then wounded by him; and Atin lies to obtain the aid of Cymochles. Canto VI. gives a most rich and exquisite picture of the temptation of Guyon by the Lady of the Idle Lake. In Canto VII. is contained the admirable description of the Cave of Mammon, who tempts Sir Guyon with riches. The VIIIth Canto depicts Guyon in his trance, disarmed by the sons of Acrates, and delivered by Arthur. Canto IX. describes the House of Temperance inhabited by Alma. This is a most ingenious and beautifully developed allegory of the human body and mind, each part and faculty being typified. Canto X. gives a chronicle of the ancient British kings down to the reign of Gloriana, or Elizabeth. In the XIth canto the Castle of Temperance is besieged, and delivered by Arthur. The XIIth and last canto of this book describes the attack of Guyon upon the Bower of Bliss, and the ultimate defeat of Acrasia or Sensual Pleasure. From this very rough and meagre analysis, which is all that my limits will permit, the reader may in some measure judge of the conduct of the fable in Spenser's great poem.

§ **6.** The versification of the work is a peculiar stanza, based upon the *ottava rima* so universally employed by the romantic and narrative poets of Italy, and of which the masterpieces of Tasso and Ariosto furnish familiar examples. To the eight lines composing this form of metre, Spenser's exquisite taste and consummate ear for harmony induced him to add a ninth, which, being of twelve instead of, as in the others, ten syllables, winds up each phrase with a long, lingering cadence of the most delicious melody. I have already observed how extensively the forms of Italian versification — as in the various examples of the sonnet and the heroic stanza — had been adopted by the English poets; and I have insisted, particularly in the case of Chaucer, on the skill with which our language, naturally rude, monosyllabic, and unharmonious, had been softened and melodized till it was little inferior, in power of musical expression, to the tongues of Southern Europe. None of our poets is more exquisitely and uniformly musical than Spenser. Indeed the sweetness and flowingness of his verse are sometimes carried so far as to become cloying and enervated. The metre he employed being very complicated, and necessitating a frequent recurrence in each stanza of similar rhymes — namely, four of one ending, three of another, and two of a third — he was obliged to take considerable liberties with the orthography and accentuation of the English language. In doing this, in giving to our metallic northern speech the flexibility of the liquid Italian, he shows himself as unscrupulous as masterly. By employing an immense mass of old Chaucerian words and provincialisms, nay, even by occasionally inventing words himself, he furnishes his verse with an inexhaustible variety of language; but at the same time the reader must remember that much of the vocabulary of the great poet was a dialect that never really existed. Its peculiarities have been less permanent than those of almost any other of our great writers.

§ 7. The power of Spenser's genius does not consist in any deep analysis of human passion or feeling, in any skill in the delineation of character; but in an unequalled richness of description, in the art of representing events and objects with an intensity that makes them visible and tangible. He describes *to the eye*, and communicates to the airy conceptions of allegory, the splendor and the vivacity of visible objects. He has the exhaustless fertility of Rubens, with that great painter's sensuous and voluptuous profusion of color. Among the most important of his other poetical writings, I must mention his *Mother Hubbard's Tale;* his *Daphnaida*, an idyllic elegy bewailing the early death of the accomplished Sidney; and above all his *Amoretti*, or love poems, the most beautiful of which is his *Epithalamium*, or Marriage-Song on his own nuptials with the "fair Elizabeth." This is certainly one of the richest and chastest marriage-hymns to be found in the whole range of literature, combining warmth with dignity, the intensest passion with a noble elevation and purity of sentiment. Here, too, as well as in innumerable passages of the *Faëry Queen*, do we see the influence of that lofty and abstract philosophical idea of the identity between Beauty and Virtue, which he borrowed from the Platonic speculations.

§ 8. The name of SIR PHILIP SIDNEY (1554–1586) occurs so frequently in the literary history of this age, and that illustrious man exerted so powerful an influence on the intellectual spirit of the epoch, that our notice of the age would be incomplete without some allusion to his life, even did not the intrinsic merit of his writings give him a place among the best poets and prose-writers of the time. He united in his own person almost all the qualities that give splendor to a character, natural as well as adventitious — nobility of birth, beauty of person, bravery, generosity, learning, and courtesy. He was almost the *beau idéal* of the courtier, the soldier, and the scholar. The jewel of the court, the darling of the people, and the liberal and judicious patron of arts and letters, his early and heroic death gave the crowning grace to a consummate character. He was born in 1554, and died at the age of thirty-two, of a wound received in the battle of Zutphen (October 19, 1586), fought to aid the Protestants of the Netherlands in their heroic struggle against the Spaniards. His contributions to the literature of his country consist of a small collection of *Sonnets*, remarkable for their somewhat languid and refined elegance; and the prose romance, once regarded as a manual of courtesy and refined ingenuity, entitled *The Arcadia*. Judging only by its title, many critics have erroneously regarded this work as a purely pastoral composition, like the *Galatea* of Cervantes, the *Arcadia* of Sannazzaro, and the multitude of idyllic romances which were so fashionable at that time; but the narrative of Sidney, though undoubtedly written on Spanish and Italian models, is not exclusively devoted to pastoral scenes and descriptions. A great portion of the work is chivalric, and the grace and animation with which the knightly pen of Sidney paints the shock of the tourney, and the noble warfare of the chase, is not surpassed by the luxurious elegance of his pastoral descriptions. In the style we see perpetual traces of that ingenious antithetical affectation which the imitation of Spanish models had rendered fashionable in England, and which became at last a kind of *Phébus* or modish jargon at the court, until it was ultimately annihilated by the ridicule of Shakspeare, just as Molière destroyed the *style précieux* which prevailed in his day in France. One charming peculiarity of Sidney is the pure and elevated view he takes of the female character, and which his example powerfully tended to disseminate throughout the literature of his day. This alone would be sufficient to prove the truly chivalrous character of his mind. The story of the *Arcadia*, though occasionally tiresome and involved, is related with considerable skill; and the reader will be enchanted, in almost every page, with some of those happy thoughts and graceful expressions which he hesitates whether to attribute to the felicity of accident or to a peculiar delicacy of fancy. Sidney also wrote a small tract entitled *A Defence of Poesy*, in which he strives to show that the pleasures derivable from imaginative literature are powerful aids not only to the acquisition of knowledge, but to the cultivation of virtue. He exhibits a peculiar sensibility to the power and genius so often concealed in rude national legends and ballads.

§ 9. The epoch which I am endeavoring to describe was fertile in a class of poets, not perhaps attaining to the highest literary merit, but whose writings are marked by a kind of solid and scholar-like dignity which will render them permanently valuable.

(i.) Such was SAMUEL DANIEL (1562–1619), whose career seems to have been tranquil and happy, and who enjoyed among his contemporaries the respect merited not only by his talents, but by a regularity of conduct then sufficiently rare among poets who, like Daniel, were connected with the stage. His works are tolerably voluminous, and all bear the stamp of that grave vigor of thought and dignified evenness of expression which, while it seldom soars into sublimity, or penetrates deep into the abysses of passion, is never devoid of sense and reflection. His most celebrated work is *The History of the Civil Wars*, a poem on the Civil Wars between the houses of York and Lancaster, in that peculiar style of poetical narrative and moral meditation the example of which had been set by Sackville's *Mirrour for Magistrates*, and which was at this time a favorite type among the literary men of England. Daniel's poem is in eight books, in stanzas of eight lines; and the talents of the writer struggle in vain against the prosaic nature of the subject, for Daniel closely adheres to the facts of history, which he can only occasionally enliven by a pathetic description or a sensible and vigorous reflection. His language is exceedingly pure, limpid, and intelligible. The poem entitled *Musophilus* is an elaborate defence of learning, cast into the form of a dialogue. The two interlocutors, Musophilus and Philocosmus, pronounce, in regular and well-turned stanzas, the usual arguments which the subject suggests. Many of Daniel's minor poems, as his *Elegies*, *Epistles*, *Masques*, and *Songs*, together with his contributions to the dramatic literature of the day, justify the reputation which he possessed. Good sense, dignity, and an equable flow of pure language and harmonious versification, are the qualities which posterity will acknowledge in his writings. He is said to have succeeded Spenser to the post of poet laureate.

(ii.) A poet somewhat similar in general character to Daniel, but endowed with a much greater originality, was MICHAEL DRAYTON (1563–1631), a voluminous writer. His longest and most celebrated productions were the topographical and descriptive poem entitled *Polyolbion*, in thirty cantos or songs, *The Barons' Wars*, *England's Heroical Epistles*, *The Battle of Agincourt*, *The Muses' Elysium*, and the delicious fancies of *The Court of Fairy*. The *Polyolbion* is a minute poetical itinerary of England and Wales, in which the affectionate patriotism of the writer has enumerated — county by county, village by village, hill by hill, and rivulet by rivulet — the whole surface of his native land; enlivening his work as he goes on by immense stores of picturesque legend and the richest profusion of allegory and personification. It is composed in the long-rhymed verse of twelve syllables, and is, both in design and execution, absolutely unique in literature. The notes attached to this work, in which Drayton was assisted by "that gulf of learning," the incomparable Selden, are a wonderful mass of curious erudition. Drayton has described his country with the painful accuracy of the topographer and the enthusiasm of a poet; and the *Polyolbion* will ever remain a most interesting monument of industry and taste. In *The Barons' Wars* Drayton has described the principal events of the unhappy reign of Edward II. The poem is composed in the stanza of Ariosto, which Drayton, in his preface, selects as the most perfect and harmonious; and the merits and defects of the work may be pretty accurately characterized by what has been said above concerning Daniel's poem on a not dissimilar subject. The *Heroical Epistles* are imagined to be written by illustrious and unfortunate personages in English history to the objects of their love. They are therefore a kind of adaptation of the plan of Ovid to English annals. It was quite natural that a poet so fertile as Drayton, who wrote in almost every form, should not have neglected the Pastoral, a species of composition at that time in general favor. His efforts in this department are certainly not inferior to those of any of his contemporaries, not even excepting Spenser himself; while in this class of his writings, as well as in his inimitable fairy poems, Drayton has never been surpassed. In the series entitled *The Muses' Elysium*, consisting of a series of nine idyls, or *Nymphals*, as he calls them, and above all in the exquisite little mock-heroic of *Nymphidia*, everything that is most graceful, delicate, quaint, and fantastic in that form of national superstition — almost peculiar to Great Britain — the fairy mythology, is accumulated and touched with a consummate felicity. The whole poem of *Nymphidia* is a gem, and is almost equalled by the *Epithalamium* in the VIIIth Nymphal, on the marriage of "our Tita to a noble Fay." It is interesting to trace the use made of these graceful superstitions in the *Midsummer Night's Dream* and the *Merry Wives of Windsor*.

(iii.) The vigorous versatility of the age, founded on solid and extensive acquirements, is well exemplified in the poems of SIR JOHN DAVIES (1570–1626), a learned lawyer and statesman, and Chief Justice of Ireland, who has left two works of unusual merit and originality, on subjects so widely different that their juxtaposition excites almost a feeling of ludicrous paradox. The subject of one of them, *Nosce Teipsum*, is the proof of the immortality of the soul; that of the other, entitled *Orchestra*, the art of dancing. The language of Davies is pure and masculine, his versification smooth and melodious; and he seems to have communicated to his metaphysical arguments in the first poem, something of the easy grace and rhythmical harmony of the dance, while he has dignified and elevated the comparatively trivial subject of the second by a profusion of classical and learned allusions.* The *Nosce*

* On the *Nosce Teipsum*, Mr. Hallam remarks, "Perhaps no language can produce a poem, extending to so great a length, of more condensation of thought, or in which fewer languid verses will be found. Yet according to some definitions, the *Nosce Teipsum* is wholly unpoetical, inasmuch as it shows no passion and little fancy. If it reaches the heart at all, it is through the reason But since strong argument, in terse and correct style, fails not to give us pleasure in prose, it seems strange that it should lose its effect when it gains the aid of regular metre to gratify the ear and assist the memory. Lines there are in Davies which far outweigh much of the descriptive and imaginative poetry of the last two centuries, whether we estimate them by the pleasure they impart to us, or by the intellectual vigor they display. Experience has shown that the facul

Teipsum, published in 1599, is written in four-lined stanzas of heroic lines, a measure which was afterwards honored by being taken as the vehicle of one of Dryden's early efforts; but Dryden borrowed it more immediately from the *Gondibert* of Davenant. The *Orchestra* is composed in a peculiarly-constructed stanza of seven lines, extremely well adapted to express the ever-varying rhythm of those dancing movements which the poet, by a thousand ingenious analogies, traces throughout all nature.

(iv.) The unanimous admiration of contemporaries placed the genius of JOHN DONNE (1573-1631), Dean of St. Paul's, in one of the foremost places among the men of letters of his day. His life, too, full of vicissitudes, and his devotion of great and varied powers, first to scholastic study and retirement, then to the service of the state in active life, and last to the ministry of the Church, by familiarizing him with all the phases of human life, furnished his mind with rich materials for poetry of various kinds. When entering upon the career of the public service, as secretary to the Treasurer Lord Ellesmere, he made a secret marriage with the daughter of Sir George Moor, a lady whom he had long ardently loved, and the violent displeasure of whose family involved Donne in severe persecution. Though distinguished in his youth for wit and gayety, he afterwards, under deep religious conviction, embraced the clerical profession, and became as remarkable for intense piety as he had previously been for those accomplishments which had made him the Pico di Mirandola of his age. The writings of Donne are very voluminous, and consist of love verses, epigrams, elegies, and, above all, satires, which latter department of his works is that by which he is now principally remembered. As an amatory poet he has been justly classed by Johnson among the *metaphysical* poets — writers in whom the intellectual faculty obtains an enormous and disproportionate supremacy over sentiment and feeling. These authors are ever on the watch for unexpected and ingenious analogies; an idea is racked into every conceivable distortion; the most remote comparisons, the obscurest recesses of historical and scientific allusion, are ransacked to furnish comparisons and illustrations which no reader can suggest to himself, and which, when presented to him by the perverse ingenuity of the poet, fill him with a strange mixture of astonishment and shame, like the distortions of the posture-master or the tricks of sleight-of-hand. It is evident that in this cultivation of the odd, the unexpected, and the monstrous, the poet becomes perfectly indifferent to the natural graces and tender coloring of simple emotion; and in his incessant search after epigrammatic turns of thought, he cares very little whether reason, taste, and propriety be violated. This false taste in literature was at one time epidemic in Spain and Italy, from whence, in all proba-

ties peculiarly deemed poetical are frequently exhibited in a considerable degree, but very few have been able to preserve a perspicuous brevity without stiffness or pedantry (allowance made for the subject and the times), in metaphysical reasoning, so successfully as Sir John Davies." — (*Lit.* ii. 129.)

bility, it infected English poets, who have frequently rivalled their models in ingenious absurdity. The versification of Donne is singularly harsh and tuneless, and the contrast between the ruggedness of his expression and the far-fetched ingenuity of his thought adds to the oddity of the effect upon the mind of the reader, by making him contrast the unnatural perversion of immense intellectual activity with the rudeness and frequent coarseness both of the ideas and the expression. In Donne's *Satires*, of which he wrote seven, and in his *Epistles* to friends, we naturally find less of this portentous abuse of intellectual legerdemain, for the nature of such compositions implies that they are written in a more easy and colloquial strain; and Donne has occasionally adapted, with great felicity, the outlines of Horace and Juvenal to the manners of his own time and country. Pope has translated some of Donne's Satires into the language of his own time, under the title of "The Satires of Dr. John Donne, Dean of St. Paul's, versified."

(v.) But the real founder of Satire in England, if we are to judge by the relative scope and completeness of his works in this department, was JOSEPH HALL (1574-1656), Bishop of Norwich, a man equally remarkable for the learning, dignity, and piety with which he fulfilled his pastoral functions, and the heroic resignation with which he supported poverty and persecution when deprived of them. He produced six books of Satires, under the title of *Virgidemiarum* (*i. e.* a harvest or collection of rods, a word modified from the similar term *Vindemiarum*, vintage), which form a complete collection, though they were not all published at the same time, the first three books, quaintly entitled by their author *toothless Satires*, having appeared in 1597, while a student at Cambridge; and the latter three, designated *biting Satires*, two years afterwards. Some of these excellent poems attack the vices and affectations of literature, and others are of a more general moral application. For the vivacity of their images, the good sense and good taste which pervade them, the abundance of their illustrations, and the ease and animation of the style, they are deserving of high admiration. Read merely as giving curious pictures of the manners and society of the day, they are very interesting in themselves, and throw frequent light on obscure passages of the contemporary drama. Hall, like Juvenal, often employs a peculiar artifice which singularly heightens the piquancy of his attacks, viz. that of making his secondary allusions or illustrations themselves satirical. Some of these satires are extremely short, occasionally consisting of only a few lines. His versification is always easy, and often elegant; and the language offers an admirable union of the unforced facility of ordinary conversation with the elevation and conciseness of a more elaborate style.*

§ 10. Space will permit only a rapid allusion to several secondary poets who adorned this period, so rich in variety and vigor. The two brothers, PHINEAS FLETCHER and GILES FLETCHER, who lived, approx-

* To Donne and Hall should be added the name of JOHN MARSTON, the dramatic poet, as one of the chief satirists of the Elizabethan era. In 1599 he published three books of Satires, under the title of *The Scourge of Villainy.*

imately, between the years 1584 and 1650, and who were connected by blood with their great contemporary the dramatist, produced, the former one of those long elaborate allegorical works which had been so fashionable at the beginning of the century, and in which science called in the aid of fiction, as in the case of Davies's poem on the Immortality of the Soul. This was *The Purple Island*, a minute description of the human body, with all its anatomical details, which is followed by an equally searching delineation of the intellectual faculties. Giles Fletcher's work is *Christ's Victory and Triumph*, in which, as in his brother's production, we see evident traces of the rich and musical diction, as well as of the lofty and philosophical tone, of the great master of allegory, Spenser. With a mere notice of the noble religious enthusiasm that prevails in the writings of CHURCHYARD, and of the unction and truly evangelical resignation of the unfortunate Jesuit SOUTHWELL, and a word of praise to the faithful and elegant translation of *Tasso* by FAIRFAX, I must conclude the present chapter.*

* For a fuller account of these poets, see Notes and Illustrations (B).

NOTES AND ILLUSTRATIONS.

A.—THE MIRROUR FOR MAGISTRATES.

(See p. 72.)

The history of this work, which is the most important poem in English literature between Surrey and Spenser, and which was very popular in its day, deserves a few words. It was projected, as stated above (p. 72), by Thomas Sackville, Lord Bathurst, about the year 1557, and its plan was to give an account of all the illustrious but unfortunate characters in English history, from the conquest to the end of the fourteenth century. The poet descends, like Dante, into the infernal regions, conducted by Sorrow. Sackville, however, wrote only the *Induction* and the legend of the fall of the Duke of Buckingham, the vision of Richard III., and then committed the completion of the work to RICHARD BALDWYNE and GEORGE FERRERS. They were both men of learning; the former an ecclesiastic, and the author of a metrical version of Solomon's Song, which he dedicated to Edward VI.; the latter a lawyer, who sat in Parliament in the reign of Henry VIII., and who filled the office of the Lord of Misrule in the palace of Greenwich at the Christmas revels appointed by Edward VI., in 1553. Baldwyne and Ferrers called in the assistance of several other writers, among whom were Churchyard and Phayer, the translator of Virgil, who took their materials chiefly from the newly published chronicles of Fabyan and Hall. The wars of York and Lancaster were their chief resource. The work was first published in 1559; and after passing through three editions was reprinted in 1587, with the addition of many new lines, under the conduct of JOHN HIGGINS, a clergyman, and the author of some school books, who wrote a new induction in the octave stanza and a new series of lives, from Albanact, the youngest son of Brutus, and the first king of Albanie, or Scotland, continued to the Emperor Caracalla. The legend of Cordelia King Lear's youngest daughter, is the most striking part of Higgins's performance. The *Mirrour* was recast, with new additions, in 1610, by the poet Richard Niccols. It continued to enjoy great popularity till superseded by the growing reputation of a new poetical chronicle, entitled *Albion's England*, published before the beginning of the reign of James I.

Warton, who has devoted considerable space to the *Mirrour for Magistrates*, remarks, "It is reasonable to suppose, that the publication of the *Mirrour for Magistrates* enriched the stores, and extended the limits, of our drama. These lives are so many tragical speeches in character. They suggested scenes to Shakspeare. Some critics imagine that Historical Plays owed their origin to this collection. At least it is certain that the writers of this Mirrour were the first who made a poetical use of the English chronicles recently compiled by Fabyan, Hall, and Hollinshed, which opened a new field of subjects and events; and, I may add, produced a great revolution in the state of popular knowledge. For before those elaborate and voluminous compilations appeared, the history of England which had been shut up in the Latin narratives of the monkish annalists, was unfamiliar and almost unknown to the general reader."

B.—MINOR POETS IN THE REIGNS OF ELIZABETH AND JAMES I.

"It was said by Ellis that nearly one hundred names of poets belonging to the reign of Elizabeth might be enumerated, besides many that have left no memorial except their songs. This, however, was but a moderate computation. Drake (*Shakspeare and his Times*, i. 674) has made a list of more than two hundred." (Hallam, *Lit.* ii. 133.) The following is a list of the most important of these poets, in addition to those already described in the text: —

THOMAS CHURCHYARD (1520-1604), a voluminous poet, was born at Shrewsbury, and served as a soldier in the armies of Henry VIII., Mary, and Elizabeth. He experienced many vicissitudes of fortune. Mr. D'Israeli describes him "as one of those unfortunate men who have written poetry all their days, and lived a long life to complete the misfortune."

RICHARD EDWARDS (1523-1566), also known as a dramatic poet, was born in Somersetshire, educated at Oxford, and was appointed by Queen Elizabeth master of the singing boys of the royal chapel. He was the chief contributor and framer of a poetical collection called *The Paradise of Dainty Devices*, which was not published till 1576, ten years after his death. It was probably undertaken in consequence of the great success of Tottel's Miscellany (see p. 70). The *Paradise of Dainty Devices* has been republished in the "British Biographer," by Sir Egerton Brydges, who remarks that the "poems do not, it must be admitted, belong to the higher classes; they are of the moral and didactic kind. In their subject there is too little variety, as they deal very generally in the commonplaces of ethics, such as the fickleness and caprices of love, the falsehood and instability of friendship, and the vanity of all human pleasures. But many of these are often expressed with a vigor which would do credit to any era." The poems of Edwards are the best in this collection, and the one entitled *Amantium Iræ* is reckoned by Brydges one of the most beautiful in the language. The poems which are next in merit in this collection are by Lord Vaux (see p. 70, A). The writer who holds the third place is WILLIAM HUNNIS (fl. 1550), one of the gentlemen of Queen Elizabeth's chapel, and the author of some moral and religious poems printed separately.

WILLIAM WARNER (1558-1609), a native of Oxfordshire, an attorney of the Common Pleas, and the author of *Albion's England*, first published in 1586, and frequently reprinted. This poem, which is written in the fourteen-syllable line, is a history of England from the Deluge to the reign of James I. It supplanted in popular favor the *Mirrour for Magistrates*. The style of the work was much admired in its day, and Meres, in his "Wit's Treasury," says, that by Warner's pen the English tongue was "mightily enriched and gorgeously invested in rare ornaments and resplendent habiliments." The tales are chiefly of a merry cast, and many of them indecent.

THOMAS WATSON (1560-1592), the author of some sonnets, which have been much admired.

JOSHUA SYLVESTER (1563-1618), a merchant, who translated *The Divine Weeks and Works* of the French poet Du Bartas, and obtained in his day the epithet of the Silver-tongued. The work went through seven editions, the last being published in 1641. It was one of Milton's early favorites.

ARTHUR BROOKE (ob. 1563), the author of *The Tragical History of Romeo and Juliet*, published in 1562, a metrical paraphrase of the Italian novel of Bandello, on which Shakspeare founded his tragedy of Romeo and Juliet. Brooke's poem is one of considerable merit.

ROBERT SOUTHWELL (1560-1595), born in Norfolk, of Catholic parents, educated at Douay, became a Jesuit, and returned to England in 1584 as a missionary. He was arrested in 1592, and was executed at Tyburn in 1595, on account of his being a Romish priest, though not involved in any political plots. His poems breathe a spirit of religious resignation, and are marked by beauty of thought and expression. Ben Jonson said that Southwell "had so written that piece of his, *The Burning Babe*, he (Jonson) would have been content to destroy many of his."

THOMAS STORER (1587-1604), of Christ Church, Oxford, the author of a poem on *The Life and Death of Thomas Wolsey, Cardinal*, published in 1599, in which he followed closely Cavendish's Life of Wolsey.

NICHOLAS BRETON (1558-1624?), the author of a considerable number of poems, and a contributor to a collection called *England's Helicon*, published in 1600, which comprises many of the fugitive pieces of the preceding twenty years. Sidney, Raleigh, Lodge, Marlowe, Greene, are among the other contributors to this collection.

FRANCIS DAVISON (1575-1618), the son of the secretary Davison, deserves mention as the editor and a contributor to the *Poetical Rhapsody*, published in 1602, and often reprinted. Like "England's Helicon" it is a collection of poems by various writers.

GEORGE CHAPMAN (1557-1634), also a dramatic poet, but most celebrated for his translation of Homer, which preserves much of the fire and spirit of the original. It is written in the fourteen-syllable verse so common in the Elizabethan era. "He would have made a great epic poet," says Charles Lamb, "if, indeed, he has not abundantly shown himself to be one; for his Homer is not so properly a translation as the stories of Achilles and Ulysses rewritten. The earnestness and passion which he has put into every part of these poems would be incredible to a reader of more modern translations." Chapman was born at Hitching Hill, in Hertfordshire. His life was a prosperous one, and he lived on intimate terms with the great men of his day.

EDWARD VERE, EARL OF OXFORD (1534-1604), the author of some verses in the *Paradise of Dainty Devices*. He sat as Great Chamberlain of England upon the trial of Mary, Queen of Scots.

HENRY CONSTABLE (1568?-1604?), was celebrated for his sonnets, published in 1592, under the name of *Diana*. It is conjectured that he was the same Henry Constable who, for his zeal in the Catholic religion, was long obliged to live in a state of banishment.

SIR FULK GREVILLE, LORD BROOKE (1554-1621), a friend of Sir Philip Sidney, was made Chancellor of the Exchequer, and a peer in 1621. He died by the stab of a revengeful servant, in 1628. His poems are a *Treatise on Humane Learning*, a *Treatise of Wars*, a *Treatise of Monarchy*, a *Treatise of Religion*, and an *Inquisition upon Fame and*

Fortune. He also wrote two tragedies, entitled *Alaham* and *Mustapha*, neither of which was ever acted, being written after the model of the ancients, with choruses, &c. Southey remarked that Dryden appeared to him to have formed his tragic style more upon Lord Brooke than upon any other author.

SAMUEL ROWLANDS (d. 1634), whose history is quite unknown, except that he was a prolific pamphleteer in the reigns of Elizabeth, James I., and Charles I. Campbell remarks that "his descriptions of contemporary follies have considerable humor. I think he has afforded in the story of Smug and Smith a hint to Butler for his apologue of vicarious justice, in the case of the brethren who hanged a 'poor weaver that was bed-rid,' instead of the cobbler who had killed an Indian.

'Not out of malice, but mere zeal,
Because he was an Infidel.'
Hudibras, Part. ii. Canto ii. l. 420."

SIR JOHN HARRINGTON (1561-1612), born at Kelston, near Bath, in Somersetshire, and celebrated as the first English translator of Ariosto's Orlando Furioso, published in 1591. Harrington also wrote a book of epigrams, and several other works. His father, John Harrington (1534-1582) was the author of some poems published in the "Nugæ Antiquæ." He was imprisoned in the Tower under Queen Mary, for holding correspondence with Elizabeth.

EDWARD FAIRFAX (fl. 1600), the translator of Tasso's Jerusalem, was a gentleman of fortune. The first edition was published in 1600, and was dedicated to Queen Elizabeth. This translation is much superior to that of Ariosto by Sir John Harrington. "It has been considered as one of the earliest works in which the obsolete English which had not been laid aside in the days of Sackville, and which Spenser affected to preserve, gave way to a style not much differing, at least in point of single words and phrases, from that of the present day." But this praise, adds Mr. Hallam, is equally due to Daniel, to Drayton, and to others of the later Elizabethan poets. The first five books of Tasso had been previously translated by CAREW in 1594. This translation is more literal than that of Fairfax, but far inferior in poetical spirit.

THOMAS LODGE (1556-1625?), also a physician and a dramatic poet, was born in Lincolnshire, was educated at Trinity College, Oxford, and first appeared as an author about 1580. Ten of Lodge's poems are contained in the "English Helicon," published in 1600. To his poem entitled *Rosalynde: Eupheus Golden Legacie* (1590), Shakspeare was indebted for the plot and incidents of his drama, *As You Like It*. For his dramatic works, see p. 126.

THOMAS CAREW (1589-1639), a poet at the court of Charles I., where he held the office of gentleman of the Privy-chamber, and server in ordinary to the king. His poems, which are mostly short and amatory, were greatly admired in their day. Campbell remarks that "the want of boldness and expansion in Carew's thoughts and subjects excludes him from rivalship with *great* poetical names; nor is it difficult, even within the narrow pale of his works, to discover some faults of affectation, and of still more objectionable indelicacy. But among the poets who have walked in the same limited path he is pre-eminently beautiful, and deservedly ranks among the earliest of those who gave a cultivated grace to our lyrical strains."

SIR HENRY WOTTON (1568-1639), a distinguished diplomatist in the reigns of Elizabeth and James I. He was secretary to the Earl of Essex; but upon the apprehension of his patron, he left the kingdom. He returned upon the accession of James, and was appointed ambassador to Venice. Later in life he was appointed Provost of Eton, and took deacon's orders. His principal writings were published in 1651, under the title of *Reliquiæ Wottonianæ*, with a memoir of his life by Izaak Walton. His literary reputation rests chiefly upon his poems. His *Elements of Architecture* were long held in esteem. The *Reliquiæ* also contain several other prose works.

RICHARD BARNFIELD (b. 1574), educated at Brasenose College, Oxford, wrote several minor poems, distinguished by elegance of versification. His ode, "As it fell upon a day," which was reprinted in the "English Helicon" under the signature of "Ignoto," in 1600, had been falsely attributed to Shakspeare in a volume entitled "The Passionate Pilgrim" (1559).

RICHARD CORBETT (1582-1635), Bishop of Oxford, and afterwards of Norwich, celebrated as a wit and a poet in the reign of James I. His poems were first collected and published in 1647. The best known are his *Journey into France* and his *Farewell to the Fairies*. They are lively and witty.

SIR JOHN BEAUMONT (1582-1628), elder brother of Francis Beaumont the dramatist, wrote in the heroic couplet a poem entitled *Bosworth Field*, which was published by his son in 1629.

PHINEAS FLETCHER (1584-1650), and his younger brother GILES FLETCHER, mentioned in the text (p. 84), deserve a fuller notice; and we cannot do better than quote Mr. Hallam's discriminating criticism respecting them. "An ardent admiration for Spenser inspired the genius of two young brothers, Phineas and Giles Fletcher. The first, very soon after the queen's death, as some allusions to Lord Essex seem to denote, composed, though he did not so soon publish, a poem, entitled The Purple Island. By this strange name he expressed a subject more strange; it is a minute and elaborate account of the body and mind of man. Through five cantos the reader is regaled with nothing but allegorical anatomy, in the details of which Phineas seems tolerably skilled, evincing a great deal of ingenuity in diversifying his metaphors, and in presenting the delineation of his imaginary island with as much justice as possible to the allegory without obtruding it on the reader's view. In the sixth canto he rises to the intellectual and moral faculties of the soul, which occupy the rest of the poem. From its nature it is insuperably wearisome, yet his language is often very poetical, his versification harmonious, his invention fertile. . . . Giles Fletcher, brother of Phineas, in Christ's Victory and Triumph, though his subject has not all the unity that might be desired, had a manifest superiority in its choice. Each uses a stanza of his own; Phineas one of seven lines, Giles one of eight. This poem was published in 1610. Each brother alludes to the work of the other, which must be owing to the alterations made by Phineas in his Purple Island, written probably the first, but not published, I believe, till 1633. Giles seems to have more vigor than his elder brother, but less sweetness, less smoothness, and more affectation in his style. This, indeed, is deformed by words neither English nor Latin, but simply barbarous, such as, *elamping*, *eblazon*, *deprostrate*, *purpured*, *glitterand*, and many others. They both bear much resemblance to Spenser; Giles sometimes ventures to cope with him, even in celebrated passages, such as the description of the Cave of Despair. And he has had the honor, in turn, of being followed by Milton, especially in the first meeting of our Saviour with Satan in the Paradise Regained. Both of these brothers are deserving of much praise; they were endowed with minds eminently poetical, and not inferior in imagination to any of their contemporaries. But an injudicious taste, and an excessive fondness for a style which the public was rapidly abandoning, that of allegorical personification, prevented their powers from being effectively displayed."

SCOTTISH POETS.

SIR ALEXANDER SCOTT (fl. 1562) wrote several amatory poems, which have procured him the title of the Scottish Anacreon.

SIR RICHARD MAITLAND (1496-1586), more celebrated as a collector of the poems which bear his name than as an original poet, but his own compositions are marked by good taste.

ALEXANDER MONTGOMERY, the author of an allegorical poem called *The Cherry and the Slae*, published in 1597, which long continued to be a favorite, and the metre of which was adopted by Burns.

ALEXANDER HUME (d. 1609), a clergyman, published in 1599 a volume of *Hymns or Sacred Songs*.

KING JAMES VI. published, in 1584, a volume of poetry, entitled *Essayes of a Prentice in the Divine Art of Poesie*, with the *Rewlis and Cautelis to be pursued and avoided*.

EARL OF ANCRUM (1578-1654), wrote some sonnets of considerable merit.

GEORGE BUCHANAN (1506-1582), celebrated for his Latin version of the Psalms, is spoken of among the prose writers (p. 107).

DR. ARTHUR JOHNSTON (1587-1641), also celebrated for his Latin version of the Psalms, was born near Aberdeen, studied medicine at Padua, and was appointed physician to Charles I. He died at Oxford. According to the testimony of Mr. Hallam, "Johnston's Psalms, all of which are in the elegiac metre, do not fall short of those of Buchanan, either in elegance of style or correctness of Latinity." Johnston also wrote several other Latin poems.

EARL OF STIRLING (1580-1640), published in 1637 a collation of his works entitled *Recreations with the Muses*, consisting of heroic poems and tragedies, of no great merit, but Campbell observes that "there is elegance of expression in a few of his shorter pieces." One of his tragedies is on the subject of Julius Cæsar.

WILLIAM DRUMMOND of Hawthornden (1585-1649), the most distinguished of the Scottish poets of this era, was the friend of Ben Jonson and Drayton. Jonson visited him in Hawthornden in 1619. His best poems are his sonnets, which Mr. Hallam describes as "polished and elegant, free from conceit and bad taste, in pure, unblemished English."

CHAPTER V.

THE NEW PHILOSOPHY AND PROSE LITERATURE IN THE REIGNS OF ELIZABETH AND JAMES I.

A. D. 1558–1625.

§ 1. Introduction. § 2. Chroniclers: STOW, HOLLINSHED, SPEED. § 3. SIR WALTER RALEIGH. § 4. Collections of Voyages and Travels: HAKLUYT, PURCHAS, DAVIS. § 5. The English Church: HOOKER'S *Ecclesiastical Polity*. § 6. Life of LORD BACON. § 7. Services of Bacon: the scholastic philosophy. § 8. History of previous attempts to throw off the yoke of the scholastic philosophy. § 9. Bacon's *Instauratio Magna.* § 10. First and Second Books: *De Augmentis Scientiarum* and the *Novum Organon:* the Inductive Method. § 11. Third Book: *Silva Silvarum:* collection and classification of facts and experiments: remaining books. § 12. Estimate of Bacon's services to science. § 13. His *Essays* and other English writings. § 14. BURTON'S *Anatomy of Melancholy.* LORD HERBERT OF CHERBURY § 15. THOMAS HOBBES.

§ 1. THE principal object of the present chapter is to trace the nature and the results of that immense revolution in philosophy brought about by the immortal writings of Bacon. It will, however, be unavoidable, in accordance with the chronological order generally adopted in our work, to sketch the character of other authors, of great though inferior importance, who flourished at the same time. Of the general intellectual character of the Age of Elizabeth, something has already been said: it may be observed that much of the peculiarly *practical* character which distinguishes the political and philosophical literature of this time is traceable to the general *laicising* of the higher functions of the public service, and is not one of the least valuable results of the Protestant Reformation. The clergy had no longer the monopoly of that learning and those acquirements which during the Catholic ages secured them the monopoly of power: and the vigorous personal character of the great queen combined with her jealousy of dictation to surround her throne with ministers chosen for the most part among the middle classes of her people, and to whom she accorded unshaken confidence, while she never allowed them to obtain any of that undue influence which the weaknesses of the woman experienced from unworthy favorites like Leicester and Essex. Such men as Burleigh, Walsingham, and Sir Thomas Smith belong to a peculiar type and class of statesmen; and their administration, though less brilliant and dramatic than might be found at other periods of our history, was incontestably more wise and patriotic than can easily be paralleled.

§ 2. In the humble but useful department of historical chronicles a few words must be said on the labors of JOHN STOW (1525–1605) and

RAPHAEL HOLLINSHED (d. 1580),* the former of whom, a London citizen of very slight literary pretensions, devoted the whole of his long life to the task of collecting materials for numerous chronicles and descriptions of London. The latter undertook a somewhat similar work, though intended to commemorate the history of England generally. From Hollinshed, it may be remarked, Shakspeare drew the materials for many of his half-legendary, half-historical pieces, such as *Macbeth*, *King Lear*, and the like; and it is curious to observe the mode in which the genius of the great poet animates and transfigures the flat and prosaic language of the old chronicler, whose very words he often quotes textually. Striking examples of this will be found in *Henry V.* and *Henry VI.*

§ 3. The most extraordinary and meteor-like personage in the literary history of this time is SIR WALTER RALEIGH (1552–1618), the brilliancy of whose courtly and military career can only be equalled by the wonderful variety of his talents and accomplishments, and by the tragic heroism of his death. He was born in 1552, and early attracted the favor of Elizabeth by an act of romantic gallantry, which has furnished the theme of a famous anecdote; and both by his military exploits and his graceful adulation, he long maintained possession of her capricious favor. He highly distinguished himself in the wars in Ireland, where he visited Spenser at Kilcolman, and was consulted by the great poet on the *Faëry Queen*, and no less as a navigator and adventurer in the colonization of Virginia and the conquest of Guiana. He is said to have first introduced the potato and the use of tobacco into England. On the accession of James I. he seems to have been, though without the least grounds, involved in an accusation of high treason connected with the alleged plot to place the unfortunate Arabella Stuart upon the throne, and he was confined for many years in the Tower under sentence of death. Proposing a new expedition to South America, he was allowed to undertake it; but, it proving unsuccessful, the miserable king, in order to gratify the hatred of the Spanish court, which Raleigh's exploits had powerfully excited, allowed him to be executed under the old sentence in 1618. During his imprisonment of twelve years Raleigh devoted himself to literary and scientific occupations; he produced, with the aid of many learned friends, among whom Jonson was one, a *History of the World*, which will ever be regarded as a masterpiece of English prose. The death of few illustrious men has been accompanied by so many traits of heroic simplicity as that of Raleigh.†

* Stow's chief works are a *Summary of English Chronicles*, first published in 1565, his *Annals* in 1573, and his *Survey of London* in 1598. To the names of Stow and Hollinshed should be added that of JOHN SPEED (1552–1629), who published in 1614 *A History of Great Britain*, from the earliest times to the reign of James I.

† Raleigh's History comes down only to the Second Macedonian War. Respecting its style, Hallam remarks that "there is little now obsolete in the words of Raleigh, nor, to any great degree, in his turn of phrase; the periods,

§ 4. The immense outburst of intellectual activity which renders the middle of the sixteenth century so memorable an epoch in the history of philosophy, was not without a parallel in the rapid extension of geographical knowledge. England, which gave birth to Bacon, the successful conqueror of new worlds of philosophical speculation, was foremost among the countries whose bold navigators explored unknown regions of the globe. Innumerable expeditions, sometimes fitted out by the state, but far more generally the undertakings of private speculation, exhibited incredible skill, bravery, and perseverance in opening new passages for commerce, and in particular in the endeavor to solve the great commercial and geographical problem of finding a north-west passage to the eastern hemisphere. The commercial rivalry between England and Spain, and afterwards between England and Holland, generated a glorious band of navigators, whose exploits, partaking of the double character of privateering and of trade, laid the foundation of that naval skill which rendered England the mistress of the seas. Drake, Frobisher, Davies, Raleigh, were the worthy ancestors of the Nelsons, Cooks, and Franklins. The recital of their dangers and their discoveries was frequently recorded by these hardy navigators in their own simple and picturesque language; and the same age that laid the foundation of the naval greatness of our country, produced also a branch of our literature which is neither the least valuable nor the least characteristic — the narration of maritime discovery. HAKLUYT (1533–1616), PURCHAS (d. 1628), and DAVIS (d. 1605) have given to posterity large collections of invaluable materials concerning the naval adventure of those times: the first two authors were merely chroniclers and compilers; the third was himself a famous navigator, the explorer of the Northern Ocean, and gave his name to the famous strait which serves as a monument of his glory. The language in all these works is simple, grave, and unadorned; the narrative, in itself so full of the intensest dramatic excitement, has the charm of a brave old seaman's description of the toils and dangers he has passed; and the tremendous dangers so simply encountered with such insignificant means are painted with a peculiar mixture of professional *sang froid* and child-like trust in Providence. The occasional acts of cruelty and oppression, which are to be mainly attributed to a less advanced state of civilization, are more than redeemed by the indomitable courage and invincible perseverance of these illustrious navigators.

§ 5. Among the various Christian sects generated by the great break-up of the Catholic Church at the Reformation, the Anglican confession appears to occupy nearly a central position, equidistant from the blind devotion to authority advocated by the Romish communion, and the extreme abnegation of authority proclaimed by the

where pains have been taken with them, show that artificial structure which we find in Sidney and Hooker; he is less pedantic than most of his contemporaries, seldom low, never affected."

Calvinistic theologians. The Church of England is essentially a compromise between opposite extremes; and it is perhaps to this moderation that it owes its solidity and its influence: it is unquestionably this moderation which recommended it to so reasonable and practical a people as the English. On its first appearance on the stage of history it was exposed to the most violent hostility and persecution at the hands of the ancient faith which it had supplanted; but no sooner had it become firmly established as the dominant and official religion of the state, than it was exposed to attacks from the very opposite point of the theological compass — attacks under whose violence it temporarily succumbed. The Catholic persecutions of Mary's reign were followed by the gradually increasing hostility of Puritanism, which had been insensibly acquiring more and more power from the middle of the reign of Elizabeth. The great champion of the principles of Anglicanism against the encroachments of the Genevan school of theology was RICHARD HOOKER (1553-1598), a man of evangelical piety and of vast learning, sprung from the humblest origin, and educated in the University of Oxford. He was for a long time buried in the obscurity of a country parsonage; but his eloquence and erudition obtained for him the eminent post of Master of the Temple in London, where his colleague in the ministry, Walter Travers, propounded doctrines in church government which, being similar to those of the Calvinistic confession, were incompatible with Hooker's opinions. The mildness and modesty of Hooker's character, rendering controversy and disputation insupportable to him, urged him to implore his ecclesiastical superior to remove him from his place, and restore him to the more congenial duties of a country parish: and it was here that he executed that great work which has placed him among the most eminent of the Anglican divines, and among the best prose writers of his age. The title of this work is *A Treatise on the Laws of Ecclesiastical Polity*, and its object is to investigate and define the fundamental principles upon which is founded the right of the Church to the obedience of its members, and the duty of the members to pay obedience to the Church. But, though the principal object of this book is to establish the relative rights and duties of the Anglican Church in particular, and to defend its organization against the attacks of the Roman Catholics on the one hand and the Calvinists on the other, Hooker has dug deep down into the eternal granite on which are founded all law, all obedience, and all right, political as well as religious. The *Ecclesiastical Polity* is a monument of close and cogent logic, supported by immense and varied erudition, and is written in a style so free from pedantry, so clear, vigorous, and unaffected, as to form a remarkable contrast with the generality of theological compositions, then generally overloaded with quotation and deformed by conceits and antithesis. It is to be regretted that this excellent work was never finished by the author, or, at least, if finished, has not descended to us as Hooker intended it to do, for the Sixth Book is supposed, though certainly the composition of the same author, to be a fragment of a quite different work.

§ 6. The political life of FRANCIS BACON (1561–1626) forms, with his purely intellectual or philosophical career, a contrast so striking that it would be difficult to find, in the records of biographical literature, anything so vividly opposed. He was the son of Sir Nicholas Bacon, long a favorite and trusted minister of Queen Elizabeth, in whose service he held the high office of Keeper of the Great Seal. Sir Nicholas was a fair specimen of that peculiar class of able statesmen with whom that great sovereign surrounded her administration, a type which we find repeated in Burleigh, Walsingham, Ellesmere, and Smith — men of great practical knowledge of the world, of powerful though not perhaps inventive faculties, and of great prudence and moderation in their religious opinions, a point of much importance at a period when the recent Reformation in the Church had exposed the country to the agitations arising from theological disputes. Francis Bacon was the nephew of Burleigh, Sir Nicholas and the great Chancellor having married two sisters; and the boy gave earnest, from his tenderest childhood, of those powers of intellect and that readiness of mind which afterwards distinguished him among men. He was born in 1561; and received a careful education, completed at an age even for that time exceedingly early, in the University of Cambridge. He is said, even as a boy, to have shown plain indications of that inquiring spirit which carried him to the investigation of natural laws, and a gravity and presence of mind which attracted the attention of the Queen; and while studying at Cambridge it is reported that he was struck with the defects of the philosophical methods, founded upon the scholastic or Aristotelian system, then universally adopted in the investigations of science. Then, perhaps, first dawned upon his mind the [illegible] outline of that great reformation in philosophy which he was afterwards destined to bring about. His father, who certainly intended to devote him to the public service, probably in the department of diplomacy, sent him to travel on the Continent; and a residence of about four years in France, Germany, and Italy, not only gave him the opportunity of acquiring a remarkable stock of political knowledge respecting the state and views of the principal European courts, but rendered him the still more valuable service of enlarging his knowledge of mankind, and making him acquainted with the state of philosophy and letters. He was recalled from the Continent by the death of his father in 1580, and found himself under the necessity of entering upon some active career. He appears to have felt that the natural bent of his genuis inclined to the study of science; and he begged his kinsman and natural protector, Burleigh, to obtain for him the means of devoting himself to those pursuits. The Chancellor, however, who was jealous of his nephew's extraordinary abilities, which he feared might eclipse or at least interfere with the talents of his own son Robert, just then entering upon that brilliant career which he so long followed, treated Francis with great harshness and indifference, and insisted on his embracing the profession of the law. He became a student of Gray's Inn; and that wonderful aptitude, to which no labor was too arduous and no subtlety too refined, very soon made him the most distinguished advocate of his day, and an admired teacher of the legal science. The jealousy of his kinsmen the Cecils, both father and son, appears to have veiled itself, in some degree perhaps unconsciously, under the pretext that Bacon was a flighty and bookish young man, too fond of projects and theories to be likely to become a useful servant of the State. But the countenance which was refused to Bacon by his uncle and cousin, he obtained from the generous and enthusiastic friendship of Essex, who used all his influence to obtain for his friend the place of Solicitor-General, and when unsuccessful in this attempt, consoled him for the disappointment by the gift of a considerable estate. During this period of his life Bacon continued to rise rapidly, both in professional reputation as a lawyer, and in fame both for philosophy and eloquence. He sat in the House of Commons, and gave evidence not only of his unequalled powers as a speaker, but also of that cowardly and interested subservience to the Court which was the great blot upon his glory, and the cause of his ultimate disgrace. There is nothing in the whole range of history more melancholy than to trace this sublime intellect truckling to every favorite who had power to help or to hurt, and betraying in succession all those to whom self-interest for the moment had attached him. After submitting, with a subserviency unworthy of a man of the least spirit, to the haughty reproaches of the Cecils, he abandoned their faction for that of Essex, whom he flattered and betrayed. On the unhappy Earl's trial for high treason, in consequence of his frantic conspiracy and revolt, Bacon, though he certainly felt for his benefactor as warm an attachment as was compatible with a mean and servile nature, not only abandoned his former friend, but volunteered with malignant eagerness among the foremost ranks of his enemies, and employed all his immense powers, as an advocate and a pamphleteer, to precipitate his ruin and to blacken his memory. Bacon was not in fact a malignant man: he was a needy, flexible, unscrupulous courtier; and showed in his after career the same ignoble readiness to betray the duties of the judge as he now did in forgetting the obligations of the friend.

On the death of Elizabeth, and the transfer of the crown to James I. in 1603, Bacon, who had been gradually and steadily rising in the service of the State, attached himself first to Carr, the ignoble favorite of that prince, and afterwards to Carr's successor, the haughty Buckingham. He had been knighted at the coronation, and at the same time married Alice Barnham, a young lady of considerable fortune, the daughter of a London alderman. He sat in more than one parliament, and was successively made Solicitor-General, Attorney-General, and at last, in 1617, chiefly by the interest of Buckingham, Lord High Chancellor of England, and Baron Verulam, which latter title was three years afterwards replaced by the still higher style of Viscount St. Alban's. Though the whole of his public career was stained with acts of the basest servility and corruption, it is not uninstructive to mention that Bacon was one of the last, if not the very last, ministers of the law in England to employ and to defend the application of torture in judicial procedure. Bacon occupied the highest office of justice during four years, and exhibited, in the discharge of his great functions, the wisdom and eloquence which characterized his mind, and the servility and meanness which disgraced his conduct; and on the assembling of Parliament in 1621, the House of Commons, then filled with just indignation against the insupportable abuses, corruptions, and monopolies countenanced by the Government, ordered a deliberate investigation into various acts of bribery of which the Chancellor was accused. The King and the favorite, though ready to do all in their power to screen a criminal who had always been their devoted servant, were not bold enough to face the indignation of the whole country; and the investigation was allowed to proceed. It was carried on before the House of Lords, and it resulted in his conviction, on the clearest evidence, of many acts of gross corruption as a judge.* Independently of the cases thus proved, it cannot be doubted that there must have existed numerous others which were not inquired into. Bacon himself fully confessed his own guilt; and in language which under other circumstances would have been profoundly pathetic, threw himself on the indulgence of his judges. The sentence, though it could not be otherwise than severe, was evidently just: it condemned him to be deprived of his place as Chancellor, to pay a fine of 40,000*l.* (a sum, be it remarked, not amounting to half the gains he was supposed to have corruptly made), to be imprisoned during the King's pleasure in the Tower, to be ever after incapable of holding any office in the State, and to be incapacitated from sitting in Parliament or coming within twelve miles of the Court In imposing so severe a punishment it must be recollected that Bacon's judges well knew that much of it would be mitigated, or altogether remitted; and the result showed how just were these anticipations. The culprit was almost immediately released from confinement; the fine was not only remitted by royal favor, but by the manner of its remission converted into a sort of protection of the fallen Chancellor against the claims of his importunate creditors; and he was speedily restored to the privilege of presenting himself at Court. There can be no doubt that James and his favorite had felt great reluctance in abandoning Bacon to the indignation of Parliament, and that they only did so in the conviction that any attempt to save their servant would not only have been inevitably unsuccessful, but must have involved the Government itself in odium, without in the least alleviating the lot of the guilty Chancellor.

The life of the fallen minister was prolonged for five years after his severe but merited disgrace; and these years were passed in intriguing, flattering, and imploring pecuniary relief in his distresses. During his whole life he had lived splendidly and extravagantly. His taste for

* Many of the charges against Bacon, related in the text, have been proved by Mr. Hepworth Dixon, in his "Personal History of Lord Bacon," to be unfounded.

magnificence in houses, gardens, and trains of domestics had been such as may generally be found in men of lively imagination; and it was to escape from the perpetual embarrassments which are the natural consequences of such tastes that he in all probability owed that gradual deadening of the moral sense, and that blunting of the sentiment of honor and self-respect, which were the original source of his crimes. Common experience shows with what fatal rapidity rises the flood of corruption in the human heart when once the first barriers are removed. Bacon's death took place, after a few days' illness, on the 9th April, 1626, and was caused by a cold and fever caught in travelling near London, and in part is attributed to an experiment which he tried, of preserving meat by freezing. He got out of his carriage, bought a fowl, and filled the inside of the bird with snow, which then lay thick upon the ground. In doing this he received a chill, which was aggravated by being put into a damp bed at Lord Arundel's house near Highgate. Bacon was buried, by his own desire, by his mother's side in St. Michael's Church, St. Alban's, near which place was the magnificent seat of Gorhambury, constructed by himself. He had no children, and left his affairs involved in debt and confusion.

§ 7. In order to appreciate the services which Bacon rendered to the cause of truth and knowledge, and which have placed his name foremost among the benefactors of the human race, two precautions are indispensable. First we must form a distinct idea of the nature of the philosophical methods which his system of investigation supplanted forever in physical research; and, secondly, we must dismiss from our minds that common and most erroneous imagination that Bacon was an inventor or a discoverer in any specific branch of knowledge. His mission was not to teach mankind a philosophy, but to teach them how to philosophize. A contrary supposition would be as gross an error as that of the clown who imagined that Newton was the discoverer of gravitation. The task which Bacon proposed to himself was loftier and more useful than that of the mere inventor in any branch of science; and the excellence of his method can be nowhere more clearly seen than in the instances in which he has himself applied it to facts which in his day were imperfectly known or erroneously explained. The most brilliant name among the ancient philosophers is incontestably that of Aristotle: the immensity of his acquirements, which extended to almost every branch of physical, political, moral, and intellectual research, and the powers of a mind unrivalled at once for grasp of view and subtlety of discrimination, have justly secured to him the very highest place among the greatest intellects of the earth: he was indeed, in the fullest sense,

"'l maestro di color che sanno."

But the instrumental or mechanical part of his system, the mode by which he taught his followers that they could arrive at true deductions in scientific investigation, when falling into inferior hands, was singularly liable to be abused. That careful examination of nature, and that wise and cautious prudence in the application to particular phenomena, of general formulas of reasoning, which are so perceptible in the works of the master, were very soon neglected by the disciples, who, finding themselves in possession of a mode of research which seemed to them to promise an infallible correctness in the results obtained, were led, by their very admiration for the genius of Aristotle, to leave out of sight his prudent reserve in the employment of his method. The synthetic mode of reasoning flatters the pride of human intellect by causing the truths discovered to appear the conquest made by its unassisted powers; and the great part played in the investigation by those powers renders the method peculiarly susceptible of that kind of corruption which arises from over-subtlety and the vain employment of words. Nor must we leave out of account the deteriorating influence of the various nations and epochs through which the ancient deductive philosophy had been handed down from the time of Aristotle himself till the days of Bacon, when its uselessness for the attainment of truth had become so apparent that a great reform was inevitable — had been indeed inevitable from a much more remote period. The acute, disputatious spirit of the Greek character had already from the very first commenced that tendency towards vain word-catching which was still further accelerated in the schools of the Lower Empire. It was from the schools of the Lower Empire that the Orientals received the philosophical system already corrupted, and the mystical and over-subtle genius of the Jewish and Arabian speculators added new elements of decay. It was in this state that the doctrines were received among the monastic speculators of the Middle Ages, and to the additional errors arising from the abstract and excessive refinements of the cloister were added those proceeding from the unfortunate alliance between the philosophical system of the Schools and the authority of the Church. The solidarity established between the orthodoxy of the Vatican and the methods of philosophy was indirectly as fatal to the authority of the one as ruinous to the value of the other. In this unhallowed union between physical science and dogmatic theology, the Church, by its arrogation to itself of the character of infallibility, put it out of its own power ever to recognize as false any opinion that it had once recognized as true; and theology being in its essence a stationary science, while philosophy is as inevitably a progressive one, the discordance between the two ill-matched members of the union speedily struck the one with impotence and destroyed the influence of the other. Independently too, of the sources of corruption which I have been endeavoring to point out, the Aristotelian method of investigation, even in its pure and normal state, had been always obnoxious to the charge of infertility, and of being essentially stationary and unprogressive. The ultimate aim and object of its speculations were, by the attainment of abstract truth, to exercise, purify, and elevate the human faculties, and to carry the mind higher and higher towards a contemplation of the Supreme Good and the Supreme Beauty: the investigation of nature was merely a means to this end. Practical utility was regarded as a result which might or might not be attained in this process of raising the mind to a certain ideal height of wisdom; but an end which, whether attained or not, was below the dignity of the true sage. Now, the aim proposed by the modern philosophy is totally different; and it follows that the methods by which that end is pursued should be as different. Since the time of Bacon all the powers of human reason, and all the energies of invention and research, have been concentrated on the object of improving the happiness of human life — of diminishing the sufferings and increasing the enjoyments of our imperfect existence here below — of extending the empire of man over the realms of nature — in short, of making our earthly state, both physical and moral, more happy. This is an aim less ambitious than that ideal virtue and that impossible wisdom which were the aspiration of the older philosophy; but it has the advantage of being attainable, while the experience of twenty centuries had sufficiently proved that the lofty pretensions of the former system had been followed by no corresponding results; nay, that the incessant disputations of the most acute and powerful intellects, during so many generations, not only had left the greatest and most vital questions where they had found them at first, but had degraded philosophy to the level of an ignoble legerdemain.

§ 8. Many attempts had been made, by vigorous and independent minds, long before the appearance of Bacon, to throw off the yoke of the scholastic philosophy; but that yoke was so riveted with the shackles of Catholic orthodoxy, that the efforts, being made in countries and at epochs when the Church was all-powerful, could not possibly be successful: all they could do was to shake the foundations of an intellectual tyranny which had so long weighed upon mankind, and to prepare the way for its final overthrow. The Reformation, breaking up the hard-bound soil, opened and softened it so that the seeds of true science and philosophy, instead of falling upon a rock, brought forth fruit a hundred fold. Long and splendid is the list of the great and liberal minds who had revolted against the tyranny of the schools before the appearance of the New Philosophy. In the writings of that wonderful monk, the anticipator of his great namesake — in the controversy between the Nominalists and Realists — in the disputes which preceded the Reformation — the standard of revolt against the tyranny of the ancient system had been raised by a succession of brave and vigorous hands; and though many of these champions had fallen in their contest against an enemy intrenched in the fortifications of religious orthodoxy, and though the stake and the dungeon had apparently silenced them forever, nevertheless the tradition of their exploits had formed a still-increasing treasury of arguments against orthodox tyranny. England, in the reign of Elizabeth and James I., was precisely the country, and a country precisely in the particular state, in which the great revolution in philosophy was possible; and it was a most providential combination of circumstances and qualities that was concentrated in Francis Bacon so as to make him, and perhaps him alone, the apostle of the new philosophical faith.

§ 9. The great object which Bacon proposed to himself, in proclaiming the advantages of the Inductive Method, was *fruit:* the improvement of the condition of mankind; and his object being different from that of the elder philosophers, the mode by which it was to be attained was different likewise. From an early age he had been struck with the defects, with the stationary and unproductive character, of the Deductive Method; and during the whole of his brilliant, agitated, and, alas! too often ignominious career, he had constantly and patiently labored, adding stone after stone to that splendid edifice which will enshrine his name when his crimes and weaknesses, his ambition and servility, shall be forgotten. His philosophical system is contained in the great work, or rather series of works, to which he intended to give the general title of *Instauratio Magna*, or Great Institution of True Philosophy. The whole of this neither was nor ever could have been executed by one man or by the labors of one age; for every new addition to the stock of human knowledge, would, as Bacon plainly saw, modify the conclusions, though it would not affect otherwise than by confirming the soundness, of the philosophical method he propounded. The *Instauratio* was to consist of six separate parts or books, of which the following is a short synoptical arrangement: —

I. *Partitiones Scientiarum:* a summary or classification of all knowledge, with indications of those branches which had been more or less imperfectly treated.

II. *Novum Organum:* the New Instrument, an exposition of the methods to be adopted in the investigation of truth, with indications of the principal sources of human error, and the remedies against that error in future.

III. *Phænomena Universi*, sive Historia Naturalis et Experimentalis ad condendam Philosophiam: a complete body of well-observed facts and experiments in all branches of human knowledge, to furnish the raw material upon which the new method was to be applied, in order to obtain results of truth.

IV. *Scala Intellectus*, sive Filum Labyrinthi: rules for the gradual ascent of the mind from particular instances or phenomena, to principles continually more and more abstract; and warnings against the danger of advancing otherwise than gradually and cautiously.

V. *Prodromi*, sive Anticipationes Philosophiæ Secundæ; anticipations or forestallings of the New Philosophy, *i. e.* such truths as could be, so to say, provisionally established, to be afterwards tested by the application of the New Method.

VI. *Philosophia Secunda*, sive Scientia activa; the result of the just, careful, and complete application of the methods previously laid down to the vast body of facts to be accumulated and observed in accordance with the rules and precautions contained in the IId and IVth parts.

Let us compare the position of Bacon, with respect to science in general, to that of an architect invited to undertake the reconstruction of a palace, ancient and splendid, but which, in consequence of the lapse of time and the changes of the mode of living, is found to be in a ruinous or uninhabitable condition. What would be the natural mode of proceeding adopted by an enlightened artist under these circumstances? He would, I think, make it his first care to draw an exact plan of the edifice in its present state, so as to form a clear notion of the extent, the defects, and the conveniences of the building as it stands; and not till then would he proceed to the demolition of the existing edifice. He would next prepare such instruments, tools, and mechanical aids, as would be likely to render the work of construction more rapid, certain, and economical. Thirdly, he would accumulate the necessary materials. Fourthly, he would provide the ladders. Lastly, he would begin to build: but should the edifice be so vast that no human life would be long enough to terminate it, he would construct so much of it as would suffice to give his successors an idea of the general plan, style, and disposition of the parts, and leave it to be completed by future generations. It will easily, I think, be seen, how accurately the mode of proceeding in Bacon's great work corresponds with common sense and with the method followed by our imaginary architect. Bacon is the builder; the great temple of knowledge is the edifice, which the labors of our race have to terminate according to his plan.

§ 10. Let us now inquire what portion of this project Bacon was able to execute. The first portion, consisting of a general view of the state of science at his time, with an explanation of the causes of its sterility and unprogressiveness, was published in 1605, in an English treatise, bearing the title of *The Proficience and Advancement of Learning:* this was afterwards much altered and extended, and republished in Latin, in 1623, under the title *De Augmentis Scientiarum.* The *Novum Organum*, the most important portion of Bacon's work, is that in which the necessity and the principles of the Inductive Method are laid down and demonstrated. It is, in short, the compendium of the Baconian logic. It was published in Latin, in 1620. The fundamental difference between the method recommended by Bacon and that which had so long been adopted by philosophers, may, I think, be rendered clear by a comparison of the accompanying little diagrams: —

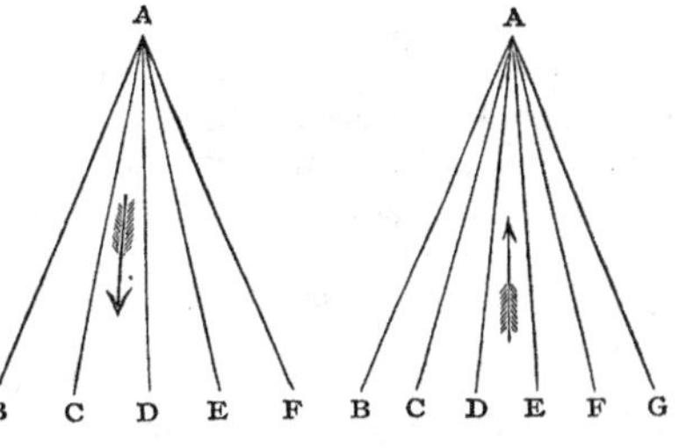

In the first of these the point A may be conceived to represent some general principle upon which depend any number of detached facts or phenomena B, C, D, E, F. Now let it be supposed that we are seeking for the explanation of one or all of these phenomena; or, in other words, desirous of discovering the law upon which they depend. It is obvious that we may proceed as the arithmetician proceeds in the solution of a problem involving the search after an unknown quantity or number; that is, we may *suppose* the law of nature to be so and so, and applying this law to one or all of the phenomena within our observation, see if it corresponds with them or not. If it does, we conclude, so far as our examination has extended, that we have hit upon the true result of which we are in search: if not, we must repeat the process, as the arithmetician would do in a like case, till we obtain an answer that corresponds with all the conditions of the problem: and it is evident, that the greater the number of separate facts to which we successfully apply our theoretical explanation, the greater will be the probability of our having hit upon the true one. Now this *application* of a preëstablished theory to the particular facts or phenomena is precisely the signification of the word *synthesis*. It is obvious that the march of the mind in this mode of investigation is from the general to the particular — that is, in the direction of the arrow, or *downwards* — whence this mode of investigation is styled *deduction*, or a *descent* from the general law to the individual example. Similarly, the Aristotelian method has received the designation *à priori*, because in it the establishment of a theory, or, at all events, the provisional employment of a theory, is *prior* to its application in practice, just as in measuring an unknown space we *previously* establish a rule, as of a foot, yard, &c., which we afterwards *apply* to the space to be so determined. In the diagram all the elements are the same as in the preceding one, with the exception that here the process follows a precisely opposite direction — that is, from a careful comparison of the different facts, the mind travels gradually upwards, with slow and cautious advances, from bare phenomena to more general consideration, till at last it reaches some point in which all the phenomena agree, and this point is the law of nature or general principle, of which we were in search. As *synthesis* signifies composition, so *analysis* signifies resolution; and it is by a continual and cautious process of resolution that the mind *ascends* — in the direction marked by the arrow — from the particular to the general. This ascending process is clearly designated by the term *induction*, which signifies an *ascent* from particular instances to a general law; and the term *à posteriori* denotes that the theory, being evolved from the examination of the individual facts, is necessarily posterior or subsequent to the examination of those facts.

All human inventions have their good and their bad sides, their advantages and their defects: and it is only by a comparison between the relative advantages and defects that we can establish the superiority of one system or mode of action over another. On contemplating the two methods of which I have just been giving a very rough and popular explanation, it will be at once obvious that the Deductive mode enables us, *when the right theory has been hit upon*, to arrive at absolute, or almost mathematical truth; while analysis, being dependent for its accuracy upon the number of phenomena which furnish the materials for our induction, can never arrive at absolute certainty; inasmuch as it is impossible to examine *all* the phenomena of a single class, and as while any phenomena remain unexamined we never can be *certain* that the discovery of some new fact will not completely overset our conclusions. The utmost that we can arrive at, therefore, by this route, is a very high degree of probability — a degree which will be higher in proportion as it is founded upon a greater number of instances, and attained by a more careful process of sifting. But the nature of the human mind is such that it is practically incapable of distinguishing between a very high probability and an absolute certainty; at least the latter is able to produce upon the reason the same amount of conviction — in some cases, perhaps, even a greater amount — than even an absolute certainty. If we consider, therefore, the enormous number of chances against any given *à priori* deduction being the right one, — for, as in an arithmetical problem, there can be only one correct solution, while the number of possible incorrect solutions is infinite, — and observe that till all the possible phenomena have been submitted to the synthetic test we never can be sure that we have the right theory, we shall easily agree that the possible certainty of a theory is dearly bought when compared with the far greater safety of the analytical method of reasoning, which, keeping fast hold of nature at each step of its progress, has the possibility, nay, even the certainty, of correcting its errors as they may arise.

The most important portion of the whole *Instauratio* is the *Novum Organum*, in which Bacon lays down the rules for the employment of Induction in the investigation of truth, and points out the origin and remedies of the errors which most commonly oppose us in our search. The earlier philosophers, and particularly Aristotle, assigning a great and almost unlimited efficacy in this research to the intellectual faculties alone, contented themselves with perfecting those logical formulas, among which the syllogism was the principal, by whose aid, as by the operation of some infallible instrument, they conceived that that result would assuredly be attained; and gave rules for the legitimate employment of their syllogism, pointing out the means of detecting and guarding against fallacies or irregularities in the *expression* of their reasoning. Bacon went far deeper than this, and showed that the most dangerous and universal sources of human error have their origin, not in the illegitimate employment of terms, but in the weaknesses, the prejudices, and the passions of mankind, exhibited either in the race or the individual. He classifies these sources of error, which in his vivid picturesque language he calls *Idols* or false appearances, in four categories; the Idols of the Tribe, of the Den, of the Market-place, of the Theatre. Under the first he warns us against those errors and prejudices which are common to the whole human race, the *tribe* to which we all belong; the idols of the Den are those which arise from the particular circumstances of the individual, as his country, his age, his religion, his profession, or his personal character; the errors of the Market-place are the result of the universal habit of using terms the meaning of which we have either not distinctly agreed on, or which we do not clearly understand. These terms are used in the interchange of thought, as money is passed from hand to hand in the market; and we accept and transfer to others coins whose real value we have not taken the trouble to test. The idols of the Theatre are the errors arising from false systems of philosophy, which dress up conceptions in unreal disguises, like comedians upon the stage. We may compare the precautions of the older logic to that of a physician who should direct his efforts to the getting rid of the external efflorescence of a disorder, and should think his duty performed when he had purified the skin, though perhaps at the cost of driving in the disease and rendering it doubly dangerous. Bacon, like the more enlightened practitioner, sought out the deep-seated constitutional source of the malady; it is to that that he addresses his treatment, certain that when the internal cause is removed, the symptoms will vanish of themselves.

§ **11.** Of the Third Book Bacon has given only a specimen, intended to show the method to be adopted in collecting and classifying facts and experiments; for in a careful examination of facts and experiments consists the whole essence of his induction, and in it are concealed the future destinies of human knowledge and power. Bacon contributed to this portion of the work a History of the Winds, of Life and Death, written in Latin; and a collection of experiments in Physics, or, as he calls it, Natural History in English. This portion of the work is alone sufficient to show how small are Bacon's claims or pretensions to the character of a *discoverer* in any branch of natural science, and how completely he was under the influence of the errors of his day; but at the same time it proves the innate merit of his method, and the power of that mind which could legislate for the whole realm of knowledge, and for sciences yet unborn. To the English fragment he gives the title of *Silva Silvarum*, i. e. a collection of materials.

The Fourth Book, *Scala Intellectus*, of which Bacon has given but a brief extract, was intended to show the gradual march to be followed by induction, in ascending from the fact perceptible to the senses to principles which were to become more and more general as we advance; and the author's object was to warn against the danger of leaping abruptly over the intermediate steps of the investigation. Of the Fifth Book he wrote only a preface, and the Sixth was never commenced.

§ **12.** Of the soundness and the fertility of Bacon's method of investigation, the best proof will be a simple and practical one: we have only to compare the progress made by humanity in all the useful arts during the two centuries and a half since induction has been generally employed in all branches of science, with the progress made during the twenty centuries which elapsed between Aristotle and the age of Bacon. It is no exaggeration to say that in the shorter interval that progress has been ten times greater than in the longer. That this progress is in any degree attributable to any superiority of the human intellect in modern times is a supposition too extravagant to deserve a moment's attention. Never did humanity produce intellects more vast, more penetrating, and more active, I will not say than Aristotle himself, but than the series of great men who wasted their powers in abstract questions which never could be solved, or in the sterile subtleties of scholastic disputation. We may remark, too, as a strong confirmation of the truth of what we are saying, that in those sciences which are independent of experiment, and proceed by the efforts of reasoning and contemplation alone, — as theology, for instance, or pure geometry, — the ancients were fully as far advanced as we are at this moment. The glory of Bacon is founded upon a union of speculative power with practical utility which were never so combined before. He neglected nothing as too small, despised nothing as too low, by which our happiness could be augmented; in him, above all, were combined boldness and prudence, the intensest enthusiasm, and the plainest common sense. He could foresee triumphs over nature far surpassing the wildest dreams of imagination, and at the same time warn posterity against the most trifling ill consequences that would proceed from a neglect of his rules. It is probable that Bacon generally wrote the first sketch of his works in English, but afterwards caused them to be translated into Latin, which was at that time the language of science, and even of diplomacy. He is reported to have employed the services of many young men of learning as secretaries and translators: amomg these the most remarkable is Hobbes, afterwards so celebrated as the author of the *Leviathan*. The style in which the Latin books of the *Instauratio* were given to the world, though certainly not a model of classical purity, is weighty, vigorous, and picturesque.

§ **13.** Bacon's English writings are very numerous: among them unquestionably the most important is the little volume entitled *Essays*, the first edition of which he published in 1597, and which was several times reprinted, with additions, the last in 1625. These are short papers on an immense variety of subjects, from grave questions of morals and policy down to the arts of amusement and the most trifling accomplishments; and in them appears, in a manner more appreciable to ordinary intellects than in his elaborate philosophical works, the wonderful union of depth and variety which characterizes Bacon. The intellectual activity they display is literally portentous; the immense multiplicity and aptness of unexpected illustration is only equalled by the originality with which Bacon manages to treat the most worn-out and commonplace subject, such, for instance, as friendship or gardening. No author was ever so concise as Bacon; and in his mode of writing there is that remarkable quality which gives to the style of Shakspeare such a strongly-marked individuality; that is, a combination of the intellectual and imaginative, the closest reasoning in the boldest metaphor, the condensed brilliancy of an illustration identified with the development of thought. It is this that renders both the dramatist and the philosopher at once the richest and the most concise of writers. Many of Bacon's essays, as that inimitable one on *Studies*, are absolutely oppressive from the power of thought compressed into the smallest possible compass. Bacon wrote also an *Essay on the Wis-*

dom of the Ancients, in which he endeavored to explain the political and moral truths concealed in the mythology of the classical ages; and in this work he exhibits an ingenuity which Macaulay justly describes as almost morbid; an unfinished romance, *The New Atlantis*, which was intended to embody the fulfilment of his own dreams of a philosophical millennium; a *History of Henry VII.*, and a vast number of state-papers, judicial decisions, and other professional writings. All these are marked by the same vigorous, weighty, and somewhat ornamented style which is to be found in the *Instauratio*, and are among the finest specimens of the English language at its period of highest majesty and perfection.

§ **14.** In every nation there may be found a small number of writers who, in their life, in the objects of their studies, and in the form and manner of their productions, bear a peculiar stamp of eccentricity. No country has been more prolific in such exceptional individualities than England, and no age than the sixteenth century. There cannot be a more striking example of this small but curious class than old ROBERT BURTON (1576–1640), whose life and writings are equally odd His personal history was that of a retired and laborious scholar, and his principal work, the *Anatomy of Melancholy*, is a strange combination of the most extensive and out-of-the-way reading with just observation and a peculiar kind of grave saturnine humor. The object of the writer was to give a complete monography of Melancholy, and to point out its causes, its symptoms, its treatment, and its cure: but the descriptions given of the various phases of the disease are written in so curious and pedantic a style, accompanied with such an infinity of quaint observation, and illustrated by such a mass of quotations from a crowd of authors, principally the medical writers of the fourteenth and fifteenth centuries, of whom not one reader in a thousand in the present day has ever heard, that the *Anatomy* possesses a charm which no one can resist who has once fallen under its fascination. The enormous amount of curious quotation with which Burton has incrusted every paragraph and almost every line of his work has rendered him the favorite study of those who wish to appear learned at a small expense; and his pages have served as a quarry from which a multitude of authors have borrowed, and often without acknowledgment, much of their materials, as the great Roman feudal families plundered the Coliseum to construct their frowning fortress-palaces. The greater part of Burton's laborious life was passed in the University of Oxford, where he died, not without suspicion of having hastened his own end, in order that it might exactly correspond with the astrological predictions which he is said, being a firm believer in that science, to have drawn from his own horoscope. He is related to have been himself a victim to that melancholy which he has so minutely described, and his tomb bears the astrological scheme of his own nativity, and an inscription eminently characteristic of the man: "Hic jacet Democritus, iunior, cui vitam dedit et mortem Melancholia."

Our notice of the prose writers of this remarkable period would be incomplete without some mention of LORD HERBERT OF CHERBURY (1581–1648), who was remarkable as a theologian and also as an historian. He was a man of great learning and rare dignity of personal character, and was employed in an embassy to Paris in 1616. There he first published his principal work, the treatise *De Veritate*, an elaborate pleading in favor of deism, of which Herbert was one of the earliest partisans in England. He also left a *History of Henry VIII.*, not published until after his death, and which is certainly a valuable monument of grave and vigorous prose, though the historical merit of the work is diminished by the author's strong partiality in favor of the character of the king. Though maintaining the doctrines of a freethinker, Herbert gives indications of an intensely enthusiastic religious mysticism, and there is proof of his having imagined himself on more than one occasion the object of miraculous communications by which the Deity confirmed the doctrines maintained in his books.

§ 15. But in force of demonstration, and clearness and precision of language, none of the English metaphysicians have surpassed THOMAS HOBBES (1588–1679), who, however, more properly belongs to a later period. Hobbes was a man of extraordinary mental activity, equally remarkable, during the whole of a long literary career, for the power as for the variety of his philosophical speculations. The theories of Hobbes exerted an incalculable influence on the opinions, not only of English, but also of Continental thinkers, for nearly a century, and though that influence has since been much weakened by the errors and sophistries mingled in many of this great writer's works, in some important and arduous branches of abstract speculation, as for example in the great question respecting Free Will and Necessity, it is doubtful whether any later investigations have thrown any new light upon the principles established by him. He was born at Malmesbury in Wiltshire in 1588, was educated at Magdalen Hall, Oxford, and subsequently travelled abroad as private tutor to the Earl of Devonshire. On his return he became intimate with the most distinguished men of his day, through the influence of his patron the Earl of Devonshire. His first literary work, the translation of Thucydides, was published in the third year of the reign of Charles I., in 1628. He subsequently passed several years in Paris and Italy, and he was in constant communication with the most illustrious minds among his contemporaries, as with Descartes for example, with Galileo, and with Harvey. Though of extreme boldness in speculation, Hobbes was an advocate for high monarchical or rather despotic principles in government: his theory being that human nature was essentially ferocious and corrupt, he concluded that the iron restraint of arbitrary power could alone suffice to bridle its passions. This theory necessarily flowed from the fundamental proposition of Hobbes's moral system; viz. that the *primum mobile* of all human actions is selfish interest. Attributing all our actions to intellectual calculation, and thus either entirely ignoring or not allowing sufficient influence to the moral elements and the affections, which play at least an equal part in the drama of life, Hobbes fell into a narrow and one-sided view of our motives which makes his theory only half true. He was a man whose reading, though not extensive, was singularly profound: and in the various branches of science and literature which he cultivated we see that clearness of view and vigor of comprehension which is found in men of few books. The most celebrated work of this great thinker was the *Leviathan* (published in 1651), an argument in favor of monarchical government: the reasonings, however, will apply with equal force to the justification of despotism. But though the *Leviathan* is the best known of his works, the *Treatise on Human Nature*, and the *Letter on Liberty and Necessity*, are incontestably those in which the closeness of his logic and the purity and clearness of his style are most visible, and the correctness of his deductions least mingled with error. Two purely political treatises, the *Elementa Philosophica de Cive*, and *De Corpore Politico*,* are remarkable for the cogency of the arguments, though many of the results at which the author struggles to arrive are now no longer considered deducible from the premises. In the latter portion of his life, Hobbes entered with great ardor upon the study of pure mathematics, and engaged in very vehement controversies with Wallis and others respecting the quadrature of the circle and other questions in which novices in those sciences are apt to be led away by the enthusiasm of imaginary discoveries. Hobbes has often been erroneously confounded with the enemies of religion. This has arisen from a misconception of the nature of his doctrines, which, in apparently lowering the moral faculties of man, have seemed to exhibit a tendency to materialism, though in reality nothing can be more opposed to the character of Hobbes's philosophical views; for the selfish theory of human actions, when divested of those limitations which confine the motive of self to those low and short-sighted views of interest with which it is generally associated, no more necessitates a materialistic line of argument than any other system for clearing up the mysteries of our moral nature.†

* These two treatises were published before the *Leviathan*, and were incorporated in the latter work.

† It may also be mentioned that Hobbes wrote, in 1672, at the age of 84 a curious Latin poem on his own life; and he also published in 1675, at the age of 87, a translation in verse of the Iliad and Odyssey. His *Behemoth*, or a *History of the Civil Wars from* 1640 to 1660, appeared in 1679, a few months after his death.

NOTES AND ILLUSTRATIONS.

MINOR PROSE WRITERS IN THE REIGNS OF ELIZABETH AND JAMES I.

WEBSTER PUTTENHAM, published in 1586 the ***Art of English Poesie;*** a writer whom Mr. Hallam considers the first who wrote a well measured prose.

RICHARD GRAFTON, a printer in the reigns of Henry VIII. and the three following sovereigns, is one of the early chroniclers. He wrote in prison, into which he was thrown for printing the proclamation of the succession of Lady Jane Grey to the throne, ***An Abridgment of the Chronicles of England***, published in 1562.

WILLIAM CECIL, LORD BURLEIGH (d. 1598), the celebrated statesman in the reign of Queen Elizabeth, wrote *Precepts, or, Directions for the well Ordering and Carriage of a Man's Life*, addressed to his son *Robert Cecil.*

JOHN LYLY, the author of the prose romance of *Euphues*, and GREENE and NASH, the authors of several pamphlets in prose, are mentioned under the dramatists (pp. 124, 125).

GEORGE BUCHANAN (1506-1582), celebrated as an elegant Latin writer, was born at Killearn, in the county of Stirling, and was educated at the Universities of St. Andrews and Paris. He was appointed by the Earl of Murray tutor to the young King James VI. His chief work is a History of Scotland, which was published in 1582, under the title of *Rerum Scoticarum Historia.* His Latin version of the Psalms has been already mentioned (p. 87). He wrote in the Scottish dialect a work called *Chamæleon*, to satirize Secretary Maitland of Lethington.

GEORGE SANDYS (1577-1643), known as a traveller and as a poet, was the youngest son of the Archbishop of York. His *Travels* in the East were very popular, and were repeatedly republished in the seventeenth century. His chief poetical production was a translation of Ovid's Metamorphoses.

WILLIAM LITHGOW (d. 1640), a native of Scotland, also celebrated as a traveller. He travelled nineteen years on foot in Europe, Asia, and Africa. The first edition of his Travels was published in 1614.

SIR JOHN HAYWARD (d. 1627), an historian, published in 1599 *The First Part of the Life and Reign of Henry IV.*, dedicated to the Earl of Essex; a work which gave such offence to the queen that the author was thrown into prison. Hayward was subsequently patronized and knighted by James I. In 1613 he published *The Lives of the three Norman Kings of England, William I., William II., and Henry I.*, dedicated to Charles, Prince of Wales. He likewise wrote *The Life and Reign of King Edward VI., with the Beginning of the Reign of Queen Elizabeth*, which was published in 1630, after his death.

RICHARD KNOLLES (d. 1610), master of the free-school at Sandwich in Kent, published in 1610 a *History of the Turks.* Johnson, in a paper in the Rambler, gives Knolles the superiority over all English historians. "He has displayed all the excellencies that narrative can admit. His style, though somewhat obscured by time and vitiated by false wit, is pure, nervous, elevated, and clear. Nothing could have sunk this author into obscurity but the remoteness and barbarity of the people he relates." Mr. Hallam thinks that Johnson has not too highly extolled Knolles's style and power of narration.

SAMUEL DANIEL, the poet of whom we have already spoken (p. 80), published in 1618 a ***History of England, from the Conquest to the Reign of Edward III.*** Mr. Hallam remarks that "this work is deserving of some attention on account of its language. It is written with a freedom from all stiffness, and a purity of style, which hardly any other work of so early a date exhibits. These qualities are indeed so remarkable that it would require a good deal of critical observation to distinguish it even from writings of the reign of Anne; and where it differs from them (I speak only of the secondary class of works, which have not much individuality of manner), it is by a more select idiom, and by an absence of the Gallicism or vulgarity which is often found in that age. It is true that the merits of Daniel are chiefly negative; he is never pedantic, or antithetical, or low, as his contemporaries were apt to be; but his periods are ill constructed; he has little vigor or elegance; and it is only by observing how much pains he must have taken to reject phrases which were growing obsolete that we give him credit for having done more than follow the common stream of easy writing. A slight tinge of archaism, and a certain majesty of expression, relatively to colloquial usage, were thought by Bacon and Raleigh congenial to an elevated style; but Daniel, a gentleman of the king's household, wrote as the court spoke, and his facility would be pleasing if his sentences had a less negligent structure. As an historian he has recourse only to common authorities; but his narration is fluent and perspicuous, with a regular vein of good sense, more the characteristic of his mind, both in verse and prose, than very commanding vigor."

WILLIAM CAMDEN (1551-1623), the antiquary and historian, was head master of Westminster School, and endowed at Oxford the chair of history, which bears his name. His most celebrated work is in Latin, entitled *Britannia*, first published in 1586, giving a topographical description of Great Britain from the earliest times. He also wrote in Latin an account of the reign of Queen Elizabeth.

SIR HENRY SPELMAN (1562-1641), also an eminent antiquary, published in Latin various works upon legal and ecclesiastical antiquities, of which one of the principal is a History [illegible] the English Councils.

CHAPTER VI.

THE DAWN OF THE DRAMA.

§ 1. Origin of the Drama. Earliest religious spectacles, called ***Mysteries* or *Miracles.*** § 2. Plays, called *Moralities* : BISHOP BALE. § 3. *Interludes* : JOHN HEYWOOD. § 4. Pageants. Latin Plays. § 5. Chronicle Plays. Bale's *King John*. First English tragedies. The tragedy of *Gorboduc*. Other early tragedies. § 6. First English comedies. *Ralph Royster Doyster*. *Gammer Gurton's Needle*. § 7. Actors. Theatres. Scenery and properties of the stage. § 8. Dramatic authors usually actors. § 9. Early English playwrights. LYLY. PEELE. KYD. NASH. GREENE. LODGE. § 10. CHRISTOPHER MARLOWE. § 11. Anonymous plays.

1. As the Drama is one of the most splendid and perhaps the most intensely national department of our literature, so its origin and development were peculiar, and totally different from anything to be found in the history of other European countries. It is only Spain and England among all the modern civilized nations, that possess a theatrical literature independent in its origin, characteristic in its form, and reflecting faithfully the features, moral, social, and intellectual, of the people among which it arose: and the nationality of Spain being strongly distinguished from that of England, it is natural that the Spanish drama should possess a character which, though, like that of Britain, strongly romantic, should be very dissimilar in its type. It is possible to trace the first dim dawning of our national stage to a very remote period, to a period indeed not very far removed from the era of the Norman Conquest: for the custom of representing, in a rude dramatic form, legends of the lives of the Saints and striking episodes of Bible History seems to have been introduced from France, and to have been employed by the clergy as a means of communicating religious instruction to the rude population of the twelfth century. There exists the record of one of these religious spectacles, which received the name of *Mysteries* or *Miracles*, from the sacred nature of their subject and personages, having been represented in the Convent of Dunstable in 1119. It was called the *Play of St. Catherine*, and in all probability consisted of a rude dramatized picture of the miracles and martyrdom of that saint, performed on the festival which commemorated her death. In an age when the great mass of the laity, from the highest to the lowest, were in a state of extreme ignorance, and when the little learning that then existed was exclusively in the hands of ecclesiastics, it was quite natural that the latter, which was then the governing class, should employ so obvious an expedient for communicating some elementary religious instruction to the people, and by gratifying the curiosity of their rude hearers, extend and strengthen the influence of the Church. It is known that this play of St. Catherine was performed in French.

which is a sufficient proof that the custom of these representations was imported from abroad; but the great and rapid extension of these performances soon showed how well this mode of religious amusement accorded with the tastes and requirements of the times. Mysteries and Miracle-plays abound in the early literature of all the Catholic countries of Europe; Spain, Germany, France, Italy possess examples so abundant that a considerable library might be formed of these barbarous pieces; and the habit of seeing them represented in public has certainly left very perceptible traces in mediæval literature and art. For example, the title, the subject, and the arrangement of Dante's immortal poem are closely connected with dramatic representations of Hell, Purgatory, and Paradise, which formed a common feature among the festivities of Florence. The *Divine Comedy*, the very name of which shows its relation to some theatrical performance, is nothing but a Miracle in a narrative form. These plays were composed and acted by monks, the cathedral was transformed for the nonce into a theatre, the stage was a species of graduated platform in three divisions rising one over the other, and placed near or over the altar, and the costumes were furnished by the splendid contents of the vestry of the church. It will appear natural enough, that on any of the high religious festivals, on the anniversary of any important religious personage or event, that personage or event should be represented in a visible form, with such details as either Scripture, legend, or the imagination of the author could supply. The childish and straightforward art of these old monkish dramatists felt no repugnance in following with strict literal accuracy every circumstance of the original narrative which they dramatized; and the simple faith of their audience saw no impropriety in the introduction of the most supernatural beings, the persons of the Trinity, angels, devils, saints, and martyrs. The three platforms into which the stage was divided represented Heaven, Earth, and Hell; and the *dramatis personæ* made their appearance on that part of the stage which corresponded with their nature. It was absolutely necessary that some comic element should be introduced to enliven the graver scenes, particularly as some of these representations were of inordinate length, there being one, for example, on the subject of the Creation and the Fall of Man, which occupied six days in the performance. Besides, the rude audience would have absolutely required some farcical or amusing episode. This comic element was easily found by representing the wicked personages, whether human or spiritual, of the drama as placed in ludicrous situations, or surrounded by ludicrous accompaniments: thus the Devil generally played the part of the clown or jester, and was exhibited in a light half terrific and half farcical. Nor were they contented with such drolleries as could be extracted from the grotesque gambols and often baffled machinations of Satan and his imps, or with the mixture of merriment and horror inspired by horns, and tails, and hairy howling mouths: the authors of these pieces introduced human buffoons; and the modern puppet-play of Punch, with his struggles with the Devil, is unquestionably a direct tradition handed down from these ancient miracles in which the Evil One was alternately the conqueror and the victim of the Buffoon, Jester, or Vice, as he was called.

Some idea may be formed of these ancient religious dramas from the titles of some of them which have been preserved; for the general reader is scarce likely to consult such of them as have been printed, though curious monuments of the faith and art of long-vanished ages. The *Creation of the World*, the *Fall of Man*, the story of *Cain and Abel*, the *Crucifixion of Our Lord*, the *Massacre of the Innocents*, the *Deluge*, besides an infinite multitude of subjects taken from the lives and miracles of the saints; such were the materials of these simple dramas. They are generally written in mixed prose and verse, and though abounding in anachronisms and absurdities both of character and dialogue, they sometimes contain passages of simple and natural pathos, and sometimes scenes which must have affected the spectators with intense awe and reverence. In an English mystery on the subject of the Deluge, a comic scene is produced by the refusal of Noah's wife to enter the Ark, and by the beating which justly terminates her resistance and scolding. But, on the other hand, a mystery on the subject of the *Sacrifice of Isaac* contains a dialogue of much pathos and beauty between Abraham and his son; and the whole action of the *Mystery of the Holy Sacrament* was capable of producing a strong impression in an age of child-like, ardent faith. These representations were *got up* with all the magnificence attainable, and every expedient was employed to heighten the illusion of the scene. Thus there is a tradition of a condemned criminal having been really crucified on the stage, in a representation of the Passion of Our Lord, in the character of the Impenitent Thief. Very evident traces of the universality of these religious dramas may be found in the early works of sculpture and painting throughout Catholic Europe. Thus the practice of representing the Deity in the costume and ornaments of a Pope or a Bishop, which appears to us an absurdity or an irreverence, arose from such a personage being generally represented, on the rude stage of the miracle-play, in a dress which was then associated with ideas of the highest reverence: and the innumerable anecdotes and apologues representing evil spirits as baffled and defeated by a very moderate amount of cunning and dexterity may easily have been generated by that peculiarity of Mediæval Christianity which pictures the wicked spirits, not as terrible and awful beings, but as mischievous goblins whose power was annihilated at the foundation of our faith.

§ 2. To trace the gradual changes which establish the affiliation from the early Mysteries of the twelfth century to the regular drama of modern times, is nothing else but to point out the steps by which the dramatic art, from an exclusively religious character acquired more and more of a lay or worldly spirit in its subjects and its personages. The Mysteries, once the only form of dramatic representation, continued to be popular from the eleventh to the end of the fourteenth century; nay, in some pastoral and remote corners of Europe, where the primitive faith glows in all its ancient ardor, and where the manners of the people have been little modified by contact with foreign civilization, something very similar to the Mysteries may be still seen even in the present day. In the retired valleys of Catholic Switzerland, in the Tyrol, and in some little-visited districts of Germany, the peasants still annually perform dramatic spectacles representing episodes in the life of Christ. The first stage in the process of *laicizing* the drama was the substitution for the Miracle-play of another kind of representation, entitled a *Morality*. This species of entertainment seems to have been popular from about the beginning of the fifteenth century, and gradually supplanted the exclusively religious Mystery. It is quite evident that the composition as well as the representation of these pieces was far less exclusively in the hands of ecclesiastics, who thus began to lose that influence over the popular mind which they derived from their monopoly of knowledge. Perhaps, however, it would be a more legitimate explanation of this change to say, that the spread of civilization among the laity, and the hostility which was gradually but rapidly undermining the foundations of Catholicism in England, had contributed to put an end to that monopoly; for many of our early Moralities, though the production of Churchmen, as in the case of Bishop Bale, were the production of Churchmen strongly tainted with the unorthodox opinions of the early reformers. The subjects of these dramas, instead of being purely religious, were moral, as their name implies; and the ethical lessons were conveyed by an action and *dramatis personæ* of an abstract or allegorical kind. Thus, instead of the Deity and his angels, the Saints, the Patriarchs, and the characters of the Old and New Testament, the persons who figure in the Moralities are Every-Man — a general type or expression of humanity — Lusty Juventus — who represents the follies and weaknesses of youth — Good Counsel, Repentance, Gluttony, Pride, Avarice, and the like. The action was in general exceedingly simple, and the tone grave and doctrinal, though of course the same necessity existed as before for the introduction of comic scenes. The Devil was far too popular and useful a personage to be suppressed; so his battles and scoldings with the Vice, or Clown, were still retained to furnish forth "a fit of mirth." Our readers may form some idea of the general character of these pieces by the analysis of one, entitled *The Cradle of Security*, the outline of which has been preserved in the narrative of an old man who had formed one of the audience in his early childhood. It was intended as a lesson to careless and sensual sovereigns. The principal personage is a King, who, neglecting his high duties and plunged in voluptuous pleasures, is put to sleep in a cradle, to which he is bound by golden chains held by four beautiful ladies, who sing as they rock the cradle. Suddenly the courtiers are all dispersed by a terrible knock at the door, and the king, awaking, finds himself in the custody of two stern and tremendous figures, sent from God to punish his voluptuousness and vice. In a similar way the action of the Morality *Lusty Juventus* contains a vivid and even humorous picture of the extravagance and debauchery of a young heir, surrounded by companions, the Virtues and the Vices, some of whom endeavor in vain to restrain his passions, while others flatter his depraved inclinations. This piece also ends with a demonstration of the inevitable misery and punishment which follow a departure from the path of virtue and religion. It is impossible to draw any strong line of demarcation, either chronological or critical, between the Mystery and Morality. The one species imperceptibly melts into the other; though the general points of distinction are clear and obvious enough. The Morality also had a strong tendency to partake of the character of the court masque, in which the Elements, the Virtues, the Vices, or the various reigns of nature, were introduced either to convey some physical or philosophical instruction in the guise of allegory, or to compliment a king or great personage on a festival occasion. Of this class is Skelton's masque, to which I have alluded in a former chapter, and to which he gave the title of *Magnificence*. A very industrious writer of these Moralities was BISHOP BALE (1495–1563), who will also be mentioned presently (p. 114) as one of the founders of our national drama.

§ **3.** Springing from the Moralities, and bearing some general resemblance to them, though exhibiting a still nearer approach to the regular drama, are the *Interludes*, a class of compositions in dialogue much shorter in extent and more merry and farcical in subject, which were exceedingly fashionable about the time when the great controversy was raging between the Catholic church and the Reformed religion in England. A prolific author of these grotesque and merry pieces was JOHN HEYWOOD, a man of learning and accomplishment, but who seems to have performed the duties of a sort of jester at the court of Henry VIII. Heywood was an ardent Catholic; and the stage at that time was used by both religious parties to throw odium and ridicule upon the doctrines of their opponents; the Catholics delighting to bring forward Luther, Catherine de Bora, and the principal figures among the reformers, in a light at once detestable and ridiculous, and the Protestants returning the compliment by showing up the corruptions and vices of the Pope and the hierarchy. The Interludes, being short, were, it is supposed, performed either in the *entr'actes* of the longer and more solemn Moralities, or represented on temporary stages between the intervals of the interminable banquets and festivities of those days.

§ **4.** In the preceding rapid sketch of the dramatic amusements of our ancestors, I have endeavored to give a general idea of these entertainments in their complete and normal form; that is, when the action selected for the subject of the piece was illustrated with dialogue, and the exhibitor addressed himself to the ears as well as to the eyes of his audience. It must not be forgotten that both the subjects of the Mysteries and those of the Moralities were sometimes exhibited in dumb show. A scene of Holy Writ or some event in the life of a saint was represented in a kind of *tableau vivant* by disguised and costumed personages, and this representation was often placed on a sort of wheeled platform and exhibited continually during those long processions which formed the principal feature of the festivities of ancient times. These *tableaux vivants* were also introduced into the great halls during the elaborate banquets which were the triumphs of ancient magnificence and thus this species of entertainment is inseparably connected with those *pageants* so often employed to gratify the vanity of citizens, or to compliment an illustrious visitor. These pageants, whether simply consisting of the exhibition, on some lofty platform, in the porch or churchyard of a cathedral, in the Town Hall or over the city gate, of a number of figures suitably dressed, or accompanying their action with poetical declamation and music, necessarily partook in all the changes of taste which characterized the age: the Prophets and Saints who welcomed the royal stranger in the thirteenth century with barbarous Latin hymns, were gradually supplanted by the Virtues and allegorical qualities; and these in their turn, when the Renaissance had disseminated a universal passion for classical imagery, made way for the Cupids, the Muses, and other classical personages whose influence has continued almost to the literature of our own time. Such spectacles as I have just been alluding to, which were so common that the chronicles of every European nation are filled with records of them, were of course frequently exhibited at the Universities: but in the hands of these bodies the shows naturally acquired a more learned character than they had elsewhere. It was almost universal in those times that the students should employ Latin on all official occasions. this was necessary, partly from the multitude of *nations* composing the body of the students, and who required some common language which they could all understand. Latin, therefore, was by a thousand different laws and regulations obligatory; and this occurred not only in the Universities, but also in many conventual and monastic societies. It was therefore natural that the public amusements of the University should partake of the same character. A large number of pieces, generally written upon the models of Terence and Seneca, were produced and represented at this time. In the great outbreak of revolt against the authority of scholasticism which preceded the Reformation, the return to classical models in dramatic composition was general, and Reuchlin boasted that he was the first to furnish the youth of Germany with comedies bearing some similarity to the masterpieces of Terence. The times of Elizabeth and James were peculiarly fertile in Latin dramas composed at the Universities; and these sovereigns, the first of whom was remarkably learned in an age of general diffusion of classical studies, while in the second erudition had degenerated into pedantry, were entertained by the students of Oxford and Cambridge with Latin plays.

§ 5. We have now traced the progress of the Dramatic art from its first rude infancy in England, and have seen how every step of that advance removed it farther and farther from a purely religious, and brought it closer and closer to a profane character. The last step of the progress was the creation of what we now understand under the term dramatic, viz. the scenic representation, by means of the action and dialogue of human personages, of some event of history or social life. As in the first appearance of this, the most perfect form which the art could attain, the influence of the great models of ancient literature must have been very powerful, dramatic compositions class themselves, by the very nature of the case, into the two great categories of Tragedy and Comedy, and even borrow from the classical models details of an unessential kind, as for example the use of the Chorus, which, originally consisting of a numerous body of performers, was gradually reduced, though its name and functions were retained to a certain degree by the old English playwrights, to a single individual, as in several of Shakspeare's dramas. It was about the middle of the sixteenth century that a considerable activity of creation was first perceptible in this department. JOHN BALE (1495–1563), the author of many semi-polemical plays, partaking in some measure of the character of the Mystery, the Morality, and the Interlude, set the example of extracting materials for rude historical dramas from the Chronicles of his native country. His drama of *King John* occupies an intermediate place between the Moralities and historical plays. But the most remarkable progress in this department of literature is to be found in a considerable number of pieces, written to be performed by the students of the Inns of Court and the Universities, for the amusement of the sovereign on high festival occasions: for it must be remembered that the establishment of regular theatres and the formation of regular theatrical troops did not take place for a considerable period after these first dramatic attempts. The great entertainments of the rich and powerful municipal corporations, of which the Lord Mayor's annual Show in London, and similar festivities in many other towns, still exist as curious relics, prove that the same circumstances which had generated the annual performance of the Chester and Coventry plays, and maintained those exhibitions uninterruptedly during a very long succession of years, still continued to exist. Contrary to what might have been expected, the first tragedies produced in the English language were remarkable for the gravity and elevation of their language, the dignity of their sentiments, and the dryness and morality of their style. They are, it is true, extremely crowded with bloody and dolorous events, rebellions, treasons, murders, and regicides: but there is very little attempt to delineate character, and certainly not the slightest trace of that admixture of comic action and dialogue which is so characteristic of the later theatre of England, in which the scene struggled to imitate the irregularity and the vastness of human life. A good example of these early plays is the Tragedy of *Gorboduc*, or *Ferrex and Porrex*, written by Thomas Sackville, Lord Buckhurst (the principal writer in the "Mirrour for Magistrates"), and Thomas Norton, and acted in 1562 for the entertainment of Queen Elizabeth, by the gentlemen of the Inner Temple. The subject of this play is borrowed from the old half-mythological Chronicles of Britain, and the principal event is similar to the story of Eteocles and Polynices, a legend which has furnished the materials not only to the genius of Æschylus, but to that of Racine and Schiller. But though the *subject* of this piece is derived from the national records, whether authentic or mythical, the *treatment* exhibits strong marks of classic imitation, though rather after the manner of Seneca than of Æschylus or Sophocles. Seneca enjoyed a most surprising reputation at the revival of Letters. The dialogue of *Gorboduc* is in blank verse,* which is regular and carefully constructed; but it is totally destitute of variety of pause, and consequently is a most insufficient vehicle for dramatic dialogue. The sentence almost invariably terminates with the line, and the effect of the whole is insupportably formal and heavy; for no weight and depth of moral and political apothegm, with which the work abounds, can compensate for the total want of life, of sentiment, and passion. Another work of a similar character is *Damon and Pythias*, acted before the Queen at Christ Church, Oxford, in 1566. This play, which is in rhyme, is a mixture of tragedy and comedy. Its author was RICHARD EDWARDS, the compiler of the miscellany called *The Paradise of Dainty Devices* (see p. 85). He also wrote *Palamon and Arcite*, the beautiful story so inimitably treated by Chaucer in *The Knight's Tale*, and afterwards in Beaumont and Fletcher's romantic play *The Two Noble Kinsmen*. In 1578 was acted *Promos and Cassandra*, by GEORGE WHETSTONE, chiefly curious as having furnished the subject of Shakspeare's *Measure for Measure*. All these plays are marked by a general similarity of style and treatment, and belong to about the same period.

§ 6. In the department of Comedy the first English works which made their appearance very little anterior to the above pieces, offer a most striking contrast in their tone and treatment. It would almost seem as if the national genius, destined to stand unrivalled in the peculiar vein of humor, was to prove that while in tragic and sublime delineations it might encounter, not indeed superiors, but rivals, — in the grotesque, the odd, the laughable, it was to stand alone. The earliest comedy in the language was *Ralph Royster Doyster*, acted in 1551, and written by NICHOLAS UDALL, who for a long time executed the duties of Master of Eton College. This was followed, about fourteen years later, by *Gammer Gurton's Needle*, composed by JOHN STILL, afterwards Bishop of Bath and Wells, and who had previously been Master of St. John's and Trinity Colleges in Cambridge. This piece was probably acted by the students of the society over which the author presided, and was long considered to have been the earliest regular comedy in the English language: but it was afterwards established that the work of Udall preceded it by a short interval. Both these works are highly curious and interesting, not only as being the oldest specimens of the class of literature to which they belong, but in some measure from their intrinsic merit. There can be no question that the former comedy is far superior to the second: it is altogether of a higher order, both in conception and execution. The action takes place in London, and the principal characters are a rich and pretty widow, her lover, and several of her suitors, the chief of whom is the foolish personage who gives the title to the play. This ridiculous pretender to gayety and

* Blank verse was first introduced by Lord Surrey in his translation of the *Æneid* (see p. 66). It was next used by Grimoald (see p. 70), who, according to Warton, gave it "new strength, elegance, and modulation." Sackville was the third writer who employed it.

love, a young heir just put into possession of his fortune, is surrounded by a number of intriguers and flatterers who pretend to be his friends, and who lead their dupe into all sorts of absurd and humiliating scrapes; and the piece ends with the return of the favored lover from a voyage which he had undertaken in a momentary pique. The manners represented are those of the middle class of the period, and the picture given of London citizen life in the middle of the sixteenth century is curious, animated, and natural. The language is lively, and the dialogue is carried on in a sort of loose doggerel rhyme, very well adapted to represent comic conversation. In general the intrigue of this drama is deserving of approbation; the plot is well imagined, and the reader's curiosity well kept alive. *Gammer Gurton's Needle* is a composition of a much lower and more farcical order. The scene is laid in the humblest rustic life, and all the *dramatis personæ* belong to the uneducated class. The principal action of the comedy is the sudden loss of a needle with which Gammer (*Commère?*) Gurton has been mending the inexpressibles of her man Hodge, a loss comparatively serious, when needles were rare and costly. The whole intrigue consists in the search instituted after this unfortunate little implement, which is at last discovered by Hodge himself, on suddenly sitting down, sticking in the garment which Gammer Gurton had been repairing.

A comparison between these early comedies, and *Gammer Gurton* in particular, and that curious and interesting piece *Maistre Pierre Pathelin*, which is regarded as the first specimen of the French comic stage, would not be uninstructive. In both the transition from the *sottie* or *farce* to regular comedy is plainly perceptible; and it must be confessed that in the humorous delineation of character, as well as in probability and variety of incident, the French piece has decidedly the advantage. The form of the dialogue, being in both cases a sort of easy doggerel verse, little removed from the real language of the classes represented, has great similarity; though the French comedy is, as far as its diction is concerned, far more archaic and difficult to a modern French reader than the English of *Gammer Gurton* to an English one. This indeed may be generally remarked, that our language has undergone less radical changes in the space of time which has elapsed from the first appearance of literary productions among us than any of the other cultivated dialects of Europe.

§ **7.** It will be inferred from what has been said respecting the custom of acting plays at Court, in the mansions of great lords, in the Universities, and in the Inns of Law, that regular public theatres were not yet in existence. The actors were to a certain degree amateurs, and were frequently literally the domestics of the sovereign and the nobles, wearing their badges and liveries, and protected by their patronage. The line of demarcation between musical performers, singers, jugglers, tumblers, and actors, was for a long period very faintly traced. The Court plays were frequently represented by the children of the royal chapel, and placed, as the dramatic profession in general was for a long time, under the peculiar supervision of the Office of the Revels, which was obliged also to exercise the duties of a dramatic censor. These bodies of actors, singers, tumblers, &c., were frequently in the habit of wandering about the country, performing wherever they could find an audience, sometimes in the mansions of rural grandees, sometimes in the town halls of provincial municipalities, sometimes in the court-yards of inns. Protected by the letters-patent and the livery of their master against the severe laws which qualified strollers as vagabonds, they generally began their proceedings by begging the countenance and protection of the authorities; and the accounts of the ancient municipal bodies, and the household registers of the great families of former times, abound in entries of permissions given to such strolling parties of actors, tumblers, and musicians, and of sums granted to them in recompense of their exertions. It is curious to remark that the amount of such sums seems to have been calculated less in reference to the talent displayed in the representation, than to the degree of respect which the grantors wished to show to the patron under whose protection the troop happened to be. This state of things, however, had existed long before; for in the accounts of the ancient monasteries we frequently meet with entries of gratuities given, not only to travelling preachers from other religious bodies, but even to minstrels, jugglers, and other professors of the arts of entertainment. Nothing was more easy than to transform the ancient hall of a college, palace, or nobleman's mansion into a theatre sufficiently convenient in the then primitive state of dramatic representation. The *dais* or elevated platform at the upper extremity was a stage ready made; it was only necessary to hang up a curtain, and to establish a few screens covered with tapestry, to produce a scene sufficient for the purpose. When the performance took place in an inn, which was very common, the stage was established on a platform in the centre of the yard; the lower classes of spectators stood upon the ground in front of it, which custom is preserved in the designation *parterre*, still given by the French to the *pit*. The latter denomination is a record of the circumstance that in England theatrical representations often took place in *cockpits*. Indeed there at one time existed in London a theatre called the Cockpit, from the circumstance of its having been originally an arena for that sport. The ancient inns, as may be seen by many specimens still in existence, were built round an open court-yard, and along each story internally ran an open gallery, upon which opened the doors and windows of the small chambers occupied by the guests. In order to witness the performance the inmates had only to come out into the gallery in front of their rooms; and the convenience of this arrangement unquestionably suggested the principal features of construction when buildings were first specifically destined for scenic performances. The galleries of the old inns were the prototypes of the circles of boxes in our modern theatres.

But the taste for dramatic entertainments grew rapidly more general and ardent; and in the course of time, in many places, particularly in London, not only did special societies of professional actors begin to come into existence, but special edifices were constructed for their exhibitions. Indeed at one period it is supposed that London and its suburbs contained at least twelve different theatres, of various degrees of size and convenience. Of these the most celebrated was undoubtedly the *Globe*, for at that time each playhouse had its sign, and the company which performed in it were also the proprietors of a smaller house on the opposite, or London side of the Thames, called the Blackfriars, situated very nearly on the spot now occupied by the gigantic establishment of the "Times" newspaper. The great majority of the London theatres were on the southern or Surrey bank of the Thames, in order to be out of the jurisdiction of the municipality of the City, which, having been from a very early period strongly infected with the gloomy doctrines of Puritanism, was violently opposed to theatrical entertainments, and carried on against the players and the playhouses a constant war, in which their opponents repelled the persecutions of authority with all the petulance of wit and caricature. Some of these theatres were cockpits or arenas for bull-baiting and bear-baiting, either transformed into regular playhouses, or alternately employed for theatrical and other spectacles: but the Globe, and probably others as well, were specifically erected for the purpose of the drama. They were all, however, very poor and squalid, as compared with the magnificent theatres of the present day, and retained in their form and arrangement many traces of the ancient model — the inn-yard. The building was octagon, and entirely uncovered, excepting over the stage, where a thatched roof protected the actors from the weather; and this thatched roof was, in 1613, the cause of the total destruction of the Globe, in consequence of the wadding of a *chamber*, or small cannon, lodging in it, fired during the representation of Shakspeare's Henry VIII. The boxes or *rooms*, as they were then styled, were of course arranged nearly as in the present day, but the musicians, instead of being placed, as now, in the orchestra, or space between the pit and the stage, were established in a lofty gallery over the scene.

The most remarkable peculiarity of the ancient English theatres was the total absence of painted scenery, which in more recent times has been carried to such a height of artistic splendor and illusion. A few *traverses*, as they were called, or screens of cloth or tapestry, gave the actors the opportunity of making their exits and entrances; and in order to give the audience an idea of the place where the action was to be supposed, they employed the singularly primitive expedient of exhibiting a placard, bearing the name of Rome, Athens, London, or Florence, as the case might be. So exceedingly rude an expedient as this is the more singular as the English drama is remarkable for its frequent changes of scene. But though they were forced to content themselves with this very inartificial mode of indicating the place of the action, the details of the locality could be represented with a much more accurate imitation. Thus, if a bedroom were to be supposed, a bed was pushed forward on the stage; a table covered with bottles and tankards, and surrounded with benches, easily suggested a tavern; a gilded chair surmounted by a canopy, and called a *state*, gave the idea of a palace, an altar of a church, and the like. At the back of the stage was erected a permanent wooden construction, like a scaffold or a high wall; and this served for those innumerable incidents where one of the *dramatis personæ* is to overhear the others without being himself seen, and also represented an infinity of objects according to the requirements of the piece, such as the wall of a castle or besieged city, the outside of a house, as when a dialogue is to take place between one person at a window and another on the exterior. Thus in the admirable garden-scene of Romeo and Juliet, Juliet probably spoke either from the summit of this wall or from a window established in it, while Romeo stood on the ground outside; in the same way the "men of Angiers" spoke to the besieging English from the top of their wall, and the storming of Harfleur divided the action between Henry and his troops upon the stage and the defenders of the city upon the platform.

In those accessories to scenic illusion which in the language of the English stage are called *properties*, the old Elizabethan theatres were better provided than could have been expected, as may be seen from very curious lists of such articles which have accidentally descended to us from the ancient greenrooms. In point of costume very little attention was paid to chronological or national accuracy. The *dramatis personæ* of all ages and countries were in general habited in the dress of the period; this was fortunately a graceful, rich, and picturesque costume; and we may judge, from the innumerable philippics of divines and moralists against the luxury of the actors, that a very considerable degree of splendor in theatrical dress was common. The employment of the contemporary costume in plays whose action was supposed to take place in Greece, Rome, or Persia, naturally led into gross anachronisms and absurdities, arming the assassins of Cæsar with Spanish rapiers, or furnishing Carthaginian senators with watches; but these anachronisms were not likely to strike in a very offensive manner the mixed and uncritical spectators of those times. It may indeed be said that the meagre material aids to the illusion of the scene which were then at the disposal of the dramatic author were in reality of the greatest service to the poetical and imaginative department of his art. Not being able to depend upon the scene-painter and the machinist, he was obliged to trust to his own resources, and to describe in words what could not be "oculis subjecta fidelibus." It is to this circumstance that we owe those inimitable pictures of natural and artificial objects and scenery with which the dramas of this age are so prodigally adorned. Though the majority of the characters were clothed in the habit of the day, there were certain conventional attributes always associated with particular supernatural personages, such as angels, devils, ghosts, and so on. Thus "a roobe for to goo invisibell" is one of the items in the lists of properties to which I have alluded above; and in all probability the spectral armor of the Ghost in Hamlet was to be found in the wardrobe of the ancient theatres. It appears that the dresses and properties belonged to persons who derived their livelihood from hiring these articles at a fixed price per night to the performers.

The curtain, that essential appendage to every theatre, is supposed to have opened perpendicularly in the middle, instead of being wound up and let down as at present; and besides this principal curtain there seem to have been others occasionally drawn so as to divide the stage into several apartments, and withdrawn to exhibit one of the characters as in a tent or closet.

The cost of admission to the theatres was small, and it was possible to secure the use of a private box or *room;* for it was then considered hardly proper for a lady to be present at the representations of the public theatres: it was certainly long before any of our sovereigns deigned to witness any of those performances. Whenever the monarch desired to see a play the actors were summoned to court; and the accounts of the chamberlain's office furnish abundant entries of the recompenses ordered to be distributed on such occasions among the performers. Several of the companies of actors were under the immediate patronage of the sovereign, of different members of the royal family and other great personages of the realm: they were bound to "exercise themselves industriously in the art and quality of stage-playing," in order to be always ready to furnish entertainment to their employer, and in return for these services they were protected against interlopers and rivals, and above all against the implacable hostility of the Puritanical municipality of London. It is perhaps to this circumstance that we may attribute the designation of *Her Majesty's Servants*, which our modern companies of actors still retain in their playbills; and the old custom of the actors at the end of the piece falling upon their knees and putting up a solemn prayer to Heaven in favor of the sovereign is perhaps commemorated in the words *Vivat Regina*, with which our modern playbills terminate. The usual hour of representation was anciently very early, in accordance with the habit of dining before midday, and the signal was given by the hoisting of a flag at the summit of the theatre, which remained floating during the whole performance.

The piece commenced with three flourishes of a trumpet, and at the *third sounding*, as it was called, the prologue was declaimed by a solemn personage whose regular costume was a long black velvet cloak. At the end of the piece, or occasionally perhaps between the acts, the clown or jester performed what was called a *jig*, a species of entertainment in which our ancestors seem to have delighted. This was a kind of comic ballad or declamation in doggerel verse, either really or professedly an improvisation of the moment, introducing any person or event which was exciting the ridicule of the day, and accompanied by the performer with tabor and pipe and with grotesque and farcical dancing. As the comic actors who performed the clowns and jesters, then indispensable personages in all pieces, tragic and comic, were allowed to introduce extemporary witticisms at their pleasure, they were probably a clever and inventive class; and the enormous popularity of several of them, as Tarlton, Kempe, and Armin, seems to prove that their drollery must have been intensely amusing.

During the representation of a deep tragedy the whole stage was sometimes hung with black; a very singular custom, to which innumerable allusions are made in our older pieces. On ordinary occasions the stage was strewed with rushes, as indeed were rooms generally in those days; and on these rushes, or on stools brought for the purpose, it was customary for the fine gentlemen to sit, amid the full business of the stage, displaying their splendid clothes, smoking clay-pipes, which was then the height of fashion, exchanging repartees and often coarse abuse with the audience before the curtain, and criticising in a loud voice the actors and the piece. In England, as in Spain, the companies of players have been generally, from time immemorial, private and independent associations. The property and profits of the theatre were divided into a number of shares, as in a joint-stock company; and the number of these shareholders being limited, whatever additional assistance the society required was obtained by engaging the services of *hired men*, who usually acted the inferior parts. Many bonds stipulating the terms of such engagements are in existence; and one of the conditions usually was, that the actor so engaged should give his services at a fixed price, and should undertake to perform for no other company during the time specified in his engagement. These men had no right to any share in the profits of the society. That these profits were very considerable and constant, and that the career of an actor of eminence was often a very lucrative one, is abundantly proved, not only by the frequent allusions to the pride, luxury, and magnificence in dress of the successful performers, which are met with in the sermons, pamphlets, and satires of the day, but still more decisively by the wills left by many of these actors, specifying the large fortunes they sometimes accumulated by the practice of their art. Examples of this will be found in the cases of Shakspeare, the great tragedian Burbage, and the well-known charitable institution due to the philanthropy and piety of Edward Alleyn.

It must never be lost sight of, by any one who wishes to form a clear notion of the state of the elder English drama, that the female parts were invariably acted by boys or young men. No woman appeared on our stage till about the time of the Restoration, and then, singularly enough, the earliest part acted by a female was the Desdemona of our great dramatist. This innovation was at first considered as something shocking and monstrous; but the evident advantages and propriety of the change soon silenced all opposition. The novelty itself first originated in Italy. We must not, however, imagine that because the parts of women were intrusted to male representatives they were necessarily ill performed: there are abundant proofs that some of the young actors who devoted themselves to this line of their art, attained by practice to a high degree both of elegance and pathos. They were often singing-boys of the royal chapel, and as long as their falsetto voice remained pure, not "cracked i' the ring," as Hamlet says, they were no unfit representatives of the graceful and beautiful heroines of Shakspeare, Ford, or Fletcher. The testimony of contemporaries proves that some of them, as for example the famous Kynaston, so admirably seized all the details of the characters they personated, that the illusion was complete; and they were no unworthy rivals of the great artists of those days. It is true that this custom of the female parts being acted by boys may have in some degree exaggerated that tendency to *double entendre* and indecent equivoque which has unfortunately been but too universally the vice of the stage: but even this objection will lose some of its weight when we reflect that the habitual appearance of women on the stage seems, so far from checking, absolutely to have aggravated the frightful profligacy and immorality which defiled the society and the literature of the country at the epoch of the Restoration, and which reached its highest intensity in compositions destined for the stage.

§ 8. Perhaps the most remarkable peculiarity of the dramatic profession at this period of our literary history was the frequent combination, in one and the same person, of the qualities of player and dramatic author. I do not mean to imply, of course, that all the actors of this splendid epoch were dramatists; but nearly all the dramatic authors were actors by profession. This circumstance must have obviously exerted a mighty influence in modifying the dramatic productions composed under such conditions — an influence not of course exclusively favorable, but which must have powerfully contributed to give to those productions that strong and individual character, that *goût du terroir*, which renders them so inimitable. It is evident that a dramatic writer, however great his genius, unacquainted practically with the mechanism of the stage, will frequently fail in giving to his work that directness and vivacity which is the essential element of popular success. Such a poet, writing in his closet under the influence not of *scenic* but of merely *literary* emotions, may produce admirable declamation, delicate anatomy of character, profound exhibition of human passion; but the most valuable element of scenic success, viz., *dramatic effect*, may be entirely absent. This precious quality may be possessed by a writer with not a tithe of the genius of the former, and for the absence of this quality no amount of abstract literary merit can compensate. A striking example of this may be found in the French theatre. All the admirable qualities of Racine and Corneille have not been able to preserve their tragedies from comparative neglect as tragedies, *i. e.* in a theatrical point of view. As literary compositions they will always be studied and admired by every one who desires to make acquaintance with the higher qualities of the French language and poetry; but as tragedies, few persons can now witness their performance without experiencing a sensation of weariness which they may attempt to disguise, but which they certainly cannot escape. It has been the fashion to explain this by attributing it to changes in the manners and habits of society; but how happens it that the scenes of Molière always retain their freshness and vivacity? The reason is, that Molière, himself a skilful actor, as well as an unequalled painter of that range of comic character which he has delineated, gave to his pieces the element of *scenic effect*; an element which will successfully replace the absence of much higher literary qualities, and which can be acquired only by the instinct of the stage. An immense majority of the dramatists of our Elizabethan theatre were actors, and this is why their writings are so often defiled by very gross faults of coarseness, violence, buffoonery, bombast, bad taste, and extravagance — such faults, in short, as were naturally to be expected from actor-authors writing in great haste, addressing themselves to a very miscellaneous public, and thinking not of future glory, but of immediate profit and success; but at the same time it is the reason why their writings, despite of all these, and even graver faults, invariably possess intense dramatic interest, and an effectiveness for the absence of which no purely literary merit can in any way compensate. But though professional actors, this brilliant constellation of writers, by a chance which has never been repeated in literary history, consisted of men of liberal and often learned education. Generally young men of strong passions, frequently of gentle birth, they in many cases left the university for the theatre, where they hoped to obtain an easy subsistence at a time when both writing for the stage and acting were well recompensed by the public, and where the joyous and irregular mode of life possessed such charms for ardent passions and lax morality. Their career was, in too many cases, a miserable succession of revelry and distress, of gross debauchery and ignoble privation; but the examples of many showed that prudence and industry would be rewarded in this career with the same certainty as in others, and the success of Burbage, Alleyn, and Shakspeare can be put forward as the contrast to the debauched lives and miserable deaths of Marlowe, Greene, and Nash. This very irregularity of life, however, may have contributed to give to the works of this time that large spirit of observation, that universality of painting, which certainly distinguished them. The career of these men, at least in its commencement and general outlines, was the same. They attached themselves, in the double quality of actors and poets, to one of the numerous companies then existing; and in many instances began their literary labors by rewriting and rearranging plays already exhibited to the public, and which a little alteration could often render more suitable to the peculiar resources of the company. Having by this comparatively humble work of making *rechauffés* acquired skill and facility, the dramatic aspirant would bring out an original work, either alone or in partnership with some brother playwright; and in this way he would be fairly started as a writer. It was of course very much to the interest of a company of actors to possess an exclusive right to the services of an able or popular dramatist; and his productions, while they remained in manuscript, continued to be the exclusive property of the company. Thus the troops of actors had the very strongest motive for taking every precaution that their pieces should *not* be printed, publication instantly annihilating their monopoly, and allowing rival companies to profit by their labors; and this is the reason why comparatively so few of the dramas of this period, in spite of their unequalled merit and their great popularity, were committed to the press during the lives, at least, of their authors. It also explains the singularly careless execution of such copies as were printed, these having been given to the public in many cases surreptitiously, and in direct contravention to the wishes and interests of the author. It must be confessed that in the sixteenth century in England theatrical writing was considered the very lowest branch of literature, if indeed it was regarded as literature at all. The profession of actor, though often profitable, and exercised by many individuals with dignity and respectability, was certainly not looked upon by society in a very favorable light. The vices and profligacy of many of its members seemed almost to justify the infamy stamped on the occupation by the old law, which classed players with "rogues and vagabonds." Placed in such a social atmosphere, and exposed to such powerful and opposing influences, the dramatic author of those times was likely to exhibit precisely the tendencies which we actually find characterizing his works, and recorded in his life.

§ **9.** I will now give a rapid sketch of the principal English playwrights anterior to Shakspeare. JOHN LYLY (b. about 1554) composed several court plays and pageants, and is supposed to have enjoyed in some degree the favor of Elizabeth, for we know that he was at one time a petitioner for the reversion of the office of Master of the Revels. His few plays were written upon classical, or rather mythological subjects, as the story of *Endymion*, *Sappho and Phaon*, and *Alexander and Campaspe*. He has a rich and fantastic imagination, and his writings exhibit genius and elegance, though strongly tinctured with a peculiar kind of affectation with which he infected the language of the Court, the aristocracy, and even to a considerable degree literature itself, till it fell under the ridicule of Shakspeare, like the parallel absurdity in France, the *Phébus* of the Hôtel de Rambouillet, under the lash of the *Précieuses Ridicules* and the *Critique de l'École des Femmes*. Lyly was the English Gongora; and his absurd though ingenious jargon, like the *estilo culto* in Spain, became the fashionable affectation of the day. It consisted in a kind of exaggerated vivacity of imagery and expression; the remotest and most unexpected analogies were sought for, and crowded into every sentence. The reader may form some notion of this mode of writing (which was called Euphuism, from Lyly's once fashionable book entitled *Euphues and his England*) by consulting the caricature of it which Scott has introduced in the character of the courtier Sir Piercy Shafton in *The Monastery*. In fact the Euphuism of Lyly was the somewhat exaggerated wit of the style of Sydney, still further *outré*. Lyly was a man of considerable classical acquirements, and had been educated at Oxford. His lyrics are extremely graceful and harmonious, and even as a playwright his merits are rather lyrical than dramatic.

GEORGE PEELE, like Lyly, had received a liberal education at Oxford. He was one of Shakspeare's fellow-actors and fellow-shareholders in the Blackfriars Theatre. He had also been employed by the City of London in composing and preparing those spectacles and shows which formed so great a portion of ancient civic festivity. His earliest work,

The Arraignment of Paris, was printed anonymously in 1584. His most celebrated dramatic works were the *Davia and Bethsabe*, and *Absolom*, in which there are great richness and beauty of language, and occasional indications of a high order of pathetic and elevated emotion; but his versification, though sweet, has little variety; and the luxurious and sensuous descriptions in which Peele most delighted are so numerous that they become rather tiresome in the end. It should be remarked that this poet was the first to give an example of that peculiar kind of historical *play* in which Shakspeare was afterwards so consummate a master. His *Edward I.* is, though monotonous, declamatory and stiff, in some sense the forerunner of such works as *Richard II.*, *Richard III.*, or *Henry V.*

THOMAS KYD, who lived about the same time, is principally noticeable as having probably been the original author of that famous play upon which so many dramatists tried their hands in the innumerable recastings which it received, and which have caused it to be ascribed in succession to almost the whole body of the elder Elizabethan dramatists. Of this piece, in spite of its occasional extravagance, even the greatest of these authors might have been proud. It is called *Hieronymo, the Spanish Tragedy.* Its popularity was very great, and furnishes incessant allusions to the playwrights of the day. The subject is exceedingly gloomy, bloody, and dolorous; but the pictures of grief, despair, revenge, and madness, with which it abounds, not only testify high dramatic power of conception, but must have been, as we know they were, exceedingly favorable for displaying the powers of a great tragic actor.

THOMAS NASH and ROBERT GREENE, both Cambridge men, both sharp, and, I fear, mercenary satirists, and both alike in the profligacy of their lives and the misery of their deaths, though they may have eked out their income by occasionally writing for the stage, were in reality rather pasquinaders and pamphleteers than dramatists — condottieri of the press, shamelessly advertising the services of their ready and biting pen to any person or any cause that would pay them. They were both unquestionably men of rare powers; Nash probably the better man and the abler writer of the two. Nash is famous for the bitter controversy he maintained with the learned Gabriel Harvey, whom he has caricatured and attacked in numerous pamphlets, in a manner equally humorous and severe. He was concerned with other dramatists in the production of a piece entitled *Summer's Last Will and Testament*, and in a satirical comedy, *The Isle of Dogs*, which drew down upon him the anger of the Government, for we know that he was imprisoned for some time in consequence.

Greene was, like Nash, the author of a multitude of tracts and pamphlets on the most miscellaneous subjects. Sometimes they were tales, often translated or expanded from the Italian novelists; sometimes amusing exposures of the various arts of *cony-catching*, *i. e.* cheating and swindling, practised at that time in London, and in which, it is to be feared, Greene was personally not unversed; sometimes moral confessions, like Nash's *Pierce Pennilesse his Supplication to the*

Devil, or Greene's *Groatsworth of Wit*, purporting to be a warning to others against the consequences of unbridled passions. Some of these confessions are exceedingly pathetic, and would be more so could the reader divest himself of a lurking suspicion that the whole is often a mere trick to catch a penny. The popularity of these tracts, we know, was very great. The only dramatic work we need specify of Greene's was *George-a-Green*, the legend of an old English popular hero, recounted with much occasional vivacity and humor.

THOMAS LODGE (1550–1625?) is described by Mr. Collier as "second to Kyd in vigor and boldness of conception; but as a drawer of character, so essential a part of dramatic poetry, he unquestionably has the advantage." His principal work is a tragedy entitled *The Hounds of Civil War, lively set forth in the Two Tragedies of Marius and Sylla* (1594). He also composed, in conjunction with Greene, *A Looking-Glass for London and England*, the object of which is a defence of the stage against the Puritanical party. (See also p. 86.)

§ 10. But by far the most powerful genius among the dramatic poets who immediately preceded Shakspeare was CHRISTOPHER MARLOWE (1563?–1593). This man, if destiny had granted to him a longer life, which might have enabled him to correct the luxuriance of an ardent temperament and an unregulated imagination, might have left works that would have placed him very high among the foremost poets of his age. As it is, his remains strike us with as much regret as admiration — regret that such rare powers should have been so irregularly cultivated. Marlowe was born at Canterbury in 1563, and was educated at Cambridge. On leaving the University he joined a troop of actors, and is recorded to have broken his leg upon the stage. His mode of life was remarkable for vice and debauchery, even in a profession so little scrupulous; and he was strongly suspected by his contemporaries of having been little better than an Atheist. His career was as short as it was disgraceful: he was stabbed in the head with his own dagger, which he had drawn in a disreputable scuffle with a disreputable antagonist, in a disreputable place: and he died of this wound at the age of thirty. His works are not numerous, but they are strongly distinguished from those of preceding and contemporary dramatists by an air of astonishing power, energy, and elevation — an elevation, it is true, which is sometimes exaggerated into bombast, and an energy which occasionally degenerates into extravagance. His first work was the tragedy of *Tamburlaine*, and the rants of the declamation in this piece furnished rich materials for satire and caricature; but in spite of this bombast the piece contains many passages of great power and beauty. Marlowe's best work is incontestably the drama of *Faustus*, founded upon the very same popular legend which Goethe adopted as the groundwork of his tragedy; but the point of view taken by Marlowe is far simpler than that of Goethe; and the English poem contains no trace of the profound self-questioning of the German hero, of the extraordinary creation of Mephistopheles, nor anything like the pathetic episode of Margaret. The witch element, which reigns so wildly and picturesquely in the German poem, is here entirely absent But, on the other hand, there is certainly no passage in the tragedy of Goethe in which terror, despair, and remorse are painted with such a powerful hand, as the great closing scene of Marlowe's piece, when Faustus, after the twenty-four years of sensual pleasure which were stipulated in his pact with the Evil One, is waiting for the inevitable arrival of the Fiend to claim his bargain. This is truly dramatic, and is assuredly one of the most impressive scenes that ever were placed upon the stage. The tragedy of the *Jew of Malta*, though inferior to *Faustus*, is characterized by similar merits and defects. The hero, Barabbas, is the type of the Jew as he appeared to the rude and bigoted imaginations of the fifteenth century — a monster half terrific, half ridiculous, impossibly rich, inconceivably bloodthirsty, cunning, and revengeful, the bugbear of an age of ignorance and persecution. Though the exploits of cruelty and retaliation upon his Christian oppressors make Barabbas a fantastic personage, the intense expression of his rage, his triumph, and his despair, give occasion for many noble bursts of Marlowe's powerful declamation. The tragedy of *Edward II.*, which was the last of this great poet's works, shows that in some departments of his art, and particularly in that of moving terror and pity, he might, had he lived, have become no insignificant rival of Shakspeare himself. The scene of the assassination of the unhappy king is worked up to a very lofty pitch of tragic pathos. Charles Lamb observes that "the reluctant pangs of abdicating royalty in Edward furnished hints which Shakspeare scarce improved in his *Richard II.*; and the death-scene of Marlowe's king moves pity and terror beyond any scene, ancient or modern, with which I am acquainted." Marlowe was the morning star that heralded the rising of the great dramatic Sun.

§ **11.** I pass over the names of a number of comparatively insignificant authors who appeared about this time, whose dramatic works have not yet been collected and printed. They in some instances, according to the custom of that age, either composed plays in partnership, or revised and altered plays written before, so that it is exceedingly difficult to assign to each playwright his just share of merit. There are, however, two or three pieces which have come down to us, either anonymous, or at least attributed to so many different authors, that it is now impossible to father them with precision. Some of these pieces are of great merit, and others are curious as being examples of the practice which afterwards became general in our theatre, of dramatizing either episodes from the chronicle history of our own or other countries (of which class we may cite the old *Hamlet*, *The Famous Victories*, and *King John*), or remarkable crimes — *causes célèbres* — which had attracted the public attention by their unusual atrocity or the romantic nature of their details. Good examples of these are *Arden of Feversham*, and *The Yorkshire Tragedy*, both founded on fact, both works of no mean merit, and both attributed, though without any probability, to the pen of Shakspeare.

CHAPTER VII.

SHAKSPEARE. A. D. 1564–1616.

§ 1. Parentage and education of Shakspeare. § 2. His early life and marriage § 3. He comes to London, joins the Globe Theatre, and turns author. § 4. Company of the Globe Theatre. § 5. Shakspeare's career at the Globe. His acting. § 6. Continuation of his life. His success and prudence. Returns to Stratford. His death. § 7. Classification of his Dramas into History and Fiction. Sources of the Dramas. § 8. His treatment of the Historical Dramas. § 9. His treatment of the Dramas founded upon Fiction. § 10. His *Venus and Adonis*, *Rape of Lucrece*, and *Sonnets*.

§ 1. WILLIAM SHAKSPEARE was born on the 23d of April, 1564, in the small county town of Stratford-on-Avon, Warwickshire, and was baptized on the 26th of the same month. His father, John Shakspeare, respecting whose trade and position in life much controversy has been raised, was, in all probability, a fellmonger and wool-dealer, to which commerce he appears to have added that of glover or manufacturer of the many articles of dress that were then made of leather. He unquestionably belonged to the burgher or shopkeeper class; but had married an heiress of ancient and even knightly descent, Isabella Arden or Arderne, the scion of a family which had figured in the courtly and warlike annals of preceding reigns; and thus in the veins of the great poet of humanity ran blood derived from both the aristocratic and popular portions of the community. Isabella Arderne had brought her husband in dowry a small freehold property; but this acquisition, though apparently advantageous, seems to have been ultimately the cause of misfortune to the family; for John Shakspeare, who had originally been a thriving and prosperous tradesman, gradually descended, during the boyhood and youth of his illustrious son, to a condition of comparative indigence. This is to be attributed, as far as may be guessed, to his acquisition of land having tempted him to engage, without experience, in agricultural pursuits, which ended disastrously in his being obliged at different times to mortgage and sell not only his farm, but even one of the houses in Stratford of which he had been owner. He at last retained nothing but that small, but now venerable dwelling, consecrated to all future ages by being the spot where the greatest of poets first saw the light, and which will ever be carefully preserved as the shrine of England's greatest glory. That John Shakspeare had been originally in flourishing circumstances is amply proved by his having long been one of the Aldermen of Stratford, and having served the office of Bailiff or Mayor in 1568. His distresses appear to have become severe in 1579, when he was excused by his brethren of the municipality from contributing a small sum at a time of public calamity, an exemption grounded, probably, on his poverty. He also, most likely from the same cause, was obliged to resign his post of Alderman; and seems at the end of his life to have been entirely dependent upon the assistance of his son, when the latter, as he speedily did, raised himself to a position of competence, and even of affluence

These details will not be regarded as trivial by any one who will reflect how closely connected they are with the important and much-agitated question of the kind and degree of education enjoyed by William Shakspeare — a question of the very deepest import in fixing our estimate of his works and our appreciation of his genius. That he could have derived even the most elementary instruction from his parents is impossible; for we know that neither John nor Isabella Shakspeare could write — an accomplishment, however, which, it should be remarked, was comparatively rare in Elizabeth's reign, in even a higher class of society than the one to which such persons belonged. But we are not to conclude from this, as is done by those who think to elevate the genius of the great poet by denying him all the advantages of regular instruction, that the poverty and ignorance of his parents necessarily deprived him of education. There existed at that time, and there exists at the present day, in the borough of Stratford, one of those endowed "free grammar-schools" of which so many country towns in England offer examples, where the pious charity of past ages has provided for the gratuitous education of posterity. In these establishments provision is always made for the children of the burgesses of the town; and to the old grammar-school in Stratford, founded in the reign of Edward IV., it is quite certain that John Shakspeare had the right, as Alderman and Past Bailiff of the town, of sending his son without expense. It is inconceivable that he should have neglected to avail himself of so useful a privilege: and that William enjoyed at all events the advantage of such elementary instruction as was offered by the grammar-schools of those days, is rendered more than probable, not only by the extensive though irregular reading of which his works give evidence, but by one among the vague traditions which have descended to us. This legend relates that the poet had been "in his youth a schoolmaster in the country," a fact which cannot, of course, be strictly true, as we know at what an early age he left his native town to enter upon his career of actor and author in the Globe Theatre in London. It may, however, be the misrepresentation of fact, namely, that after passing through the lower classes of Stratford Grammar-School he may have been employed, as a lad of his aptitude would not improbably have been, in assisting the master in instructing the junior pupils.

§ 2. Among the various legends connected with the early life of so great a man, and which posterity, in the singular absence of more trustworthy details, swallows with greediness, the most celebrated and romantic is that which represents his youth as irregular and even profligate, and in particular recounts his deer-stealing expedition, in company with other riotous young fellows, to Sir Thomas Lucy's park at Charlcote, near Stratford. The young poacher, who had "broken the park, stolen the deer, and kissed the keeper's daughter," is said to have been seized, brought before the indignant Justice of the Peace, and treated with so much severity by Sir Thomas, that he revenged himself on the rural magnate by affixing a doggerel pasquinade to the gates of Charlcote. The wrath of the magistrate is said to have blazed so high at this additional insolence that Shakspeare was obliged to withdraw himself from more serious persecution by escaping to London. Here, continues the legend, which is so circumstantial and picturesque that we cannot but regret its total want of proof and probability, the young poet arrived in such deep poverty, as to be for some time reduced to earn a livelihood by holding horses at the doors of the theatres, where "his pleasant wit" attracting the notice of the actors, he ultimately obtained access "behind the scenes," and by degrees became a celebrated actor and valuable dramatic author. Eager as we are for every scrap of personal information which can help to *realize* so great a man as Shakspeare, we are naturally reluctant to renounce our belief in so striking a story; but, though the deer-stealing story may very possibly be not altogether devoid of foundation, the romantic incidents connected with his leaving Stratford and embracing the theatrical career, are to be explained in a different and much less improbable manner. It is quite certain that he left his native town in 1586, at the age of twenty-two; and it is quite possible that the distressed situation in which his parents then were, and, what is no less likely, the imprudence and irregularity of his own youthful conduct, may have contributed to render a longer stay in Stratford disagreeable, if not impossible. One event, which had occurred about four years before, most probably contributed more powerfully to send him forth "to seek his fortune," than the ire of Sir Thomas Lucy, or the perhaps not very enviable reputation which his boyish escapades had probably acquired among the steady burgesses of the little town, who probably shook their heads at the young scapegrace, prophesying that he would never come to any good. This event was his marriage, contracted when he was only eighteen, in 1582, with Anne Hathaway, the daughter of a small farmer, little above the rank of a laboring man, who resided at the hamlet of Shottery, about two miles from Stratford. Anne Hathaway was seven years and a half older than her boy-husband; and the marriage appears to have been pressed on with eager haste, probably by the relatives of the bride, who may have forced young Shakspeare to heal a breach which he had made in the young woman's reputation. There is still in existence the undertaking, legally signed by the parties, giving Shakspeare, then a minor, the power of contracting marriage. The whole of this important episode in the poet's life bears strong trace of a not over reputable family mystery. The fruit of this union was first a daughter Susanna, the poet's favorite child, born in 1583, and in the following year twins, Judith and Hamnet. The latter, the poet's only son, died at twelve years of age; his two daughters survived him. After these he had no more children; and there are several facts which seem to point, significantly though obscurely, to the conclusion that the married life of the poet was not marked by that love and confidence which is the usual result of well-considered and well-assorted unions. Thus, though Shakspeare passed the most active portion of his life, from 1586 to 1611, almost constantly in London, there is evidence to show that his wife, during the whole of that long period, never resided with her husband, but with his parents in Stratford; and therefore could only have seen him on the occasions, probably pretty frequent, of his flying visits to his native place. In the great poet's Will, too, which invaluable document gives us so many details concerning his private life, Mrs. Shakspeare appears to be treated in a manner very different from that which a beloved and respected wife might have expected from so generous and gentle a character as William Shakspeare's unquestionably was. To his wife the poet leaves only "his second-best bed, with the hangings," a very slighting and inconsiderable legacy when we reflect that he died comparatively rich.*

Concerning the boyhood and youth of the great painter of nature and of man we know little or nothing. It is more than probable that his education was neglected, his passions strong, and his conduct far from regular: yet we may in some sort rejoice at the destiny which allowed him to draw his earliest impressions of nature from the calm and graceful scenery of Warwickshire, and placed him in a situation to study the passions and characters of men among the unsophisticated inhabitants of a small provincial town. Perhaps, too, the very imperfection of his intellectual training was an advantage to his genius, in allowing his gigantic powers to develop themselves, untrammelled by the bonds of regular education. It is not improbable that at one period of his youth he had been placed in the office of some country practitioner of the law: in all his works he shows an extraordinary knowledge of the technical language of that profession, and frequently draws his illustrations from its vocabulary. Besides, such terms as he employs he almost always employs correctly; which would hardly be possible but to one who had been professionally versed in them: add to which in one of the few ill-natured and satirical allusions made to Shakspeare by his contemporary rivals, there is a distinct indication of the poet's having in his youth exercised "the trade of Noverint," that is, the occupation of a lawyer's clerk, this word being the usual commencement of writs — "noverint universi."

§ 3. At the age of twenty-two, therefore, Shakspeare, now the father of three children, in all probability not enjoying in his native place a very enviable reputation, without means of support, his father having at this time descended to a very low ebb of worldly fortunes, for we know that at this period, 1586, he was obliged to retire altogether from the municipal council, determined upon the great step of leaving Stratford altogether, and embarking on the wide ocean of London theatrical life. The story of his being reduced to hold horses at the doors of theatres is

* On the other hand, it should be recollected that, as Shakspeare's property was chiefly freehold, his wife was entitled to dower.

too absurd to deserve a moment's consideration. In the first place it is established by a thousand passages and allusions in the dramatic compositions of that day, that the audiences universally visited the theatres either on foot or in boats, for which facility these establishments were built upon the banks of the Thames, then a much more convenient highway than the narrow and tortuous streets of London of the sixteenth century. Consequently there could be no horses to hold. Secondly, it is not conceivable that a young man endowed with such talents as Shakspeare, talents of which he had most certainly given evidence in his early poems, many of them probably written before this time, should have found the least difficulty in entering a profession so easy of access as the theatre then was. The companies of actors were always glad to enlist among them such men of ready genius as could render themselves useful as performers and dramatists; and this combined occupation Shakspeare, like Ben Jonson, Marlowe, and many others of his contemporaries, fulfilled with an aptitude of which the proofs are evident. Besides, theatrical performances had before this time been popular in Warwickshire. Various companies had visited Stratford in their summer peregrinations, and had performed for the amusement of the corporation. The greatest tragic actor of that day, Richard Burbage, was a Warwickshire man, and Thomas Greene, a distinguished member of the troop of the Globe, then the first theatre in London, was a native of Stratford, and is by many supposed to have been even a relation of Shakspeare. Nothing, therefore, is more probable than that the young adventurer, whose talents could not have been unknown, received an invitation to throw in his lot with the company of the Globe. It is certain that he joined that undertaking; for we find him in 1589, that is, only three years after his arrival in London, enrolled among the shareholders of the above theatre, his name being the eleventh in a list of fifteen. It will be remembered, as I have indicated in a preceding chapter, that the number of shareholders in the Elizabethan theatrical companies was generally small, and that the profits of the representation were divided among them; the additional actors necessary for the performance being "hired men," receiving a fixed salary, and having no claim upon the general profits of the undertaking. Like other young men of that time, he rendered himself useful to his company in the double capacity of *actor and arranger of pieces*: and there is no reason to suppose that his professional career differed from that of Marlowe, Jonson, Fletcher, Ford, and others, in any respect save in the industry and success with which he pursued his double calling, and the prudence with which he accumulated the pecuniary results of that activity. He began, in all probability, by adapting old plays to the exigencies of his theatre, and while engaged in this humble employment acquired that consummate knowledge of stage effect which distinguished him, and which first struck out the spark of that inimitable dramatic genius which places him above all other poets in the world. His connection with the theatre continued from 1586 to his retirement in 1611, a period of twenty-five years, embracing the splendor of his youth and the vigor of his manhood. It is between these dates that were produced the thirty-seven dramas which compose his best-known works.

It would evidently be no less curious than useful could we establish, with some degree of accuracy, the dates and sequence of these thirty-seven plays: such an investigation would furnish us with inestimable materials for tracing the intellectual and artistic development of the greatest of all dramatists; but though many such attempts have been made, some of them with extraordinary acuteness and erudition, none of them have resulted even in an approach to a satisfactory chronology of Shakspeare's dramatic history. The notices of the first performance of some of these wonderful works, the minute examination of possible historical allusions contained in them, the order of their sequence in the first complete edition of the plays, which was not given to the world till 1623, that is, seven years after the poet's death, all these apparently promising materials for establishing a sound theory of their order of composition, will be found on trial not to be relied on. Internal evidence founded upon shades of style and a higher or lower degree of artistic perfection in treatment, is a test of a still more tempting but even more visionary nature; and from the employment of all these methods combined we may indeed sometimes class the plays of Shakspeare into certain great but not very accurately marked periods, but we can never hope to attain anything like an exact chronological order. This is of course to be deeply regretted, but cannot be an object of surprise; for during the whole of his literary career our great dramatic master-workman, in all likelihood, continued to adapt and arrange old plays as well as to compose original pieces; and working for bread, and probably with great rapidity, he was not scrupulous as to how far the inferior composition of an earlier and ruder poet passed for his own production. This consideration will also explain the extraordinary difference in point of merit, literary as well as theatrical, which even the least critical reader may discern in his performances, some of them, as *Othello* for example, being specimens of the most consummate perfection both in style and construction, while others, as *Titus Andronicus*, *Pericles*, and parts of *Henry VI.*, are not only markedly inferior to his other compositions, but are unworthy of a dramatist even of the humblest pretensions.

§ 4. The Company of the Globe Theatre, to which Shakspeare remained attached as an actor and shareholder during the whole of his London career, was, as I have said, the richest and most prosperous of the numerous troops that then furnished amusement to the capital. Their principal place of representation was the playhouse which gave them their name, so called from its sign bearing the effigy of Atlas supporting the globe, with the motto "Totus Mundus agit Histrionem," and was situated on the Bankside in Southwark near the Surrey extremity of London Bridge. Most of the theatres of that day were placed on the river's bank in the southern suburb of the capital, partly, no doubt, for the convenience of access by water, but mainly to place them out of the jurisdiction of the Corporation of London, which, being at that time deeply infected with Puritan doctrines, used all its efforts to discountenance and crush the players. The enmity between the "witty vagabonds" of the theatre and the fanatic Aldermen was envenomed by incessant jokes and pasquinades on the part of the former, and by constant persecution from the latter: and on the ultimate triumph of the Puritans at the outbreak of the Civil War, the vindictive bigotry of the city succeeded in completely annihilating the theatre. The Globe company was undoubtedly the most respectable as well as the most prosperous of the then theatres, and partly by prudently avoiding to give offence by political allusions, and partly by securing powerful protection at Court, as for instance that of Lord Keeper Egerton and the accomplished Earl of Southampton, the liberal patron and personal friend of Shakspeare himself, this society obtained the unusual permission of opening, as a theatre, a private house altered for the purpose, in the forbidden precincts of London itself. This was the Blackfriars playhouse, situated nearly on the exact spot now occupied by the printing-house of the *Times* newspaper. This edifice, much smaller than the Globe, was entirely roofed over, and the company were in the habit of performing here in the winter, whereas during the summer their representations were given on the Bankside, the inclemency of the weather being then less inconvenient.

§ **5.** Guided by the faint and feeble lights of tradition and occasional obscure allusions in the writings of the day, we may trace Shakspeare's professional and literary career from his joining the Globe company in 1589 till his retirement from active life in 1611. That career appears to have been a highly successful one. During the first years he probably rendered himself useful to his theatre as an actor; and here arises the question of the degree of talent he displayed in this branch of his profession; some maintaining him to have been a tragic and comic performer of the first class, while others accord him only a very moderate amount of talent. That he was better acquainted than perhaps any man has ever been with the theoretic principles of the actor's art is unquestionable from many passages in his writings; it will suffice to allude to the inimitable "directions to the players" put into the mouth of Hamlet, which, in incredibly few words, contain the whole system of the art. But in all probability the truth, as far as regards his own personal proficiency as a performer, lies between the two extremes. From some clear and other obscure indications, we may guess at certain parts which he acted in his own dramas as in those of other poets. Thus we have good authority for supposing that he acted the Ghost in his tragedy of *Hamlet;* the secondary, but graceful and touching character of Adam, the faithful old servant, in his *As You Like It;* the passionate and deeply pathetic impersonation of grief and despair in Kyd's popular tragedy of *Hieronymo;* and the sensible citizen, Old Knowell, in Ben Jonson's *Every Man In His Humor.* Such parts, it is evident, would never have been intrusted, in a company so rich in talent as was that of the Globe, to an incompetent actor: at the same time they all belong to a particular and perhaps secondary type, from which we may conclude that Shakspeare's *line* or *emploi*, as it is now called in the technical jargon of the English and French stages, was that of the old men — the *pères nobles*. It is probable, however, that he soon abandoned the practice of appearing, except perhaps occasionally, on the stage, and found that his services as an adapter and arranger of plays, and then as an original author, were more valuable to his troop than his exertions as an actor. Burbage, we know, was the original and most popular performer of his comrade's great tragic creations, Richard III., Hamlet, Othello, and the like.

§ 6. Shakspeare's first original poems were not dramatic; he must be regarded as the creator of a peculiar species of narrative composition which was destined to achieve an immediate and immense popularity. *Venus and Adonis*, which, in his dedication to Lord Southampton, he calls "the first heir of his invention," was published in 1593. It is highly probable that this poem — exhibiting all the luxuriant sweetness, the voluptuous tenderness, of a youthful genius — was conceived, if not composed, at Stratford. The *Rape of Lucrece*, a somewhat similar but inferior work, written, like its companion, in a species of Italian stanza, enjoyed a great but inferior popularity. The former of these works was reissued in five several editions between the years 1593 and 1602; while the *Lucrece*, during nearly the same lapse of time, appeared in three. The first years of Shakspeare's theatrical life were probably devoted to mere arrangement and adaptation of old plays; and the traces of his pen might perhaps be found in an immense number of works of earlier dramatists — Kyd, Marlowe, Lyly, &c. Even among his published and collected works, several — as *Pericles*, *Titus Andronicus*, *Henry VI.*, perhaps much of *Henry VIII.* — seem to be examples of this; and though difficult, it would not be impossible to track his genius here and there through the rude and undigested chaos of the older playwright, vivifying some stroke of passion or character, or interspersing one of those inimitable touches of description and reflection which glow and sparkle like gems amid the rubbish of the original piece. At what period he began to be fully conscious of his own vast powers, and abandoned such adaptation for original dramatic composition, it is quite impossible to ascertain; for some of those immortal works which bear the strongest and deepest impress of his wondrous genius were undoubtedly based upon former productions by former hands, and had undergone repeated recastings and alterations by himself and others. As examples of this I may mention *Hamlet*, *Henry V.*, and *King John*. Shakspeare must have speedily risen to so much importance in the Globe company as sufficed to call down upon him the attacks of envious or disappointed rivals; for the learned and witty but disreputable Nash makes bitter allusions unmistakably pointing at Shakspeare's name and alleged want of learning, as well as at his activity in "bolstering out a blank verse," and producing "whole *Hamlets*, or handfuls, of tragical speeches." He is "Johannes Factotum," and on the strength of a few blustering commonplaces fancies himself "the only Shakescene [Shakspeare] in a country."

That he gradually and steadily rose in importance among his "fellows" is proved by his name, which in 1589 was eleventh in a list of fifteen shareholders, being found seven years afterwards fifth in a list of eight; and again in the license renewed to the company on the accession of James I., Shakspeare stands second. In the scurrilous pamphlet entitled Greene's *Groatsworth of Wit*, published by Chettle after the death of that unhappy but clever profligate, there was a libellous attack upon Shakspeare, evidently dictated by the envy of a disappointed rival; but for this unfounded calumny Chettle was speedily obliged to apologize in the fullest manner, and in terms which bear high testimony not only to the great poet's genius as a writer, but to his respectability as a man, and to his amiable, gentle, and generous disposition — a quality which all contemporary notices conspire in attributing to our bard.

But it is not only from the effusions of spite and literary jealousy that we can gain some feeble insight into Shakspeare's personal history. It is quite certain that the accomplished Pembroke and the generous Southampton were his admirers and patrons. The former, indeed, is related to have made the poet a present of 1000*l.* — an immense sum, if we take into consideration the far higher value of money in those days; but though this princely gift was in all probability not a personal gratuity to Shakspeare, but rather a generous contribution to the support of the drama as represented by Shakspeare's company, and designed to assist them in building a new theatre, the action, nevertheless, shows the high respect which the poet had inspired. That Shakspeare, in his business relations with the theatre and the public, exhibited great good sense, prudence, and knowledge of the world, seems proved by the skill with which the actors of the Globe managed to steer clear of the various dangers arising from the puritanic opposition of the London Corporation, and the still more serious perils incurred by offending, in political or satirical allusions, the susceptibility of the Court and the Censorship, then so severe that almost all the other companies of players suffered more or less for their imprudences, some in the forcible closing of their theatres, some in the imprisonment of their authors and performers. That the singular good fortune of the Globe company in this respect was in no small degree attributable to Shakspeare's prudence, or to the powerful patronage he had secured among the great, is rendered probable by the fact that no sooner had he retired from an active interference in the concerns of the theatre than repeated causes of complaint arose from the petulance of his comrades, and were punished with considerable severity. Shakspeare's worldly prosperity seems to have gone on steadily increasing, and he appears to have carefully invested his gains; for in 1597, when he was aged thirty-three, he purchased the landed estate of New Place in Stratford, and either built entirely or partially reconstructed a house long considered the most considerable in the town, and to which he determined to retire as soon as the state of his fortune would permit, to pass the evening of his life far from the turmoils of the stage, in the competency he had so wisely earned. During the whole of his London life he no doubt made frequent visits to his native place, keeping up a lively interest in the public and private affairs of his townsmen. He was able to afford a tranquil asylum to his parents, who appear to have closed their lives under the protection of his roof. The death of his only son, Hamnet, in 1596, when the boy was in his twelfth year, must have been a severe shock to so loving a heart; but in general his life seems to have been one of continued prosperity. In 1602 he purchased one hundred and seven acres of land, and most probably engaged in farming speculations, with the assistance of his brother Gilbert. Two years after this we get a curious insight into his private life, by finding him the plaintiff in an action for the delivery of a certain quantity of malt, in which affair the justice of the case seems to have been entirely on his side. About the same time he purchased a share in the tithes of Stratford, as a means of securing a safe revenue; and there is extant an interesting note in which some of his townsmen employed him, as a man resident in London and well versed in business, to obtain a favorable hearing from the legal authorities in a matter concerning the enclosure of some lands near Stratford. In 1607 (the poet now aged forty three) his favorite daughter Susanna married Dr. Hall, and in the following year she brought into the world a granddaughter to the dramatist. Both at the marriage and at the christening it is highly probable that Shakspeare visited Stratford. He certainly was godfather, at the latter period, to William Walker, the child of one of his friends and fellow-townsmen. In 1611, the poet, having disposed of most of his interest in the Globe, finally retired to New Place, where he lived with his daughter Mrs. Hall and her husband, who enjoyed a considerable provincial reputation for medical skill, and who most probably treated his illustrious father-in-law in his last illness. Shakspeare did not long enjoy the retirement which he had labored for so long. He died, after a short illness, on the 23d April, the anniversary of his birthday, in 1616, having exactly completed his fifty-second year. A short time before his death his second daughter, Judith, was married to Thomas Quiney; but her career in life appears to have been altogether humbler than her sister's. Respecting the details of Shakspeare's last illness and decease we have no information. Dr. Hall indeed has left us a curious record of some of the most remarkable cases occurring in his practice, but unluckily his notes exhibit a void for the years before and after this precise period. There exists indeed a tradition that the great poet had been suffering from fever, when, desiring to entertain with his usual hospitality Ben Jonson and Drayton, who had come down from London to visit him, he imprudently arose from his bed, and brought on a relapse by sharing too freely in conviviality. He was buried in the parish church of Stratford, the registers of which furnish the greater part of the meagre though trustworthy information we possess concerning the family vicissitudes of the Shakspeares. Over his grave is erected a mural monument in the Italianized taste of that day, which is chiefly remarkable as containing a bust of the poet — an authentic though not very well executed portrait. Indeed the likenesses of Shakspeare, whether sculptured, painted, or engraved, are neither very numerous nor altogether to be relied on. The bust just mentioned, and the coarse engraving by Droeshout, prefixed to the first folio edition of his works in 1623, appear to have the best claims to our confidence. The latter, in particular, is vouched for as a faithful resemblance in the eulogistic verses placed under it by Ben Jonson, who knew intimately his great contemporary, and was not a man to assert what he did not think.

The tomb and the birthplace of Shakspeare will ever be sacred spots — shrines of loving pilgrimage for all the nations of the earth. The house of New Place has long been destroyed, but the garden in which it stood, as well as the house where the poet was born, will be preserved to the latest ages by the piety of his countrymen and the veneration of the civilized world. A short time before his death Shakspeare made his will; and thus we have, singularly enough, a very exact account of the nature and extent of his property at the time of his decease. In the mode of its disposal we see evident traces of that kind and affectionate disposition which every proof seems to establish as having characterized him — a careful remembrance of his old comrades and "fellows," to each of whom he leaves some token of regard, generally a ring. This document is unspeakably precious to us on another ground, viz. from its containing his signature twice repeated. These and one or two more autographs, consisting likewise of nothing more than the signature, are literally the only specimens that have been preserved of the writing of that immortal hand.

§ **7.** It is with the most unfeigned diffidence — diffidence arising from a veneration which no words can express — that I approach the difficult but delightful task of examining the writings of Shakspeare. From the number, no less than the excellence, of the dramatic portion of these works, it will be absolutely necessary to employ some method of classifying them into groups. This would possess the advantage of conciseness in the treatment, as well as of assisting the memory of the student. The most valuable principle of classification would be one based upon the chronological order of production, because such a method would give us a chart of the intellectual and artistic development of Shakspeare's mind, enabling us to trace the course of that majestic river from its first sparkling but irregular sources to the full flow of its calm and mighty current: but this mode, as has already been pointed out, though it has exercised the ingenuity and research of many laborious and acute investigators, has furnished no results which can be depended upon — a fact evidenced by the extreme discrepancy among the various systems of chronological arrangement which have hitherto been given to the world. Upon the order of the pieces as given in the first folio edition, published in 1623 by Hemings and Condell, Shakspeare's friends and "fellows," it is evident no reliance can be placed. Independently of the many contradictions and impossibilities involved in the adoption of their order as the true order of composition — impossibilities which are obvious on a superficial examination — the extreme negligence of the printing of that edition, in evincing a total absence of care in the editing and correction of the press, leads us inevitably to the conclusion that, in spite of the assurances of the editors as to its having been based upon the "papers" of their immortal colleague, the publication must be regarded as little better than a hasty speculation, carelessly entered into for the purpose of snatching a momentary and not very honorable profit, without much regard to the literary reputation of the great poet.

Another mode of classifying Shakspeare's dramas is founded on the principle of ranging them respectively under the heads of Tragedies, Comedies, and Histories or Historical Plays, without attempting to enter into the question of the order of their production; and this system has at all events the advantage of clearness, as well as that of dividing them into manageable groups, easily retained in the memory. This is the principle upon which are based most of the editions of the dramas. But this method is in some measure open to objection. Though some of the pieces (such as *Othello*, *Lear*, *Hamlet*) are distinctly tragedies, in the ordinary sense of that word, — a sense common to the critical nomenclature both of the Classical and Romantic types of the drama, — and though others (as *As You Like It*, the *Merry Wives of Windsor*, the *Taming of the Shrew*, or *Twelfth Night*) are as evidently comedies, there exists a considerable number of the plays which, from their tone and incidents, might be ranged equally under both heads. Nay, in all the pieces of Shakspeare we find such a mixture of the tragic and comic elements as would withdraw them equally from the strongly marked boundaries appropriated, as in the French theatre for instance, respectively to Tragedy and Comedy; and where Thalia and Melpomene are never permitted to intrude upon each other's domains. Indeed, as has been said some pages back, it is precisely this mixture of tragedy and comedy in the same piece, the same character, the same scene, and in even the same phrase, which constitutes the peculiar distinguishing trait of the noble romantic drama of England in the Shakspearian Age; and not only its distinguishing trait, but also, in the opinion of the English reader, as well as of the most profound art-critics of Germany, its peculiar excellence and title of superiority, as a picture of life and nature, over the national drama of every other country.

There remains a third mode of classification, which we may adopt as not devoid either of convenience or of philosophic truth; and this is based upon the *sources* from which Shakspeare drew the materials for his dramatic creations. If we follow the classification according to the three heads we have just been alluding to, we shall find that the thirty-seven plays composing the collection will range themselves as follows: eleven tragedies, two tragi-comedies, ten historical plays, and fourteen comedies. But the classification according to sources will give somewhat different results. The sources in question will naturally divide themselves first into the two great genera — History and Fiction, *Wahrheit und Dichtung*; while the former of these two genera will naturally subdivide into different classes or degrees of historical authenticity, ranging from vague and half-poetical legend to the comparatively firm ground of recent historical events. Again, the legendary category may be referred to the different countries from whose chronicles the events were borrowed: thus *Hamlet* is taken from the Danish chronicler Saxo-Grammaticus; *Macbeth*, *Lear*, and *Cymbeline* refer respectively to the legends, more or less fabulous, of Scottish and British history; while *Coriolanus*, *Julius Cæsar*, and *Antony* and *Cleopatra* are derived from the annals of ancient Rome. Many of the historical dramas of Shakspeare are intended to depict the events of the more recent and consequently more reliable details of the history of his own country; and these, beginning with *King John* and terminating with *Henry VIII.*, embrace materials possessing various shades of authenticity, from what may be called the semi-legendary to a degree of precision as great as could be expected in the then state of historical literature. For these pieces Shakspeare mainly drew his materials from the old annalist Hollinshed; and both in their form and peculiar excellences this class of dramas, though not perhaps invented by Shakspeare, was certainly carried by him to a wonderful degree of perfection. These pieces are not tragedies or comedies in the strict sense of the word, but they are grand panoramas of national glory or national distress, embracing often a very considerable space of time, even a whole reign, and retracing — with apparent irregularity in their plan, but with an astonishing unity of general feeling and sentiment — great epochs in the life of the nation. Examples of such will be found in *Richard II.*, *Richard III.*, the two unequalled dramas on the reign of *Henry IV.*, and the glorious chant of patriotic triumph embodied in *Henry V.*, in which Shakspeare has completed the type of the Hero-King. To such pieces is applied the particular designation of Histories; and of such histories Shakspeare, though not the inventor, was certainly the most prolific author.

The second general category, that of pieces derived from fiction, need not detain us long. The materials for this — the largest — class of his dramas, Shakspeare derived from the Italian novelists and their imitators, who supplied the chief element of light literature in the sixteenth century. The most brilliant type of this species of writer was Boccaccio, whose *Novelle*, translated and copied into all the tongues of Europe, furnished a mass of excellent materials, from Chaucer down to Lafontaine. These short tales, which so long formed the predominant type of the literature of amusement in many countries, were in many instances derived from a still more ancient source — the *fabliaux* and piquant stories with which the narrative poets, the moralists, and theologians of the middle ages enlivened their compositions; but in the form which they ultimately attained in Boccaccio and his innumerable imitators they were most singularly adapted to furnish an appropriate canvas or groundwork upon which Shakspeare was to construct his humorous or pathetic actions. In the first place, these tales were, from the nature of the case, exceedingly short; they depended for their popularity rather upon amusing and surprising incidents than upon any development of character, which would have been impracticable within the narrow limits of a few pages. In dramatizing such stories, therefore, the playwright enjoyed full liberty for the exercise of his peculiar talent of portraying human character, while at the same time he had ready prepared to his hand a series of striking events which he could compress or expand as best suited his purpose; he was left free just where freedom was most essential to his particular form of art, and spared the necessity of invention precisely where the task of invention would be likely to embarrass him. It is susceptible of proof that in no one instance has Shakspeare taken the trouble of inventing the plot of a piece for himself; certainly from no want of genius, but simply from his consummate knowledge of his art. He knew that he would act more profitably for his dramatic success by combining materials already prepared, and directing all his energies to that department in which he has never met an equal — the exhibition of human nature and human passion. How nobly he performed his task may be perceived by a simple comparison of the original novel or legend which he selected as the groundwork of his pieces, with such creations as *Othello*, the *Tempest*, or the *Merchant of Venice*. The number of Shakspeare's pieces derived from fiction amounts to eighteen; by far the majority of these are traceable, as already remarked, to the Italian novelists and their French or Spanish imitators. We are not, however, to infer that the great poet necessarily consulted the tales in the original language. From a careful examination of his works it seems to result that our great dramatist has rarely, if ever, made use, whether in the way of subjects for his plays or quotations introduced into the dialogue, of any ancient or foreign materials *not then existing in English translations:* and this important fact, while it does not necessarily lead to the monstrous conclusion of his having been a totally illiterate man, yet furnishes proof that Ben Jonson was neither an envious carper nor a malicious perverter of the truth when, in his exquisite tribute to the genius and virtues of his departed friend, he qualifies him as having "small Latin and less Greek." We may also remark that what Jonson, one of the most learned men of his day, may have expressed by *small* may have been in reality no inconsiderable tincture of scholarship.

The following general classification may be found not altogether useless nor uninteresting: in it I have endeavored to combine, together with a rough indication of the class to which each piece belongs, the particular origin whence Shakspeare drew his materials: —

I. History.

Legendary: —

Hamlet (Tragedy). The Chronicle of Saxo-Grammaticus, and an older play.

King Lear (Tragedy). Hollinshed, and older dramas.

Cymbeline (Tragi-comedy). Hollinshed, and old French romances.

Macbeth (Tragedy). Hollinshed.
Julius Cæsar (Tragedy). Plutarch.
Antony and Cleopatra (Tragedy). Plutarch.
Coriolanus (Tragedy). Plutarch.
Titus Andronicus (Tragedy). Probably an older play on the same subject.

ii. *Authentic:* —

Henry VI., Part I. ——— Part II. ——— Part III. } Various old plays, among which The *Contention between the famous Houses of York and Lancaster*.
King John. Founded on an older play on the same subject.
Richard II. The Chronicles of Hall, Fabian, and Hollinshed.
Richard III. The Chronicles, and an older but very inferior play.
Henry IV., Part I. ——— Part II. *Henry V.* } An old play of The *Famous Victories of Henry V.*
Henry VIII.

All these belong to the department of "Histories," or Historical dramas

II. FICTION.

Midsummer Night's Dream (Comedy). Chaucer's *Knight's Tale*.
Comedy of Errors (Comedy). The *Menæchmi* of Plautus.
Taming of the Shrew (Comedy). An old English piece of the same name.
Love's Labor's Lost (Comedy). Unknown; probably an Italian play.
Two Gentlemen of Verona (Comedy). Exact origin unknown.
Romeo and Juliet (Tragedy). Paynter's *Palace of Pleasure*.
Merchant of Venice (Comedy). The *Pecorone* and the *Gesta Romanorum*.
All's Well that Ends Well (Comedy). The *Palace of Pleasure*, translated from Boccaccio.
Much Ado about Nothing (Comedy). An episode of the *Orlando Furioso*.
As You Like It (Comedy). Lodge's *Rosalynde*, and the *Coke's Tale of Gamelyn*.
Merry Wives of Windsor (Comedy). Exact origin unknown
Troilus and Cressida (Tragedy) Chaucer, and the *Recuyell of Troye*.
Measure for Measure (Comedy). Cinthio's *Hecatommithi*, Dec. viii. Nov. 5.
Winter's Tale (Comedy). Greene's tale of *Dorastus and Fawnia*.
Timon of Athens (Tragedy). Plutarch, Lucian, and *Palace of Pleasure*.

Othello (Tragedy). Cinthio's *Hecatommithi*, Dec viii. Nov. 7
Tempest (Comedy). Exact origin unknown, probably Italian.
Twelfth Night (Comedy). A novel by Bandello, imitated by Belleforest.
Pericles (Comedy). Twine's translation of the *Gesta Romanorum.*

§ 8. In the historical department of the above classification it will be seen that many plays were based upon preceding dramatic works treating of the same, or nearly the same subjects; and in some few cases we possess the more ancient pieces themselves, exhibiting different degrees of imperfection and barbarism. We thus are in a position to compare the changes introduced by the consummate art of Shakspeare into the rude draughts of his theatrical predecessors, and to appreciate the wise economy he showed in retaining what suited his purpose, as well as the skill he exhibited in modifying and altering what did not. In one or two examples we have more than one edition of the same play in its different stages towards complete perfection under the hand of Shakspeare, instances of which may be cited in the cases of *Hamlet* and *Lear*. A careful and minute collation of such various editions furnishes us with precious materials for the investigation of the most interesting and profitable problem that literary criticism can approach — the tracing of the different phases of elaboration through which every great work must pass. It is no mean privilege to be thus admitted, as it were, into the studio of the mighty painter, the laboratory of the mighty chemist — to mark the touches, sometimes bold, sometimes almost imperceptible in their delicacy, which transform the rugged sketch into the highly-finished picture, the apparently insignificant operations by which the rude ore is transformed into the consummate jewel. It is like being admitted into the penetralia of nature herself. The first impression which strikes the reader when he makes acquaintance with the Historical and Legendary category of Shakspeare's dramas, is the astonishing force and completeness with which the poet seized the general and salient peculiarities of the age and country which he undertook to reproduce. With the limited and imperfect scholarship that he probably possessed, this power is the more extraordinary, and shows that his vast mind must have proceeded in a manner eminently synthetic; he first made his characters true to general and universal humanity, and then gave them the peculiar distinguishing traits appropriate to their particular period and country. His persons are true portraits of Romans, for example, because they are first true portraits of men. His great contemporary Jonson has shown a far more accurate and extensive knowledge of the details of Roman manners, ceremonies, and institutions; but his personages, admirable as they are, are entirely deficient in that intense human reality which Shakspeare never fails to communicate to his *dramatis personæ.* The nature of the Historical Play, as it was understood by Shakspeare, admitted, and even required, the adoption of an extensive epoch as the subject, and a numerous crowd of agents as the material, of such pieces; and it is not too much to say, that in all the personages so introduced, from the most prominent down to the most obscure, the reader may detect, if he takes the necessary pains, that every one had, in the mind of the author, a separate and distinct individuality, equally true to universal and to particular nature. Nay, in comparing such subjects as are drawn from different periods in the history of his own or other nations, in ancient or modern times, we may remark the singular felicity with which this great creator has *differentiated*, so to say, various phases in the character, social or political, of a people: thus the Romans in *Coriolanus* are very different from the Romans in *Julius Cæsar* or *Antony and Cleopatra*, though equally true to general human nature and to the particular nature of the Roman people at the different epochs selected. The same extraordinary power of *differentiating* is equally perceptible in the English historical plays, as will plainly be seen on comparing *King John*, for example, with *Henry IV.* or *Henry V.* This power of throwing himself into a given epoch is, in Shakspeare, carried to a degree which cannot be justly qualified as anything short of superhuman. It is true that in these plays we find instances of gross anachronism in detail; but these anachronisms never touch the essential truth of the delineation; they are mere external excrescences, which can be instantly got rid of by the imaginative reader, and which, though they may excite a passing smile, do not affect for a moment the sense of verisimilitude. Shakspeare may make a hero of the Trojan War quote Aristotle, or he may arm the Romans of Pharsalia with the Spanish rapier of the sixteenth century; but he never infects the language and sentiments of classical times with the conceits of gallant and courtly compliment that were current in the age of Louis XIV. In the scenes of private and domestic life which he has freely intermingled with the stirring and heroic episodes of war or policy, his knowledge of human nature enables him to paint with an equally firm and masterly touch the hero and the man. The delicate task of giving glimpses into the private life of great historical personages, which we find generally evaded in all other authors who have treated such subjects, is a proof of the supremacy of Shakspeare's genius. The same thing may be said of the boldness with which he has introduced comic incidents and characters amid the most lofty and solemn events of history, and as frequently and successfully in his Roman as in his English plays. In the two parts of *Henry IV.* the heroi and familiar are side by side, and the Prince's adventures with the inimitable Falstaff and his other pleasant but disreputable companions, are closely intermingled with the majestic march of the great historical events. This shows that Shakspeare, far from fearing, as an inferior artist would have done, the juxtaposition of the familiar and the sublime, the wildest and most fantastic comedy with the loftiest and gravest tragedy, not only made such apparently discordant elements mutually heighten and complete the general effect which he contemplated, but in so doing teaches us that in human life the sublime and the ridiculous are side by side, and that the source of laughter is placed close by the fountain of tears.

Even a cursory examination of these wonderful plays will supply us with another and not less remarkable evidence of Shakspeare's creative power. In them, though the chief characters may be historical, the action requires the introduction of a multitude of other personages; and these are not always necessarily subordinate ones, which the poet must unavoidably have created out of his own observation. Now, in such cases the most difficult trial of a dramatic talent would be the *callida junctura* which should make the imaginary harmonize with the historical personages; and this ordeal would be equally arduous whether the subject upon which it was exercised were persons or events. Walter Scott, with all his power of delineation, has not always been successful in hiding the *joining on* of the real with the imaginary. In Shakspeare, on the contrary, we never see a deficiency: indeed, whether by his consummate skill in realizing the ideal, or in idealizing the real, both the one and the other stand before us in the same solidity; and it is not too much to say that to us his imaginary persons are as much real entities — nay, often far more so — than the authentic figures of history itself. Thus, to our intimate consciousness, Othello and Shylock are persons as real as Coriolanus and Wolsey.

In the department of Shakspeare's works which we are now treating, as well as in the other category which we shall examine presently, there are unquestionably some pieces manifestly inferior to others. Thus among the English Histories the three plays upon the subject of Henry VI. bear evident marks of an inferior hand, and were in all probability older dramas which Shakspeare retouched and revivified here and there with some of his inimitable strokes of nature and poetic fancy. The last of the English historical plays, at least the latest in the date of its action, is *Henry VIII.* This piece bears many traces of having been in part composed by a different hand: in the diction, the turn of thought, and in particular in the peculiar mechanism of the versification, there is much to lead to the conclusion that Shakspeare, in its composition, was associated with one other, if not more, poets. This kind of collaboration was an almost universal practice in that age; and the circumstance that the play was written with a particular intention and contained very pointed and graceful compliments both to Elizabeth and her successor seem to indicate that it was composed with great rapidity, and that therefore Shakspeare was likely to have worked upon it in partnership with others.

§ 9. But a general conception of the dramatic genius of Shakspeare must be founded upon an examination of *all* his pieces; and while the historical dramas show how he could free his mind from the trammels imposed by the necessity of adhering to real facts and persons, the romantic portion of his pieces, or those founded upon Fiction, will equally prove that the freedom of an ideal subject did not deprive him of the strictest fidelity to general nature. The characters that move through the action of these latter dramas exhibit the same consummate appreciation of the general and the individual in humanity; and though he has occasionally stepped over the boundary of ordinary human nature, and has created a multitude of supernatural beings, fairies, spirits, witches, and other creatures of the imagination, even in these the severest consistency and the strictest verisimilitude never for a moment abandon him. They are always *constantes sibi;* we know that such beings do not and cannot exist; but we irresistibly feel, in reading the scenes in which they appear, that if they did exist, they could not exist other than as he has painted them. The data being established, the consequences, to the most remote and trivial details, flow from them in a manner that no analysis can gainsay. In the *mode* of delineating passion and feeling Shakspeare proceeds differently from all other dramatic authors. They, even the greatest among them, create a personage by accumulating in it all such traits as their reading and observation show to usually accompany the fundamental elements which go to form its constitution: and thus they all, more or less, fall into the error of making their personages embodiments of such and such a moral peculiarity. They give us admirable and complete *monographies* of ambition, of avarice, of hypocrisy, and the like. Moreover, in the expression of their feelings, whether tragic or comic, such characters almost universally *describe* the sensations they experience. This men and women in real life never do: nay, when under the influence of strong emotion or other powerful moral impression, we indicate to others what we feel, rather, and far more powerfully, by what we suppress than by what we utter. In this respect the men and women of Shakspeare exactly resemble the men and women of real life, and not the men and women of the stage. Nor has he ever fallen into the common error of forgetting the infinite complexity of human character. If we analyze any one of the prominent personages of Shakspeare, though we may often at first sight perceive in it the predominance of some one quality or passion, on a nearer view we shall find that the complexity of its moral being goes on widening and deepening with every new attempt on our part to grasp or sound the whole extent of its individuality. Macaulay has excellently observed that it is easy to say, for example, that the primary characteristic of Shylock is revengefulness; but that a closer insight shows a thousand other qualities in him, the mutual play and varying intensity of which go to compose the complex being that Shakspeare has drawn in the terrible Jew. Thus Othello is no mere impersonation of jealousy, nor Macbeth of ambition, nor Falstaff of selfish gayety, nor Timon of misanthropy, nor Imogene of wifely love: in each of these personages the more closely we analyze them the deeper and more multiform will appear the infinite springs of action which make up their personality. Shakspeare has shown, in a manner that no one has either equalled or approached, how a given character will act under the stimulus of some overmastering passion; but he has painted ambitious and revengeful men, not ambition and revenge in human form. Nothing is more childish than the superficial judgment which identifies the great creations of Shakspeare with some prominent moral or intellectual characteristic. His conceptions are as multiform as those of nature herself; and as the physiologist knows that even in the plant or mollusk of apparently the simplest construction there are depths of organization which bid defiance to all attempts to fathom them, so in the characters of the great painter of humanity, there is a variety which grows more and more bewildering the more earnestly we strive to penetrate its mysteries. This wonderful power of conceiving complex character is at the bottom of another distinguishing peculiarity of our great poet; namely, the total absence in his works of any tendency to self-reproduction. Possessing only the dramas of Shakspeare, it would be totally impossible for us to deduce any notion of what were the sympathies and tendencies of the author. He is absolutely impersonal; or rather he is all persons in turn: for no poet ever possessed to a like degree the portentous power of successively identifying himself with a multitude of the most diverse individualities, and of identifying himself so completely that we cannot detect a trace of preference. Let us suppose a man capable of conceiving and delineating such a picture of jealousy as we have in the tragedy of Othello. Would not such a man be irresistibly impelled to do a second time what he had so admirably done the first? But Shakspeare, when he has once thrown off such a character as Othello, never recurs to it again. Othello disappears from the stage as completely as a real Othello would have done from the world, and leaves behind him no similar personage. True, Shakspeare has given us a number of other pictures of jealous men; but their jealousy is as different from that of Othello as in real life the jealousy of one man is different from that of another. Leontes, Ford, Posthumus, are all equally jealous; but how differently is the passion manifested in each of these! In the female characters, too, what a wonderful range, what an inexhaustible variety! Perhaps in no class of his impersonations are the depth, the delicacy, and the extent of Shakspeare's creative power more visible than in his women: for we must not forget that in writing these exquisitely varied types of female character, he knew that they would be intrusted, in representation, to boys or young men — no female having acted on the stage till long after the age which witnessed such creations as Hermione, Lady Macbeth, Rosalind, or Juliet. We may conceive what a chill it must have been to the imagination of a poet to be conscious that a marvel of female delicacy, grandeur, or passion would be personated on the stage by a performer of the other sex, and that the author would feel what Shakspeare has so powerfully expressed in the language of his own Cleopatra: —

> "The quick comedians
> Extemporary shall stage us: Antony
> Shall be brought drunken forth, and I shall see
> Some squeaking Cleopatra *boy* my greatness."

Surely the power of ideal creation has never undergone a severer ordeal. Shakspeare's triumph over this great practical difficulty is the more surprising as there is, perhaps, no class of his personages more varied, more profound, and more exquisitely delicate than his female characters, which possess a far higher tone of sentiment than can be found in the most beautiful conceptions of womanly qualities which even the greatest of his contemporaries — as Beaumont, Massinger, and Ford — have given to the drama. Some critics, indeed, have traced his superior refinement in this respect to the imitation of the pure and lofty feminine ideal which he found in the *Arcadia* of the illustrious Sidney and the graceful purity of the *Faerie Queene.*

In the expression of strong emotion, as well as in the delineation of character, Shakspeare is superior to all other dramatists, superior to all other poets. He never finds it necessary, in order to produce the effect he desires, to have recourse in the one case to violent or declamatory rhetoric, or in the other to unusual or abnormal combinations of qualities. In him we meet with no sentimental assassins, no moral monsters,—

"Blessed with one virtue and a thousand crimes."

Without overstepping the ordinary limits of human experience, he is always able to interest or to instruct us with the exhibition of general passions and feelings, manifesting themselves in the way we generally see them in the world. He is like the great painter of antiquity, who produced his ever-varying effects by the aid of four simple colors. In the expression, too, he uniformly draws, at least in his finest passages, his illustrations from the most simple and familiar objects, from the most ordinary scenes of life. When a great occasion presents itself, he ever shows himself equal to that occasion. There are, indeed, in his works many passages where he has allowed his taste for intellectual subtleties to get the better of his judgment, and where his passion for playing upon words — a passion which was the literary vice of his day, and the effects of which are traceable in the writings of Bacon as well as in his — is permitted to cool the enthusiasm excited by the situation or the feelings of the speaker. But this indulgence in conceits generally disappears in the great culminating moments of intense passion: and while we are speaking of this defect with due critical severity, we must not forget that there are occasions when the intensest moral agitation is not incompatible with a morbid and feverish activity of the intellect, and that the most violent emotion sometimes finds a vent in the intellectual contortions of a conceit. Nevertheless, it cannot be denied that Shakspeare very often runs riot in the indulgence of this tendency, to the injury of the effect designed and in defiance of the most evident principles of good taste. His style is unquestionably a very difficult one in some respects; and this obscurity is not to be attributed, except of course in some particular instances, to the corrupt state in which his writings have descended to us, and still less to the archaism or obsoleteness of his diction. Many of the great dramatists his contemporaries, for example Massinger and Ford, are in this respect as different from Shakspeare as if they had been separated from him by two centuries of time — their writings being as remarkable for the limpidity and clearness of expression as his are occasionally for its complexity. It is not therefore to the remoteness of the period that we must ascribe this peculiarity. Indeed in this respect Shakspeare's language will present nearly as much difficulty to an English as to a foreign student. We must look for the cause of this in the enormously developed intellectual and imaginative faculty in the poet; leading him to make metaphor of the boldest kind the ordinary tissue of his style. The thoughts rise so fast under his pen, and successively generate others with such a portentous rapidity, that the reader requires almost as great an intellectual vivacity as the poet, in order to trace the leading idea through the labyrinth of subordinate illustration. In all figurative writing the metaphor, the image, is an ornament, something extraneous to the thought it is intended to illustrate, and may be detached from it, leaving the fundamental idea intact: in Shakspeare the metaphor is the very fabric of the thought itself and entirely inseparable from it. His diction may be compared to some elaborate monument of the finest Gothic architecture, in which the superficial glance loses itself in an inextricable maze of sculptural detail and fantastically fretted ornamentation, but where a close examination shows that every pinnacle, every buttress, every moulding is an essential member of the construction. This intimate union of the reason and the imagination is a peculiarity common to Shakspeare and Bacon, in whose writings the severest logic is expressed in the boldest metaphor, and the very titles of whose books and the very definitions of whose philosophical terms are frequently images of the most figurative character. There is assuredly no poet, ancient or modern, from whose writings may be extracted such a number of profound and yet practical observations applicable to the common affairs and interests of life; observations expressed with the simplicity of a casual remark, yet pregnant with the condensed wisdom of philosophy; exhibiting more than the acuteness of De Rochefoucauld, without his cynical contempt for humanity, and more than the practical good sense of Molière, with a far wider and more universal applicability. In the picturing of abnormal and supernatural states of existence, as in the delineation of every phase of mental derangement, or the sentiments and actions of fantastic and supernatural beings, Shakspeare exhibits the same coherency and consistency in the midst of what at first sight appears altogether to transcend ordinary experience. Every grade of folly, from the verge of idiotcy to the most fantastic eccentricity, every shade of moral perturbation, from the jealous fury of Othello to the frenzy of Lear or the not less touching madness of Ophelia, is represented in his plays with a fidelity so complete that the most experienced physiologists have affirmed that such intellectual disturbances may be studied in his pages with as much profit as in the actual patients of a madhouse.

§ **10.** The non-dramatic works of Shakspeare consist of the two narrative poems, written in the then fashionable Italian stanza, entitled *Venus and Adonis*, and the ***Rape of Lucrece***, the volume of beautiful *Sonnets* whose internal signification has excited so much controversy, and a few lyrics, some of which appear to have good and others but indifferent claims to be attributed to the great poet. *Venus and Adonis*, which the author himself, in his dedication to the Earl of Southampton, calls "the first heir of his invention," was undoubtedly one of his earliest productions, and though the date of its composition is not precisely known, was possibly written by Shakspeare before he left Stratford, at all events at the very outset of his poetical career. It is stamped with the strongest marks of youthful genius, exhibiting all the flush and voluptuous glow of a fervent imagination. The story is the common mythological episode of the loves of Venus and the hunter; and both in its form and substance, it must be regarded as an original attempt at a new kind of poetry, in which the extraordinary success of Shakspeare afterwards induced a multitude of other poets to follow his example. It ran through an unusual number of editions in a very short time, and was indeed one of the most successful literary ventures of the age. In the rich and somewhat sensual love-scenes in this poem, in the frequent inimitable touches of description which give earnest of Shakspeare's miraculous power of painting external nature, and in the delicious but somewhat effeminate melody of the verse, we see all the marks of youth, but it is the youth of a Shakspeare. The *Rape of Lucrece*, though less popular than its predecessor, a circumstance which may be attributed to the repulsive nature of the subject, is yet a poem of very great merit. The *Sonnets* of Shakspeare possess a peculiar interest, not only from their intrinsic beauty, but from the circumstance of their evidently containing carefully veiled allusions to the personal feelings of their author, allusions which point to some deep disappointment in love and friendship suffered by the poet. They were first printed in 1609, though, from allusions found in contemporary writings, many of them were composed previously. They are one hundred and fifty-four in number, and some are evidently addressed to a person of the male sex, while others are as plainly intended for a woman. The poet bitterly complains of the treachery of the male, and the infidelity of the female object of his affection, while he speaks both of the one and of the other in the most ardent language of passionate yet melancholy devotion. Throughout the whole of these exquisite but painful compositions there runs a deep undercurrent of sorrow, self-discontent, and wounded affection, which bears every mark of being the expression of a real sentiment. No clew, however, has as yet been discovered by which we may hope to trace the persons to whom these poems are addressed, or the painful events to which they allude. The volume was dedicated, on its first appearance, by the publisher, Thomas Thorpe, to "Mr. W. H.," who is qualified as the only begetter of these sonnets, and some hypotheses suppose that this mysterious "Mr. W. H." was no other than William Herbert, Earl of Pembroke, one of Shakspeare's most powerful patrons, and a man of great splendor and accomplishments. It is, however, difficult to suppose that a personage so high-placed could easily have interfered to destroy the happiness of the comparatively humble player and poet of the Globe, or, if he had, that a bookseller would have ventured to allude to him under so familiar a designation as "W. H." In fact the whole production is shrouded in mystery; and we must content ourselves with admiring the deep tenderness, the melancholy grace, and the inimitable touches of poetical fancy and moral reflection which abound in these poems, without endeavoring to solve the enigma — unquestionably a painful and personal one — involved in the circumstances under which they were composed.

CHAPTER VIII.

THE SHAKSPEARIAN DRAMATISTS.

§ 1. BEN JONSON. His life. § 2. His tragedies and comedies. § 3. His masques and other works. § 4. BEAUMONT and FLETCHER. § 5. MASSINGER. § 6. FORD. § 7. WEBSTER. § 8. CHAPMAN, DEKKER, MIDDLETON, MARSTON, and other minor Dramatists. § 9. SHIRLEY. § 10. Remarks on the Elizabethan drama.

§ 1. THE age of Elizabeth and James I. produced a galaxy of great dramatic poets, the like of whom, whether we regard the nature or the degree of excellence exhibited in their works, the world has never seen. In the general style of their writings, they bear a strong family resemblance to Shakspeare; and indeed many of the peculiar merits of their great prototype may be found scattered among his various contemporaries, and in some instances carried to a height little inferior to that found in his writings. Thus intensity of pathos hardly less touching than that of Shakspeare may be found in the dramas of Ford, gallant animation and dignity in the dialogues of Beaumont and Fletcher, deep tragic emotion in the sombre scenes of Webster, noble moral elevation in the graceful plays of Massinger; but in Shakspeare, and in Shakspeare alone, do we see the consummate union of all the most opposite qualities of the poet, the observer, and the philosopher.

The name which stands next to that of Shakspeare in the list of these illustrious dramatists is that of BEN JONSON (1573-1637), a vigorous and solid genius, built high with learning and knowledge of life, and whose numerous works, dramatic as well as other, possess an imposing and somewhat monumental weight. He was born in 1573, and was consequently nine years younger than Shakspeare. His career was full of strange vicissitudes. Though compelled by a step-father to follow the humble trade of a bricklayer, he succeeded in gratifying an intense thirst for learning. He passed some short time, probably with the assistance of a patron, at the University of Cambridge, and there, as well as after leaving college, continued to study with a diligence that certainly rendered him one of the most learned men of his age — an age fertile in learned men. He is known to have served some time as a soldier in the Low Countries, and to have distinguished himself by his courage in the field; but his theatrical career seems to have begun when he was about twenty years of age, when we find him attached as an actor to one of the minor theatres, called the Curtain. His success as a performer is said to have been very small, arising most probably from want of grace and beauty of person; and there is no reason to suppose that his theatrical career differed from the almost universal type of the actor-dramatists of that age. While still a very young man he fought a duel with one of his fellow-actors, whom he had the misfortune to kill, receiving at the same time a severe wound; and for this infringement of the law, which at that particular period was punished with extreme severity, the poet was condemned to death, though afterwards pardoned. Among other vicissitudes of life, Jonson is related to have twice changed his religion, having been converted by a Jesuit to the Roman Catholic faith, and to have afterwards again returned to the bosom of his mother-Church, on which last occasion he is said, when receiving the Sacrament on his reconversion to have drunk out the whole chalice, in sign of the sincerity of his recantation.

His first dramatic work, the Comedy of *Every Man in his Humor*, is assigned to the year 1596. This piece, the action and characters of which were originally Italian, failed in its first representation; and there is a tradition, far from improbable in itself, that Shakspeare, who was then in the full blaze of his popularity, advised the young aspirant to make some changes in the piece and to transfer its action to England. Two years afterwards the comedy, with considerable alterations, was brought out a second time, at Shakspeare's theatre of the Globe, and then with triumphant success. One of the few parts which Shakspeare is known to have personated on the stage is that of Old Knowel, the jealous merchant, in this comedy. Thus was probably laid the foundation of that warm and solid friendship between Jonson and Shakspeare, which appears to have continued during their whole lives, and the existence of which is proved not only by many pleasant anecdotes recording the gay and witty social intercourse of the two great poets, but by the enthusiastic, and yet discriminating, eulogy in which Jonson — who was not a man to give light or unconsidered praise — has honored the memory and described the genius of his friend. From the moment of this second representation of his comedy Ben Jonson's literary reputation was established; and during the remainder of his very active career, though the success of particular pieces may have fluctuated, Jonson undoubtedly occupied a place at the very head of the dramatic authors of his day. His social and generous, though coarse and somewhat overbearing character, the extraordinary power and richness of his conversation, contributed to make him one of the most prominent figures in the literary society of that day. His "wit-combats" at the famous taverns of the Mermaid, the Devil, and the Falcon, have been commemorated in many anecdotes; and he even appears to have been regarded at last as a sort of intellectual potentate, much as his great namesake Samuel Johnson was afterwards, and to have conferred upon his favorites the title of his *sons;* "sealing them," as he says in one of his epigrams, "of the tribe of Ben."

His first comedy was followed in the succeeding year by *Every Man Out of his Humor*, and his literary activity continued to be very great, for in 1603 he gave to the world his tragedy of *Sejanus*, and in 1605 he appears to have had some share, with Chapman, Marston, Dekker, and other dramatists, in the piece of *Eastward Hoe!* a comedy which called down upon all connected with it a severe persecution from the Court, which was bitterly offended by certain satirical allusions to the favor then accorded by King James to his Scottish countrymen Jonson was involved in this persecution; and there is a story that the guilty wits having been condemned to have their noses slit, Jonson generously refused to abandon his associates, and that his mother had prepared for herself and him "a strong and lusty poison," to enable him to escape the ignominy of such a disfigurement. With the frank and violent character of Jonson it was impossible that he could escape continual quarrels and disputes, so difficult to avoid in a literary career and particularly in the dramatic profession. Thus we have notices of violent feuds between him and Dekker, Chapman, Marston, and others, as well as Inigo Jones, the Court architect and arranger of festivities and masques, whose favor seems to have given great umbrage to the proud and self-confident nature of old Ben. Many of these literary quarrels may be traced in the dramatic works of Jonson and his contemporaries, who used the stage as a vehicle for mutual attack and recrimination. In rapid succession between 1603 and 1619 followed some of Jonson's finest works, *Volpone*, *Epicene*, the *Alchemist*, and the tragedy of *Catiline*. In the latter year he was appointed Laureate or Court poet, and was frequently employed in getting up those splendid and fantastic entertainments called masques, in which magnificence of scenery, decoration, and costume, ingenious, allegorical, and mythological personages, exquisite music, dancing, and declamation were made the instruments for paying extravagant compliments to the king and the great personages of the Court, on occasion of any festivity at the palace or in the mansions of the great. These charming compositions, in which Jonson exhibited all the stores of his invention and all the resources of his vast and elegant scholarship, were represented sometimes by actors, but often by the ladies and gentlemen of the Court, and were performed, not in the public theatres, but in palaces and great houses, both in London and the country. Many of Jonson's later pieces were entirely unsuccessful, and in one of the last, the *New Inn*, acted in 1630, the poet complains bitterly of the hostility and bad taste of the audience. Towards the end of his life Ben Jonson appears to have fallen into poverty, aggravated by disappointment and ill health, the latter probably caused by his too great fondness for copious libations of sack. He died in 1637, in the twelfth year of the reign of Charles I., and was buried, it is said, in a vertical position, in the churchyard of Westminster, the stone over his grave having been inscribed with the excellent and laconic words, "O rare Ben Jonson."

§ 2 The dramatic as well as the other works of this great poet are so numerous that I must content myself with a very cursory survey of them. They are of various degrees of merit, ranging from an excellence not surpassed by any contemporary excepting Shakspeare, to the lowest point of laborious mediocrity. Two of them are tragedies, the *Fall of Sejanus* and the *Conspiracy of Catiline*. The subjects of both these plays are borrowed from the Roman historians, and the dialogue and action in both may be regarded as a mosaic of striking and brilliant extracts from the Latin literature, reproduced by Jonson with such a consummate force and vigor that we may call him a Roman author who composed in English. Nothing can exceed the minute accuracy with which all the details of the Roman manners, ceremonies, religion, and sentiments are reproduced; and yet the effect of the whole is singularly stiff and unpleasing, partly perhaps from the absence of pathos and tenderness which characterizes Jonson's mind, and partly from the unmanageable nature of the subjects, the hero in both cases being so odious that no art can secure for his fate the sympathy of the reader. Many of the scenes, however, particularly those of a declamatory character, as the trial of Silius and Cremutius Cordus before the abject Senate, the appearance of Tiberius, and the magnificent oration in which Petreius describes the defeat and death of Catiline, are of extraordinary power and grandeur. Of comedies, properly so called, Jonson composed fifteen, the best of which are incontestably ***Every Man in his Humor***, ***Volpone***, ***Epicene*** or the ***Silent Woman***, and the ***Alchemist*** The plots or intrigues of Jonson are far superior to those of the generality of his contemporaries: he always constructed them himself, and with great care and skill. Those of ***Volpone*** and the ***Silent Woman*** for example, though some of the incidents are extravagant, are admirable for the constructive skill they display, and for the art with which each detail is made to contribute to the catastrophe. The general effect, however, of Jonson's plays, though abundantly satisfactory to the reason, is hard and defective to the taste. The character of his mind was eminently analytic; he dissected the vices, the follies, and the affectations of society, and presented them to the reader rather like anatomical preparations than like men and women. His observation was extensive and acute; but his mind loved to dwell rather upon the eccentricities and monstrosities of human nature than upon those universal features with which all can sympathize, as all possess them. His mind was singularly deficient in what is called ***humanity***; his point of view is invariably that of the satirist, and thus, as he fixed his attention chiefly upon what was abnormal, many of his most elaborately-drawn portraits are a sort of dry, harsh, abstruse caricatures of absurdities which were peculiar to the manners and society of that day, and appear to us as strange and quaint as the pictures of our ancestors in their stiff and fantastic dresses. The satiric tendency of Jonson's mind, too, induced him to take his materials, both for intrigue and character, from odious or repulsive sources; thus the subject of two of his finest pieces, ***Volpone*** and the ***Alchemist***, turns entirely upon a series of ingenious cheats and rascalities; all the persons, without exception, being either scoundrels or their dupes. Nevertheless, in spite of these peculiarities, the knowledge of character displayed by Jonson is so vast, the force and vigor of expression are so unbounded, he has poured forth into his dialogue such a wonderful wealth of illustration drawn from men as well as books, that his comedies form a study eminently ***substantial***

In some of them, as in *Poetaster, Bartholomew Fair*, and the *Tale of a Tub*, Jonson has attacked particular persons and parties, as Dekker in the first, the Puritans in the second, and Inigo Jones in the third; but these pieces can have but little interest for the modern reader. The tone of morality which prevails throughout Jonson's works is high and manly, and he is particularly remarkable for the lofty standard he invariably claims for the social value of the poet, the dramatist, and the satirist. Though he has too often devoted his great powers to the delineation of those oddities and absurdities which were then called *humors*, and which may be defined as natural follies and weaknesses exaggerated by affectation, he has traced more than one truly comic personage, the interest of which must be permanent; thus his admirable type of coward braggadocio in Bobadill will always deserve to occupy a place in the great gallery of human folly. The want of tenderness and delicacy which I have ascribed to Jonson will be especially perceived in the harsh and unamiable characters which he has given to his female persons. Without stamping him as a woman-hater, it may be said that there is hardly one female character in all his dramas which is represented in a graceful or attractive light, while a great many of them are absolutely repulsive from their coarseness and their vices.

§ 3. It is singular that while Jonson in his plays should be distinguished for that hardness and dryness which I have endeavored to point out, this same poet, in another large and beautiful category of his works, should be remarkable for the elegance and refinement of his invention and his style. In the *Masques* and *Court Entertainments* which he composed for the amusement of the king and the great nobles, as well as in the charming fragment of a pastoral drama entitled *The Sad Shepherd*, Jonson appears quite another man. Everything that the richest and most delicate invention could supply, aided by extensive, elegant, and recondite reading, is lavished upon these courtly compliments, the gracefulness of which almost makes us forget their adulation and servility. This servility, it should be remarked, was the fashion of the times; and was carried quite as far towards the pedantic and imbecile James as it had been towards his great predecessor, Elizabeth. Of such masques and entertainments, Jonson composed about thirty-five, many of which exhibit a richness and playfulness of invention which have never been surpassed. These productions were, of course, generally short, and depended in a great measure for their effect upon the scenes, machinery, costumes, dances, and songs, with which they were thickly interspersed. The magnificence sometimes displayed in these spectacles was extraordinary, and forms a striking contrast with the beggarly *mise en scène* of the regular theatres of those days. Among the most beautiful of these masques we may mention *Paris Anniversary*, the *Masque of Oberon*, and the *Masque of Queens*. In the dialogue of these slight pieces, as well as in the lyrics which are frequently introduced, we see how graceful and melodious could become the genius of this great poet, though generally attuned to the severer notes of the satiric muse. Besides his dramatic works Jonson left a very large quantity of literary remains in prose and verse. The former portion contains many curious and valuable notes made by Jonson on books and men, among which are particularly interesting the references to Shakspeare and Bacon; and the latter consists chiefly of *epigrams* written in the manner of Martial, and sometimes containing interesting notices of contemporary persons and things. All these are pregnant with wit fancy, and solid learning, and confirm the idea which we derive from Jonson's dramas of the power, richness, and variety of his genius.

§ 4. Superior to Ben Jonson in variety and animation, though hardly equal to him in solidity of knowledge, were the two illustrious dramatists who worked together with so intimate a union that it is impossible, in the works composed before their friendship was dissolved by death, to separate their contributions. These were BEAUMONT (1586-1615) and FLETCHER (1576-1625), both men of a higher social status, by birth and by education, than the generality of the dramatists of this splendid epoch; for Beaumont was of noble family, and the son of a judge, while Fletcher was son to Bishop Fletcher, an ecclesiastic, however, of no very enviable reputation, in the reign of Elizabeth. John Fletcher was born in 1576; Thomas Beaumont ten years later, but he died early, in 1615, at the age of thirty, and his friend survived him ten years, and was one of the victims to the plague in 1625. Concerning the details of their lives and characters we possess but vague and scanty information; it is, however, evident from their works that they had both received a learned education. They were accomplished men, possessing a degree of scholarship far inferior, perhaps, in depth and accuracy to that of Jonson, but amply sufficient to furnish their writings with rich allusions and abundant ornaments. The dramatic works of these brilliant fellow-laborers, in spite of the very short existence of the one, and the not very long life of the other, are extraordinary not only for their excellence and variety, but also for their number, their collected dramas — which were not printed in a complete form till 1647 — amounting to fifty-two. Some of these, it is certain, were acted before Beaumont's death; and of the remainder many are attributed to Fletcher alone, and this probably with justice, though it is impossible to know how far Fletcher, in those works which are to be ascribed to the period succeeding that event, may have profited by the unfinished sketches thrown off by them both in partnership. The common tradition relates that Beaumont possessed more of the elevated, sublime, and tragic genius, while Fletcher was rather distinguished by gayety and comic humor; but so intimately interwoven is the glory of these two excellent poets, that neither in their names nor in their writings does biography or criticism ever separate them. Such imperfect notices, however, as have come down to our time upon this subject I will introduce here, as they will assist the memory in judging of such a multiplicity of pieces, by dividing them into comparatively manageable groups. Dryden, who has spoken with just enthusiasm of the works of these great dramatists, to whom he himself owed so much, has asserted that the first successful piece they placed upon the stage was the charming romantic drama of

Philaster, though they had composed several before this production raised their names to a high pitch of popularity. Among the pieces performed anterior to 1615 may be mentioned, besides *Philaster*, the *Maid's Tragedy*, *A King and No King*, the *Laws of Candy*, all of a lofty or tragic character; while among the dramas belonging to the same early period may be specified the following, as exhibiting the comic genius of the two illustrious fellow-laborers: the *Woman-hater*, the *Knight of the Burning Pestle* (one of their richest and most popular extravaganzas), the *Honest Man's Fortune*, the *Captain*, and the *Coxcomb*. Of those attributed, with more or less show of probability, to Fletcher alone, it will be seen that a large proportion possess a character in which the comic tone is predominant. I will specify the following: the excellent comedies of the *Chances*, the *Spanish Curate*, *Beggars' Bush*, and *Rule a Wife and Have a Wife*. But a mere enumeration of the principal dramas of these animated and prolific playwrights will be found tiresome and unsatisfactory. I will therefore, after making a few general remarks on the genius and manner of Beaumont and Fletcher, note such peculiarities in their principal plays as my limited space will permit. The first quality which strikes the reader in making acquaintance with these poets is the singularly airy free, and animated manner in which they exhibit incident, sentiment, and action. They evidently wrote with great ease and rapidity; and their productions, though occasionally offending against the rules of good taste and propriety, are never deficient in the tone of good society. Their dialogue, far less crowded with thought than that of Shakspeare, and less burdened with scholar-like allusion than that of Jonson, is singularly vivacious and flowing. Their style, though not altogether free from affectation, is wonderfully limpid, and will generally be found much easier to understand at the first glance than that of Shakspeare — a clearness which arises from less complexity in the ideas. They often attain, in their more poetical and declamatory passages, a high elevation both of tragic and romantic eloquence. In the delineation of character and passion they are inferior to the great artist with whom they have not seldom ventured to measure their strength; and if ever they have deserved the high honor of being compared for a moment with Shakspeare, it must be remembered that we must select, as the subject of such comparison, not the deeper and vaster creations of the great master's genius, —

"For in that circle none durst walk but he," —

not, in short, such works as *Hamlet*, *Lear*, *Othello*, but rather what may be called his secondary pieces, such as *Much Ado about Nothing*, *Measure for Measure*, or the *Tempest* — works in which the graceful, fantastic, and romantic elements predominate. In this department Beaumont and Fletcher are no unworthy rivals to the greatest of dramatists. They possess high comic powers in the delineation of violently farcical and extravagant characters. Their portraiture of bragging cowardice in Bessus is one of the finest and completest delineations which the stage has given; while in such quaint and outrageously ludicrous impersonations as those of Lazarillo, the hungry courtier who is in vain pursuit of the "umbrana's head," which is the object of his idolatry, they have touched the very brink to which humorous extravagance can be carried. Their plots, like those of Shakspeare, are often carelessly constructed and improbable in incident; but the curiosity of the reader is always kept alive by striking situations and amusing turns of fortune. Their materials are similar to those which the romantic dramatists of that age generally employed — Italian and French novels, and sometimes legendary or authentic history. It should be remarked, however, that they have never once attempted, like Shakspeare, the historical drama, founded upon the annals of their own country, though they have freely used materials derived from Roman chronicles — as in their tragedy of the *False One*, in which they seem to have intended to try their strength against *Julius Cæsar;* and from the legendary history of the middle ages, as in *Rollo*, *Thierry and Theodoret*, and other pieces. They are singularly happy in the delineation of noble and chivalrous feeling, the love and friendship of young and gallant souls; and their numerous portraits of valiant veterans may be pronounced unequalled. As examples of the former I may cite the personages of Philaster, of Arbaces, of Palamon and Arcite, of Arcas in the *Loyal Subject*, and, above all, of Caratach in the tragedy of *Bonduca*. They possess the art of rendering a character vicious, and even criminal, without making it forfeit all claims to our sympathy; and thus exhibit a true sense of humanity. A striking example of this is the erring but generous hero of *A King and No King*. Their pathos, though frequently exhibited, is rather tender than deep: among the most striking instances of this I may refer to the *Maid's Tragedy*, one of their most admired and elaborate works. The grief of Aspasia and the despair of Evadne are worked up to a high pitch of tragic emotion. In the *Two Noble Kinsmen*, the subject of which is borrowed from the *Knight's Tale* of Chaucer, the dignity of chivalric friendship is portrayed with the highest and most heroic spirit. In this play the scenes exhibiting the love and madness of the Gaoler's Daughter show an evident imitation of the character of Ophelia; and there can be no higher praise to Beaumont and Fletcher than to confess that they come out of the contest beaten indeed, but not disgraced. Excellent too are they in pictures of simple tenderness and sorrow: there are few things in dramatic literature mor pathetic than the character and death of the little heroic Prince Henge in the tragedy of *Bonduca*. But it is perhaps in their pieces of mixed sentiment, containing comic matter intermingled with romantic and elevated incidents, that Beaumont and Fletcher's genius shines out in its full effulgence. It is on such occasions that we see them rise without effort and sink without meanness. Perhaps no better examples of this — the most charming — phase of their peculiar talent can be selected than the comedies of the *Elder Brother*, *Rule a Wife and Have a Wife*, *Beggars' Bush*, and the *Spanish Curate*. In the third-mentioned piece the romantic and the farcical intrigues are combined in a most masterly manner, while in the first and second the force of innate worth and courage is made to shine out brilliantly amid the most apparently adverse circumstances. In the more violently farcical intrigues and characters, such as are to be found in the *Little French Lawyer*, the *Woman-hater*, the *Humorous Lieutenant*, the *Scornful Lady*, *Wit at Several Weapons*, and the like, we willingly forget the eccentricity, or even absurdity, of the idea, in consideration of the inexhaustible series of laughable extravagancies in which it is made to develop itself. Such extravagancies are very different from the dry, persevering, analytical method in which Jonson works out to its very last dregs the exhibition of one of those "humors" which he so delighted to portray — a process which may almost be called scientific, like the destructive distillation of the chemist, leaving nothing behind but a *caput mortuum*. The fools and grotesques of Beaumont and Fletcher are "lively, audible, and full of vent;" and the authors seem to enjoy the amusement of heaping up absurdity upon absurdity, out of the very abundance of their humorous conception. The language in which the poet clothes their droll extravagancies is often highly figurative, full of imagery, and of a rich and generous music; sometimes the simple change of a few words will transform one of these passages of ludicrous and yet picturesque exaggeration into a noble outburst of serious poetry. Some of the pieces of Beaumont and Fletcher furnish us with a store of curious antiquarian and literary materials: thus the excellent romantic play of *Beggars' Bush* contains, in the humorous scenes where the "mumping" fraternity is introduced, valuable materials illustrating that singular subject the *slang* dialect, or the professional jargon of thieves, beggars, and such like offscourings of society; and it is curious to see how long much of this *argot* has been in existence, and how slight are the changes it has undergone. In the same way the fantastic extravaganza of the *Knight of the Burning Pestle* is an absolute storehouse preserving a multitude of popular chivalric legends and fragments, sometimes beautiful and always interesting, of ancient English ballad poetry. In a good many passages of Fletcher we meet with evident parodies or caricatures of scenes and speeches of other dramatists, and particularly of Shakspeare, in which latter case the interest of such passages is of course very high; but it must be remembered that such caricatures or parodies are marked by a playful spirit, and bear no trace of malignity or envy. Examples of this will be found in the play I have just mentioned, in the droll, pathetic speech on the installation of Clause as King of the Gypsies, an evident and good-natured jest at Cranmer's speech in the last scene of *Henry VIII*. Many others might be adduced. The pastoral drama of the *Faithful Shepherdess* is unquestionably one of the most exquisite combinations of delicate and tender sentiment with description of nature and lyrical music that the English or any other literature can boast. Originally imitated from the Italian, this mixture of the eclogue and the drama forms a peculiar subdivision of poetry. Though the characters, sentiments, language, and incidents have little relation to real life, the charm of such idyllic compositions, from the days of Theocritus to those of Guarini and Tasso, has always been felt; and the refined ideal and half-mythologic beauty of the "fabled life" of Tempe seems to gratify that craving of the imagination which makes us all hunger after something purer, sweeter, and more innocent than the atmosphere of our ordinary "working-day world." The pictures of nature which crowd this exquisite Arcadian drama have never been surpassed for their truth, their delicacy, and the melody of their expression; and it is not the least glory of Beaumont and Fletcher that in this exquisite poem they are the victorious rivals of Ben Jonson, whose delicious fragment of the *Sad Shepherd* was undoubtedly suggested by the drama I am speaking of; while Fletcher also furnished to Milton the first prototype of one of the most inimitable of his works — the pastoral drama of *Comus.*

§ 5. Of the personal history of PHILIP MASSINGER (1584-1640) little is known. This excellent poet was born in 1584, and died, apparently very poor, in 1640. His birth was that of a gentleman, his education good, and even learned; for though his stay in the University of Oxford, which he entered in 1602, was not longer than two years, his works prove, by the uniform elegance and refined dignity of their diction, and by the peculiar fondness with which he dwells on classical allusions, that he was intimately penetrated with the finest essence of the great classical writers of antiquity. His theatrical life, extending from 1604 to his death, appears to have been an uninterrupted succession of struggle, disappointment, and distress; and we possess one touching document proving how deep and general was that distress in the dramatic profession of the time. It is a letter written to Henslowe, the manager of the Globe Theatre, in the joint names of Massinger, Field, and Daborne, all poets of considerable popularity, imploring the loan of an insignificant sum to liberate them from a debtor's prison. Like most of his fellow-dramatists, Massinger frequently wrote in partnership with other playwrights, the names of Dekker, Field, Rowley, Middleton, and others being often found in conjunction with his. We possess the titles of about thirty-seven plays either entirely or partially written by Massinger, of which number, however, only eighteen are now extant, the remainder having been lost or destroyed. These works are tragedies, comedies, and romantic dramas partaking of both characters. The finest of them are the following: the *Fatal Dowry*, the *Unnatural Combat*, the *Roman Actor*, and the *Duke of Milan*, in the first category; the *Bondman*, the *Maid of Honor*, and the *Picture*, in the third; and the *Old Law* and *A New Way to Pay Old Debts* in the second. The qualities which distinguish this noble writer are an extraordinary dignity and elevation of moral sentiment, a singular power of delineating the sorrows of pure and lofty minds exposed to unmerited suffering, cast down but not humiliated by misfortune. In these lofty delineations it is impossible not to trace the reflection of Massinger's own high but melancholy spirit. Female purity and devotion he has painted with great skill; and his plays exhibit many scenes in which he has ventured to sound the mysteries of the deepest passions, as in the *Fatal Dowry* and the *Duke of Milan*, the subject of the latter having some resemblance with the terrible story of Mariamne. It was unfortunately indispensable, in order to please the mixed audiences of those days, that comic and farcical scenes should be introduced in every piece; and for comedy and pleasantry Massinger had no aptitude. This portion of his works is in every case contemptible for stupid buffoonery, as well as odious for loathsome indecency; and the coarseness and obscenity of such passages forms so painful a contrast with the general elegance and purity of Massinger's tone and language that we are driven to the supposition of his having had recourse to other hands to supply this obnoxious matter in obedience to the popular taste. Massinger's style and versification are singularly sweet and noble. No writer of that day is so free from archaisms and obscurities; and perhaps there is none in whom more constantly appear all the force, harmony, and dignity of which the English language is susceptible. From many passages we may draw the conclusion that Massinger was a fervent Catholic. The *Virgin Martyr* is indeed a Catholic mystery; and in many plays — as, for example, the *Renegado* — he has attributed to Romanist confessors, and even to the then unpopular Jesuits, the most amiable and Christian virtues. If we desire to characterize Massinger in one sentence, we may say that dignity, tenderness, and grace are the qualities in which he excels.

§ 6. If Massinger, among the Elizabethan dramatists, be peculiarly the poet of moral dignity and tenderness, JOHN FORD (1586–1639) must be called the great painter of unhappy love. This passion, viewed under all its aspects, has furnished the almost exclusive subject matter of his plays. He was born in 1586, and died in 1639; and does not appear to have been a professional writer, but to have followed the employment of the law. He began his dramatic career by joining with Dekker in the production of the touching tragedy of the *Witch of Edmonton*, in which popular superstitions are skilfully combined with a deeply-touching story of love and treachery; and the works attributed to him are not numerous. Besides the above piece he wrote the tragedies of the *Brother and Sister*, the *Broken Heart* (beyond all comparison his most powerful work, a graceful historical drama on the subject of Perkin Warbeck), and the following romantic or tragi-comic pieces: the *Lover's Melancholy*, *Love's Sacrifice*, the *Fancies*, *Chaste and Noble*, and the *Lady's Trial*. His personal character, if we may judge from slight allusions found in contemporary writings, seems to have been sombre and retiring; and in his works sweetness and pathos are carried to a higher pitch than in any other dramatist. In the terrible play of the *Brother and Sister* the subject is love of the most unnatural and criminal kind; and yet Ford fails not to render his chief personages, however we may deplore and even abhor their crime, objects of our sympathy and pity. In the *Broken Heart* we have in the noble Penthea, in Orgilus, Ithocles, and Calantha, four phases of unhappy passion; and in the scenes between Penthea and her cruel but repentant brother, between Penthea and the Princess (in which the dying victim makes her will in such fantastic but deeply-touching terms), and last of all in the tremendous accumulation of moral suffering with which the piece concludes, we cannot but recognize in Ford a master of dramatic effect. His lyre has but few tones, but his music makes up in intensity for what it wants in variety; and at present we can hardly understand how any audience could ever have borne the harrowing up of their sensibilities by such repeated strokes of pathos. Ford, like the other great dramatists of that era of giants, never shrank from dealing with the darkest, the most mysterious enigmas of our moral nature. His verse and dialogue are even somewhat monotonous in their sweet and plaintive melody, and are marked by a great richness of classical allusion. His comic scenes are even more worthless and offensive than those of Massinger. One proof of the consummate mastery which Ford possessed over the whole gamut of love-sentiment is his skill in making attractive the characters of unsuccessful suitors, in proof of which may be cited Orgilus and the noble Malfato.

§ 7. But perhaps the most powerful and original genius among the Shakspearian dramatists of the second order is JOHN WEBSTER. His terrible and funereal Muse was Death; his wild imagination revelled in images and sentiments which breathe, as it were, the odor of the charnel: his plays are full of pictures recalling with fantastic variety all associations of the weakness and futility of human hopes and interests, and dark questionings of our future destinies. His literary physiognomy has something of that dark, bitter, and woful expression which makes us thrill in the portraits of Dante. The number of his known works is very small: the most celebrated among them is the tragedy of the *Duchess of Malfy* (1623); but others are not inferior to that strange piece in intensity of feeling and savage grimness of plot and treatment. Besides the above we possess *Guise, or the Massacre of France*, in which the St. Barthelemy is, of course, the main action, the *Devil's Law Case*, the *White Devil*, founded on the crimes and sufferings of Vittoria Corombona, *Appius and Virginia;* and we thus see that in the majority of his subjects he worked by preference on themes which offered a congenial field for his portraiture of the darker passions and of the moral tortures of their victims. In selecting such revolting themes as abounded in the black annals of mediæval Italy, Webster followed the peculiar bent of his great and morbid genius; in the treatment of these subjects we find a strange mixture of the horrible with the pathetic. In his language there is an extraordinary union of complexity and simplicity: he loves to draw his illustrations not only from "skulls, and graves, and epitaphs," but also from the most attractive and picturesque objects in nature, and his occasional intermingling of the deepest and most innocent emotion and of the most exquisite touches of natural beauty produces the effect of the daisy springing up amid the festering mould of a graveyard. Like many of his contemporaries, he knew the secret of expressing the highest passion through the most familiar images; and the dirges and funeral songs which he has frequently introduced into his pieces possess, as Charles Lamb eloquently expresses it, that intensity of feeling which seems to resolve itself into the very elements they contemplate. His dramas are generally composed in mingled prose and verse; and it is possible that he may have had a share in the production of many other pieces besides those I have enumerated above.

§ **8.** As the dramatic form was the predominant type of popular literature at this splendid period, the student must expect to be bewildered by the great though subordinate glory of a multitude of minor lights of the theatrical heaven, whose genius our space will enable u to analyze but in a very rapid and cursory manner. The works of these playwrights, each of whom has, when closely examined, his peculiar traits, have, however, such a strong family resemblance both in their merits and defects, that this cursory appreciation will not lead the reader into any considerable error; one star of the bright constellation may somewhat differ from another in glory, but the general character and composition of their rays are the same. Chapman, Dekker, Middleton, and Marston are all remarkable for their fertility and luxuriance. GEORGE CHAPMAN, who has been previously mentioned as the translator of Homer (p. 85), is, however, more admirable for his lofty, classical spirit, and for the power with which he communicated the rich coloring of romantic poetry to the forms borrowed by his learning from Greek legend and history. THOMAS DEKKER, one of the most inexhaustible of the literary workers of his age, though he generally appears as a fellow-laborer with other dramatists, yet in the few pieces attributed to his unassisted pen shows great elegance of language and deep tenderness of sentiment. THOMAS MIDDLETON is admired for a certain wild and fantastic fancy which delights in portraying scenes of witchcraft and supernatural agency. JOHN MARSTON, on the contrary, deserves applause less by a purely dramatic quality of genius than by a lofty and satiric tone of invective in which he lashes the vices and follies of mankind, and in particular the neglect of learning. Nor can he who would make acquaintance with the dramatic wealth of this marvellous age pass without attention the works of Taylor, Tourneur, Rowley, Broome, and Thomas Heywood. Tourneur has some resemblance, in the sombre and gloomy tone of his works, to the terrible genius of Webster, while Broome is remarkable for the immense number of pieces in whose composition he had a greater or less share; an observation which may also be applied to Heywood. This latter poet must not be confounded with his namesake John, who was one of the earliest dramatic authors, and flourished in the reigns of Henry VIII. and Mary (see p. 112). Thomas Heywood exhibits a graceful fancy, and one of his plays, *A Woman Killed with Kindness*, is among the most touching of the period. Broome was originally Ben Jonson's domestic servant, but afterwards attained considerable success upon the stage.

§ **9.** The dramatic era of Elizabeth and James closes with JAMES SHIRLEY (1594–1666), whose comedies, though in many respects bearing the same general character as the works of his great predecessors, still seem the earnest of a new period. He excels in the delineation of gay and fashionable society, and his dramas are more laudable for ease, nature, and animation than for profound tracings of human nature, or for vivid portraiture of character. He passed through the whole of the Civil War, the Commonwealth, and the Revolution, and is the link which connects the great dramatic school of Shakspeare with the very different form of the drama which revived at the Restoration in 1660. In proportion as the Puritan party grew in influence and acrimony, in precisely equal degree grew the hostility to the theatre; and at last, when fanaticism was rampant, the theatre was formally and legally suppressed, the play-houses were pulled down by bigoted mobs of citizens and soldiers, and the performance of plays, nay, the simple witnessing of theatrical representations, made a penal offence. This took place September 2, 1642, and the dramatic profession may be regarded as remaining under the frown of government during about fourteen years from that date, when the theatre was revived, but revived, as we shall afterwards see, under a completely different form, and with totally different tendencies, moral as well as literary. Of the nature and causes of this dramatic revolution, not less profound than the great political and social revolution of which it was a symptom and a result, I shall speak in another place.

§ 10. The Elizabethan drama is the most wonderful and majestic outburst of genius that any age has yet seen. It is characterized by marked peculiarities; an intense richness and fertility of imagination, such as was natural in an age when the stores of classical antiquity were suddenly thrown open to the popular mind; and this richness and splendor of fancy are combined with the greatest force and vigor of familiar expression. We have an intimate union of the common and the refined, the boldest flights of fancy and the most scrupulous fidelity to actual reality. The great object of these dramatists being to produce intense impressions upon a miscellaneous audience, they sacrificed everything to strength and nature. The circumstance that most of these writers were actors tended to give their productions the peculiar tone they exhibit: to this we must attribute some of their gravest defects as well as many of their most inimitable beauties — their occasional coarseness, exaggeration, and buffoonery, as well as that instinctive knowledge of *effect* which never abandons them. But besides being actors, they were, almost without exception, men of educated and cultivated minds; and thus their writings never fail to show a peculiar *aroma* of style and language, which is perceptible even in the least fragment of their dialogue. They were also *men*, men of strong passions and often of irregular lives; and what they felt strongly, and what they had seen in their wild lives, they boldly transferred to their writings; which thus reflect not only the faithful images of human character and passion under every conceivable condition, not only the strongest as well as the most delicate coloring of fancy and imagination, but the profoundest and simplest precepts derived from the practical experience of life. It should never be forgotten that they all resemble Shakspeare in the general texture of their language and the prevailing principles of their mode of dramatic treatment, and only differ from him in the degree to which they possess separately those high and varied qualities which he alone of all human beings carried to an almost superhuman degree of intensity.

NOTES AND ILLUSTRATIONS.

OTHER DRAMATISTS.

ANTHONY MUNDAY (1553-1633) was said by Meres to be the "best plotter" among the comic poets. Fourteen plays were written either partly or wholly by him. The first of importance was *Valentine and Orson*, published in 1598. Drayton and others assisted him in *Sir John Oldcastle*, which was referred by some to Shakspeare. In 1601 he published *Robert Earl of Huntingdon's Downfall*, and *Robert Earl of Huntingdon's Death*, in the last of which he was assisted by Chettle. His writings extended over the period 1580-1621. He died August 10, 1633, and is styled on his monument in St. Stephen's, Coleman Street, "citizen and draper of London."

HENRY CHETTLE was a most industrious writer of plays. Thirty-eight are said to bear an impress from his hand. With Haughton and Dekker he produced *Patient Grissil* in 1603. According to Mr. Collier he wrote for the stage before 1592. Three only of his plays have been preserved. He wrote too largely to produce works of more than passing interest.

GEORGE COOKE produced *Green's Tu quoque* in 1599, and was the author of fifty epigrams.

THOMAS NABBES wrote in the reign of Charles I. A third-rate poet, but original. None of his dramatic pieces are extant, the chief of which were *Microcosmus*, *Spring's Glory*, *Bride*. *Charles the First*, a tragedy, and *Swetnam*, a comedy, are proved not to be his. Nabbes was secretary to some noble or prelate near Worcester. He also wrote a continuation of Knolles's *History of the Turks*.

THOMAS RANDOLPH (1605-1634), born near Daventry. A scholar and poet of some worth, but whose pieces have sunk into an obscurity ill deserved. He studied at Cambridge, and through too great excess shortened his life, and died at the early age of twenty-nine. His chief plays were *The Muses' Looking-Glass*, and *The Jealous Lovers*.

NATHANIEL FIELD, in the reigns of James I. and Charles I., wrote *A Woman's a Weathercock*, 1612; *Amends for Ladies*, 1618.

JOHN DAY wrote between 1602 and 1654. Studied at Caius College, Cambridge, was associated with Rowley, Dekker, Chettle, and Marlowe, and is said to have been the subject of the satirical lines on the flight of *Day*. His chief works were *Bristol Tragedy*, 1602, *Law Tricks*, 1608, and the *Blind Beggar of Bethnal Green*, 1659.

HENRY GLAPTHORNE lived in the reign of Charles I. Winstanley calls him "one of the chiefest dramatic poets of that age." There is much ease and elegance in his verse, but little force and passion. His plays numbered nine, five of which are preserved. *Albertus Wallenstein*, 1634 *The Hollander*, 1640, &c.

CHAPTER IX.

THE SO-CALLED METAPHYSICAL POETS. A. D. 1600-1700

§ 1. Characteristics of the so-called metaphysical poets. § 2. WITHER and QUARLES. § 3. HERBERT and CRASHAW. § 4. HERRICK, SUCKLING, and LOVELACE. § 5. BROWNE and HABINGTON § 6. WALLER. § 7. DAVENANT and DENHAM. § 8. COWLEY.

§ 1. THE seventeenth century is one of the most momentous in English history. A large portion of it is occupied by an immense fermentation, political and religious, through which were worked out many of those institutions to which the country owes its grandeur and its happiness. The Civil War, the Commonwealth, the Protectorate, and the Restoration, fill up the space extending from 1630 to 1660, while its termination was signalized by another revolution, which, though peaceful and bloodless, was destined to exert a perhaps even more beneficial influence on the future fortunes of the country. In its literary aspect this agitated epoch, though not marked by that marvellous outburst of creative power which dazzles us in the reigns of Elizabeth and her successor, yet has left deep traces on the turn of thought and expression of the English people; and confining ourselves to the department of poetry, and excluding the solitary example in Milton of a poet of the first class, who will form the subject of a separate study, we may say that this period introduced a class of excellent writers in whom the intellect and the fancy play a greater part than sentiment or passion. Ingenuity predominates over feeling; and while Milton owed much to many of these poets, whom I have ventured, in accordance with Johnson, to style the *metaphysical* class, nevertheless we must allow that they had much to do with generating the so-called correct and artificial manner which distinguishes the classical writers of the age of William, Anne, and the first George. I propose to pass in rapid review, and generally according to chronological order, the most striking names of this department, extending from about 1600 to 1700.

§ 2. GEORGE WITHER (1588–1667) and FRANCIS QUARLES (1592–1644) are a pair of poets whose writings have a considerable degree of resemblance in manner and subject, and whose lives were similar in misfortune. Wither took an active part in the Civil War, attained command under the administration of Cromwell, and had to undergo severe persecution and long imprisonment. His most important work is a collection of poems, of a partially pastoral character, entitled the *Shepherd's Hunting*, in which the reader will find frequent rural descriptions of exquisite fancifulness and beauty, together with a sweet and pure tone of moral reflection. The vice of Wither, as it was generally of the literature of his age, was a passion for ingenious turns and unexpected conceits, which bear the same relation to really beautiful thoughts that plays upon words do to true wit. He is also often singularly deficient in taste, and frequently deforms graceful images by the juxtaposition of what is merely quaint, and is sometimes even ignoble. Many of his detached lyrics are extremely beautiful, and the verse is generally flowing and melodious; but in reading his best passages we are always nervously apprehensive of coming at any moment upon something which will jar upon our sympathy. He wrote, among many other works, a curious series of *Emblems*, in which his puritanical enthusiasm revels in a system of moral and theological analogies at least as far-fetched as poetical. Quarles, though a Royalist as ardent as Wither was a devoted Republican, exhibits many points of intellectual resemblance to Wither; to whom, however, he was far inferior in poetical sentiment. One of his most popular works is a collection of *Divine Emblems*, in which moral and religious precepts are inculcated in short poems of a most quaint character, and illustrated by engravings filled with what may be called allegory run mad. For example, the text, "Who will deliver me from the body of this death?" is accompanied by a cut representing a diminutive human figure, typifying the soul, peeping through the ribs of a skeleton as from behind the bars of a dungeon. This taste for extravagant yet prosaic allegory was borrowed from the laborious ingenuity of the Dutch and Flemish moralists and divines; and Otto Van Veen, the teacher of Rubens, is answerable for some of the most extravagant pictorial absurdities of this nature. Quarles, however, in spite of his quaintness, is not destitute of the feeling of a true poet; and many of his pieces breathe an intense spirit of religious fervor. In spite of their antagonism in politics, Quarles and Wither bear a strong resemblance: the one may be designated as the most roundhead of the Cavaliers, the other as the most cavalier of the Roundheads.

§ 3. If Quarles and Wither represent ingenuity carried to extravagance, GEORGE HERBERT (1593–1632) and RICHARD CRASHAW (circa 1620–1650) exhibit the highest exaltation of religious sentiment, and are both worthy of admiration, not only as Christian poets, but as good men and pious priests. George Herbert was born in 1593, and at first rendered himself remarkable by the graces and accomplishments of the courtly scholar; but afterwards entering the Church, exhibited, as parish priest of Bemerton in Wiltshire, all the virtues which can adorn the country parson — a character he has beautifully described in a prose treatise under that title. He died in 1632, and was known among his contemporaries as "holy George Herbert." He was certainly one of the most perfect characters which the Anglican Church has nourished in her bosom. His poems, principally religious, are generally short lyrics, combining pious aspiration with frequent and beautiful pictures of nature. He decorates the altar with the sweetest and most fragrant flowers of fancy and of wit. Herbert's poems are not devoid of that strange and perverted ingenuity with which I have reproached Quarles and Wither; but the tender unction which reigns throughout his lyrics serves as a kind of antidote to the poison of perpetual conceits. In his most successful efforts he has almost attained the perfection of devotional poetry, a calm and yet ardent glow, a well-governed fervor, which seem peculiarly to belong to the Church of which he was a minister, equally removed from the pompous and childish enthusiasm of Catholic devotion and the gloomy mysticism of Calvinistic piety. His best collection of sacred lyrics is entitled the *Temple, or Sacred Poems and Private Ejaculations.*

Crashaw's short life was glowing throughout with religious enthusiasm. The date of his birth is not exactly known, but probably was about 1620; and he died, a canon of the Cathedral of Loretto, in 1650. He was brought up in the Anglican Church, and received a learned education at Oxford; but during the Puritan troubles he embraced the Romish faith, and carried to the ancient Church a singularly sensitive mind, very extensive erudition, and a gentle but intense devotional mysticism. He had been employed in negotiation by Charles I., and seems to have possessed among his contemporaries a high reputation for ability. The mystical tendency of his mind was increased by his misfortunes and by his change of religion, and in his later works we find the fervor of his pietism reaching a pitch little short of extravagance. He is said to have been an ardent admirer of the ecstatic writings of St. Theresa; and that union of the sensuous fervor of human affection with the wildest flights of theological rapture which we see in the writings of the great Catholic mystics, is faithfully reproduced in Crashaw. That he possessed an exquisite fancy, great melody of verse, and that power over the reader which nothing can replace, and which springs from deep earnestness, no one can deny. The reader will never regret the time he may have employed in making some acquaintance with Crashaw's poetry, among the most favorable specimens of which I may cite the *Steps to the Temple*, and the beautiful description entitled *Music's Duel*, borrowed from the celebrated *Contention between a Nightingale and a Musician*, composed by Famianus Strada, of which there is a most exquisite imitation in Ford's play of the *Lover's Melancholy.*

§ 4. Love, romantic loyalty, and airy elegance find their best representatives in three charming poets whose works may be examined under one general head. These are ROBERT HERRICK (1591–1674), SIR JOHN SUCKLING (1609–1641), and SIR RICHARD LOVELACE (1618–1658). The first of these writers, after beginning his career among the brilliant but somewhat debauched literary society of the town and the theatre, took orders, and, like Herbert, passed the latter portion of his life in the obscurity of a country parish. Unlike Herbert, however, he continued to exhibit in his writings, after this change of life, the same graceful but voluptuous spirit which distinguished his early writings; and unlike the holy pastor of Bemerton, he seems never to have ceased repining at the fate which obliged him to exchange the gay conversation of poets and wits for the unsympathizing companionship of the rural "salvages" among whom he was condemned to live. His poems are all lyric, generally songs; and love and wine form their invariable topics. In Herrick we find the most unaccountable mixture of sensual coarseness with exquisite refinement. Like the Faun of the ancient sculpture, his Muse unites the bestial and the divine. In fancy, in genius, in power over the melody of verse, he is never deficient; and it is easy to see that in his union of tenderness with richness of imagination he had been inspired by the lovely pastoral and lyric movements of Fletcher and of Heywood. Suckling and Lovelace are the types of the Cavalier poet: both underwent persecution, and were reduced to poverty. Lovelace was long and often imprisoned for his adherence to the loyal doctrines of his party, and is said to have died in abject distress. Both were men of elegant if not profound scholarship, and both exemplify the spirit of loyalty to their king, and gallantry to the ladies. Many of Suckling's love songs are equal, if not superior, to the most beautiful examples of that mixture of gay badinage and tender if not very deep-felt devotion which characterizes French courtly and erotic poetry in the seventeenth century; and his thoughts are expressed with that cameo-like neatness and refinement of expression which is the great merit of the minor French literature from Marot to Béranger. But his most exquisite production is his *Ballad upon a Wedding*, in which, assuming the character of a rustic, he describes the marriage of a fashionable couple, Lord Broghill and Lady Margaret Howard. In this inimitable gem, if we exclude one or two allusions of a somewhat too warm complexion, the reader will find the perfection of grace and elegance, rendered only the more piquant by the well-assumed naïveté of the style. Lovelace is more serious and earnest than Suckling: his lyrics breathe rather devoted loyalty than the half-passionate, half-jesting love-fancy of his rival. Some of his most charming lyrics were written in prison; and the beautiful lines to Althea, composed when the author was closely confined in the Gate-house at Westminster, remind us of the caged bird which learns its sweetest and most plaintive notes when deprived of its woodland liberty.

The gay and airy spirit which we see running through the minor poetry of this epoch may be traced back to a period considerably earlier — to the contemporaries of Ben Jonson and the great dramatists. The pleasant and facetious BISHOP CORBET (p. 86), CAREW, one of the ornaments of the court of Charles I. (p. 86), and even DRUMMOND (p. 87), though the genius of the latter is of a more serious turn, all exhibit a tendency to intellectual ingenuity which was afterwards gradually divested of that somewhat pedantic character which Drummond, for example, had imbibed from his models, the masters of the Italian sonnet. It is curious to observe that the Scots should in this time have distinguished themselves in their writings by a learned and artificially classical spirit strangely at variance with the unadorned graces of the "native woodnotes wild" that thrill so sweetly through their national and popular songs. This learned character was perhaps derived from, as it is chiefly exemplified in, Buchanan, one of the purest and most truly classical writers in Latin verse among those who have appeared since the destruction of Roman literature (p. 107). The Scots have generally been a learned people, and much of their national annals was written in Latin, sometimes in Latin of great elegance. This may perhaps be in some degree attributed to the fact that their vernacular dialect, when they employed it, was, though certainly far too cultivated to be stigmatized as a *patois* of English, yet at all events no better than a provincial mode of speech; and the naïveté which is charming in a song or poem runs great risk of exciting contempt when coloring historical or philosophical matter.

§ 5. WILLIAM BROWNE (1590–1645) was the author, besides a large number of graceful lyrics and shorter poems, of a work entitled *Britannia's Pastorals*, undoubtedly suggested, as far as their style and treatment are concerned, by the example of Spenser and Giles Fletcher. They contain much agreeable description of rural life, but they are chargeable with that ineradicable defect which accompanies all idyllic poetry, however beautiful may be its details, namely, the want of probability in the scenes and characters, when the reader tests them by a reference to his own experience of what rustic life really is. His verse is almost uniformly well knit, easy, and harmonious; and the attentive reader could select many passages from this poet, now little read, exhibiting great felicity of thought and expression.

WILLIAM HABINGTON (1605–1654) is a poet of about the same calibre as Browne, though his writings are principally devoted to love. He celebrates, with much ingenuity and occasional grace, the charms and virtues of a lady whom he calls Castara, and who — a fate rare in the annals of the love of poets — was not only his ideal mistress, but his wife. Habington, like Crashaw, was a Catholic; and his poems are free from that immorality which so often stains the graceful fancies of the poets of this age. Though generally devoted to love, Habington's collected works exhibit some of a moral and religious tendency.

§ 6. The most prominent and popular figures of the period we are now considering, and the writers who exerted the strongest influence on their own time, I have reserved till the end of this chapter: they are Waller and Cowley, to which may be added the secondary but still important names of Denham and Davenant.

EDMUND WALLER (1605–1687) was unquestionably one of the leading characters in the literary and political history of England during the momentous period embraced by his long life. He was of ancient and dignified family, of great wealth, and a man of varied accomplishments and fascinating manners; but his character was timid and selfish, and his political principles fluctuated with every change that menaced either his safety or his interest. He sat for many years in Parliament, and was the "darling of the House of Commons" for the readiness of his repartees and the originality and pleasantness of his speeches. It was unfortunate for a man endowed with the light talents formed to adorn a court to be obliged to take part in public affairs at so serious a crisis as that of the Long Parliament, the Civil War, and the Restoration; but Waller seems for a while to have floated scathless through the storms of that terrible time, trusting, like the nautilus, to the very fragility which bears it safely among rocks and quicksands where an argosy would be wrecked. He exhibited repeated indications of tergiversation in those difficult times, professing adherence to Puritan and Republican doctrines while really sympathizing with the Court party; and on more than one occasion was accused of something very like distinct military treachery. Even his consummate adroitness did not always succeed in securing impunity; and in 1643 he was convicted by the House of a plot to betray London to the King, and narrowly escaped a capital punishment, being imprisoned, fined 10,000*l*., and obliged to exile himself for some time, which he passed in France. His conduct at this juncture is said to have been mean and abject. Though distantly related by birth to the great and good Hampden, and to Oliver Cromwell himself, whom he has celebrated in one of his finest poems, Waller was ready to hail with enthusiasm every new change in the political world; and he panegyrized Cromwell and Charles II. with equal fervor, though not with equal effect. He lived to see the accession of James II., whose policy he prophesied would lead to the fatal results that afterwards occurred. During the whole of his life Waller was the idol of society, but neither much trusted nor much respected — a pliant, versatile, adroit partisan, joining and deserting all causes in succession, and steering his bark with address through the dangers of the time. In his own day, and in the succeeding generation, his poetry enjoyed the highest reputation. He was said to have carried to perfection the art of expressing graceful and sensible ideas in the clearest and most harmonious language; but his example, which acted so powerfully on Dryden and Pope, has ceased to exert the same influence, which it owed rather to the good sense and good taste by which Waller avoids faults than to the ardor and enthusiasm which can alone attain beauties. Regular, reasonable, well-balanced, well-proportioned, the lines of Waller always gratify the judgment, but never touch the heart or fire the imagination. Here and there in his works may be found strokes of happy ingenuity which we know not whether to attribute more to accident or to genius; as in the passage where he laments the cruelty of his mistress Sacharissa (Lady Dorothy Sidney), and boasts that his disappointment as a lover had given him immortality as a poet, he makes the following delicious allusion to the fable of Apollo and Daphne: —

> "I caught at love, but filled my arms with bays."

Most of his poems are love verses, but his panegyric on Cromwell contains many passages of great dignity and force. He was less felicitous in his longer work, the *Battle of the Summer Islands*, in which, in a half-serious, half-comic strain, he described an attack upon a stranded whale in the Bahamas.

§ 7. SIR WILLIAM DAVENANT (1605–1668), born in the same year with Waller, was one of the most active literary and political personages of his day. He is principally interesting to us at the present day as being connected with the revival of the theatre after the eclipse it had suffered during the severe Puritan rule; and nothing can more clearly indicate the immense change which literary taste had undergone, than the fact that Davenant, who was a most ardent worshipper of the genius of Shakspeare and Shakspeare's mighty contemporaries, should, in attempting to revive their works, have found it necessary to alter their spirit so completely, that a reader who admires the originals must regard the adaptations with a feeling little less than disgust. Yet there can be no doubt that Davenant's veneration was sincere. He was long connected with the Court Theatre, and both in the dramas which he composed himself, and in those which he adapted and placed upon the stage, we see how far the taste for splendor of scenery, dances, music, and decoration had usurped the passion of the earlier public for truth and intensity in the picturing of life and nature. Declamation and pompous tirades had now taken the place of the ancient style of dialogue, so varied, so natural, touching every key of human feeling, from the wildest gayety to the deepest pathos. The mechanical accessories of the stage had been immensely improved; actresses, young, beautiful, and skilful, usurped the place of the boys of the Elizabethan scene, and in every respect the stage had undergone a complete revolution. We see the influence of that French or classical taste which was brought into England by the exiled court of Charles II., and which afterwards completely metamorphosed the character of our dramatic literature, which, in the time of Dryden and Congreve, was destined to produce much that was imposing and vigorous in tragedy and much that was inimitable in comedy, but which was, in all its essentials, something totally different from the great productions of the preceding era. Davenant was a most prolific author, not only in the dramatic department, in which his most popular productions were ***Albovine***, the ***Siege of Rhodes***, the ***Law against Lovers***, the ***Cruel Brother***, and many others, but also as a narrative poet. He was also one of the most active, virulent, and unscrupulous party-writers of that period. There is a ridiculous story of Davenant being in the habit of giving out that he was a natural son of William Shakspeare by a handsome Oxford landlady, but neither the supposition itself nor the fact of Davenant's exhibiting such a strange, perverted kind of vanity, is at all deserving of credit. One of Davenant's principal non-dramatic works is the poem of ***Gondibert***, narrating a long series of lofty and chivalric adventures in a dignified but somewhat monotonous manner. It is written in a peculiar four-lined stanza with alternate rhymes, afterwards employed by Dryden in his ***Annus Mirabilis.*** It is, however, a form of versification singularly unfitted for continuous narration, and its employment may be one cause of the neglect into which the once-admired work of Davenant has fallen — a neglect so complete that perhaps there are not ten men in England now living who have read it through.

Sir John Denham (1615–1668) was the son of the Chief Baron of the Exchequer in Ireland, and a supporter of Charles I. Though a poet of the secondary order, when regarded in connection with Cowley, one work of his, *Cooper's Hill*, will always occupy an important place in any account of the English Literature of the seventeenth century. This place it owes not only to its specific merits, but also in no mean degree to the circumstance that this poem was the first work in a peculiar department which English writers afterwards cultivated with great success, and which is, I believe, almost exclusively confined to our literature. This department is what may be called local or topographic poetry, and in it the writer chooses some individual scene as the object round which he is to accumulate his descriptive or contemplative passages. Denham selected for this purpose a beautiful spot near Richmond on the Thames, and in the description of the scene itself, as well as in the reflections it suggests, he has risen to a noble elevation. Four lines, indeed, in which he expresses the hope that his own verse may possess the qualities which he attributes to the Thames, will be quoted again and again as one of the finest and most felicitous passages of verse in any language.

§ 8. One of the most accomplished and influential writers of the period was ABRAHAM COWLEY (1618–1667). He exhibits one of the most perfect types of the ideal man of letters. He was a remarkable instance of intellectual precocity, for he is said to have published his first poems, filled with enthusiasm by the *Fairy Queen* of Spenser, when only thirteen years of age. He received a very complete and learned education, partly at Oxford, and afterwards, when obliged by religious and political troubles to leave that academy, in the sister University of Cambridge; and he early acquired and long retained among his contemporaries the reputation of being one of the best scholars and most distinguished poets of his age. During the earlier part of his life he had been confidentially employed, both in England and in France, in the service of Charles I. and his queen, and on attaining middle age he determined to put in execution the philosophical project he had long fondly cherished, of living in rural and lettered retirement. He was disappointed in obtaining such a provision as he thought his services had deserved; but receiving a grant of some crown leases producing a moderate income, he quitted London and went to reside near Chertsey. But his dreams of ease and tranquillity were not fulfilled: he was involved in continual squabbles with the tenants, from whom he could extort no rents; and he speaks with constant querulousness of the hostility and vexations to which he was subjected. He died of a fever caused by imprudence and excess, but not before he had learned the melancholy truth that annoyances and vexations pursue us even into the recesses of rural obscurity.

Cowley is highly regarded among the writers of his time both as a poet and an essayist. Immense and multifarious learning, well digested by reflection and polished into brilliancy by taste and sensibility, renders his prose works, in which he frequently intermingles passages of verse, reading little less delightful than the fascinating pages of Montaigne. Cowley, like Montaigne, possesses the charm arising from the intimate union between reading and reflection, between curious erudition and original speculation, the quaintness of the scholar and the practical knowledge of the man of the world. There are few writers so substantial as Cowley; few whose productions possess that peculiar attraction which grows upon the reader as he becomes older and more contemplative. As a poet, the reputation of Cowley, immense in his own day, has much diminished, which is to be attributed to that abuse of intellectual ingenuity, that passion for learned, far-fetched, and recondite illustrations which was to a certain extent the vice of his age. He has very little passion or depth of sentiment; and in his love-verses — a kind of composition then thought obligatory on all who were ambitious of the name of poet — he substitutes the play of the intellect for the unaffected outpouring of the feelings. He was deeply versed both in Greek and Latin literature, and his imitations, paraphrases, and translations show perfect knowledge of his originals and great mastery over the resources of the English language. He translated the *Odes of Anacreon*, and attempted to revive the boldness, the picturesqueness, and the fire of the Pindaric poetry; but his odes have only an external resemblance with those of the "Theban Eagle." They have the irregularity of form — only an apparent irregularity in the case of the Greek originals, which, it must be remembered, were written to be accompanied by that Greek music of whose structure nothing is now known; but they have not that intense and concentrated fire which burns with an inextinguishable ardor, like the product of some chemical combustion, in the great Bœotian lyrist. Cowley seems always on the watch to seize some ingenious and unexpected parallelism of ideas or images; and when the illustration is so found, the shock of surprise which the reader feels is rather akin to a flash of wit than to an electric stroke of genius. Cowley lived at the moment when the revolution inaugurated by Bacon was beginning to produce its first fruits. The Royal Society, then recently founded, was astonishing the world, and astonishing its own members, by the immense horizon opening before the bold pioneers of the Inductive Philosophy. In this mighty movement Cowley deeply sympathized; and perhaps the finest of his lyric compositions are those in which, with a grave and well-adorned eloquence, he proclaims the genius and predicts the triumphs of Bacon and his disciples in physical science.

One long epic poem of great pretension Cowley meditated but left unfinished. This is the *Davideis*, the subject of which is the sufferings and glories of the King of Israel. But this work is now completely neglected. Biblical personages and events have rarely, with the solitary and sublime exception of Milton, been transported with success out of the majestic language of the Scripture; and it may be maintained, without much fear of contradiction, that the rhymed heroic couplet — the measure employed by Cowley — is not a form of versification capable of supporting the attention of the reader through a lofty epic narrative. The genius of Cowley was far more lyric than epic;

and in his shorter compositions he exerted that influence upon the style of English poetry which tended very much, during nearly two centuries, to modify it very perceptibly, and which is especially traceable in the writings of Dryden, Pope, and generally in the next succeeding generations.

NOTES AND ILLUSTRATIONS.

OTHER POETS.

WILLIAM CHAMBERLAYNE (1619-1689), a physician at Shaftesbury, in Dorsetshire, wrote *Pharonnida*, an heroic poem, in five books, which contains some vigorous passages, but the versification is rugged, and the style slovenly and quaint. Chamberlayne is also the author of a tragi-comedy entitled *Love's Victory*, acted after the Restoration under the new title of *Wits led by the Nose, or the Poet's Revenge.*

CHARLES COTTON (1630-1687), best known as the friend of Izaak Walton, had an estate in Derbyshire upon the river Dove, celebrated for its trout. He wrote several humorous poems, and his *Voyage to Ireland*, Campbell remarks, seems to anticipate the manner of Anstey in the *Bath Guide.*

HENRY VAUGHAN (1614-1695), a native of Wales, born in Brecknockshire, first bred to the law, which he afterwards relinquished for the profession of physic. He published in 1651 a volume of miscellaneous poems. Campbell says of him that "he is one of the harshest even of the inferior order of the school of conceit; but he has some scattered thoughts that meet our eye amid his harsh pages, like wild flowers on a barren heath."

DR. HENRY KING (1591-1669), chaplain to James I., and afterwards Bishop of Chichester, wrote chiefly religious poetry. His thoughts are elevated, and his language is choice. His style is not free from the conceits so fashionable in the writers of this age, but the little fancies he indulges are chaste and full of beauty.

JOHN CLEVELAND (1613-1658), son of a Leicestershire clergyman, distinguished himself as a soldier and poet on the king's side during the Civil War. In 1647 he published a severe satire on the Scotch; was imprisoned in 1655, released by Cromwell, but died soon after. Some of his writings are amatory, and though conceited contain true poetry. It is said that Butler borrowed no little from him in his 'Hudibras.'

SIR RICHARD FANSHAWE (1607-1666), brother of Lord Fanshawe, and secretary to Prince Rupert. He was made ambassador to Spain by Charles II., and died at Madrid. He translated Camoens' *Lusiad*, and the *Pastor Fido* of Guarini. He wrote also some minor poems. His song, *The Saint's Encouragement*, 1643, is full of clever satire, and all his verse is forcible, with here and there a touch of the true poet's beauty.

THOMAS STANLEY (1625-1678), a native of Hertfordshire, studied at Cambridge, and entered the Middle Temple. In 1651 he published some poems chiefly on the tender passion, full of beautiful thought and happy fancy, but marked by the too common quaintness of the times.

DUCHESS OF NEWCASTLE (d. 1673), daughter of Sir Charles Lucas, and maid of honor to Queen Henrietta Maria. In 1653 she published *Poems and Fancies* — was assisted by her husband in many of her writings, according to Horace Walpole in the *Royal and Noble Authors.* Twelve folio volumes were issued by the industrious marquis and his wife, but the value of the writings is not great.

MRS. KATHERINE PHILIPS (1631-1664), a Cardiganshire lady, known by the name of *Orinda*, exceedingly popular as a writer with her contemporaries. Her style is more free than that of most of the poets of the age from quaintness and conceit.

CHAPTER X.

THEOLOGICAL WRITERS OF THE CIVIL WAR AND THE COMMONWEALTH.

§ 1. Theological Writers. JOHN HALES and WILLIAM CHILLINGWORTH. § 2. SIR THOMAS BROWNE. § 3. THOMAS FULLER. § 4. JEREMY TAYLOR. His Life. § 5. His *Liberty of Prophesying* and other works. § 6. His style compared with Spenser. § 7. RICHARD BAXTER. The Quakers: FOX, PENN, and BARCLAY.

§ 1. THE Civil War, which led to the temporary overthrow of the ancient monarchy of England, was in many respects a religious as well as a political contest. It was a struggle for liberty of faith at least as much as for liberty of civil government. The prose literature of this time, therefore, as well as of a period extending considerably beyond it, exhibits a strong religious or theological character. The blood of martyrs, it has been said, is the seed of the Church; and the alternate triumphs and persecutions, through which passed both the Anglican Church and the multiplicity of rival sects which now arose, naturally developed to the highest degree both the intellectual powers and the Christian energies of their adherents. The most glorious outburst of theological eloquence which the Church of England has exhibited, in the writings of Jeremy Taylor, Barrow, and the other great Anglican Fathers, was responded to by the appearance, in the ranks of the sectaries, of many remarkable men, some hardly inferior in learning and genius to the leaders whose doctrines they opposed, while others, with a ruder yet more burning enthusiasm, were the founders of dissenting communions, as in the case of the Quakers.

JOHN HALES (1584–1656), surnamed "the ever-memorable John Hales," was a man who enjoyed among his contemporaries an immense reputation for the vastness of his learning and the acuteness of his wit. He was born in 1584, and in the earlier part of his life had acquired, by travel and diplomatic service in foreign countries, a vast amount not only of literary knowledge, but practical acquaintance with men and affairs: he afterwards retired to the learned obscurity of a fellowship of Eton College, where he passed the sad and dangerous years filled with civil contention. During part of this time his writings and opinions rendered him so obnoxious to the dominant party that a price was set upon his head, and he was obliged to hide, being at the same time reduced to the extremest privations. He for some time subsisted by the sale of his books. He died in 1656, and left behind him the reputation of one of the most solid and yet acutest intellects that his country had produced. The greater part of his writings are controversial, treating on the politico-religious questions that then agitated men's minds. He had been present at the Synod of Dort, and has given an interesting account of the questions debated in that assembly. While attending its sittings as an agent for the English Church he was converted from the Calvinistic opinions he had hitherto held to those of the Episcopalian divines. Both in his controversial writings and in his sermons he exhibits a fine example of that rich yet chastened eloquence which characterizes the great English divines of the seventeenth century, and which was carried to the highest pitch of gorgeous magnificence by Taylor and of majestic grandeur by Barrow.

WILLIAM CHILLINGWORTH (1602–1644), also an eminent defender of Protestantism against the Church of Rome, was converted to the Roman Catholic faith while studying at Oxford, and went to the Jesuits' College at Douay. But he subsequently returned to Oxford, renounced his new faith, and published in 1637 his celebrated work against Catholicism, entitled *The Religion of the Protestants a Safe Way to Salvation*, in reply to a treatise by a Jesuit, named Knott, who had maintained that unrepenting Protestants could not be saved. "In the long parenthetical periods," observes Mr. Hallam, "as in those of other old English writers, in his copiousness, which is never empty or tautological, there is an inartificial eloquence springing from strength of intellect and sincerity of feeling that cannot fail to impress the reader. But his chief excellence is the close reasoning which avoids every dangerous admission, and yields to no ambiguousness of language. He perceived and maintained with great courage, considering the times in which he wrote and the temper of those whom he was not unwilling to keep as friends, his favorite tenet, that all things necessary to be believed are clearly laid down in Scripture. . . . In later times his book obtained a high reputation; he was called the immortal Chillingworth; he was the favorite of all the moderate and the latitudinarian writers, of Tillotson, Locke, and Warburton."

§ 2. The writings of SIR THOMAS BROWNE (1605–1682), though not exclusively theological, belong, chronologically as well as by their style and manner, to this department. Both as a man and a writer this is one of the most peculiar and eccentric of our great prose-authors; and the task of giving a clear appreciation of him is unusually difficult. He was an exceedingly learned man, and passed the greater part of his life in practising physic in the ancient city of Norwich. It should be remembered that the great provincial towns at that time had not been degraded to that insignificance to which the modern facility of intercourse has reduced them in relation to the Metropolis: they were then so many little capitals, possessing their society, their commercial activity, and their local physiognomy, and had not yet been swallowed up by the monster London. Browne was born in 1605, and his life was unusually prolonged, as he died in 1682. His writings are of a most miscellaneous character, ranging from observations on natural science to the most arduous subtleties of moral and metaphysical speculation. Among the most popular of his works are the treatise entitled *Hydriotaphia, or Urn-Burial*, and the Essays on *Vulgar Errors*, which bear the name of *Pseudoxia Epidemica*. The first of these treatises was suggested by the digging up in Norfolk of some Roman funeral urns, and the other is an attempt to overthrow many of the common superstitions and erroneous notions on various subjects. But a mere specification of the subject will altogether fail to give an idea of Browne's strange but fascinating writings. They are the frank and undisguised outpourings of one of the most original minds that ever existed. With the openness and discursive simplicity of Montaigne, they combine immense and recondite reading: at every step the author starts some extraordinary theory, which he illustrates by analogies so singular and unexpected that they produce upon the reader a mingled feeling of amusement and surprise, and all this in a style absolutely bristling with quaint Latinisms, which in another writer would be pedantic, but in Browne were the natural garb of his thought. His diction is stiff with scholastic terms, like the chasuble of some mediæval prelate, thick-set with pearl and ruby. The contrast between the simplicity of Browne's character and the out-of-the-way learning and odd caprices of theory in which he is perpetually indulging, makes him one of the most amusing of writers; and he very frequently rises to a sombre and touching eloquence. Though deeply religious in sentiment he is sometimes apparently sceptical, and his sudden turns of thought and strange comparisons keep the attention of the reader continually awake. He stands almost alone in his passion for pursuing an idea through every conceivable manifestation; and his ingenuity on such occasions is absolutely portentous. For instance, in a treatise on the *Quincunx* he finds quincunxes on the earth, in the waters, and in the heavens, nay, in the very intellectual constitution of the soul. He has a particular tendency to dwell on the dark mysteries of time and of the universe, and makes us thrill with the solemnity with which he suggests the nothingness of mortal life, and the insignificance of human interests when compared to the immeasurable ages that lie before and behind us. In all Sir Thomas Browne's works an intimate companionship is established between the writer and the reader; but the book in which he ostensibly proposes to communicate his own personal opinions and feelings most unreservedly, is the *Religio Medici*, a species of Confession of Faith. In this he by no means confines himself to theological matters, but takes the reader into his confidence in the same artless and undisguised manner as the immortal Montaigne. The images and illustrations with which his writings are crowded, produce upon the reader the same effect as the familiar yet mysterious forms that make up an Egyptian hieroglyphic: they have the same fantastic oddity, the same quaint stiffness in their attitude and combination, and impress the mind with the same air of solemn significance and outlandish remoteness from the ordinary objects of our contemplation.

§ 3. THOMAS FULLER (1608–1661) is another great and attractive prose-writer of this period, and has in some respects a kind of intellectual resemblance to Browne. Unlike him, however, he passed a very active life, having taken a not unprominent part in the Great Civil

War, in which he embraced the cause of the royalists. He was born in 1608, and survived till 1661, and it is said was to have been rewarded for his services with a bishopric, had the intention of the restored court not been defeated by his death. He studied first at Queen's and afterwards at Sidney College, Cambridge, and, entering the Church, rendered himself conspicuous in the pulpit. In the course of time he was nominated preacher at the Savoy in London, and in 1642, just at the outbreak of the Civil War, offended the Parliament by a sermon delivered at Westminster, in which he advised reconciliation with the King, who had left his capital and was on the eve of declaring war against his subjects. Fuller after this joined Charles at Oxford, and is said to have displeased the court party by a degree of moderation which they called lukewarmness. Having thus excited the dissatisfaction of both factions, we may, I think, fairly attribute to reasonable and moderate views the double unpopularity of Fuller. During the war he was attached, as chaplain, to the army commanded by Sir Ralph Hopton, in the West of England; and he took a distinguished part in the famous defence of Basing House, when the Parliamentary army under Sir William Waller was forced to abandon that siege. During his campaigning Fuller industriously collected the materials for his most popular work, the *Worthies of England and Wales*, which, however, was not published until after the author's death. This, more than his *Church History*, is the production with which posterity has generally associated the name of Fuller; but his *Sermons* frequently exhibit those singular peculiarities of style which render him one of the most remarkable writers of his age. His writings are eminently *amusing*, not only from the multiplicity of curious and anecdotic details which they contain, but from the odd and yet frequently profound reflections suggested by those details. The *Worthies* contain biographical notices of eminent Englishmen, as connected with the different counties, and furnish an inexhaustible treasure of curious stories and observations. But whatever the subject Fuller treats, he places it in such a number of new and unexpected lights, and introduces in illustration of it such a number of ingenious remarks, that the attention of the reader is incessantly kept alive. He was a man of a pleasant and jovial as well as an ingenious turn of mind: there is no sourness or asceticism in his way of thinking; flashes of fancy are made to light up the gravest and most unattractive subjects, and, as frequently happens in men of a lively turn, the sparkle of his wit is warmed by a glow of sympathy and tenderness. His learning was very extensive and very minute, and he drew from out-of-the-way and neglected corners of reading illustrations which give the mind a pleasant shock of novelty. One great source of his picturesqueness is his frequent use of antithesis; and, in his works, antithesis is not what it frequently becomes in other authors, as in Samuel Johnson for example, a bare opposition of *words*, but it is the juxtaposition of apparently discordant *ideas*, from whose sudden contact there flashes forth the spark of wit or the embodiment of some original conception. The shock of his antithetical oppositions is like the action of the galvanic battery — creative. He has been accused of levity in intermingling ludicrous images with serious matter, but these images are the reflex of his own cheerful, ingenious, and amiable nature; and though their oddity may sometimes excite a smile, it is a smile which is never incompatible with serious feeling. He is said to have possessed an almost supernatural quickness of memory, yet he has given many excellent precepts guarding against the abuse of this faculty, and in the same way he has shown that wit and ingenuity may be rendered compatible with lofty morality and deep feeling. In a word, he was essentially a wise and learned humorist, with not less singularity of genius than Sir Thomas Browne, and with less than that strange writer's abstract indifference to ordinary human interests.

§ 4. But by far the greatest theological writer of the Anglican Church at this period was JEREMY TAYLOR (1613–1667). He was of good but decayed family, his father having exercised the humble calling of a barber at Cambridge, where his illustrious son was born in 1613. The boy received a sound education at the Grammar-School founded by Perse, then recently opened in that town, and afterwards studied at Caius College, where his talents and learning soon made him conspicuous. He took holy orders at an unusually early age, and is said to have attracted by his youthful eloquence, and by his "graceful and pleasant air," the notice of Archbishop Laud, the celebrated Primate and Minister, to whose narrow-minded bigotry and tyrannical indifference to the state of religious opinion among his countrymen so much of the confusion of those days is to be ascribed. Laud, who was struck with Taylor's merits at a sermon preached by the latter, made the young priest one of his chaplains, and procured for him a fellowship in All Souls' College, Oxford. His career during the Civil War bears some semblance to that of Fuller, but he stood higher in the favor of the Cavaliers and the Court. He served, as chaplain, in the Royalist army, and was taken prisoner in 1644 at the action fought under the walls of Cardigan Castle; but he confesses that on this occasion, as well as on several others when he fell into the power of the triumphant party of the Parliament, he was treated with generosity and indulgence. Such traits of mutual forbearance, during the heat of civil strife, are honorable to both parties, and as refreshing as they are rare. Our great national struggle, however, offered many instances of such noble magnanimity. The King's cause growing desperate, Taylor at last retired from it, and Charles, on taking leave of him, made him a present of his watch. Taylor then placed himself under the protection of his friend Lord Carbery, and resided for some time at the seat of Golden Grove, belonging to that nobleman, in Carmarthenshire. Taylor was twice married; first to Phœbe Langdale, who died early, and afterwards to Joanna Bridges, a natural daughter of Charles I., with whom he received some fortune. He was unhappy in his children, his two sons having been notorious for their profligacy, and he had the sorrow of surviving them both. During part of the time which he passed in retirement, Taylor kept a school in Wales, and continued to take an active part in the religious controversies of the day. The opinions he expressed were naturally distasteful to the dominant party, and on at least three occasion subjected him to imprisonment and sequestrations at the hands of the Government. In 1658, for example, he was for a short time incarcerated in the Tower, and on his liberation migrated to Ireland, where he performed the pastoral functions at Lisburn. On the Restoration his services and sacrifices were rewarded with the Bishopric of Down and Connor, and during the short time he held that preferment he exhibited the brightest qualities that can adorn the episcopal dignity. He died at Lisburn of a fever, in 1667, and left behind him a high reputation for courtesy, charity, and zeal — all the virtues of a Christian Bishop.

§ 5. Taylor's works are very numerous and varied in subject: I will content myself with mentioning the principal, and then endeavor to give a general appreciation of his genius. In the controversial department his best known work is the treatise *On the Liberty of Prophesying*, which must be understood to refer to the general profession of religious principles and the right of all Christians to toleration in the exercise of their worship. This book is the first complete and systematic defence of the great principle of religious toleration; and in it Taylor shows how contrary it is, not only to the spirit of Christianity but even to the true interests of Government, to interfere with the profession and practice of religious sects. Of course, the argument, though of universal application, was intended by Taylor to secure indulgence for what had once been the dominant Church of England, but which was now proscribed and persecuted by the rampant violence of the sectarians. An *Apology for Fixed and Set Forms of Worship* was an elaborate defence of the noble ritual of the Anglican Church. Among his works of a disciplinary and practical tendency I may mention his *Life of Christ, the Great Exemplar*, in which the details scattered through the Evangelists and the Fathers are co-ordinated in a continuous narrative. But the most popular of Taylor's writings are the two admirable treatises *On the Rule and Exercise of Holy Living*, and *On the Rule and Exercise of Holy Dying*, which mutually correspond to and complete each other, and which form an Institute of Christian life and conduct, adapted to every conceivable circumstance and relation of human existence. This devotional work has enjoyed in England a popularity somewhat similar to that of the *Imitation of Jesus Christ* among Catholics; a popularity it deserves for a similar eloquence and unction. The least admirable of his numerous writings, and the only one in which he derogated from his usual tone of courtesy and fairness, was his *Ductor Dubitantium*, a treatise of questions of casuistry. His *Sermons* are very numerous, and are among the most eloquent, learned, and powerful that the whole range of Protestant — nay, the whole range of Christian — literature has produced. As in his character, so in his writings, Taylor is the ideal of an Anglican pastor. Our Church itself being a middle term or compromise between the gorgeous formalism of Catholicism and the narrow fanaticism of

Calvinistic theology, so our great ecclesiastic writers exhibit the union of consummate learning with practical simplicity and fervor.

§ 6. Taylor's style, though occasionally overcharged with erudition and marked by that abuse of quotation which disfigures a great deal of the prose of that age, is uniformly magnificent. The materials are drawn from the whole range of profane as well as sacred literature, and are fused together into a rich and gorgeous unity by the fire of an unequalled imagination. No prose is more melodious than that of this great writer; his periods, though often immeasurably long, and evolving, in a series of subordinate clauses and illustrations, a train of images and comparisons, one springing out of another, roll on with a soft yet mighty swell, which has often something of the enchantment of verse. He has been called by the critic Jeffrey, "the most Shakspearian of our great divines;" but it would be more appropriate to compare him with Spenser. He has the same pictorial fancy, the same voluptuous and languishing harmony; but if he can in any respect be likened to Shakspeare, it is firstly in the vividness of intellect which leads him to follow, digressively, the numberless secondary ideas that spring up as he writes, and often lead him apparently far away from his point of departure, and, secondly, the preference he shows for drawing his illustrations from the simplest and most familiar objects, from the opening rose, the infant streamlet, "the little rings and wanton tendrils of the vine," the morning song of the soaring lark, or the "fair cheeks and full eyes of childhood." Like Shakspeare, too, he knows how to paint the terrible and the sublime no less than the tender and the affecting; and his description of the horrors of the Judgment-Day is no less powerful than his exquisite portraiture of married love. Nevertheless, with Spenser's sweetness he has occasionally something of the luscious and enervate languor of Spenser's style. He had studied the Fathers so intensely that he had become infected with something of that lavish and Oriental imagery which many of those great writers exhibited — many of whom, it should be remembered, were Orientals, not only in their style, but in their origin. Taking his personal character and his writings together, Jeremy Taylor may be called the English Fénélon; but in venturing to make this parallel, we must not forget that each of these excellent writers and admirable men possessed the characteristic features of his respective country: if Fénélon's productions, like those of Taylor's, are distinguished by their sweetness, that sweetness is allied in the former to the neat, clear, precise expression which the French literature derives not only from the classical origin of the language, but from the antique writers who have always been set up as models for French imitation; while Jeremy Taylor, with a sweetness not inferior, owes that quality to the same rich and poetic susceptibility to natural beauty that gives such a matchless coloring to the English poetry of the sixteenth and seventeenth centuries.

§ 7. Having thus given a rapid sketch of some of the great figures whose genius adorned the Church, it may complete our view of the religious aspect of that time to mention some of the more remarkable men who appeared in the opposing party. The greatest names among the latter class — Milton and Bunyan — will be discussed in subsequent chapters; but a few words may now be added respecting the excellent Baxter and the fanatical founder of the sect of the Quakers, George Fox, together with his more cultivated, yet not less earnest, follower William Penn, and Barclay, who defended with the arms of learning and argument a system originally founded by half-frantic enthusiasm.

RICHARD BAXTER (1615–1691) was during nearly the whole of his long life the victim of unrelenting persecution. Few authors have been so prolific as he; the multitude of his tracts and religious works almost defies computation. He was the consistent and unconquerable defender of the right of religious liberty; and in those evil days when James II. endeavored forcibly to re-establish the Roman Catholic religion in England, Baxter was exposed to all the virulence and brutality of the infamous Jeffries and his worse than inquisitorial tribunal. He was a man of vast learning, the purest piety, and the most indefatigable industry. In prison, in extreme poverty, chased like a hunted beast, suffering from a weak constitution and a painful and incurable disease, this meek yet unconquerable spirit still fought his fight, pouring forth book after book in favor of free worship, and opposing the quiet sufferance of a primitive martyr to the rage and tyranny of the persecutor. His works, which have little to recommend them to a modern reader but the truly evangelical spirit of toleration which they breathe, are little known in the present day, with the exception of the *Saints' Everlasting Rest*, and *A Call to the Unconverted*.

GEORGE FOX (1624–1690), the founder of the Quaker sect, was a man born in the humblest rank of life in 1624, and so completely without education that his numerous writings are filled with unintelligible gibberish, and in many instances, even after having been revised and put in order by disciples possessed of education, it is hardly possible, through the mist of ungrammatical and incoherent declamation, to make out the drift of the author's argument. The life of Fox was like that of many other ignorant enthusiasts; believing himself the object of a special supernatural call from God, he retired from human companionship, and lived for some time in a hollow tree, clothed in a leathern dress which he had made with his own hands. Wandering about the country to preach his doctrines, the principal of which were a denial of all titles of respect, and a kind of quietism combined with hostility not only to all formal clerical functions and establishments, but even to all institutions of government, he met with constant and furious persecution at the hands of the clergy, the country magistrates, and the rabble, whose manners were, of course, much more brutal than in the present day. He has left curious records of his own adventures, and in particular of two interviews with Cromwell, upon whose mind the earnestness and sincerity of the poor Quaker seemed to have produced an impression honorable to the goodness of the Protector's heart. Fox's claims to the gift of prophecy and to the power of detecting witches bear witness at once to his ignorance and simplicity, and to the universal prevalence of gross superstition; but we cannot deny to him the praise of ardent faith, deep, if unenlightened, benevolence, and a truly Christian spirit of patience under insults and injuries.

WILLIAM PENN (1644–1718), the founder of the colony of Pennsylvania, played a very active and not always very honorable part at the court of James II. when that prince, under a transparent pretext of zeal for religious liberty, was endeavoring, by giving privileges to the dissenting and nonconformist sects, to shake the power and influence of the Protestant Church, and thus to pave the way for the execution of his darling scheme, the re-establishment of Romanism in England. Penn was a man of good birth and academical education, but early adopted the doctrines of the Quakers. His name will ever be respectable for the benevolence and wisdom he exhibited in founding that colony which was afterwards destined to become a wealthy and enlightened state, and in the excellent and humane precepts he gave for the conduct of relations between the first settlers and the Indian aborigines. The sect of Quakers has always been conspicuous for peaceable behavior, practical good sense, and much acuteness in worldly matters. Their principles forbidding them to take any part in warfare, and excluding them from almost all occupations but those of trade and commerce, they have generally been thriving and rich, and their numbers being small they have been able to carry out those excellent and well-considered plans for mutual help and support which have made their charitable institutions the admiration of all philanthropists.

ROBERT BARCLAY (1648–1690) was a Scottish country-gentleman of considerable attainments, who published a systematic defence of the doctrines of the sect founded by the rude zeal of Fox. His celebrated *Apology* for the Quakers was published, originally in Latin, in 1676.

NOTES AND ILLUSTRATIONS.

OTHER THEOLOGICAL AND MORAL WRITERS.

JOSEPH HALL (1574-1656), Bishop of Norwich, whose satires have been already mentioned (p. 83), was also a distinguished theological writer. His *Contemplations* and his *Art of Divine Meditation* are the most celebrated of his works. As a devotional writer he is second only to Jeremy Taylor.

ROBERT SANDERSON (1587-1663), Bishop of Salisbury, one of the most celebrated of the High-Church Divines, wrote works on casuistry, and sermons distinguished by great learning.

OWEN FELTHAM (circa 1610-1677) lived in the house of the Earl of Thomond. His work entitled *Resolves, Divine, Moral, and Political*, was first published in 1628, and enjoyed great popularity for many years. But Mr. Hallam's judgment is that "Feltham is not only a labored and artificial, but a shallow writer." He owed much of his popularity to a pointed and sententious style.

SIR THOMAS OVERBURY (1581-1613), who was poisoned in the Tower in the reign of James I., wrote a work entitled *Characters*, which displays skill in the delineation of character. His description of the *Fair and happy Milkmaid* has been often quoted, and is one of the best of his characters. He also wrote two didactic poems entitled *The Wife* and the *Choice of a Wife*.

JOHN EARLE (1601-1665), Bishop of Worcester, and afterwards of Salisbury, the reputed author of a work, *Microcosmography, or a Piece of the World Discovered, in Essays and Characters*, published anonymously about 1628. "In some of these short characters Earle is worthy of comparison with La Bruyère; in others, perhaps the greater part, he has contented himself with pictures of ordinary manners, [illegible] occupation, rather than of [illegible], simply. In all, however, we find an acute observation and a happy humor of expression. The chapter entitled the Sceptic is best known; it is witty, but an insult throughout on the honest searcher after truth, which could have come only from one that was content to take up his own opinions for ease or profit. Earle is always gay and quick to catch the ridiculous, especially that of exterior appearances; his style is short, describing well with a few words, but with much of the affected quaintness of that age. It is one of those books which give us a picturesque idea of the manners of our fathers at a period now become remote, and for this reason, were there no other, it would deserve to be read." (Hallam.)

PETER HEYLIN (1600-1662), a divine and historian, deprived of his preferments by the Parliament, was the author of many works, of which the most popular was his *Microcosmus, or a Description of the Great World*, first published in 1621.

JOHN SELDEN (1584-1654), one of the most learned men of his age, and the author of numerous historical and antiquarian works; but the one by which he is best known in English literature is his *Table-Talk*, published after his death, containing many acute sayings, and well worth reading.

JAMES USSHER (1581-1656), Archbishop of Armagh, likewise distinguished for his great learning, is best known by his chronological work, entitled *Annals*, containing chronological tables of universal history from the creation to the time of Vespasian. The dates in the margin of the authorized version of the Bible are taken from Ussher.

JOHN GAUDEN (1605-1664), Bishop of Exeter, and afterwards of Worcester, was the author of *Ikon Basilikè*, a work professing to be written by Charles I. The authorship of this book has been the subject of much controversy; but there can be no doubt that it was written by Gauden, who, after the Restoration, claimed it as his own.

CHAPTER XI.

JOHN MILTON, A. D. 1608–1674.

§ 1. JOHN MILTON. His early life and education. § 2. Travels in Italy. § 3. Returns to England. Espouses the popular party. His *Areopagitica.* § 4 Made Latin Secretary to the Council of State. His *Defensio Populi Anglicani*, and other Prose Works. His *Tractate of Education.* § 5. History of his life after the Restoration. His death. § 6. Three periods of Milton's literary career. FIRST PERIOD: 1623–1640. *Hymn on the Nativity. Comus.* § 7. *Lycidas.* § 8. *L'Allegro* and *Il Penseroso.* § 9. Milton's Latin and Italian writings. His English Sonnets. § 10. SECOND PERIOD: 1640–1660. Style of his prose writings. § 11. THIRD PERIOD: 1660–1674. *Paradise Lost.* Analysis of the poem. Its versification. § 12. Incidents and personages of the poem. Conduct and development of the plot. § 13. *Paradise Regained.* § 14. *Samson Agonistes.*

§ 1. ABOVE the seventeenth century towers, in solitary grandeur, the sublime figure of JOHN MILTON (1608–1674). It will be no easy task to give even a cursory sketch of a life so crowded with literary as well as political activity; still less easy to appreciate the varied, yet all incomparable, works in which this mighty genius has embodied its conceptions. He was born, on the 9th December, 1608, in London, and was sprung from an ancient and gentle stock. His father, an ardent republican, and who sympathized with the Puritan doctrines, had quarrelled with his relations, and had taken his own independent part in life, embracing the profession of a money-scrivener, in which, by industry and unquestioned integrity, he had amassed a considerable fortune, so as to be able to retire to a pleasant country-house at Horton, near Colne, in Oxfordshire. It was undoubtedly from his father that the poet first imbibed his political and religious sympathies, and perhaps also something of that lofty, stern, but calm and noble spirit which makes his character resemble that of the heroes of ancient story. The boy evidently gave indications, from his early childhood, of the extraordinary intellectual powers which distinguished him from all other men; and his father, a person of cultured mind, seems to have furthered the design of Nature, by setting aside the youthful prophet and consecrating him — like Samuel — to the service of the Temple — the holy temple of patriotism and literature. Milton enjoyed the rare advantage of an education specially training him for the career of letters; and the proud care with which he collected every production of his youthful intelligence, his first verses and his college exercises, shows that he was well aware that everything proceeding from his pen, "whether prosing or versing," as he says himself, "had certain signs of life in it," and merited preservation. What in other men would have been a pardonable vanity, in him was a duty he owed to his own genius and to posterity. He was most carefully educated, first at home, then at St. Paul's School, London, whence he entered Christ's College, Cambridge, yet a child in years, but already a consummate scholar. We may conceive with what admiration, even with what awe, must have been regarded by his preceptors both in the School and in the University the first efforts of his Muse, which, though taking the commonplace form of academical prolusions, exhibit a force of conception, a pure majesty of thought, and a solemn and organ-like music of versification that widely separate them from even the matured productions of contemporary poets. He left Cambridge in 1632, after taking his Master's degree, and there are many allusions in his works which prove that the doctrines and discipline of the University at that time contained much that was distasteful to his haughty and uncontrolled spirit. His first attempts in poetry were made as early as his thirteenth year, so that he is as striking an instance of precocity as of power of genius; and his sublime *Hymn on the Nativity*, in which may plainly be seen all the characteristic features of his intellectual nature, was written, as a college exercise, in his twenty-first year. On leaving the University he resided for about five years at his father's seat at Horton, continuing his multifarious studies with unabated and almost excessive ardor, and filling his mind with those sweet and simple emanations of rural beauty which are so exquisitely reflected in his poetry. His studies seem to have embraced the whole circle of human knowledge the literature of every age and of every cultivated language, living and dead, gave up all its stores of truth and beauty to his all-embracing mind: the most arduous subtleties of philosophy, the loftiest mysteries of theological learning, were familiar to him: there is no art, no science, no profession with which he was not more or less acquainted; and however we may wonder at the majesty of his genius, the extent of his acquirements is no less astounding. It was during this, probably happiest, period of his life that he wrote the more graceful, fanciful, and eloquent of his poems, the pastoral drama, or Masque, of *Comus*, the lovely elegy on his friend King entitled *Lycidas*, and in all probability the descriptive gems *L'Allegro* and *Il Penseroso*. At this epoch his mind seems to have exhibited that exquisite susceptibility to all refined, courtly, and noble emotions which is so faithfully reflected in these works, emotions not incompatible in him with the severest purity of sentiment and the loftiest dignity of principle. He was at this time eminently beautiful in person, though of a stature scarcely attaining the middle size; but he relates with pride that he was remarkable for his bodily activity and his address in the use of the sword. During the whole of his life, indeed, the appearance of the poet was noble, almost ideal: his face gradually exchanged a childish, seraphic beauty for the lofty expression of sorrow and sublimity which it bore in his blindness and old age. When young he was the type of his own angels, when old of a prophet, a patriot, and a saint.

§ 2. In 1638 the poet, now about thirty, set out upon his travels on the continent — the completion of a perfect education. He visited the most celebrated cities of Italy, France, and Switzerland; was furnished with powerful introductions, and received everywhere with marked respect and admiration. "Johannes Miltonus, Anglus," seems to have struck the learned and fastidious Italians with unusual astonishment; and wherever he went the youthful poet gave proofs, "as the manner was," of his profound skill in Italian and Latin verse. He appears everywhere to have made acquaintance with all who were most illustrious for learning and genius; he had an interview with Galileo, "then grown old, a prisoner in the Inquisition," and he laid the foundation of solid friendships with the learned Deodate, originally of an illustrious house of Lucca, but now retired, for the free profession of Protestant opinions, to Geneva, where he was a celebrated professor of theology, and the noble Manso, the distinguished poet and friend of poets, who had been the friend of Torquato Tasso, and now—

"With open arms received one poet more."

During his residence abroad the young poet gave proofs not only of his learning and genius, but also of the ardor of his religious and political enthusiasm, so hostile to Catholicism and monarchy; and though he had at starting received from the wise diplomatist Wotton the prudent recommendation of maintaining "il volto sciolto ed i pensieri stretti," his anti-papal zeal exposed him at Rome and other places to considerable danger, even, it is supposed, of assassination. The friendships Milton formed with virtuous and accomplished foreigners were in some degree the suggesting motive for many of his Italian and Latin poems; for in the former language he wrote at least as well as the majority of the contemporary poets of any but the first class, and in the latter his compositions have never been surpassed by any modern writer of Latin verse.

§ **3.** After spending about fifteen months on the continent he was abruptly recalled to England by the first mutterings of that social and political tempest which was for a time to overthrow the Monarchy and the Church. So fervid a patriot and so inveterate an enemy of episcopacy was not likely to remain an inactive spectator of the momentous conflict: he threw himself into the struggle with all the ardor of his temperament and convictions; and from this period begins the second phase of his many-sided life. His father was dead, and Milton now began the career of a vehement and even furious controversialist. He was one of the most prolific writers of that agitated time, producing works on all the most pressing questions of the day. Chiefly the advocate of republican principles in the state, he was the most uncompromising enemy of the Episcopal Church. His fortune being small, he opened a school in 1640, and among those who had the honor of his instructions, only two persons are at all celebrated, his nephews John and Charles Phillips, who have contributed some details to the history of English Poetry. The commencement of Milton's career as a prose writer may be referred to about the year 1641, and it continued almost without interruption till the Restoration defeated all his hopes, and left him, in blindness, poverty, and danger, nothing but the proud consciousness of having done his duty as a good citizen, and the leisure to devote the closing years of his life to the composition of his sublimest poems, the *Paradise Lost* and the *Paradise Regained.*

Milton's first prose writings were directed against the Anglican Church Establishment, but he soon took a very active part in agitating an important question involving the Law of Divorce. This was suggested by his own conjugal infelicity. His first marriage was an unfortunate one. In 1643 he was united to Mary Powell, the daughter of a spendthrift and ruined country gentleman of strong Royalist sympathies, to whom Milton's father had lent sums of money which he was unable to repay, and who appears to have sacrificed his daughter to an unsuitable and unpromising match in order to escape from his embarrassments. Mary Powell, soon disgusted with the austerity of Milton's life, fled to her father's house, and was only recalled to the conjugal roof by a report that her husband, basing his determination upon the Levitical law, was meditating a new marriage with another person. The lady was forgiven by her husband, but the remaining years of her marriage were probably not happy, though three daughters were the fruit of the union. We shall by and by see that Milton was twice married after the death of his first wife. The finest of the prose compositions produced at this epoch was the *Areopagitica*, an oration after the antique model, addressed to the Parliament of England in defence of the Liberty of the Press. It is the sublimest pleading that any age or country has produced, in favor of the great fundamental principle of Freedom of Thought and Opinion. In this, as in many other of his prose works, Milton rises to an almost superhuman elevation of eloquence. It was published in 1644. About this time he began his *History of England*, a work which he abandoned quite at its commencement; he used the subject merely as a vehicle for attacking the abuses of Catholicism and the monastic orders.

§ 4. In 1649 Milton received the appointment of Latin Secretary to the Council of State, a post in which his skill in Latin composition was employed in carrying on the diplomatic intercourse between England and other countries, such correspondence being at that time always couched in the universally-understood language of ancient Rome; but in these duties, probably in consideration of his rapidly-increasing infirmity of sight, were joined with him in his office first Meadowes, and afterwards the excellent and accomplished Marvell. The loss of the great poet's sight became total in 1662, though the *gutta serena* which caused it had been gradually coming on during ten years. His eyes, even from early youth, had been delicate; and in his intense devotion to study he had greatly overtasked them. In one of the noblest of his Sonnets he alludes, in a strain of lofty self-consciousness and religious resignation, to the fact of his loss of sight, which he proudly attributes to his having overtasked it in the defence of truth and liberty; and in the character of the blinded Samson, he undoubtedly shadows forth his own infirmity and his own feelings.

Connected with Milton's engagement in the service of the Republican Government are passages, both in prose and verse, in which he expresses his sympathy with the glorious administration and great personal qualities of Cromwell: but his eulogy, though warm and enthusiastic, is free from every trace of adulation. He probably, though disapproving of the despotic and military character of the Protector's rule, gave his adherence to it as the least in a choice of many evils, and pardoned some of the unavoidable severities of a revolutionary government, in consideration of the great benefits which accompanied, and the patriotic spirit which animated it. It made England, for the time, the terror of the Continental nations and the representative of the Protestant interest.

Milton's most celebrated controversy was that with Salmasius (de Saumaise) on the subject of the right of the English people to make war upon, to dethrone, and to decapitate their King, on the ground of his attempts to infringe the Constitution in virtue of which he reigned. The misfortunes and the tragic death of Charles I. naturally excited in the minds of sovereigns at that time something of the same horror and alarm as the execution of Louis XVI. afterwards spread throughout Europe: and the eccentric Christian of Sweden employed de Saumaise, one of the most learned men of that day, to write what may be called a ponderous Latin pamphlet — for Latin was the language universally employed at that time in diplomacy, in controversy, and in science — invoking the vengeance of Heaven upon the regicide Parliament of England. Milton replied in his *Defensio Populi Anglicani*, maintaining the right and justifying the conduct of his countrymen. His invectives are not less violent than those of his antagonist, his Latinity is not less elegant, but the controversy is as little honorable to the one as to the other combatant. The tone of literary warfare was then coarse and ferocious; and in their vehemence of mutual vituperation these two great scholars descend to personal abuse, in which exquisite Latinity forms but a poor excuse for brutal violence.

It would be tiresome to the reader, and inappropriate to a work like the present, to give a detailed list of all Milton's Prose writings. Their subjects, for the most part, had only a temporary interest; and their style, whether Latin or English, generally resembles, in its wonderful power, grandeur, and picturesqueness, and in a sort of colossal and elaborate involution, that of the writings which I have already mentioned. I may, however, note the *Apology for Smectymnuus*, in which Milton defends the conclusions of that famous pamphlet, the strange name of which is a kind of anagram composed of the initials of its five authors, the chief of whom was Thomas Young, Milton's deeply-venerated Puritan preceptor, the book called *Iconoclastes* — or the *Image-breaker* — intended to neutralize the effect of the celebrated *Icon Basilike*, written by Bishop Gauden in the character of Charles I., in which the piety, resignation, and sufferings of the Royal martyr were represented in so lively a manner that this work probably contributed more than anything else to excite the public commiseration. Other treatises, among which may be mentioned ***The Reason of Church Government Urged against Prelacy***, *A Ready and Easy Way to Establish a True Commonwealth*, sufficiently exhibit in their titles the nature of their subjects. What is now most interesting to us in these controversial writings of Milton is firstly the astonishing grandeur of eloquence to which he occasionally rises in those outbursts of enthusiasm that are intermingled with drier matter, and secondly the frequent notices of his own personal feelings, studies, and mode of life, which, in his eagerness to defend himself against calumnious attacks on his moral character, he has frequently interspersed. For example, both the *Areopagitica* and his pamphlet against Prelacy, contain a most glorious epitome of his studies, his projects, and his literary aspirations. The only work that I need particularly mention, besides those already enumerated, is his curious *Tractate of Education*. In this Milton has drawn up a beautiful, but entirely Utopian, scheme for remodelling the whole system of training and reducing it to something like the antique pattern. Milton proposes the entire abolition of the present system both of School and University; he would bring up young men with as much attention to physical as to intellectual development, by a mechanism borrowed from the *prytaneia* of the ancient Greeks, public institutions in which instruction should have an encyclopædic character, and where all the arts, trades, and sciences should be taught, so as to produce sages, patriots, and soldiers. This treatise was published in 1644.

§ 5. With the Restoration, in 1660, begins the last, the most gloomy, and yet the most glorious period of the great poet's career. That event was naturally the signal of distress and persecution to one who by his writings had shown himself the most consistent, persevering, and formidable enemy of monarchy and episcopacy, and who had attacked, with particular vehemence, the character of Charles I. Milton was excepted, together with all those who had taken any share in the trial and execution of the king, from the general amnesty. He was imprisoned, but liberated after a confinement of some months; and the indulgence with which he was treated may be attributed either to consideration for his learning, poverty, and blindness, or, perhaps, to the intercession of some who knew how to appreciate his virtues and his genius. It is said that Sir W. Davenant successfully used his influence to spare the aged poet any further persecution. From this period till his death he lived in close retirement, busily occupied in the composition of *Paradise Lost* and *Paradise Regained*. The former of these works was finished in 1665, and had been his principal employment during about seven years. The companion epic, a work of much shorter extent, as well as the noble and pathetic tragedy of *Samson Agonistes*, are attributed to the year 1671. On the 8th of November, 1674, Milton died, at the age of sixty-six, and was buried in Cripplegate churchyard. He had been thrice married, first to Mary Powell, by whom he had three daughters, all of whom survived him, and who are said to have treated him in his old age with harshness and disrespect. There is a tradition of his having employed his daughters to read to him and to write under his dictation, but this is hardly probable, as there are documents which prove them to have been almost entirely without education. His second wife, Katharine Woodcock, he espoused in 1656, and this union, though of short duration, appears to have been far better suited than the first; his wife Katharine died two years after, in childbed, and Milton had alsc the grief of losing his infant. He married for the third time at the advanced age of fifty-five, probably with a view of obtaining that comfort and care which his helpless state so much required. The lady was Elizabeth Minshull, and was much younger than the poet, whom she survived.

§ 6. Milton's literary career divides itself naturally into three great periods — that of his youth, that of his manhood, and that of his old age. The first may be roughly stated as extending from 1623 to 1640; the second from 1640 to 1660, the date of the Restoration; and the third from the Restoration to the poet's death in 1674. During the first of these he produced the principal poetical works marked by a graceful, tender character, and on miscellaneous subjects; during the second he was chiefly occupied with his prose controversies; and in the third we see him slowly elaborating the *Paradise Lost*, the *Paradise Regained*, and the *Samson Agonistes*. I will now examine, somewhat more in detail, the works belonging to each phase of his intellectual development, premising only that the first epoch is mainly characterized by grace, the second by force and vehemence, and the third by unapproachable sublimity.

In the early, almost boyish productions of Milton's muse — as the *Verses at a Solemn Music*, the poetical exercises written at school and college, the *Hymn on the Nativity* — no reader can fail to remark that this author already exhibits qualities of thought and expression which distinguish him from all poets of any age or country. The chief of these qualities is a peculiar majesty of conception, combined with consummate though somewhat austere harmony and grace. His poetry is like his own Eve — a consummate type of loveliness, uniting the severe yet sensuous beauty of classical sculpture with the ideal and abstracted elevation of Christian art. In all these works we see a scholarship so vast and complete that it would have overwhelmed and crushed a power of original conception less mighty than that of Milton, and a power of original conception that derives a duly subordinate adornment from the inexhaustible stores of erudition. Above all there is visible, in even the least elaborate of Milton's poems, a peculiar solemn weighty melody of versification that fills and satisfies the ear like the billowy sound of a mighty organ. How wonderfully has he, in the *Hymn on the Nativity*, combined with the pictures of simple rural innocence the shepherds sitting ere the break of dawn, the picturesque legends connected with the cessation of the Pagan oracles at the period of our Lord's incarnation, the pictures of the horrible rites of Moloch and Osiris, the grand image of universal peace that then reigned throughout the world, with the kings sitting still with "awful eye" of expectation, and the glimpse into the unspeakable splendors of heaven, the "helmed cherubim and sworded seraphim harping in loud and solemn quire' before the throne of the Almighty! This magnificent ode is a fitting prelude to the *Paradise Lost*.

In my remarks upon the dramatic literature of the age of Elizabeth and James I., I took occasion to speak of that peculiar and exquisitely fanciful species of entertainment called the *Masque*, of which Ben Jonson and other poets had produced such delicious examples. It was reserved to Milton to equal the great poets who preceded him in the elegance and refinement which characterize this kind of half-dramatic, half-lyric composition, while he far surpassed them in loftiness and purity of sentiment. They had exhausted their courtly and scholar-like fancy in inventing elaborate compliments to some of the most worthless and contemptible of princes; Milton communicated to what was originally a mere vehicle for elegant adulation a pure and lofty ethical tone that soars into the very empyrean of moral speculation. The Masque of *Comus* was written to be performed at Ludlow Castle, in the presence of the Earl of Bridgewater, then Governor-General of the Welsh Marches, an accomplished nobleman, and one of the most powerful personages of the time. His daughter, Lady Alice Egerton, and his two sons had lost their way in the woods when walking; and out of this simple incident Milton created the most beautiful pastoral drama that has hitherto been produced. It was represented by the young people who were the heroes of the incident on which it was founded, and the other characters were filled by Milton's friend, Henry Lawes, a composer who had studied in Italy, and who furnished the graceful music that accompanied its lyric portions. The characters are few, consisting of the Lady, the two Brothers, Comus (a wicked enchanter, the allegorical representative of vicious and sensual pleasure, a personage enacted by Lawes), and the Guardian Spirit, disguised as a shepherd, which part one pleases one's self in fancying may have been filled by the poet. The plot is exceedingly simple, rather lyric than dramatic. The delineation of passion forms no part of the poet's aim; and perhaps the very abstract and ideal nature of the characters — their impersonality, so to say — adds to the intended effect by raising the mind of the reader into the pure and ethereal atmosphere of philosophical beauty. The dialogues are inexpressibly noble, not however as dialogues, for they must rather be regarded as a series of exquisite soliloquies setting forth, in pure and musical eloquence, like that of Plato, the loftiest abstractions of love and virtue. They have the severe and sculptural grace of the Grecian drama, but combined with the warmest coloring of natural beauty; for the frequent descriptions of rural objects possess the richness, the accuracy, and the fancifulness of Fletcher, of Jonson, or of Shakspeare himself. Though the dialogue itself be lyrical in its character, the songs interspersed are of consummate melody. For instance, the drinking chorus of Comus's rout, the Echo-song, and the admirable passages with which the Attendant Spirit opens and concludes the piece. The general character of this production Milton undoubtedly borrowed from Fletcher's *Faith-*

ful Shepherdess, from Jonson's *Masques* and his delicious fragment of a pastoral drama, and probably also from the same Italian sources as had suggested to those great poets the general tone and construction of the pastoral allegory; but in elevation, purity, and dignity, if not also in exquisite delineation of natural beauty, Milton has surpassed Fletcher and Jonson as much as they surpassed Tasso, or as Tasso had surpassed Guarini. In a somewhat similar strain to *Comus*, Milton composed a fragment entitled *Arcades*, performed at Harefield before the Countess of Derby by different members of that illustrious family. In this masque Milton wrote only the poetical portion, the rest of the entertainment, as was frequently the case on such occasions, being made up of dances, music, and scenic transformations. Though the portion contributed by the poet is comparatively inconsiderable, it exhibits all his usual characteristics.

§ 7. The pastoral elegy entitled *Lycidas* was a tribute of affection to the memory of Milton's friend and fellow-student Edward King, lost at sea in a voyage to Ireland, where he was about to undertake the duties of a clergyman. He was a young man of virtue and accomplishments, and the pastoral form of elegy was not inappropriate either to symbolize early conformity of studies between him and his elegist, or to the profession to which he was about to devote himself. In the general tone of the poem, and in the irregular and ever-varying music of the verse, Milton imitated those Italian models with whose scholarlike and elaborate spirit he was so deeply saturated. The poem is a *Canzone*, and one of which even the greatest poets of Italy might well have been proud. Throughout we meet with a mixture of rural description, classical and mythological allegory, and theological allusions borrowed from the Christian system; and nothing is more singular than the skill with which the poet has combined such apparently discordant elements into one harmonious whole. The shock given to the reader's taste by this apparent incongruity is in a great measure softened away by the abstract and poetical air of the whole, by the art with which the transitions are managed, and in some degree by the exquisite descriptions of natural scenery, flowers, and the famous rivers immortalized by the great pastoral poets of antiquity. Nevertheless the ordinary reader is somewhat surprised to find St. Peter making his appearance among the sea-nymphs, and allusions to the corruptions of the Episcopal Church and the happiness of just men made perfect brought into connection with the fables of Pagan mythology. But the force of imagination and the exhaustless beauty of imagery which is displayed from the beginning to the end make the truly sensitive reader entirely forget what are inconsistencies only to the logical reasoning. In this poem we see how great was Milton's mastery over the whole scale of melody of which the English language is capable. From a solemn and psalm-like grandeur to the airiest and most delicate playfulness, every variety of music may be found in *Lycidas;* and the poet has shown that our northern speech, though naturally harsh and rugged, may be made to echo the softest melody of the Italian lyre.

§ 8. The two descriptive poems *L'Allegro* and *Il Penseroso*, as they form a sort of pair of cabinet pictures, the one the complement and counterpart of the other, will be most advantageously examined under one head. They are of nearly the same length, written in the same metre, and consisting, with the exception of a few longer and irregular lines of invocation at the beginning of each, of the short-rhymed octosyllabic measure. In the *Allegro* the poet describes scenery and various occupations and amusements as contemplated by a man of joyous and cheerful temperament; in the *Penseroso* not dissimilar objects viewed by a person of serious, melancholy, and studious character. The individuality of the poet is seen in the calm and somewhat grave cheerfulness of the one, as well as in the tranquil though not sombre meditativeness of the other. His joy is without frivolity, as his melancholy is without gloom. It would be interesting to compare these two poems with minute detail, paragraph by paragraph; for every picture, almost every phrase, in the one corresponds, with close parallelism, to something similar in the other. Thus the beautiful opening lines in which the poet drives away Melancholy to her congenial dwelling in hell, correspond to the opening of the *Penseroso;* and the invocation to Joy and her retinue of Quips and Cranks and wanton Wiles, Sport, Liberty, and Laughter, forms the pendant to the sublime impersonation of Melancholy, which is indeed in poetry what the Night of Michael Angelo is in sculpture. The Cheerful Man is awakened by the lark, the cock, and the hunter's horn; and walks out, "by hedge-row elms and hillocks green," to see the gorgeous sunrise. The sounds and sights of early morning are represented with wonderful beauty and reality; and the gradual unfolding of the landscape, under the growing radiance of the dawn, is perfectly magical. We then have a charming picture of rustic life; and this is succeeded by a village festival, where every line seems to bound responsive to the joyous bells and the sound of the rebeck. The day terminates with ghost stories and fairy legends related over the "nut-brown ale," round the farm-house fire. Having completed the picture of rural pleasures (in which, however, it should be remarked, the amusements of the chase forms no part), the poet goes on to describe the more courtly and elaborate pastimes of the great city—the tourney, the dance, the marriage feast; and the poem terminates with one of the most admirable of those many passages in which Milton has at once celebrated and exemplified the charms of music. Music was his favorite art: he inherited from his father an intense love for and no mean skill in it; it was afterwards his best—perhaps his highest—consolation in his poverty and blindness; and assuredly no poet in any language has shown such a deep sensibility to its enchantments. The passage in the *Allegro* in which he speaks of it is the most perfect representation that words have ever given of the consummate execution of the highest Italian vocal music. Among the pleasures of the city Milton has not forgotten the glories of the stage; and here he pays a compliment to Jonson's "learned sock," and to the "wood-notes wild" of Shakspeare. In the *Penseroso* we have, instead of the walk by the bright dawn, the contemplative wandering in the moonlit forest; the song of the nightingale, and the solemn sound of the curfew "over some wide-watered shore, swinging slow with sullen roar;" and the meditation over the glowing embers in some solitary chamber. The contemplative man passes the long watches of the night in penetrating the sublime mysteries of philosophy with Plato, in studying the solemn scenes of the great dramatists of Greece, in following the wild and wondrous legends of chivalric tradition and poetry; and the daily walk is amid the deep recesses of some fairy-haunted forest, where the imagination is filled with the half-seen glories beside some stream round which floats a mysterious music. The poem ends with an aspiration after an old age of hermit-like repose and contemplation.

No analysis will give any idea of the immense riches of description with which these poems are crowded. There is hardly an aspect of external nature, beautiful or sublime, terrible or smiling, which is not expressed here; sometimes, as is ever the case in poetry of the highest order, in an incredibly condensed form. There are many examples of a whole picture exhibited in a single word, stamped with one inimitable expression, by a single stroke: as, for example, the "dappled dawn;" the cock which "stoutly struts his dames before;" the sun, at his rising, "robed in flames and *amber* light;" the hill "hoar with the floating mists of dawn;" the "fallows gray;" the towers of the ancient manor "*bosomed* high in tufted trees;" the "*tanned* haycock;" the peasants "dancing in the *chequered* shade." In like manner does the *Penseroso* abound with inimitable examples of picturesque word-painting What a figure is that of Melancholy! "all in a robe of darkest grain flowing with majestic train," fixed in holy rapture, till she "forgets herself to marble;" and the song of Philomel "smoothing the rugged brow of night;" "the *wandering* moon *riding* near her highest noon," and "*stooping* through a fleecy cloud!" All have seen this: how few have embodied it in verse! The glowing embers that "teach light to counterfeit a gloom;" or Tragedy "*sweeping by* in sceptred pall;" the "iron tears" drawn down the cheek of Pluto by the song of Orpheus; and "minute drops" falling as the shower passes away; the "high-embowed roof" and "storied windows" of a Gothic cathedral, with their "dim religious light." What poet has so vividly painted all that is most striking in nature and in art? Be it remembered, too, that the strokes so rapidly enumerated are merely examples of happy expressions concentrated into a single word. The two poems abound in pictures not inferior in beauty to these, but developed at a length which precludes my quoting them here. Indeed to quote the beauties of these two works would be to transcribe them from beginning to end. The *Allegro* and *Penseroso* have been justly called not so much poems as stores of imagery from which might be drawn materials for volumes of picturesque description. Like all Milton's works, admirable as they are in themselves, they are a thousand times more valuable for their peculiarly *suggestive* character — filling the mind, by allusion to other images, natural and artificial, with impressions of tenderness or grandeur.

§ 9. The Latin and Italian productions of Milton may not unsuitably be considered in this place, as their composition belongs principally to the youth of the poet. In the felicity with which he has reproduced the diction of classical antiquity, Milton has never had an equal among the modern writers of Latin verse. Not even Buchanan, far less such authors as Johannes Secundus, has reached a more consummate purity of expression, or attained — which is far more difficult — the style of antique *thought*, and avoided the intrusion of modern ideas. He not only writes like Tibullus and Propertius, but he also *feels* like them: we never meet with the incongruity of modern ideas clumsily masquerading in classical costume. The *Elegies* of Milton, however, graceful as they are, are less interesting than the *Epistolæ* addressed to his literary friends: as, for example, the exquisite *Mansus*, and the Latin verses to Charles Deodate. These, from their personal and intimate character, possess the charm of bringing us nearer to the thoughts, the tastes, and the individual occupations of the poet. They are totally free from that air of being a *cento* or a *pasticcio*, which is the prevailing defect of modern Latin poetry; their author seems always to think and feel as well as to write in the language he employs. In many passages, too, of these poems we see striking examples of that powerful conception which distinguishes Milton; as in his verses on the *Gunpowder Plot* there are impersonations which give us a foretaste of the *Paradise Lost*. The Italian poems of Milton are chiefly sonnets, and exhibit the same acquaintance with the forms and spirit of that species of composition, though perhaps hardly so much ease as the Latin works.

As a writer of sonnets it would be unjust to try Milton by any other standard than by his English productions in this department. Though a few are playful and almost ludicrous in their subject, the majority of the sonnets are of that lofty, grave, and solemn character which seems most congenial to the spirit of Milton. In the universal taste for imitating the types of Italian poetry, English writers, almost from the beginning of our literature, had cultivated this delicate exotic. Sidney, Spenser, Shakspeare, and a host of inferior poets, had written sonnets, some of a very high degree of beauty; but it was reserved to Milton to transport into his native country the Italian sonnet in its highest form. Macaulay justly observes that Milton's sonnets have none of that enamel-like brilliancy of expression which marks the sonnets of Petrarch: they are also free from the cold and pedantic conceits, and from that tone of scholastic ingenuity, which frequently deform the conceptions of the lover of Laura. Milton's sonnets are hardly ever on the subject of love; religion, patriotism, domestic affection, are his themes; and the great critic I have just quoted has most happily compared them to the Collects of the English Liturgy. Among the finest of them I may specify the following: I. *To the Nightingale*, VII. and VIII. containing a noble anticipation of his poetical glory; XIII. addressed to his friend Lawes, in which Milton at once describes and exemplifies the sweetness of Italian song; XVI. a noble recapitulation of Cromwell's victories; XVIII. on the *Massacre of the Piedmontese Protestants;* XIX. *on his own blindness*, one of the sublimest as well as the most interesting from its personal subject; XX. a charming invitation to his friend Lawrence, describing the pleasures of an Attic and philosophic festivity. Both Horace and Juvenal have similar passages; and I know not whether Milton, though infinitely more concise, has not described more beautifully than they the unbending of a wise and cultivated mind. The XXIId. sonnet is on the same subject as the XIXth., and the poet has treated his blindness in a no less awful spirit of religious resignation mingled with patriotic pride. In the XXIIId. sonnet, which in spirit is not unlike many passages in the *Vita Nuova* of Dante, and will fully bear a comparison with the famous *Levòmmi il mio Pensier* of Petrarch, the poet describes a dream in which he saw in a vision his second wife, whose death he so deeply deplored.

§ **10.** The second period of Milton's literary life is filled with political and religious controversy. In the very voluminous prose works belonging to this epoch we see at once the ardor of his convictions, the loftiness of his personal character, and the force and grandeur of his genius. Those who are unacquainted with his prose works are utterly incapable of forming an idea of the entire personality of Milton. Whether written in Latin or in English, these productions bear the stamp of his mind. They are crowded with vast and abstruse erudition; and the learning is, as it were, *fused* into a burning mass by the fervor of enthusiasm. The prose style of Milton is remarkable for a weighty and ornate magnificence, which in any other hands would be cumbrous and pedantic, but under the burden of which he moves with as much ease as did the champions of the Round Table under their ponderous panoply. When lashed to anger by the calumnies directed against the purity of his personal life, he gives us, in majestic eloquence, a picture of his own studies, labors, and literary aspirations, interesting in themselves, and striking from the beauty of the language. Glorious bursts of piety and patriotism, "a sevenfold chorus of halleluias and harping symphonies," show him ever and anon rising to a superhuman height. No style presents so hopeless a subject for imitation as that of Milton's prose. The immense length and involution of the sentences, its solemn and stately march, defy all mimicry; consequently there is no style so characteristic of its author — none which so completely stands alone in literature. Even when writing English, Milton seems to think in Latin. His frequent inversions, and his general preference for words of Latin origin, contribute to make him in some respects the most Roman of all English authors. This quality, however, while it testifies to his learning and his originality, has undoubtedly tended to exclude Milton's prose writings from that place among the popularly-read English classics to which their eloquence undoubtedly entitles them. There is no doubt that they are becoming every day better known to the general reader, and that their popularity is certain to extend still farther. The finest of them, at least the most calculated to attract the notice of the literary student, are the *Areopagitica*, the *Defensio Secunda*, the *Defensio Populi Anglicani*, the *Reasons of Church Government urged against Prelaty*, the *Apology for Smectymnuus*, and the *Tractate on Education.*

§ 11. There is no spectacle in the history of literature more touching and sublime than Milton blind, poor, persecuted, and alone, "fallen upon evil days and evil tongues, with dangers and with darkness compassed round," retiring into obscurity to compose those immortal Epics which have placed him among the greatest poets of all time. The calm confidence with which he approached his task was the fruit of long meditation, profound study, and fervent prayer. The four great Epic Evangelists, if we may so call them without irreverence, respectively symbolize the four great phases of the history of mankind. Homer is the poetical representative of the boyhood of the human race, Virgil of its manhood. These two typify the glory and the greatness of the antique world, as exhibited under its two most splendid forms — the heroic age in Greece, and the majesty of Roman empire. Christianity is the culminating fact in the history of mankind: it is like the mountain ridge from which diverge two rivers running in opposite directions. As the antique world produced two great epic types, so did Christianity — Dante and Milton. Dante represents the poetical side of Catholic, Milton of Protestant Christianity; Dante its infancy, its age of faith and heroism; Milton its virile age, its full development and exaltation. Dante is the Christian Homer, Milton the Christian Virgil. If the predominant character of Homer be vivid life and force, and of Virgil majesty and grace, that of Dante is intensity, that of Milton is sublimity. Even in the mode of representing their creations a strong contrast may be perceived: Dante produces his effect by realizing the ideal, Milton by idealizing the real.

The *Paradise Lost* was originally composed in ten Books or Cantos, which were afterwards so divided as to make twelve. Its composition, though the work was probably meditated long before, occupied about seven years; that is, from 1658 to 1665. I will give a rapid analysis of the poem, condensed from Milton's own plan prefixed to the various cantos. In *Book I.*, after the proposition of the subject, the Fall of Man, and a sublime invocation, are described the council of Satan and the infernal angels, their determination to oppose the designs of God in the creation of the Earth and the innocence of our first parents, and the description of the erection of Pandemonium, the palace of Satan. *Book II.* describes the debates of the evil spirits, the consent of Satan to undertake the enterprise of temptation, his journey to the Gates of Hell, which he finds guarded by Sin and Death. *Book III.* transports us to Heaven, where, after a dialogue between God the Father and God the Son, the latter offers himself as a propitiation for the foreseen disobedience of Adam. In the latter portion of this canto Satan meets Uriel, the angel of the Sun, and inquires the road to the new-created Earth, where, disguised as an angel of light, he descends. *Book IV.*

brings Satan to the sight of Paradise, and contains the picture of the innocence and happiness of Adam and Eve. The angels set a guard over Eden, and Satan is arrested while endeavoring to tempt Eve in a dream. He is, however, allowed to escape. In *Book V.* Eve relates her dream to Adam, who comforts her; and they, after their morning prayer, proceed to their daily employment. They are visited by the angel Raphael, sent to warn them; and he relates to Adam the story of the revolt of Satan and the disobedient angels. In *Book VI.* the narrative of Raphael is continued, and the triumph of the Son over the rebellious spirits. *Book VII.* is devoted to the account given by Raphael, at Adam's request, of the creation of the world. In *Book VIII.* is pursued the conference between the angel and Adam, who describes his own state and recollections, his meeting with Eve, and their union. The action of *Book IX.* is the temptation first of Eve, and then, through her, of Adam. *Book X.* contains the judgment and sentence, by the Son, of Adam and Eve, who are instructed to clothe themselves. Satan, triumphant, returns to Pandemonium, but not before Sin and Death construct a causeway through Chaos to Earth. Satan recounts his success, but is with all his angels transformed into serpents. Adam and Eve bewail their fault, and determine to implore pardon. *Book XI.* relates the acceptance of Adam's repentance by the Almighty, who, however, commands him to be expelled from Paradise. The angel Michael is sent to reveal to Adam the consequences of his transgression. Eve laments her exile from Eden, and Michael shows Adam in a vision the destiny of man before the Flood. *Book XII.* continues the prophetic picture shown to Adam by Michael of the fate of the human race from the flood. Adam is comforted by the account of the Redemption and rehabilitation of man, and by the destinies of the Church. The poem terminates with the wandering forth of our first parents from Paradise.

The peculiar form of blank verse in which this poem, as well as the *Paradise Regained*, is written, was, if not absolutely invented by Milton, at least first employed by him in the narrative or epic form of poetry. Though consisting mechanically of precisely the same elements as the dramatic metre employed by Shakspeare and his contemporaries, this kind of verse acquires, in the hand of Milton, a music of a totally different tone and rhythm. It is exceedingly solemn, dignified, and varied with such inexhaustible flexibility that the reader will hardly ever be able to find two verses of similar structure and accentuation — at least except at a considerable distance from each other. Every modification of metrical foot, every conceivable combination of emphasis, is employed to vary the harmony; and in this respect Milton has given to his metrical structure an ever-changing cadence, as beautiful in itself, and as delicately responsive to the impressions required to be conveyed, as can be found in the multitudinous billow-like harmonies of the Homeric hexameter, whose regular yet varied cadence has been so well compared to the roll of the ocean.

§ 12. In the incidents and personages of the poem we find extreme simplicity united with the richest complexity and inventiveness. Where it suited his purpose, Milton closely followed the severe condensation of the scriptural narrative, where the whole history of primitive mankind is related in a few sentences; and where his subject required him to give a loose to his invention, he showed that no poet ever surpassed him in fertility of conception. The description of the fallen angels, the splendors of Heaven, the horrors of Hell, the ideal yet natural loveliness of Paradise, exhibits not only a perception of all that is awful, sublime, or attractive in landscape and natural phenomena, but the power of overstepping the bounds of our earthly experience, and so realizing scenes of superhuman beauty or horror, that they are presented to the reader's eye with a vividness rivalling that of the memory itself. The characters introduced, the Deity and His celestial host, Satan and his infernal followers, and, perhaps, above all the ideal and heroic, yet intensely human personages of our first Parents in their state of innocence, bear witness alike to the fertility of Milton's invention, the severity of his taste, and the loftiness of what we may style his artistic morality. In Dante and Tasso the evil spirits, powerfully and picturesquely as they may be described, are composed of the common elements of popular superstition: they are monsters and bugbears, with horns, and tails, and eyes of glowing braise: and in their action we see nothing but savage malignity exaggerated to colossal proportions. Milton's Satan is no caricature of the popular demon of vulgar superstition: he is not less than Archangel, though archangel ruined; and in him, as well as in his attendant spirits, the poet has given sublimity as well as variety to his infernal agencies, by investing them with the most lofty or terrible attributes of the divinities of classical mythology. In employing this artifice he was able to pour out upon this department of his subject all the wealth of his incomparable learning, and to make his descriptions as suggestive as they are beautiful. Indeed, the mode by which he impresses the imagination is partly derived from the power, grandeur, and completeness of his own conceptions, and partly by the indirect allusions wherein his subsidiary illustrations revive in our minds all the impressions left in them by natural beauty, by the finest passages of other poets, and by all that is most striking in art, in history, and in legend. Milton is pre-eminently the poet of the learned; for however imposing may be his pictures even to the most uncultivated intellect, it is only to a reader familiar with a large extent of classical and Biblical reading that he displays his full powers. Of him may be eminently said that "he who reads, and to his reading brings not" a spirit, if not equal yet trained at least in somewhat similar discipline as his own, the half of his beauties will be imperceptible. In the personages and characters of Adam and Eve he has solved perhaps the most difficult problem presented by his undertaking — that of representing two human beings in a position which no other human beings ever did or ever can occupy; and endowed with such feelings and sentiments as they alone could have experienced. They are beings worthy of the Paradise they inhabit;

and though raised to heroic and ideal proportions, their moral and intellectual qualities are such as we can understand and consequently sympathize with. There is nothing more admirable than the intense humanity with which Milton has clothed them; while at the same time they are truly ideal impersonations of love, innocence, and worship. Like the finest relics of ancient sculpture, or the consummate works of early Italian painting, they reach the full majesty of the divine without forfeiting the human and the real.

In the conduct and development of the plot of his poem Milton unites the merits of simplicity and complexity. He follows closely, when it suits his purpose, the severe concision of the Biblical narrative, and at the same time gives a loose to his mighty invention in the scenes of Hell, of Heaven, and particularly in the episodical description of the revolt and punishment of the Fallen Angels. It has been objected that Adam is only the nominal hero of *Paradise Lost*, and that the real protagonist is Satan; and it is certainly true that the necessarily inferior nature of man, as compared with the tremendous agencies of which he is the sport, reduces him, apparently at least, to a secondary part in the drama; but this difficulty is surmounted by the dignity and *moral* elevation which Milton has given to his human personages, and by his making them the central pivot round which revolves the whole action. To speak of particular passages, either of sentiment or description, in which Milton exhibits beauty or sublimity, would be quite inappropriate in an essay whose limits are confined: I may remark, that in every instance where his imagination and plastic power are seen at work, we find him at once soaring from the sensible into the abstract.

If the genius of Dante be eminently analytic, that of Milton is as obviously synthetic: where the former takes captive your credulity by the intense realization — often attained by the most matter-of-fact details of measurement or comparison — of the awful objects which he sets, as it were, before your bodily eye, the latter hurries your imagination into the realms of the ideal by suggesting what you dimly conceive rather than have ever seen. Thus in a somewhat parallel passage of the two poets, Dante, wishing to convey the conception of the size of a monstrous giant, gives you an exact measurement of some of its parts, and compares them to some well-known and familiar object; Milton, on the other hand, makes the giant bulk of the thunder-smitten demon lie extended "many a rood" upon the burning billows, and instantly goes off into picturesque details of the "small night-foundered skiff moored to the scaly rind of the whale to which Satan is compared: or again, in that passage of unequalled grandeur where the evil spirit defies the archangel who has detected him: —

> "On the other side, Satan, alarmed,
> Collecting all his might, dilated stood,
> Like Teneriffe or Atlas, unremoved.
> His stature reached the sky, and on his crest
> Sat horror plumed."

The whole poem is crowded with similar examples of the idealizing tendency, which no poet ever possessed in an equal degree, and which is always united with Milton's peculiar taste for illustrating his pictures by means of subsidiary allusions suggesting the finest and most imposing objects in art, in legend, in nature, and in poetry.

§ 13. The companion-poem to the great Epic, the Odyssey to the Christian Iliad, is the *Paradise Regained*. It is much shorter than the first work, and consists of only Four Books or Cantos. The subject is the Temptation of Christ by Satan in the Wilderness; and the poet has closely followed the narrative of that incident, as recorded in the fourth chapter of St. Matthew's Gospel. It is, however, evident that the only event comparable in importance to the Fall of Man was the Redemption of Man through the voluntary sacrifice of the Saviour; and that the Cross is the natural counterpart to the Tree of the Knowledge of Good and Evil; Calvary the true *pendant* to Eden. It is uncertain whether to attribute to advanced age or the consciousness of failing powers Milton's selection for the subject of his second epic, of an event in the history of Our Lord which, however important in itself, is unquestionably far less momentous than the consummation of the great act of human redemption. Some have ascribed this choice to certain modifications of belief experienced by the poet in the decline of life, and which prevented him from selecting the Crucifixion as a subject. Into this mysterious question it would be misplaced to enter here; I will content myself with noting that the universal consent of readers places the *Paradise Regained*, in point of interest and variety, very far below the *Paradise Lost*. The inferiority of interest is, of course, attributable to its want of action; the whole poem being occupied with the arguments carried on between Christ and the Tempter, and the description of the kingdoms of the earth as contemplated from the summit of the mountain. Even in *Paradise Lost* the long and sublime dialogues, frequently turning on the most arduous subtleties of theology, though they probably enjoyed a great popularity in Milton's own day, when such subjects formed topics of universal discussion, are now often found to be tedious; but in that poem they are relieved by the perpetual interference of action. In *Paradise Regained* the genius of Milton appears in its ripest and completest development: the self-restraint of consummate art is everywhere apparent; and in the descriptions of Rome, Athens, Babylon, and the state of society and knowledge, the great poet has reached a height of solemn grandeur which shows him to have lost nothing either of imagination or of learning. Nevertheless the effect of the poem upon the general reader is less powerful than that of *Paradise Lost*. A rapid analysis of the poem would be as follows: — *Book I.* After being baptized, Jesus offers to undertake the defeat of the plans meditated by Satan. He retires into the wilderness. Satan appears under the disguise of an old peasant, and endeavors to justify himself. *Book II.* contains a consultation of the evil spirits, after which Satan tempts Our Lord with a banquet and afterwards with riches. In *Book III.* Satan pursues his attempts, endeavoring to excite ambition in the mind of the Saviour, and shows him the kingdoms of

Asia. *Book IV.* exhibits the greatness of Rome and the intellectual glories of Athens; and Our Lord, after being conveyed back to the desert, is exposed to a pitiless storm; Satan again appears, and, after carrying him to the pinnacle of the Temple, is again defeated and reduced to silence. The poem terminates with a triumphant hymn of the angels ministering to our Lord after His fast. In grandeur, elevation, and a kind of subdued sentiment, the *Paradise Regained* in no sense yields to its immortal companion; but in brilliancy of coloring and intensity of interest it is inferior. It may be said that the beauties of *Paradise Regained* will generally be more perceptible as the reader advances in life, and to those minds in which the contemplative faculty is more developed than the imagination.

§ **14.** To this, the closing period of Milton's literary career, belongs the Tragedy of *Samson Agonistes*, constructed according to the strictest rules of the Greek classical drama. In the character of the hero, his blindness, his sufferings, and his resignation to the will of God, Milton has given a most touching embodiment of himself. As in the Greek tragedies, the action is simple, the persons few, the statuesque severity of the dialogue is relieved by majestic outbursts of lyric verse placed in the mouth of the Chorus, and the catastrophe, which could not be represented worthily on the stage, is, after the Greek fashion, related by a messenger. The whole piece breathes the somewhat harsh but lofty patriotism and religion of the Old Testament, and the lyric-choruses are sometimes inexpressibly sublime. So closely has Milton copied all the details, literary as well as mechanical, of the ancient dramas, that there is no exaggeration in saying that a modern reader will obtain a more exact impression of what a Greek tragedy was, from the study of *Samson Agonistes*, than from the most faithful translation of Sophocles or Euripides. The ancient tragedies had always a religious or mythological element; and the Biblical character, for us, has a sanctity like that of the heroic legends for a Greek; and therefore Samson is to us a personage not dissimilar to what Prometheus or Hercules would have been to a Greek.

NOTES AND ILLUSTRATIONS.

CONTEMPORARIES OF MILTON.

Closely connected, principally in a political, but in some degree also in a literary relation, with Milton, is the truly venerable name of ANDREW MARVELL (1620-1678). He was born in 1620, educated at Cambridge, and employed the earlier part of his life in the diplomatic service, having been for some time attached to the English embassy at Constantinople. He afterwards gave instruction in the family of Fairfax, and was recommended by Milton to the President Bradshaw as a person very fit to be joined with himself in the execution of his office of Latin Secretary. This appointment he obtained though not till some time after, in 1657; and Marvell appears to have all along entertained the strongest admiration for his great colleague; an admiration founded on community of taste as well as conformity in political and religious opinions. Not long before the Restoration Marvell was sent to the House of Commons as representative for the town of Hull, and down to his death, in 1678, he continued to fulfil the duties of a good patriot and an honest man. Many striking anecdotes are related of his incorruptible integrity, of the constancy with which he resisted both the menaces and the caresses of the

Court, of whose arbitrary proceedings he was a vigorous opponent. But though many of these stories do not rest upon very good authority, their general similarity proves the character he enjoyed not only for virtue but for a pleasant and festive wit. He is said not to have been eloquent, but to have been listened to by all parties with respect; and his character seems to have conspicuously combined the severest rectitude with good nature and intelligence. He took an active part in the controversies of the day, and in several pamphlets powerfully denounced the arbitrary and papistical tendencies of the government. His works contain many interesting details of his long and familiar intercourse with Milton. He also deserves an honorable place among the minor poets of his time. His *Lamentation of the Nymph on the Death of her Fawn*, his song of *The Emigrants* (the Puritan exiles) *to Bermuda*, his *Thoughts in a Garden*, are full of sweet and pleasant fancies, and exhibit a great delicacy of expression, often exquisite from its very quaintness; as, for example, where he represents the oranges hanging in the tropic shade "like golden lamps in a green light," or, again, the fawn which "trod as if on the four winds," a most delicate hyperbole. In his satirical verses on the Dutch he has a droll exaggeration and ingenious buffoonery; many of the ideas are worthy of the quaint and learned fancy of Butler. It is difficult to find a more complete contrast than that presented by the conduct of Marvell as compared with that of Waller. They were both men of rare attainments; but while Marvell will always remain the type of the honest, incorruptible politician, faithful to his convictions, and the warm advocate of liberty and toleration, Waller is the ideal of the cowardly and selfish time-server.

Another political writer of this period is JAMES HARRINGTON (1611-1677), the author of the once famous republican theory embodied in the *Oceana*, which may be regarded as forming the counterpart to Hobbes's monarchical scheme of the *Leviathan*. He was learnedly brought up at Oxford, where he is said to have been the disciple of Chillingworth, and for a long time resided abroad in the diplomatic service, being at various times attached to the legations in Holland, Denmark, the Hague, and Venice. He was appointed one of the attendants upon King Charles I., when that unfortunate prince was a prisoner in the hands of the Parliament in 1647; and succeeded in inspiring the captive sovereign with feelings of confidence and attachment. He himself felt strong admiration for those high qualities of patience and magnanimity which misfortune developed in Charles's character. His great work, the *Oceana*, was published in 1656. It contains an elaborate project for the establishment of a pure republic upon philosophical principles, carried out to those minute details which are so frequently met with in paper constitutions, and which are so impracticable when attempted to be put in actual execution. His organization is based upon landed property, which, he maintains, is the only solid foundation for power; and the distinguishing characteristic of his plan is the principle of an elective administration, whose members are to go out of office by a complicated system of rotation. His exposition is clear and logical, but the method he proposes has the never-failing defect of all these scientific systems of ideal constitution-makers, viz., that of calculating upon results as if they could be predicted with unerring certainty upon mathematical premises. Political projectors from Plato down to the Abbé Siéyès, invariably forget that they have to do with the capricious elements of human nature and not with ciphers or the unvarying forces of inanimate nature. Harrington was the founder of the celebrated Rota Club; a society of political enthusiasts who met to discuss their theories, and to which belonged most of the philosophical republicans of that day — the Girondins of our English Revolution. In these discussions Harrington's mind was so heated that at last his reason gave way while undergoing an imprisonment to which he had been condemned; and in 1677 he died, after having been liberated from confinement and restored to the care of his friends in consideration of his insanity.

ALGERNON SIDNEY (1621-1683), another celebrated republican writer, the son of Robert, Earl of Leicester, and executed in the reign of Charles II., wrote a work entitled *Discourses on Government*, which was not published till 1698. It is a refutation of the patriarchal theory which is most fully propounded in the *Patriarcha* of SIR ROBERT FILMER, written in the reign of Charles I., but not published till 1680. Filmer's fundamental principle is, that the paternal authority is absolute, and that the first kings, being fathers of families, have transmitted this power to their descendants. Filmer's work was answered by Locke immediately after the Revolution (p. 272).

Our Revolution, so fertile in striking events and great orators, statesmen, and soldiers, was not without many noble instances of virtue and intellect exhibited by women. On the side of the friends of liberty appear two female figures glowing with the purest radiance — those of LADY RACHEL RUSSELL, wife of the illustrious patriot and martyr, and of LUCY HUTCHINSON, perhaps the most perfect idea of conjugal affection and constancy. Both occupy an honorable place in the literature of their times, the former by the admirable collection of letters written to her friends after the cruel bereavement she so nobly supported, and the latter by the memoirs which are among the most valuable and interesting documents of that agitated time. Lady Russell, whose husband was executed in 1683, survived till 1725, and her correspondence was collected and published after her death.

CHAPTER XII.

THE AGE OF THE RESTORATION.

§ 1. SAMUEL BUTLER: his life. § 2. Subject and nature of *Hudibras*. § 3. Butler's miscellaneous writings. § 4. JOHN DRYDEN: his life. § 5. His dramas § 6. His poems. *Absalom and Achitophel.* The *Medal.* *Mac-Flecknoe* § 7. *Religio Laici* and the *Hind and Panther*. § 8. *Odes.* Translations of *Juvenal* and *Virgil.* § 9. *Fables.* § 10. Dryden's prose works. § 11. JOHN BUNYAN: his life. § 12. His works. *Grace abounding in the Chief of Sinners.* § 13. *The Pilgrim's Progress.* § 14. *The Holy War.* § 15. EDWARD HYDE, EARL OF CLARENDON. § His *History of the Great Rebellion.* § 17. IZAAK WALTON. His *Lives* and *Complete Angler*. § 18. MARQUESS OF HALIFAX. JOHN EVELYN. § 19. SAMUEL PEPYS. § 20. SIR ROGER L'ESTRANGE.

§ 1. IF the greatest name among the Puritan and Republican party be that of Milton, the most illustrious literary representative of the Cavaliers is certainly SAMUEL BUTLER (1612-1680). However opposed in political opinions, and however different in the nature of their works, these two men have some points of resemblance, in the vastness of an almost universal erudition, and in the immense quantity of *thought* which is embodied in their writings. The life of Butler was melancholy; the great wit was incessantly persecuted by disappointment and distress; and he is said to have died in such indigence as to have been indebted for a grave to the pity of an admirer. He was born of respectable but not wealthy parentage in 1612, and began his education at Worcester Free School. Great obscurity rests upon the details of his career: thus there are contradictory traditions as to whether he studied at Oxford or at Cambridge, or even whether he enjoyed the advantages of a University training at all. In all probability the latter supposition is the truth, and lack of means deprived him of any lengthened opportunity of acquiring, at either University, any portion of that immense learning which his works prove him to have possessed. As a young man he performed the office of clerk to Jeffries, a country Justice of the Peace; and there is no doubt that he made himself acquainted with the details of English law procedure. He was afterwards — most likely by the protection of Selden, who knew and admired his talents, and who is said to have employed him as an amanuensis — preferred to the service of the Countess of Kent, in whose house Selden long resided, and to whom indeed he is said to have been secretly married. Here Butler enjoyed one of the few gleams of sunshine that cheered his unhappy lot; he possessed good opportunities for study in tranquil retirement, and he had the advantage of conversing with accomplished men. It is nearly certain that he was for some time in the service — in the capacity of tutor or clerk — of Sir Samuel Luke, a wealthy and powerful county magnate, and who figured prominently in those troubled times as a violent republican member of Parliament, and as one of Cromwell's provincial satraps, half military and half political. In the house of Luke, who was an ardent fanatic, Butler had the opportunity of accumulating those innumerable traits of bigotry and absurdity which he afterwards interwove into his great satire on the Puritans and Independents; and Luke himself, it seems almost indubitable, was the original of Butler's inimitable caricature of Hudibras, in which he embodies all that was odious, ridiculous, and vile in the politics and religion of the dominant party. His great work, the burlesque satire of *Hudibras*, was published in detached portions and at irregular intervals: the first part, containing the first three cantos, in 1663, the second part in the following year, and the third not until 1678. Though composed, in all probability, long before, the first instalment of this inimitable satire was obliged to await the Restoration to make its first appearance; for it was only that event, by inaugurating the triumph of Butler's loyal opinions, that could have secured the author from serious danger. The poem instantly became the most popular book of the age; for it gratified at once the taste for the highest wit and ingenuity, and the vindictive triumph of the Royalists over their enemies and tyrants. Charles II., with all his vices, was a man who could appreciate wit and learning. He carried about *Hudibras* in his pocket, was incessantly quoting and admiring it, and Butler's poem became as fashionable at court as the not superior satire of Rabelais had been in a former age. Very little solid recompense, however, accrued to Butler for his work. He was named Secretary to Lord Carbury, and in that capacity held for some time the office of Steward of Ludlow Castle, where the *Comus* of Milton had been presented before the Earl of Bridgewater by his accomplished children; but soon after Butler lost this place. It is said that Clarendon, then Chancellor, and Buckingham, as well as the King, had intended to do something for the illustrious supporter of their cause; but that a sort of fatality combined with the usual ingratitude of that profligate court to leave Butler in his former poverty; and the great wit is reported to have died, in extreme poverty, in a miserable lodging in Rose Street, Covent Garden (1680). He was buried, at the expense of his friend and admirer, Longueville, in the churchyard of St. Paul's in that poor neighborhood.

§ **2.** Butler's principal title to immortality is his burlesque poem of *Hudibras*, a satire upon the vices and absurdities of the fanatic or republican party, and particularly of the two dominant sects of the Presbyterians and Independents. It is indeed to the English Commonwealth Revolution what the satire Menippee is to the troubles and intrigues of the League. Its plan is perfectly original, though the leading idea may be in some measure referred to the *Don Quixote* of Cervantes; but as the object of Butler was totally different from that of the immortal Spanish humorist, so the execution is so modified as to leave the English work all the glory of complete novelty. The aim of Cervantes was to make us laugh at the extravagances of his hero, but without losing our love and respect for his noble and heroic character;

that of Butler was to render his personages as odious and contemptible as was compatible with the sentiment of the ludicrous. Don Quixote, though never ceasing to be laughable, is in the highest degree amiable and respectable: indeed it is only the discordance between his lofty chivalric sentiments and the low and prosaic incidents which surround him, that makes him ridiculous at all. Transport him to the age of the Round Table, and he is worthy to ride by the side of Lancelot or Galahad. Butler's hero — the combination of all that is ugly, cowardly, pedantic, selfish, and hypocritical — is on the very verge of being an object, not of ridicule, but of hatred and detestation; and hatred and detestation are tragic and not comic feelings. Butler has shown consummate skill in stopping short just where his aim required it. All comic writing, the object of which is to excite laughter, attains its effect by the principle of discordance or disharmony between its subject and treatment; for as harmony is a fundamental principle of the beautiful, so is discord a fundamental principle of the ludicrous: consequently comic representations, whether written, painted, or sculptured, naturally divide themselves into two categories, both attaining their end by the same principle, though exhibiting that principle in two different ways. In one we have a lofty and elevated subject intentionally treated in a low and prosaic manner; in the other a low and prosaic subject treated in a lofty and pompous manner; and in either case the contrast, or discord, between the subject and the treatment, being suddenly presented to the imagination, provokes that mysterious emotion which we call the sense of the ludicrous. In the former case is produced what we name *Burlesque*, in the second what we designate *Mock-heroic*.

The poem of *Hudibras* describes the adventures of a fanatic Justice of the Peace and his clerk, who sally forth to put a stop to the amusements of the common people, against which the Rump Parliament had in reality passed many violent and oppressive acts. Not only were the theatres suppressed, and all cheerful amusements proscribed, during that gloomy time, but the rougher pastimes of the lower classes, among which bear-baiting was one of the most favorite, were violently suppressed by authority. The celebrated story of Colonel Pride causing the bears to be shot by a file of soldiers furnished the enemies of the Puritan government with inexhaustible materials for epigram and caricature. Be it observed that these severe measures were in no degree prompted by any motive drawn from the brutal cruelty of the sport, but simply from a systematic hostility to everything that bore a semblance of gayety and amusement. Sir Hudibras, the hero of Butler, and who, as already remarked, is in all probability a caricature of Sir Samuel Luke, is described, both in his person and equipment, and in his moral and intellectual features, as a combination of pedantry, cowardice, ugliness, and hypocrisy, such as, for completeness, oddity of imagery, and richness of grotesque illustration, no comic writer, neither Lucian, nor Rabelais, nor Voltaire, nor Swift, has surpassed. He is the type or representative of the Presbyterian party. His clerk Ralph

— the Sancho Pança of this odious Quixote — is the satiric portrait of the sour, wrong-headed, but more enthusiastic Independent sect. The versification adopted by Butler, as well as the name of his hero, is drawn from the old Anglo-Norman Trouvère poets, and the Legends of the Round Table; and the baseness of the incidents, the minuteness of the details, and the long dialogues between the personages, form a parody the comic impression of which is heightened when we think of the stately incidents of which the poem is a burlesque. Sallying forth to stop the popular amusements, Sir Hudibras and his Squire encounter a procession of ragamuffins conducting a bear to the place of combat. They refuse to disperse at the summons of the knight, when a furious mock-heroic battle ensues, in which, after varying fortunes, Hudibras is victorious, and succeeds in incarcerating in the parish stocks the principal delinquents. Their comrades return to the charge, liberate them, and place in durance in their stead the Knight and Squire, who are in their turn liberated by a rich widow, to whom Sir Hudibras, purely from interested motives, is paying his court. Hudibras afterwards visits the lady, and receives a sound beating from her servants disguised as devils; and he afterwards consults a lawyer and an astrologer to obtain revenge and satisfaction. The merit, however, and the interest of this extraordinary poem by no means consist in its plot. Such incidents as are introduced are indeed described with extraordinary animation and a grotesque richness of invention; but there is a complete want of unity and connection of interest, and there cannot be traced any general combination of events into an intrigue, or leading to a catastrophe.

A long interval elapsed between the publication of the first and last canto, and in that interval the politics of the day had undergone a complete change. Butler, whose main object was to satirize the follies and wickedness of the reigning party, was obliged to direct his shafts against quite other vices and totally different persons: thus in the last canto he describes the general breaking up of the Rump Parliament, and the events immediately preceding the Restoration. His poem in general, like the adventure of the Bear and Fiddle which it contains, "begins, and breaks off in the middle." But no reader probably ever regretted the irregular and undecided march of the story; for the pleasure given by *Hudibras* is quite independent of the gratification of that kind of curiosity which finds its aliment in a well-developed intrigue. The astonishing fertility of invention displayed in the descriptions both of things and persons, the analysis of character exhibited in the long and frequent dialogues (principally between Hudibras and Ralph), the vivid and animated painting of the incidents, and above all the immeasurable flood of witty and unexpected illustration which is poured forth throughout the whole poem — these are the qualities which have made Butler one of the great classics of the English language. Wit is the power of tracing unexpected analogies, whether of difference or resemblance; the faculty of bringing together ideas, apparently incongruous, but between which, when so brought together, the ordinary mind, though itself totally incapable of bringing them into contact, at once perceives their relation; and this perception, suddenly excited, is accompanied by a flash of pleasure and surprise. From the juxtaposition of the two poles of the galvanic wire, each previously cold and inert, darts forth a lightning-like spark of heat and radiance. The reader, being made the conducting body of this magic flash of wit, feels for the moment all the pleasure of the discoverer of the hidden relation. This power of associating ideas and images apparently incongruous, no author ever possessed in so high a degree as Butler; his learning was portentous in its extent and variety: and he appears to have accumulated his vast stores, not only in the beaten tracks, but in the most obscure corners and out-of-the-way regions of books and sciences. The amount of *thought* as well as reading he displays is almost terrifying to the mind; and he surprises not only by the unexpected images supplied by his immense reading, but quite as often by what is suggested by his fertile and ever-working imagination. The effect of the whole is augmented by the easy, rattling, conversational tone of his language, in which the most colloquial, familiar, and even vulgar expressions are found side by side with the pedantic terms of art and learning. The metre, too, is singularly happy; the short octosyllable verse carries us on with unabating rapidity; and the perpetual recurrence of odd and fantastic rhymes, whose ingenuity is artfully concealed under an appearance of the most unstudied ease, produces a series of pleasant shocks that awaken and satisfy the attention.

Butler is at once intensely concise and abundantly rich. His expressions, taken singly, have the pregnant brevity of proverbs; while the fertility of his illustrations is perpetually opening new vistas of comic and witty association. He is as suggestive in his manner of writing as Milton himself; but while our great epic poet fills the mind, by indirect allusion, with all images that are graceful, awful, or sublime, Butler brings to bear upon his satiric pictures an unbounded store of ideas drawn from the most recondite sources. Milton leads the reader's mind to wander through all the realms of nature, philosophy, and art; Butler brings the stores of his knowledge and reading to our door. It is this marvellous condensation in his style, combined with the quaintness of his rhymes, that have caused so many of Butler's couplets to become proverbial sayings in common conversation, and to be frequently employed by people who perhaps do not know whence these sparkling fragments of wit and wisdom are derived. The contrast of characters in Hudibras and Ralph is of course far less dramatic than that between Don Quixote and his inimitable Squire; yet the delicacy and vivacity with which Butler has distinguished between two cognate varieties of pedantry and fanaticism are worthy of great admiration. The sophistries and rascally equivocations which abound in the long arguments between the Knight and his attendant are admirable. It is not to be expected that Butler, whose object was exclusively satirical, should have taken into consideration any of the nobler qualities of the fanatics whom he attacked; and therefore we must not be surprised to find their intense religious zeal painted otherwise than as hypocritical greed, and their undoubted courage transformed into cowardice. The poem is crowded with allusions to particular persons and events of the Civil War and Commonwealth; and consequently its merits can be fully appreciated only by those who are acquainted with the minute history of the epoch, for which reason Butler is eminently one of those authors who require to be studied with a commentary; yet the mere ordinary reader, though many delicate strokes will escape him, may gather from *Hudibras* a rich harvest of wisdom and of wit. However specific be the direction of much of the satire, a very large proportion will always be applicable as long as there exist in the world hypocritical pretenders to sanctity, and quacks in politics or learning. Many of the scenes and conversations are universal portraitures; as, for example, the consultation with the lawyer, the dialogues on love and marriage with the lady, the scenes with Sidrophel, and a multitude of others. From Butler's writings alone there would be no difficulty in drawing abundant illustrations of all the varieties of wit enumerated in Barrow's famous enumeration: the "pat allusion to a known story, the seasonable application of a trivial saying; the playing in words and phrases, taking advantage from the ambiguity of their sense, or the affinity of their sound. Sometimes it is wrapped in a dress of humorous expression sometimes it lurks under an odd similitude; sometimes it is lodged in a sly question, in a smart answer, in a quirkish reason, in a shrewd intimation, in cunningly diverting or cleverly retorting an objection; sometimes it is couched in a bold scheme of speech, in a tart irony, in a lusty hyperbole, in a startling metaphor, in a plausible reconciling of contradictions, or in acute nonsense; sometimes an affected simplicity, sometimes a presumptuous bluntness, giveth it being; sometimes it riseth only from a lucky hitting upon what is strange, sometimes from a crafty wresting obvious matter to the purpose."

§ 3. A large mass of Butler's miscellaneous writings has been published; and a curious discovery was made, long after his death, of the commonplace book in which he entered the results of his reading, and such thoughts and expressions as he intended to work up into his writings. The posthumous miscellanies consist of prose and verse. Among the former are sketches of a series of characters somewhat in the manner of Theophrastus, Fuller, More, and Feltham. They are marked by that extreme pregnancy of wit and allusion which is so characteristic of his genius. The poems are in many instances bitter ridicule of the puerile pursuits which he attributes to the physical investigations of that day, and he is particularly severe upon the then recently-founded Royal Society; but he seems to be unjust to the ardor and success with which such researches were then carried on, and to have confounded with the sublime outburst of experimental philosophy the quackery and pedantry with which such movements are necessarily accompanied.

§ 4. The great name of JOHN DRYDEN (1631–1700) forms the connecting link between the English literature of the seventeenth century and the completely different turn of thought and style of writing which were introduced at the Restoration. His life in its general features occupies the quarter of a century succeeding that of Butler. He was born, of an ancient and wealthy county family, in 1631, and his father being an ardent Puritan, it is not surprising that he should have entered upon his literary career a partisan of the same religious and political doctrines, and gained his first laurels by composing, in heroic stanzas, a warm eulogium on Cromwell. He was solidly educated, first under the famous Busby at Westminster School, and afterwards at Trinity College, Cambridge. At the approach of the Restoration he abandoned, as was to be expected, his predilections in favor of Puritanism, and attached himself thenceforward to the Royalist party, which was not only more likely to reward literary and poetical merit, but the spirit of which was an atmosphere far more congenial to his character. The whole life of Dryden is filled with vigorous and unremitting literary labor, and presents but few events unconnected with the successive composition of his works. Theatrical pieces were then the best-rewarded and productive form of intellectual labor, and, therefore, though conscious of his own deficiency in some important elements of dramatic genius, Dryden principally devoted himself to the stage, making a legal engagement with the King's Company of Players to supply them regularly with three dramas every year. It proves his wonderful readiness and fertility, as well as his extraordinary industry, that he was long able to fulfil so arduous a contract; and the mind is struck with astonishment on contemplating the rapid succession of dramatic works in which, by majestic versification, brilliant dialogue, striking situations, romantic and picturesque incidents, he contrived to compensate for his want of pathos and delicate analysis of human nature. His dramatic works constitute a very large portion of his entire compositions, and both in their merits and their faults they are at once strikingly characteristic of the peculiar genius of their author, and of the state of taste at the period when they were written. His dramatic career began about the year 1662, with the *Duke of Guise*, the *Wild Gallant*, the *Rival Ladies*, the *Indian Emperor*, and many other pieces, tragic, comic, and romantic.

In 1663 the poet married Lady Elizabeth Howard, daughter of the Earl of Berkshire, a union which is not supposed to have much contributed to his happiness, the lady having been of a sour and querulous disposition; and whether from his own unfavorable experience, or from natural disposition, Dryden generally exhibits himself in the light if not of a professed misogynist, yet of one who delighted to gird at marriage. In 1667 he produced his first great poem of a kind other than dramatic, the *Annus Mirabilis*, intended to commemorate the great events, or rather the great calamities, of the preceding year, the terrible Plague and Fire of London, and the War with the Dutch, then the rivals of England for supremacy by sea. This poem, written in the peculiar four-lined stanza which Davenant had employed in his poem of *Gondibert*, Dryden made the vehicle for much ill-deserved eulogium upon the King, and much equally ill-founded glorification of the conduct of a naval war which was one of the most humiliating episodes of our history. The poem, however, gave abundant proof of the vigor, majesty, and force of Dryden's style, and proved him to be the rightful heir to the vacant throne of English poetry. At this time he wrote his *Essay on Dramatic Poetry*, in which he formally maintains the superiority of rhyme in theatrical dialogue, thus ranging himself openly on the side of the then dominant literary party, who endeavored to subject the English stage to the rules and principles of French tragedy. The theory he maintained in argument he at this time exemplified in practice, by composing many pieces, as *Tyrannic Love*, in rhyme. His good taste, however, afterwards enabled him to shake off the shackles of prejudice in this respect, and he returned to the far finer and more national system of blank verse which had been consecrated by the authority of the great dramatists of the Elizabethan era. At this period Dryden was appointed Poet Laureate, and Historiographer to the King, and for some time enjoyed the moderate salary of 200*l.* attached to the office.

During the whole of his life Dryden was engaged in literary and political squabbles, sometimes with envious rivals, as with Settle, a bad poet, whom the public and patrons sometimes preferred to him, sometimes with more powerful and dangerous adversaries, as with the eccentric and infamous Duke of Buckingham, who not only caricatured him with the assistance of zealous poetasters, on the stage in the famous burlesque of the *Rehearsal*, but on one occasion revenged himself on the poet by causing him to be waylaid by night and severely beaten by a number of bravoes or bullies, such as were often in the pay of the great men in those odious times. The incident, like the slitting of Sir John Coventry's nose, is disgracefully characteristic of a state of society, the tone of which, particularly in the higher and more fashionable classes, was, to use a popular but expressive term, eminently *blackguardly*.

In 1681 appeared the first part of one of Dryden's noblest and most original works, the political satire of *Absalom and Achitophel*, in which, under a transparent disguise of Hebrew names and allusions, he attacks the factious policy of the Chancellor Shaftesbury, and his intrigues with the Duke of Monmouth on the subject of the succession of the Duke of York. The second part of this poem was published three years after, but was principally written by Tate, Dryden having only contributed two hundred lines, and probably also revised the rest. To the same period belongs also the *Medal*, directed against the same bold and unscrupulous politician. The purely literary Satire, *Mac-Flecknoe*, in which Dryden takes a terrible revenge upon Settle and Shadwell, and which is as original in design as it is forcible in execution, belongs to the year 1682. Dryden's fertility was almost inexhaustible. In 1684 he produced the *Religio Laici*, an eloquent and vigorous defence of the Anglican Church against the Dissenters, and one of the finest controversial poems in any language. In 1686 Dryden abandoned the faith he had so powerfully defended, and embraced the Catholic doctrines, in which act he is unfortunately suspected of having been swayed in some degree by interested motives, as the change most suspiciously coincides with the efforts made by the King, James II., to convert every one, by threats or corruption, to the faith of which he was so bigoted a professor Dryden, nevertheless, may have been sincere in thus changing his religion; at all events he produced in defence of it a polemical poem, which, in spite of the fundamental absurdity of its plan, exhibits in a high degree his unequalled power of combining vigorous reasoning with sonorous verse and rich illustration. The poem was entitled the *Hind and Panther*, and will form the subject of some critical remarks in our general review of his works. It was published in 1687. In the following year the Revolution deprived the poet of that court favor which no Catholic or partisan of absolute monarchy could hope to retain; but this event was incapable of arresting the activity or chilling the fire of the great poet. He continued to write dramatic pieces, and gave to the world his excellent translation of Juvenal and Persius, with the former of which satirists his genius had many points of similarity. His translation of Virgil appeared in 1697, and seems to have been one of his most profitable literary ventures; it has been said that he gained 1200*l.* by this publication. At the same time he composed his *Ode on St. Cecilia's Day*, one of the noblest lyrics in the English language. Old age and broken health seem not to have been able to interrupt his career; for in 1700 he produced his *Fables*, a collection of tales either borrowed and modernized from Chaucer or versified from Boccaccio, in which his invention, fire, and harmony appear in their very highest power. In this year he died of a mortification in the leg, combined with dropsy; and was buried in Westminster Abbey, followed to the grave by the admiration of his countrymen, who saw that in him they had lost incomparably the greatest poet of the age.

§ 5. In considering the voluminous writings of Dryden, it will be advisable to review, first his dramas, then his various works in other departments of poetry, and lastly his prose.

In the drama Dryden is the chief representative of that great revolution in taste which followed the Restoration, when the sweet and powerful style of the romantic drama of the Elizabethan type was supplanted by an imitation of French models. The comic pieces of Dryden are marked by all and more than all the profound immorality which corrupted fashionable society at that odious period: and at the same time his deficiency in humor renders his pieces dull and stupid in spite of their extravagance, giving the reader no pleasantry to compensate for their grossness. The most flagrant instance of his ill-success in this branch was his comedy of *Limberham*, while it is but fair to remark that in the *Spanish Friar* there are scenes and characters of considerable merit. As the most popular and fashionable species of entertainment, the theatre was, of course, exposed to the full influence of the prevailing immorality, which was the reaction after the exaggerated severity of the Puritan times; and being a vice to which the stage is always of itself especially prone, this immorality was further intensified by the shameless profligacy of the court. Dryden, in yielding to this detestable tendency, merely followed the prevailing fashion; and though not perhaps personally a man of high spirit, showed, by the submission with which he received Jeremy Collier's well-merited rebuke on the indecency and irreligion of his plays, that he had the grace to be ashamed of faults which he had not the virtue to avoid.

The tragedy of this period forms a most amusing contrast to the comedy; while in the latter the vilest indecency was paraded with unblushing impudence, tragedy affected a tone of romantic enthusiasm and superhuman elevation far removed from nature and common sense. The heroes were incessantly represented as supernaturally brave, as involving themselves in the most abstruse casuistry of amorous metaphysics, originally traceable to the wire-drawn subtleties of the romances of the sixteenth century, and which in their turn had their origin in the Arrêts d'Amour of the Provençal troubadours. Self-sacrifice is pushed to the verge of caricature, and all the ordinary feelings of nature are violated to attain a sort of impossible ideal of heroic and amorous perfection. In the *Rival Ladies*, the *Indian Emperor*, *Tyrannic Love*, *Aureng-zebe*, *All for Love*, *Cleomenes*, *Don Sebastian*, and similar pieces, we see Dryden's dramatic genius, as we see the dramatic spirit of the age, in its power and in its weakness. Dryden had very little mastery over the tender emotions, and very little skill in the delineation of character: nor was he ignorant of his deficiencies in this respect: he tried, and with no mean success, to compensate for them by striking, unexpected, and picturesque incidents, by powerful declamatory dialogue, and by a majesty, ease, and splendor of versification. The kind of scenes in which Dryden exhibits his nearest approach to dramatic excellence are dialogues in which the speakers begin by violent recriminations and finish with reconciliation; scenes, in short, similar to the quarrel between Brutus and Cassius in the *Julius Cæsar* of Shakspeare. Conscious of his power, Dryden has frequently repeated situations of this kind; examples of which are the dispute between Antony and Ventidius in *All for Love*, a piece founded upon *Antony and Cleopatra*, and the still finer specimen of the same kind of writing between Dorax and the King in *Don Sebastian*. In such scenes Dryden reaches if not the level of Shakspeare, at least that of Massinger or Fletcher. In his eagerness to supply constant food to the craving for novelty, Dryden sometimes forgot that veneration for the genius of his predecessors which on other occasions he has eloquently expressed; thus, in conjunction with Davenant, he condescended to make alterations and additions to Shakspeare's *Tempest*, transforming that pure and ideal creation into a brilliant and meretricious opera, full of scenic effects, and containing, besides Miranda, the addition of a young man who has never seen a woman, giving full opportunity for those prurient allusions which were then so vehemently applauded. Similarly he did not scruple to transform the *Paradise Lost* into an operatic entertainment, in which the sublimity and purity of Milton are strangely disfigured. This piece was styled the *State of Innocence.* In those days *Prologues* and *Epilogues* formed an essential and favorite accompaniment to theatrical pieces; and they were written with great skill, containing either allusions to the topics of the moment or judgments on the great authors of the earlier stage; and, when delivered by a fascinating actress or a graceful tragedian, were received with enthusiastic applause. Dryden was equally adroit and fertile in this class of composition, and many of his prologues and epilogues are masterpieces both in the comic and elevated style. In many of the comic productions of this nature he unfortunately panders to the prevailing taste for loose allusion and equivoque, particularly in those which were delivered by Nell Gwynne and other frail but fascinating beauties.

§ 6. Even in the earliest productions of this poet, as in his *Heroic Stanzas* in praise of Cromwell, it is easy to perceive that force, vigor, and majestic melody of style which distinguish him above all the writers of his age, above all the writers of any age, perhaps, in the English literature. In some of his first attempts he adopted the form of the stanza, generally, as in his *Annus Mirabilis*, the four-lined alternately-rhymed stanza of the *Gondibert* of Davenant. But he ultimately preferred the rhymed heroic couplet of ten-syllabled lines, a measure which he carried to the highest perfection of which it is capable; and even in his stanzas we may clearly see that they possess the essential elements of this last form of versification, as each can be resolved into two sonorous couplets. This kind of metre Dryden wielded with singular force and mastery: whether he reasons, or describes, or declaims, or narrates, he moves with perfect freedom; and the regularity of the structure of his verse, and the recurrence of the rhyme, so far from appearing to shackle his movements, seem only to give majesty and impetus to his march. He frequently intersperses a third line, rhyming with the two preceding, and forming a triplet, and this third line, which is often an Alexandrine of twelve instead of ten syllables, winds up the period with a roll of noble harmony, —

> "A long-resounding march and melody divine."

Perhaps the greatest among his longer poems are those in which the subject is half-polemic and half-satirical. The *Absalom and Achitophel* contains a multitude of admirably drawn portraits, among which those of Shaftesbury, the Duke of Buckingham, Settle, Shadwell, and the infamous Titus Oates, remain in the memory of every reader. Nothing can better prove the extreme difference between the descriptive and dramatic manner of drawing characters than a comparison between the astonishing vivacity of these delineations and Dryden's weakness when endeavoring to represent human beings on the stage. In order to fully appreciate all the merits of this poem it is necessary to read it in connection with the history of the time, and to follow Dryden into his innumerable allusions to the questions and persons of the day; but even the general student, who will examine it from a purely literary point of view, will find in it the noblest examples of moral painting, always vigorous though not always just, and will perceive all the highest qualities of the English language as a vehicle for reasoning and description. The *Medal*, a satire directed, like the former, chiefly against the factious turbulence of Shaftesbury, contains passages not inferior.

Dryden has given us, in *Mac-Flecknoe*, the first example of purely literary and personal satire. Its object was his rival Shadwell; and the poet supposes his victim to be the successor in the supremacy of stupidity to a wretched Irish scribbler named Flecknoe, giving him to indicate this succession the title of Mac, the Celtic or Irish form of the patronymic. The satire is undoubtedly coarse and violent, but it contains numerous interesting details concerning the literature, and particularly the drama, of the day; and many passages are powerfully and bitterly original.

§ **7.** The two great controversial poems *Religio Laici* and the *Hind and Panther* exhibit in its highest perfection Dryden's consummate mastery in perhaps the most difficult species of writing, namely, poetry in which close reasoning on an abstract subject like theology should be combined with rich illustration and picturesque imagery. With the nature of his arguments it is not necessary to meddle; they are, both on the Protestant and Catholic side, the same that naturally present themselves to the disputant; and are based upon Scripture or tradition, upon induction or experience, as may best serve the writer's purpose. But the powerful and unfettered march of the reasoning, the abundance of picturesque illustration, and the noble outbursts of enthusiasm make us alternately converts to the one faith and to the other, and prove Dryden to be one of the greatest of ratiocinative poets. In the *Hind and Panther* we very soon get over the preliminary absurdity of the fable, in which the two animals that give the title to the poem are represented as engaging in an elaborate argument in favor of the two churches whose emblems they are — the "milk-white Hind" the Catholic, and the Panther the Church of England — as well as the representation of the other sects under the guise of wolves, bears, and a whole menagerie of animals. The opening of the *Religio Laici* is incomparably fine, as well as the allusions more than once made in both poems to the writer's own religious convictions. What is very curious is that Dryden, though unquestionably a man of strong pious aspirations, has always given a very unfavorable character of the clergy; and does not confine his satirical invectives to the priests of any one religion, but classes pagan augurs, Turkish imams, Egyptian hierophants in one common reprobation with Christian ministers of all sects, orthodox as well as sectarian.

§ **8.** The lyric productions of this poet are not numerous in proportion to their excellence. Interspersed among the scenes of his romantic dramas are many beautiful and harmonious songs; but his most celebrated production of this kind is his *Ode on St. Cecilia's Day*, written for music, and celebrating the powers and the triumph of the art. The narrative portion of this noble lyric is a description of the various passions excited by the Greek harper Timotheus in the mind of Alexander the Great, as he is feasting with his victorious chieftains in the royal halls of Persepolis. Joy, pleasure, pride, pity, terror, and revenge successively arise under the "mighty master's" touch, and the various strophes at once describe and exemplify the sentiment they paint. The poem concludes with an allusion to the fabled invention of sacred music by St. Cecilia. Dryden is said to have written this admirable poem at a single jet, and in the space of a few hours. It will always be regarded as one of the most energetic lyrics in the English language. In spite of some inequalities of expression, it rushes on with a flow and a swing like that of Pindar himself, and in many places the sound is an echo to the sense. It is the *Sinfonia Eroica* of Beethoven in words.

The translation into English verse of the *Satires of Juvenal and Persius* exhibits Dryden's power of transferring to his own language, not perhaps the exact sense of those difficult authors, but their general spirit. There was a considerable similarity between the tone of Dryden's mind and that of Juvenal; the same force, the same somewhat declamatory character, and the same unscrupulous boldness in painting what was odious and detestable: but the plain-spoken frankness of the Roman, in delineating the incredible corruption of the times of Domitian, degenerates into licentiousness in Dryden, who seems sometimes to gloat over descriptions which Juvenal introduced purely with an intention of exhibiting in all its horror the vice which he lashes. Our poet's most extensive work of poetical translation was his English version of *Virgil;* and though he has produced what will always be regarded as one of the great standard monuments of our literature, it may be regretted that the author he selected for translation was not one more accordant with his peculiar genius. Virgil's predominant quality is majesty indeed, but majesty always tempered with consummate grace; and Dryden, however characterized by majesty, was certainly deficient in grace and elegance. He seems himself to have become conscious of his error, and to have lamented that he had not rather chosen Homer. Two of our most illustrious poets, Dryden and Pope, have respectively translated Virgil and Homer: their glory would have been greater had they exchanged subjects. The robust and somewhat masculine genius of Dryden could not perfectly assume the virginal and ideal refinement of the Diana-like Muse of Mantua.

§ 9. The highest qualities of Dryden's literary genius never blazed out with greater splendor than when about to set forever in the grave. His *Fables*, as he called them, though they are in no sense fables, but rather tales in verse, exhibit all his noblest qualities, and are in general free from his defect of occasional coarseness. The subjects of these narratives are either modernized and paraphrased from Chaucer, or taken from the same sources whence Chaucer drew his materials, the Decameron of Boccaccio, and other French and Italian *novelle.* Among the revivals of Chaucer may be specified *Palamon and Arcite* (the

Knight's Tale), *January and May* (the Doctor's Tale), the *Cock and the Fox* (the Nun's Priest's Tale), and a paraphrase of Chaucer's character of the Good Parson; among the latter category the stories of *Cymon and Iphigenia* and *Theodore and Honoria.* These works are for the most part of considerable length; and it is curious to see how Dryden, with all his deep and sincere veneration for Chaucer, has failed to reproduce the more delicate and subtler qualities of his model. The splendor, the force, the picturesqueness of the original are indeed there; but the tender *naiveté*, the almost infantine pathos of the original, have quite evaporated, like some subtle perfume, in the process of transfusion. How far this is to be attributed to Dryden's own character — always deficient in tenderness — how far to the general tone of the age in which he lived, an age the very antipodes of sentiment, it is difficult to decide: in some degree, perhaps, that evanescent and subtle fragrance may be intimately connected with Chaucer's archaic language: but all who have attempted to modernize the father of our poetry have in a greater or less degree encountered the same insuperable difficulty. The diminution of tenderness is peculiarly perceptible in such passages as the dying speech of Arcite, and in many traits of the portrait of the Parson, to whom Dryden has communicated quite a modern air. These narratives, therefore, in order to produce their full effect, should be read as independent works of Dryden, without any reference either to Chaucer or Boccaccio; in which case they cannot fail to excite the liveliest admiration. The flowing ease with which the story is told, the frequent occurrence of beautiful lines and happy expressions, will ever make them the most favorable specimens perhaps of Dryden's peculiar merits.

§ **10.** Besides poetry, Dryden produced a very large quantity of prose, much of it of great value, not only for the style, but in many instances also for the matter. The form of his prose works was generally that of *Essays or Prefaces* prefixed to his various poems, and discussing some subject in connection with the particular matter in hand. Thus in his *Essay on Dramatic Poetry* he investigates the then hotly-argued question as to the employment of Rhyme in Tragedy; his Juvenal was accompanied with a most amusing treatise on Satire; indeed few of his poetical works appeared without some prose disquisition. In this way he has travelled over a vast field of critical inquiry, and given us invaluable appreciations of poets of his own and other countries. Dryden must be regarded as the first enlightened critic who appeared in the English language. His judgments concerning Chaucer, Shakspeare, and his mighty contemporaries, Milton and a multitude of other authors, do equal honor to the catholicity of his taste and the courage with which he expressed his opinions. His decisions may, indeed, sometimes be erroneous, but they are always based upon reflection and a ground, specious at least, if not solid. These works, besides, are admirable specimens of lively, vigorous, idiomatic English, of which no man, when he chose to avoid the occasional pedantic employment of fashionable French words, was a great master. The *Dedica* *tions* of many of his works to great and influential patrons, however little honor they may do to Dryden's independence of character, are singularly ingenious and well-turned; and in judging the tone of servility which such things display, we must not forget that it was the fashion of the time, and that a professional author, who lived by his pen, could hardly afford to sacrifice his interest to an assertion of dignity which no one at that time could understand.

§ **11.** Literature presents no more original personality than that of JOHN BUNYAN (1628–1688), the greatest master of allegory that ever has existed. He was born at the village of Elstow, near Bedford, in 1628. His father was a tinker, and the son in his youth followed the same humble calling. Though born in the very lowest rank of social life, and consequently enjoying very limited advantages of education, which appear in Bunyan's case to have extended no farther than simple reading and writing, he had before him the example of piety and morality, and at about the age of eighteen entered the military service in the Parliamentary army. In the strange and interesting religious autobiography which he wrote under the title of *Grace Abounding in the Chief of Sinners*, Bunyan has given a curious picture of his internal struggles, his despair, his conversion, and his acceptance by God; and the whole range of mystical literature does not offer a more touching confession. Like all enthusiasts, he much exaggerates the sinfulness of his original state; and the peace and confidence in Divine mercy, which he attained at the price of agonies such as almost overthrew his reason, and which are of themselves an evidence of the natural strength of his feelings, form a contrast with the gloom and despair from which he imagined himself to have been rescued by a miraculous interposition of heavenly grace. But it is certain that the irregularities he so deeply deplores were venial, if not altogether trifling, and that his conduct had always in the main been virtuous and moral. He married very young, and his worst vices appear to have been a habit of swearing, and a taste for ale-drinking and the pastime — always so popular among the English peasantry — of bell-ringing and playing at hockey and tip-cat. After experiencing the fearful internal struggles usual when strongly imaginative and impressionable minds are first brought under religious conviction, he joined, in 1655, the sect of the Baptists one of the most enthusiastic among the innumerable Calvinistic sects with which England was then seething; and he gradually attracted notoriety by the fervor of his piety and the rude eloquence of his discourses. Deeply sincere himself, and of a benevolent and loving disposition, he was eager to communicate to others those "glad tidings of great joy" which had been, as he imagined, divinely brought home to his own soul; and his powerful genius, combined with his religious ardor, must have given him vast power over the humble enthusiasts who composed his congregations.

At the time of the Restoration the government began to persecute with extreme severity the dissenting sects, which were in most cases identified with the political doctrines of the recently overthrown Com monwealth; and Bunyan, as a leading man among the Baptists, was necessarily exposed to these trials. After undergoing some minor persecutions, he was convicted of frequenting and upholding conventicles, and imprisoned for upwards of twelve years in the jail of Bedford. During this long confinement, the rigor of which, however, was gradually much relaxed towards its close, he supported himself by making tagged laces, and acquired the veneration of his companions by the benevolence with which he consoled them, and by the fervor of his religious exhortations. In prison, too, he enjoyed the society of his family, and particularly of his little blind daughter, of whom he was passionately fond. It was during this confinement that he composed his immortal allegory the *Pilgrim's Progress.* In the eleventh year of his imprisonment, when he was frequently allowed to leave the jail, he was chosen preacher of the Baptist congregation. The persecution against the sects having been gradually relaxed, in consequence of the Jesuitical policy of James II., who under the mask of general toleration wished insensibly to relieve the proscription that weighed upon the Catholics, Bunyan was at last liberated altogether; and in 1672 he had become a venerated and influential leader in his sect, preaching frequently both in Bedford and London. His sufferings, his virtues, his genius as a writer, and his eloquence as a pastor contributed to his fame. He died in 1688, in London, it is said in consequence of a cold caught in a journey undertaken by him in inclement weather with the object of reconciling a father and a son. His character appears to have been essentially mild, affectionate, and animated by a truly evangelical love to all men. He was kind and indulgent, and free from that narrow-minded sectarian jealousy which loves to confine the privileges of salvation to its own little *coterie;* and, though a leading member of a most fanatical and enthusiastic persuasion, he exhibited a rare example of Christian charity and a truly catholic love for all mankind. In spite, however, of the real mildness and gentleness of his character, his external manners and appearance, as he has himself recorded, had something austere and forbidding; but this was only apparent, and, apart from a few of those childish and almost technical scruples in matters really indifferent, which may be called the badges of sectarian societies, Bunyan showed none of the sour and peevish narrowness which is the vice of such bodies. This is as honorable to him as it is extraordinary in itself, when we reflect upon his limited education and upon the almost irresistible tendency of the circumstances which surrounded him.

§ 12. The works of Bunyan are numerous; but there are only three among them upon which it will be necessary for us to dwell. These are the religious autobiography entitled *Grace Abounding in the Chief of Sinners*, to which I have slightly alluded above, and the two religious allegories, the *Pilgrim's Progress* and the *Holy War*. In the first of these works Bunyan has given the minutest and most candid account of his own spiritual struggles and conversion. It is a book of the same order with the mystic writings of St. Theresa, with the Confessions of

St. Augustine, and not inferior in interest and originality to the Confessions of Rousseau. The author lays bare before us all the recesses of his heart, and admits us to the tremendous spectacle of a human soul working out by unspeakable agonies its liberation from the bonds of sin and worldliness. It is evident that Bunyan has enormously exaggerated the criminality of his unregenerate state, and that the enthusiasm of his character has, though in perfect simplicity and good faith, intensified both the lights and shades of the picture. The delineation, however, can never fail to possess interest either for the religious student or for the philosopher who loves to investigate the mysterious problems of our moral and spiritual nature. The gloom and the sunshine, the despair and the triumph, are alike reflected in the simple and fervent language of Bunyan; and the book abounds with those little inimitable touches of natural feeling and description which have placed its author among the most picturesque of writers.

§ 13. But it is in his allegories that Bunyan stands unrivalled, and particularly in the *Pilgrim's Progress.* This book, which is in two parts, the first beyond comparison the finest, narrates the struggles, the experiences, and the trials of a Christian in his passage from a life of sin to everlasting felicity. "Mr. Christian," dwelling in a city, is incited by the consciousness of his lost state, typified by a heavy burden, to take a journey to the New Jerusalem — the city of eternal life. All the adventures of his travel, the scenes which he visits, the dangers which he encounters, the enemies he combats, the friends and fellow-pilgrims he meets upon his road, typify, with a strange mixture of literal simplicity and powerful imagination, the vicissitudes of religious experience. Shakspeare is not more essentially the prince of dramatists that Bunyan is the prince of allegorists. So intense was his intellectual vision that abstract qualities are instantly clothed by him with personality, and we sympathize with his shadowy personages as with real human beings. In the fair or terrible scenes which he sets before us we feel our belief captivated as with real incidents and places. Thousands of readers, from the child to the accomplished man, have trembled and rejoiced, have smiled and wept, in sympathy with the joys and sufferings of Bunyan's personages. Dante possesses a somewhat similar power of *realizing* the conceptions of the imagination; but Dante took for his subjects real human beings, whom he placed in extraordinary positions, where they still retain their personality; while Bunyan clothes with flesh and blood the abstract and the imaginary. Spenser was a great master of allegory; but it is not with his persons, so much as with the brilliant and picturesque accessories that surround them, that we interest ourselves. The Red-Cross Knight, Una, Malbecco, and Britomart do not excite any very lively anxiety about their fate as persons; we follow their adventures with pleasure and curiosity, as we follow the unfolding incidents of a dramatic spectacle; but we no more identify ourselves with their fate than we do with that of so many actors after the fall of the curtain. But Bunyan's *dramatis personæ* we follow with a breathless sympathy, something like that with which we read *Robinson Crusoe* for the first time. This result is indeed in some degree to be ascribed to the simple, direct, unadorned style in which Bunyan wrote, and to the reality with which he himself conceived his persons and adventures.

The popularity of the *Pilgrim's Progress* was immediate and immense: it has continued to the present day; and the tale is one of the most fascinating to children and peasants. Indeed, there is hardly a cottage in England or Scotland where Bunyan's fiction does not find a place on the scanty book-shelf, between the Bible and the Almanac. Encouraged by the success of the first part, Bunyan was induced to compose a continuation, in which the wife and children of Christian go over nearly the same ground and meet with nearly similar adventures. The charm, however, of the second part is far inferior to that of the first; the invention displayed, though remarkable, is devoid of the freshness which marks the persons and incidents of Christian's journey. A great many scenes and characters in Bunyan's books, though intended to embody allegorical meanings, are evidently drawn from real life. The description of Vanity Fair, many of the landscapes so beautifully and vividly painted, and a large number of the personages and dialogues, bear all the marks of being transcripts from Bunyan's actual experience. The agitated times in which the book was written were abundant in strongly-marked characters, both good and bad; and we may accept, for example, the life-like scene of the accusation before the court of justice as a faithful picture of the incredible brutality and corruption of the tribunals of those evil days. Bunyan, like all great creators, was gifted with a lively sense of the humorous, and in the characters and adventures we frequently see a comic element of no inconsiderable merit. The sublime and the grotesque, the tender, the terrible, and the humorous, were alike tasted by this truly *popular* genius. In the largeness of his nature, as well as in the forcible and idiomatic picturesqueness of his language, he perfectly sympathizes with the people; and he has expressed their sentiments in their natural tongue. His knowledge of books was very small; but the English version of the Bible, in which our language exhibits its highest force and perfection, had been studied by him so intensely that he was completely saturated with its spirit. He wrote unconsciously in its style, and the innumerable scriptural quotations with which his works are incrusted like a mosaic, harmonize, without any incongruity, with the general tissue of his language. Except the Bible, from which he borrowed, consciously or unconsciously, the main groundwork of his diction, he probably was little acquainted with books. Fox's *Martyrs* and a few popular legends of knights errant, such as have ever been a favorite reading among the English peasantry, probably furnished all such materials as he did not find in the Scriptures. The Bible, indeed, he is reported to have known almost by heart.

With such intellectual training, applied to a mind naturally sensitive and enthusiastic, the style of a writer might be rude, harsh, nay, even sometimes ungrammatical, but it was sure to be perfectly free from vulgarity and meretricious ornament; and Bunyan is the most perfect representative of the plain, vigorous, idiomatic, and sometimes picturesque and poetical language of the common people. It resembles in its masculine breadth and solidity that ancient style of architecture which is improperly called Saxon; its robust pillars and stout arches, its combination of rugged stone and imperishable heart of oak, giving earnest of illimitable duration. It is surprising how universally Bunyan's diction is drawn from the primitive Teutonic element in our language: for pages together we sometimes meet with nothing but monosyllable and dissyllable words; with the exception of a few theological terms, his structure is built up of the solid granite that lies at the bottom of our speech. Of course it was impossible that the allegory could always be maintained; in a work of such length the spiritual type could not always be kept distinct from the bodily antitype; but the reader seldom experiences any difficulty from this cause, being carried forward by the vivacity of the narrative. The long spiritual discussions, expositions of theological questions, and exhortations addressed by one interlocutor to the others, not only afford curious specimens of the religious composition of those days, but increase the verisimilitude of the persons. These passages, too, show Bunyan's profound acquaintance with the language and the spirit of the Scriptures, and place in the strongest light his benevolent and evangelical Christianity. In his descriptions he is equally powerful whether the object he paints be terrible or attractive: the Valley of the Shadow of Death is placed before us with the same astonishing reality as the Delectable Mountains — a reality strongly recalling the Hell and Paradise of Dante. No religious writer has analyzed more minutely and represented more faithfully every phase of feeling through which the soul passes in its struggles with sin: the clearness of these pictures is rather increased than diminished by the allegorical dress in which they are clothed. In them Bunyan did but draw upon his own memory, and narrate his own experiences. He exhibits, too, that inseparable characteristic of the higher order of creative power, a constant sympathy with the simpler objects of external nature, and a preference of the great fundamental elements of human character.

§ **14.** The *Holy War* is an allegory typifying, in the siege and capture of the City of Mansoul, the struggle between sin and religion in the human spirit. Diabolus on the one hand and Immanuel on the other are the leaders of the opposing armies. In this narrative we see frequent traces of Bunyan's personal experience in military operations, such as he had witnessed while serving in the ranks of Cromwell's stout and God-fearing army. The narrative, viewed as a tale, is far less interesting than the *Pilgrim's Progress*, our sympathies not being excited by the dangers and escapes of a single hero; and in many points the allegory is too refined and complicated to be always readily followed. The style, though similar in its masculine vigor to that of the former allegory, is less fresh and animated.

§ 15. One of the most prominent figures in the Long Parliament and the Restoration was EDWARD HYDE, afterwards Chancellor, better known by his title of EARL OF CLARENDON (1608–1674). Not only was he an actor in the political drama of that momentous epoch, but he holds an honorable place among English historians by means of his history of the events in which he had taken part. Descended from a gentle stock, and educated at Oxford, he soon abandoned the profession of a barrister for the more exciting struggles of political life. He sat in the Short Parliament of 1640, when he was a member of the moderate party in opposition to the court, and afterwards, in the same year, was a conspicuous orator in the Long Parliament, at first supporting opposition principles, but after a violent quarrel with Hampden and the more advanced adherents of the national cause, he gradually passed over to the Royalist side. Finding himself at last in open rupture with the constitutional party, and even in imminent danger of arrest, he fled from London and joined the king at York. From this time Clarendon must be regarded among the most faithful, though certainly among the most moderate adherents of the Royalist cause. In 1644 he was appointed member of the Council named to advise and take charge of the prince, whom he accompanied to Jersey, and whose exile and vicissitudes he shared from the execution of Charles I. to the Restoration in 1660. During the Republic and Protectorate Hyde remained abroad, generally in close attendance upon the exiled prince and his little disreputable court, and generally giving such advice, as, if followed by his master and his companions, would have spared them much disgrace and many embarrassments. He was also rewarded with the title — then but an empty name — of Chancellor, and he was employed in several diplomatic services, one to the Court of Madrid, with the object of inducing the European cabinets to interfere actively on behalf of the exiled house. In this mission he was unsuccessful, so great was the terror inspired by the vigor of the great soldier and statesman who then swayed the destinies of England, and who first placed his country among the first-class powers of Europe. During this time Hyde had frequently, like many of his companions, and like the king himself while wandering in France and Holland, to support extreme poverty and privation. With the death of Cromwell crumbled to pieces the structure maintained as well as raised by his genius and patriotism. The Restoration took place; and in the frenzy of triumph which greeted the re-established monarchy, it was natural that Hyde should reap the reward of his services. He was installed in the high office of Chancellor, made first a Baron, and afterwards, in 1661, Earl of Clarendon, and for some time was among the most powerful advisers of the court. His popularity, however, as well as his favor with the king, soon began to decline; for both his virtues and his faults were such as to render him disliked. The gravity and austerity of his morals formed a strong contrast to the extreme profligacy of the court; his advice, generally in favor of prudence and economy, could not but be distasteful to the king; and his lectures had the additional disadvantage of being tedious; while, like many other statesmen who have returned to power after a long exile, he was not able to accommodate himself to the altered state of opinion. At the same time the people looked with envy and distrust upon the great wealth which he was accumulating, not always by the most scrupulous means, and upon the spirit of nepotism which was making the House of Hyde one of the richest and most splendid in the country. The magnificence, too, of his palaces and gardens gave additional umbrage to public dislike, which was carried to the highest pitch when a secret marriage was divulged between his daughter Anne and the Duke of York, brother and heir-apparent of the king. This alliance between a family that every one remembered to have risen from the rank of country gentleman and the Royal House was looked upon with strong displeasure. Clarendon, by it, became the progenitor of two queens of England, Mary and Anne. The minister's unpopularity was completed by the share he had in advising Charles to sell Dunkirk to Louis XIV., a measure which excited the intensest feeling of national humiliation; and Clarendon was accused by popular rumor of receiving a share of the proceeds of this disgraceful compact: his splendid palace in London received the bitter nickname of "Dunkirk House." Charles was not a man to sacrifice an atom of popularity for the purpose of screening a minister, even had he been personally attached to Clarendon. The Chancellor was impeached for High Treason, went into exile, and passed the remainder of his life in France, where he died, at Rouen, in 1674.

§ **16.** Clarendon was the author of many state papers and other official documents, which exhibit a grave and dignified eloquence; but his great work is the *History of the Great Rebellion*, as he naturally, in his quality of a Royalist, designated the Civil War. This review of events embraces a detailed account, rather in the form of Memoirs than regular history, of the proceedings from 1625 to 1633, together with a narrative of the incidents which led to the Restoration. As the materials were derived from the author's personal experience, the work is of high value, and places Clarendon among the leading historical writers of his age; while the dignity and liveliness of the style, in spite of occasional obscurity, will ever rank him among the great classical English prose-writers. Impartial he cannot be expected to be; but his partiality is less frequent and less flagrant than could fairly have been anticipated. The moderation of his character has occasionally led him to hesitate between two conclusions, and even when convicted of partiality he may be said to be rather negatively than positively unfair. If we take into consideration the number and complexity of the events he had to treat, we shall find fewer serious inaccuracies than could have been looked for in his account of facts. Above all he is excellent in the delineation of character. These are the parts of his work most carefully elaborated, and in them we often find penetration in judging and skill in portraying varieties of human nature.

§ **17.** There is perhaps no character, whether personal or literary, more perfectly enviable than that of IZAAK WALTON (1593–1683). He was born at Stafford in 1593, and passed his early manhood in London, where he carried on the humble business of a "sempster" or linen-draper. At about fifty he was able to retire from trade, probably with such a competency as was sufficient for his modest desires, and lived till the great age of ninety in ease and tranquillity, enjoying the friendship of many of the most learned and accomplished men of his time, and amusing himself with literature and his beloved pastime of the angle. His marriage with a sister of the truly apostolic Bishop Ken probably brought him into contact with such men as Donne, Hales, Wotton, Chillingworth, Sanderson, and Ussher; and the exquisite modesty and simplicity of his character soon ripened such acquaintance into solid friendships. He produced at different times the *Lives* of five persons, all distinguished for their virtues and accomplishments, namely, Donne, Wotton, Hooker, Herbert, and Bishop Sanderson, with the first, second, and last of whom he had been intimate. These biographies are unlike anything else in literature; they are written with such a tender and simple grace, with such an unaffected fervor of personal attachment and simple piety, that they will ever be regarded as masterpieces. But Walton's great work is the *Complete Angler*, a treatise on his favorite art of fishing, in which the precepts for the sport are combined with such inimitable descriptions of English river scenery, such charming dialogues, and so prevailing a tone of gratitude for God's goodness, that the book is absolutely *unique* in literature. The passion of the English for all kinds of field-sports and out-of-door amusements is closely connected with sensibility to the loveliness of rural nature; and the calm home-scenes of our national scenery are reflected with a loving truth in Walton's descriptions of those quiet rivers and daisied meadows which the good old man haunted rod in hand. The treatise, with a quaint gravity that adds to its charm, is thrown into a series of dialogues, first between Piscator, Venator, and Auceps, each of whom in turn proclaims the superiority of his favorite sport, and afterwards between Piscator and Venator, the latter of whom is converted by the angler, and becomes his disciple. Mixed up with technical precepts, now become a little obsolete, are an infinite number of descriptions of angling-days, together with dialogues breathing the sweetest sympathy with natural beauty and a pious philosophy that make Walton one of the most eloquent teachers of virtue and religion. The expressions are as pure and sweet and graceful as the sentiment; and the occasional occurrence of a little touch of old-fashioned innocent pedantry only adds to the indefinable fascination of the work, breaking up its monotony like a ripple upon the sunny surface of a stream. No other literature possesses a book similar to the *Complete Angler*, the popularity of which seems likely to last as long as the language. A second part was added by CHARLES COTTON (see p. 176), a clever poet, the friend and adopted son of Izaak, and his rival in the passion for angling. The continuation, though inferior, breathes the same spirit, and, like it, contains many beautiful and simple lyrics in praise of the art.

§ 18. GEORGE SAVILE, MARQUESS OF HALIFAX (1630-1695), one of the most illustrious statesmen of the Restoration, deserves notice on account of his political tracts, which, says Macaulay, "well deserve to be studied for their literary merit, and fully entitle him to a place among English classics."

One of the most charming, as well as solid and useful, writers of this period was JOHN EVELYN (1620–1706), a gentleman of good family and considerable fortune, whose life and character afford a model of what is most to be envied and desired. Virtuous, accomplished, and modest, he distributed his time between literary and philosophical occupations and the never-cloying amusements of rural life. He was one of the founders of the delightful art, so successfully practised in England, of gardening and planting. His principal works are *Sylva*, a treatise on the nature and management of forest-trees, to the precepts of which, as well as to the example of Evelyn himself, the country is indebted for its abundance of magnificent timber; and *Terra*, a work on agriculture and gardening. In both of these books we see not only the practical good sense of the author, but the benevolence of his heart, and an exquisite sensibility to the beauties of nature, as well as a profound and manly piety. In his feeling for the art of gardening he is the worthy successor of Bacon and predecessor of Shenstone. Evelyn has left also a Diary, giving a minute account of the state of society in his time and his pictures of the incredible infamy and corruption of the court of Charles II., through the abominations of which the pure and gentle spirit of Evelyn passed, like the Lady in *Comus*, amid the bestial rout of the enchanter. His description of the tremendous fire of London in 1665, of which he was an eye-witness, is the most detailed as well as trustworthy and picturesque account of that awful calamity. It was at the country house of Evelyn, at Sayes Court, near Deptford, that Peter the Great was lodged during his residence in England; and Evelyn gives a lamentable account of the dirt and devastation caused in the dwelling and the beautiful garden by the barbarian monarch and his suite. Indeed he obtained from Government compensation for the injury done to his property. The Diary, as well as all the other works of this good man, abounds in traits of personal character. He, his family, and his friends, seem to have formed a little oasis of piety, virtue, and refinement, amid the desert of rottenness offered by the higher society of those days; and his writings will always retain the double interest derived from his personal virtues, and the fidelity with which they delineate a peculiar phase in the national history.

§ 19. An original and even comic personality of this era is SAMUEL PEPYS (1632–1703), whose individual character was as singular as his writings. He was the friendless cadet of an ancient family, but born in such humble circumstances that, after receiving some education at the University, he is supposed to have for some time exercised the trade of a tailor; and during his whole life he retained a most ludicrous passion for fine clothes, which he is never weary of describing with more than the gusto of a man-milliner. By the protection of a distant connection, Sir Edward Montagu, he was placed in a subordinate office in the Admiralty; and by his punctuality, honesty, and knowledge of business, he gradually rose to the important post of Secretary in that department. He remained many years in this office, and must be considered as almost the only honest and able public official connected with the Naval administration during the reigns of Charles II. and James II. In the former of these the English marine was reduced, by the corruption and rapacity of the Court, to the very lowest depth of degradation and inefficiency. The successor of Charles was by profession a seaman, and on his accession employed all his efforts to restore the service to its former vigor. Perhaps the only portion of that miserable King's administration which can be regarded with anything but contempt and horror, is the effort he made to improve the condition of the Fleet. To this object the honesty and activity of Pepys contributed; and after acquiring a sufficient fortune without any serious imputation on his integrity, the old Secretary retired from the service to pass the evening of his life in well-earned ease. During the whole of his long and active career, Pepys had amused himself, for the eternal gratitude of posterity, in writing down, day by day, in a sort of cipher or short hand, a *Diary* of everything he saw, did, or thought. After having been preserved for about a century and a half, this curious record has been deciphered and given to the world; and the whole range of literature does not present a record more curious in itself, or exhibiting a more singular and laughable type of human character. Pepys was not only by nature a thorough gossip, curious as an old woman, with a strong taste for occasional jollifications, and a touch of the antiquity and curiosity hunter, but he was necessarily brought into contact with all classes of persons, from the King and his ministers down to the poor half-starved sailors whose pay he had to distribute. Writing entirely for himself, Pepys, with ludicrous *naiveté*, sets down the minutest details of his gradual rise in wealth and importance, noting every suit of clothes ordered by either himself or his wife, which he describes with rapturous enthusiasm, and chronicling every quarrel and reconciliation arising not of Mrs. Pepys's frequent and not unfounded fits of jealousy; for he is suspiciously fond of frequenting the pleasant but profligate society of pretty actresses and singers. The *Diary* is a complete scandalous chronicle of a society so gay and debauched that the simple description of what took place is equal to the most dramatic picture of the novelist. The statesmen, courtiers, players, and demireps actually live before our eyes; and there is no book that gives so lively a portraiture of one of the extraordinary states of society that then existed. All the minutiæ of dress, manners, amusements, and social life are vividly presented to us; and it is really alarming to think of the uproar that would have taken place if it had come to light that a careful hand had been chronicling every scandal of the day. Pepys's own character — an inimitable mixture of shrewdness, vanity, good sense, and simplicity — infinitely exalts the piquancy of his revelations; and his book possesses the double interest of the value and curiosity of its matter, and of the coloring given to that matter by the oddity of the narrator.

§ **20.** As a type of the fugitive literature of this age may be mentioned the writings of SIR ROGER L'ESTRANGE (1616-1704), an active pamphleteer and hack writer in favor of the Royalist party. His savage diatribes against the opponents of the Court are now almost forgotten, but they are curious as exhibiting a peculiar force of *slang* and vulgar vivacity which were then regarded as smart writing. His works are full of the familiar expressions which were current in society; and though low in taste, are not without a certain fire. Like another writer of the same stamp, TOM BROWN, he has given an example of how ephemeral must always be the success of that *soi-disant* humorous style which depends for its effect upon the employment of the current jargon of the town. In every age there are authors who trust to this for their popularity; and the temporary vogue of such writers is generally as great as is the oblivion to which they are certain to be condemned. L'Estrange has curiously exemplified his mode of writing in a sort of prose paraphrase of the ancient Fables attributed to the mysterious name of Æsop; and his Life of that imaginary person is a rare specimen of the pert familiarity which at that time passed for wit.

NOTES AND ILLUSTRATIONS.

OTHER WRITERS.

DR. WALTER CHARLETON (1619-1707), physician o Charles II. and President of the College of Physicians. He was a man of science and a theologian, a philosopher and an antiquarian. In 1675 he published *A brief Discourse concerning the different Wits of Men.* One of his best productions was a translation of Epicurus's *Morals*, 1670. The rendering is accurate and the English idiomatic. He was among the first who accounted for the differences in men's minds by the size and form of the brain.

WILLIAM WALSH (1663-1708), chiefly a critic, scholar, and patron of men of letters, but he himself published some fugitive pieces. He was member of Parliament for Worcestershire, and is mentioned by Pope in the well-known lines,—

"But why then publish? Granville the polite,
And knowing Walsh, would tell me I could write."

CHARLES MONTAGU, EARL OF HALIFAX (1661-1715), a great patron of letters during the reigns of William III. and Anne. He himself wrote some poems, but oftenest his name appeared on the early pages of authors' works, "fed with soft dedication all day long." He assisted Prior in the *City Mouse and the Country Mouse.* He rose to great distinction as a politician in the reign of William III., when he filled the office of Chancellor of the Exchequer, and was raised to the peerage in 1714, soon after the accession of George I.

CHAPTER XIII.

THE NEW DRAMA AND THE CORRECT POETS.

§ 1. Contrast between the drama of Elizabeth and that of the Restoration. § 2. SIR GEORGE ETHEREGE. § 3. WILLIAM WYCHERLEY: his life and works. The *Country Wife* and the *Plain Dealer*. § 4. SIR JOHN VANBRUGH. The *Relapse*, the *Provoked Wife*, the *Confederacy*, and the *Provoked Husband*. § 5. GEORGE FARQUHAR. The *Constant Couple*, the *Inconstant*, the *Recruiting Officer*, and the *Beaux' Stratagem*. § 6. WILLIAM CONGREVE: his life. 7. His works. The *Old Bachelor*. The *Double Dealer*. *Love for Love*. The *Mourning Bride*. § 8. JEREMY COLLIER'S attack of the stage: Congreve's reply. Congreve's *Way of the World*. § 9. THOMAS OTWAY. The *Orphan* and *Venice Preserved*. § 10. NATHANIEL LEE. THOMAS SOUTHERNE. *Isabella, or the Fatal Marriage*, and *Oroonoko*. JOHN CROWNE. § 11. NICHOLAS ROWE. *Jane Shore* and the *Fair Penitent*. 12. MRS. APHRA BEHN, THOMAS SHADWELL, and GEORGE LILLO. Lillo's *George Barnwell*, the *Fatal Curiosity*, and *Arden of Faversham*. § 13. Character of English poetry of this era. Noble poets: EARL of ROSCOMMON. EARL of ROCHESTER. SIR CHARLES SEDLEY. DUKE of BUCKINGHAMSHIRE. EARL of DORSET. § 14. JOHN PHILIPS and JOHN POMFRET.

§ 1. IN a previous chapter I have endeavored to sketch the immense revolution in dramatic literature, which is exemplified in the contrast between the age of Elizabeth and that of the Restoration. The theatre of the latter period, representing, as the theatre always must, the prevailing tone of sentiment and of society, is marked by the profound corruption which distinguishes the reign of Charles II., and which was the natural reaction after the strained morality of the Puritan dominion. The new drama differed from the old not only in its moral tone, but quite as widely in its literary form. The aim of the great writers who are identified with the dawn of our national stage was to delineate nature and passion; and therefore, as nature is multiform, they admitted into their serious plays comic scenes and characters, as they admitted elevated feelings and language into their comedies. But at the Restoration the artificial distinction between tragedy and comedy was strongly marked, and generally maintained with the same severity as upon the stage of France, which had become the chief model of imitation. In the place of the Romantic Drama arose the exaggerated, heroic, and stilted Tragedy on the one hand, and on the other the Comedy of artificial life, which, drawing its materials not from nature but from society, took for its aim the delineation not of character but of *manners*, which is indeed the proper object of what is correctly termed comedy in the strictest sense. Wit, therefore, now supplanted Humor; and England produced, during the seventeenth and part of the eighteenth centuries, a constellation of splendid dramatists. Their works are, it is true, now become almost unknown to the general reader; which is to be attributed to their abominable profligacy; but no one can have any conception of the powers of the English language and the brilliancy of English wit, who has not made acquaintance with these pieces.

§ 2. This class of writers may be said to begin with SIR GEORGE ETHEREGE (1636–1694), who was a man of fashion, and employed as a diplomatist. He died of a fall at Ratisbon, where he was residing as plenipotentiary. His principal work was entitled the *Man of Mode* or *Sir Fopling Flutter*, that character being the impersonation of the fashionable coxcomb of the day. Great vivacity of dialogue, combined with striking and unexpected turns of intrigue, form the general peculiarity of all the comedies of this time. Dryden and his once popular rival Shadwell must be regarded as the link connecting the elder drama with the new style; and Etherege is the first who embodied the merits and defects of the latter; though Etherege was destined to be far outstripped both in the wit and gayety and in the immorality of his scenes.

§ 3. A greater writer than Etherege, but exhibiting similar characteristics, was WILLIAM WYCHERLEY (1640–1715), born in 1640, of a good Shropshire family. His father, probably disgusted with the gloomy Puritanism of the reigning manners, sent the future dramatist to be educated in France, where he was brought up in the brilliant household of the Duke of Montausier. Here the young man abandoned his national faith and embraced Catholicism, probably regarding the latter as more especially the religion of a gentleman and man of fashion. Returning to England, adorned with all the graces of French courtliness, and remarkable for the beauty of his person, Wycherley, while nominally studying the Law, became a brilliant figure in the gay and profligate society of the day. In his literary career we do not find indications of any great precocity of genius: his first comedy *Love in a Wood*, was not acted until he had reached the age of about thirty-two; and the small number of his dramatic works, as well as the style of their composition, seems to prove that he was neither very original in conception, nor capable of producing anything otherwise than by patient labor and careful revision. *Love in a Wood* was followed, in 1673, the next year, by the *Gentleman Dancing-Master*, the plot of which was borrowed from Calderon. His two greatest and most successful comedies are the *Country Wife*, acted in 1675, and the *Plain Dealer*, in 1677. Moving in the most brilliant society of his time, Wycherley was engaged in many intrigues, the most celebrated being that with the infamous Duchess of Cleveland, one of the innumerable mistresses of Charles II. His grace and gayety attracted the notice of the king; and he was selected to superintend the education of the young Duke of Richmond, Charles's natural child; but a secret marriage which he contracted with the Countess of Drogheda caused him to lose the favor of the court. His union with the lady, which commenced in an accidental and even romantic manner, was not such as to secure either his happiness or his interest; and after her death

Wycherley fell into such distress as to have remained several years in confinement for debt. He was at last liberated partly by the assistance of James II.; and on this occasion, probably to gratify the king, he again rejoined the Catholic church, from which he had been temporarily reconverted. The remainder of Wycherley's life is melancholy and ignoble. Having long survived the literary types which were in fashion in his youth, with a broken constitution and an embarrassed fortune, he continued to thirst with vain impotence after sensual pleasure and literary glory. With the assistance of Pope, then a mere boy, but who had blazed out upon the world with sudden splendor, Wycherley concocted a huge collection of stupid and obscene poems, which fell dead upon the public. The momentary friendship and bitter quarrel of the old man and the young critic form a curious and instructive picture. Wycherley died in 1715, at an advanced age, having, on his very death-bed, married a young girl of sixteen, with the sole purpose of injuring his family, and preventing them from receiving his inheritance.

It is by the *Country Wife* and the ***Plain Dealer*** that posterity will judge the dramatic genius of Wycherley. Both these plays indicate great deficiency of original invention; for the leading idea of the first is evidently borrowed from the *École des Femmes* of Molière, and that of the second from the same author's *Misanthrope*. As Macaulay has excellently observed, nothing can more clearly indicate the unspeakable moral corruption of that epoch in our drama, and the degree in which that corruption was exemplified by Wycherley, than to observe the way in which he has modified, while he borrowed, the data of the great French dramatist. The character of Agnès is so managed as never to forfeit our respect, while the corresponding personage, Mrs. Pinchwife, is in the English comedy a union of the most incredible immorality with complete ignorance of the world; while the leading incident of the piece, the stratagem by which Horner blinds the jealousy of the husband, is of a nature which it is absolutely impossible to qualify in decent language. Nevertheless the intrigue of the piece is animated and amusing; the sudden and unexpected turns seem absolutely to take away one's breath; and the dialogue, as is invariably the case in Wycherley's productions, is elaborated to a high degree of liveliness and repartee. In the ***Plain Dealer*** is still more painfully apparent that bluntness of feeling, or rather that total want of sensibility to moral impressions, which distinguishes the comic drama of the Restoration, and none of the writers in that drama more signally than Wycherley. The tone of sentiment in Molière, as in all creators of the highest order, is invariably pure in its general tendency Alceste, in spite of his faults, is a truly respectable, nay, a noble character. Those very faults indeed are but a proof of the nobility of his disposition: "di vino dolce e l' aceto forte," says the Italian adage; and a generous heart, irritated past endurance by the smooth hypocrisy of social life, and bleeding from a thousand stabs inflicted by a cruel coquette, claims our sympathy even in the outbursts of its outraged feeling. But Wycherley borrowed Alceste; and in his hands the virtuous and injured hero of Molière has become "a ferocious sensualist, who believes himself to be as great a rascal as he thinks everybody else." "And to make the whole complete," proceeds our admirable critic, "Wycherley does not seem to have been aware that he was not drawing the portrait of an eminently honest man. So depraved was his moral taste, that, while he firmly believed that he was producing a picture of virtue too exalted for the commerce of this world, he was really delineating the greatest rascal that is to be found, even in his own writings."

§ 4. The second prominent name in this constellation of brilliant comic writers, the stars of which bear a strong general resemblance to each other, is that of SIR JOHN VANBRUGH (1666–1726). He was the son of a rich sugar-baker in London, probably, as his name indicates, of Dutch descent; and was born, it is not quite certain whether in France or England, in 1666. He unquestionably passed some part of his youth in the former country; and he united in his own person the rarely combined talents of architect and dramatist. As an architect he is one of the glories of the English school of the seventeenth century; and to his picturesque imagination we owe many works which, though open to criticism on the score of irregularity and a somewhat meretricious luxuriance of style, will always be admired for their magnificent and princely richness of invention. Among the most remarkable of these are Castle Howard and Blenheim, the latter being the splendid palace constructed at the national expense for the Duke of Marlborough. While engaged in this work Vanbrugh was involved in violent altercations with that malignant old harpy, the Duchess Sarah; and his account of the quarrel is almost as amusing as a scene in one of his own comedies. Vanbrugh was appointed King-at-Arms, and was employed, both in this function and as an architect, in many honorable posts. Thus he was deputed to carry the insignia of the Garter to the Elector of Hanover, and was afterwards knighted by that prince when he became King of England as George I., who also appointed him Comptroller of the Royal Works. He died in 1726, just before the close of that reign.

Vanbrugh's comedies, the production of which commenced in 1697, are the *Relapse*, the *Provoked Wife*, *Æsop*, the *Confederacy*, and the first sketch of the *Provoked Husband*, left unfinished, and afterwards completed by Colley Cibber. It still keeps possession of the stage, and is one of the best and most popular comedies in the language. Vanbrugh's principal merit is inexhaustible liveliness of character and incident. His dialogue is certainly less elaborate, less intellectual, and less highly finished than that of Wycherley: but he excels in giving his personages a ready ingenuity in extricating themselves from sudden difficulties; and one great secret of the comic art he possesses to a degree hardly surpassed by Molière himself, viz., the secret depending upon skilful repetition — an infallible talisman for exciting comic emotions. His fops, his booby squires, his pert chambermaids and valets, his intriguing ladies, his romps and his blacklegs are all drawn from the life, and delineated with great vivacity; but there is a good deal of exaggeration in his characters, an exaggeration which we easily pardon in consideration of the amusement they afford us and the consistency with which their personality is maintained — the more easily perhaps, as these types no longer exist in modern society, and we look upon them with the same sort of interest as we do upon the quaint costumes and fantastic attitudes of a collection of old portraits. In the *Relapse* Lord Foppington is an admirable impersonation of the pompous and suffocating coxcomb of those days. Sir Tunbelly Clumsy, the dense, brutal, ignorant country squire, a sort of prototype of Fielding's Western, forms an excellent contrast with him, and in Hoyden Vanbrugh has given the first specimen of a class of characters which he drew with peculiar skill, that of a bouncing rebellious girl, full of animal spirits and awaiting only the opportunity to break out of all rule. A variety of the same character is Corinna in the *Confederacy*, with the difference that Hoyden has been brought up in the country, while Corinna, in spite of her inexperience, is already thoroughly corrupted, and, as she says herself, "a devilish girl at bottom." The most striking character in the *Provoked Wife* is Sir John Brute, whose drunken, uproarious blackguardism was one of Garrick's best impersonations. The *Confederacy* is perhaps Vanbrugh's finest comedy in point of plot. The two old usurers and their wives, whose weakness is played upon by Dick Amlet and his confederate sharper Brass, Mrs. Amlet, the *marchande de la toilette*, the equivocal mother of her graceless scamp, Corinna, and the maid Flippanta — all the dramatis personæ are amusing in the highest degree. We feel indeed that we have got into exceedingly bad company; for all the men are rascals, and the women no better than they should be; but their life and conversation, "pleasant but wrong," are invariably animated and gay: and perhaps the very profligacy of their characters, by forbidding any serious sympathy with their fate, only leaves us freer to follow the surprising incidents of their career. The unfinished scenes of the comedy left by Vanbrugh, and afterwards completed under the title of the *Provoked Husband*, promised to be elaborated by the author into an excellent work. The journey to London of the country squire, Sir Francis Wronghead, and his inimitable family, is worthy of Smollett himself. The description of the cavalcade, and the interview between the new "Parliament-Man" in search of a place and the minister, are narrated with the richest humor. All the sentimental portions of the piece, the punishment and repentance of Lady Townley, and the contrast between her and her "sober" sister-in-law Lady Grace, were the additions of Collev Cibber, who lived at a time when the moral or sermonizing element was thought essential in comedy. This part of the intrigue, however, had the honor of being the prototype of Sheridan's delightful scenes between Sir Peter and Lady Teazle in the *School for Scandal*. In brilliancy of dialogue Vanbrugh is inferior to Wycherley; but his high animal spirits, and his extraordinary power of contriving sudden incidents, more than compensate for the deficiency. In Vanbrugh perhaps there is more of *mind*, but less of intellect.

§ 5. GEORGE FARQUHAR (1678–1708) was born at Londonderry in Ireland in 1678, and in his personal as well as his literary character he exemplifies the merits and the defects of his nation. He received some education at college, but at the early age of eighteen embraced the profession of an actor. Having accidentally wounded one of his comrades in a fencing-match, he quitted the stage and served for some time in the army, in the Earl of Orrery's regiment. His military experience enabled him to give very lively and faithful representations of gay, rattling officers, and furnished him with materials for one of his pleasantest comedies. His dramatic productions, which were mostly written after his return to his original profession, are more numerous than those of his predecessors, and consist of seven plays: *Love and a Bottle*, the *Constant Couple*, the *Inconstant*, the *Stage Coach*, the *Twin Rivals*, the *Recruiting Officer*, and the *Beaux' Stratagem*. These were produced in rapid succession, for the literary career of poor Farquhar was compressed into a short space of time — between 1698, when the first of the above pieces was acted, and the author's early death about 1708. The end of this brief course, which terminated at the age of thirty, was clouded by ill health and poverty; for Farquhar was induced to marry a lady who gave out, contrary to truth, that she was possessed of some fortune.

The works of Farquhar are a faithful reflection of his gay, loving, vivacious character; and it appears that down to his early death, not only did they go on increasing in joyous animation, but exhibit a constantly augmenting skill and ingenuity in construction, his last works being incomparably his best. Among them it will be unnecessary to dwell minutely on any but the *Constant Couple* (the intrigue of which is extremely animated), the *Inconstant*, and chiefly the *Recruiting Officer* and the *Beaux' Stratagem*. In Farquhar's pieces we are delighted with the overflow of high animal spirits, generally accompanied, as in nature, by a certain frankness and generosity. We readily pardon the peccadillos of his personages, as we attribute their escapades less to innate depravity than to the heat of blood and the effervescence of youth. His heroes often engage in deceptions and tricks, but there is no trace of the deep and deliberate rascality which we see in Wycherley's intrigues, or of the thorough scoundrelism of Vanbrugh's sharpers. The *Beaux' Stratagem* is decidedly the best constructed of our author's plays; and the expedient of the two embarrassed gentlemen, who come down into the country disguised as a master and his servant, though not perhaps very probable, is extremely well conducted, and furnishes a series of lively and amusing adventures. The contrast between Archer and Aimwell and Dick Amlet and Brass in Vanbrugh's *Confederacy*, shows a higher moral tone in Farquhar, as compared with his predecessor; and the numerous characters with whom they are brought in contact — Boniface the landlord, Cherry, Squire Sullen, and the inimitable Scrub, not to mention Gibbet the highwayman, and Father Foigard the Irish-French Jesuit — are drawn with never-failing vivacity. Passages, expressions, nay, sometimes whole scenes, may be found among the dramas of Farquhar, stamped with that rich humor and oddity which engrave them on the memory. Thus Boniface's laudation of his ale, "as the saying is," Squire Sullen's inimitable conversation with Scrub: "What day of the week is it? *Scrub*. Sunday, sir. *Sul.* Sunday? *Then* bring me a dram!" And Scrub's suspicions. "I am sure they were talking of me, for they laughed consumedly!"—such traits prove that Farquhar possessed a true comic genius. The scenes in the *Recruiting Officer*, where Sergeant Kite inveigles the two clowns to enlist, and those in which Captain Plume figures, are also of high merit. In those plays upon which I have not thought it necessary to insist, as the *Constant Couple* and the *Inconstant*, the reader will not fail to find scenes worked up to a great brilliancy of comic effect; as, for example, the admirable interview between Sir Harry Wildair and Lady Lurewell, when the envious coquette endeavors to make him jealous of his wife, and he drives her almost to madness by dilating on his conjugal happiness. Throughout Farquhar's plays the predominant quality is a gay geniality, which more than compensates for his less elaborate brilliancy in sparkling repartee. He seems always to write from his *heart;* and therefore, though we shall in vain seek in his dramas for a very high standard of morality, his writings are free from that inhuman tone of blackguard heartlessness which disgraces the comic literature of the time.

§ 6. The dramatic literature of this epoch naturally divides itself into the two heads of Comedy and Tragedy; and having now to speak of an author whose reputation in his own day was unrivalled in both departments, I shall place him here as a sort of link connecting them together. This was WILLIAM CONGREVE (1670–1729), who will always stand at the very head of the comic dramatists, while he certainly occupies no undistinguished place among the tragedians. He was born in Yorkshire of an ancient and honorable family, in 1670; and his father being employed in a considerable post in Ireland, the youth received his education in that country, first at a school in Kilkenny, and afterwards at the University of Dublin. Here he acquired a degree of scholarship, particularly in the department of Latin literature, which placed him far above the generality of contemporary writers of *belles lettres*, and he came to London, nominally to study the law in the Temple, but really to play a distinguished part in the fashionable and intellectual circles of the time. During his whole life he seems to have been the darling of society; and possessing great personal and conversational attractions, together with a cold and somewhat selfish character, was the perfect type of what Thackeray, adopting the expressive slang of our day, has qualified as the "fashionable literary *swell*." He thirsted after fame as a man of elegance and as a man of letters; but as the literary profession was at that time in a very degraded social position, he was tormented by the difficulty of harmonizing the two incompatible aspirations: and it is related that when Voltaire paid him a visit he affected the character of a mere gentleman, upon which the French wit, with equal acuteness and sense, justly reproved his vanity by saying

"If you had been a mere gentleman I should not have come to see you." Congreve's career was singularly auspicious: the brilliancy of his early works received instant recompense in solid patronage. Successive and hostile ministers rivalled each other in rewarding him: he obtained numerous and lucrative sinecures; and by his prudence was able not only to frequent, as an honored guest, the society of the greatest and most splendid of his time, but to accumulate a large fortune A disorder of the eyes, under which he long suffered, ultimately terminated in blindness; but neither this infirmity nor the gout could diminish the grace and gayety of his conversation, or render him less acceptable in company. He was regarded by the poets, from Dryden to Pope, with enthusiastic admiration: the former hailed his entrance upon the literary arena with fervent praise, and in some very beautiful and touching lines named Congreve his successor in that poetical throne he had so long and gloriously filled, imposing upon his friendship the task of defending his memory from slander; and Pope, when publishing his great work of the translation of Homer, passed over the powerful and the illustrious to dedicate his book to the patriarch of letters. Congreve, like most men of fashion at that time, was celebrated for many *bonnes fortunes*: his most durable connection was with the fascinating and generous Mrs. Bracegirdle, so famous for the excellency of her acting and the beauty of her person. In his old age, however, Congreve appears to have neglected her for the Duchess of Marlborough, daughter and inheritress of the great Duke; and at his death he bequeathed the bulk of his fortune, amounting to the large sum of 10,000*l.*, not to the comparatively needy actress, nor to his own relatives, then comparatively poor, but to the Duchess, in whose immense revenue such a legacy was but as a drop in the ocean. This circumstance furnishes an additional proof that Congreve was more remarkable for ostentation than for generosity or warmth of heart. He died in 1729, and was honored with a magnificent and almost national funeral. His body lay in state in the Jerusalem Chamber, and was followed to the tomb in Westminster Abbey by all that was most illustrious in England.

§ 7. The literary career of Congreve begins with a novel of insignificant merit, which he published under the pseudonyme of Cleophil; but the real inauguration of his glory was the representation, in 1693, of his first comedy, the *Old Bachelor*. This work, the production of a young man of twenty-three, was received by the public and by the critics with a tempest of applause. In spite of the bad construction and improbability of the intrigue, and of the conventional and so to say mechanical conception of the characters, it was easy to foresee in it all the peculiar merits which belong to the greatest comic dramatists of the eighteenth century. The chief of these is the unrivalled ease and brilliancy of the dialogue. Congreve's scenes are one incessant flash and sparkle of the finest repartee; the dazzling rapier-thrusts of wit and satiric pleasantry succeed each other without cessation; and the wit, as is always the case when of the highest order, s allied to shrewd sense and acute observation of mankind. Indeed the main defect of Congreve's dialogue is a plethora of ingenious allusion; for he falls into the error of making his fools and coxcombs as brilliant as his professed wits — a fault common to most of the authors of his school. But the quality in which he stands alone is his skill in divesting this brilliant intellectual sword-play of every shade of formality and constraint. His conversations are an exact copy of refined and intellectual conversation, though of course containing far more brilliancy than any real conversation ever exhibited. This air of consummate ease and idiomatic vivacity gives to his style a peculiar flavor which no other author has attained; and perhaps no English write furnishes so many examples of the capacity of our language as a vehicle for intellectual display. I have said that the characters in the *Old Bachelor* are conventional; they are nevertheless exceedingly amusing: as, for example, Captain Bluff, a reproduction of the bullying braggadocio so frequently placed upon the stage. This hero's mention of Hannibal is deliciously comic: "Hannibal was a very pretty fellow in those days, it must be granted. But, alas! sir, were he alive now he would be nothing — nothing in the earth!" This is of the strain of Parolles, of Bessus, and of Bobadil. We can hardly wonder at, though we may not confirm, the enthusiasm of Congreve's contemporaries, when, with Dryden at their head, they hailed this brilliant débutant as the successor and the more than rival of Fletcher and Shakspeare.

Congreve's second theatrical venture was the *Double Dealer*, acted in 1694. The success of this comedy was much less than that of its predecessor; and the comparative failure is to be attributed to the admixture, in the plot, of characters and incidents too gloomy and tragic to harmonize with the follies and vanities that form the woof of comedy. The wickedness of Lady Touchwood is of a tint too funereal to harmonize with the brilliant and shifting colors of comedy; and the villanous plots of Maskwell are so intricate and complex that the puzzled reader is unable to follow them. As in Shakspeare's *Comedy of Errors*, the confusion between the two pairs of twins is so complete that the reader, as much embarrassed as the personages in the piece, loses the thread of the story, and therefore the interest which is the source of pleasure, so in Congreve's play the abstruseness of the intrigue defeats its own purpose. Many of the minor scenes and characters, however. are full of comic verve.

Congreve's masterpiece is *Love for Love*, which was acted in 1695. This is one of the most perfect comedies in the whole range of literature. The intrigue is effective, and the characters exhibit infinite variety, and relieve each other with unrelaxing spirit. The pretended madness of Valentine, the unexpected turns in his passion for Angelica, Sir Sampson Legend, the doting old astrologer Foresight, Mrs. Frail, Miss Prue (a character something like Vanbrugh's Corinna, or Wycher ley's Hoyden), and above all the inimitable Ben — the first attempt to portray on the stage the rough, unsophisticated sailor — the whole *dramatis personæ*, down to the most insignificant, are a crowd of picturesque and well-contrasted oddities. The scene in which Sir Sampson endeavors to persuade his son to renounce his inheritance, that between Valentine and Trapland the old usurer (almost as good as Don Juan's reception of M. Dimanche), the arrival of Ben from sea, and his conversation with Miss Prue, — these, and many more, are the highest exaltation of comedy. Sir Sampson is one of those big, blustering characters that make their way by noise and confidence; he has something in common with Ben Jonson's Mammon, and was the model whence Sheridan afterwards copied his Sir Anthony Absolute.

Two years after this triumph Congreve burst forth upon the world in a completely new department of the drama — that of tragedy. He produced the *Mourning Bride*, which was received with no less ardent encomiums than the comedies. This piece is written in that pompous, solemn, and imposing strain which the adoption of French or classical models had rendered universal, and which Dryden had adopted as far as his bold and muscular genius, so rebellious to authority, permitted. The distress in this tragedy is extremely deep, but Congreve does not succeed in touching the heart. The chief merits of the piece consist in dignified passages of declamation, or what the French call *tirades;* and there are several descriptive passages of considerable power and melody, though their merit is rather that of narrative than dramatic poetry. Of this kind is the perpetually quoted description of a temple, which the extravagant eulogy of Johnson, by absurdly comparing it to pictorial passages in Shakspeare, has deprived of its due meed of applause. If "faint praise" "damns," exaggerated laudation damns still more fatally.

§ 8. About this time took place an event of equal importance to Congreve and to the literary character of that age. This was the attack directed by JEREMY COLLIER (1650–1726), an ardent nonjuring clergyman, against the profaneness and immorality of the English stage. His pamphlet was written with extraordinary fire, wit, and energy; and the evil which he combated was so general, so inveterate, and so glaring, that he immediately ranged upon his side all moral and thinking men in the nation. He anatomized with a vigorous and unsparing scalpel the foul ulcer of theatrical immorality, and cauterized it with such merciless satire that Dryden, powerful as he was in controversy, remained silent out of shame. The gauntlet thrown down by Collier, and which conscious guilt prevented Dryden from lifting, was taken up by Congreve; but the defence he made was poor, and the victory remained, both as regards morality and wit, on the side of Collier. The controversy had the effect of inaugurating a better tone in the drama and in lighter literature in general; and from that period dates the gradual but rapid improvement which has ended in rendering the literature of England the purest and healthiest in Europe.

Congreve's last dramatic work was the *Way of the World*, performed in 1700. Its success was not great, although its dialogue exhibits the rare charm which never deserted him, and though it contains in Millamant one of the most delicious portraits of a gay, triumphant beauty, coquette, and fine lady ever placed upon the stage. It is like the porcelain figures in old Dresden china; crisp, sparkling, highly yet delicately colored, filling the mind with images of grace and fancy. In his old age the poet produced a volume of fugitive and miscellaneous trifles, which do not much rise above the level of a class of composition extremely fashionable at that period.

§ 9. Among the exclusively tragic dramatists of the age of Dryden the first place belongs to THOMAS OTWAY (1651-1685), who died, after a life of wretchedness and irregularity, at the early age of thirty-four. He received a regular education at Winchester School and Oxford, and very early embraced the profession of the actor, for which he had no natural aptitude, but which familiarized him with the technical requirements of theatrical writing. He produced in the earlier part of his career three tragedies, *Alcibiades*, *Don Carlos*, and *Titus and Berenice*, which may be regarded as his first trial-pieces; and about 1677 he served some time in a dragoon regiment in Flanders, to which he had been appointed by the protection of a patron. Dismissed from his post in consequence of irregularities of conduct, he returned to the stage, and in the years extending from 1680 to his death, he wrote four more tragedies, *Caius Marcius*, *the Orphan*, *the Soldier's Fortune*, and *Venice Preserved.* All these works, with the exception of the *Orphan* and *Venice Preserved*, are now nearly forgotten; but the glory of Otway is so firmly established upon these latter, that it will probably endure as long as the language itself. The life of this unfortunate poet was an uninterrupted series of poverty and distress; and his death has frequently been cited as a striking instance of the miseries of a literary career. It is related that, when almost starving, the poet received a guinea from a charitable friend, on which he rushed off to a baker's shop, bought a roll, and was choked while ravenously swallowing the first mouthful. It is not quite certain whether this painful anecdote is strictly true, but it is incontestable that Otway's end, like his life, was miserable. How far his misfortunes were unavoidable, and how far attributable to the poet's own improvidence, it is now impossible to determine. Otway, like Chatterton, like Gilbert, like Tasso, and like Cervantes, is generally adduced as an example of the miserable end of genius, and of the world's ingratitude to its greatest benefactors.

As a tragic dramatist Otway's most striking merit is his pathos; and he possesses in a high degree the power of uniting pathetic emotion with the expression of the darker and more ferocious passions. The distress in his pieces is carried to that intense and almost hysterical pitch which we see so frequently in Ford and Beaumont and Fletcher, and so rarely in Shakspeare. The sufferings of Monimia in *the Orphan*, and the moral agonies inflicted upon Belvidera in *Venice Preserved*, are carried to the highest pitch, but we see tokens of the essentially second-rate quality of Otway's genius the moment he attempts to delineate madness. Belvidera's ravings are the expression of a disordered fancy, and not, like those of Lear or of Ophelia, the lurid flashes of reason and consciousness lighting up for an instant the tossings of a mind agitated to its profoundest depths. In *Venice Preserved* Otway has not attempted to preserve historical accuracy, but he has succeeded in producing a very exciting and animated plot, in which the weak and uxorious Jaffier is well contrasted with the darker traits of his friend and fellow-conspirator Pierre, and the inhuman harshness and cruelty of the Senator Priuli with the ruffianly thirst for blood and plunder in Renault. The frequent declamatory scenes, reminding the reader of Dryden, as, for instance, the quarrels and reconciliation of Pierre and Jaffier, the execution of the two friends, and the despair of Belvidera, are worked up to a high degree of excellence; and Otway, with the true instinct of dramatic fitness, has introduced, as elements of the deep distress into which he has plunged his principal characters, many of those familiar and domestic details from which the high classical dramatist would have shrunk as too ignoble. Otway in many scenes of this play has introduced what may be almost called comic matter, as in the amorous dotage of the impotent old senator and the courtesan Aquilina; but these, though powerfully and naturally delineated, are of too disgusting and odious a nature to be fit subjects for representation. Otway's style is vigorous and racy; the reader will incessantly be reminded of Dryden, though the author of *Venice Preserved* is far superior to his great master in the quality of pathos; and in reading his best passages we are perpetually struck by a sort of flavor of Ford, Heywood, Beaumont, and other great masters of the Elizabethan era.

§ **10.** No account of the drama of this period would be complete without some mention of NATHANIEL LEE (d. 1692), a tragic poet who not only had the honor of assisting Dryden in the composition of several of his pieces, but who, in spite of adverse circumstances, and in particular of several attacks of insanity, one of which necessitated his confinement during four years in Bedlam, possessed and deserved a high reputation for genius. He was educated at Westminster School and Cambridge, and was by profession an actor: he died in extreme poverty in 1692. His original dramatic works consist of eleven tragedies, the most celebrated of which is *The Rival Queens, or Alexander the Great*, in which the heroic extravagance of the Macedonian conqueror is relieved by amorous complications arising from the attachment of the two strongly-opposed characters of Roxana and Statira. Among his other works may be enumerated *Theodosius*, *Mithridates*, and the pathetic drama of *Lucius Junius Brutus*, the interest of which turns on the condemnation of the son by the father. In all these plays we find a sort of wild and exaggerated tone of imagery, sometimes reminding us of Marlowe: but Lee is far superior in tenderness to the author of Faustus; nay, in this respect he surpasses Dryden. In the beautiful but feverish bursts of declamatory eloquence which are frequent in Lee's plays, it is possible to trace something of that violence and exaggeration which are perhaps derived from the tremendous malady of which he was so long a victim.

THOMAS SOUTHERNE (1659–1746) was born at Dublin, but passed the greater part of his life in England. He studied the Law in the Temple, but quitted that profession for the army: it is known that he served as a captain in one of the corps employed in the suppression of the unfortunate Duke of Monmouth's rebellion, and in all probability was present at the battle of Sedgemoor. The close of his life was tranquil and surrounded with competence. Southerne was the author of ten plays, the most conspicuous of which are the tragedies of *Isabella, or the Fatal Marriage*, and the pathetic drama of *Oroonoko*. The latter is founded upon the true adventures of an African prince: the subject is said to have been given to Southerne by Aphra Behn, of whom we shall have to say a few words presently, and who, being the daughter of a governor of Surinam, where the events took place, was personally acquainted both with the incidents and the individuals which form the groundwork of the story. The sufferings of the generous and unhappy African, torn by the slave-trade from his country and his home, and his love for Imoinda, furnish good materials to the pathetic genius of Southerne, who was the first English author to hold up to execration the cruelties of that infernal traffic that so long remained a stain upon our country The distress in *Isabella* is also carried to a high degree of intensity, and tenderness and pathos may be asserted to be the primary characteristics of Southerne's dramatic genius.

Another minor, but not unimportant, name among the dramatists of this period is that of JOHN CROWNE (1661–1698). Among the seventeen pieces which he produced, I may mention the tragedy of *Thyestes* and the comedy entitled *Sir Courtly Nice*. Both of these works possess considerable merit, though the revolting nature of the legend which forms the subject of the first is of a nature that ought to exclude it from the dramatist's attempt. We may remember that these dreadful Greek traditions had previously been preferred by Chapman. Crowne is remarkable for the beauty of detached passages of sentiment and description, and in particular bears some resemblance to his predecessor in the dignity and elegance with which he inculcates those moral precepts which Euripides was so fond of introducing, and which in the Greek Drama are called γνῶμαι.

§ 11. In success in life and social position NICHOLAS ROWE (1673–1718) was a happy contrast to the wretched career of many dramatists by no means his inferiors in talent. He was born in 1673, and studied in the Temple, employing his leisure hours in writing for the stage. He was cordially received in the brilliant and literary society of his day, and was a member of that intellectual society which surrounded Pope, Swift, Arbuthnot, and Prior, and who were bound together by such strong ties of intimacy and friendship. It is said, however, that Rowe, though much admired for his social accomplishments, was regarded as of a somewhat cold and selfish nature; in short, there seem to be many elements of character in common between him and Congreve. He was not only in possession of an independent fortune, but was splendidly rewarded for his literary exertions by the gift of many lucrative places in the patronage of Government. Thus he was Poet Laureate and Surveyor of the Customs, Clerk of the Council in the service of the Prince of Wales, and Clerk of the Presentations. He was an example of that mode which for some time was general in England, of rewarding with profitable or sinecure appointments merit of a literary kind. The profession of letters enjoyed a transient gleam of prosperity and consideration; the period preceding and that following this epoch being remarkable for the want of social consideration — nay, the degradation attaching to the author's profession. It was not till the vast extension of the reading public, by offering the writer the most honorable form of recompense and the purest motives for exertion, that he could be relieved from the humiliation of a servile dependence on individual patrons on the one hand, and the fluctuations of temporary success and prevailing poverty, on the other. Rowe was the first who undertook an edition of Shakspeare upon true critical and philological principles, and, though his work is marked by the inevitable deficiency of an age when the art of the commentator, as applied to an author of the sixteenth century, was still in its infancy, yet his edition gives some earnest of better things, and has, at all events, the merit of exhibiting a profound and loyal admiration of the great poet's genius. Rowe died in 1718. His dramatic productions amount to seven, the principal being *Jane Shore*, the *Fair Penitent*, and *Lady Jane Grey*, all, of course, tragedies. Tenderness is Rowe's chief dramatic merit; in the diction of his works we incessantly trace the influence of his study of the manner of the great Elizabethan playwrights. This imitation is often only superficial; and in some cases, as, for example, in *Jane Shore*, extends little farther than an aping of the quaintness of the elder authors; but in many points Rowe did all that a nature, I suspect not very impressionable, could do to catch some echo of those deep tones of pathos and passion that thrill through the writings of the great elder dramatists. In the *Fair Penitent* we have an almost intolerable load of sorrow accumulated on the head of the heroine. It is curious that the character of the seducer in this play, "the gallant, gay Lothario," should have become the proverbial type of the faithless lover — just as Don Juan has been in our own time — and should have furnished Richardson with the outline which that great painter of character afterwards filled up so successfully in his masterly portrait of Lovelace.

§ 12. Mrs. Aphra Behn (d. 1689), celebrated in her day under the poetical appellation of Astræa, enjoyed some reputation for the gayety, and, I may add, for the immorality, of her comedies. She was one of those equivocal characters, half literary, half political adventurers, who naturally appear in times of public agitation. The daughter of a governor of Surinam, she had passed her youth in that colony, and, coming to Europe, was much mixed up in the obscurer intrigues of the Restoration. She resided some time in Holland, and seems to have rendered services to Charles II. as a kind of political spy. She died in 1689, and her novels, as well as comedies, though now forgotten, may be consulted as curious evidences of the state of literary and social feeling that prevailed at that agitated epoch.

The only other names that need be cited among the dramatists of this period are those of Shadwell and Lillo. THOMAS SHADWELL (1640-1692) wrote seventeen plays, but is now chiefly known by Dryden's satire as the hero of *Mac-Flecknoe*, and the Og of *Absalom and Achitophel.* On the Revolution, he succeeded Dryden as Poet Laureate. GEORGE LILLO (1693-1739) is in many respects a remarkable and singular literary figure. He was a jeweller in London, and appears to have been a prudent and industrious tradesman, and to have accumulated a fair competence. His dramatic works, which were probably composed as an amusement, consist of a peculiar species of what may be called tragedies of domestic life, in some respects resembling those *drames* which are at present so popular in France. The principal of them are *George Barnwell*, the *Fatal Curiosity*, and *Arden of Feversham.* Lillo composed sometimes in verse and sometimes in prose; he based his pieces upon remarkable examples of crime, generally in the middle ranks of society, and worked up the interest to a high pitch of intensity. In *George Barnwell* is traced the career of a London shopman — a real person — who is lured by the artifices of an abandoned woman and the force of his own passion first into embezzlement, and then into the murder of an uncle. The hero of the play, like his prototype in actual life, expiates his offences on the scaffold. The subject of the *Fatal Curiosity*, Lillo's most powerful work, is far more dramatic in its interest. A couple, reduced by circumstances, and by the absence of their son, to the lowest depths of distress, receive into their house a stranger, who is evidently in possession of a large sum; while he is asleep, they determine to assassinate him for the purpose of plunder, and afterwards discover in their victim their long-lost son. It will be remembered that the tragic story of *Arden of Feversham*, a tissue of conjugal infidelity and murder, was an event that really took place in the reign of Elizabeth, and had furnished materials for a very popular drama, attributed, but on insufficient evidence, to Shakspeare among other playwrights of the time. It was again revived by Lillo, and treated in his characteristic manner — a manner singularly intense in spirit, though prosaic in form. Indeed, the very absence of imagination in this writer may have contributed to the effect he produced, by augmenting the air of reality in his conceptions. He has something of the gloom and sombre directness which we see in Webster or Tourneur, but he is entirely devoid of the wild, fantastic fancy which distinguishes that great writer. He is real, but with the reality, not of Walter Scott, but of Defoe.

§ 13. From the time of Dryden to about the end of the first quarter of the eighteenth century English poetry exhibits a character equally removed from the splendid brilliancy of the epoch of Elizabeth and the picturesque intensity of the new Romantic school. Correctness and good sense were the qualities chiefly aimed at; and if the writers avoid the abuse of ingenious allusion which disfigures the productions of

Cowley, Donne, and Quarles, they are equally devoid of the passionate and intense spirit which afterwards animated our poetry. It is remarkable how many of the writers of this time were men of rank and fashion: their literary efforts were regarded as the elegant accomplishment of amateurs; and, though their more ambitious productions are generally didactic and critical, and their lighter works graceful and harmonious songs, they must be regarded less as the deliberate results of literary labor than as the pastime of fashionable dilettanti. EARL OF ROSCOMMON (1634–1685), the nephew of the famous Strafford, produced a poetical *Essay on Translated Verse* and a version of the *Art of Poetry* from Horace, which were received by the public and the men of letters with an extravagance of praise attributable to the respect then entertained for any intellectual accomplishment in a nobleman. EARL OF ROCHESTER (1647–1680), so celebrated for his insane debaucheries and the witty eccentricities which made him one of the most prominent figures in the profligate court of Charles II., produced a number of poems, chiefly songs and fugitive lyrics, which proved how great were the natural talents he had wasted in the most insane extravagance: his death-bed conversion and repentance produced by the arguments of Bishop Burnet, who has left an interesting and edifying account of his penitent's last moments, show that, amid all his vices, Rochester's mind retained the capacity for better things. Many of his productions are unfortunately stained with such profanity and indecency, that they deserve the oblivion into which they are now fallen.

SIR CHARLES SEDLEY (1639–1701) was another glittering star in the court firmament; he was a most accomplished gentleman, and his life was far more regular, as well as more tranquil, than that of Rochester: his comedy, the *Mulberry Garden*, is not devoid of gayety and wit, and contains several songs of merit. Many other slight lyrics prove that Sedley possessed the grace, airiness, and ingenuity, which are the principal requisites of this species of writing.

To the same category may be ascribed the DUKE of BUCKINGHAM (Sheffield) (1649–1720) and EARL of DORSET (1637–1705), perfect specimens of the aristocratic literary dilettante of those days. The former is best known by his *Essay on Poetry*, written in the heroic couplet; the latter by his charming, playful song—*To all you ladies now on land*, said to have been written at sea on the eve of an engagement with the Dutch fleet under Opdam. It is addressed by the courtly volunteer to the ladies of Whitehall, and breathes the gay and gallant spirit that animates the *chanson militaire*, in which the French so much excel.

§ 14. The only poets of any comparative importance, not belonging to the higher classes of society, were Philips and Pomfret, both belonging to the end of the seventeenth century. JOHN PHILIPS (1676–1708) is the author of a half-descriptive, half-didactic poem on the manufacture of *Cider*, written upon the plan of the Georgics of Virgil; but he is now known to the general reader by his *Splendid Shilling*, a pleasant *jeu d'esprit*, in which the learned and pompous style of Milton is agreeably parodied, by being applied to the most trivial subject. Such parodies are common, and by no means difficult of execution; but among them there will always be some which, either from their originality as first attempts in a particular style, or from the peculiar felicity of the imitation, will excite and retain a higher popularity than generally rewards trifles of this nature. Such has been the peculiar good fortune of Philips. JOHN POMFRET (1667–1703) was a clergyman, and the only work by which he is now remembered is his poem of *The Choice*, giving a sketch of such a life of rural and literary retirement as has been the *hoc erat in votis* of so many. The images and ideas are of that nature that will always come home to the heart and fancy of the reader; and it is to this naturalness and accordance with universal sympathy, rather than to anything very original either in its conception or its execution, that the poem owes the hold it has so long retained upon the attention.

CHAPTER XIV.

THE SECOND REVOLUTION.

§ 1. JOHN LOCKE: his life. § 2. His works. *Letters on Toleration, Treatise on Civil Government.* § 3. *Essay on the Human Understanding.* § 4. *Essay on Education. On the Reasonableness of Christianity. On the Conduct of the Understanding.* § 5. ISAAC BARROW: his life and attainments. His *Sermons.* § 6. Characteristics of the Anglican divines. JOHN PEARSON. § 7. ARCHBISHOP TILLOTSON. § 8. ROBERT SOUTH. EDWARD STILLINGFLEET. THOMAS SPRAT. WILLIAM SHERLOCK. § 9. Progress of the physical sciences towards the end of the seventeenth century. Origin of the Royal Society. DR. JOHN WILKINS. § 10. Scientific writers. § 11. SIR ISAAC NEWTON. § 12. JOHN RAY. ROBERT BOYLE. THOMAS BURNET. § 13. BISHOP BURNET. His *History of the Reformation*, and other works.

§ 1. THE period of the great and beneficent revolution of 1688 was characterized by the establishment of constitutional freedom in the state, and no less by a powerful outburst of practical progress in science and philosophy. It was this period that produced Newton in physical and Locke in intellectual science. The latter, in his character and career, offers the most perfect type of the good man, the patriotic citizen, and the philosophical investigator. JOHN LOCKE (1632-1704) was born in 1632, educated at Westminster School and Christ-Church, Oxford, where he particularly devoted himself to the study of the physical sciences, and especially of medicine. He undoubtedly intended to practise the latter profession, but was prevented from doing so by the weakness of his constitution, and a tendency to asthma, which in after life obliged him to retire from those public employments for which his integrity and talents so well fitted him. The direction of his studies at Oxford must have tended to inspire him with distaste and contempt for that adherence to the scholastic method which still prevailed in the University, and to excite in him a strong hostility to that stationary or rather retrograde spirit which sheltered itself under the venerable and much-abused name of Aristotle. There is no question that Locke's investigations during the thirteen years of his residence at Oxford had been much turned to metaphysical subjects, and that he had seen the necessity of applying to this branch of knowledge that experimental or inductive method of which his great master Bacon was the apostle. In 1664 he accompanied Sir Walter Vane, as his secretary, on a diplomatic mission to Brandenburg, and returning to Oxford in the following year, refused a flattering offer made him by the Duke of Ormond of considerable preferment in the Irish Church. His reasons for declining to take orders were equally honorable to Locke's good sense and to his high conscientious feeling. He declined the favor on the ground of his not experiencing that internal vocation without which no man should enter the priestly profession. In 1666 Locke became acquainted with Lord Ashley, afterwards Earl of Shaftesbury, and subsequently so celebrated for his political talents and for his unprincipled and factious conduct when Chancellor and the head of the parliamentary opposition. He is said to have rendered himself useful to this statesman by his medical skill, and unquestionably secured his intimacy and respect by the charms of his conversation and the virtues of his character. He attached himself intimately both to the domestic circle and to the political fortunes of this statesman, in whose house he resided several years, having undertaken the education first of the Chancellor's son and afterwards of his grandson, the latter of whom has left no unworthy name as an elegant, philosophical, and moral essayist. Locke's acquaintance with Shaftesbury brought him into daily and intimate contact with many of the most distinguished politicians and men of letters of the day, among whom I may mention the all-accomplished Halifax, Sheffield, Duke of Buckinghamshire, and many others. Locke fully shared in the frequent and violent vicissitudes of Shaftesbury's agitated career. He was nominated, on his patron becoming Chancellor in 1672, Secretary of the Presentations, with which he combined another appointment; but these he lost in the following year on the first fall of his patron. In 1675 he visited France for his health, and his journals and letters are not only valuable for the accurate but very unfavorable account they give of the then state of French society, but are exceedingly amusing, animated, and gay. In 1679 Locke returned to England and rejoined Shaftesbury on his second accession to power during that stormy period when he was at the head of the furious agitation in favor of the Exclusion-Bill depriving the Duke of York, afterwards James II., and then Heir-Apparent, of the right of succeeding to the throne, on the ground of his notorious sympathies with the Roman Catholic religion. The Chancellor again fell from power, was arraigned for High Treason, and though the bill of indictment was ignored by a patriotic jury, fled to Holland, where he died in 1683.

During the evil days of tyranny and persecution which followed this event, Locke found a safe and tranquil retreat in Holland, a country which had so long been the asylum of all who were brought, by the profession of free opinions on politics or religion, under the frown of power; and he enjoyed the friendship and society of Le Clerc and many other illustrious exiles for conscience' sake. During this time Locke, whose bold expression of constitutional opinions and whose ardent attachment to free investigation must have made him peculiarly obnoxious to the bigotry of Oxford, was deprived of his Studentship at Christ-Church, and denounced as a factious and rebellious agitator, and as a dangerous heresiarch in philosophy. The Revolution of 1688 was the triumph of those free principles of which Locke had been the preacher and the martyr; and he returned to England in the same fleet which conveyed Queen Mary from Holland to the country whose crown she had been called to share. From this period his career was eminently useful, active, and even brilliant. He was appointed a member of the Council of Trade, and in that capacity took a prominent part in carrying out Montague's difficult and most critical operation of calling in and reissuing the silver coinage — an operation of the most vital importance at the moment, and of which Macaulay has given in his history a narrative of the most dramatic interest. After a short service Locke retired from public employment, and resided during the remainder of his life with his friend Sir F. Masham at Oates in Essex. Lady Masham, an accomplished and intellectual woman, was the daughter of the philosopher Cudworth, tenderly loved and respected by her illustrious guest, who enjoyed under her roof the ease and tranquillity he had so nobly earned. Locke died in 1704; and his personal character seems to have been one of those which approach perfection as nearly as can be expected from our fallible and imperfect nature. On his return to England in 1688 Locke became acquainted with the illustrious Newton, who, like himself, was employed in the public service; but somewhere about 1692 certain untoward events, among which one of the principal was the unfortunate accidental burning of his papers, seem to have shaken, if not overthrown for a season the balance of the great philosopher's mind; and his querulous and suspicious irritation appears to have vented itself in a most unfounded misunderstanding with Locke, whom he accuses of "embroiling him with women and other things." It is pleasing to think that Locke's conduct in the affair was delicate and forbearing, and that his manly expostulations and wise advice re-established a good understanding that was never again interrupted.

§ **2.** The writings of this excellent thinker are numerous, varied in subject, all eminently useful, and breathing a constant love of humanity. In 1689 were published the ***Letters on Toleration***, originally composed in Latin, but immediately translated into French and English. The author goes over somewhat the same ground as had been occupied by Jeremy Taylor in his ***Liberty of Prophesying***, and by Milton in the immortal ***Areopagitica;*** but Locke deduces his arguments less from scriptural and patristic authority than was done by the former, and depends more upon close reasoning and considerations of practical utility than Milton. Of course in Locke's work there is no trace of that gorgeous and imposing eloquence which glows and blazes through the ***Speech on Unlicensed Printing;*** but perhaps Locke's calm and logical proofs have not less powerfully contributed to fix the universal conviction as to the justice of his cause. The ***Treatise on Civil Government*** was undertaken to overthrow those slavish theories of Divine Right which were then so predominant among the extreme monarchical parties, and nowhere carried to such extravagance as in the University of Oxford. Locke's more special object was the refutation of Sir John Filmer's once famous book entitled ***Patriarcha***, in which these principles were maintained in all their crudeness, and supported with some learning and much ill-employed ingenuity. Filmer maintains that the monarchical form of government claims from the subject an unlimited obedience, as being the representative of the patriarchal authority in the primitive ages of mankind, while the patriarchal authority is in its turn the image of the power naturally possessed over his offspring by the parent, that again being the same in nature as the power of the Creator over his creature. The last-named of these being essentially infinite, it follows, according to Filmer, that all the others are so likewise. Locke combats and overthrows this monstrous theory, and seeks for the origin of government, and consequently the ground of authority on the one hand and obedience on the other, in the common interest of society; showing that any form of polity which secures that interest may lawfully be acquiesced in, while none that does not secure it can claim any privilege of exemption from resistance. He investigates the origin of society, and finds it based — as it can only be solidly based — upon the great and fertile principle of property and individual interest.

§ 3. The greatest, most important, and most universally known of Locke's works is the *Essay on the Human Understanding*. In this book, which contains the reflections and researches of his whole life, and which was in the course of composition during eighteen years, Locke shows all his powers of close deduction and accurate observation. His object was to give a rational and clear account of the nature of the human mind, of the real character of our ideas, and of the mode in which they are presented to the consciousness. He attributes them all, whatever be their nature, to two, and only two, sources; the first of these he calls Sensation, the second Reflection. He thus opposes the notion that there are any innate ideas, that is, ideas which have existed in the mind independently of impressions made upon the senses, or of the comparison, recollection, or combination of those impressions made by the judgment, the memory, or the imagination. Locke is eminently an inductive reasoner, and was the first to apply the method of experiment and observation to the obscure phenomena of the mental operations; and he is thus to be regarded as the most illustrious disciple of Bacon, whose mode of reasoning he adopted in a field of research till then considered as totally unamenable to the *à posteriori* logic. The most striking feature in this, as in all Locke's philosophical works, is the extreme clearness, plainness, and simplicity of his language, which is always such as to be intelligible to a plain understanding. He is the sworn foe of all technical and scientific terms, and his reasonings and illustrations are of the most familiar kind; indeed he never scruples to sacrifice elegance to the great object of making himself understood. The following brief analysis of the work may be found not unacceptable to the reader: —

In Book I., consisting of four chapters, Locke inquires into the nature of the understanding, and demonstrates that there exist neither innate speculative nor innate practical principles. Book II., containing thirty-three chapters, is devoted to an examination into the nature of ideas, respectively treated as simple, as of solidity, of space, of duration, of number, of infinity, and the like. He then considers the ideas of pleasure and of pain, of substance, of relations, as of cause and effect, and finally treats the important question of the association of ideas. Book III., divided into eleven chapters, is a most original and masterly investigation of the nature and properties of Language, of its relation to the ideas of which it is the vehicle, and of its abuses and imperfections. This is, in the present day, when some parts of Locke's general theory are regarded as no longer tenable, the most valuable portion of the work. Book IV., including twenty-one chapters, discusses knowledge in general, its degrees, its extent, and its reality. The philosopher then proceeds to consider the nature of truth, of our knowledge of existence, of our knowledge of the existence of a God, and of other beings. Then are investigated various important questions relating to judgment, probability, reason, faith, and the degrees of intellectual assent, and after some reflections on enthusiasm and on wrong assent, or error, Locke terminates with some valuable considerations on the Division of the Sciences.

It was unavoidable that the portion of the work devoted to the investigation of sensation should be more interesting and satisfactory than the portion treating of the obscure phenomena of reflection; but however we may dissent from particular details of Locke's theory, we cannot fail to render full justice to the inimitable clearness of his exposition, and to the multitude of well-observed and well-arranged facts which form the groundwork of his arguments.

§ 4. The *Essay on Education* has, like the book just examined, a practical tendency, and may be said to have mainly contributed to bring about that beneficial revolution which has taken place in the training of the young. Locke powerfully discountenances that exclusive attention to mere philology which prevailed in the education of the seventeenth century, and in no country more than in England. He advocates a more generous, liberal, and practical system, both in the choice of the subject-matter to be taught and in the mode of conveying instruction. He is therefore in favor of making the pupil's own conscientiousness a substitute for that tyranny of force and authority which formerly disgraced our schools. Much of what is humane and philosophical in Rousseau's celebrated *Emile* is plainly borrowed from Locke, who is not responsible for the absurdities and extravagances ingrafted upon his plans by the Genevese theorist. Indeed both the educational and metaphysical works of Locke were unceremoniously ransacked by many French writers of the end of the seventeenth century, who were frequently not solicitous to point out the sources whence they drew their ideas.

Besides the above works may be mentioned a treatise *On the Reasonableness of Christianity*, in which the calm piety and benevolence of the sentiments form a triumphant refutation of those bigots who, like De Maistre, have accused Locke of irreligious and materialistic tendencies, and a small but admirable little book *On the Conduct of the Understanding*, which was not published until after the author's death. It contains a kind of manual of reflections upon all those natural defects or acquired evil habits of the mind, which unfit it for the task of acquiring and retaining knowledge. It shows an acuteness and scope of observation not inferior to that exhibited in his great anterior work, together with the same calm but ardent spirit of humanity and benevolence which animates all the writings, as it did the whole life, of this great and excellent man.

§ 5. I have now to consider a series of excellent writers, who will always retain the place of classics in English prose, and who are equally worthy of admiration as Protestant theologians and as models of logical and persuasive eloquence. At the head of them stands ISAAC BARROW (1630-1677), a man of almost universal acquirements, and whose sermons are still studied as the most powerful and majestic prose compositions that the seventeenth century has produced. He was born in 1630, educated at the Charter-house, whence he passed to Trinity College, Cambridge, of which he was one of the most illustrious alumni. He is said to have been, as a boy, remarkable for a violent and quarrelsome disposition, and to have been perpetually fighting with his schoolfellows: of this temper nothing remained in after life save great energy and vigor of character, and a degree of personal courage of which he gave a striking proof in a sea-fight against an Algerine pirate, when returning from his travels in the East. At the University his studies seem to have embraced every branch of knowledge, not only Philology, of which he became so great a proficient as to have been first an unsuccessful and afterwards a successful candidate for the Greek professorship, but all the range of the mathematical sciences, together with Anatomy, Chemistry, and Botany. After some time he left Cambridge, and travelled through the greater part of Europe to the East, revisiting France and Italy on his way to Smyrna and Constantinople, and returning home by way of Germany and Holland in 1645. It was while sailing in the Mediterranean that he gave that proof of intrepidity to which I have alluded above. During his residence in the East he pursued his studies in Natural History, and obtained some acquaintance with the Oriental Languages, so useful in biblical research. On returning to Cambridge he was appointed Professor of Greek, to which he added the chair of Geometry in Gresham College, and afterwards the Lucasian professorship of Mathematics in the University. He was one of the ablest and profoundest mathematicians of his day, and cultivated with distinguished success those same departments of science in which his illustrious pupil and successor, Newton, gained his undying glory — as Optics, Mechanics, and Astronomy. Indeed it has been the misfortune of Barrow that his mathematical fame, though brilliant and solid, has been eclipsed by the superior splendor of his great contemporary's renown. Had he not lived at the same time with Newton, and pursued nearly the same branches of investigation, the name of Barrow would have stood among those of the foremost mathematicians of England. Newton was, indeed, a pupil of Barrow, who warmly appreciated and befriended him; and it was to him that he resigned his Lucasian professorship. This transfer took place in 1669; before which period Barrow had taken orders, and devoted himself to that career of theology and Christian eloquence in which he assuredly had no rival to fear. His sermons, many of which were preached in London, now became famous. He was named one of the king's chaplains, and in 1672 was elected Master of Trinity College; and having in his turn filled the high office of Vice-Chancellor of the University, he died of a fever at the early age of forty-six, in 1677.

It is related that though Barrow's appearance in the pulpit was far from imposing at the first glance, his influence as an orator was irresistible, and that notwithstanding the dignity and Demosthenic grandeur of his eloquence, he at commencing suffered painfully from diffidence and timidity. His pulpit orations are not only filled and almost overladen with thought, so that even the most powerful intellect must use all its force and employ all its attention to follow his reasoning, but they were, as compositions, elaborated with the greatest care, and revised and rewritten with scrupulous anxiety before he was satisfied with his work. His sermons are numerous; and many of the most valuable of them form series, devoted to the exhaustive explanation of some particular department of religious knowledge or belief: thus there is an excellent series of discourses commenting upon the Lord's Prayer, which is anatomized, clause by clause; each article forming the text of a separate discourse. A similar set of sermons is devoted to the Creed, another to the Decalogue, another to the Sacraments, and so on. The predominant quality of Barrow's style is a weighty majesty of thought and diction; every line that he produced bears a peculiar stamp of unconscious power — the vigor of a mind to which no subtlety was too arduous, no deduction too obscure. Whatever subject he approaches he seems to handle with a giant grasp, and to manage the most ponderous difficulties of theology with an heroic ease, like that of Homer's champions hurling stones that "nine degenerate men" of modern times would fail to lift. Though full of truly Christian and evangelical meekness, his writings have not that flush of beauty, that almost effeminate prodigality of images, that lingering and somewhat enervate melody that make the writings of Jeremy Taylor so poetical and so enchanting. Nor does he fall into Taylor's error of overloading his sermons with quotation. If Taylor be of the Corinthian, Barrow is of the Doric order, not devoid of appropriate ornament, but chiefly distinguished for solidity and justness of proportion. If Taylor be the English Isocrates, Barrow is the Demosthenes of the Church. In some general features of style the reader will trace a resemblance between Barrow and Bossuet. It is true that the grand tone of denunciation is seldom heard from the lips of the Protestant divine; but both exhibit a similar loftiness of conception, a similar might and grasp of intellect, and a similar severity and purity of taste. There is perhaps no English prose writer, the study of whose works would be more invigorating to the mind, and more adapted to the formation of a pure taste, than Barrow; nor can there be a better proof that the most capable critics have agreed in this opinion, than the fact that Chatham recommended Barrow, as the finest model of eloquence.

to his son, and the accomplished Landor has not hesitated to place him above all the greatest of the ancient thinkers and philosophers. "Plato and Xenophon," he makes one of his personages assert, "as men of thought and genius, might walk without brushing their skirts between these two covers," striking his hand on a volume of Barrow.

§ 6. It will be necessary to pass rapidly over the names of a considerable number of able divines who adorn the Church and literature of their country during the period of which I am now treating. Their works are distinguished by merits varying both in kind and in degree; but they are all characterized in common by a spirit which I may call Protestant, or rather Anglican; a mixture of Christian fervor and extensive learning with a practical acquaintance with the requirements and dangers of real life — a spirit equally remote from the fanatical gloom and mysticism of the Calvinistic extreme, and the dogmatic pedantry of the Romish writers. The first I shall mention is JOHN PEARSON (1613–1686), originally Professor of Theology and Master of Trinity College, Cambridge, and afterwards Bishop of Chester. His most celebrated work is his *Exposition of the Creed*, which is still regarded as one of the most complete and searching treatises investigating the great fundamental principles of our faith. In our examination of the English divines we shall see that they are pretty equally shared between our two great Universities. The theological and political tendencies which predominated at one or another period in these two learned bodies are faithfully reflected in the writings of their children; for in that agitated epoch political and theological tendencies were intimately connected together, most of the great and exciting questions being tinged with a strong leaven of either spirit; but our Universities have no reason to be ashamed either of the learning or the conduct of their *alumni*.

§ 7. Next after Barrow, JOHN TILLOTSON (1630–1694) perhaps enjoys the highest and most durable popularity among the pulpit orators of this time: indeed the popularity of his sermons has extended to the present day, and they are frequently read by pious Churchmen even now. But Tillotson, though a sound and classical English prose-writer, was a man of a calibre far inferior to Barrow. He studied at Cambridge, where he at first rendered himself conspicuous for his decided Puritan sympathies. He, however, afterwards made no difficulty in conforming to the rules and discipline of the Anglican Church, and ultimately rose to the dignity of Archbishop of Canterbury. He was a person of easy, good-natured, and amiable character; and his change of party seems to have left no other effect upon him than that of increasing his candor and indulgence for all shades of sincere opinion. In his conduct as a pastor and as a prelate he exhibited much zeal in correcting the abuses which had crept into the Church, and gave a notable example of liberal charity and episcopal virtue. He was renowned as a preacher; and his sermons, though falling far short of Barrow's in grasp of mind and vigor of expression, are precisely of such a nature as is most likely to command popularity. They show an easy flow of style, sometimes, it is true, carrying too far the affectation of familiarity, in consequence of which the images and illustrations are occasionally trivial; but there is a good deal of artifice, and even sophistry, in the reasoning, cunningly concealed under an air of candor which never deserts Tillotson. His sentences, too, are often singularly unmusical, and are evidently made as colloquial in tone as possible. Tillotson often preached to the higher classes; and in addressing such congregations he strove to conquer their fashionable indifference by adopting, as far as possible, the tone and air of a man of the world.

§ 8. ROBERT SOUTH (1633-1716) enjoyed in his day the reputation of being the "wittiest Churchman" of the time. His character was far less deserving of admiration than that of Tillotson, as he exhibited extreme violence in attacking opinions from which he had apostatized. Like the Archbishop, he began his career as a partisan of Puritan doctrines, and produced an extravagant poetical eulogy of Cromwell; but at the University he imbibed the extreme Tory or monarchical opinions which had become prevalent at Oxford, where he filled the post of Public Orator, and indeed became one of the most characteristic specimens of that bigoted and unreasonable class of Churchmen who were called *highfliers* in the party jargon of the day, and who went all lengths in maintaining the outrageous doctrines of passive obedience and non-resistance. He often preached before Charles II., and was much admired by the courtly audiences of those days for the animation, and even gayety, of his manner, and the pleasant stories and repartees which he sometimes introduced into his sermons. Many witty and jocose anecdotes are related of him; but in these cases it is necessary to accept such stories with some reserve, as there exists in the world a vast floating capital of such pleasantries, which are successively fathered upon any man who possesses a reputation for humor. The gross adulation with which he was not ashamed to address Charles II., and in which he lauded the virtues of Charles I., proves that South, with all his talents, has no claim to the character of a high-spirited man, particularly when we contrast the furious personal abuse he lavished on Cromwell with the extravagant praise that he had previously given him. His denunciations of the principles and convictions of his former party, too, are so unmeasured and illiberal as to destroy our belief in their sincerity, and we feel involuntarily constrained to attribute them to the got-up fervor of an interested convert.

EDWARD STILLINGFLEET (1635-1699), Bishop of Worcester, is another name which must not be passed over without notice. He is principally remembered for his controversy with Locke, some of whose propositions he attacked, on the ground of their being, as he maintained, hostile to the doctrine of the immateriality, and consequently of the immortality, of the soul. Locke triumphantly replied to these objections; and the philosopher was so generally considered as having been victorious in this contest of argument over the divine, that the mortification of defeat is said to have shortened Stillingfleet's life.

THOMAS SPRAT (1636-1713), Bishop of Rochester, was a man re

nowned in his time for the brilliancy and variety of his talents. He was an ardent cultivator of physical science, which had just then made its first sudden bound forwards in that splendid career of observation and discovery which has ever since gone on progressing with such portentous rapidity. He was one of the members of the Royal Society, then recently founded, and to which the glory of English science owes so much. He was distinguished as a poet, though his writings in this department are now little read; and as a biographer of poets, as the author of an excellent and interesting *Life of Cowley*. Besides these he was a theologian and preacher of no mean ability, and a very active contributor to the polemical and political literature of his day. Sprat was a member of the University of Oxford; and that his high reputation for brilliancy of eloquence and ardor of imagination was not to be entirely attributed to the partiality of contemporary admiration, may be proved by the honorable terms in which his talents are spoken of by two such critics as Johnson and Macaulay.

I shall conclude the present category of authors with the name of WILLIAM SHERLOCK (1678–1761), Dean of St. Paul's, whose expositions of scriptural doctrine have always been regarded with approval, and who in his own time was conspicuous as a polemic writer against the Dissenters. His best-known work is a ***Practical Discourse concerning Death***.

§ 9. Though the aim of these pages is to give an account of Literature in its strict and proper sense, the subject of Science comes in contact with that object at so many points, that I should but ill perform my task without offering some notice of the writers who, though they devoted their chief attention to physical researches, yet occupy a place among English authors. It is true that at the period of which we are treating, important scientific works were generally given to the world in Latin, that language being then the universal medium, the intellectual money, so to say, current among the learned in all parts of Europe; but many of the great men who carried to so unequalled a height the glory of the human intellect and the honor of their native country, composed a portion of their works in their vernacular tongue, or at least published English versions of their learned labors, and thus deserve some mention in their capacity of English writers. There are few episodes in the history of human knowledge more surprising than the sudden and dazzling progress made in the physical sciences towards the end of the seventeenth century. This progress is visible in Germany, in Holland, in France, and in England; in none of these nations, indeed, more so than in our own. It was just and natural that the vivifying effect produced by the writings and by the method of Bacon should be peculiarly powerful in that country which gave birth to the great reformer of philosophy; and there is no doubt that the development of free institutions and open discussion exercised a powerful influence in facilitating research, in promoting a spirit of inquiry, and in rendering possible the open expression of opinion.

A very prominent part in the cultivation and dissemination of experimental research, in all branches of physics and natural history, was played by the Royal Society, that illustrious body which, originating in the meetings of a few learned and ingenious men at each other's houses, was incorporated by Charles II., in 1662, into the Society to the labors of which human knowledge owes so much.

Among the founders of this corporation one of the most active was DR. JOHN WILKINS (1614–1672), Bishop of Chester, a most energetic and ingenious man, whose vivacious inventiveness sometimes bordere upon extravagance, but who rendered great services, both in his writings and his conversation, to the cause of science. He was essentially a projector, and at a period when the first wonderful results of the employment of the experimental method had made even the calmest minds in some degree lose their balance, and become unable to distinguish between what was practicable and what was visionary, we can hardly feel surprised that the ardor of his genius should have carried him beyond the bounds of good sense, so far as to seriously propose, among other Utopian schemes, a plan by which it would be possible to fly to the moon. Wilkins was a theological writer and a preacher of high reputation; but his name is now chiefly associated with his projects and inventions, and in particular with the prominent part he took, together with Boyle and others, in the organization of the Royal Society.* He married the sister of Oliver Cromwell, and his stepdaughter was married to Tillotson.

§ **10.** The progress of physical science had been very rapid before this time. The labors of WILLIAM GILBERT (1540–1603), whose researches in magnetism laid the foundation for all future investigations in that science, and the immortal discovery of WILLIAM HARVEY (1578–1658), the first demonstrator of the circulation of the blood, belong to an earlier period; but the concentration of the labors of many separate investigators upon one special branch of research was a result mainly to be attributed to the institution of our great scientific corporation. As a proof of this I may mention the contemporary, or nearly contemporary labors of Newton in optics, astronomy, and celestial mechanics, and those of Flamsteed, Halley, and others, in the combined departments of careful observation and the application of new and convenient mathematical formulas to the practical solution of problems in astronomy and navigation; while Boyle, embracing a wide extent and vast variety of research, particularly devoted himself to the investigation of chemical and pneumatic science; and Ray, Derham, Willoughby, and Sydenham brought valuable contributions to physiology, natural history, and medicine. Most of these great men, independently of their purely scientific writings, which, as in the case of the immortal *Principia* of the most illustrious among them, were in Latin, contributed in

* The chief works of Wilkins are:—1. *Discovery of a New World: or a discourse tending to prove that it is probable that there may be another habitable World in the Moon; with a discourse concerning the possibility of a passage thither.* Published in 1638. 2. *An Essay towards a Real Character and a Philosophical Language* printed by order of the Royal Society in 1668.

a greater or less proportion to the vernacular literature of their country. Thus Newton wrote, in English, upon the Prophecies, and other subjects connected with biblical knowledge; and Boyle enjoyed a high reputation for his moral and religious writings. It is remarkable and consoling to see with what unanimous consent these illustrious philosophers, all men of extraordinary acumen and caution, and all accustomed, from the nature of their pursuits, to take nothing for granted, to weigh and balance evidence with the severest exactness, agreed in the intensity of their religious convictions. Those habits of physical investigation which are so often ignorantly accused of being unfavorable to the habi of belief, seem to have led the most powerful and inquiring minds only the more irresistibly to a firm conviction of the truths of revealed religion.

§ **11.** SIR ISAAC NEWTON (1642–1727) was born in 1642, of a respectable but not opulent family, at Woolsthorpe in Lincolnshire. From his earliest boyhood he showed the greatest taste and aptitude for mechanical invention, and entering the University of Cambridge, in 1660, he made such rapid progress in mathematical studies that in nine years Barrow resigned in his favor the Lucasian professorship. The greater part of Newton's life was passed within the quiet walls of Trinity, of which College he is the most glorious ornament; and it was here that he elaborated those admirable discoveries and demonstrations in Mechanics, Astronomy, and Optics which have placed his name in the very foremost rank of the benefactors of mankind. He sat in more than one parliament as member for his university; but he appears to have been of too reserved and retiring a character to take an active part in political discussion: he was appointed Master of the Mint in 1695, and presided over that establishment at the critical period of Montagu's bold recall and reissue of the specie. It is delightful to see with what simplicity and readiness this illustrious philosopher abandoned all those sublime researches in which he stands almost alone among mankind, and devoted all his energy and attention to the public duties that had been committed to his charge. He even writes with a kind of pettish querulousness to upbraid friends who had consulted him about "mathematical things," as he calls them, when he was entirely occupied with the public service. In 1703 he was made president of the Royal Society, and knighted two years afterwards by Queen Anne. He died in 1727. His character, the only defects of which appear to have been a somewhat cold and suspicious temper, was the type of those virtues which ought to distinguish the scholar, the philosopher, and the patriot. His modesty was as great as his genius, and he invariably ascribed the attainment of his discoveries rather to patient attention than to any unusual capacity of intellect. His English writings, which are chiefly discourses upon the prophecies and chronology of the Scriptures, are composed in a manly, plain, and unaffected style, and breathe an intense spirit of piety, though his opinions seem to have in some measure inclined towards the Unitarian type of theology. His glory, however, will always mainly rest upon his purely scientific works, the chief of which are so well known that it is almost superfluous to enumerate them — the *Philosophiæ Naturalis Principia Mathematica* and the invaluable treatise on *Optics*, of which latter science he may be said to have first laid the foundation.

§ **12.** JOHN RAY (1628-1705), together with Derham and Willoughby, combined the descriptive department of Natural History with moral and religious eloquence of a high order: they seem never to be weary of proclaiming the wisdom and goodness of that Providence whose works they had so attentively studied. Ray was the first who elevated Natural History to the rank of a science. ROBERT BOYLE (1627-1691) was an able writer as well as a distinguished philosopher. "No Englishman of the seventeenth century, after Lord Bacon," observes Mr Hallam, "raised to himself so high a reputation in experimental philosophy as Robert Boyle: it has even been remarked that he was born in the year of Bacon's death, as the person destined by nature to succeed him — a eulogy which would be extravagant if it implied any parallel between the genius of the two, but hardly so if we look on Boyle as the most faithful, the most patient, the most successful disciple who carried forward the experimental philosophy of Bacon. His works occupy six large volumes in quarto. They may be divided into theological or metaphysical and physical or experimental. The metaphysical treatises — to use that word in a large sense — of Boyle, or rather those concerning Natural Theology, are very perspicuous, very free from system, and such as bespeak an independent lover of truth. His Disquisition on Final Causes was a well-timed vindication of that palmary argument against the paradox of the Cartesians, who had denied the validity of an inference from the manifest adaptation of means to ends in the universe to an intelligent Providence. Boyle takes a more philosophic view of the principle of final causes than had been found in many theologians, who weakened the argument itself by the presumptuous hypothesis that man was the sole object of Providence in the creation. His greater knowledge of physiology led him to perceive that there are both animal and what he calls cosmical ends in which man has no concern."

One of the most extraordinary writers of this period — at least in a purely literary sense — was THOMAS BURNET (1635-1715), Master of the Charter-house, author of the eloquent and poetic declamation *Telluris Theoria Sacra*, giving a hypothetical account of the causes which produced the various irregularities and undulations which we see in the earth's surface. These he attributes to the action of fire and water, and in language of indescribable picturesqueness he first describes the convulsions and cataclysms which have given to our earth its present form, and then goes on to picture the final destruction that is awaiting our globe in the mysterious abysses of the future. The geological and physical theories of Burnet are fantastic in the extreme; but the pictures which he has drawn of the devastation caused by the great unbridled powers of Nature are grand and magnificent, and give Burnet a claim to be placed among the most eloquent and poetical of prose-writers. In richness of fancy and melody of language he is no unworthy rival of Jeremy Taylor, with whose noble description of the final destruction of the earth Burnet's sublime painting will bear a comparison.

§ **13.** This writer must not be confounded with GILBERT BURNET (1643-1715), born in Edinburgh, in 1643, and who was one of the most active politicians and divines during the period embracing the reigns of Charles II., James II., and the accession of William of Orange. By birth and personal predilections he occupies a middle space between the extreme Episcopalian and Presbyterian parties, and though a man of ardent and busy character, he was possessed of rare tolerance and candor. He was much celebrated for his talents as an extempore preacher, and was the author of a very large number of theological and political writings. Among these his *History of the Reformation* is still considered as one of the most valuable accounts of that important revolution. The first volume of this was published in 1679, and the work was afterwards completed by the author. He also gave to the world an account of the *Life and Death* of the witty and infamous *Rochester*, whose last moments he attended as a religious adviser, and whom his pious arguments recalled to a sense of repentance. He at one time enjoyed the favor of Charles II., but soon forfeited it by the boldness of his remonstrances against the profligacy of the king and by his defence of Lord William Russell, whose execution was one of the great political crimes of that reign. Burnet also published an *Exposition of the XXXIX Articles.* On falling into disgrace at court he travelled on the Continent, and afterwards attached himself closely to the service of William of Orange at the Hague, where he became the religious adviser of the Princess Mary, afterwards Queen. At the Revolution Burnet accompanied the deliverer on his expedition to England, took a very active part in controversy and political negotiation, and was raised to the Bishopric of Salisbury, in which function he gave a noble example of the zeal, tolerance, and humanity which ought to be the chief virtues of a Christian pastor. He died in 1715, leaving the MS. of his most important work, the *History of My Own Times*, which he directed to be published after the lapse of six years. This work, consisting of Memoirs of the important transactions of which Burnet had been contemporary, is of a similar nature and not inferior value to Clarendon's, which represents the events of English history from a nearly opposite point of view. Burnet is minute, familiar, and gossiping, but lively and trustworthy in the main as to facts; and no one who desires to make acquaintance with a very critical and agitated period of our annals can dispense with the materials he has accumulated. It is from him that we learn the true greatness and energy of William's character, and the milder virtues of his queen; and the very ardor of Burnet's predilections gives a vivacity and a value to his pictures of men and things.

NOTES AND ILLUSTRATIONS.

(A.)—OTHER THEOLOGICAL WRITERS.

HENRY MORE (1614-1687), known by the name of the Platonist, spent his whole life at Cambridge engaged in metaphysical and philosophical studies. He is a writer of genius and power, but he adopted the mystical views not only of the later Platonists, but even of the cabalistic writers. His most important works are *The Mystery of Godliness*, *The Mystery of Iniquity*, and *A Discourse on the Immortality of the Soul*. He also wrote a volume of *Philosophical Poems*.

RALPH CUDWORTH (1617-1688), a contemporary of More at Cambridge, and Regius Professor of Divinity at that University, is a writer of still greater power than More. In 1678 Cudworth published the first part of his great work, entitled *The True Intellectual System of the Universe*. "Cudworth," observes Mr. Hallam, "was one of those whom Hobbes had roused by the atheistic and immoral theories of the Leviathan; nor did any antagonist perhaps of that philosopher bring a more vigorous understanding to the combat. This understanding was not so much obstructed in its own exercise by a vast erudition, as it is sometimes concealed by it from the reader. Cudworth has passed more for a recorder of ancient philosophy, than for one who might stand in a respectable class among philosophers; and his work, though long, being unfinished, as well as full of digression, its object has not been fully apprehended. This object was to establish the liberty of human actions against the fatalists. Of these he lays it down that there are three kinds: the first atheistic; the second admitting a Deity, but one acting necessarily and without moral perfections; the third granting the moral attributes of God, but asserting all human actions to be governed by necessary laws which he has ordained. The first book of the Intellectual System, which alone is extant, relates wholly to the proof of the existence of a Deity against the atheistic fatalists, his moral nature being rarely or never touched; so that the greater and more interesting part of the work, for the sake of which the author projected it, is wholly wanting, unless we take for fragments of it some writings of the author preserved in the British Museum. . . . . Cudworth is too credulous and uncritical about ancient writings, defending all as genuine, even where his own age had been sceptical. His terminology is stiff and pedantic, as is the case with all our older metaphysicians, abounding in words which the English language has not recognized. He is full of the ancients, but rarely quotes the schoolmen. Hobbes is the adversary with whom he most grapples; the materialism, the resolving all ideas into sensation, the low morality of that writer, were obnoxious to the animadversion of so strenuous an advocate of a more elevated philosophy. In some respects Cudworth has, as I conceive, much the advantage; in others, he will generally be thought by our metaphysicians to want precision and logical reasoning; and upon the whole we must rank him, in philosophical acumen, far below Hobbes, Malebranche, and Locke, but also far above any mere Aristotelians or retailers of Scotus and Aquinas." He was, however, most unfairly accused of favoring the atheists, because he fairly stated their arguments. He left an only daughter, who married Sir Francis Masham, and who is known as the friend of Locke (see p. 251).

RICHARD CUMBERLAND (1632-1718), made Bishop of Peterborough by William III., is best known by his Latin work, *De Legibus Naturæ Disquisitio Philosophica*, published in 1672, in opposition to the philosophical principles of Hobbes. Cumberland was also the author of an *Essay on Jewish Weights and Measures*.

ROBERT LEIGHTON (1613-1684), Archbishop of Glasgow, whose commentary on the First Epistle of St. Peter may be regarded as a classic, both for profoundness of thought and felicity of expression. Attention has been drawn to it in modern times by Coleridge in his "Aids to Reflection."

THEOPHILUS GALE (1628-1678), Fellow of Magdalen College, Oxford, but ejected at the Restoration, is known by a learned work, called *The Court of the Gentiles*, published between 1669 and 1677, in which he attempts to prove that all heathen philosophy was borrowed from the Scriptures, or at least from the Jews.

GEORGE BULL (1634-1710), Bishop of St. David's, a great opponent of the Augustinian theology, and still regarded as one of the pillars of the Anglican Church. In his *Harmonia Apostolica*, published in 1669, he maintains that we are to interpret St. Paul by St. James, and not St. James by St. Paul, because St. James was the latest authority. Another of Bull's celebrated works was the *Defensio Fidei Nicenæ* published in 1685, for which he received the thanks of an assembly of the French clergy, through the influence of Bossuet.

JOHN OWEN (1616-1683), Vice-Chancellor of the University of Oxford under Cromwell, and one of the most eminent of the Independent divines, published a large number of theological works, of which *An Exposition on the Epistle to the Hebrews* is the best known. Owen's style is dull, heavy, and confused.

JOHN HOWE (1630-1705), chaplain to Cromwell, and also an eminent Independent divine, wrote various theological works, the style of which is far superior to Owen's.

JOHN FLAVEL (1627-1691), a Nonconformist divine at Dartmouth, whose theological writings are chiefly devotional, characterized by much fervor, and of the Calvinistic theology. They are still popular with persons of that school.

MATTHEW HENRY (1662-1714), son of Philip Henry, and like his father an eminent Nonconformist divine. He is best known by his Commentary on the Bible, written in a perspicuous and pointed style.

EDMUND CALAMY (1600-1666), originally a clergyman of the Church of England, but afterwards a dissenting minister in London. He took part in the *Smectymnus*, an attack on Episcopacy. His sermons are practical, though now and then we find political feelings overmastering the calmer style of the divine.

THOMAS ELLWOOD (1639-1713), a pupil of Milton and when the great poet became blind, he read to him. He turned Quaker, and labored diligently to extend the principles of his Society. He wrote an autobiography and several polemical tracts, such as that against *Tithes*, 1682, and on the *Histories of the Old and New Testament*, 1705-9.

DR. WILLIAM LOWTH (1661-1732), a celebrated classic and theologian, prebend of Winchester, and rector of Buriton. His writings on the *Inspiration of the Old and New Testaments*, and *Commentaries*, were valuable additions to the theology of the age. He was the father of the well-known Bishop Lowth.

SCOTTISH DIVINES.

SAMUEL RUTHERFORD (1600-1661).
THOMAS HALYBURTON (1674-1712).
THOMAS BOSTON (1676-1732).

In this age occurred "the great Marrow controversy," occasioned by a book of Edward Fisher, a Calvinistic minister in Wales, entitled *The Marrow of Modern Divinity*, 1645. This work was warmly received by a section of the church, while another portion rejected it. It gave rise to much disturbance and contest.

The three writers mentioned above, who took an active part in this controversy, were severe and sombre in their divinity; but there was a massiveness of thought and a richness of expression which still make this age one of the most remarkable and valuable in the history of Christian theology.

(B.) OTHER PROSE WRITERS.

BULSTRODE WHITELOCKE (1605-1676), an able lawyer, was sent by Cromwell as ambassador to Sweden, and held other high offices under the Protector. He wrote *Memorials of English Affairs*, from the beginning of the reign of Charles I. to the Restoration, which work was first published in 1682.

HENRY NEVILE (1620-1694), the friend of Harrington, the author of the Oceana, and a member of the republican party, published in 1681 an able work, entitled *Plato Redivivus, or a Dialogue concerning Government*. The dialogue is between a Venetian nobleman, an English doctor (supposed to be Harvey), and an English gentleman. Though formerly belonging to the republican party, Nevile in this work advocates a monarchical form of government.

SIR WILLIAM DUGDALE (1605-1686), a learned antiquary, who published the *Baronage of England, The Antiquities of Warwickshire Illustrated, A History of St. Paul's Cathedral*, &c.

ELIAS ASHMOLE (1617-1692), also a learned antiquary, who married the daughter of Sir William Dugdale, published in 1672 *The Institutions, Laws, and Ceremonies of the Most Noble Order of the Garter*. He wrote numerous other works, and was the founder of the Museum at Oxford which still bears his name.

ANTHONY WOOD (1632-1695), published in 1691 his *Athenæ Oxonienses*, an account of the eminent men educated at Oxford.

JOHN AUBREY (1626-1697) collected materials for many works, but published only one, in 1696, entitled *Miscellanies*, containing an account of popular superstitions, from which it appears that Aubrey was very credulous.

SIR MATTHEW HALE (1609-1676), the celebrated Chief-Justice of the King's Bench in the reign of Charles II., wrote several works, many of them of a moral and religious character, of which his *Contemplations, Moral and Divine*, are the best known.

SIR GEORGE MACKENZIE (1636-1691), Lord-Advocate in the reigns of Charles II. and James II., was well acquainted with polite literature, but was held in execration by the Covenanters for his enforcement of the cruel laws against them. His prose is better than his verse, and his *Moral Essays* may still be read with pleasure.

CHAPTER XV.

POPE, SWIFT, AND THE AUGUSTAN POETS.

§ 1. ALEXANDER POPE: his early life. Publication of his *Pastorals, Essay on Criticism, Rape of the Lock, Windsor Forest.* Versions from Chaucer. § 2. Translation of the *Iliad* and *Odyssey*. § 3. Publication of the *Elegy on an Unfortunate Lady*, the *Epistle from Sappho to Phaon*, the Epistle of *Eloisa to Abelard*. His life at Twickenham. His edition of Shakspeare. Collection of *Miscellanies*. § 4. Publication of the *Dunciad*, of his *Epistles, Essay on Man*, and *Imitations of Horace*. § 5. His death, character, and other works. § 6. Criticism of the *Rape of the Lock*. § 7. JONATHAN SWIFT: his early life. His connection with Sir William Temple. § 8. Settles in Ireland. His *Tale of a Tub*. § 9. Returns to England and joins the Tories. Made Dean of St. Patrick's, Dublin. § 10. Takes up his residence in Ireland. *Drapier's Letters. Travels of Gulliver.* His Death. § 11. His relation to Stella and Vanessa. § 12. Criticism of the *Travels of Gulliver*. § 13. Of the *Tale of a Tub*, and other works. Comparison between Swift, Rabelais, and Voltaire. § 14. DR. JOHN ARBUTHNOT. His *History of John Bull*. § 15. MATTHEW PRIOR. § 16. JOHN GAY. The *Beggar's Opera*. § 17. GARTH, PARNELL, and TICKELL. § 18 EDWARD YOUNG. The *Night Thoughts*. § 19. ALLAN RAMSAY.

§ 1. SENSE, vigor, harmony, and a kind of careless yet majestic regularity were the characteristics of that powerful school of poetry which was introduced into England at the Restoration, and of which Dryden is the most eminent type. These qualities were, in the so-called Augustan reign of Queen Anne, succeeded by a still higher polish, and an elegance sometimes degenerating into effeminacy. The slender and somewhat enervate grace of the Corinthian order succeeds the more masculine beauties of the Ionic. Far above all the poets of this epoch shines the brilliant name of ALEXANDER POPE (1688-1744). He was born in London of a respectable Catholic family of good descent, in 1688. His father had been engaged in trade as a linen-draper, and retired to a pleasant country house at Benfield, near Windsor, so that the childish imagination of the future poet imbibed impressions of rural beauty from the lovely scenery of the Forest. The boy was of almost dwarfish stature, and so deformed that his after life was "one long disease," which not only precluded the possibility of his embracing any active profession, but could be preserved only by constant care and nursing. Like many other deformed and diminutive persons, he possessed a singularly intellectual and expressive countenance, and his eyes were remarkable for their tenderness and fire. He exhibited an extraordinary precocity of intellect, and the literary ambition by which he was devoured even from his early boyhood at once pointed out the poetical career to which he was destined. He has said of himself, "I lisped in numbers, for the numbers came," and the earliest attempts at poetry were made by him when he had hardly emerged from the nursery. His father had acquired a competent fortune, which enabled the boy poet to indulge that taste for study and poetical reading which continued to be the passion of his life. At the age of twelve he was so struck with reverence for the glory of Dryden, that he is said to have persuaded a friend to accompany him to Will's Coffee-house, which the glorious veteran was in the habit of frequenting, and to obtain a glance of the illustrious patriarch, whose death took place in that year. At sixteen he commenced his literary career by composing a collection of *Pastorals* and by translating portions of *Statius*, which were published in 1709. From this period his activity was unremitting, and an uninterrupted succession of works, equally varied in their subjects and exquisite in their finish, placed him at the head of the poets of his age. His *Essay on Criticism*, published in 1711, and highly praised by Addison, was perhaps the first poem that fixed his reputation, and gave him a foretaste of that immense popularity which he enjoyed during his whole life. The precepts of this work are the same as those inculcated by Horace, and repeated by Boileau, and all the poets and critics of the classical school, but they are expressed by Pope with such a union of force and delicacy, such ripeness of judgment and such grace of expression and melody of verse, that the poem appears less like the effort of a young writer than the result of consummate experience and practice in composition. It is to this period of Pope's career that we must ascribe the conception and first sketch of the most original and charming production not only of Pope, but of the century in which he lived; a perfect gem, or masterpiece, equally felicitious in its plan and execution; one of those happy thoughts that are to be attributed half to genius and half to rare and favorable accident. This was the mock-heroic poem *The Rape of the Lock*, justly described by Addison as "*merum sal*, a delicious little thing," to which I shall presently recur and analyze in detail. This poem is the victorious rival of the *Lutrin* and of *Vert-vert*, and is indeed incomparably superior to every heroic comic composition that the world has hitherto seen. In 1713 appeared his pastoral eclogues entitled *Windsor Forest*, in which beauty of versification and neatness of diction do all they can to compensate for the absence of that deep feeling for nature which the poetry of the eighteenth century did not possess. The plan of this work is principally borrowed from Denham's *Cooper's Hill*, but Pope has hardly any passage to be compared with those few but unequalled lines which have preserved the vitality of the latter work. The frequent descriptions introduced by Pope, though beautiful in their way, have the same artificial air which forms so fatal a defect in almost all pastoral poetry, from Virgil to Sannazzaro. In 1715 Pope published several modernized versions from Chaucer, as if he were desirous in all things to parallel his great master Dryden. He produced the *Temple of Fame*, and the not over moral story of *January and May*, which is in substance the *Merchant's Tale* of the great patriarch of our literature.

§ 2. At this time, too, Pope undertook the laborious enterprise of translating into English verse the Iliad and the Odyssey. The work was to be published by subscription, and Pope was at first reduced almost to despair when brought face to face with the vastness of his undertaking: but with practice came facility, and the whole of the Iliad was successfully given to the world by the year 1720, and excited a frenzy of admiration which found a vent in some laudatory epigrams which by the very extravagance of their eulogy of Pope only prove how little the writers understood of Homer. In a pecuniary sense this was a most successful venture: Pope received for his labor upwards of 3200*l.*, and laid the foundation of that competence which he enjoyed with good sense and moderation. The Odyssey did not appear till five years later: and of this he himself translated only twelve of the twenty-four books, employing for the remaining half the assistance of the respectable contemporary poets WILLIAM BROOME (1689–1745) and ELIJAH FENTON (1683–1730), to whom he of course paid a proportionable share of the proceeds. Pope selected for the form of his version that rhymed decasyllabic verse of which he was so consummate a master, but which, however beautiful as a medium for appropriate subjects, is quite unfitted, from the regularity of its pauses, the neatness of its structure, and the irresistible tendency to terminate the sense with the couplet, to reproduce in English the solemn, ever-varied, resounding swell of the billow-like hexameter of Homer. The old Ionian bard is stripped of his flowing chlamys and his fillets, and imprisoned in the high-heeled shoes, the laced velvet coat and flowing periwig, of the eighteenth century. Mechanically, indeed, Pope's translation is far from unfaithful; but in the spirit, the atmosphere, so to say, of the original, the ballad-like version of Chapman is far superior. Bentley's criticism is, after all, the best and most comprehensive that has yet been made on this work: "It is a pretty poem, Mr. Pope, but you must not call it Homer." It will nevertheless be always regarded as a noble monument of our national literature; and it is difficult to imagine how many readers, to whom the original Greek was inaccessible, have filled their minds with the brilliant though refracted effulgence of the great Sun of Poetry, by studying the graceful couplets of Pope. It is unfortunate that in their selection of the two great epic writers as subjects of translation, Dryden and Pope had not exchanged parts: Dryden, though perhaps incapable of reproducing the wonderful freshness and grandeur of Homer, still possessed most of the Homeric quality of fire and animation; while Pope, in whom consummate grace and finish is the prevailing merit, would have far more successfully reproduced the unsurpassed dignity, the chastened majesty, of Virgil.

§ 3. About 1717 Pope probably composed the *Elegy on an Unfortunate Lady*, the *Epistle from Sappho to Phaon*, borrowed from the *Heroïdes* of Ovid, and the *Epistle of Eloisa to Abelard*, a poem on a similar plan, but taking its subject from the romantic and touching story of mediæval times. These works are all artificial in their arrangement, and in some degree also in their diction; but the passion they express is so intense, and illustrated with such varied, pathetic, and beautiful imagery, that they will ever be considered masterpieces. The subject of the first is very obscure, but it seems to have been derived from a real tale of disappointed love and suicide; though many passages in the Elegy are of consummate beauty, the *Eloisa*, as a whole, is a finer and more sustained composition. The intense glow of unhappy passion lights up the gloom and horror of the cloister with a lurid splendor, like that of the fabled lamps in sepulchres. During this part of his life Pope was living, with his father and mother, to whom he always showed the tenderest and most dutiful affection, at Chiswick; but on the death of the former parent he removed with his mother to a villa he had purchased at Twickenham, on a most beautiful spot on the banks of the Thames. Here he passed the remainder of his life, in easy, if not opulent circumstances; his taste for gardening, and his grotto and quincunxes, in which he delighted, amused his leisure, and he lived in familiar intercourse with almost all the most illustrious statesmen, orators, and men of letters of his day — Swift, Atterbury, Addison, Bolingbroke, Prior, Gay, and Arbuthnot. He was perhaps a little too fond of talking of his own independence, and alluding, with affected indifference, to the great and titled guests whom he received, and like most men who live in a narrow clique, was very apt to treat all those who were outside the charmed bounds as wretches deserving only of contempt, and as if all virtue, wit, and honor were exclusively confined to his own set. In 1725 he published an *Edition of Shakspeare* in six volumes, in the compilation of which he exhibited a deficiency in that peculiar kind of knowledge which is absolutely indispensable to the commentator on an old author. His work was judged by the public to be far inferior to the contemporary edition of Theobald's, who, though destitute of poetic genius, possessed more critical discernment, and produced a much more valuable result. For this Pope's jealous envy could never forgive Theobald, and we shall see by and by how savagely he revenged himself. During the three following years he was engaged, together with Swift and Arbuthnot, in composing that famous collection of *Miscellanies*, to which each of the friends contributed. The principal project of the fellow-laborers was the extensive satire on the abuses of learning and the extravagances of philosophy, entitled Memoirs of *Martinus Scriblerus*. This was intended to be for literature something like what Don Quixote was for chivalry: but the idea, though happily enough carried out in some of its parts by the festive and humorous wit of Arbuthnot, was not a very happy one. The contributors, and chiefly Pope, whose admirable satiric genius instantly deserted him when he abandoned verse for prose, often descend to personality and buffoonery, and perhaps, with the exception of Arbuthnot's inimitable burlesque *History of John Bull*, the prose portions of the Miscellanies are hardly worthy of the fame of their authors. Pope, however, supplied to this publication some of the finest and most brilliant of his poetical pieces, particularly in the department of satire.

§ 4. The brilliant success of Pope, his steady popularity, the tinge

of vanity and malignity in his disposition, and above all the supercilious tone in which he speaks of the struggles of literary existence, then at a very low ebb of social respectability, all conspired to raise around him a swarm of enemies, animated alike by envy and revenge. He had been frequently engaged in squabbles, in some of which his conduct was far from estimable, and he determined to inflict upon his innumerable enemies, the gnats and mosquitos of the press, a severe and memorable castigation. Under the mask of zeal for reason and good taste he could indulge to the extreme the pleasure of chastising men whom he feared or hated: and in many cases there is no reason to doubt that he was in good faith when he identified the expression of personal spite with the indignant voice of taste and morality. He composed the satire of the *Dunciad*, the primary idea of which may have been suggested by Dryden's Mac-Flecknoe, but which is incomparably the fiercest, most sweeping, and most powerful literary satire that exists in the whole range of literature. In it he flays and boils and roasts and dismembers the miserable scribblers he attacks, with the ferocity of a Mohock execution, and with more than the ingenuity of Orcagna's pictures of the Last Judgment. Most of the persons attacked are so obscure that their names are now rescued from oblivion by being embalmed in Pope's satire, like worthless rubbish preserved in the lava of a volcano: but in the latter part of the poem, and particularly in the portion added in the editions of 1742 and 1743, the poet has given a sketch of the gradual decline and corruption of taste and learning in Europe, which is one of the noblest outbursts of his genius. The plot of the poem — the Iliad of the Dunces — is not very ingenious, and was borrowed from Dryden. Pope supposes that the throne of Dulness is left vacant by the death of Shadwell, and that the various aspirants to "that bad eminence" engage in a series of trials, like the Olympic Games of old, to determine who shall inherit it. In the original form of the poem, as it appeared in 1728 and 1729, the palm of pedantry and stupidity was given to Theobald, Pope's successful rival in commenting Shakspeare. In the new edition of 1743, published just before the poet's death, Theobald is degraded from the throne, and the crown is given to Colley Cibber, an actor, manager, and dramatic author of the time, and who, whatever were his vices and frivolity, certainly was in no sense an appropriate King of the Dunces But in this, as in numberless other instances, Pope's bitterness of enmity entirely ran away with his judgment. The poem is an admirable — almost a fearful — example of the highest genius applied to the most selfish of ends — the lightning of genius, under the guise of chastising bad literature, burning, searing, and devouring the victims of self-love.

In the four years extending from 1731 to 1735 Pope was engaged in the composition of his *Epistles*, addressed to Burlington, Cobham, Arbuthnot, Bathurst, and other distinguished men. These poems, half satirical and half familiar, were in their manner a reproduction of the charming productions of Horace. Indeed Pope may not unjustly be called the English Horace, as Dryden is the English Juvenal. With less good-humored epicurean philosophy than the great Augustan satirist, Pope possesses a finer and more elaborate poetical spirit; in good sense, clearness, and neatness of diction it is difficult to give the palm of superiority. At the same period was produced the *Essay on Man*, in four epistles, addressed to Bolingbroke — a work of more pretension, and aiming at the illustration of important ethical and metaphysical principles. In the First Epistle Man is regarded in his relation to the Universe, in the Second in his relation to himself, in the Third in his relation to society, and in the Fourth with respect to his ideas of and pursuit after happiness. In the whole poem the exquisite neatness and concision of the language, the unvarying melody of the verse, and the beauty and felicity of the illustrations, are far more perceptible than the orignality or even soundness of the theory: but the *Essay* is an incomparable example of the highest skill in the art of so treating an abstract philosophical subject as to render it neither dry nor unpoetical. I have now arrived nearly at the end of Pope's well-filled and brilliant literary life. The death of his mother, of whose "declining age" he had "rocked the cradle" with the tenderest assiduity, the loss of many friends, among whom was Swift, now sinking into hopeless idiocy, the increased complication of his own maladies, to whose number asthma and dropsy were now added — all these causes threw a gloom over his declining years and warned him of his approaching end. He gave to the world his highly-finished and brilliant *Imitations of Horace*, in which, like so many previous writers of his own and other countries, from Bishop Hall down to Boileau, he adapted the topics of the Roman satirist to the persons and vices of modern times.

§ 5. On the 30th of May, 1744, this great poet died, unquestionably the most illustrious writer of his age, hardly if at all inferior to Swift in the vigor, the perfection, and the originality of his genius. As a man he was a strange mixture of selfishness and generosity, malignity and tolerance: he had a peculiar tendency to indirect and cunning courses; and the intense literary ambition by which, like Voltaire, he was kept in an incessant fever, sometimes showed itself in personal and sometimes in literary meannesses and jealousies. Of this his quarrel with Addison is a characteristic specimen; while his dishonorable conduct towards Bolingbroke will ever be a blot upon his memory as a man. Among his works few of any importance have, I think, been left unnoticed. I should perhaps mention his Eclogue of the *Messiah*, a happy adaptation of the Pollio of Virgil to a sacred subject, the *Ode on St. Cecilia's Day*, in which he was bold enough to try his strength with Dryden, and though defeated, yet without disgrace. Pope has selected as his illustration of the powers of Music the story of Orpheus, and particularly his descent into Hades for Eurydice. He composed a considerable number of *Epitaphs*, some of which are remarkable as exemplifying his consummate skill in the art of paying a compliment. In a multitude of passages throughout his works we find instances of this, and we may apply to him what Macaulay has so gracefully said of Voltaire: "No man ever paid compliments better than he. His sweetest confectionery had always a delicate, yet stimulating flavor, which was delightful to palates wearied by the coarse preparations of inferior artists." The *Rape of the Lock*, the *Epistles*, and even the *Satires*, abound in examples of the most artful and ingenious flatteries, often veiled, for greater piquancy, under an air of blame: one of the most perfect instances is in the closing lines in the Epitaph of young Harcourt.

§ 6. The subject of the *Rape of the Lock*, perhaps the most inimitable of Pope's productions, is the rather cavalier frolic of Lord Petre, a man of fashion at the court of Queen Anne, in cutting off a lock of hair from the head of Arabella Fermor, a beautiful young maid of honor. This incident Pope treated with so much grace and delicate mock-heroic pleasantry, that on consulting Addison on the first sketch of the poem, the latter strongly advised him to refrain from altering a "delicious little thing," that any change would be likely to spoil. Pope, however, fortunately for his glory, though the critic's counsel was as prudent as it certainly was sincere, incorporated into his poem the delicious supernatural agency of the Sylphs and Gnomes, beings which he borrowed from the fantastic theories of Paracelsus and the Rosicrucian philosophers. The action of these miniature divinities, being exquisitely proportioned to the frivolous persons and events of the poem, delightfully replaces the classical deities, some of whom favor, while others oppose, the heroes of epic story from Homer downwards; and is far more graceful, as well as original, than the hackneyed personification of Sloth and other abstract qualities in the famous mock-heroic of Boileau. The poem is a little dwarf epic in five books, and bears the same relation to the lofty and serious works of which it is a parody, as a Dresden china figure does to the Venus or the Apollo. It is all sparkling with the flash of diamonds and roguish glances, all a flutter with hoop-petticoats, brocades, and powdered wigs. Book I., after a due Invocation, describes the counsel given by Ariel in a dream to Belinda, whose toilet is then inimitably described. Canto II. relates the sacrifice offered by "the adventurous Baron" in the hope of succeeding in his designs on the Lock; after which Belinda goes upon the water, and there is a solemn council of the Sylphs, in which their chief, Ariel, warns them of the impending danger. In Canto III. the courtly party arrives at Hampton Court, where they take coffee, and a game of Ombre is described with the minutest detail, and in the manner of a solemn tournament. After this the tremendous catastrophe is described, and the fatal scissors, furnished by a rival beauty, divide the fatal lock "from the fair head, forever, and forever!" Canto IV. transports us to the gloomy abode of Spleen, and introduces us to the Gnomes. Sir Plume, "with earnest eyes and round, unthinking face," is sent by Belinda to demand the restitution of the lock, which is refused. Canto V. describes a terrific combat — in metaphor — between the beaux and belles. Many of the former perish by the cruel glances of their fair opponents, when in the midst of the carnage, the

Lock, the *causa teterrimæ belli*, is suddenly snatched up into the skies, where it has ever since glittered as the constellation called the Tress of Berenice.

§ 7. The most original genius, as well as the most striking character of this period, was JONATHAN SWIFT (1667–1745), who, whether as a man or as a writer, occupies a foremost place in the literary and political history of the time. He was born in Dublin, in 1667, of English family and descent, his father having the appointment of Steward of the King's Inns. His entrance into life was unfortunate, and tended to aggravate a natural tendency towards haughty misanthropy and bitter self-reliance. His father died in very embarrassed circumstances, and Swift, a posthumous child, found himself from his earliest years a dependant upon the charity of distant relations. He passed three years of his infancy in England, and was afterwards sent to a school at Kilkenny, whence he proceeded, in 1682, to Trinity College, Dublin. Here he occupied himself with irregular and desultory study, and at last received his degree with the unfavorable notice that it was conferred "speciali gratia," indicating that his conduct had not satisfied the academical authorities. In 1688 he entered the household of Sir William Temple, a distant connection of his family, who was then residing in luxurious retirement at his beautiful villa of Moor Park in Surrey where the cautious and sybaritical old diplomatist amused himself with gardening and dilettante literature. Swift remained in Temple's service as a sort of humble hanger-on, secretary, and literary subordinate, and there is no doubt he deeply felt the miseries of dependence which must have intensely rankled in the memory of so proud and ambitious a character. Temple was frequently visited and consulted by King William, from whom Swift, who had occasionally been employed as a messenger between his patron and that prince, expected, but in vain, some advancement. It is said that William offered Swift a commission in a troop of horse, and taught him the Dutch way of cutting and eating asparagus. Swift's residence at Moor Park continued down to Temple's death in 1699, with, however, one or two intervals, in which he took the degree of M. A. at Oxford, and entered into holy orders on the Irish Church establishment, having obtained a small preferment on which he found it impossible to live. These temporary absences were caused by quarrels with his patron, whose easy yet supercilious condescension his bitter and haughty spirit could not brook; but he swallowed his humiliation, and begged pardon in terms which show how he chafed against the yoke of dependence, and explain the mingled shame and anger with which in after life he recalled his connection with Temple. During this period of his life he was industriously employed in study; and steady and extensive reading corrected the defects of his earlier education. His acquaintance with history, poetry, and science was considerable, and he possessed in the highest degree the power of rendering instantly available for a specific purpose the stores he had acquired. On Temple's death he became the literary executor of his patron, and prepared for the press the numerous works he left, which he presented, with a preface and dedication written by himself, to William III.

§ 8. Failing in obtaining any preferment from that sovereign, never remarkable for much sympathy with letters, Swift went to Ireland as chaplain to Earl Berkeley, the Viceroy, and received the small livings of Laracor and Rathbeggan, altogether amounting to about 400*l.* a year. At Laracor he lived till 1710, amusing himself with gardening and repairing his church and parsonage, and making yearly visits to England, where the brilliancy of his conversation, his vigorous aptitude for affairs, and his connection with Temple, rendered him acceptable to the leading Whig statesmen who were the ministers of the day. He became the familiar companion of the most illustrious men of the time, Halifax, Godolphin, Somers, as well as Addison, equally famous in letters and in politics. Congreve he had met when visiting Temple at Moor Park, and Dryden was a distant relation of Swift's family. Swift's persevering dislike to Dryden, whom he constantly underrated in after life, is said to have originated in the great poet's unfavorable estimate of some of Swift's verses which were submitted to him, on which occasion he said, "Cousin Swift, you will never be a poet!" His connection with William III. and Temple, as well as the predominance at that moment of Whig policy, naturally caused Swift to enter public life under the Whig banner; but he very soon gave proof that his adherence to any party was merely a matter of interest and ambition, and that his sole motive was his own personal aggrandizement, the gratification of his malignant pride, and the delight of inflicting pain upon his opponents. In 1704 was published his first important work, unquestionably his production, though never formally owned by him, the savage and yet exquisitely humorous pasquinade entitled *The Tale of a Tub.* Temple had actively engaged in the furious controversy that had originally been raised in England between Boyle and Atterbury on the one hand and the illustrious Bentley on the other, respecting the genuineness of certain letters ascribed to the tyrant Phalaris. These letters had been edited with great parade by a clique of Oxford wits and pretended philologers; and the unequalled knowledge and acumen of the greatest of English, perhaps the greatest of all Hellenists, had instantly pronounced them spurious, and completely unmasked the quackery and sciolism of the Oxford scholars. The dispute originating in a mere personal squabble with Bentley, who had been, though unjustly, accused of discourtesy in his capacity of librarian to the University of Cambridge, soon embraced the then violently-contested question of the relative superiority of the Ancients and the Moderns. This was a dispute which involved almost all the nations of the Continent, and Temple had engaged in the discussion on the side of the Ancients, exhibiting a lamentable deficiency of knowledge and common sense.* Swift became the champion of the same side, and gave a striking foretaste of those tremendous powers of sarcasm and vitupera-

* For a fuller account of this controversy, see Notes and Illustrations to Ch. XVI.

tion which made him the most formidable pamphleteer that ever existed. The merits of the case he does not attempt to touch; but with the wildest and most grotesque oddity of invention, and the unscrupulous use of everything coarse, familiar, and ludicrous in language, he strives to cover his opponents with ignominy and contempt. The plan of the pamphlet is in no respect original; it describes a general engagement between the Ancients and the Moderns, in a sort of parody of the Homeric battles; but the boldness and fertility of the abuse show how great a master had appeared of the whole vocabulary of insult. Like a Chinese piratical junk, he gains his victory by the loathsome offensiveness of the stink-pots which he hurls.

In 1708 Archbishop King, Primate of Ireland, employed Swift to negotiate, in the name of the Irish clergy, with the English government, for the abandonment of their claim to the first-fruits and tenths, a species of fines paid on the institution to benefices in the Church: and with this intention he visited England, and exhibited great activity and intelligence, but without obtaining the result he desired. He had now rendered himself a prominent person both in his profession and in the general world of politics, was known and feared as a powerful and unscrupulous pamphleteer, and was the familiar associate of those who were at the head of affairs; but his hopes of preferment were not fulfilled. At this time he regarded Ireland with a mixture of contempt and detestation, and was eager for any advancement that would enable him to reside in England, near the focus of literary and political activity; and his failure urged him to an act characteristic of his temper. He unceremoniously abandoned his former party, and began to write, to intrigue, and to satirize, with even greater force, vehemence, and success, on the side of the Tories.

§ 9. Harley, afterwards created Earl of Oxford, and St. John, better known as the brilliant but unprincipled Bolingbroke, were now at the head of affairs. So formidable a political condottiere as Swift they naturally received with open arms; as a deserter from the enemy's camp he brought with him not only the zeal of the apostate, but a damaging knowledge of the secrets of the adversary's tactics, and Swift was not a man to scruple to use any advantage he possessed. He became more useful to his present than he had ever been to his former party, and was caressed and flattered by the great, the fair, the witty, and the wise. He affected to treat men of the highest rank with the freedom and familiarity of an equal, and this somewhat *parvenu* air was forgiven in consideration of his undoubted talents and the services which he rendered with his terrible pen. His negotiation about the first-fruits and tenths was successfully terminated, and he poured forth with unexampled rapidity squib after squib and pamphlet after pamphlet, employing all the stores of his unequalled fancy and powerful sophistry to defend his party and to blacken and ridicule his antagonists. The great object of his ambition was an English bishopric, and the ministers would have been willing enough to gratify him; but he encountered secret hostility, such as a man of such a stamp could not fail to have aroused. Sharp, then Archbishop of York, represented to the Queen that high preferment could not with propriety be conferred upon a man whose writings, as in the case of the *Tale of a Tub*, verged upon the very brink of profanity and indecency; but a still more fatal hostility was that of the Queen's favorite, the Duchess of Somerset, whom Swift had lampooned in a manner that the meekest of her sex could not forgive. Swift's bitter and cruel verses had indeed been suppressed as soon as printed, but the Duchess threw herself at the Queen's feet with a copy of the pasquinade, and he learned *furens quid femina possit* In spite of the strongest desire to do more for their supporter, the ministers were obliged to confine his recompense to the deanery of St. Patrick's, Dublin, to which he was nominated, to his extreme disappointment, in 1713. He was soon recalled from Ireland, whither he had been called by the business of his installation, by the news of an irremediable breach between Harley and Bolingbroke. Swift vainly interfered to reconcile the statesmen, upon whose union depended the whole stability of the government: he found Harley timid, pompous, and reserved, and St. John volatile and insolent, and after intense but fruitless efforts to heal their dissension Swift again retired. This took place in 1714. Bolingbroke, combining with Mrs. Masham, the Queen's favorite, who, rising from a humble and almost menial position, had gradually succeeded in ousting the imperious Duchess of Marlborough from the favor of that weak princess, succeeded in turning out Harley, whom the Queen abandoned under pretext of his having appeared before her flustered with wine. But St. John's triumph was short. The death of Anne and the accession of the Elector of Hanover recalled the Whigs to power; the ministry were accused, and with strong grounds of probability, of a plot for bringing back the Pretender, and thus nullifying the Protestant succession; Oxford and Atterbury were committed to the Tower, Bolingbroke fled beyond the sea, and soon made his appearance in the exiled court of St. Germains, and Swift retired to Ireland, where he was received with a universal yell of contempt and execration.

§ **10.** During his long and repeated visits to England Swift's company and conversation had always been sought after by men of letters as well as statesmen. He founded, together with Harley and other friends, a sort of Club called the Society of Brothers, in which many of his most amusing political squibs were concocted; and with Pope, Gay, and Arbuthnot, he formed what was called the Scriblerus Club, the members of which were united by the closest intimacy, and threw into a common stock their ideas embodied in the famous *Miscellanies*. From 1714 to 1720 Swift resided principally in Ireland, and from being an object of detestation raised himself to a height of popularity which has never been surpassed even in the stormy political atmosphere of that country. The condition of Ireland, always a cancer and a disgrace to Britain, was just then unusually deplorable; the population torn by bitter rivalry and mutual persecution between the dominating Protestant and the enslaved and impoverished Catholics, while the national evil of absenteeism had reduced the agricultural classes to the lowest abyss of misery and degradation. In some degree, perhaps, from motives of philanthropy, but far more, probably, out of a desire to annoy and embarrass the English government, Swift boldly proclaimed the misery of the country, and the force and bitterness of his pamphlets soon drew down the persecution of the Ministers. A State prosecution was instituted against the printer, which the Government made desperate but unavailing efforts, by means of subservient judges and packed juries, to carry to a conviction. But the highest point of Swift's Irish popularity was attained by the seven famous letters which he wrote, signed *M. B. Drapier* (draper), and inserted in a Dublin newspaper. The occasion was the attempt, on the part of the English ministry, to force in Ireland the circulation of a large sum of copper money, the contract for coining which had been undertaken by William Wood, a Birmingham speculator. This money Swift endeavored to persuade the people was enormously below its nominal value, and he counselled all true patriots not only to refuse to take it, but to refrain from using any English manufactures whatever. The force and animation of his arguments, and the exquisite skill with which he wore his mask of a plain, honest, patriotic tradesman, excited the impressionable Irish almost to frenzy. As Swift afterwards boasted to Archbishop Boulter, he would have had but to lift his finger to cause the ministry to be torn in pieces. The government was obliged to renounce the project of Wood's coinage, and the attorney-general's indictment of Harding, the printer of the letters, though maintained by all the violence of Whitshed, was ignored by the jury. Swift was known to be the real author of the letters, and his defence of the rights of the Irish people made him from this moment the idol of that warm-hearted and impressionable race.

From 1724 to 1737 Swift was occupied with the production not only of his greatest and most immortal work, the *Travels of Gulliver*, but with an infinity of pamphlets and occasional compositions. He visited England in 1726, when *Gulliver* was brought out, exciting a universal burst of delight and admiration. The death of Stella, one of the few beings that Swift ever really loved, happened in 1728, and the loss of many friends further contributed to darken and intensify the gloom of this proud and sombre spirit. He had from an early period suffered more or less constantly from giddiness and pain in the head; and the fearful anticipations of insanity which had constantly haunted him were destined to be cruelly verified. In 1741 he was afflicted with a painful inflammation which necessitated restraint, and which gradually merged into a state of idiocy that lasted without interruption till his death in 1745. During the last three years of this period he is said never to have spoken, and to have shown an almost complete unconsciousness; and there is nothing recorded more melancholy or more instructive than the spectacle of this great wit and satirist, without any attendance save that of mercenary hands, — for his own unaccountable and selfish conduct had deprived him of the comforts of a family, —

expiring, "a driveller and a show." He is buried in his own cathedral of St. Patrick's, and over his grave is inscribed that epitaph which he composed for himself, and which is one of the most tragic and terrible of human compositions: in it he speaks of resting "ubi sæva indignatio ulterius cor lacerare nequit;" a fearfully vivid portraiture of his own character.

§ 11. My account of Swift would be imperfect without some mention of those extraordinary events which are connected with his relations towards the two unhappy women whose love for him was the glory and the misery of their lives. While residing in Temple's family he became acquainted with Esther Johnson, a beautiful young girl brought up as a dependant in the house, and who, though passing for the daughter of Sir William's steward, appears really to have been a natural child of the old diplomatist. To her, while hardly in her teens, Swift gave instruction; and the bond between master and pupil ripened into the deepest and tenderest passion on the part of the maiden, and as much attachment on that of the former as the proud and bitter nature of Swift was capable of feeling. Having inherited a small fortune, Swift induced Stella — such was the poetical name he gave her — to settle with her friend Mrs. Dingley in Ireland, where he maintained with both of them — though Mrs. Dingley was merely a mask to save appearances — that long, curious, and intimate correspondence which has since been published as his *Journal to Stella.* In it we see the unbending of this haughty spirit: he addresses his correspondent in the fondest puerilities of his "little language," and while giving the minutest account of his thoughts and doings from day to day, he interests us with a thousand details concerning the political and literary life of the time. The journal is full of the most affectionate aspirations after a tranquil retreat in the society of "little M. D.," and there can be hardly any doubt that Swift anticipated marrying Stella, while Stella's whole life was filled with the same hope. During one of his visits to London Swift became intimate with the family of a rich merchant named Vanhomrigh, over whose daughter Hester, to whom he gave the name of Vanessa, he exerted the same kind of enchantment as he had exhibited in gaining the affections of Stella, a power indeed which Swift seems to have eminently possessed over the imagination of women, however inexplicable it may be, when we think of the bitterness and coldness of his nature. From at first directing her studies he succeeded, perhaps involuntarily on his part at first, in inspiring an ardent, beautiful and accomplished girl with a passion so deep and intense, that the difference of age only makes more difficult to explain. He seems to have played with this attachment, alternately exciting and discouraging hopes in poor Vanessa; while his letters to Stella in Ireland grow gradually colder and more formal. On the death of her father Miss Vanhomrigh, who possessed an independent fortune, retired to a villa at Celbridge in Ireland, where Swift continued his visits, but without clearing up to one of these unhappy ladies the nature of his relations with the other. At last Vanessa, driven almost to madness by suspense and irritation, wrote to Stella to inquire into the nature of Swift's position with regard to her. The letter was intercepted by Swift, and brought back by him, and thrown down without a word, but with a terrible countenance, before the unhappy writer. Swift left her, and never saw her more; and poor Vanessa died a few weeks afterwards (1723), being one of the rare examples of death of a broken heart. Stella, whose health was entirely broken, implored Swift to render her the poor justice of calling her his wife; and it is said that the ceremony of marriage was privately performed in the garden, though Swift never either recognized her in public, or changed his strange rule of never living in the same house with her, or even seeing her otherwise than in the presence of a third person. This rule had been observed ever since Stella's first settlement in Ireland. This unhappy victim of Swift's eccentric selfishness — the second — died in 1728; and in the notices he wrote of her, while smarting under the agony of her recent loss, it is impossible not to see a love as intense as its manifestation had been singular and inexplicable.

§ **12.** The greatest and most characteristic of Swift's prose works is the *Voyages of Gulliver*, a vast and all-embracing satire upon humanity itself, though many of the strokes were at the time intended to allude to particular persons and contemporary events. The general plan of this book is the following: It is written in the character of a plain, unaffected, honest ship-surgeon, who describes the strange scenes and adventures through which he passes with that air of simple, straightforward, prosaic good faith that gives so much charm to the narratives of our brave old navigators, and which Defoe has so successfully mimicked in *Robinson Crusoe*. The contrast between the extravagance of the inventions and the gravity with which they are related, forms precisely the point of the peculiar humor of Swift, and is equally perceptible in other works, while it was the distinguishing feature of that singular saturnine kind of pleasantry which made his conversation so sought after. He is said never to have been known to laugh; but to have poured forth the quaintest and most fantastic inventions with an air of gravity and sternness that kept his audience in convulsions of merriment. This admirable fiction consists of four parts or voyages: in the first Gulliver visits the country of Lilliput, whose inhabitants are about six inches in stature, and where all the objects, houses, trees, ships, and animals, are in exact proportion to the miniature human beings. Indeed, one of the principal secrets of Swift's humor, as well as of the power he possesses over the imagination — I had almost said the belief — of the reader, is the exquisite and watchful manner in which these proportions are preserved. The author never forgets himself in this respect; nay, he has managed to give to the passions, the ambition, the ceremonies, and the religion of his diminutive people an air of the same littleness as invests the physical objects. The invention displayed in the droll and surprising incidents is as unbounded as the natural and *bonâ-fide* air with which they are recounted; and we can hardly wonder at the exclamation of the learned bishop, who is said to have cried out, "That there were *some* things in Gulliver that he could *not* quite believe!" The second voyage is to Brobdingnag, a country of enormous giants, of about sixty feet in height; and here Gulliver plays the same part as the insect-like Lilliputians had played to him. As in the first voyage, the contemptible and ludicrous side of human things is shown by exhibiting how trifling they would appear in almost microscopic proportions, so in Brobdingnag we are made to perceive how odious and ridiculous would appear our politics, our wars, and our ambitions, to the gigantic perceptions of a more mighty race. The lesson is the same; but we learn it by looking through the other end of the telescope. The Third Part, which is generally found inferior, from the want of unity in the objects of representation, to the preceding voyages, carries Gulliver to a series of strange and fantastic countries. The first is Laputa, a flying island inhabited by philosophers and astronomers. Here Swift intended to satirize the follies and abuses of learning and science; but independently of the fact that much of this part, as the Academy of Lagado, is borrowed from Lucian, Rabelais, and other satirists, his strokes of ridicule are not always very well directed, and fall pointless, being levelled against imaginary follies. From Lagado the traveller goes to Glubbdubdrib and then to Luggnagg, which latter episode introduces the terrific description of the Struldbrugs, wretches who are cursed with bodily immortality without preserving at the same time their intellects or their affections.

Gulliver's last voyage is to the country of the Houyhnhnms, a region in which horses are the reasoning, civilized, and dominant beings; and where men, under the name of Yahoos, are degraded to the rank of noxious, filthy, and unreasoning brutes. The manner in which Swift has described the latter, retaining a resemblance to man in their propensities which only renders them more horrible and loathsome, shows how intense were his hatred and scorn of humanity. The satire goes on, deepening as it advances; playful and amusing in the scenes of Lilliput, it grows blacker and bitterer at every step, till in the Yahoos it reaches a pitch of almost insane ferocity, which there is but too much reason to believe faithfully embodied Swift's real opinion of his fellow-creatures.

§ **13.** In the ***Tale of a Tub*** he gives a burlesque allegorical account of the three great sects of Christianity, the Roman Catholic, the Lutheran, and the Calvinistic churches. These are represented with the wildest and most farcical extravagance of incident, under the form of three brothers, Peter, Jack, and Martin; and their squabbles and ultimate separation figure the Reformation and its consequences. Between the chapters of narrative are interposed what Swift calls *digressions*, in which the most ludicrous fancies are embodied in a degree of out-of-the-way learning not to be met with in any other of his works. Everything that is droll and familiar in ideas and language is concentrated in this extraordinary production, and many of the pleasantries are sufficiently irreverent to justify the accusation of his religious belief not being very firmly fixed. The innumerable pamphlets and political and historical tracts poured forth by Swift, as his *Conduct of the Allies*, the *Public Spirit of the Whigs*, the *Last Years of Queen Anne*, his contributions to journals, his *Sentiments of a Church of England Man*, his remarks on the *Sacramental Test*, and a multitude of others, being written on local and temporary subjects, are now little consulted; they all exhibit the vigor of his reasoning, the admirable force and directness of his style, and his unscrupulous ferocity of invective. They are all, whatever be their nature, party pamphlets of the most virulent kind, in which the author was never restrained by any feeling of his own dignity, or of candor and indulgence for others, from overwhelming his opponents with ridicule and abuse. He is like the Indian savage, who, in torturing his captive at the stake, cares little how he wounds and burns himself, so long as he can make his victim writhe; or, like the street ruffian, who, in hurling ordure on his antagonist, is indifferent to the filth that may stick to his own fingers. The bitterness, as well as the power, of these writings is often something almost diabolical. Many of his smaller prose writings are purely satirical, as his *Polite Conversation* and *Directions to Servants*. In the former he has combined in a sort of comic manual all the vulgar repartees, nauseous jokes, and *selling of bargains*, that were at that time common in smart conversation; and in the latter, under the guise of ironical precepts, he shows how minute and penetrating had been his observations of the lying, pilfering, and dirty practices of servants. Perhaps the pleasantest, as they are the most innocent, of his prose pleasantries, are the papers written in the character of Isaac Bickerstaff, where he shows up, with exquisite drollery, the quackery of the astrologer Partridge. His letters are very numerous; and those addressed to his intimate friends, as Pope and Gay, and those written to Sheridan, half-friend and half-butt, contain inimitable specimens of his peculiar humor, which has been excellently described by Coleridge as "anima Rabelæsii habitans in sicco." The three greatest satirical wits of modern times possess each a peculiar manner. Rabelais, with his almost frantic animal spirits, pours forth a side-shaking mixture of erudition and ingenious buffoonery; Voltaire, with his sly grin of contempt, makes everything he attacks appear at once odious and despicable; but Swift inspires us with loathing as well as with contempt. We laugh with Rabelais, we sneer with Voltaire; with Swift we despise and we abhor. He will not only be ever regarded as one of the greatest masters of English prose, but his poetical works will give him a prominent place among the writers of his age. They are, however, most strongly contrasted in their style and manner to the type most prevalent at the time, and of which Pope is the most complete representative. They have no pretension to loftiness of language, are written in the *sermo pedestris*, in a tone studiously preserving the familiar expression of common life. In nearly all of them Swift adopted the short octosyllable verse that Prior and Gay had rendered popular. The poems show the same wonderful acquaintance with ordinary incidents as the prose compositions, the same intense observation of human nature, and the same profoundly misanthropic view of mankind. The longest of the narrative writings, *Cadenus* (Decanus, an anagram indicating the Dean himself) *and Vanessa,* is at the same time the least interesting. It gives an account, though not a very clear one, of the love-episode which terminated so fatally for poor Hester Vanhomrigh. The most likely to remain popular are the *Verses on my own Death,* describing the mode in which that event, and Swift's own character, would be discussed among his friends, his enemies, and his acquaintances; and perhaps there is no composition in the world which gives so easy, animated a picture, at once satirical and true, of the language and sentiments of ordinary society. He produced an infinity of small burlesques and pleasantries, in prose and verse, as for example, *The Grand Question Debated,* in which he has, with consummate skill and humor, adopted the maundering style of a vulgar servant-maid. Shakspeare himself, in Mrs. Quickly and in Juliet's Nurse, has not more accurately seized the peculiarities of the lower class. A thousand parodies, jests, punning Latin and English letters, epigrams and descriptions might be cited. Many of them are slight toys of the fancy, but they are toys executed with the greatest perfection, and in some, as the *Legion Club,* the verses on Bettesworth and Lord Cutts, the ferocious satire of Swift is seen in its full intensity: they are little sparkling bubbles, but they are blown from vitriolic acid.

§ **14.** No member of the brilliant society of which Pope and Swift were the chief luminaries, deserves more respect, both for his intellectual and personal qualities, than Dr. John Arbuthnot (1667–1735). He was of Scottish origin, and enjoyed high reputation as a physician, in which capacity he remained attached to the court from 1709 till the death of Queen Anne. He was one of the most lovable, as well as the most learned and accomplished wits of the day, and was a chief contributor to those *Miscellanies* of which I have so often spoken in connection with Pope. He is supposed to have conceived the plan of that extensive satire on the abuses of learning, embodied in the *Memoirs of Martinus Scriblerus,* and to have indeed executed the best portions of that comprehensive though fragmentary work, and in particular the description of the pedantic education given to his son by the learned Cornelius. But the fame of Arbuthnot is more intimately connected with the inimitable *History of John Bull,* in which the intrigues and Wars of the Succession are so drolly caricatured. The object of the work was to render the prosecution of the war by Marlborough unpopular with the nation; but the adventures of Squire South (Austria), Lewis Baboon (France), Nic. Frog (Holland), and Lord Strutt (the King of Spain), are related with fun, odd humor, and familiar vulgarity of language. There is much of the same kind of humor as we find in the *Tale of a Tub,* and in *Gulliver;* but Arbuthnot is always good-natured, and there is no trace of that fierce bitterness and misanthropy which tinge every page of Swift. In the latter part of the *History* Arbuthnot details with great humor some of the political intrigues of the English ministry, and in particular the way in which the Scottish Presbyterian party were tricked by the Earl of Nottingham into assenting to the bill for Occasional Conformity. The characters of the various nations and parties are conceived and maintained with consummate spirit; and perhaps the popular ideal of John Bull, with which Englishmen are so fond of identifying their personal and national peculiarities, was first stamped and fixed by Arbuthnot's amusing burlesque. Besides these well-known pleasantries Arbuthnot's fertile and festive genius produced others in the same manner, as the *Art of Political Lying*, and the *Memoirs of P. P. Clerk of this Parish*, intended to caricature the trifling and egotistic details of Brunet's History. He was also the author of many learned tracts both in general literature and in subjects more immediately professional; and he seems to have fully deserved the admiration lavished upon him by all his friends, as an accomplished scholar, an able and benevolent physician, and a wit of singular brilliancy and fertility.

§ **15.** MATTHEW PRIOR (1664–1721) was a poet and diplomatist of this time, who played a prominent part on the stage of politics as well as on that of literature. He was of humble origin, and after receiving a commencement of education in Westminster School, is said to have been obliged to pass some time with an uncle who kept a tavern in London, and in whose house the lad was employed in serving the customers. His scholarship is related to have attracted the notice of the splendid and generous Dorset, who enabled him to finish his studies at St. John's College, Cambridge, where he distinguished himself and obtained a small fellowship. He took part with Montagu, another of his patrons, in the composition of the *Country Mouse and City Mouse*, a poem intended to ridicule Dryden's *Hind and Panther;* and the door of public employment was soon opened to him. His career in the diplomatic service was brilliant: after accompanying Berkeley, Ambassador to the Hague, as Secretary, he became Secretary of Legation at the Peace of Ryswick, and received a considerable pecuniary gratification from the Government. He twice resided at Versailles in the capacity of envoy, and by his talents in negotiation as well as by his wit and accomplishments in society appears to have been very popular among the French. Many stories are related of his address in polished repartee, in which he showed himself not inferior to the Parisian wits and men of letters. On returning to England he was made a Commissioner of Trade, and in 1701 became a member of the House of Commons. Though he had entered public life as a partisan of the Whigs he now deserted them for the Tories, on the occasion of the impeachment of Lord Somers; and he again went to Paris, where he lived in great splendor during the negotiations in which Bolingbroke acceded to the disgraceful Treaty of Utrecht. In 1715 he was ordered into custody by the Whigs, on a charge of high treason, and remained two years in confinement. The worst result to Prior of this political persecution was the loss of all his fortune, his means of subsistence being now nearly reduced to the small revenue of his college fellowship, which in the days of his splendor he had refused to give up, prudently calculating that the time might come when he would be glad to possess even so small an income. However, with the assistance of his friends, he published by subscription a collection of his works, the proceeds of which amounted to a considerable sum. Prior was an easy Epicurean philosopher of the Horatian stamp, and accommodated himself with facility to every change of fortune. His longer and more ambitious poems are *Alma*, a metaphysical discussion carried on in easy, unembarrassed Hudibrastic verse, exhibiting a good deal of thought and learning disguised under an easy conversational garb; and the Epic entitled *Solomon*, a poem somewhat in the manner, and with the same defects as the *Davideis* of Cowley. A work of considerable length, and ambitious in its character, is the dialogue entitled *Henry and Emma*, modernized, and spoiled in the modernizing, from the exquisite old ballad of the *Nutbrowne Maide*. The transference to modern times, and the expression in the smooth verse of the correct school of poets, of the simple passion and picturesque sentiment of the ancient poem, is like the appearance of Homer in the version of Pope. Prior's two claims to admiration are his easy, animated, half-tender, half-libertine love-songs, many of which exhibit the same union of natural though not profound sentiment with a sort of philosophic gayety and carelessness that form the peculiar charm of the French chansonniers. Prior composed a number of Tales in verse, in the same style as the *Contes* of La Fontaine, showing much similarity with that class of productions of the inimitable fabulist, but open to the same objection — an objection which will now exclude them from the reading of our more fastidious age — of occasional immorality in their subjects and treatment.

§ **16.** The name of JOHN GAY (1688–1732) is one of the most attractive among the brilliant literary stars that make up the constellation of which Pope and Swift were the leading luminaries. He was one of those easy, amiable, good-natured men who are the darlings of their friends, and whose talents excite admiration without jealousy, while their characters are the object rather of fondness than respect. He was born 1688, and carried off prematurely by an inflammatory fever, in 1732; and his death filled the jealous Pope with sorrow, and forced tears even from the hard and cynical eyes of Swift. He entered life in a humble station, as a linen-draper's shopman, but soon exchanged this occupation for a dependence upon the great, which was not more favorable either to happiness or self-respect, and for a vain pining after public employment and court favor for which his indolent and self-indulgent habits rendered him singularly unfit. His most important poetical productions at the beginning of his career were the collection of Eclogues entitled *The Shepherd's Week*, and the original and charmingly executed mock-didactic poem, *Trivia, or the Art of Walking the Streets of London*. In the former, consisting of seven pastorals, he originally intended a parody on Ambrose Philips, whose writings were the general butt or ridicule to Pope and his friends; but the work of Gay is so fresh and pleasant, and his descriptions of real English rural nature and peasant life are so agreeable that his composition will always be read with pleasure for its intrinsic merit. Like Spenser before him, Gay gave a national color to his personages and to his landscape, but his incidents and the general tone of his dialogues are comic. He has shown great address in applying the topics of Theocritus and Virgil to the customs, employments, and superstitions of English peasants, and he has endeavored to heighten the effect by the occasional employment of antiquated and provincial expressions. The *Trivia* is interesting, not only for its ease and quiet humor, but for the curious details it gives us of the street scenery, costume, and manners of that time. Gay produced several dramatic works, principally of a comic nature, and interspersed with songs, for the composition of which he showed an almost unrivalled talent: I may mention *What d'ye Call it?* a sort of half-pastoral extravaganza, and the farce of *Three Hours after Marriage*. Gay's pieces generally contained, or were supposed to contain, occasional political allusions, the piquancy of which greatly contributed to their popularity. They are also seldom free from a somewhat loose and immoral tendency. His most successful venture was the *Beggars' Opera*, the idea of which is said to have been first suggested by Swift, when residing, in 1726, at Pope's villa at Twickenham. The idea of this piece is eminently happy: it was to transfer the songs and incidents of the Italian Opera — then almost a novelty in England, and in the blaze of popularity — to the lowest class of English life. The hero of the Beggars' Opera is a highwayman, and gaolers, pickpockets, and prostitutes form the dramatis personæ, while the scene is principally in Newgate. In a word, to use Swift's expression, it was a kind of Newgate pastoral, and was a sort of parody of the opera then in vogue, while it became the origin of the English Opera. The beauty and charming voice of Elizabeth Fenton, who first acted Polly, the satirical allusions plentifully scattered through the dialogue, and eagerly caught up by the parties of the day, the novelty and oddity of the whole spectacle, and above all, the exquisite beauty of the songs plentifully interspersed throughout, gave the *Beggars' Opera* an unparalleled success. Polly became the idol of the town, and was removed from the stage to share the coronet of a duke; and Gay acquired from the performance of his piece the very large sum of nearly 700*l.* He was encouraged by success to endeavor to continue in the same strain, and produced a kind of continuation called *Polly*, which, though far inferior, was even more profitable, for being prohibited on the ground of political allusions, by the authority of the Lord Chamberlain, the opposition party, in order to spite the court, contributed so liberally to its publication that Gay is said to have cleared about 1100*l.* The poet, with that sanguine improvidence which characterized him, had previously met with severe losses in the famous South Sea mania; but grown wiser by experience, and profiting by the advice of friends who possessed more practical common sense than himself, he determined to husband the little fortune he had accumulated. He was received into the family of the Duke and Duchess of Queensberry, where he seem to have been petted like some favorite lapdog, till his death in 1732. He was the author of a collection of *Fables* in easy octosyllable verse, which he wrote to contribute to the education of William Duke of Cumberland; and though these are the best-known and most frequently cited works of the kind in our language, they will be found immeasurably inferior in wit, profound sense, picturesqueness, and above all in the rare, precious quality of intense national spirit, to the immortal fables of La Fontaine and of Krinloff. They retain their popularity from their figuring in every collection of poetry for the young, their style rendering them peculiarly adapted for reading and learning by heart. Gay's songs and ballads, whether those introduced into the Beggars' Opera and other dramatic works, or those written separately, are among the most musical, touching, playful, and charming that exist in the language. The diction and subject are often of the most familiar kind, but the grace of the expression, and the flowing harmony of the verse, make them, whether pathetic or lively, masterpieces of skill. They have, too, invariably that rare and high attribute of the best song-writing, that the very march of the number irresistibly suggests the air to which they are to be sung.

§ **17.** My space will only permit a cursory mention of SIR SAMUEL GARTH (died in 1718), a Whig physician of eminence, whose poem of *The Dispensary*, written on occasion of a squabble between the College of Physicians and the Apothecaries' Company, was half satirical and half a plea in favor of giving medical assistance to the poor; THOMAS PARNELL (1679–1718), a friend of Pope and Swift, who held a living in Ireland, and is known chiefly by his graceful but somewhat feeble tale of *The Hermit*, a versified parable founded on a striking story originally derived from the *Gesta Romanorum*; and THOMAS TICKELL (1686–1740), celebrated for his friendship with the accomplished Addison, whose death suggested a noble elegy, the only work of Tickell which rises above the elegant mediocrity that marks the general tone of the minor poetry of that age. Tickell contributed papers to the *Spectator*, and also published a translation of the first book of the Iliad, which led to a misunderstanding between Addison and Pope (see p. 293). Tickell published a collected edition of Addison's works.

§ **18.** I now come to EDWARD YOUNG (1681–1765), the most powerful of the secondary poets of the epoch. He began his career in the unsuccessful pursuit of fortune in the public and diplomatic service of the country. Disappointed in his hopes and somewhat soured in his temper, he entered the church, and serious domestic losses still further intensified a natural tendency to morbid and melancholy reflection. He obtained his first literary fame by his satire entitled the *Love of Fame, the Universal Passion*, written before he had abandoned a secular career. It is in rhyme, and bears considerable resemblance to the manner of Pope, though it is deficient in that exquisite grace and neatness which distinguish the latter. In referring the vices and follies of mankind chiefly to vanity and the foolish desire of applause, Young exhibits a false and narrow view of human motives; but there are many passages in the three epistles which compose this satire, that exhibit strong powers of observation and description, and a keen and vigorous expression which, though sometimes degenerating into that tendency to paradox and epigram which are the prevailing defect of Young's genius, are not unworthy of his great model. The Second Epistle, describing the character of women, may be compared, without altogether losing in the parallel, to Pope's admirable work on the same subject. But Young's place in the history of English poetry — a place long a very high one, and which is likely to remain a far from unenviable one — is due to his striking and original poem *The Night Thoughts*. This work, consisting of nine *nights* or meditations, is in blank verse, and consists of reflections on Life, Death, Immortality, and all the most solemn subjects that can engage the attention of the Christian and the philosopher. The general tone of the work is sombre and gloomy, perhaps in some degree affectedly so, for though the author perpetually parades the melancholy personal circumstances under which he wrote, overwhelmed by the rapidly-succeeding losses of many who were dearest to him, the reader can never get rid of the idea that the grief and desolation were purposely exaggerated for effect. In spite of this, however, the grandeur of Nature and the sublimity of the Divine attributes are so forcibly and eloquently depicted, the arguments against sin and infidelity are so concisely and powerfully urged, and the contrast between the nothingness of man's earthly aims and the immensity of his immortal aspirations is so pointedly set before us, that the poem will always make deep impression on the religious reader. The prevailing defects of Young's mind were an irresistible tendency to antithesis and epigrammatic contrast, and a want of discrimination that often leaves him utterly unable to distinguish between an idea really just and striking, and one which is only superficially so: and this want of taste frequently leads him into illustrations and comparisons rather puerile than ingenious, as when he compares the stars to diamonds in a seal-ring upon the finger of the Almighty. He is also remarkable for a deficiency in continuous elevation, advancing, so to say, by jerks and starts of pathos and sublimity. The march of his verse is generally solemn and majestic, though it possesses little of the rolling, thunderous melody of Milton; and Young is fond of introducing familiar images and expressions, often with great effect, amid his most lofty bursts of declamation. The epigrammatic nature of some of his most striking images is best testified by the large number of expressions which have passed from his writings into the colloquial language of society, such as "procrastination is the thief of time," "all men think all men mortal but themselves," and a multitude of others. A sort of quaint solemnity, like the ornamentation upon a Gothic tomb, is the impression which the *Night Thoughts* are calculated to make upon the reader in the present time; and it is a strong proof of the essential greatness of his genius, that the quaintness is not able to extinguish the solemnity.

§ 19. The poetry of the Scottish Lowlands found an admirable representative at this time in ALLAN RAMSAY (1686–1758), born in a humble class of life, and who was first a wigmaker, and afterwards a bookseller in Edinburgh. He was of a happy, jovial, and contented humor, and rendered great services to the literature of his country by reviving the taste for the excellent old Scottish poets, and by editing and imitating the incomparable songs and ballads current among the people. He was also the author of an original pastoral poem, the *Gentle* (or Noble) *Shepherd*, which grew out of two eclogues he had written, descriptive of the rural life and scenery of Scotland. The complete work appeared in 1725, and consists of a series of dialogues in verse, written in the melodious and picturesque dialect of the country, and interwoven into a simple but interesting love-story. The pictures of nature given in this charming work, equally faithful and ideal, the exact representation of real peasant life and sentiment, which Ramsay, with the true instinct of a poet, knew how to make strictly true to reality without a particle of vulgarity, and the light but firm delineations of character, render this poem far superior in interest, however inferior in romantic ideality, to the *Pastor Fido*, the *Galatea*, or the *Faithful Shepherdess*. The songs he has occasionally interspersed, though they may sometimes be out of place by retarding the march of the events, are often eminently beautiful, as are many of those scattered through Ramsay's voluminous collections, in which he combined the revival of older compositions with imitations and originals of his own. It is impossible to overrate the influence which Ramsay exerted in producing, in the following century, the unequalled lyric genius of his great successor, Burns. The treasures of tenderness, beautiful description, and sly humor which Ramsay transmitted from Dunbar, James I., David Lyndsay, and a thousand nameless national bards, were concentrated into one splendid focus in the writings of the author of a *Tam O'Shanter*.

NOTES AND ILLUSTRATIONS.

MINOR POETS.

RICHARD SAVAGE (1696–1743), so well known for Johnson's account of him, was the bastard child of Richard Savage, Earl Rivers, and the Countess of Macclesfield. He led a dissipated and erratic life, the victim of circumstances and of his own passions. In his miscellaneous poems the best are *The Wanderer* and *The Bastard*.

SIR RICHARD BLACKMORE (1658?–1729), a physician in extensive practice, and knighted by William III. wrote several epic poems, of which *The Creation*, published in 1712, has been admitted into the collections of the British Poets. Johnson remarks, that "Blackmore, by the unremitted enmity of the wits, whom he provoked more by his virtue than his dulness, has been exposed to worse treatment than he deserved." And he adds, that "the poem on *Creation* wants neither harmony of numbers, accuracy of thought, nor elegance of diction."

AMBROSE PHILIPS (1675–1749), educated at St. John's College, Cambridge, was a friend of Addison and Steele, but was violently attacked by Pope. He wrote three tragedies and some *Pastorals*, which were much admired at the time, but are now deservedly forgotten. "The pieces of Philips that please best," observes Johnson, "are those which, from Pope and Pope's adherents, procured him the name of *Namby Pamby*, the poems of short lines, by which he paid his court to all ages and characters, from Walpole, the 'steerer of the realm,' to Miss Pulteney in the nursery. The numbers are smooth and sprightly, and the diction is seldom faulty. They are not much loaded with thought, yet, if they had been written by Addison, they would have had admirers."

GEORGE GRANVILLE, LORD LANSDOWNE (1665–1735), some of whose poems are included in the collection of the British Poets, a distinction to which they are hardly entitled. His early pieces were commended by old Waller, whose faults he imitated. Pope designates him as "Granville the polite." His verses to *Mira* are best known.

ANNE COUNTESS OF WINCHELSEA (d. 1720). The writings of this lady, with all the smoothness and elegance of the age, gave indications of the better days that were coming upon English poetry. Between the *Paradise Lost* and the *Seasons*, Mr. Wordsworth says that there is not a "single new image of external nature," except in the *Windsor Forest* of Pope and the *Nocturnal Reverie* of this poetess. She was the daughter of Sir William Kingsmill, Southampton.

DR. ISAAC WATTS (1674–1748) was born at Southampton, July 17, 1674, and educated among the dissenters by the Rev. Thomas Rowe. In 1698 he became minister of the Independent congregation at Stoke Newington, where he labored, under declining health, until 1712, when he entered the house of Sir Thomas Abney of Abney Park, and continued the guest of the baronet, and afterwards of his widow, preaching occasionally, but chiefly devoting himself to study and literature until his death on the 25th November, 1748. Dr. Watts's talents were of a high order, and his efforts bore him over a most extended field of study. His style is easy and graceful, and his poetic diction gives him a high place among the religious poets of England. His *Psalms and Hymns*, whilst full of imperfections, are yet acknowledged to contain some of the finest specimens of praise in the English tongue, whilst his prose writings, embracing theological, philosophical, and polemical works, have exercised an extensive and wholesome influence, especially upon the more popular classes of the community. "It was therefore, with great propriety," said Dr. Johnson, "that in 1728 he received from Edinburgh and Aberdeen an unsolicited diploma by which he became a Doctor of Divinity. Academical honors would have more value if they were always bestowed with equal judgment."

His chief works were — *Logic*, 1725, once used as a text book at Oxford. *Astronomy and Geography*, 1726. *Works for Young Children*. Essays and theological writings.

CHAPTER XVI.

THE ESSAYISTS.

§ 1. JOSEPH ADDISON: his life. *The Campaign. Travels in Italy. Rosamond. The Drummer.* § 2. His connection with STEELE: life of the latter. The *Tatler, Spectator,* and *Guardian.* § 3. Addison's *Cato.* Made Secretary of State. His death. His quarrel with Pope. His character. § 4. His contributions to the *Tatler, Spectator,* and *Guardian.* § 5. His poetry. § 6. SIR WILLIAM TEMPLE. § 7. BISHOP ATTERBURY. § 8. LORD SHAFTESBURY His *Characteristics* § 9. LORD BOLINGBROKE. His works. His connection with David Mallet. § 10. BERNARD MANDEVILLE. His *Fable of the Bees.* § 11. BISHOP BERKELEY. His *Minute Philosopher* and *Theory of Vision.* § 12. LADY MARY MONTAGU. Her letters. Compared with those of Madame de Sévigné.

§ 1. THE class of writers who form the subject of this chapter are identified with the creation of a new and peculiar form of English literature, which was destined to exert a powerful and most beneficial influence on the manners and intellectual development of society. The mode of publication was periodical, and a kind of journals made their appearance, many of them enjoying an immense popularity, combining a small modicum of public news with a species of short essay or lively dissertation on some subject connected with morality or criticism, and inculcating principles of virtue in great, and good taste and politeness in small things. The *Essay* was first made popular by Montaigne, and the taste for this easy and desultory form of composition became general throughout Europe. It was in England that it was first combined with the principle of journalism. The first establishment of this species of publication is due to Sir Richard Steele, of whom we shall give some account presently. His most illustrious fellow-laborer in the task of disseminating among the higher and middle classes a better tone of manners and a taste for intellectual enjoyments was JOSEPH ADDISON (1672–1719). This great writer and excellent man was the son of Lancelot Addison, a divine of some reputation for learning, and was born in 1672. He was educated at the Charter-house, from whence he passed to Queen's and ultimately to Magdalen College, Oxford; and here he distinguished himself by the regularity of his conduct, the assiduity of his application, and his exquisite taste in Latin verse. Indeed his knowledge of the Roman literature, and especially of the poets, was accurate and profound. His graceful exercises in this elegant branch of letters, and in particular his poems on Punch and Judy (the *Machinæ Gesticulantes*) and on the Barometer, made him the hope and pride of his College. His first essays in English verse were a eulogistic poem on the King, which was honored with the high approval of Dryden; and it was under Dryden's wing that Addison continued his trial-flight, translating the IVth Georgic of Virgil. Lord Somers procured for the rising neophyte a pension of 300*l.*, which enabled him to travel in France and Italy, and he gave speedy proof how well he had profited by these opportunities of employing and extending his classical and philosophical acquirements. During his sojourn in France he had an interview with the aged Boileau, then the patriarch of poetry and criticism, and the literary lawgiver not only to his own country but to England. The accession of King William deprived Addison of his pension; and he passed some time in London very poor in purse, but exhibiting that dignified patience and quiet reserve which made his character so estimable. In his retirement he was found out by the Ministers, who being desirous that the recent triumphs of Marlborough should be celebrated in verse in a worthy manner, Godolphin was deputed to propose to him that he should write a poem on the immortal campaign which had just terminated in the victory of Blenheim. Addison readily undertook the task; and the unfinished portion, containing the once celebrated comparison of the great leader to the Destroying Angel, being shown to the Ministers, they were in raptures; and the work, when it appeared, under the title of *The Campaign*, was universally pronounced superior not only to Boileau, but to anything that had hitherto been written in the same style. The verses appear to modern readers stiff and artificial enough; but Addison deserves credit for having been the first to abandon the absurd custom of former poets, who praise a military hero for mere personal courage, and paint him slaughtering whole squadrons with his single arm, and to place the glory of a great general on its true basis — power of conceiving and executing profound intellectual combinations, and calmness and imperturbable foresight in the hour of danger. Literary services were at that time often rewarded with political advancement, and from this moment the career of Addison was a brilliant and successful one. He was appointed Under-Secretary of State, and Chief Secretary for Ireland, besides which high posts he at different times received various other places, both lucrative and honorable. The publication of the *Campaign* had been followed by that of his *Travels in Italy*, exhibiting proofs not only of Addison's graceful and accomplished scholarship, but also of that quiet yet delicate humor, that humane and benevolent morality, and that deep though not bigoted religious spirit, which so strongly mark his character and his writings. In 1707 he gave to the world his pleasing and graceful opera or musical entertainment entitled *Rosamond;* and about this time he in all probability sketched out the comedy of the *Drummer*, which, however, was not published till after his death when it was brought out by his friend Steele, who is said to have had some share in its composition. It is deficient in plot and vivacity of interest; but many of the scenes exhibit much comic power, and the character of Vellum, the old steward, is in particular extremely amusing.

§ 2. It was about this period of his career that Addison embarked in that literary venture first launched by his friend Steele, and with his share in which is connected the most durable element of his fame; and I shall introduce here, incidentally, a short account of Steele himself. **Sir Richard Steele** (1675-1729) was of Irish origin, but had been the schoolfellow of Addison, upon whom, both at the Charter-house and afterwards during his short stay at Oxford, he seems to have looked with a curious and most affecting mixture of veneration and love. His life was full of the wildest vicissitudes, and his character was one of those which it is equally impossible to hate and to respect. His heart was inordinately tender, his benevolence deep, and his aspirations lofty; but his passions were strong, and he had so much of the Irish impressionableness that his life was passed in sinning and repenting, in getting into scrapes and making projects of reformation which a total want of prudence and self-control prevented him from executing. Passionately fond of pleasure, and always ready to sacrifice his own interest for the whim of the moment, he caused himself to be disinherited for enlisting in the Horse-Guards as a private; and when afterwards promoted to a commission, astonished the town by his wild extravagance, in the midst of which he wrote a moral and religious treatise entitled the *Christian Hero*, breathing the loftiest sentiments of piety and virtue. He was a man of ready though not solid talents and being an ardent partisan pamphleteer, was rewarded by Government with the place of Gazetteer, which gave him a sort of monopoly of official news at a time when newspapers were still in their infancy He determined to profit by the facilities this post afforded him, and to found a new species of periodical which should combine ordinary intelligence with a series of light and agreeable essays upon topics of universal interest, likely to improve the taste, the manners, and morals of society. It should be remarked that this was a period when literary taste was at its lowest ebb among the middle and fashionable classes of England. The amusements, when not merely frivolous, were either immoral or brutal. Gambling, even among women, was frightfully prevalent; and the sports of the men were marked with a general stamp of cruelty, and of an indulgence in drunkenness which I will venture to call — for I know no more appropriate word — *blackguardly*. In such a state of things intellectual pleasures and acquirements were regarded either with wonder or contempt. The fops and fine ladies actually prided themselves on their ignorance of spelling, and any allusion to books was scouted as pedantry. Such was the disease which Steele desired to cure, and he determined to treat it, not with formal doses of moral declamation, but with homœopathic quantities of good sense, good taste, and pleasing morality, disguised under an easy and fashionable style. In 1709 he founded the *Tatler*, a small sheet which appeared thrice a week at the cost of 1*d.*, each number containing a short essay, generally extending to about a couple of octavo pages, and the rest filled up with news and advertisements. The popularity of this new kind of journal was instant and immense; no tea-table, no coffee-house — in that age of coffee-houses — was without it; and the authors writing with the ease, pleasantry, and knowledge of life, rather of men of the world and men about town, than mere literary recluses, soon gained the attention of the class they addressed. The *Tatler* continued about a year, when it was remodelled into the far more celebrated and successful *Spectator*. This was carried on upon the same plan, with the difference that it appeared every day; and after reaching five hundred and fifty-five numbers was discontinued for a short time, after which it was resumed in 1714, and extended to about eighty numbers more. A third journal, the *Guardian*, was commenced in 1712, and reached one hundred and seventy-five numbers, but was strikingly inferior to the *Spectator* both in talent and success. Though master of a singularly ready and pleasant pen, Steele was of course obliged to obtain as much assistance as he could from his friends; and many writers of the time furnished hints or contributions — Swift, Berkeley, Budgell, and others. But the most constant and powerful aid was supplied by Addison, who entered warmly into the project; and even while absent in Ireland contributed a very considerable and certainly the most valuable proportion of papers, amounting in the *Tatler* to about one sixth, in the *Spectator* to more than one half, and in the *Guardian* to one third of the whole quantity of matter. Addison's contributions to the *Spectator* are generally signed with one of the letters composing the word *Clio*. After dissipating more than one fortune, and committing all kinds of extravagant follies, poor Steele, who had thrown himself with his usual headlong zeal into politics, died in great poverty at Carmarthen in Wales, in 1729.

§ 3. In 1713 Addison brought out his tragedy of *Cato*, which, partly from the eminence of its author, partly from the avidity with which the political allusions were caught up and applied by furious parties, and in some degree, also, it is but fair to add, from the stately dignity of the declamation, enjoyed an enormous popularity. It is a solemn, cold, and pompous series of tirades in the French taste, and is written in scrupulous adherence to the severest rules of the imaginary classical unities; but the intrigue is totally devoid either of interest or probability, and the characters, including Cato himself, are mere frigid embodiments of patriotic and virtuous rhetoric. The declamation, however, is in parts dignified and noble; and the famous soliloquy on suicide, pronounced by the hero, is a passage of much merit, though by no means merit of a dramatic nature. In 1716 Addison married the Dowager Countess of Warwick, to whose son he had in former days been tutor; but this union does not seem to have added much to his happiness. The lady was of a haughty and irritable character; and Addison probably enjoyed far more of that friendly and lettered ease which he so prized, when a poor adventurer haunting the coffee-houses, than when residing under the fantastic roofs of Holland House, to which historic abode he has bequeathed the glory of his presence. Neither in the House of Commons, of which he was for some time a member, nor in Government offices where he performed important duties, was Addison distinguished for eloquence or ready business talents, though there is no reason to believe the common anecdotes which make him incapable of writing an ordinary official paper; but his invincible timidity prevented him from speaking, if ever, at least frequently or with effect; and his powers of conversation, which were extraordinary, are said to have quite deserted him in the presence of more than one or two hearers; and it was necessary, too, that they should be intimate friends, with whom he felt himself perfectly at ease. To conquer his natural diffidence, and to give flow and vivacity to his ideas, Addison is said, both for conversation and composition, to have had recourse to wine; and this is almost the only defect with which his otherwise almost perfect character can be reproached. In making the accusation we must not forget that excessive drinking was rather the fashion than regarded as the vice of the age in England.

In 1717 Addison reached the highest point of his political career: he was made Secretary of State, and in this eminent position he exhibited the same liberality, modesty, and genuine public spirit that had characterized his whole life. Nothing is more honorable to him than that, in an age when political struggles were carried on with the most unscrupulous perfidy and intolerant violence, he should never have been induced, either by interest or cowardice, to desert his friends who might be ranged under opposing banners; and in his controversies, which he actively carried on principally in the journals entitled the *Freeholder* and the *Examiner*, he never departed from a tone of candor, moderation, and good breeding, which he was almost the first to introduce into political discussion. Of this noble feature in his character, his fidelity to his old personal friendship with Swift, in spite of the latter's apostasy and defeat, is a striking example. He did not retain his post of Secretary of State for a long period: he soon retired, with a handsome pension of 1500*l.* a year, and determined to devote the evening of his days to the composition of an elaborate work on the evidences of the Christian religion. In this task he was interrupted by death, which cut short his career in 1719. One of the most interesting literary events in his life is his quarrel, or rather misunderstanding, with Pope. The latter, who was of a singularly malignant and insincere nature, suspected Addison of being jealous of his fame, and of employing, under the mask of friendship, disingenuous arts to depreciate his works. He particularly made use of a natural source of misunderstanding, really arising out of Addison's extreme delicacy, to accuse him of unfair conduct respecting his translation of the *Iliad*, of which Addison's friend Tickell had also translated a portion, and taken his advice respecting it: moreover he alleged that Addison, in dissuading any alteration in the first sketch of the *Rape of the Lock*, had been actuated by unworthy motives of envy and jealousy. But whoever knows the characters of the two persons must feel convinced that the whole tenor of Addison's life and conduct was such as to rebut these accusations, while the details of Pope's career are irresistible arguments in favor of his meanness, his irritable vanity, and his irrepressible spirit of intrigue. His enmity to Addison, however, produced one of the finest and most finished passages of his works, the unequalled lines drawing the character of Atticus, and unquestionably meant for Addison. Of all the accusations so brilliantly launched against him, Addison might plead guilty to none save the very venial one of loving to surround himself with an obsequious circle of literary admirers: but all the blacker portions of the portrait are traceable to the pure malignity of the venomous but sparkling satirist. The character of Addison seems to have approached, as near as the frailties and imperfections of our nature will allow, to the ideal of a perfectly good man. In him indulgence in detail did not exclude severity of principle, and tolerance and fervor were united in his religious sentiments. Everybody knows the story of his sending for the young Earl of Warwick, his former pupil, when on his death-bed, and telling him that he had asked his presence that he might see how a Christian can die. The scene must have made a deep impression, even upon that wild and worthless reprobate, who was the scandal of his time for his profligate adventures.

§ **4.** Of the works of this admirable man and excellent writer, it is the prose portion which gives him the right to the very high place he holds in the English Literature of the eighteenth century; and among the prose works, almost exclusively those Essays which he contributed to the *Tatler*, *Spectator*, and *Guardian*. The immense fertility of invention displayed in these charming papers, the variety of their subjects, and the singular felicity of their treatment, will ever place them among the masterpieces of fiction and of criticism. The variety of them is indeed extraordinary; and though we know that the primary hints for some of them may have been given by Swift, yet enough, and more than enough, remains to testify to the richness and inventiveness of Addison's own genius. These papers are of all kinds: sometimes we have an apologue like the *Vision of Mirza*, sometimes the *Transmigrations* of the Monkey, or the judgment of women in Hades; at other times we have calm and yet fervent religious musings on the starry heavens or in Westminster Abbey; then a playful mock criticism, or a description of Mr. Penkethman, the Puppet-show, or the Opera; then a noble appreciation of the half-neglected grandeur of Milton, or the rude, energetic splendor of the old ballad of Chevy Chase. Nothing is too high, nothing too low, to furnish matter for amusing and yet profitable reflection: from the patched and cherry-colored ribbons of the ladies, to the loftiest principles of morality and religion, everything is treated with appropriate yet unforced appositeness. Addison was long held up as the finest model of elegant yet idiomatic English prose; and even now, when a more lively, vigorous, and colored style has supplanted the neat and somewhat prim correctness of the eighteenth century, the student will find in Addison some qualities that never can become obsolete — a never-failing clearness and limpidity of expression, and a singular appropriateness between the language and the thought. Like the Pyrrha of Horace, the style of this author is *simplex munditiis*. The age of the *Tatler*, *Spectator*, and *Guardian* was the age of clubs in England; and Steele, in order to give vivacity and individuality to his journals, supposed that they were edited by some imaginary person, the philosophic spectator of the gayeties and follies of society, some Isaac Bickerstaff, or some short-faced gentleman. None of these are of much felicity, except the invention of the Club in the *Spectator*, consisting of representatives of the chief classes of town and rural society. Thus we have Sir Andrew Freeport as the type of the merchants, Captain Sentry of the soldiers, Sir Roger de Coverley of the old-fashioned country-gentlemen, and Will Honeycomb of the men of fashion and pleasure: while linking them all together is Mr. Spectator himself, the short-faced gentleman who looks with a somewhat satirical yet good-humored interest on all that he sees going on around him. In the conception and impersonation of these characters, which were in all probability first thought of by Steele, there is nothing very happy or very extraordinary, with the exception of the inimitable personage of Sir Roger de Coverley, and the adventures and surroundings of the worthy old knight. It is a perfect, finished picture, worthy of Cervantes or of Walter Scott; and the manner in which the foibles and the virtues of the old squire are combined is a proof that Addison possessed humor in its highest and most delicate perfection. The account of Sir Roger's visit to London, of his conduct at the Club, of his expedition by water to Westminster Abbey, of his remarks on the statues and curiosities he sees there, is the perfection of tender, delicate, loving humor; and Mr. Spectator's description of his visit to the old provincial magnate in his Gothic Hall, his exhibition of his picture-gallery, his behavior at church and upon the bench of the *quorum*, his long-standing amour with the widow, and the inimitable sketches of his dependants, the chaplain, the butler, and Will Wimble, the poor relation, — all these traits of character and delicate observation of nature must ever place Addison very high among the great painters of human nature.

§ **5.** Addison's poetry, though rated very high in his own time, has since fallen in public estimation to a point very far below that occupied by his prose. His Latin productions are remarkable for their elegance and a classic purity of turn and diction, and they show very great address in that difficult department in the art of the modern imitator of ancient verse, the rendering in graceful and idiomatic Latinity ideas and objects purely modern. Nevertheless, Addison's Latin poetry, like that of all moderns, labors under the fatal defect of being, after all, but a skilful *cento*, and an artificial reproduction of thought in a language which was not the real language of the writer. The songs in *Rosamond* are very pleasing and musical; and, had Addison continued to write in that manner, he would undoubtedly have left something which rival authors would have found it very difficult to surpass. Perhaps the portion of his poetical works which is destined to survive longest the dangers of complete oblivion is his *Hymns*, which not only breathe a fervent and tender spirit of piety, but are in their diction and versification stamped with great beauty and refinement: the verses beginning

"When all Thy mercies, O my God," and the well-known adaptation of the noble psalm, "The Heavens declare the Glory of God," derive, at least, as much of their effect from the sincere worship of a devout mind, of which they are the eloquent outpourings, as they do from any merely literary merits, though the latter are far superior to what is found in the general run of religious verse. The earlier and more ambitious poems of Addison, even including the once-lauded *Campaign*, have little to distinguish them from the vast mass of regular, frigid, irreproachable composition which was poured forth under the influence of Pope and the Classical school, when a certain refined mediocrity could be attained by a practice little better than mechanical, and when, of course, such mechanical address was fatal to the existence of any vigorous or original creation.

§ 6. The name of SIR WILLIAM TEMPLE (1628–1698) has already occurred in connection with the early life of Swift, who was for some time his dependant. He played an important part in the political and diplomatic history of the reigns of Charles II. and William III., and in particular negotiated with the great and good De Witt the treaty of alliance by which England, Holland, and Sweden opposed a barrier to the encroaching ambition of France. In middle life he retired from that active political life for which his timidity and selfishness, as well as his self-indulgent habits and weak health, unfitted him during a stormy and factious period, and amused himself, in his villa at Sheen, and afterwards at his lovely retreat of Moor Park, in Surrey, with gardening and elegant and somewhat dilettante literary pursuits. He produced a number of easy and graceful though superficial *Essays*, which were extravagantly lauded at a time when the rank of a writer much increased the public admiration of his works; but which are now read with interest principally on account of their easy good sense, their pleasing reflections on nature, and the agreeable and *gentlemanly* style in which they are written. He took part in the famous controversy suggested by the publication of the spurious *Letters of Phalaris*, but which had its origin in a discussion respecting the relative superiority of the Ancients or the Moderns; and he was treated by Bentley, not, indeed, with contempt, but with less respect than his contemporaries were in the habit of paying to the statesman and ambassador who condescended to enter the arena of literature. His writings upon this subject exhibit a degree of childish ignorance and presumption that would have warranted much more severe treatment at the hands of the great scholar, whose profound and accurate knowledge settled the question which his wit and pleasantry had so much enlivened.*

§ 7. No name, among the brilliant circle which surrounded Pope and Swift, is more remarkable than that of BISHOP ATTERBURY (1662–1732). A Tory and Jacobite of the extreme Oxford type, he played a prominent part, both on the political and literary scene. He was

* For a full account of this controversy, see Notes and Illustrations (B) at the end of this chapter.

a man of great intellectual activity, of considerable though by no means profound learning, and of a violent, imperious, and restless temper. He took an active part in the controversy between Boyle and Bentley, and was for a time considered, by the people of fashion who knew nothing of the subject, to have completely demolished the dull, ill-bred Cambridge pedant. He was the principal author of the reply written in the name of Boyle, whose tutor he had been at Christ-Church. Of this great and illustrious college Atterbury was for some time dean; but his violent and overbearing spirit, as well as his extravagant Tory opinions, soon excited general confusion and dispute. He was in 1713 raised to the see of Rochester, and became conspicuous not only as a controversialist, but for the force and eloquence of his speeches in Parliament. Though he had solemnly sworn to conform to the Protestant and Hanoverian dynasty upon which the throne was now settled, he began, in disgust at the coldness and suspicion with which the Court regarded him, to engage in that secret and treasonable correspondence with the party of the exiled Stuarts, that ultimately caused his well-merited fall. He had been known as an ardent favorer of the project for reinstating the Pretender at the death of Queen Anne, and in 1722 he was openly impeached by Parliament, convicted of treasonable practices, committed to the Tower, deprived of his bishopric, and condemned to exile. He resided first at Brussels, afterwards at Paris, and ultimately at Montpellier, and continued to show his attachment to the hopeless cause of the exiled family, though he refused an invitation to Rome, where the Pretender was residing. His conduct throughout appears to have been disingenuous, if not treacherous, in the highest degree. The private and personal side of Atterbury's character is far more attractive and respectable than his public conduct. His friendship for Pope was tender and sincere, and he was not only the great poet's most affectionate companion, but guided him with wise and valuable literary counsel. His fondness, too, for his daughter is a redeeming trait in his feverish and unhappy life; and there are few stories more pathetic than her hasty journey, to receive her father's blessing, to take the sacrament from his hand, and to die in his embrace. His taste in literature appears to have been sound, and the intense admiration he always showed for the genius of Milton is the more honorable to his judgment, as his extreme Tory opinions must have made it difficult for him to sympathize with the Puritan and Republican poet.

§ **8.** Lord Shaftesbury (1671–1713), grandson of the famous chancellor, who was the friend and patron of Locke, himself enjoyed the tuition of that great and excellent man. His political and private conduct affords a striking contrast to the factiousness and profligacy of the chancellor; and his literary reputation, though now become comparatively obscure, stood very high both as a moralist and metaphysician, and also as an elegant and classical model of English prose. His collected works bear the title of *Characteristics*, and may still be read with interest Shaftesbury's style is refined and regular, though somewhat ambitious and finical; but he sometimes, as in his dialogue entitled the *Moralists*, rises to a lofty height of limpid eloquence, reminding the reader of the Platonic manner. His delineations of characters show much acuteness and observation, and have obtained for him the honor of comparison with La Bruyère, to whose neat antithetical mode of portrait-painting the thoughts and language of Shaftesbury bear no inconsiderable resemblance. As a writer on ethics he is remarkable for having strongly insisted on the existence in human nature of a distinct moral sense, enabling us to distinguish almost instinctively between good and evil actions. He is indeed by some considered the discoverer of this principle, antagonistic to those reasoners who maintain that the difference between virtue and vice is only relative and experimental.

§ 9. HENRY ST. JOHN, VISCOUNT BOLINGBROKE (1678–1751), presents a strong contrast to the last-mentioned writer. His career as a statesman and orator was meteoric, and he astonished his age with the splendor and versatility of his talents. In early life he was notorious for his dissipation; but, addicting himself to politics, he became celebrated for his eloquence as a speaker and his vivacity as a party-writer. He was a member of the brilliant coterie of Pope and Swift, and was joined in the administration with Harley. The collision between his ardent and flighty character and the slow and plodding nature of his colleague produced a rupture which all the efforts of Swift could not heal; and on the death of Queen Anne, Bolingbroke, who had engaged in treasonable correspondence with the Court of St. Germains, was obliged to go into exile to escape the dangers of a formal impeachment. He had rendered himself odious to the nation by his share in the unpopular Treaty of Utrecht. In France he actually entered the service of the Pretender, but was soon dismissed through intrigue, and on receiving a pardon in 1723 returned to England, when he again made himself conspicuous for the virulence with which he opposed Walpole. He again retired to France for some time, and amused the declining years of life in the composition of many political, moral, and philosophical essays. One of these, the *Idea of a Patriot King*, he gave in MS. to Pope, and affected great anger when he discovered, after the poet's death, that the latter had caused a large impression to be printed, contrary to a solemn promise. Of his other works, his *Letter to Sir William Windham* in defence of his political conduct, and his *Letters on the Study and Use of History*, are the most important. The language of Bolingbroke is lofty and oratorical, but the tone of philosophical indifference to the usual objects of ambition generally strikes the reader as artificial and affected. It was to Bolingbroke that Pope addressed and dedicated the *Essay on Man*, and some of the not very orthodox positions maintained in that poem were borrowed from his brilliant writings, the poet being too unfamiliar with such speculations to be always able to distinguish the results to which they logically led; and Pope was indebted to the vigorous sophistry of Warburton, by which they were, in appearance at least, reconciled with orthodoxy. Bolingbroke's writings against revealed religion were bequeathed by him to his friend DAVID MALLET, the publisher and an unbeliever, who brought them out together with Bolingbroke's other works, in 1754. Mallet, who died in 1765, was himself an author, but is now chiefly known by his *Ballads*, of which *William and Margaret* is the most striking and beautiful. It was to Mallet's house that Gibbon was taken by his father, when he had embraced Catholicism at Oxford, with the view of weaning him from his new faith.

§ **10.** A similarly irreligious tendency is objected to the essays of BERNARD MANDEVILLE (1670–1733), a physician and voluminous writer, remarkable for the boldness of his theories and the vivacity with which he supported them. The most celebrated of his productions is the *Fable of the Bees*, in which he endeavors to prove that private vices may be public benefits, or, in other words, that the play of human passions and propensities, however immoral or flagitious some of them may be in the relations between man and man, works unconsciously and harmoniously towards the welfare of that complex body which we call society. In this theory there is undoubtedly much that is true, for the limits between virtue and vice are so fluctuating, when viewed in a general or social point of view, that the suppression of what is beyond the middle line on the one side would be as fatal to the existence of society, nay, of humanity itself, as the annihilation of what is beyond it on the other. Society would be as inconceivable without the existence of vice, as it would be impossible without the existence of virtue.

§ **11.** The chief opponent of Mandeville was the accomplished and almost ideally virtuous BISHOP BERKELEY (1684–1753), equally famous for the evangelic benevolence of his character and the acuteness of his genius. His mind was ever full of projects for increasing the virtue and happiness of his fellow-creatures; and the Utopian character of some of these plans only proves the intensity of his philanthropic humanity. One of them was the establishment of a sort of missionary college in the Bermudas, for the purpose of converting and civilizing the Carib savages. He was made Bishop of Cloyne in Ireland, and presents one of the rare instances of a prelate, out of pure love for his flock and an unaffected contentment with his lot, obstinately refusing any further promotion. His writings are exceedingly numerous, and embrace a wide field of moral and metaphysical discussion. He is one of the most brilliant, as well as one of the earliest maintainers of the extreme spiritualistic theory, and thus in some degree an opponent of Locke. His celebrated argument that we have no more grounds for doubting the existence of spirit than we have for denying the existence of matter has been perverted or exaggerated by people who talk loosely into a supposition that he argued against the existence of matter altogether. The truth is, that in investigating the very obscure and arduous question of the nature of that evidence upon which we base our convictions of material objects external to and independent of our selves, he has shown to how much abuse that conviction is liable when once we apply the evidence to the establishment of a metaphysical proof. Berkeley frequently wrote in the form of dialogue, which indeed, as the great examples of Plato and Cicero prove, is well adapted to the purpose of philosophical discussion: and one of the most characteristic and popular of his works is entitled *The Minute Philosopher* In the connection between the physical and metaphysical branches of investigation, Berkeley's writings occupy an important place: thus his *Theory of Vision* established several valuable facts, and drew conclusions from several striking phenomena, concerning that subtle subject. In all his arguments his aim was to refute the materialist theoricians: but in his eagerness to do this he has sometimes involuntarily struck at the very root of those notions which are indispensable to all reasoning, as when he describes ideas as something foreign to or independent of the mind; whereas the only conceivable mode of accounting for the existence of ideas is to suppose that they are states or modifications of the mind, or rather impressions, more or less permanent, made upon the thinking faculty itself.

§ **12.** The last author whom I shall mention in the present chapter is LADY MARY MONTAGU (1690–1762), the most brilliant letter-writer of this period, when Pope and many other distinguished men of letters assiduously cultivated the epistolary form of composition. She was the daughter of the Duke of Kingston, and celebrated, even from her childhood, as Lady Mary Pierrepont, for the vivacity of her intellect, her precocious intellectual acquirements, and the beauty and graces of her person. Her education had been far more extensive and solid than was then usually given to women: her acquaintance with history, and even with Latin, was considerable, and her studies had been in some degree directed by Bishop Burnet. She was, even as a clever and beautiful child, the pet and darling of the accomplished Whig society of the day, and she has recorded the intense delight she felt at the admiration of the members of the Kit-cat Club, by whom she was elected a *toast*. In 1712 she married Mr. Edward Wortley Montagu, a grave and saturnine diplomatist, with whose character the sprightly and airy woman of fashion and literature could have had nothing in common. She accompanied her husband on his embassy to the court of Constantinople, and described her travels over Europe and the East in those delightful *Letters* which have given her in English literature a place resembling that of Madame de Sévigné in the literature of France. Lady Mary was the first traveller who gave a familiar, picturesque, and animated account of Oriental society, particularly of the internal life and manners of the Seraglio, to which her sex and her high position gave her unusual facilities of access. She returned from her travels in 1718, and separating, with mutual consent, from her husband, again went abroad, and resided in Italy till his death: this portion of her life embraced a period from 1739 to 1761. She then returned to her native country, where she died in the following year. Her family life, not only with relation to her husband, but still more so with regard to her only son, was uncomfortable and unhappy. The latter was a man whose talents were considerable, but whose vices and eccentricities were such as to justify the supposition of madness, and his career was one of the most extraordinary adventure and singularity. Lady Mary, however, was of a cold and unimpressionable nature, and seems to have borne her private misfortunes with philosophical equanimity. She was perhaps in some degree indemnified for the pain her son's conduct gave her, by the affection of her daughter, for whom she probably felt as much tenderness as she had to bestow, and to whom some of her liveliest and most amusing letters are addressed. Admirable common sense, observation, vivacity, extensive reading without a trace of pedantry, and a pleasant tinge of half-playful sarcasm, are the qualities which distinguish her correspondence. The style is perfection: the simplicity and natural elegance of the high-born and high-bred lady combined with the ease of the thorough woman of the world. The moral tone, indeed, is far from being high, for neither the character nor the career of Lady Mary had been such as to cherish a very scrupulous delicacy. But she had seen so much, and had been brought into contact with so many remarkable persons, and in a way that gave her unusual means of judging of them, that she is always sensible and amusing. I have compared her to Madame de Sévigné, but the differences between the two charming writers are no less striking than the resemblances. In Lady Mary there is no trace of that intense and even morbid maternal affection which breathes through every line of the letters addressed to Madame de Grignan; nor is there any of that fetish-like worship of the court which seems to pervade everything written in the chilling and tinsel atmosphere that surrounded Louis XIV. In wit, animation, and the power of hitting off, by a few felicitous touches, a character or a scene, it is difficult to assign the palm of superiority. Lady Mary was unquestionably a woman of far higher intellectual calibre, and of a much wider literary development. She can reason and draw inferences where Madame de Sévigné can only gossip, though it must be allowed that her gossip is the most delicious in the world. The successful introduction of inoculation for the smallpox is mainly to be attributed to the intelligence and courage of Lady Mary Montagu, who not only had the courage to try the experiment upon her own child, but with admirable constancy resisted the furious opposition of bigotry and ignorance against the bold innovation. She was at one time the intimate friend of Pope, and the object of his most ardent adulation; but a violent quarrel occurred between them, supposed to have originated in a rather warm outburst of admiration on the part of the poet, received by the great lady, as might indeed have been expected when we consider Pope's personal peculiarities, with a contemptuous ridicule which transformed his admiration into the bitterest and most persevering malignity. She was the author of a small miscellaneous collection of poems, exhibiting the ease, regularity, and fluency which generally marked the lighter verses of that day, and also a rather lax and epicurean tone of philosophy, which is sometimes expressed with inimitable felicity. Nothing can more strongly mark the wide difference between the social condition of England in the seventeenth and eighteenth centuries than a comparison between the tone and the topics of the admirable Memoirs of Lucy Hutchinson, and the gay, worldly, satirical letters of Lady Mary Montagu. Both the one and the other are types of the female character as modified by the respective influences of the two so strongly-contrasted epochs.

NOTES AND ILLUSTRATIONS.

A.—MINOR ESSAYISTS, &c.

EUSTACE BUDGELL (1685-1736), a friend of Addison, who obtained for him many important posts under Government. He contributed to the *Spectator* all the papers marked with the letter X. Having lost almost his whole fortune in the South Sea scheme, and large sums of money in unsuccessful attempts to obtain a seat in Parliament, he became a ruined man. He was accused of having forged in his favor Tindal's Will, a charge to which Pope alludes in the lines,—

"Let Budgell charge low Grub Street on my quill,
And write whate'er he please—except my will."

Budgell was supposed to have assisted Tindal in his infidel works. His circumstances having become desperate, Budgell committed suicide, by leaping from a boat into the Thames. In his house was found a slip of paper, on which he had written—

"What Cato did, and Addison approved,
Cannot be wrong."

Budgell published a weekly periodical called the *Bee*.

JOHN HUGHES (1677-1720) contributed some papers to the *Spectator*, *Tatler*, and *Guardian*. He also published some miscellaneous poems, a tragedy called the Siege of Damascus, several translations from the French, and an edition of Spenser's Works.

TOM BROWN (d. 1704) and TOM D'URFEY (d. 1723) two facetious but immoral writers, frequently mentioned in the lighter literature of the period. D'URFEY wrote several plays of a licentious character. In No. 67 of the Guardian Addison solicits his readers to attend a play for D'Urfey's benefit.

B.—BOYLE AND BENTLEY CONTROVERSY.

This celebrated controversy, which has been alluded to more than once in the preceding chapters, arose out of another upon the comparative merits of the ancient and modern writers. The dispute had its origin in France, where Fontenelle and Perrault claimed for the moderns a general superiority over the writers of antiquity. A reply to their arguments was published by Sir William Temple in 1692, in his *Essay on Ancient and Modern Learning*, written in elegant language, but containing much puerile matter, and exhibiting great credulity. Not content with pointing out the undoubted merits of the great writers of antiquity, he undervalued the labors and discoveries of the moderns, and passed over Shakspeare, Milton, and Newton without even mentioning their names. A far abler and an impartial estimate of the controversy was made by Wotton in his *Reflections upon Ancient and Modern Learning*, published in 1694. WILLIAM WOTTON (1666-1726) had been a boy of astonishing precocity, and was admitted in his tenth year to Catherine Hall, Cambridge. When he took his degree, at the age of thirteen, he was acquainted with twelve languages. In his "Reflections" he discusses the subject with great impartiality and learning; and, while assigning to the ancients their real merits, he points out the superiority of the moderns in physical science.

Sir William Temple, in his Essay, among other arguments for the decay of humor, wit, and learning, had maintained "that the oldest books extant were still the best in their kind;" and in proof of this assertion had cited the Fables of Æsop and the Epistles of Phalaris. This led to the publication of a new edition of the Epistles of Phalaris by the scholars of Christ-Church, Oxford (1695). The nominal editor was Charles Boyle, brother of the Earl of Orrery, who, in his Preface, inserted a bitter reflection upon RICHARD BENTLEY (1662-1742), the King's Librarian, on account of the supposed refusal of the latter to grant him the loan of a MS. in the King's Library. Bentley, who appears to have been unjustly blamed in this matter, soon had an opportunity of retaliation. In the second edition of Wotton's Reflections, published in 1697, Bentley added a dissertation, in the form of letters to his friend, in which he proved that the author of the Epistles of Phalaris was not the Sicilian tyrant, but some sophist of a later age. Sir William Temple, who had been greatly annoyed at Wotton's Reflections, was still more incensed at Bentley's Dissertation; and Swift, who then resided in Temple's house, made his first attack upon Bentley in the

Battle of the Books, in which he ridiculed the great scholar in the most ludicrous manner; though the work was not printed till some years after.

At Christ Church the indignation was, if possible, even greater. Bentley's attack was considered an affront to the whole College, and it was resolved to crush, at once and forever, the audacious assailant. All the strength of Christ Church was enlisted in the contest; but the chief task of the reply was undertaken by Atterbury. He was assisted by George Smalridge, Robert Friend, afterwards head-master of Westminster School, his brother John Friend, and Anthony Alsop. "In point of classical learning," observes the biographer of Bentley, "the joint-stock of the confederacy bore no proportion to that of Bentley; their acquaintance with several of the books upon which they comment appears only to have begun upon that occasion, and sometimes they are indebted for their knowledge of them to their adversary; compared with his boundless erudition, their learning was that of school-boys, and not always sufficient to preserve them from distressing mistakes. It may be doubtful whether Busby himself, by whom every one of the confederate band had been educated, possessed knowledge which could have qualified him to enter the lists in such a controversy." But their deficiency in learning they made up by wit and raillery; and when the book appeared, in 1698, it was received with extravagant applause. It was entitled *Dr. Bentley's Dissertations on the Epistles of Phalaris and the Fables of Æsop, examined by the Honorable Charles Boyle, Esq.* It is usually known by the familiar title of *Boyle against Bentley;* though Boyle, whose name it bears, had no share in the composition of the work. It was generally supposed that Bentley was silenced and crushed. "All accounts agree in stating the applause which the book met with to have been loud and universal; and the general interest excited by this controversy, properly a business of dry learning, appears to us almost incredible. This state of public feeling is attributable in some degree to the vein of wit and satire which pervades the Christ Church performance, but still more to extraneous causes. The numbers and ability of the members of that distinguished society, who appear to have felt as one man in this common cause, had a powerful influence over public opinion. Again, the extreme popularity of Sir W. Temple, who was represented as rudely attacked, and the interest excited in behalf of Mr. Boyle, a young scholar of noble birth, who appeared in the field of controversy as the champion of an accomplished veteran, disposed people at all hazards to favor his cause. Added to this, an opinion which had been industriously circulated of Bentley's incivility, and a certain haughty carriage which undoubtedly belonged to him, gave a violent prejudice to the public mind. Severe and accurate erudition being rare in those days, people were so far deluded as to believe that on most, if not all points, Boyle was successful: we learn from Bentley himself, that the book was at first generally regarded as unanswerable; and this even among his own friends. Nobody suspected that he would venture to reply; still less that he could ever again hold up his head in the republic of learning: the blow was thought to be fatal; and many persons, as usual, eagerly joined the cry against the devoted critic." — (Monk's *Life of Bentley*, i. p. 108.)

Among the many other attacks made upon Bentley at this period, the only one which continues to be known is Swift's *Battle of the Books*, in which he pours forth upon Bentley all the embittered vehemence of his satire.

In the midst of this outcry Bentley remained unmoved. Conscious of his own learning, he could afford to despise the ignorant malice of his enemies; and he set himself resolutely to work to prepare an answer, which should not only silence his opponents, but establish his reputation as one of the greatest scholars that ever lived. His work appeared in 1699, under the title of *A Dissertation upon the Epistles of Phalaris: with an Answer to the Objections of the Hon. Robert Boyle, by Richard Bentley, D. D.;* but it is frequently called *Bentley against Boyle.* "The appearance of this work is to be considered an epoch not only in the life of Bentley, but in the history of literature. The victory obtained over his opponents, although the most complete that can be imagined, constitutes but a small part of the merits of this performance. Such is the author's address, that, while every page is professedly controversial, there is embodied in the work a quantity of accurate information relative to history, chronology, antiquities, philology, and criticism, which it would be difficult to match in any other volume. The cavils of the Boyleans had fortunately touched upon so many topics, as to draw from their adversary a mass of learning, none of which is misplaced or superfluous: he contrives, with admirable judgment, to give the reader all the information which can be desired upon each question, while he never loses sight of his main object. Profound and various as are the sources of his learning, everything is so well arranged, and placed in so clear a view, that the student who is only in the elementary parts of classical literature may peruse the book with profit and pleasure, while the most learned reader cannot fail to find his knowledge enlarged. Nor is this merely the language of those who are partial to the author; the eminently learned Dodwell, who had no peculiar motive to be pleased with a work by which he was himself a considerable sufferer, and who as a nonjuror was prejudiced against Bentley's party, is recorded to have avowed 'that he had never learned so much from any book in his life.' This learned volume owes much of its attraction to the strain of humor, which makes the perusal highly entertaining. The advocates of Phalaris, having chosen to rely upon wit and raillery, were now made to feel in their turn the consequences of the warfare which they had adopted. So well sustained is the learning, the wit, and the spirit of this production, that it is not possible to select particular parts as objects of admiration without committing a sort of injustice to the rest. And the book itself will long continue to be in the hands of all educated persons, as long as literature maintains its hold in society." — (Monk's *Life of Bentley*, i. pp. 120-123.)

With this dissertation the controversy came to an end, for Bentley's reply was so complete and crushing that it was hopeless to attempt a rejoinder. Sir William Temple died a few weeks before the publication of Bentley's work, and was thus spared the mortification of witnessing the utter discomfiture of his friends.

OTHER WRITERS.

SIR ANDREW FLETCHER OF SALTOUN (1653-1716) was a member of Parliament in the reign of Charles II., and afterwards engaged in the various political events of the reigns of James II., William and Mary, and Anne. His writings were chiefly in the form of political tracts. He is the author of the saying, "If a man were permitted to make all the ballads, he need not care who should make the laws of a nation."

MRS. MANLEY (1724), in the reign of Anne, was a dramatist, novelist, and political writer, popular, but of no very good character as regards either her life or her writings. She was the author of *Atalantis*, a political satire of some force, published about 1709. She conducted the *Examiner* for some time after it had been given up by Swift. She was the daughter of Sir Roger Manley, governor of Guernsey.

JOHN STRYPE (1643-1737), son of a refugee from Brabant, was brought up at Cambridge, and entered the Church. He was an extensive historian and biographer. He wrote lives of *Cranmer*, 1694, *Grindal*, 1710, *Parker*, 1711, and other archbishops; *Annals of the Reformation*, 1709-31; and was editor of the "Survey of London," by Stow, besides other works of historical and antiquarian interest. He died at Hackney, aged 94.

LAWRENCE ECHARD (1671-1730). An extensive compiler and careful annalist. His histories of *England*, *Rome*, the *Church*, &c., were valuable collections in their day. Several editions of the Ecclesiastical History have been published.

He was educated at Cambridge, and became Archdeacon of Stowe and prebend of Lincoln.

CHAPTER XVII.

THE GREAT NOVELISTS.

§ 1. History of Prose Fiction. The Romance and the Novel. § 2. DANIEL DEFOE. His life and political career. § 3. *Robinson Crusoe.* § 4. Defoe's other works. § 5. SAMUEL RICHARDSON. *Pamela, Clarissa Harlowe,* and *Sir Charles Grandison.* § 6. HENRY FIELDING. His life and publications. § 7. Characteristics of his writings. *Joseph Andrews, Jonathan Wild, Tom Jones,* and *Amelia.* § 8. TOBIAS SMOLLETT. His life and publications. § 9. Characteristics of his novels. Compared with Fielding. § 10. LAWRENCE STERNE. *Tristram Shandy* and the *Sentimental Journey.* § 11. OLIVER GOLDSMITH. His life and publications. § 12. Criticism of his works. *The Traveller* and *The Deserted Village. The Vicar of Wakefield. The Good Natured Man* and *She Stoops to Conquer.*

§ 1. MOST departments of literature were cultivated earlier in England than that of Prose Fiction. We have, it is true, the romantic form of this kind of writing in the *Arcadia* of Sidney, and the philosophical form in the *Utopia* and the *Atlantis;* but the exclusive employment of prose narrative in the delineation of the passions, characters, and incidents of real life was first carried to perfection by a constellation of great writers in the eighteenth century, among whom the names of Defoe, Richardson, Fielding, Smollett, Sterne, and Goldsmith, are the most brilliant luminaries. Originally appearing, as do all types of literature, in a poetical form, the rhymed narratives of chivalry, poured forth with such inexhaustible fertility by the Trouvères of the Middle Ages, were in course of time remodelled and clothed in prose, and in their turn gave birth to the long, pompous, and unnatural romances of the time of Louis XIII. and Louis XIV., which formed the principal light reading of the higher classes. In the *Grand Cyrus,* the *Astrée,* and the *Princesse de Clèves,* a class of writers of whom D'Urfé, Scudéri, Calprenède, and Madame de la Fayette, may be considered the types, imitated in descriptions of the adventures of classically-named heroes, the lofty, heroic, stilted language and sentiments which they borrowed from the Castilian writers. The absurdities and exaggerations of this kind of story naturally produced a reaction; and Spain and France gave birth to the Comic Romance originally intended as a kind of parody of the superhuman elevation and hair-splitting amorous casuistry of the popular fictions. *Don Quixote* was in this way as much a caricature of Montemayor as the *Roman Comique* of Scarron of the *Clélie,* or *Grand Cyrus.* In England, where the genius of the nation is eminently practical, and where the immense development of free institutions has tended to encourage individuality of character, and to give importance to private and domestic life, the literature of Fiction speedily divided into two great but correlative branches, to which our language alone has given specific and distinct appellations — the Romance and the Novel. Both these terms are indeed ultimately derived, like the things they represent, from the nations of the South; the former originally signifying the dialect of the Trouvères and Troubadours, and thence, by a natural transition, that species of narrative fiction which was most abundantly produced in the dialect: the second, the *Novella*, *Nouvelle*, or short amusing tale, of which such a multitude of examples are to be found in the Italian, Spanish, and French literature of the fifteenth and sixteenth centuries. It will be sufficient merely to mention the *Decamerone* of Boccaccio and the *Cent Nouvelles Nouvelles* of Marguerite of Navarre. This latter, the lighter or more comic form of narrative, is a type traceable ultimately to the *Fabliaux* of the old Provençal poets. But in modern English the Romance and the Novel both express varieties of prose and fiction of considerable length and elaborateness of construction: the former word indicating a narrative, the characters and incidents of which are of a lofty, historical, or supernatural tone, while the latter expresses a recital of the events of ordinary or domestic life, generally of a contemporary epoch. It is the latter department in which English writers, from the time of its first appearance in our literature down to the present time, have encountered few rivals and no superiors.

§ 2. The founder of the English Novel is DANIEL DEFOE (1661–1731), a man of extraordinary versatility and energy as a writer, and one of the most fertile authors of narrative and controversial productions; for his complete works are said to comprise upwards of two hundred separate writings. His life was agitated and unfortunate. He was the son of a butcher in London, and by family as well as personal sympathies an ardent Whig and Dissenter. Indeed, he was educated for the ministry in a dissenting sect, but embraced a mercantile career, having at various periods carried on the business of a hosier, a tile-maker, and a woollen-draper. But his real vocation was that of a writer, and the ardor with which he maintained, in innumerable pamphlets, the principles of constitutional liberty, not only distracted his attention from his commercial pursuits, but exposed him, in those evil times, to repeated persecutions from the Government. He carried his devotion to Protestant principles so far, as to join the abortive insurrection under the Duke of Monmouth, though from this danger he escaped with impunity. He was at different times punished on charges of sedition, with all the inhuman brutality of those days, having been exposed in the pillory, sentenced to have his ears cut off, severely fined, and on two occasions imprisoned in Newgate, his confinement on one occasion extending to nearly two years. Nothing, however, could daunt or silence this indefatigable champion of liberty, and he continued to pour forth pamphlet after pamphlet, full of irony, logic, and patriotism. Among the most celebrated of his works in this class are his *Trueborn Englishman*, a poem in singularly tuneless rhymes, but full of strong sense and vigorous argument, in which he defends William of Orange and the Dutch against the prejudices of his countrymen, the *Hymn to the Pillory*, and the famous pamphlet *The Shortest*

Way with the Dissenters, in which, to show the folly and cruelty of the recent Acts persecuting the Sectarians, he with admirable sarcasm adopts the tone of a violent persecutor, and advises Parliament to employ the stake, the pillory, and the halter, with unrelenting severity The mask of irony is so well worn in this pamphlet, that it was at first considered a serious defence of the parliamentary measure, and when the trick was discovered the fury of the dominant party knew no bounds The purely political career of Defoe was, generally, from 1687 to 1715 and it was during one of his imprisonments that he carried on the *Review*, a literary journal which may be regarded as the prototype of our modern semi-political, semi-literary periodicals. It appeared thrice a week, and was written with great force and ready vigor of language. During the negotiations which preceded the union of Scotland to the British crown, Defoe was employed as a confidential agent in Edinburgh, and acquitted himself with ability. He afterwards published a narrative of that important event. Defoe's mercantile speculations were so unfortunate that he says in one of his poems, —

"Thirteen times have I been rich and poor;"

and he probably employed the unequalled facility of his pen in fiction, principally as a means of supplying daily bread to his family, to which he was tenderly attached.

§ 3. In 1719 Defoe published the first part of *Robinson Crusoe*, the success of which, among that comparatively humble class of readers which Defoe generally addressed, was instantaneous and immense. Indeed, if perfect originality in the plan, and the highest perfection in the execution of a fiction, be sufficient to establish a claim of creative genius, Defoe must be regarded as a creative genius of no common order. The primary idea of *Robinson Crusoe* may have been derived from the authentic narrative of Alexander Selkirk, a sailor who had been *marooned*, as the term then was, by his captain on the uninhabited island of Juan Fernandez, where he passed several years in complete solitude. Selkirk, who, by a most singular coincidence, was taken off the island by the very same captain — Woods Rogers — who had abandoned him there, published on his return to England an account of his sufferings and adventures. By this narrative he appears to have gradually descended to the condition, if not of a wild beast, at least of a savage very little superior in intelligence; for when discovered he had almost entirely lost the use of language, which he only obtained again after a considerable time. The intense interest of *Robinson Crusoe* partly arises from the simplicity and probability of the events, the *unforeseenness* of many of which completely annihilate the reader's suspicion of the truth of what he is perusing, the skill with which Defoe identifies himself with the character of his Recluse, who is always represented as a commonplace man, without any pretensions to extraordinary knowledge or intelligence. He is, therefore, just such a person as every reader, ignorant or cultivated, old or young, can thoroughly sympathize with, and can fancy, while reading of his difficulties and embarrassments, setting about remedying them, as he himself would do, under similar circumstances. Thus Robinson Crusoe is never endowed with more ingenuity or forethought than the generality of mankind: and thus, for example, when he cuts down a huge tree and after incredible labor shapes it into a boat, he finds that it is too heavy for him to launch. It is evident that the majority of readers acutely sympathize with this, because ninety-nine out of a hundred feel that they would be likely to commit a similar oversight. It is perhaps somewhat injurious that this book is generally read when we are very young; for the impressions it leaves upon the memory and the imagination, among the strongest that we can recall, are so deep and permanent that we do not return to the work when increased intellectual development would make us better able to appreciate Defoe's wonderful art. The raft, the goats, the dog, cats, and parrots, the palisaded fortification, the cave, the wrecked ships, the circumnavigation of the island, the fishing, turtle-catching, and planting of corn; every scene, every episode, is indelibly fixed upon the mind. It would be difficult to guess how many boys *Robinson Crusoe* has turned into sailors, or how many projects of living with a faithful Friday in a desert island, have been generated in childish fancies by this incomparable tale. The second part, which the success of the first encouraged Defoe to produce, is manifestly inferior to the first: indeed the moment the solitude of the island is invaded by more strangers than Friday, the charm is evidently diminished. Scott has well remarked that a striking evidence of Defoe's skill in this kind of fiction is the studiously low key, both as regards style and incidents, in which the whole is pitched. Defoe's object was not to instruct, but to amuse; to captivate that mysterious faculty by which we identify ourselves with imaginary events; and this he most successfully did by imitating not only the plain, straightforward, unaffected narratives of the old navigators, but their simple, idiomatic, unadorned diction.

§ 4. Among Defoe's numerous other works of fiction may be mentioned the *Memoirs of a Cavalier*, supposed to have been written by one who had taken part in the great Civil War; in which many historical facts are dressed up with that intense personal reality which Defoe knew so well how to communicate, and which made Lord Chatham cite the book as an authentic narrative. A not less remarkable narrative is the *Journal of the Great Plague in London*, where the imaginary annalist, a respectable London shopkeeper, — a character which Defoe assumed with consummate skill, — describes the terrible sights of that fearful time. The air of verisimilitude in this book is so complete, that grave medical and statistical writers have quoted it as authentic; and it is only the application of the tests of modern science that have proved it to be a tissue of inventions in which the devastation caused by the scourge is most enormously exaggerated. Nothing can exceed the quiet yet not unpicturesque vividness with which episodes of the city life during the great calamity are set before us, and in some passages, as in the description of the maniac fanatic Solomon Eagle, the Great Pit in Aldgate, and the long line of anchored ships stretching far down the Thames, Defoe rises into a very lofty and powerful strain of description. A number of stories, the *Adventures of Colonel Jack*, *Moll Flanders*, *Roxana*, *Captain Singleton*, show the same quiet power of imitating reality. They are generally the lives of thieves, robbers, and other offscourings of society, and were written, I imagine, purely for profit: but Defoe has never pandered to the false taste of his readers by holding up to admiration the characters and exploits of such personages, and has faithfully represented their lives as being for the most part as miserable as they are flagitious. In one remarkable tract he has described the *Apparition of one Mrs. Neal to her friend Mrs. Bargrave at Canterbury;* and this is one of the boldest experiments ever made upon human credulity. It was composed to help off the sale of a dull book of Sermons, and had the effect of instantly causing the whole edition to quit the bookseller's shelves; for *Drelincourt on Death* was powerfully recommended by the visitor from another world.

§ **5.** If *Robinson Crusoe* is less a novel than a tale, being excluded, at least in its finer parts, by the solitude of the chief character from that play of human interest which properly constitutes the Novel, SAMUEL RICHARDSON (1689–1761) must be regarded as the real founder of the romance of private life in English Literature. His life presents few materials for comment: it was the career of a careful, prudent, industrious tradesman, who raised himself to opulence by the exercise of the most laudable though somewhat prosaic assiduity. He was far advanced in life — nearly fifty years of age, indeed — before he entered upon that literary path which led him to immense and well-deserved popularity. He was born of very humble rustic parentage, and came to London when a lad to be apprenticed to a printer. In this calling he distinguished himself by so much diligence that in the course of time he was taken into partnership by his employer, and gradually rose to the highest place in his business, being appointed first printer of the Journals of the House of Commons, and then, in 1754, Master of the Stationers' Company, and in 1760 becoming the purchaser of a half share in the lucrative patent office of Printer to the King. Having accumulated an easy fortune, he retired to a pleasant suburban house at Parson's Green, near London, where he passed an honorable old age in literary employment, surrounded by a little knot of female worshippers, whose adulatory incense his intense vanity made him greedily receive. The correspondence and literary remains of Richardson, which have been published, give a curious picture of his timid, sensitive, effeminate character, and of the enervating atmosphere of twaddling flattery with which he loved to surround himself. The works of Richardson are three in number, *Pamela*, published in 1741, *Clarissa Harlowe*, in 1749, and *Sir Charles Grandison*, in 1753. These three novels are all written upon one plan, that is, the story is entirely told in letters which are supposed to be written by the various persons in the action — a mode of fictitious composition which has frequently been employed since Richardson's time, and which is attended with advantages and disadvantages of a very evident kind. In the first place it gives the author the opportunity of successively identifying himself with his different characters and exhibiting the minutest shades of their feelings and sensations, and this he can do subjectively. On the other hand this method of writing is open to the objection of necessitating a very slow, minute, and painful evolution of the story; and the improbability of any real letters being sufficiently minute and voluminous to detail all that is essential for the reader's understanding of the plot is so great, that it is in general found insurmountable. But the peculiar genius of Richardson is seen rather in the evolution of character by slow and delicate touches of self-betrayal, than by any vigor of description — that is, objective description — of persons or events; and, therefore, in spite of the innate improbability attached to a whole story told in letters, he selected the mode best suited to his peculiar genius.

Pamela describes the sufferings, trials, and vicissitudes undergone by a poor, but beautiful and innocent, country girl who enters the service of a rich gentleman. She triumphantly resists all the seductions and all the violence by which he essays to overcome her virtue, and what is still more difficult, the promptings of her own heart in his favor; for Richardson represents her as passionately attached to her unworthy master, to whom, by way of a moral inculcating the reward of virtue, she is ultimately married. The letters in which this story is told are principally written by Pamela herself; and Richardson exhibits throughout the work that profound and wonderful knowledge of the female character, which he is said to have acquired in his boyhood, by being the amanuensis for carrying on the love-correspondence of three young women in humble life. The pathetic power exhibited in Pamela is very great, and is an earnest of that intense mastery over the tender emotions which he afterwards exhibited in his *Clarissa Harlowe*. *Pamela* originally sprang from a collection of familiar letters which Richardson, at the request of his publishing firm, had undertaken to write as a manual to improve the style and the morality of the middle classes of readers; and while engaged on it he was struck with the happy idea of making his letters tell a continuous story. The success of the tale was prodigious; and we cannot wonder at it when we think of the immense contrast between the nature, reality, and living interest of *Pamela* and the far-fetched, wire-drawn, impossible caricatures which then formed the only light reading of the world — feeble exaggerations of the already exaggerated conceptions of the old French romances of the seventeenth century. The popularity of *Pamela* was so great that five editions were exhausted in one year, although this, like all Richardson's works, is extremely voluminous, according to our modern ideas: for example, his third romance, *Sir Charles Grandison*, as originally written, would have filled about a dozen octavo volumes.

Clarissa Harlowe is incontestably Richardson's greatest work. Whether we consider the interest of the story, the variety and truth of the characters, or the intense and almost unendurable pathos of the catastrophe, to which every incident artfully and imperceptibly leads, we must not only accord it a decisive superiority over his other produc tions, but must give it one of the foremost places in the history of prose fiction. It is the story of a young lady who falls a victim to the treachery and profligacy of a man of splendid talent and attractions, but of complete and almost diabolical corruption. Though Richardson, both by natural disposition and circumstances, is far more successful in the delineation of female than of male characters, Lovelace, the seducer, is one of the most perfect and finished portraits that literature has to show. There is no better proof of this than the fact that the name has become in all languages the synonyme of the brilliant and unprincipled seducer. This circumstance also gives us a record of the immense popularity which Richardson still enjoys throughont Europe, though its splendor in England has been in some measure eclipsed by later novelists, some of whom address themselves, like Fielding and Scott, more exclusively to national sympathies, whereas Richardson's delineations possess the lasting interest attached to *general* pictures of human nature. The prevailing tone of feeling in *Clarissa* is sombre and mournful, and the sufferings of the pure but injured heroine are worked up at the end to a pitch of intensity reminding us of Ford or Webster. The interest in this, as in the other works of Richardson, is generated by the accumulation of a thousand little imperceptible touches, and the characters are elaborated with the slow and painful minuteness of the Dutch painters. The reader finds himself in an atmosphere of trifling, tedious, and artificial details, but the gentle, equable current of passion and incident carries him onward in spite of himself, till he feels its force to be irresistible.

The last work in this famous trilogy is *Sir Charles Grandison*, in which the author, who never relinquished the idea of incorporating a moral in his fictions, intended to give an ideal portrait of a character which should combine consummate ethical and religious perfection with the graces and accomplishments of a man of fashion. In his three successive novels Richardson essayed to portray three different orders in the social scale: in *Pamela* the lower, in *Clarissa* the middle, and in *Grandison* the aristocratic class of society. But he was, from education and position, totally unacquainted with the real manners and modes of thought and feeling prevalent in the fashionable world, and in describing what he so imperfectly guessed at he fell into the error natural to men of imperfect education and inexperienced in the manners of the great world. He is perpetually straining after fine language, and his stiff and labored expression forms a ludicrous contrast with the really easy, unaffected tone of circles, where, as they have no superiors to ape, they are at least free from the vice of vulgar pretension of manner. The characters he wishes to hold up to admiration — the ultra-perfect Sir Charles, with his eternal bowing and solemn hand-kissing, and the heroine, Miss Harriet Byron, who is in all respects his worthy counterpart — are of that most insupportable category of people who are expressively though coarsely designated as *prigs*, a class equally insupportable in fiction and in reality. Indeed the only personages with whom we sympathize in Sir Charles Grandison are those in which some alloy of human weakness tempers their tiresome perfections: thus Clementina, whose madness and despair are delineated with a pathetic force that Fletcher might have been proud to own, is far more interesting than either. Richardson, with that feminine turn of disposition which I have noted in him, shows an extreme tendency to dwell upon long and minute description; and Hazlitt tells a pleasant story that he had been disposed to murmur at about a dozen pages being devoted to the wedding clothes of Sir Charles and his bride, till he found that a young lady had actually copied out the whole passage as one of the most striking episodes of the story. It is said that Richardson consulted a great lady as to the tone and language of high life; and that she found so many errors and inconsistencies that he abandoned in despair the hope of correcting them. In patient analysis of the human mind and passions, particularly in the female sex, in a tendency to accumulate minute incident and microscopic description, and in a sickly and morbid tone of sentiment, there is considerable resemblance, allowing, of course, for differences of nation and of age, between Richardson and Balzac; nor is Clarissa an unworthy rival of the enchanting portrait of Eugènie Grandet.

§ 6. The second great name among the novelists of this period is that of HENRY FIELDING (1707–1754), qualified by Byron, with extreme but hardly undeserved praise, "the prose Homer of human nature." In his personal character, as well as in his literary career, in everything, indeed, but the power of his genius, he was the exact opposite of Richardson. He was descended from the illustrious house of Denbigh, itself an offshoot from the counts of Habsburg, and his father was General Fielding, a man of fashion, ruined by his extravagance. The novelist was born in 1707, and received his education first at Eton, and afterwards at the University of Leyden, whither he went, like many young men of fashion, to study the law. His father dying, with his affairs in inextricable confusion, he returned to England in absolute want of money, and though he nominally inherited an income of 200*l.* a year, he found himself dependent upon his own resources for a livelihood. Of gay and festive inclinations, a favored guest among men of pleasure and enjoyment, he naturally betook himself to the stage, and at the age of twenty became a dramatic author and a lively writer in the *Covent Garden Journal*. He produced a considerable number of pieces, now entirely forgotten, which show that his talent was in no way adapted to the theatre. Indeed it seems an established fact that no great writer of narrative fiction ever succeeded on the stage. The only exceptions I can remember to this rule are the cases of Cervantes and Le Sage, while the examples of Walter Scott and a multitude of others prove the universality of the principle. The dramatic works of Fielding constitute a large portion of his writings; but none of them have either retained possession of the stage or attracted the curiosity of the reader. Always passionately fond of gayety and joyous company, Fielding struggled on, and married a lady of great beauty and excellence, Mrs. Craddock, with whom he received a portion of about 1500*l.*

This he dissipated in a very short time, for he was of an extremely sanguine and volatile temper, and was assisted in running through his little fortune by the desperate project of speculating in the Haymarket Theatre, which completed the ruin of his affairs. He then resumed the study of the Law, and was called to the bar in the Temple. Meeting with no professional success, he continued his career as a dramatic writer, producing a number of pieces exhibiting vivacity and carelessness rather than any depth of ability, and also took an active part in political controversy. In numerous pamphlets and articles for journals he maintained liberal and anti-jacobite principles; and it was about this period of his life (1742) that he struck out that vein of humorous writing in which he never had, nor is ever likely to have, a rival. His first novel was *Joseph Andrews*, which was in some sense intended as a parody or caricature, ridiculing the timid and fastidious morality, the shop-keeper tone and the somewhat preaching *good-boy* style of *Pamela*, just then in the full blaze of success. Richardson's jealous vanity could never forgive the wicked wit of Fielding in ridiculing his heroine; and he shows in all his correspondence not only an intense soreness, but an absolute inability to appreciate Fielding's genius. Like the *Roman Comique* of Scarron, which, though written to laugh at a particular class of works, became the prototype of a new and original department of Fiction, Fielding's novel at once received the honor due to a great original creation; and in pretty rapid succession he produced his *Journey from this World to the Next*, full of political allusions that have now lost their piquancy, and his truly remarkable satirical tale, *The Life of Jonathan Wild the Great.* In 1749 he was appointed to the laborious and then far from respectable post of a London police magistrate, a function in which he showed distinguished zeal and intelligence, and which was useful to his literary glory by giving him opportunities of observing the manners of the lowest of the people. While engaged in this ignoble occupation he composed the finest, completest, and profoundest of his works, the incomparable *Tom Jones*, which was followed, after a brief interval, by *Amelia*, in which he unquestionably intended to portray some of his own follies and irregularities, but with the principal object of paying a tribute to the virtues and affection of his wife. Her he had the misfortune to lose, and he soon supplied her place by marrying her maid, with whom he had "frequently bewailed the angel they had lost." In spite of the seeming oddity of this second choice, she made him a prudent and loving partner, and an excellent mother to his children. Fielding's health was now completely ruined by labor and excesses: he was attacked with dropsy, and ordered to try a warmer climate. He sailed for Lisbon in 1754, and after passing a short time died in that city, and was buried in the Protestant cemetery there towards the end of the same year.

§ 7. The qualities which distinguish Fielding's genius are close and accurate observation of character, and an extraordinary power of deducing the actions and expressions of his personages from the elements of their nature, a constant sympathy with the vigorous, unrestrained characters, in all ranks of society, but especially in the lowest, which he loved to delineate. With the vast and motley field of English society, so strongly marked at that time, he was minutely acquainted, and his spirit of analysis, at once learned and picturesque, delighted in the reproduction of the oddities and eccentricities of man. He is intensely English in his subject as in his mode of treatment. Hogarth himself is not more powerfully national: painter and novelist exhibit the same direct and practical vigor, which, however, is always compatible with an appreciation of the subtlest shades of character. In the construction of his plots he is masterly. That of *Tom Jones* is perhaps the finest example to be met with, in fiction, of a series of events probable yet surprising, each of which inevitably leads to the ultimate catastrophe. He combined an almost childish delight in fun and extravagantly ludicrous incident, with a philosophic closeness of analysis of character and an impressive tone of moral reflection, the latter often masked under a pleasant air of satire and irony. His novels breathe a sort of fresh *open-air* atmosphere, a strong contrast to the close, artificial medium which pervades the romances of Richardson. When we are reading the latter we seem to be surrounded with the close, breathless atmosphere of a city parlor: taking up Fielding is like emerging into the bracing, sun-shiny air of a high-road. A large proportion of the scenes and adventures in Fielding takes place in inns and in the course of travelling: this is to be explained by the much greater proportion of time then passed on the road, when men proceeded from place to place on foot, on horseback, in the humble wagon, or in the aristocratic coach and six, and were consequently brought more closely and frequently into contact with the miscellaneous crowd of travellers.

Joseph Andrews was originally written as a kind of parody upon *Pamela*, and for this purpose the chief character was represented as the brother of Richardson's heroine; and Pamela's virtuous resistance to seduction was transferred, with great humor, to the person of a young footman. Joseph, on being expelled from the household of Squire Booby, in consequence of the jealous rage of his mistress, — the "spretæ injuria formæ," — wanders about England in company with his friend and humble companion Parson Adams, one of the richest, most humorous, and truly genial conceptions of this great painter of character. Adams's learning, simplicity, and courage, together with his innumerable and always consistent oddities, make him as truly humorous a character as Sancho Panza himself. There is no doubt that in the low social estimation, as well as in the ignorance and coarseness of many of his clerical personages, Fielding has faithfully represented the degraded state of the rural clergy at the time when he wrote.

The adventures of *Jonathan Wild the Great* were intended to be a satire upon the false estimate generally formed of glory, and the whole book is written in a tone of irony. The hero was a real person, originally a thief, housebreaker, and highwayman, and afterwards a spy and secret agent of the police; he became celebrated as a receiver of stolen goods, and after committing a thousand crimes was most justly hanged

The exploits of this consummate scoundrel are related in a tone of ironical admiration; but though the story contains some powerful and many humorous scenes, the reader becomes weary of the uninterrupted meanness and depravity of the persons and events.

In *Tom Jones* it is difficult to know what most to admire, the artful conduct of the plot, the immense variety, truth, and humor of the personages, the gayety of the incidents, or the acute remarks and reflections which the author has plentifully interspersed, in most cases in the introduction to his chapters. The character of Squire Western, the type of the violent, brutal rural magnate of those days, is one which remains forever fixed on the memory, and thousands of inferior personages might be cited, each marked ineffaceably, though often lightly, with the stamp of truth and nature. Tom Jones himself and the fair Sophy, though elaborated by the author with peculiar care, as types of all that he thought attractive, are generally found to be tinged with much coarseness and vulgarity. Fielding's standard, whether for grace or morality, was not a very high one, and the time when he wrote was remarkable for the low tone of manners and sentiment — perhaps the lowest that ever prevailed in England; for it was precisely a juncture when the romantic spirit of the old chivalric manners was extinguished, and before the modern standard of refinement was introduced.

The interest of *Amelia* is entirely domestic and familiar: the errors and repentance of Captain Booth, and the inexhaustible love and indulgence of the heroine, are strongly contrasted; but we never can get rid of the conviction that Booth is but a sorry scamp, and are hardly compensated for our indifference to the principal character by the extraordinary vividness, nature, and reality of the subordinate ones. Fielding had little or no power over the pathetic emotions; there are, however, in this novel several episodes and strokes of character which are touching, and exhibit that peculiar and essential characteristic of truly humorous conceptions, namely, the power of touching the heart while exciting the sense of the ludicrous. It is a curious contradiction that while Richardson, a man of the humblest birth and career, should have chiefly described aristocratic life, Fielding, the man of fashion and of lofty origin, should have preferred to paint the manners of the lowest of the people. Fielding, in spite of much coarseness and indecency, is fundamentally sound in his moral principles, though he excuses, if he does not justify, a considerable degree of laxity. He seems inclined to pardon any escapade, if rendered venial by high spirits, youth, and passion, and accompanied with courage, frankness, and generosity.

§ 8. Tobias George Smollett (1721–1771), descended from an ancient and respectable family in Scotland, was educated, first at Dumbarton, and afterwards at the University of Glasgow. Being totally without fortune, he determined to embrace the medical profession, and was apprenticed to a practitioner in Glasgow of the name of Gordon. After remaining a short time in this man's service, the future poet and novelist, then only nineteen years of age, and burning with literary ambition, proceeded to London with the MS. of a tragedy, entitled the *Regicide*, in his pocket. Failing in his attempt to bring out this work, he entered the naval service in the humble capacity of surgeon's mate on board a man-of-war, and was present at the inglorious and unfortunate expedition to Carthagena, under the command of Admiral Knowles. Here he had the opportunity of studying the oddities of sea-characters, which he afterwards so admirably reproduced in his fictions, and of learning by experience the atrocious cruelty, corruption, and incompetency which then reigned in the naval administration. He left the service and resided for some time in the West Indies, whence he returned in 1744, and began to unite literary pursuits with the practice of his profession in London. He was the author of several satires and other poetical pieces now forgotten, but in 1748 he began his career of a novelist with *Roderick Random*, in some respects the most vigorous of his fictions. In the manner and construction of his novels he follows the models of Le Sage and of those Spanish authors, in the style called *picaresca*, whom Le Sage himself imitated; and he relied for success rather on a lively series of grotesque adventures than on any elaboration of intrigue or deep analysis of character. *Peregrine Pickle* was published in 1751, and Smollett, meeting with but small success as a physician, now devoted himself to the career of a writer and politician. For the task of controversy he was well qualified by the vigor and readiness of his style, by the ardor of his opinions, and the patriotic elevation of his principles; but he was rash, violent, and impulsive, and more than once changed his side, not from any interested or unworthy motive, but under the influence of his personal feelings. In 1753 he produced his third great romance, *The Adventures of Ferdinand, Count Fathom*, describing, with a higher moral intention than is usually found in his works, the career of an unprincipled scoundrel, cheat, and swindler. This book forms a sort of counterpart or parallel to Fielding's *Jonathan Wild*, and is open to the same objections. Two years later this indefatigable worker brought out his translation of *Don Quixote*, in which he clearly shows himself utterly unable to appreciate the higher, more poetical, and ideal side of the great conception of Cervantes, and has confined himself solely to the grotesque and farcical side of that vast creation. About this time the violence of Smollett's political opinions brought him in collision with the law; the terrible picture he had given of maladministration in the Navy and his severe strictures on the conduct of Admiral Knowles caused him to be defeated in an action for libel. He was fined 100*l.* and imprisoned for three months, during which time he continued the management of the *Critical Review*, in the pages of which the obnoxious strictures had appeared, and in his capacity of literary censor he managed to raise up against himself a whole swarm of angry politicians, writers, and doctors. He now produced his novel of *Sir Lancelot Greaves*, a most unfortunate and feeble effort to adapt the plot and leading idea of *Don Quixote* to English contemporary life; and wrote, with extraordinary rapidity, his *History of England*, in which his ardent and partial judgments are no less remarkable than the consummate elegance and calm prophetic spirit which charm in the pages of Hume. In a *Tour in France and Italy*, which he undertook to divert his grief under the loss of a beloved child, Smollett exhibits a painful, and almost ludicrous incapacity to appreciate the beautiful, sublime, or interesting objects he met with: he "travelled from Dan to Beersheba, and found all barren." In a now-forgotten tale, *The Adventures of an Atom*, he attacked Bute, who had formerly been his patron. This work may be said to correspond with the *Journey from this World to the Next*, in the not very dissimilar literary career of Fielding. Smollett's health was now completely broken up through incessant labor and continual agitation, and he was, like his illustrious contemporary, obliged to try the effect of a more genial climate. He resided a short time at Leghorn, and there, in spite of weakness, exhaustion, and suffering, the dying genius gave forth its most pleasing flash of comic humor. This was the novel of *Humphrey Clinker*, the only fiction in which Smollett adopted the epistolary form, and the most cordial, comic, and laughable of them all. Like Fielding he died and was buried in a foreign land and two of the most intensely national of our painters of character were doomed, nearly at the same time, to lay their bones under the soil of the stranger.

§ 9. In the structure of his fictions Smollett is manifestly inferior both to Richardson and Fielding: he does not possess the slow but exquisitely logical evolution of the former, or the skilful combination and planning of connected incidents which distinguish the latter. His novels are a series of striking, grotesque, farcical, and occasionally pathetic scenes, which have little other bond of union than the fact of their being threaded, so to say, on the life of a single person. Yet his books are eminently *amusing;* the reader's attention is kept awake by a lively succession of persons and events, some of which, though they may be coarse and low-lived, are invariably vivid and life-like, while the tendency to florid description and sentimental exaggeration does not deprive others of the charm of freshness and earnestness. The characters in Smollett are extraordinarily numerous and animated, but they are not analyzed with the profound psychological anatomy of Fielding: some prominent feature is seized, some oddity is placed in a strong light and exhibited in full development, and the reader asks for nothing more. This external or superficial mode of delineation makes Smollett very careless about maintaining the consistency of his personages. He never scruples to sacrifice that consistency, whether it refer to their bodily or mental qualities, when it stands in his way in placing them under ridiculous points of view: thus Roderick Random is sometimes represented as gawky, ugly, and even mean and cowardly, and at other times as eminently handsome and brave. There can be no doubt that Smollett was frequently in the habit of transferring to his novels real adventures of his own life: thus Random's miseries at school, his apprenticeship with the apothecary, his journey to London, his experiences in the fleet have the strongest air of being transcripts of reality: many of the persons introduced, and no small proportion of the scenes, as for example the medical examination, and the abominable tyranny and abuses on board ship, were unquestionably drawn from the life. The same may be said of his inimitable and exquisitely varied sailor-characters, from Lieutenant Bowling and Ap Morgan in the first novel, through the rich gallery of oddities in his later works, particularly Commodore Trunnion and Pipes in *Peregrine Pickle.* Smollett's heroes are generally a little too much of the picaresque, or Lazarillo de Tormès type: they have but little to attract the reader's sympathy, being generally hard, impudent, selfish, and ungrateful adventurers; but in the subordinate persons, and especially in those of grotesque but faithful followers, like Strap or Pipes, Smollett shows a greater warmth of sentiment. His style is lively and picturesque; much more careless than that of Fielding, who occasionally produces passages of considerable length that are noble specimens of English prose, and he allows the fire of his imagination to seduce him into the faults of tawdriness and sentimentality. Many of his most laughable scenes — and such abound in his writings — depend for their effect upon what may be called mechanical humor, blows and kicks and extravagant terrors: but these low episodes are not made the occasion, as they often are in Fielding, of educing profound traits of human character. With the laugh he has excited, Smollett's use of them is at an end. In *Humphrey Clinker*, though running over with fun and grotesque incident, there is a riper and mellower tone of character-painting than is to be found in his preceding works: the personages of Lismahago and Tabitha Bramble are inimitably carried out: the latter is indeed perhaps the most finished portrait in Smollett's whole gallery. This latter novel contains a great deal of what is merely descriptive, being the travelling-journal of the droll and original party whose various letters make up the work; and the modern reader may gather from Smollett's descriptions of the country and the various watering-places in England and Scotland visited during the imaginary tour, most curious and interesting details concerning the state of the country and the manners of our forefathers. Smollett, like Fielding, and indeed like most authors of those days, was in the habit, probably in imitation of the practice of Cervantes and the old masters, of occasionally introducing long episodical narratives into the midst of his novels; a most injudicious custom, and equally injurious to the effect of the intercalary tale and of the work in which it was set. Examples of what I mean will be found in the history of the *Fair Marcelia* in Don Quixote, the absurd and unnatural story of the *Man of the Hill* introduced into *Tom Jones*, and the *Story of the Lady of Quality*, which Smollett is said to have been bribed to insert in one of his novels.

Smollett possessed considerable poetical talents: he wrote the powerful verses entitled the *Tears of Scotland*, which breathed the patriotic indignation of a generous mind, horror-struck by the cruelties inflicted by the orders of the Duke of Cumberland after the battle of Culloden. This little poem is equally honorable to the civil courage of Smollett as to his genius, for so free an expression of outraged patriotism was then dangerous, and it is recorded that the poet, when warned of that danger after composing six stanzas of vigorous denunciation, instantly sat down and added a seventh, more bitter and stinging than those which had gone before.

§ **10.** Laurence Sterne (1713-1768) was a brilliant literary comet. His character was as eccentric as his works, both the one and the other being marked by strange inconsistency, equally attractive to the imagination and incompatible with severe principle. He was born in Ireland, but educated, with the assistance of some relations of his mother's, at Cambridge. Entering the Church, he enjoyed, through their interest, considerable preferment in the north, having long held the living of Sutton, to which he afterwards added a prebend's stall in the Cathedral of York; and he was ultimately advanced to the rich living of Coxwold. His private life was little in harmony with his profession: he appears to have been a fanciful, vain, self-indulgent humorist, perpetually at war with the neighboring clergy, and masking caprice and harshness under a pretence of extreme sensibility. His conduct to his wife was base and selfish. The first two volumes of his novel of *Tristram Shandy* were published in 1761, and the novelty and oddity of his style instantly raised him to the summit of popularity: two more volumes appeared in the following year, and Sterne became the pet and lion of fashionable London society, where he gratified his morbid appetite for flattery and indulged in a series of half-immoral, half-sentimental intrigues, some of them with married women. He made two tours on the Continent, the first in France, and the second in France and Italy, where he accumulated the materials incorporated in his delightful *Sentimental Journey*, intended to form a part of his romance, but which is generally read as an independent work. In this book he personates his favorite character Yorick, a mixture of the humorist and the sentimental observer. The *Sentimental Journey*, with all its faults of taste and morality, has the merit of breathing a tone of complacency, candor, and appreciation of the good qualities of foreign nations, equally rare and laudable at a time when Englishmen regarded all other countries, and especially France, with the most narrow-minded prejudice and hostility. Sterne's health had always been precarious; he had all his life been consumptive, and the feverish life of London society broke up a constitution naturally sickly. He died alone and friendless in a Bond Street lodging-house, attended in his last illness by mercenaries, who are said to have plundered him of such trifles as he possessed — a comfortless and gloomy ending, which he had himself desired.

His works consist of the novel of *Tristram Shandy*, of the *Sentimental Journey*, and of a collection of *Sermons*, written in the odd and fantastic style which he brought into temporary vogue. It is not an easy task to give an intelligible account of the plan, the merits, and the defects of his writings. *Tristram Shandy*, though nominally a romance in the biographical form, is intentionally irregular and capricious, the imaginary hero never making his appearance at all, and the story consisting of a series of sketches and episodes introducing us to the interior of an English country family, one of the richest collections of oddities that genius has ever delineated. The narrative is written partly in the character of Yorick (Sterne himself), supposed to be a clergyman and a humorist, and partly in that of the phantom-like Tristram; and the most prominent persons are Walter Shandy, a retired merchant, the father of the supposed hero, his mother, his uncle Toby Shandy (a veteran officer), and his servant Corporal Trim. These are all conceived and executed in the finest and most Shaksperian spirit of humor, tenderness, and observation; and they are supported by a crowd of minor yet hardly less individual portraitures — Obadiah, Dr. Slop, the Widow Wadman, Susanna, nay, down to the "foolish fat scullion." Mr. Shandy, the restless, crotchety philosopher, is delineated with consummate skill, and admirably contrasted with the simple benevolence and professional enthusiasm of the unequalled Uncle Toby, a personage belonging to the same category of creative genius as Sancho or as Parson Adams. The characters in Sterne are not delineated descriptively, but rather *allusively;* and thus the reader incessantly enjoys the pleasure of making out their pleasant and eccentric features, not through the medium of the author, but by himself, as if they were real personages. The conversations, the incidental episodes, all introduce us to the eccentricities and amiable oddities of the persons; and perhaps the very absence of all regular construction, the abrupt transitions, the complete confusion of all order, the exclamations, parenthetical chapters, and the abrupt and interjectional character of the style, contribute to the effect of the whole. In all Sterne's writings there is a great parade of obscure and quaint erudition, which passed off at the time these books appeared, when the elder authors were but rarely studied, as indicative of immense learning; but he is known at present to have been a most unscrupulous plagiarist, pillaging Burton, Rabelais, and the seldom-consulted pages of the old lawyers and canonists. All this, however, tends powerfully to give an original flavor to his style. His humor and his pathos are often truly admirable; and he possesses in a high degree that rare power, found only in the greatest humorists, of combining the ludicrous and the pathetic, but both his humor and his pathos are very often false and artificial, the one degenerating into buffoonery, indecency, and even profanity in more than a single instance, and the other into a morbid and sickly sentimentality. He is always trembling on the verge of an obscene allusion; and many passages, both in *Shandy* and the *Sentimental Journey*, are quite unjustifiable as coming from the pen of a clergyman. In this mixture of pruriency and theatrical sentiment Sterne resembles certain of the most brilliant French authors; and even the rapidity and abruptness of his style cause him to be perhaps the only one of our great humorists who can be adequately translated into French. His episodes, as the often-quoted *Story of Le Fevre*, are related with consummate art and tenderness; but in Sterne -- probably from his vanity and deficiency of discrimination — there is no medium between excellence and failure. He is an acute and just observer of the little turns of gesture and expression, and makes his characters *betray* their idiosyncrasies by involuntary touches, just as men do in real life.

§ 11. The most charming and versatile, and certainly one of the greatest writers of the eighteenth century, is OLIVER GOLDSMITH (1728-1774), whose works, whether in prose or verse, bear a peculiar stamp of gentle grace and elegance. He was born at the village of Pallas in the county of Longford, Ireland, in 1728. His father was a poor curate of English extraction, struggling, with the aid of farming and a miserable stipend, to bring up a large family. By the assistance of a benevolent uncle, Mr. Contarine, Oliver was enabled to enter the University of Dublin in the humble quality of sizar. He, however, neglected the opportunities for study which the place offered him, and became notorious for his irregularities, his disobedience to authority, and above all for a degree of improvidence carried to the extreme, though excused by a tenderness and charity almost morbid. The earlier part of his life is an obscure and monotonous narrative of ineffectual struggles to subsist, and of wanderings which enabled him to traverse almost the whole of Europe. Having been for a short time tutor in a family in Ireland, he determined to study medicine; and after nominally attending lectures in Edinburgh, he began those travels — for the most part on foot, and subsisting by the aid of his flute and the charity given to a poor scholar — which successively led him to Leyden, through Holland, France, Germany, and Switzerland, and even to Pavia, where he boasted, though the assertion is hardly capable of proof, that he received a medical degree. His professional as well as his general knowledge was of the most superficial and inaccurate character. It was while wandering in the guise of a beggar in Switzerland that he sketched out the plan of his poem of the *Traveller*, which afterwards formed the commencement of his fame. In 1756 he found his way back to his native country; and his career during about eight years was a succession of desultory struggles with famine, sometimes as a chemist's shopman in London; sometimes as an usher in boarding-schools, the drudge of his employers and the butt and laughing-stock of the pupils; sometimes as a practitioner of medicine among the poorest and most squalid population — "the beggars in Axe Lane," as he expressed it himself; and more generally as a miserable and scantily-paid bookseller's hack. More than once, under the pressure of intolerable distress, he exchanged the bondage of the school for the severer slavery of the corrector's table in a printing-office, and was driven back again to the bondage of the school. The grace and readiness of his pen would probably have afforded him a decent subsistence, even from the hardly-earned wages of a drudge-writer, but for his extreme improvidence, his almost childish generosity, his passion for pleasure and fine clothes, and above all his propensity for gambling. At one time, during this wretched period of his career, he failed to pass the examination qualifying him for the humble medical post of a hospital mate; and, under the pressure of want and improvidence, committed the dishonorable action of pawning a suit of clothes lent him by his employer, Griffiths, for the purpose of appearing with decency before the Board. His literary apprenticeship was passed in this severe school — writing to order, and at a moment's notice, school-books, tales for children, prefaces, indexes, and reviews of books; and contributing to the Monthly, Critical, and Lady's Review, the British Magazine, and other periodicals. His chief employer in this way appears to have been Griffiths, and he is said to have been at one time engaged as a corrector of the press in Richardson's service. In this period of obscure drudgery he composed some of his most charming works, or at least formed that inimitable style which makes him the rival, and perhaps more than the rival, of Addison. He produced the *Chinese Letters*, the plan of which is imitated from Montesquieu's Lettres Persanes, giving a description of English life and manners in the assumed character of a Chinese traveller, and containing some of those little sketches and humorous characters in which he was unequalled; a *Life of Beau Nash;* and a short and gracefully-narrated *History of England*, in the form of Letters from a Nobleman to his Son, the authorship of which was ascribed to Lyttleton. It was in 1764 that the publication of his beautiful poem of the *Traveller* caused him to emerge from the slough of obscure literary drudgery in which he had hitherto been crawling. The universal judgment of the public pronounced that nothing so harmonious and so original had appeared since the time of Pope; and from this period Goldsmith's career was one of uninterrupted literary success, though his folly and improvidence kept him plunged in debt, which even his large earnings could not enable him to avoid, and from which indeed no amount of fortune would have saved him. In 1766 appeared the *Vicar of Wakefield*, that masterpiece of gentle humor and delicate tenderness; in the following year his first comedy, the *Good-natured Man*, which failed upon the stage in some measure from its very merits, some of its comic scenes shocking the perverted taste of an audience which admired the whining, preaching, sentimental pieces that were then in fashion. In 1768 Goldsmith composed, as taskwork for the booksellers — though taskwork for which his now rapidly rising popularity secured good payment — the *History of Rome*, distinguished by its extreme superficiality of information and want of research no less than by enchanting grace of style and vivacity of narration. In 1770 he published the *Deserted Village*, the companion poem to the *Traveller*, written in some measure in the same manner, and not less touching and perfect; and in 1773 was acted his comedy *She Stoops to Conquer*, one of the gayest, pleasantest, and most amusing pieces that the English stage can boast. Goldsmith had long risen from the obscurity to which he had been condemned: he was one of the most admired and popular authors of his time; his society was courted by the wits, artists, statesmen, and writers who formed a brilliant circle round Johnson and Reynolds, —

Burke, Garrick, Beauclerk, Percy, Gibbon, Boswell, — and he became a member of that famous Club which is so intimately associated with the intellectual history of that time. Goldsmith was one of those men whom it is impossible not to love, and equally impossible not to despise and laugh at: his vanity, his childish though not malignant envy, his more than Irish aptitude for blunders, his eagerness to shine in conversation, for which he was peculiarly unfitted, his weaknesses and genius combined, made him the pet and the laughing-stock of the company. He was now in the receipt of an income which for that time and for the profession of letters might have been accounted splendid; but his improvidence kept him plunged in debt, and he was always anticipating his receipts, so that he continued to be the slave of booksellers, who obliged him to waste his exquisite talent on works hardly thrown off, and for which he neither possessed the requisite knowledge nor could make the necessary researches: thus he successively put forth as task-work the *History of England*, the *History of Greece*, and the *History of Animated Nature*, the two former works being mere compilations of second-hand facts, and the last an epitomized translation of Buffon. In these books we see how Goldsmith's never-failing charm of style and easy grace of narration compensate for total ignorance and a complete absence of independent knowledge of the subject. In 1774 this brilliant and feverish career was terminated. Goldsmith was suffering from a painful and dangerous disease, aggravated by disquietude of mind arising from the disorder in his affairs; and relying upon his knowledge of medicine he imprudently persisted in employing a violent remedy against the advice of his physicians. He died at the age of forty-six, deeply mourned by the brilliant circle of friends to which his very weaknesses had endeared him no less than his admirable genius, and surrounded by the tears and blessings of many wretches whom his inexhaustible benevolence had relieved. He was buried in the Temple Churchyard, and a monument was erected to his memory in Westminster Abbey, for which Johnson wrote a Latin inscription, one passage of which gracefully alludes to the versatility of his genius: "qui nullum fere scribendi genus non tetigit, nullum quod tetigit non ornavit."

§ **12.** In everything Goldsmith wrote, prose or verse, serious or comic, there are a peculiar delicacy and purity of sentiment, tinging, of course, the language and diction as well as the thought. It seems as if his genius, though in its earlier career surrounded with squalid distress, was incapable of being sullied by any stain of coarseness or vulgarity Though of English descent, he had in an eminent degree the defects as well as the virtues of the Irish character; and no quality in his writings is more striking than the union of grotesque humor with a sort of pensive tenderness, which gives to his verse a peculiar character of gliding melody and grace. He had seen much, and reproduced with singular vivacity quaint strokes of nature, as in his sketch of Beau Tibbs and innumerable passages in the Vicar of Wakefield. The two poems of the ***Traveller*** and the ***Deserted Village*** will ever be regarded as masterpieces of sentiment and description. The light yet rapid touch with which, in the former, he has traced the scenery and the natural peculiarities of various countries will be admired long after the reader has learned to neglect the false social theories embodied in his deductions; and in spite of the inconsistency, pointed out by Macaulay, between the pictures of the village in its pristine beauty and happiness, and the same village when ruined and depopulated by the forced emigration of its inhabitants, the reader lingers over the delicious details of human as well as inanimate nature which the poet has combined into the lovely pastoral picture of "sweet Auburn." The touches of tender personal feeling which he has interwoven with his description, as the fond hope with which he dwelt on the project of returning to pass his age among the scenes of innocence which had cradled his boyhood, the comparison of himself to a hare returning to die where it was kindled, the deserted garden, the village alehouse, the school, and the evening landscape, are all touched with the pensive grace of a Claude; while, when the occasion demands, Goldsmith rises with easy wing to the height of lofty and even sublime elevation, as in the image of the storm-girded yet sunshine-crowned peak to which he compares the good pastor.

The *Vicar of Wakefield*, in spite of the extreme absurdity and inconsistency of its plot, an inconsistency which grows more perceptible in the latter part of the story, will ever remain one of those rare gems which no lapse of time can tarnish. The gentle and quiet humor embodied in the simple Dr. Primrose, the delicate yet vigorous contrasts of character in the other personages, the atmosphere of purity, cheerfulness, and gayety which envelops all the scenes and incidents, will contribute, no less than the transparency and grace of the style, to make this story a classic for all time. Goldsmith's two comedies are written in two different manners, the *Good-natured Man* being a comedy of character, and *She Stoops to Conquer* a comedy of intrigue. In the first the excessive easiness and generosity of the hero are not a quality sufficiently reprehensible to make him a favorable subject for that satire which is the essential element of this kind of theatrical painting; and the merit of the piece chiefly consists in the truly laughable personage of Croaker, and in the excellent scene where the disguised bailiffs are passed off on Miss Richland as the friends of Honeywood, whose house and person they have seized. But in *She Stoops to Conquer* we have a first-rate specimen of the comedy of intrigue, where the interest mainly depends upon a tissue of lively and farcical incidents, and where the characters, though lightly sketched, form a gallery of eccentric pictures. The best proof of Goldsmith's success in this piece is the constancy with which it has always kept possession of the stage; and the peals of laughter which never fail to greet the lively bustle of its scenes and the pleasant absurdities of Young Marlow, Mr. and Mrs. Hardcastle, and above all the admirable Tony Lumpkin, a conception worthy of Vanbrugh himself.

Some of Goldsmith's lighter fugitive poems are incomparable for their peculiar humor. The *Haunch of Venison* is a model of easy narrative and accurate sketching of commonplace society; and in *Retaliation* we have a series of slight yet delicate portraits of some of the most distinguished literary friends of the poet, thrown off with a hand at once refined and vigorous. In how masterly a manner, and yet in how few strokes, has Goldsmith placed before us Garrick, Burke, and Reynolds! and how deeply do we regret that he should not have given us similar portraits of Johnson, Gibbon, and Boswell! Several of the songs and ballads scattered through his works are remarkable for their tenderness and harmony, though the *Edwin and Angelina* which has been so often lauded, has always appeared to me mawkish, affected, and devoid of the true spirit of the mediæval ballad.

NOTES AND ILLUSTRATIONS.

OTHER NOVELISTS.

SARAH FIELDING (1714–1768) was sister of the celebrated novel-writer, and herself well known as an authoress. Her best known novels were *David Simple* and *The Cry*. She also translated Xenophon's *Memorabilia*.

CHARLES JOHNSTONE (d. 1800) was the author of the once popular *Adventures of a Guinea*, 1760, and other now unknown works. The former is a severe satire on the sins and follies of the age. We lay it down "with a feeling of relief." It exhibits the "baser sides of literature and life."

CHAPTER XVIII.

HISTORICAL, MORAL, POLITICAL, AND THEOLOGICAL WRITERS OF THE EIGHTEENTH CENTURY.

§ 1. DAVID HUME His life and publications. *Treatise on Human Nature* an *History of England.* § 2. WILLIAM ROBERTSON. *Histories of Scotland, Charles V.*, and *America.* § 3. EDWARD GIBBON. His life and works. § 4. Criticism of the *Decline and Fall of the Roman Empire.* § 5. SAMUEL JOHNSON. His early life and struggles. *London. Life of Savage.* § 6. *English Dictionary. Vanity of Human Wishes.* Tragedy of *Irene.* § 7. The *Idler* and *Rambler. Rasselas.* Johnson receives a pension from the government. § 8. His acquaintance with Boswell. Edition of Shakspeare. *Journey to the Hebrides. Lives of the Poets.* Johnson's death. § 9. EDMUND BURKE. His life and writings. *Essay on the Sublime and Beautiful.* His impeachment of Warren Hastings. *Letter to a Noble Lord. Reflections on the French Revolution. Letter on a Regicide Peace.* § 10. *Letters of Junius.* § 11. ADAM SMITH. *Inquiry into the Nature and Causes of the Wealth of Nations.* § 12. SIR WILLIAM BLACKSTONE. *Commentaries on the Laws of England.* § 13. BISHOP BUTLER and WILLIAM PALEY. § 14. GILBERT WHITE. *Natural History of Selborne.*

§ 1. IN accordance with that peculiar law which seems to govern the appearance, at particular epochs, of several great names in one department of art or literature, like the sculptors of the Periclean age, the romantic dramatists in that of Elizabeth, and the novelists who appeared in England in the days of Richardson and Fielding, the eighteenth century was signalized by a remarkable wealth of historical genius, and gave birth to Hume, Robertson, and Gibbon.

DAVID HUME (1711–1776) was born, of an ancient Scottish family, in 1711, and received his education in the University of Edinburgh. His desires and ambition were irresistibly set upon literary fame, and after reluctantly trying the profession of law and the pursuit of commerce, he lived abroad some years, devoting himself, by means of prudence and economy, to the cultivation of moral and metaphysical science, and to the preparation of his mind for future historical labors. His intellect was calm, philosophical, and sceptical, and he imbibed that strong disbelief in the possibility of miracles which, when expressed in his subtle logic and refined purity of style, has rendered him one of the most dangerous enemies of revealed religion. In 1737 he returned to England, and was so much discouraged with the coldness of the public towards his first moral and metaphysical productions that he at one time meditated changing his name and expatriating himself forever. In 1746 and the following year a gleam of success shone upon him, for he had hitherto lived in such narrow circumstances that his extreme prudence and economy scarcely enabled him to subsist respectably, and he was even at one time reduced to the painful and uncongenial office of taking charge of the young Marquis of Annandale, who was insane. He now entered the public service, and was employed as Secretary to General St. Clair in various diplomatic missions. When again residing at Edinburgh, in 1752, he accepted the post of Librarian to the Faculty of Advocates, for which he received no salary, but which placed at his disposal a large and excellent collection of books. With the aid thus furnished he began his great work, the *History of England* from the accession of the Stuart Dynasty to the Revolution of 1688, to which he afterwards added in successive volumes the earlier history from the invasion of Julius Cæsar to the reign of James I. Though the first volumes were received with the same neglect as had encountered his previous publications, the extraordinary merits of the plan and the incomparable clearness and beauty of the narration soon overcame the indifference of the public, and the history gradually and rapidly rose to the highest popularity, and took that place among the prose classics of the language which it has ever since retained. The admiration excited by the *History*, by a natural consequence, reacted also upon his previous works, which now began to enjoy a high degree of popularity, in spite of the heterodox tenets which they were accused of maintaining. Hume's reputation was now solidly established: he was again employed in the public service, and accompanied as secretary the embassy of General Conway to Paris, where he became one of the lions of the fashionable society of the French capital, a popularity which he owed more to his literary glory and to the sceptical theories — then so prevalent in France — of which he was one of the apostles, than to any personal aptitude for the society of wits and fine ladies; for Hume was heavy and inelegant in appearance, and possessed few charms of conversation or readiness of repartee. He afterwards fulfilled for a short time the still higher functions of Under-Secretary of State, and retiring with a pension passed the evening of his life in philosophic and intellectual tranquillity, enjoying the respect and affection which his virtuous and amiable qualities attracted, and which not even his scepticism could repel. Hume died in 1776. He was distinguished by great benevolence of heart, and by a spirit of candor and indulgence to the opinions of others, which might have been advantageously imitated by many of those who controverted his opinions.

As a moral and metaphysical writer Hume certainly deserves a high place in the history of philosophy. The prominent feature of his *Treatise on Human Nature*, published in 1738, was the attempt to deduce the operations of the mind entirely from the two sources of impressions and ideas, which he looks upon as distinct, and his denying the existence of any fundamental difference between such actions as we call virtuous and vicious, other than as they are practically found to be conducive to or destructive of the advantage of the individual or the species. In other words Hume is the assertor of the theory of Utility, as the only one capable of satisfactorily explaining the mysterious question — What is the essential difference between good and evil? Such a theory was received with intense dissatisfaction by the orthodox: but seldom has the controversialist to encounter a tougher antagonist than Hume, the clearness of whose exposition, and the subtlety of whose arguments, a subtlety the more formidable as it is always veiled under an air of philosophic candor, were but too often met with declamation and unfair attacks on a personal character which was above reproach. But the chief danger of Hume's philosophical doctrines lies in his famous argument on the impossibility of miracles, based upon the two propositions: first, that it is contrary to all human experience that miracles should be true, both reason and facts tending to show the invariable nature of the laws which govern all physical phenomena; and secondly, that the improbability of a miracle ever having taken place is far greater than the improbability of the testimony to such an event being false, the witnesses being likely either to have been duped themselves or to dupe others.

The *History of England* is a book of very high value. In a certain exquisite ease and vivacity of narration it certainly has never been surpassed; and in the analysis of characters and the appreciation of great events, Hume's singular clearness and philosophic elevation of view give him a right to one of the foremost places among modern historians. But its defects are no less considerable. Hume's indolence induced him to remain contented with taking his facts at second-hand from preceding writers, without troubling himself about accuracy Thus legendary and half-mythological stories are related with the same air of belief as the more well-authenticated events of recent times; a fault pardonable enough in Herodotus and Livy, but less venial in a writer who ought to have applied his powerful critical faculty to the sifting of truth from tradition. Hume, essentially a classicist of the Voltaire and Diderot type, too much despised the barbarous monkish chroniclers to think of consulting them as authorities, or of separating the germ of fact which they envelop in a mass of superstitious and imaginative detail. Moreover, the history of England is essentially the history of the conflict of opinion on religious and political questions; and Hume was indifferent to religion, and a partisan of extreme monarchical opinions in politics. Thus he shows a strong leaning to the Stuart dynasty, and even to the Catholic church as opposed to Protestantism; for he belonged to the aristocratical section of the Scottish people, who were almost uniformly Jacobites, while the middle and lower classes were as ardent supporters of liberal principles. The sceptical and philanthropic reasoner was, by a singular paradox, inclined from personal sympathies to opinions precisely contrary to those which he might have been expected to maintain, and struggles by sophistry to excuse the crimes and follies of the arbitrary Stuarts, while he exhibits an indifference, strange in a man so benevolent by nature, to the sufferings and heroism of those who, in Parliament or on the field of battle, fought the great fight for political and religious freedom.

§ 2. Contemporary with Hume was his countryman WILLIAM ROB-

ERTSON (1721-1793), distinguished, like him, by the eloquence of his narrative, by the luminous dissertations on great historical questions introduced into his works, by the picturesque power of delineating characters and events, and also by a singular dignity and purity of style, which is almost free from Scotticisms. His personal career was that of a Presbyterian pastor, and he was highly celebrated for his eloquence in the pulpit. In 1762 he was elected Principal of the University of Edinburgh, where he had received his education, and he exhibited remarkable powers as a speaker and debater in the Scottish General Assembly of Divines. He produced three great historical works, the *History of Scotland*, embracing the reigns of the unfortunate Mary and of her son James VI. down to the accession of the latter to the throne of England, the *History of the Reign of Charles V.*, and the *History of the Discovery*, and first Colonization by the Spaniards, *of America.* These three productions appeared respectively in 1759, 1769, and 1777.* In all of them we perceive a rich and melodious though somewhat artificial style, great though not always accurate research, and a strong power of vivid and pathetic description. The *History of Scotland* is perhaps the work most honorable to Robertson's genius, for in the other two the grandeur and dramatic interest of the subject were such that, in the hands even of an inferior author, the reader's curiosity could not but be excited and gratified. Moreover though many of the general disquisitions prefixed to or introduced in Robertson's history are marked by largeness of view and lucidity of arrangement, his account of many episodes of the life of Charles V., and in particular of his retirement to San Yuste, contains much of the romantic and theatrical inaccuracy which recent investigations have dispelled: and in this work, as well as in the wondrous story of Columbus and the Conquestadors, he either knew not or neglected vast stores of information which would have thrown a very different light upon the characters and events he had to portray. This assertion will be amply proved by comparing Robertson's account of these great events with the more recent labors of Prescott, Motley, and others. In spite of these defects, Robertson's name will always retain an honorable place among the prose-writers and historians of England.

§ **3.** But by far the greatest name in English historical literature — indeed one of the very foremost names in all historical literature — is that of EDWARD GIBBON (1737-1794). Descended from an ancient family, he was born at Putney near London in 1737, and was the grandson of a merchant of large fortune. His health, during his boyhood and early youth, was exceedingly precarious, and he owed the gradual fortifying of his constitution, and the first development of his intellectual faculties, to the more than maternal care of an aunt, Catherine Porten. His education was at first neglected, but he gradually acquired an insatiable appetite for reading of all kinds, which at length

* Robertson also published, in 1791, an *Historical Disquisition concerning the Knowledge which the Antients had of India*; a work of great merit, though now superseded by more recent investigations.

concentrated itself upon historical literature. He passed a short time at Westminster school, and was intrusted to several successive private tutors, but at the early age of fifteen was placed at Magdalen College, Oxford, where he remained only fourteen months, still pursuing his studies in a vague and desultory manner. An ardent fit of controversial reading, and the arguments he found in Pascal and Bossuet, overthrew his attachment to the doctrines of Protestantism, and on his formally embracing the Catholic faith, his father, shocked at such apostasy, sent him to Lausanne, where he was placed under the care of M. Pavillard, an eminent Swiss theologian. The arguments of his tutor so far prevailed as to induce him to re-enter the Protestant Church, though his religious belief from this time forward was little more than a sort of philosophical Deism. In Switzerland, however, he commenced that course of regular and systematic study, which gradually filled his mind with immeasurable stores of sacred and profane learning: and here too his mind acquired that strong sympathy with French modes of thought that make him the least national of all our great authors. While in Switzerland he conceived a passion for Susanne Curchod, afterwards the wife of Necker, and the mother of Madame de Staël; but Gibbon's sensibility was never very ardent, and he acquiesced, with decent readiness, in the refusal of his father to permit the union. Returning to England, he passed some time in the frivolous pleasures of a young gentleman of fortune; but without relaxing in his intense diligence of study, which he found means to maintain even during the five years he passed in military service as captain of the Hampshire militia. It was at this period that he gave to the world the first-fruits of his pen in the excellent little essay, written in French, on the *Study of Literature*. Between 1763 and 1765 he travelled over France, Switzerland, and Italy, and while at Rome, in 1764, the first idea of writing the history of the *Decline and Fall* of the mighty empire first flashed upon his mind. He has given a most striking and picturesque description of the moments of the generation and the completion of his great work. The sudden shock of conception given amid the sunset ruins of the Capitol, "while the barefooted friars were singing vespers in the Temple of Jupiter," found its picturesque consummation in the "valley of acacias" by the moonlit lake of Geneva in 1787. Gibbon returned to England in 1765, and set strenuously to work on the composition of his history, the first volume of which appeared in the following year, and was received not only with the applause of the learned, but with universal popularity among the fashionable world and the ladies. The praises of Hume found an echo in the gayest and most frivolous circles. At various intervals appeared the successive volumes, each of which excited the admiration and enthusiasm which the grandeur of the work was so calculated to inspire. Gibbon has related the hesitation, and almost terror, with which the immense extent and difficulty of his enterprise at first filled him, and the fastidious care with which he revised and re-revised the opening chapters, the first of which he wrote thrice, and the second twice over, before he was satisfied with the style; but as he advanced, the various parts of his gigantic subject took form and symmetry, and the increasing facility of composition enabled him to advance with steady speed.

With the year 1774 begins Gibbon's political career: he sat in several successive Parliaments as member for Liskeard, and supported, with a silent vote — for both modesty and vanity prevented him from trying his fortune as a speaker — the ministry, during the whole course of the American War, down to the formation of the Coalition Cabinet. Lord North rewarded his constant adhesion with the post of one of the Lord Commissioners of Trade, which Gibbon enjoyed for about three years, till the abolition of the office in 1782. In 1783 Gibbon determined to settle altogether at Lausanne. He established himself in the comfortable house which he had purchased on the lovely shore of Lake Leman, a spot forever memorable from the residence of this great genius. This was perhaps the happiest part of his life; he was able to devote himself in tranquillity to his mighty task, and his leisure hours were enlivened with intellectual society and the companionship of his friend Deyverdun. At length his residence at Lausanne becoming disagreeable in consequence of the agitation which heralded the outbreak of the French Revolution, he returned to London in 1793, and died there in the following year. The personal character of Gibbon was rather respectable than attractive. Of a cold and somewhat selfish disposition, he played a prominent part in the brilliant intellectual circle which surrounded Burke and Johnson; his immense acquirements and refined manners rendered his conversation interesting and valuable, and his vanity, though concealed by good breeding and knowledge of the world, was not incompatible with generosity and benevolence.

§ 4. His *History of the Decline and Fall of the Roman Empire* is undoubtedly one of the greatest monuments of industry and genius. The task he undertook, to give a connected narrative of one of the most eventful periods in the annals of the world, —

"Res Romanas, perituraque regna," —

was colossal. It embraced, exclusive of the introductory sketch of Roman history from the time of Augustus, of itself a noble monument of philosophical research, a period of upwards of thirteen centuries, that is, from about 180 to 1453 A. D. This immense space included not only the manhood and the decrepitude of the Roman Empire, but the irruption of the Barbarian nations, the establishment of the Byzantine power, the reorganization of the European nations, the foundation of the religious and political system of Mahometanism, and the Crusades. The enormous scope of the undertaking rendered indispensable not only the most vast and accurate knowledge of the whole range of classical, Byzantine, mediæval, and Oriental literature, but such a largeness of view as should give a clear and philosophical account of some of the greatest religious and social changes that have ever modified the destinies of our race; the rise of Christianity, the Mussulman dominion, and the institutions of Feudalism and Chivalry. Nor was the complexity of the subject less formidable than its extent; while the materials for much of its treatment were to be painfully sifted from the rubbish of the Byzantine annalists, and the wild exaggerations of the Eastern chroniclers. From this immense chaos were to be deduced light, order, and regularity, and the historian was to be familiar with the whole range of philosophy, science, politics, and war. Gibbon has confessed that his experience of parliamentary tactics and the knowledge of military affairs which he had acquired in the House of Commons and in the Hampshire militia, had been of signal service to him in describing the deliberations of senates and the movements of immense armies; for man is everywhere the same, and the historian possessed the rare art of bringing home to our sympathies and understanding the sentiments and actions of remote ages and distant peoples. Gibbon is one of the most dangerous enemies by whom the Christian faith was ever assailed — he was the more dangerous because he was insidious. The following is the plan of his tactics. He does not formally deny the evidence upon which is based the structure of Christianity, but he indirectly includes that system in the same category with the mythologies of paganism. The rapid spread of Christianity he explains by merely secondary causes; and in relating the disgraceful corruptions, persecutions, and superstitions which so soon supplanted the pure morality of the primitive church, he leads the reader to consider these less as the results of human crime, folly, and ambition, than as the necessary consequences of the system itself. He either did not or would not distinguish between the *parceque* and *quoique;* and represents what is in reality an abuse as an inevitable consequence. Byron well described him as

"Sapping a solemn creed with solemn sneer,
The lord of irony, that master-spell."

But the accusations of having intentionally distorted facts or garbled authorities he has refuted in the Vindication in which he replied to his opponents. In the full and complete references and quotations with which he scrupulously fortifies his assertions and his deductions, we see a panoply which offers few weak places to the adversary. The deliberate opinion of Guizot, whom no one can accuse of indifference to religion, will be conclusive as to Gibbon's merit on this point. His style is remarkably pompous, elaborate, and sonorous: originally artificial, it had gradually become the natural garb of his thoughts. In the antithetical and epigrammatic structure of his phrases, and in the immense preponderance of the Latin over the Teutonic element in his diction, Gibbon is the least English of all our writers of the first class: and the ease with which whole pages of his writings may be translated almost without a change of words or grammar, into French, render credible the statement of his having for some time hesitated whether to compose his work in that language or his mother-tongue. He was so fastidious in his search after elegance, that to avoid the repetition, at close intervals, of a name or event, he is apt, each time it occurs after the first, to express it by a periphrasis or an incidental allusion, to understand which often demands from the reader a degree of knowledge which few readers possess, and this is sometimes the cause of obscurity. His descriptions of events, as of battles, of nations, of individual characters, are wonderfully life-like and animated; and his chief sin against good taste is a somewhat too gorgeous and highly-colored tone. His imagination was sensuous, and he dwells with greater enthusiasm upon material grandeur than upon moral elevation; for his moral susceptibilities do not appear of a very lofty order. He had in common with Voltaire a peculiar and most offensive delight in dwelling upon scandalous and immoral stories, and this tendency, which in Voltaire's light and fleering style is less repulsive, becomes doubly odious when exhibited in combination with Gibbon's solemn and majestic language.

§ 5. Perhaps the most striking figure in the social and literary history of this period is that of SAMUEL JOHNSON (1709-1784). His career was eminently that of a man of letters; and the slow and laborious efforts by which, in spite of every obstacle, personal as well as material, he raised himself to the highest intellectual supremacy present a spectacle equally instructive to us and honorable to him. He was born in 1709, the son of a learned, but poor and struggling provincial bookseller in Lichfield; and he exhibited, from his very childhood, the same singular union of mental power and constitutional indolence, ambition and hypochondriacal gloom, which distinguished him through life. He was disfigured and half blinded by a scrofulous disorder, which seamed and deformed a face and figure naturally imposing, and at the same time afflicted him with strange and involuntary contortions, reacting also upon his mind and temper, and making him sombre, despondent, and irritable. In the various humble seminaries, where he received his early education, he unfailingly took the first place; and being assisted by a benevolent patron with the means of studying at the University, he carried to Pembroke College, Oxford, an amount of scholarship very rare at his age. Here he remained about three years, remarkable for the roughness and uncouthness of his manners, and no less for his wit and insubordination, as well as for that sturdy spirit of independence which made him reject with indignation any offer of assistance. The story of his throwing away a pair of new shoes, which some one, pitying the poverty of the ragged student, had placed at his door, is striking, and even pathetic. His father's affairs being in hopeless confusion, and the promises of assistance not being fulfilled, he was obliged to leave the University without a degree; and receiving, at his father's death, only 20*l*. as his share of the inheritance, he abandoned it to his mother's use, for he was ever a most dutiful and generous son, and entered upon the hard career of teacher and usher in various provincial schools. For success in this profession he was equally unfitted by his person, his nature, and the peculiar character of his mind and acquirements; and after unsuccessfully attempting to keep a school himself at Edial, near Lichfield, he began that tremendous struggle with labor and want, which continued during thirty years. His first literary undertaking was a translation of Father Lobo's *Travels in Abyssinia*, but his hopes of success meeting with little but disappointment, he determined to launch upon the great ocean of London literary life. In 1736 he had married Mrs. Porter, a widow old enough to be his mother, but whom, notwithstanding her defects of person and cultivation, he always loved with the energy of his masculine and affectionate character. In 1737 he travelled to London in company with David Garrick, one of the few pupils he had had under his charge at Edial, who was destined, in another path, to follow a brilliant career. Garrick's ambition was to appear on the stage, where he speedily took the first place, and Johnson carried with him the unfinished MS. of his tragedy *Irene*. Without fortune, without friends, of singularly uncouth and forbidding exterior, Johnson entered upon the career—then perhaps at its lowest ebb of profit and respectability—of a bookseller's hack, or literary drudge. He became a contributor to divers journals, and particularly to the *Gentleman's Magazine*, then carried on by its founder, Cave; and as an obscure laborer for the press he furnished criticisms, prefaces, translations, in short all kinds of humble literary work, and ultimately supplied reports of the proceedings in Parliament, though the names of the speakers, in obedience to the law which then rendered it penal to reproduce the debates, were disguised under imaginary titles. He first emerged into popularity in 1738, by the publication of his satire entitled *London*, an admirable paraphrase or reproduction of the thirteenth satire of Juvenal, in which he adapts the sentiments and topics of the great Roman poet to the neglect of letters in London, and the humiliations which an honest man must encounter in a society where foreign quacks and native scoundrels could alone hope for success. During this miserable and obscure portion of his career, when he dined in a cellar upon sixpenny-worth of meat and a pennyworth of bread, when he signed himself, in a note to his employer, "yours, *impransus*, S. Johnson," when his ragged coat and torn shoes made him ashamed to appear at the table of his publisher, and caused him to devour his dinner behind a screen, he retained all his native dignity of mind and severe honesty of principle. There is something affecting in the picture of this great and noble mind laboring on through toil and distress which would have crushed most men, and which, though it roughened his manners, only intensified his humanity, and augmented his self-respect. In 1744 he published the *Life of Savage*, that unhappy poet whose career was so extraordinary and whose vices were not less striking than his talents. Johnson had known him well, and they had often wandered supperless and homeless about the streets at midnight. The vigorous and manly thought expressed in Johnson's sonorous language rendered this biography popular; but the improvement in the author's circumstances was very tardy in making its appearance: no literary life was ever a more correct exemplification than that of Johnson, of the truth of his own majestic line: "Slow rises worth by poverty depressed."

§ 6. During the eight years extending from 1747 to 1755 Johnson was engaged in the execution of his laborious undertaking, the compilation of his great *Dictionary of the English Language*, which long occupied the place among us of the Dictionary of the Academy in France and Spain. The etymological part of this great work, in consequence of Johnson sharing the then almost universal ignorance of the Teutonic languages, is totally without value; but the accuracy and comprehensiveness of the definitions, and above all the interesting quotations adduced to exemplify the different senses of the words, render it a book that may always be read with pleasure. The compilers of the French and Spanish Dictionaries do, indeed, quote passages, in support of the meanings they assign to words, from the great classical writers of their respective literature; but these quotations have no further interest, or even sense, than is necessary to exhibit the particular meaning of the word illustrated, while Johnson's are either some striking passage of poetry and eloquence, or some historical fact or scientific axiom or definition. Thus a page of Johnson's Dictionary always gratifies a curiosity quite independent of mere philological research. When we think of this solitary scholar with painful industry compiling a great national work, at least not inferior to productions which in other countries have occupied the attention of learned and richly endowed societies during a great number of years, we cannot but feel deep admiration for our countryman. While engaged in this laborious task he diverted his mind by the publication of the *Vanity of Human Wishes*, a companion to his *London*, being a similar imitation of the tenth satire of his Roman prototype. This is written in a loftier, more solemn and declamatory style than the preceding poem, and is a fine specimen of Johnson's dignified but somewhat gloomy rhetoric. The illustrations, drawn from history, of the futility of those objects which men sigh for, literary, military, or political renown, beauty, wealth, long life, or splendid alliances, Johnson has reproduced with kindred vigor; but he has added several of his own, where he shows a power and grandeur in no sense inferior to that of Juvenal. Thus to the striking picture of the fall of Sejanus, related with such grim humor by the Roman satirist, Johnson has added the not less impressive picture of the disgrace of Wolsey, and his episode of Charles XII. is no unworthy counterpart to the portrait of Hannibal. At about the same time Johnson brought out upon the stage, principally through the friendly interest of Garrick, who was now the principal theatrical manager, the tragedy of *Irene*, which had long been in vain awaiting the opportunity of representation. Its success was insignificant, and indeed could not have been otherwise, for the plot of the piece is totally devoid of interest and probability; there is no discrimination of character, no painting of passion, and the work consists of a series of lofty moral declamations in Johnson's labored and rhetorical style.

§ **7.** Johnson founded, and carried on alone, two periodical papers in the style that Addison and Steele had rendered so popular. These were the *Idler*, which lasted but a short time, and the *Rambler*, appearing twice a week and sold at a low price. The ease, grace, pleasantry, and variety which gave such charm to the *Tatler* and *Spectator* are totally incompatible with the heavy, antithetical, ponderous manner of Johnson; and his good sense, piety, and sombre tone of morality are but a poor substitute for the *mite ingenium* and knowledge of the world displayed in his models. Yet though bearing every mark of labor, Johnson's essays were written with great rapidity, and often despatched to the press without revisal. This species of periodical essay-writing, which exerted so powerful an influence on taste and manners in the eighteenth century, may be said to terminate with the *Rambler*, though continued with gradually increasing want of originality by other writers, till it finally died out with Hawkesworth, Moore, and Bonnell Thornton,* the former of whom was but a feeble mimic of the Johnsonian manner. Johnson's mother died in 1759, and he wrote with extraordinary rapidity, and for the purpose of raising funds for her funeral, his once-celebrated moral tale, *Rasselas, Prince of Abyssinia*. The manners and scenery of this story are neither those of Oriental nor of any other known country, and the book is little else but a series of dialogues and reflections, embodying the author's ideas on an immense variety of subjects connected with art, literature, society, and philosophy, and his lofty, but gloomy and discouraging principles of ethics and religion. It has sometimes been fancifully contrasted with the *Candide* of Voltaire, and indeed it would be difficult to find two nearly contemporary works presenting a more complete antagonism in tendency and manner.

At various periods of his career Johnson had given to the world several political pamphlets, generally distinguished for the violence with which arbitrary doctrines are maintained, and for a strange mixture of sense and vigor and narrow prejudice. Thus he was an ardent opponent of the rights of the American colonies to revolt against oppression, and through his whole life exhibited an ardent advocacy of extreme Tory doctrines, singularly at variance with his liberality in other respects. It was not till 1762, when the philosopher had reached the age of fifty-three, that he emerged from the constant poverty which had hitherto almost overwhelmed him, and against which he had so valiantly struggled. At the accession of George III. the government hoped to gain popularity by showing some favor to art and letters; and Johnson, who now occupied an honorable and leading position as a

* JOHN HAWKESWORTH (1715–1773) edited *The Adventurer*, which appeared twice a week from 1752 to 1754. Hawkesworth also translated *Telemachus*, and wrote an account of Captain Cook's voyages.

EDWARD MOORE (1712–1757) edited *The World*, which appeard weekly from 1753 to 1756, and in which he was assisted by Lord Lyttelton, the Earl of Chesterfield, Horace Walpole, and other distinguished literary men. Moore likewise wrote a tragedy called *The Gamester*.

BONNELL THORNTON (1724–1768) wrote, in conjunction with his friend George Colman the elder, *The Connoisseur*, which appeared from 1754 to 1756. Thornton was the author of several other works; but he is best known by his translation of Plautus, which he made in conjunction with Warner and Colman.

moralist and poet, was gratified by Lord Bute with a pension of 300*l.* a year. Johnson now found himself, for the first time in his life, placed above want, and was able to indulge not only his constitutional indolence, but that noble charity and benevolence which transformed his dwelling into a sort of asylum for helpless indigence. In spite of his own poverty he had maintained under his roof a strange assembly of pensioners on his bounty, whose only claims upon him were their infirmities and their distress. There was Anna Williams, a blind poetess, Mrs. Desmoulins, and Levett, a sort of humble practitioner of medicine among the most miserable classes of London; and a thousand anecdotes are related of the generosity of Johnson to these inmates, with whose quarrels and repinings he bore, and over whom he watched with unrelaxing kindness.

§ 8. At this period of his life Johnson became acquainted with JAMES BOSWELL (1740–1795), whose biography of the old sage is perhaps the most perfect and interesting account of a literary life and a literary epoch which the world has yet seen. Boswell was a young Scottish advocate of good family and fortune; he belonged to a nation which Johnson regarded with unreasonable and almost ludicrous aversion; he was vain, tattling, frivolous, and contemptible in the highest degree, totally deficient both in self-respect, tact, and solidity of principle; yet his sincere admiration for Johnson established a lasting friendship between these incompatible characters, and Boswell has produced not only the most lively and vivid portrait of the person, manners, and conversation of Johnson, but the most admirable picture of the society amid which he played so brilliant a part. Among the most celebrated social meetings of that age of clubs was the society founded by Johnson, and in which his friends Reynolds, Burke, Garrick, Bishop Percy, Goldsmith, Bennet Langton, Beauclerc, and others, were prominent figures. Indeed from its very foundation the most distinguished artists, conversers, and men of letters have been members of this club; and Boswell's delight was to record the "wit combats" which were incessantly taking place among them, as well as to preserve every fragment that he could collect by hearsay and observation, of the manners and converse of his idol. Thus he has given us, with a consummate skill only the more astonishing from what we know of his character, the most accurate yet lively transcript of the intellectual society of Johnson's day. Johnson's powers of conversation were extraordinary: he delighted in discussion, and had acquired by constant practice the art of expressing himself with pointed force and elegance, while the ponderous antitheses and sesquipedalian diction of his written style were replaced by a muscular and idiomatic expression which formed an appropriate vehicle for his weighty thoughts, his apt illustrations, and his immense stores of reading and observation. He often argued for victory; and the ingenious paradox and sledge-hammer repartees with which he sometimes overwhelmed opposition, are by no means the least interesting traits of his wonderful skill in social contest. Hardly any subject was broached on which Johnson had not something ingenious, if not admirable, to say. This was perhaps the most brilliant and the happiest portion of his life. He made the acquaintance of the family of Thrale, a rich brewer and member of the House of Commons, who, like most of his contemporaries, was filled with admiration by the varied and imposing talents of the great wit and writer, and whose wife was equally famous for her own talents and for the bright intellectual society she loved to assemble round her. At Thrale's house in London, as well as at his luxurious villa at Streatham, Johnson was for many years a frequent and an honored guest. His comfort was studied, his sickness was nursed, his coarseness of manner forgiven, and down to the time of Thrale's death Johnson enjoyed under his roof all that friendship and respect, aided by boundless wealth, could give. This connection, which lasted about fourteen years, gave Johnson the opportunity of frequenting refined society; and in the company of the Thrales he made several excursions to different parts of England, and once indeed as far as Paris. He undertook, unfortunately for his fame, the task of preparing a new edition of Shakspeare, an enterprise for which he was unfitted not only by his little sympathy with that romantic class of poetry of which Shakspeare is the chief representative, but by an almost total want of acquaintance with the writings of Shakspeare's age, an accurate knowledge of which is of course a primary requisite for any one who wishes to explain the obscurities of the poet. The edition, with the exception of an occasional happy remark, and a sensible selection from the commentaries of preceding annotators, is quite unworthy of Johnson's reputation. In 1773 Johnson undertook, in company with his friend Boswell, an expedition to the Hebrides, a journey which would in those days have appeared almost as enterprising as would now an exploration of the interior of Africa; and this voyage not only enabled him to make acquaintance with Scotland and the Scots, and thus to dissipate many of his old prejudices against the country and the people, but gave him the opportunity of exercising his observation and curiosity on a region entirely new to him and rarely visited by travellers. The volume in which he gives an account of his impressions contains many interesting and characteristic passages. His last work of any consequence, and which is also unquestionably his best, was the *Lives of the Poets*, originating in the proposal made to him by several publishers that he should write a few lines of biographical and critical preface to the collected works of the English poets, of which they were preparing an edition. Johnson accepted the task, but the work far outgrew the limits originally proposed, and he furnished an invaluable series of literary portraits. Unfortunately the plan altogether excluded the greatest poets that our literature has produced, and admitted no names, excepting those of Milton, Butler, Dryden, and Pope, which can be ranked in the first, or even very high in the second class. It seemed as if the plan had been purposely designed to embrace what was undoubtedly the least poetical epoch of our literature. But Johnson performed his task with such skill, and poured forth so abundantly the stores of his sound sense and acute reflection, that there lives are not only one of the most amusing books in the language, but contain, in spite of the narrowness of the author's literary creed, innumerable passages of the happiest and most original criticism, particularly in the appreciation of those writers who, belonging to what is called the classical or artificial school, exhibit characteristics which Johnson was capable of appreciating. His remarks upon the poetry of Cowley, Waller, and Pope are admirable; and his immense knowledge of life, and sharp and weighty sense, have filled his pages with striking and valuable observations. He incorporated with this work his previously written Life of Savage; and on comparing the style of this book with his preceding productions, we are struck by its comparative freedom from that pompous and rhetorical tone which disfigures his earlier prose-writings, in which the abuse of antithesis, of carefully balanced sentences, and of the employment of long Latinized words, had been carried so far as almost to justify his writing being denied the title of idiomatic English. In 1784 this good man and vigorous writer died, after suffering severely from dropsy and a complication of disorders; and it is consoling to reflect that the morbid and almost hypochondriac horror of death which had tormented him during his whole existence gave way, under the influence of his strong religious sentiments, and at the approach of the moment he had so dreaded, to a calm and resignation worthy of so wise and so benevolent a character. Few literary men have enjoyed so much deference as Johnson: both his virtues and his defects, his talents and his weaknesses, contributed to make him the king of his circle; and it is less a matter of surprise that the hardships of his early life should have left a stamp of coarseness and ferocity upon his manners and demeanor, than that the causes which made him rough and bearish in argument, and careless of the minor decencies of social intercourse, should never have sullied the undeviating purity of his moral principles, nor diminished the tenderness of his heart. He was a singular mixture of prejudice and liberality, of scepticism and credulity, of bigotry and candor: and with that paradoxical strangeness which pervades all his personality, we know him better, and admire him more, in the unadorned records which Boswell has given of his conversational triumphs, than in those rhetorical and elaborate writings which his contemporaries thought so magnificent, but which more recent generations seem likely to condemn to comparative oblivion.

§ 9. The name of Edmund Burke (1731–1797) has already occurred more than once as connected with Johnson and the accomplished literary society of that day. Burke was a man of powerful and versatile genius, carrying the fervor and imagery of a great orator into philosophical discussion, and uniting in himself the highest qualities of the statesman, the writer, and the philosopher. His predominant quality was a burning and dazzling enthusiasm for whatever object attracted his sympathies, and in the service of this enthusiasm he impressed all the disciplined forces of his learning, his logic, and his historical and political knowledge. His mind resembled the Puritan regiments of

Cromwell, which moved to battle with the precision of machines, while burning with the fiercest ardor of fanaticism. His sympathies were indeed generally excited by generous pity for misfortune, and horror at cruelty and injustice; but, as in the case of his rupture with Fox, his splendid oratorical display in the impeachment of Warren Hastings, and his furious denunciation of the French Revolution, the very excess of his tenderness made him cruel, and the vehemence of his detestation of injustice made him unjust. He was the son of a Dublin attorney, came early to England to study law, but commenced his career as a miscellaneous writer in magazines. He was the founder and first author of the *Annual Register*, a useful epitome of political and general facts, and gained his first reputation by his *Essay on the Sublime and Beautiful*, a short treatise in which ingenuity is more perceptible than solidity of reasoning, and he became one of the most constant and brilliant ornaments of the club where Johnson, Reynolds, and Goldsmith used to assemble. Burke's powers of conversation were most extraordinary; his immense and varied stores of knowledge were poured forth in language unequalled for its splendor of illustration; and Johnson, jealous as he was of his own social supremacy, confessed that in Burke he encountered a fully equal antagonist. Burke's political career commenced as Secretary to Hamilton in Ireland, and he was afterwards attached in the same capacity to Lord Rockingham. He sat in the House of Commons successively for Wendover, Bristol, and Malton, and was one of the most prominent debaters during the agitated period of the American War and the French Revolution. He formed part of more than one ministry, and was successively either in power or in opposition in the successive administrations of Rockingham, North, Grenville, and others. For a short time he held the lucrative post of Paymaster of the Forces in the Rockingham cabinet. The culminating points of his political life were his share in the famous India Bill, which was to entirely change the administration of our Eastern dependencies, and in the trial of Warren Hastings, which lasted from 1786 to 1795, and terminated with the acquittal of the accused. In this majestic and solemn scene, where a great nation sat in public judgment upon a great criminal, Burke played perhaps the most prominent part: he was one of the managers of the impeachment in the name of the Commons, and his speech is one of the sublimest philippics that ancient or modern oratory can show. He had heated his imagination in contemplating the vast, gorgeous, and picturesque nations and history of the East, and his almost morbid philanthropy was intensified by the consciousness of his proud position as a defender of ancient and oppressed populations before the venerable bar of history and the English people. It is curious to observe how gradually his speeches and writings increase in vividness of coloring and in intensity of passion as he advanced in life: his powerful mind almost lost its balance under the shock of that bitter disappointment caused by the horrors of the French Revolution, in which his unrivalled political sagacity could foresee nothing but unmingled evil. The Reign of

Terror transformed Burke from a constitutional Whig into a Tory, but at the same time animated his genius to some of its most unrivalled bursts of eloquence. The close of this great and good man's life was melancholy; the loss of his son, a youth of great promise, crushed all his hopes, and elicited one of the noblest monuments of pathetic oratory. His finest written compositions are his ***Letter to a Noble Lord***, in which he defends himself against the aspersions of the Duke of Bedford, who had attacked him for accepting a pension, his ***Reflections on the French Revolution***, and his ***Letter on a Regicide Peace.*** In Parliament, though his speeches were perhaps unequalled for splendor of illustration, for an almost supernatural acuteness of political foresight, and for the profoundest analysis of constitutional principles, he was often less popular than many inferior debaters: he spoke ***over the heads*** of his audience, but he will ever be regarded as one of the greatest orators and statesmen of any age or country.

§ **10.** The last half of the eighteenth century was a very gloomy and agitated crisis. The dispute between Great Britain and her American colonies, the lowering and ominous looming of the great revolutionary tempest of France, and many internal subjects of dissension involving important constitutional questions, rendered the political atmosphere gloomy and thunder-charged. From about the beginning of 1769, and with occasional interruptions down to 1772, there appeared in the "Public Advertiser," one of the leading London journals, then published by Woodfall, a series of ***Letters*** for the most part signed ***Junius.*** They exhibited so much weight and dignity of style, and so minute an acquaintance with the details of party tactics, and breathed such a lofty tone of constitutional principle, combined with such a bitterness, and even ferocity, of personal invective, that their influence was unbounded. Government made the most violent, but fruitless efforts to discover the writer, and Woodfall submitted to severe punishment, though there is every reason to believe that he too was kept in perfect ignorance of the real name of his correspondent. The chief objects of the attack of Junius were the Dukes of Grafton and Bedford, and he strongly pronounced himself against the infringement of constitutional liberty in the expulsion of Wilkes from the House of Commons and the seizure of his papers: but the concealed writer does not confine himself to great public questions, but exhibits minute knowledge of disputes and intrigues in the subordinate department of the War-office and shows all the rancor of a man who felt himself personally aggrieved. The whole annals of political controversy show nothing so bitter and terrible as the personalities and invectives of ***Junius***, which are rendered more formidable by the lofty dignity of the language, and by the moderate and constitutional principles which he professes to maintain. These letters will always be regarded as masterpieces in their particular style. Many efforts, some very learned, ingenious, and elaborate, have been employed to clear up the riddle of the real authorship of these letters: but the enigma still remains one of the most mysterious in the history of letters. Burke, Hamilton, Francis.

Lyttelton, and Lord George Sackville, have been successively fixed upon as the writer; and the mingled glory and shame — glory for the high merits of the composition, and shame for the atrocious spirit of calumny — have been transported by successive demonstrations to one or to the other. Among the numerous claimants to the doubtful honor Sir Philip Francis appears to have the strongest suffrages: the opinion of Macaulay, whose knowledge of the history of the time was unrivalled, is unconditionally in favor of Francis: but a recent investigator has brought forward some ingenious arguments in favor of Lyttelton. It is hardly probable that this curious and much-vexed question will now ever be settled by anything more conclusive than more or less strong presumptive evidence; and the authorship of the *Letters of Junius* will remain a singular example of an unsolved political mystery, like the Man in the Iron Mask or the Executioner of Charles I. However this may be, the letters themselves will ever be a monument of the finest but fiercest political invective.

§ **11.** ADAM SMITH (1723–1790) was the founder, in England, of the science of Political Economy. He was a Scotchman, and exhibited in a high degree that aptitude for moral, metaphysical, and economic investigation which seems to be so general in his country. He was successively Professor of Logic and of Moral Philosophy in the University of Glasgow. At one period of his life he lectured with success at Edinburgh on rhetoric and *belles lettres*, and was persuaded to travel with the young Duke of Buccleuch, whose education he superintended. His most important work is the *Inquiry into the Nature and Causes of the Wealth of Nations*, the fruit of ten years of study and investigation, and which laid the foundation for modern economic science. It was the first systematic treatise produced in England upon a most important subject, and though not free from erroneous deductions, was the most valuable contribution ever made to a science then almost in its infancy, and which was destined, thanks in a great measure to his clear and logical reasoning and abundant and popular illustration, to exert an immense and beneficial influence on legislation and commerce. The fundamental principles taught by Adam Smith are chiefly, that gold and silver are by no means wealth either to individuals or communities, being only symbols and conventional representatives of value; that labor is the true source of riches, and that any state interference with the distribution or production of commodities can only aggravate the evils it is intended to cure. He was the first to show, by apt and picturesque illustration, the wonderful results of the division of labor, both as regards the quantity and quality of the product. His moral and metaphysical theories are now nearly forgotten, but his *Inquiry* will ever remain the alphabet or text-book of the important science of which he was the pioneer.

§ **12.** Something similar to what Adam Smith performed for political economy, SIR WILLIAM BLACKSTONE (1723–1780) did for the vast and complicated study of the Constitution and the Laws of England. He was by profession a lawyer, though he mingled a strong taste for elegant literature with the graver studies of his profession: and he ultimately became a Justice of the Common Pleas. His *Commentaries on the Laws of England* gave the first example of a systematic work combining and popularizing all the elementary and historical knowledge requisite for the study; and this book, which is written in a singularly easy and pleasant style, is the groundwork of every legal education, nay, the accidence, so to say, of the grammar of English law. Numerous editions have been published, bringing up the work to the existing state of legal knowledge, and showing such modifications as from time to time have been made in our legislation; and Blackstone's *Commentaries* still continue the best and completest outline of the history and principles of English law. The great questions of right and property which lie at the bottom of all social organization are lucidly treated, and the mingled web of Teutonic, Feudal, Parliamentary, and Ecclesiastical legislation is carefully unravelled and disposed with luminous distinctness.

§ 13. The most prominent names in the English theological philosophy of the eighteenth century are those of BISHOP BUTLER (1692-1752) and WILLIAM PALEY (1743-1805). The former is more remarkable for the severe and coherent logic with which he demonstrates his conclusions, the latter for the consummate skill with which he popularized the abstruser arguments of his predecessors. Butler's principal work is his *Analogy between Natural and Revealed Religion*, in which, neglecting the question of the historical credibility of the miracles, he examines into the resemblance between the existence and attributes of God, as proved by arguments drawn from the works of Nature, and shows that that existence and those attributes are in no way incompatible with the notions conveyed to us by Revelation. The writings of Butler have filled the greatest thinkers with admiration, and their study has contributed to form some of the most accomplished dialecticians: but the closeness of his reasoning, which necessitates an unusual degree of attention and a rare faculty of following his analysis, places his writings out of the reach of ordinary readers. His moral theory is mainly based upon the existence, in every mind, of a guiding and testing principle of conscience, furnishing an infallible and supreme criterion of the goodness or wickedness of our actions.

Many of Butler's arguments are rendered more accessible in the easy and animated pages of Paley, who was, like Butler, an ornament of the Church. His books are numerous, and all excellent: the principal of them are *Elements of Moral and Political Philosophy*, the *Horæ Paulinæ*, the *Evidences of Christianity*, and the wonderful production of his old age, the *Treatise on Natural Theology*. It will be seen from the titles of these books over what an immense extent of moral and theological philosophy Paley's mind had travelled; for in the first of the above books he investigates the principles of human action whether exhibited in the individual or the community; in the second he examines questions of specific theology by the light of Scripture; and in the third he demonstrates the inherent credibility of the Christian miracles, and of the inspired narrative of those miracles, defending them against the arguments of scepticism, and in particular against the scepticism of Hume. The *Natural Theology* deduces the existence and the benevolence of God from the evidence afforded by the phenomena of nature in favor of design, power, and beneficence: and to supply himself with materials, Paley studied physiology, and has described the structure and functions of animated beings with a vivacity and a knowledge that give him a very honorable place among writers on anatomy. For clearness, animation, and easy grace, the style of Paley has rarely been equalled.

§ **14.** If the palm of merit is to be awarded less to the pretension of a literary work than to a universal popularity arising from a consummate charm of execution, then the fame of GILBERT WHITE (1720–1793) is to be coveted little less eagerly than that of Izaak Walton. The greater portion of his life was passed in the sequestered village of Selborne, in Hampshire, which he has immortalized in one of the most enchanting books in the world. White was educated at Oxford, where he became a student of Christ Church, but succeeding to the living of Selborne, which had been held by his father, he devoted his happy and tranquil life to the observation of nature. In a series of letters to Pennant and Daines Barrington, he has registered every phenomenon both of animal and vegetable life as well as of scenery and meteorology which came under the eye of a most curious, patient, and loving observer, and a thousand details so slight or so familiar as to escape the attention of previous naturalists, have been chronicled with exquisite grace, and form valuable contributions to science. Every change of weather, every circumstance in the habits of birds, beasts, and insects, were noted by him with an interest and enthusiasm that captivates the dullest reader; and the *Natural History of Selborne* has made at least as many naturalists as *Robinson Crusoe* has made sailors. The benevolent playfulness which overflows in White's remarks, the pleasant touches of credulity, as in his obstinate desire to find proofs that swallows hibernate under water, the intense personality with which he is associated with the beautiful scenes he loved so well, the ardent fondness for natural objects — every feature of his character heightens the charm of this most fascinating book.

NOTES AND ILLUSTRATIONS.

THEOLOGICAL WRITERS.

DR. HUMPHREY PRIDEAUX (1648-1724), one of the best known and most valuable theological writers, author of the *Connection of the Old and New Testaments*, 1715-17. He was a scholar of great research, and professor of Hebrew at Oxford.

DR. WILLIAM NICHOLSON (1655-1727), an Irish prelate and learned antiquary, wrote on *Border Laws, Laws of Anglo-Saxons*. In 1706 he produced a catalogue of books and MSS., the *Historical Libraries of England, Scotland, and Ireland*.

DR. BENJAMIN HOADLEY (1670-1761) occupied successively the sees of Bangor, Hereford, Salisbury, and Winchester. He espoused the cause of the Whigs, and was a great controversialist on the more liberal side both in the Church and in politics. His chief works were *On the Nature of the Kingdom or Church of Christ*, which gave rise to the celebrated Bangorian controversy; *Reasonableness of Conformity; Terms of Acceptance; Treatise on the Sacrament*.

CHARLES LESLIE (1650-1722), a clergyman and controversialist, chiefly known for *A Short and Easy Method with the Deists*. The whole of his works were published at Oxford in 1832.

WILLIAM WHISTON (1667-1752), a mathematician of the school of Newton, whom he succeeded as professor at Cambridge. He was at first a clergyman, but was expelled the Church on account of his Arian opinions, became lecturer on astronomy in London, and before his death held the principles of the Baptist body, and the millenarian doctrines. His chief works are — *Theory of the Earth*, 1696; *Essay on the Revelation of St. John*, 1706; *Sermons*, 1708; *Primitive Christianity Revived*, 1712; *Memoirs*, 1749-50.

BISHOP WARBURTON (1698-1779), one of the celebrated writers of his day; but the value of his works was ephemeral, and, with the exception of his *Divine Legation of Moses*, they are almost forgotten. He was born at Newark, received no education for the Church, yet, by assiduous and brilliant use of the pen, obtained presentations to livings, and at last was raised to the See of Gloucester. He enjoyed the friendship and assistance of the leading men of the day; but his love of paradox and startling hypotheses did much to lessen the lasting value and influence of his writings. Warburton was a man of force and genius, but spoiled his efforts for real success by his display and arrogance. A modern critic applies Gibbon's epithet of the Legation to the life and works of the author: "A splendid ruin" — "not venerable from cherished associations, but great, unsightly, and incongruous."

DR. ROBERT LOWTH (1710-1787), successively Bishop of St. David's, Oxford, and London, was a man of great learning. His chief works are — *Translation of Isaiah* and *Prelections on Hebrew Poetry*, the latter being in Latin, delivered by him when he was Professor of Hebrew at Oxford.

REV. WILLIAM LAW (1686-1761), a Jacobite Nonconformist, whose *Serious Call to a Higher Life* deserves mention, not only from its being popular, but also because the reading of it is said by Dr Johnson to have been "the first occasion of his thinking in earnest of religion after he became capable of rational inquiry."

DR. RICHARD WATSON (1737-1816), Bishop of Llandaff, and author of replies to Paine and Gibbon. The *Apologies* for Christianity and the Bible are well known.

DR. SAMUEL HORSLEY (1733-1806), Secretary of the Royal Society, and successively Bishop of St. David's, Rochester, and St. Asaph. His principal works are translations of the Psalms, and his controversial writings with Priestley.

DR. JOHN JORTIN (1698-1770), Prebendary of St. Paul's and Archdeacon of London, author of works on *Ecclesiastical History*, 1751-4; *Life of Erasmus*, 1758; which are written in a striking, lively style.

DR. RICHARD HURD (1720-1808), successively Bishop of Lichfield and Coventry, and of Worcester, a great friend of Warburton, and an elegant scholar, wrote, among other things, *Discourses on the Prophecies*, and a *Life of Warburton*.

DR. GEORGE HORNE (1730-1792), Bishop of Norwich, wrote the well-known *Commentary* on the Psalms, 1776.

DR. NATHANIEL LARDNER (1684-1768), a Presbyterian divine, the author of a very learned work on *The Credibility of the Gospel History*, 1730-57. He also wrote a work similar to the above entitled *A Large Collection of Ancient, Jewish and Heathen Testimonies to the Truth of the Christian Religion*.

DR. PHILIP DODDRIDGE (1702-1751), one of the most distinguished Nonconformist divines. He was born in London, was educated among the Dissenters, became minister at Northampton, and died at Lisbon, whither he had departed for the benefit of his health. Doddridge was a man of learning and earnest piety. He was beloved and admired by all the religious bodies of the country. His style is plain, simple, and forcible. He was a critic of some acumen, and a preacher of great distinction. But his name lives from his practical works and expository writings, the chief of which are — *Discourses on Regeneration*, 1741; *Rise and Progress of Religion in the Soul*, 1745; and his greatest and most extensive work, *The Family Expositor*, one of the most widely circulated works of its class.

DR. GEORGE CAMPBELL (1709-1796), Professor of Divinity at Aberdeen, was one of the most celebrated of the clergymen of the Scotch Church. His *Dissertation on Miracles* was in reply to Hume. *The Philosophy of Rhetoric* is one of the ablest works that has appeared on that subject. He also wrote *A Translation of the Four Gospels*, and *Lectures on Ecclesiastical History*. Few men have shown greater skill in polemical writing, combined with a gentleness and regard for the opponent; and a modern critic places him next to Robertson the historian at the head of the clergy of the Scottish Church.

The following are authors of works of no high literary value, but yet have been of great service in shaping the moral and religious thought of the country.

GEORGE WHITEFIELD (1714–1770).

JOHN WESLEY (1703–1791), the founder of the sect of Wesleyan Methodists, and author of several practical works, chiefly homiletic.

JAMES HERVEY (1714–1758), author of *The Meditations*, *Theron and Aspasia*, &c.

EBENEZER ERSKINE (1680–1754); and RALPH ERSKINE (1685–1752).

PHILOSOPHICAL WRITERS.

DR. FRANCIS HUTCHESON (1694–1747), a native of Ireland, studied at Glasgow, and became Professor of Moral Philosophy in that University. He did much to restore the study of philosophy in Scotland, and is considered as the founder of the Scotch School of Metaphysics. In 1726 he published an *Inquiry into Beauty and Virtue*. His chief work was *A System of Moral Philosophy*, which was given to the world by his son after his death.

DR. MATTHEW TINDAL (1657–1733) turned Roman Catholic under James II., but afterwards became an unbeliever, and is well known for his attack on Christianity, entitled *Christianity as old as the Creation*. Dr. Tindal's nephew, NICHOLAS TINDAL (1687–1774), was the continuer of the *History of England* left incomplete by Rapin.

HENRY HOME, LORD KAMES (1696–1782), a lawyer, judge, and mental philosopher, resided in Edinburgh, and there drew round him many of the leading thinkers and writers. His chief works were — *Essays on the Principles of Morality and Religion*; *Introduction to the Art of Thinking*; *The Elements of Criticism*; *Sketches of the History of Man*; the last of which works is a collection of anecdotes and miscellaneous facts picked up in the course of his reading.

DR. SAMUEL CLARKE (1675–1729), one of the ablest metaphysicians that England has produced. He was a native of Norwich, was educated at Caius College, Cambridge, and became chaplain to Bishop Moore of Norwich. In 1704 he delivered the Boyle Lectures, in which he brought forward his celebrated argument *a priori* for the being of a God, grand in conception, but, like all arguments of that class, really resting on the *à posteriori* expressed or implied. He wrote on the *Immateriality and Immortality of the Soul*, and translated *Newton's Optics* into Latin. In 1709 he was presented to the rectory of St. James's, and was appointed one of the Queen's chaplains. His controversies with the Trinitarians arose from his espousal of the Arian doctrine in his treatise on the *Trinity*. He defended the Newtonian philosophy against Leibnitz, and in 1717 the papers were published. In 1724 he published seventeen sermons, partly metaphysical and partly practical. He refused the offer of the Mastership of the Mint in 1727. He died on the 17th of May, 1729. He has not the extensive grasp and original views of Locke, but he exhibits more of the accuracy of the dialectician. Many of his speculations are too refined. His moral system, which makes the rule of virtue consist in the fitness of things, or a "congruity of relations," and neglects the distinction and prior discernment of good ends from bad, has been condemned by the Butlerian school and modern moralists as too limited and confined. Dr. Clarke's style is simple, and free from meretricious adornment, vigorous, and at times really eloquent, a model of philosophical and controversial writing.

DR. ADAM FERGUSON (1724–1816), a native of Perthshire, educated at St. Andrew's, Professor of Natural and Moral Philosophy in the University of Edinburgh, author of several works on philosophy and history, the chief of which are — *A History of the Roman Republic*, 1783; *Principles of Moral and Political Science*, 1792.

JAMES BURNET, LORD MONBODDO (1714–1799), a Scotch Judge, and an eccentric but learned writer, author of an *Essay on the Origin and Progress of Language*, 1771–3, and a *Work on Ancient Metaphysics*, 1779. Monboddo is best known for his theory of mankind having at one time possessed tails like other monkeys, but which by a long course of sitting have been worn away.

DAVID HARTLEY (1705–1757), was educated at Jesus College, Cambridge, and practised medicine. He was the founder of a school embracing at one time a large number of English thinkers. He explained the various states of the mind by the principle of association. His chief work was *Observations on Man, &c.*, which appeared in 1749.

DR. RICHARD PRICE (1723–1791), a Nonconformist minister and writer on morals, who endeavored in his *Review of the Principal Questions and Difficulties in Morals*, 1758, to revive the Cudworth school, which traced moral obligation to the perceptions of the understanding. He wrote several able works on financial subjects, and was invited by the United States, in 1778, to settle in America, in order to assist them in regulating their finances. He was a warm advocate of civil and religious liberty, and is best known in the history of literature by the attack made upon him by Burke, in his *Reflections on the Revolution in France*.

ABRAHAM TUCKER (1705–1774), an English country-gentleman, who devoted himself to metaphysical studies. He held for the most part the Hartleian doctrines, and received the praise of Paley and Mackintosh. His celebrated work was entitled *The Light of Nature Pursued*, 1768.

DR. JOSEPH PRIESTLEY (1733–1804), an eminent Nonconformist minister, who went over from the Calvinistic school of theology to the Unitarian. He was settled in Birmingham for some time, and it was there that the rioters set fire to his house at the time of the French Revolution in 1791. His philosophical opinions were opposed to the Scotch school. In *Matter and Spirit* (1777) he inclined to materialism and necessity. A large number of tracts issued from his pen, which was ever kept at work from the assiduity of his opposers. Priestley shines most, however, in experimental physics. He was one of the fathers of chemistry, and made several discoveries in relation to light and color. He left England for America in 1794, and died in Northumberland, Pennsylvania, in 1804.

DR. THOMAS REID (1710–1796), one of the founders of the Scotch School of Metaphysics, was a Presbyterian clergyman, and Professor of Moral

Philosophy, first at King's College, Aberdeen, and afterwards at Glasgow, where he succeeded Adam Smith. His *Inquiry into the Human Mind* (1764) was directed against the ideal system, and the scepticism of Hume. In 1785 he published his *Essays on the Intellectual Powers*, and in 1788 his *Essays on the Active Power of the Human Mind*.

DUGALD STEWART (1753-1828), a pupil of Reid, whose philosophical system he adopted and taught with great elegance of style, was Professor of Moral Philosophy in the University of Edinburgh from 1785 to 1810. His *Elements of the Philosophy of the Human Mind* appeared in 1792, and his *Philosophical Essays*, on which his fame chiefly rests, in 1810. Sir James Mackintosh remarks that "it is in Essays of this kind that Stewart has most surpassed other cultivators of mental philosophy. His remarks on the effect of casual associations may be quoted as a specimen of the most original and just thoughts conveyed in the best manner."

DR. THOMAS BROWN (1778-1820), who properly belongs to the next century, is mentioned here on account of his close connection with Reid and Stewart. He succeeded the latter in the chair of Modern Philosophy at Edinburgh in 1810. As a philosopher he was distinguished by the power of analysis. He was also the author of several poems which are now forgotten.

HISTORIANS AND SCHOLARS.

LORD LYTTELTON (1709-1773), the first lord of this title, and Chancellor of the Exchequer in 1756, is the author of a *History of Henry II.* (1764-1767), a work of learning and research, but is perhaps best known by his *Observations on the Conversion of St. Paul*. His poetry has gained for him a place in Johnson's Lives, but it is of slender merit.

THOMAS CARTE (1686-1754), the author of a *History of England*, coming down to 1654, and a *Life of the Duke of Ormond*, was a strong Jacobite in politics.

DR. CONYERS MIDDLETON (1683-1750), librarian of the University of Cambridge, and one of the opponents of the celebrated Bentley. Indeed, he is said to have been the only adversary whom Bentley really feared. When the latter was deprived of his degree by the University, Middleton addressed to him a letter entitled "The Rev. Richard Bentley, late D. D." Middleton is now best known for his *Life of Cicero* — a work of research, and written in an elegant and perspicuous style; but he also wrote several works on ecclesiastical history. His *Free Inquiry into the Miraculous Powers possessed by the Christian Church* advocates many of the views adopted by what is called the school of the modern Rationalists.

LORD HERVEY (1696-1743), the author of *Memoirs of the Reign of George II.*, published first in 1848, under the editorship of Mr. Croker. Hervey was in constant attendance upon Queen Caroline, the wife of George II., was a friend of Lady Mary Wortley Montagu, and the object of Pope's severest satire, by the name of Sporus.

The Universal History, in 23 vols., was completed in 1760, under the care of Bower, Campbell, William Guthrie, and Psalmanazar. Goldsmith wrote a preface for it, and received three guineas for the work.

WILLIAM TYTLER (1711-1792), the father of Alexander Fraser Tytler, the author of *Elements of General History*, was himself the author of an *Inquiry into the Evidence against Mary Queen of Scots*, and an *Examination into the Histories of Robertson and Hume*.

DR. THOMAS BIRCH (1705-1766), a clergyman was the author of many laborious historical works relating to modern history. He also published a *General Dictionary, Historical and Critical*, and edited *Thurloe's State Papers*.

DR. ROBERT HENRY (1718-1790), a native of Stirlingshire, and clergyman in Edinburgh, published a *History of Great Britain*, which was popular in its day. It extended to the reign of Henry VIII., and treated at some extent, with the internal events, the manners and customs of the people.

DR. POTTER (1674-1747), born at Wakefield in Yorkshire, educated at University College, Oxford, Archbishop of Canterbury, best known for his work on the *Antiquities of Greece*, which was for a long time the chief authority on the subject.

BASIL KENNETT (1674-1714) was educated at Oxford, and became English chaplain at Leghorn; is known for his work on *Roman Antiquities*.

RICHARD PORSON (1759-1808), was born in Norfolk, of humble parents, but became one of the greatest Greek scholars of the country, and in 1790 was appointed Greek Professor at Cambridge. Besides his well-known contributions to classical literature, Porson deserves a place in English literature, on account of the admirable style of his *Letters to Archdeacon Travis* (1790) upon the disputed verse in 1 John v. 7. His *Adversaria* were published after his death by Monk and Blomfield.

JOHN LOUIS DE LOLME (1740-1806), published in 1775 a work on the *Constitution of England*. It was of value and an authority in its day, but is now supplanted by more modern works. Its interest to the student of English literature arises from the ease and skill with which a native of Geneva wrote our language.

MRS. CATHARINE MACAULAY (1733-1791), the wife of a physician, called by Walpole "the hen-brood of faction," was the authoress of the celebrated Republican *History of England during the Stuart Dynasty*. This work received considerable attention at the time. It is of no great historical value, but the style is vigorous and popular. Mrs. Macaulay crossed the Atlantic and had an interview with George Washington. She even ventured to measure her strength against Burke, and attacked his work on the French Revolution.

WILLIAM ROSCOE (1753-1831) was born in Liverpool, and spent his early years at the desk of an attorney. In 1806 he was chosen member of Parliament, but soon retired from public life, and steadily refused all applications which were made him to return. In 1796 he published *The Life of Lorenzo de Medici*, which was one of the most popular works of the day. The style was easy, graceful, and pleasing. *Leo X.*, which was published in 1805, did not attain the same popularity. There were questions of a most delicate nature to be discussed; the reformation presented points of deepest interest to Papist and to Protestant, and the historian had to guard against offending either party.

NATHANIEL HOOKE (d. 1764), a Roman Cathslic, and a friend of Pope, the author of a *Roman History*, which was for a long time the standard work on the subject, but is deficient in criticism, and is now entirely superseded. Hooke was a warm partisan of the plebeians in their struggles with the patricians.

JACOB BRYANT (1715–1804), secretary to the Duke of Marlborough, who gave him a lucrative place in the Ordnance Office, was the author of several works on classical and mythological subjects. His fancy carried him often too far in paradox and speculation, but he established and defended his theories with great ingenuity and research. His leading works were *A New System or Analysis of Ancient Mythology*, 1774–76; *On the Plain of Troy*, 1795; and *On the Trojan War*, 1796.

GILBERT WAKEFIELD (1756–1801), a well-known writer on divinity, and a classical scholar. He left the church from Unitarian views, and published a translation of the New Testament, and a work on the Evidences of Christianity, in answer to Paine. He was found guilty of libel in his reply to the Bishop of Llandaff in defence of the revolution in France, and imprisoned for two years. He was a hasty but honest man, "as violent against Greek accents as he was against the Trinity, and anathematized the final *v* as strongly as episcopacy."

DR. GILBERT STUART (1742–1786), born in Edinburgh, was an active writer in the Reviews, in which he attacked many of his contemporaries with extreme bitterness. He wrote a *History of the Reformation of Religion in Scotland*, and a *History of Scotland*, in which he vehemently attacks Robertson.

DR. WARNER (d. 1767) and Dr. LELAND (1722–1785) published histories of Ireland. The latter was author of the well-known translation of Demosthenes.

The *History of Manchester*, and *Vindication of Mary Queen of Scots*, by JOHN WHITAKER (1735–1808), deserve a passing mention.

REV. JAMES GRANGER'S (d. 1776) *Biographical History of England*, which was continued by Noble, may still be consulted with advantage.

JAMES MACPHERSON (1738–1796), mentioned in the next chapter in connection with the poems of Ossian (p. 394), appeared as an historian and defender of the Tories in his *History of Great Britain from the Restoration to the Accession of the House of Hanover*, 1775, a work of some value from the private history which it reveals.

LORD HAILES, SIR DAVID DALRYMPLE (1726–1792), was a well-known lawyer and judge, a man of great erudition, and author of *Annals of Scotland*, published in 1776, and other legal and historical works.

Robertson's *History of Charles V.* was continued by ROBERT WATSON (d. 1780), Professor of Logic at St. Andrew's, in a *History of Philip II.*, a work of no merit.

DR. WILLIAM RUSSELL (1741–1793), born at Selkirk, the author of a history of *Modern Europe*, which is now superseded by Mr. Dyer's.

MALCOLM LAING (1762–1818), born in Orkney, which he represented for some time in Parliament, wrote a *History of Scotland*, from the Union of the Crowns on the accession of James VI. to the throne of England, to the Union of the Kingdoms in the reign of Queen Anne.

JOHN PINKERTON (1758–1826), born in Edinburgh, a laborious and learned writer, the author of numerous works, among which may be mentioned a *History of Scotland*, *Modern Geography*, *Voyages and Travels*, &c.

MISCELLANEOUS WRITERS

PHILIP DORMER STANHOPE, EARL OF CHESTERFIELD (1694–1773), was one of the most accomplished men in the Court of the Georges, but his only lasting contribution to literature is his *Letters* containing advice to his son. The style is agreeable, but the moral tone is low; Dr. Johnson said it taught the morals of a courtesan and the manners of a dancing-master; but something of this severity must be set down to the relation which subsisted between Johnson and Chesterfield. The speeches essays, &c., with memoir of Chesterfield, were published by Dr. Maty, in 1774. The copyright of Chesterfield's Letters realized 1500*l.*, and in the year succeeding their publication five editions were distributed.

THOMAS AMORY (1692–1789), a native of Ireland was educated as a physician, and resided in Westminster. As a writer he is humorous, but pedantic. His chief works were—*Memoirs, containing the Lives of several Ladies of Great Britain*, 1755; and the *Life of John Buncle, Esq.*, 1756–66. This last is in the form of an autobiography, full of humor, quotation, and thought, reminding the reader of Burton's quaint work.

SIR WILLIAM JONES (1746–1794), a celebrated Oriental scholar, and the author of many works in various branches of literature, was the son of a mathematician of some eminence. He was educated at Harrow, and University College, Oxford, was called to the bar in 1774, and was appointed in 1783 a judge of the Supreme Court at Calcutta, where he died in 1794, after a residence of eleven years. He was one of the first Europeans who studied Sanskrit, and he contributed many valuable papers to the "Asiatic Researches." While in India he translated from the Sanskrit *Sacuntalâ* a dramatic poem by Kalidasa, and the *Hitopadêsa*, a collection of fables. He has obtained a place among the English poets on account of two small volumes of poems, containing a few original pieces, and several translations from the Eastern writers.

JOHN HORNE TOOKE (1736–1812) was born in London, son of a poulterer named Horne. He received his education at Westminster, Eton, and St. John's, Cambridge. He entered the church, but threw himself into the great political struggles of those days, and wrote in 1765 in favor of Wilkes. In 1773 he resigned his preferment in the church, in order to study for the bar, but the benchers refused to call him because he was a clergyman. Mr. Tooke, of Purley, whose name he afterwards adopted, left him his fortune. In 1794 he was tried for high treason, and was defended by Erskine. In 1796 he was returned to Parliament as member for Westminster, and again in 1801 for Sarum. The declining years of his life were passed at Wimbledon, a literary retreat, whither friends often resorted to enjoy the hospitality, humor, and philosophy of the hale and witty old man. He wrote *The Diversions of Purley*, 1786–1805, a series of dialogues upon language. He reduces all parts of speech to nouns and verbs. The book should be carefully consulted by every student of the English language, but many of the etymologies are fanciful and far-fetched.

DR. JOHN LANGHORNE (1735–1779) was born in Westmoreland, and held a living in Somersetshire. He was a preacher of some popularity, and author of some tales and poems, and with his brother published a translation of *Plutarch's Lives.*

DR. RICHARD FARMER (1735–1797), Master of Emmanuel College, Cambridge, published in 1766 an *Essay on the Learning of Shakspeare*, which discussed with some skill the historic and classic authorities of the great dramatist.

Another celebrated Shakspearian critic was GEORGE STEEVENS (1736–1800), who was joint editor with Johnson of the edition of Shakspeare published in 1773. He afterwards remodelled the text, and brought out a new edition in 1793, in which he took great liberties with the text.

The chief rival of Steevens was EDMOND MALONE (1741–1812), who had previously contributed some notes to Steevens's earlier edition of Shakspeare, but brought out one of his own in 1790. His posthumous edition was published by Boswell in 1821, in twenty-one volumes. Malone had not Steevens's ability but was a more cautious editor, and paid more respect to the text of the first folio.

During the latter part of the eighteenth century some of the most interesting English travels were published. The chief writers were, —

LORD MACARTNEY (1737–1806) and

SIR GEORGE L. STAUNTON (1737–1801), whose mission to China was narrated in two interesting works, *Macartney's Journal* and *Staunton's Account of the Embassy.*

The two greatest names, however, are those of JAMES BRUCE (1730–1794), who penetrated far into Abyssinia and Central Africa in search of the source of the Nile; and

MUNGO PARK (1771–1805), whose literary achievements are far greater than those of Bruce. Park was drowned whilst escaping from an attack of the natives, but his second narrative was preserved, and published posthumously in 1815.

NOVELISTS.

FRANCES SHERIDAN (1724–1766), mother of Richard Brinsley Sheridan, was authoress of *Nourjahad* and *Sidney Biddulph*, and two comedies not so able as the novels, entitled *The Discovery* and *The Dupe.* *Sidney Biddulph* was greatly admired by Dr. Johnson.

MRS. CHARLOTTE LENNOX (1720–1804), authoress of the once popular novels, *Harriot Stuart*, 1751: and the *Female Quixote*, 1752.

CHAPTER XIX.

THE DAWN OF ROMANTIC POETRY.

1. Revolution in popular taste. The *Minstrel* of BEATTIE. The *Grave* by BLAIR. The *Spleen* by GREEN. § 2. JAMES THOMSON. *The Seasons. The Castle of Indolence.* Ode to *Liberty.* Tragedy of *Sophonisba.* § 3. The *Schoolmistress* of SHENSTONE. The *Odes* of COLLINS. The *Pleasures of the Imagination* by AKENSIDE. § 4. THOMAS GRAY. *Ode on Eton College. Elegy written in a Country Churchyard. Pindaric Odes.* § 5. JOSEPH and THOMAS WARTON. *History of English Poetry.* § 6. WILLIAM COWPER. His life. *The Task, Table-Talk, Tirocinium, Translation of Homer.* Characteristics of his poetry. § 7. Poems of a technical character. The *Shipwreck* by FALCONER. *Loves of the Plants* by DARWIN. § 8. Literary forgeries. MACPHERSON'S *Ossian.* § 9. CHATTERTON'S forgeries. IRELAND'S forgeries. § 10. GEORGE CRABBE. His life and writings. § 11. ROBERT BURNS. His life and writings. § 12. JOHN WOLCOT, better known as PETER PINDAR. § 13. History of the Comic Drama from the middle of the eighteenth century. GARRICK, FOOTE, CUMBERLAND, the two COLMANS, and SHERIDAN. The *Rivals,* the *School for Scandal,* the *Critic,* and the *Rehearsal.*

§ 1. THE great revolution in popular taste and sentiment which substituted what is called the romantic type in literature for the cold and clear-cut artificial spirit of that classicism which is exhibited in its highest form in the writings of Pope was, like all powerful and durable movements, whether in politics or in letters, gradual. The mechanical perfection of the poetry of the age of Queen Anne had been imitated with such success that every versifier had caught the trick of melody and the neat antithetical opposition of thought; and indications soon began to be perceptible of a tendency to seek for subjects and forms of expression in a wider, more passionate, and more natural sphere of nature and emotion. In the *Minstrel* of JAMES BEATTIE (1735–1803), in the striking meditative lines entitled *The Grave* by ROBERT BLAIR (1699–1746), this tendency is perceptible, and may be in some measure ascribed to the weariness inspired by the eternal repetition of the neat and epigrammatic ingenuity which had gradually become a mere far-off echo of Pope. Under the influence of this weariness, poets began to seek for materials in a more direct and picturesque reproduction of nature, and endeavored to give freshness to their diction by rebaptizing it in the deep and sparkling fountains of our older literature.

The principal agent, however, in this revolution was Bishop Percy, whose publication in 1765 of the *Reliques of Ancient English Poetry,* of which I shall speak more fully in the next chapter, showed the world what treasures of beauty, pathos, and magnificence lay buried in the old Minstrel ballads of the Middle Ages. In the poets who will form the subject of this chapter, extending from Thomson to Burns, we shall see how gradual the movement was. I cannot omit all mention of MATTHEW GREEN (1696–1737), whose pleasant and truly original poem *The Spleen* was written to point out the mode of remedying that insupportable species of moral depression. It is written in easy octosyllabic verse, and contains a multitude of passages where new ideas are expressed in singularly felicitous images. The prevailing tone is cheerful and philosophic, and is highly honorable not only to the talents but to the principles of the author. Green was originally a dissenter, but his work shows no traces of sectarian gloom and narrow-mindedness. He is said to have been himself a sufferer from the malady he describes, which was long satirically supposed to be peculiarly common in England: and, like Burton, he wrote on melancholy to divert his mind from its sufferings.

§ 2. JAMES THOMSON (1700–1748) is the poet who connects the age of Pope with that of Crabbe, and it is delightful to think of the sympathy and appreciation shown to his gorgeous and picturesque genius by the former of these great writers, who hailed his appearance with warm admiration. Thomson was born in a rural and retired corner of Scotland, in 1700, and after receiving his education at Edinburgh, came to London, as Smollett had done before him, "smit with the love of sacred song," and eager to try his fortune in a literary career. He carried with him the unfinished sketch of his poem of *Winter*, which he showed to his countryman Mallet, then enjoying some authority as a critic, and was advised by him to complete and publish it. Thomson at first adopted the profession of private tutor, and was intrusted with the care of the son of Lord Binning, after which he entered the family of the Chancellor Talbot, and travelled with the son of that dignitary in Italy. The poem of *Winter* appeared in 1726, and was received with great favor, obtaining the warm suffrages of Pope, then supreme in the literary world, and who not only gave advice to the young aspirant, but even corrected and retouched several passages in his works. *Summer* was given to the world in the succeeding year, and Thomson then without delay issued proposals for the completion of the whole cycle of poems, *Spring* and *Autumn* being still wanting to fill up the round of the *Seasons*. The patronage of Talbot, by conferring on Thomson a place in the Chancellor's gift, assisted the poet in attaining independence; but losing this post on the death of the minister, its loss was afterwards supplied first with one, and afterwards with another sinecure post which soon placed the poet out of the reach of difficulty. Though somewhat sensual and extraordinarily indolent and self-indulgent, Thomson was not devoid of the prudence so general among his countrymen. He purchased a snug cottage near Richmond, and lived in modest luxury and literary ease. He was of an extremely kind and generous disposition, and his devotion to his relations is an amiable trait in his character: he was also generally loved, and does not appear to have had a single enemy or ill-wisher. His death was premature; for, catching cold in a boating-party on the Thames, he died of a fever in the forty-eighth year of his age. During the years of his happy retirement he had not only revised and corrected innumerable passages of his *Seasons*, but had time to compose his delightful half-serious, half-playful poem of the *Castle of Indolence*, the most enchanting of the many imitations of the style and manner of Spenser, and a work which, at the same time, possesses the finest qualities of Thomson's own natural genius. He was also the author of a somewhat declamatory and ambitious poem on the tempting but impracticable subject of *Liberty*, and of a few tragedies, some of which, as *Sophonisba*, were acted with temporary success. The *Seasons*, consisting of the four detached poems, *Spring*, *Summer*, *Autumn*, and *Winter*, must be considered as the corner-stone of Thomson's literary fame. It is a poem, in plan and treatment, entirely original, and gives a general, and at the same time a minute description of all the phenomena of Nature during an English year. Perhaps the very uncertainty of our climate, by giving greater variety to our scenery and greater vicissitudes to our weather than can be seen in more apparently favored countries, as Italy or Greece, was favorable to Thomson's undertaking, which could hardly have prospered in the hands of a poet who might have been born in more genial climes. It is certain that he has watched every fleeting smile or frown on the ever-changing face of Nature with a loving and an observant eye: there is hardly a phase of external appearance, hardly an incident in the great drama of the seasons, which he has not depicted with consummate success. He is especially happy in sketching the manners of birds and domestic animals; and every line of his poem breathes an ardent benevolence and a deep sense of the majesty and goodness of God. The metre is blank-verse, which, though seldom showing anything of the Miltonic swell or tenderness, is rich and harmonious. Thomson's chief defect is a kind of pompous struggle after fine language, which sometimes degenerates into ludicrous vulgarity. In order to relieve the monotony of a poem entirely devoted to description, he has occasionally introduced episodes or incidental pictures more or less naturally suggested by the subject. Thus, in his *Winter* he gives the famous description of the shepherd losing his way and perishing in the snow, in *Summer* the story of Musidora bathing, in *Autumn* the narrative of Lavinia, which is borrowed, and spoiled in the borrowing, from the exquisite pastoral story of Ruth and Boaz. In such of these episodes as involve the passion of love, it must be confessed that Thomson's mode of delineating that feeling is far more ardent than ideal. In point of literary finish the *Castle of Indolence* is superior to the Seasons. The idea and treatment of this poem are Spenserian; and the versification, borrowed from the languid and dreamy melody of the *Fairie Queene*, corresponds admirably with the rich and luxurious imagery in which Thomson revelled. The allegory of the enchanted "Land of Drowsihead," in which the unhappy victims of Indolence find themselves hopeless captives, and their delivery from durance by the Knight Industry, whose pedigree and training are given in an exact imitation of Spenser's manner, are relieved with occasional touches of a sly and pleasant humor, as in those passages where Thomson has drawn portraits of himself and of his friend. Hardly has Spenser himself surpassed the rich and dreamy loveliness or the voluptuous melody of the description of the enchanted Castle and its gardens of delight, and the strains of the Æolian harp, then a recent invention, are described in stanzas whose music forms a most appropriate echo to its harmonies.

§ 3. A passing notice will suffice for WILLIAM SHENSTONE (1714–1763), whose popularity, once considerable, has now given place to oblivion, but whose pleasing and original poem the *Schoolmistress* will deserve to retain a place in every collection of English verse. He is still more remarkable as having been one of the first to cultivate that picturesque mode of laying out gardens, and developing by well-concealed art the natural beauties of scenery, which, under the name of the English style, has supplanted the majestic but formal manner of Italy, France, and Holland. In the former Nature is followed and humored, in the latter she is forced. The *Schoolmistress* is in the Spenserian stanza and antique diction, and with a delightful mixture of quaint playfulness and tender description, paints the dwelling, the character, and the pursuits of an old village dame who keeps a rustic day-school. The Pastoral ballads of Shenstone are melodious, but the thin current of natural feeling which pervades them cannot make the reader forget the improbability of the Arcadian manners, such as never existed in any age or country, or the querulous and childish tone of thought.

The career of WILLIAM COLLINS (1721–1759) was brief and unhappy. He exhibited from very early years the strong poetical powers of a genius which, ripened by practice and experience, would have made him the first lyrical writer of his age; but his ambition was rather feverish than sustained; he led a life of projects and dissipation; and the first shock of literary disappointment drove him to despondency, despondency to indulgence, and indulgence to insanity. This gifted being died at thirty-eight, after suffering the cruelest affliction and humiliation that can oppress humanity. He was educated at Winchester School, and afterwards at Magdalen College, Oxford, and entered upon the career of professional literature, full of golden dreams, and meditating vast projects. His first publication was a series of Eclogues, transferring the usual sentiments of pastoral to the scenery and manners of the East. Oriental, or Persian, incidents were for the first time made the subjects of compositions retaining in their form and general cast of thought and language the worn-out type of pastoral. Thus the lamentation of the shepherd expelled from his native fields is replaced by a camel-driver bewailing the dangers and solitude of his desert journey; and the dialogues so frequent in the bucolics of Virgil or Theocritus are transformed into the amœbæan complaints of two Circassian exiles. The national character and sentiments of the East, though every effort is made by the poet to give local coloring and appropriate costume and scenery, are in no sense more true to nature than in the majority of pictures representing the fabulous Arcadia of the poets, and though these eclogues exhibit traces of vivid imagery, and melodious verse, the real genius of Collins must be looked for in his *Odes*. Judged by these latter, though they are but few in number, he will be found entitled to a very high place: for true warmth of coloring, power of personification, and dreamy sweetness of harmony, no English poet had till then appeared that could be compared to Collins His most commonly quoted lyric is the ode entitled *The Passions*, in which Fear, Rage, Pity, Joy, Hope, Melancholy, and other abstract qualities are successively introduced trying their skill on different musical instruments. Their respective choice of these, and the manner in which each Passion acquits itself, is very ingeniously conceived. Nevertheless, many of the less popular odes, as that addressed to *Fear*, to *Pity*, to *Simplicity*, and that *On the Poetical Character*, contain happy strokes, sometimes expressed in wonderfully laconic language, and singularly vivid portraiture. Collins possessed, to an unusual degree, the power of giving life and personality to an abstract conception, and that this power is exceedingly rare may be seen by the predominant coldness and pedantry which generally prevail in modern lyric poetry, where personification has been abused till it has become a mere mechanical artifice. In Collins the prosopopœia is always fresh and vivid. In the unfinished *Ode on the Superstitions of the Highlands* there are many fine touches of fancy and description; but the reader cannot divest himself of a consciousness that the pictures are rather transcripts from books than vivid reflection from personal knowledge. Collins writes of the Highlands and their inhabitants not like a native, but like an English hunter after the picturesque. Some of the smaller and less ambitious lyrics, as the *Verses to the Memory of Thomson*, the *Dirge in Cymbeline*, and the exquisite verses *How sleep the brave*, are perhaps destined to a more certain immortality: for a tender, luxuriant richness of reverie, perhaps there is nothing in the English language that surpasses them. All the qualities of Collins's finest thought and expression will be found united in the lovely little *Ode to Evening*, consisting of but a few stanzas in blank verse, but so subtly harmonized that they may be read a thousand times without observing the absence of rhyme, and exhibiting such a sweet, soothing, and yet picturesque series of images, all appropriate to the subject, that the sights and sounds of evening seem to be reproduced with a magical fidelity. The whole poem seems dropping with dew and breathing the fragrance of the hour. It resembles a melody of Schubert.

MARK AKENSIDE (1721–1770) is one of the examples, so frequent in the English literature of the last age, of the united worship of Medicine and Poetry. Like Arbuthnot, Garth, Smollett, and Blackmore, he was a physician as well as a writer, and a man of considerable learning, as well as of pure, lofty, and classical turn of genius. His chief work is the philosophical poem entitled *The Pleasures of the Imagination*, in which he seeks at once to investigate and illustrate the emotions excited by beautiful objects in art and nature upon the human mind. Like the still nobler poem of Lucretius, the philosophical merit of his theories is very often but small; but the beauty of the imagery and the language will ever secure for this lofty, thoughtful, and noble work, the admiration of those readers who can content themselves with elevated thoughts, without looking for passages of strong human interest, in which Akenside is deficient. He wrote in musical and sonorous blank verse, reminding the reader of Thomson; but he is less sensuous, less vivid, and less picturesque, than the latter, and at the same time less liable to offend against severe principles of taste in diction. The abstract nature of his subject will confine his readers to small number, but the beauty and dignity of his illustrations will compensate them for the cold and sculptural character of his writings. Few English poets, since Milton, have been more deeply saturated with the spirit of classical antiquity, which is partly to be attributed, as in the case of the author of *Paradise Lost*, to very extensive learning, and partly to that Puritan spirit of haughty resistance to authority which filled the minds of both with splendid dreams of liberty and tyrannicide.

§ **4.** The greatest of the exclusively lyrical poets that England had hitherto produced was THOMAS GRAY (1716–1771), a man of vast and varied acquirements, and whose life was devoted to the cultivation of letters. He was the son of a respectable London money-scrivener, but his father was a man of violent and arbitrary character, and the poet was early left to the tender care of an excellent mother, who had been obliged to separate from her tyrannical husband. He received his education at Eton, and afterwards settled in learned retirement at Cambridge, where he passed nearly the whole of his life. He travelled in France and Italy as tutor to Horace Walpole, but quarrelling with his pupil he returned home alone. Fixing himself at Cambridge, he soon acquired a high poetical reputation by his beautiful *Ode on a Distant Prospect of Eton College*, published in 1747, which was followed, at pretty frequent intervals, by his other imposing and highly-finished works, the *Elegy written in a Country Churchyard*, the *Pindaric Odes*, and the far from numerous but splendid productions which make up his works. His quiet and studious retirement was only broken by occasional excursions to the North of England, and other holiday journeys, of which he has given in his letters so vivid and animated a description. His correspondence with his friends, and particularly with the poet Mason, is remarkable for interesting details, descriptions, and reflections, and is indeed, like that of Cowley, among the most delightful records of a thoughtful and literary life. Gray refused the offer of the Laureateship which was proposed to him on the death of Cibber, but accepted the appointment of Professor of Modern History in the University, though he never performed the functions of that chair, his fastidious temper and indolent self-indulgence keeping him perpetually engaged in forming vast literary projects which he never executed. He appears not to have been popular among his colleagues; his haughty, retiring, and somewhat effeminate character prevented him from sympathizing with the tastes and studies that prevailed there;

and he was at little pains to conceal his contempt for academical society. His industry was untiring, and his acquirements undoubtedly immense; for he had pushed his researches far beyond the usual limits of ancient classical philology, and was not only deeply versed in the romance literature of the Middle Ages, in modern French and Italian, but had studied the then almost unknown departments of Scandinavian and Celtic poetry. Constant traces may be found in all his works of the degree to which he had assimilated the spirit not only of the Greek lyric poetry, but the finest perfume of the great Italian writers: many passages of his works are a kind of mosaic of thought and imagery borrowed from Pindar, from the choral portions of the Attic tragedy, and from the majestic lyrics of the Italian poets of the sixteenth and seventeenth centuries: but though the substance of these mosaics may be borrowed from a multitude of sources, the fragments are, so to say, fused into one solid body by the intense flame of a powerful and fervent imagination. His finest lyric compositions are the Odes entitled *The Bard*, that on the *Progress of Poetry*, the *Installation Ode* on the Duke of Grafton's election to the Chancellorship of the University, and the short but truly noble *Ode to Adversity*, which breathes the severe and lofty spirit of the highest Greek lyric inspiration. The *Elegy written in a Country Churchyard* is a masterpiece from beginning to end. The thoughts indeed are obvious enough, but the dignity with which they are expressed, the immense range of allusion and description with which they are illustrated, and the finished grace of the language and versification in which they are embodied, give to this work something of that inimitable perfection of design and execution which we see in an antique statue or a sculptured gem. In the *Bard*, starting from the picturesque idea of a Welsh poet and patriot contemplating the victorious invasion of his country by Edward I., he passes in prophetic review the whole panorama of English History, and gives a series of most animated events and personages from the thirteenth to the eighteenth century. It is true that he is occasionally turgid, but the general march of the poem has a rush and a glow worthy of Pindar himself. The phantoms of the great and the illustrious flit before us like the shadowy kings in the weird procession of Macbeth; and the unity of sentiment is maintained first by the gratified vengeance with which the prophet foresees the crimes and sufferings of the oppressors of his country and their descendants, and by the triumphant prediction of the glorious reign of the Tudor race in Britain. In the odes entitled *The Fatal Sisters*, and the *Descent of Odin*, Gray borrowed his materials from the Scandinavian legends. The tone of the Norse poetry is not perhaps very faithfully reproduced, but the fiery and gigantic imagery of the ancient Scalds was for the first time imitated in English; and though the chants retain some echoes of the sentiment and versification of more modern and polished literature, these attempts to revive the rude and archaic grandeur of the mythological traditions of the Eddas deserve no niggardly meed of approbation. In general Gray may be said to overcolor his language, and to indulge occasionally in an excess of ornament and personification; he will nevertheless be always regarded as a lyric poet of a very high order, and as one who brought an immense store of varied and picturesque erudition to feed the fire of a rich and powerful fancy.

§ **5.** The poetical instinct must have been unusually strong in the family of the Wartons, to have made three of its members more or less distinguished at the same time. The two brothers, JOSEPH WARTON (1722–1800) and THOMAS WARTON (1728–1790) were the sons of a Professor of Poetry at Oxford, and both brothers, especially the younger, deserve a place in the annals of our literature. Joseph was head master of Winchester School, and his brother Thomas, an Oxford Fellow, and during some time poet laureate, was a pleasing writer, one of the firs to infuse into his writings a taste for the romantic sentiment. He rendered great service to literature by his agreeable but unfinished *History of English Poetry*, which unfortunately comes to an abrupt termination just as the author is about to enter upon the glorious period of the Elizabethan era; but the work is valuable for research and a warm tone of appreciative criticism. Thomas Warton exhibited his knowledge of and fondness for Milton in an excellent edition of that poet, enriched with valuable notes. The best of his own original verses are sonnets, breathing a peculiar tender softness of feeling and showing much picturesque fancy. His brother's talent, though inferior, has a strong family resemblance to his.

§ **6.** The progress which carried our national taste most rapidly from the correct and artificial type of Pope in the direction of the real sympathies of general humanity is most strongly exemplified in the writings of WILLIAM COWPER (1731–1800). He is eminently the poet of the domestic affections and the exponent of that strong religious feeling which, originating in the revival of Evangelical piety generated by the preaching of Wesley and Whitefield, began to penetrate and modify all the relations of social life. His story is singularly sad. He was of ancient and even illustrious race, the grandson of Lord Chancellor Cowper, and was born with an extremely tender and impressionable character. After being cowed by bullying at a private school, he was sent to Westminster, and afterwards placed in an attorney's office, where one of his desk companions was Thurlow, afterwards celebrated as Chancellor for his sternness and political bigotry; and here he acquired some knowledge of the law, though he was destined never to practise it as his profession. His early life was frivolous and somewhat dissipated. Obtaining the nomination to a comfortable and lucrative post, that of Clerk of the Journals to the House of Lords, Cowper's sensitive and morbid disposition was so terrified at the idea of making a public appearance, that he fell into a gloomy despondency, and attempted to put an end to his existence. An attack of madness rendered it necessary that he should be confined in an asylum, from whence he was after some time discharged, with his intellect restored indeed, but with his sensitive nature so deeply shaken that any active career in life had become an impossibility. Possessing a small income, and assisted by his family, he retired into the country, and passed the remainder of his life in privacy, being first placed under the care of the family of Mr. Unwin, a clergyman in Huntingdon. His virtues and accomplishments inspired every person in the small circle with which he was in contact with the tenderest attachment; and with Mrs. Unwin in particular he laid the foundation of a tender and life-long friendship. Cowper's mind, always impressionable, and still smarting under the tremendous affliction which it had undergone, became morbidly susceptible of enthusiastic religious impressions; and in the occasional relapses of his dreadful malady his hallucinations took that most unhappy form of mental disease — a form unfortunately the most common in England — of religious despair. The strong and elastic mind of Bunyan, and his natural cheerfulness of disposition, was able to triumph over these gloomy phantoms; but Cowper's more feminine organization succumbed in the trial. On the death of Unwin, he removed, with the widow, to Olney, where he resided in the house of John Newton, a man of great eloquence, and who professed the theology of the more Calvinistic section of the English Church. A more fatal companionship for a man in Cowper's situation could not have been imagined. By perpetually dwelling upon mysterious and gloomy religious questions, and by encouraging the fatal habit of analyzing his own internal sensations, the poet's tendency to enthusiasm was aggravated; and, though it could not diminish the charm of his genius or the benevolence of his heart, this religious fanaticism entirely destroyed the happiness of his life. He began to cultivate literature at first merely as a pastime, and as a means of distracting his attention from his own more than half-imaginary sufferings; but the force, originality, and grace of his genius soon acquired popularity, and he pursued as a profession what he had at first taken up as a diversion. His poetical talent did not flower until late: his first important publication did not appear till he had reached middle life. In 1773 and the two following years he suffered a relapse of his malady; on recovering from which he endeavored to calm his shattered spirits with a variety of innocent amusements — gardening, carpentering, and taming hares. His first poems were given to the world in 1782, and his friend Lady Austen, a woman of cheerful, accomplished mind, playfully gave him the Sofa as a subject. Upon this he composed his poem of *The Task*, which became so popular that he was encouraged to follow up his success with other works in a similar style — the *Table-Talk*, *Tirocinium*, and many others. His most laborious but least successful undertaking was the translation into English blank verse of the Iliad. He justly considered that the neat and artificial style of Pope had done but scant justice to the father of Greek poetry; but in endeavoring to give greater force and vigor to his own version, he fell into the opposite fault to that of Pope, and made his translation harsh and rugged, without approaching one whit nearer to the true character of his original. From Olney he removed to Weston, where Mrs. Unwin died, and the pain of this loss clouded the remaining days of the unhappy poet with redoubled gloom and despondency.

The longer and more important poems of Cowper are written in a peculiar and entirely original manner, and on a plan then entirely new in literature. They contain a union of reflection, satire, description, and moral declamation. Some of them are in blank verse, while in others he has employed rhyme. His aim was to keep up a natural and colloquial style, and he is the declared enemy of all the pomp of diction which was at that time regarded as essential to poetry. His pictures of life and nature, whether of rural scenery or of in-door life, have seldom been surpassed for truth and picturesqueness, and his satirical sketches of the follies and absurdities of manners, and his indignant denunciations of national offences against piety and morality, are equally remarkable, in the one case, for sharpness and humor, and in the other for a lofty grandeur of sentiment. The district in which he lived is one of the least romantic in England; yet nothing more victoriously proves that true poetical genius can give a charm and an interest to the most unpromising subjects, than the fact that Cowper has communicated to the level banks of the Ouse a magic that will never pass away. Similarly the quiet home circle of middle English life, the tea-table, the newspaper, and the hearth, have derived from him a beauty and a dignity which other men have failed to communicate to the proudest scenes of camps and courts. Though the morbid and fanatical religious system of Cowper has here and there tinged his works, the natural goodness and benevolence of his disposition more than neutralize the impression such passages produce, and in many of his comic and humorous delineations we see in full effulgence a playful gayety which no cloud can dim. Of all our poets Cowper is essentially the painter of domestic life, and his writings have deeply incorporated themselves into the tissue of our household existence. Their mixture of worldly observation, delicate painting of nature, and intense religious feeling peculiarly endears them to the great middle class in England. Many of Cowper's songs and shorter lyrics are elegant and sportive, and his beautiful lines *On Receiving my Mother's Picture*, will ever be read with delight. His comic ballad *John Gilpin* is a pleasant drollery, and his last verses, *The Castaway*, give a painful reflection of his despairing and unhappy creed. Cowper's letters are perhaps the most charming in the language; they show the poet in his most amiable light, and invest every trifle which surrounds him with a sort of halo of purity and goodness.

§ 7. Several poems have appeared in England possessing what may be called a technical character, being either devoted to the teaching of some art, or describing some special sport or amusement. I may mention ARMSTRONG'S *Art of Preserving Health*, GRAINGER'S *Sugar-Cane*, PHILIPS'S *Cyder*, and SOMERVILLE'S *Chase*. Many of these works, in spite of the impracticable nature of their subjects, show considerable power of execution, and contain passages of excellence; but the most popular and successful work of this kind is the *Shipwreck* of WILLIAM FALCONER (1730–1769), a self-taught poet, who, as a professional seaman, had himself witnessed the calamity he describes so well. He was born about 1730, and perished at sea in a man-of-war which sailed on a cruise in 1769, and was never more heard of. Falconer's principal work, the *Shipwreck*, is a narrative poem in three cantos, detailing the danger and ultimate loss of a merchant-ship on a voyage to Venice, which is cast away, after experiencing a violent gale in the Greek archipelago, on the dangerous rocks of Cape Colonna, the ancient Sunium. The description of the vessel, of her various manœuvres during the hurricane, and of the ultimate destruction which she encounters, are all strictly in accordance with nautical experience: every detail of seamanship is given in its proper technical language, and the poem has not only the merit of vigorous and correct painting of Nature under her wildest aspects of storm and terror, but is minutely accurate in point of seamanship. Falconer wisely and with good taste did not scruple to use the terms of his art, and has thus not only given truth and vivacity to his picture, but has produced a work that may serve the young navigator as a sort of grammar of his art. He was the author of a useful *Dictionary of Marine Terms*, and the accurate practical knowledge which he possessed of the details of his noble profession he has in his poem clothed with the charm of no ignoble verse. The least interesting portions of the poem are the romantic and sentimental details with which he clothes the persons of his officers: but no one ever read the *Shipwreck* without following, with breathless interest, the course of the fated ship from Candia to her death-struggle among the breakers of Cape Colonna.

To the department of technical poetry belongs also ERASMUS DARWIN (1731–1802), who endeavored to clothe in dazzling and somewhat tinsel splendor the principles of the Linnæan sexual system of vegetable physiology. Darwin was a man of unquestionable genius, and even of large scientific acquirements; but he unfortunately guided himself by the notion that poetry must address itself to the senses rather than to the sentiments, and produced a series of pictures which strike the fancy, but never touch the heart. Every object he struggled to present vividly, as it were, to the eye: and his abuse of personification, which is repeated so as to become as wearisome as it is generally fantastical, together with his meretricious and tawdry diction, though it gave him a great momentary popularity, has condemned him to neglect within half a century. His principal work is a poem the first part of which was entitled the *Botanic Garden*; the second soon after followed under the name of the *Loves of the Plants*, and the work was afterwards completed by a third canto. The system which he wrote to illustrate gave him but too abundant opportunity of indulging in that highly-colored and somewhat sensual vein of description and impersonation which he carried to excess, and the elaborate and ambitious melody of his versification has not sufficed to compensate for the over-wrought and fatiguing monotony of his imagery. The decline of his fame, once very great, may also in some degree be attributed to a tendency in his doctrines, which some readers blame as not slightly tinged with materialism. Many of his episodes and subordinate descriptions exhibit a great force of language and a powerful faculty of the picturesque.

§ **8.** The middle of the eighteenth century was remarkable for several nearly contemporaneous attempts at literary imposture — the poetical forgeries of Macpherson, Chatterton, and Ireland. The first of these three has alone survived, in some part, the ordeal of strict critical examination; and that because, though the totality of the works palmed upon the public as Ossian's have no claim whatever to the character arrogated for them by their pretended translator, they are nevertheless filled with names, incidents, and allusions really traceable to Celtic antiquity. James Macpherson (1738–1796) was a Scotchman, and a sort of literary adventurer of rather equivocal reputation. Originally a country schoolmaster, and afterwards a tutor, he pretended to have accumulated, in his travels through the Highlands of Scotland, an immense mass of fragments of ancient poetry composed in the Gaelic or Erse dialect common to that country and Ireland. The first portion of these — not, however, a very large one — he showed to Home, the author of the once-admired Tragedy of *Douglas*, and they were printed, exciting an intense enthusiasm, and soon giving ground to one of the most vehement controversies that have ever raged among antiquarians and literary men. The translations, which Macpherson professed to have made from the originals, were composed in a pompous and declamatory rhetorical sort of prose, something like the versions of the poetical portions of the Scriptures. The Highlanders, eager for the honor of their country, maintained the authenticity of these poems, and asserted that the name of Ossian, the supposed author, as well as innumerable persons, descriptions, and historical events mentioned in them, had been familiar to their memories as the legends of their childhood. The Southern critics, however, among whom Johnson occupied a foremost place, expressed the strongest scepticism, basing their disbelief upon the want of evidence that there existed among the Scottish Celts any written literature approaching in antiquity to the date assigned to the fragments, and also upon the impossibility of such a state of society and such refined and chivalrous sentiments ever having prevailed among so rude a people as the Highlanders were at the supposed period. Macpherson might at once have settled the question by producing the supposed originals, a philological and critical examination of which would, of course, have instantly decided their degree of authenticity and the age and country which produced them; but this Macpherson, after much shuffling, refused to do, under the pretext that his honor had been impeached. He afterwards published two long poems in the same style, *Fingal* in six, and *Temora* in eight books, which he attributed, like the preceding fragments, to the genius of the Celtic Homer. The regularity of construction in these works, the numerous passages in them as well as in their predecessors evidently plagiarized from the whole range of literature, from the Bible and Homer down to Shakspeare, Milton, and even Thomson, the artificial and monotonous though strained and highly-wrought diction, and above all the sentiments in constant discordance with the real manners of the ancient Highlanders, would have sufficed, even in the general ignorance of the Gaelic language, to undeceive all except those who were ignorantly carried away by the imposing but hollow magnificence of the style. More accurate investigation established that though these poems are crowded with names and allusions which really abound in the old Irish and Highland legends, no entire poem, nay, no considerable fragment of a poem, has ever been found in the least corresponding with any of Macpherson's pretended discoveries. Yet more, the scanty remains of Celtic verse attributed upon more solid grounds to Ossian, have a character totally different, and evidently belong to an age considerably later than that assigned by him; for they contain allusions to Christianity, of which there is no trace in the pretended antiquities of Macpherson. The wild and overstrained style and imagery of Ossian long made Macpherson's forgeries enormously popular throughout Europe; poetry and painting, and even the stage, were filled with the "daughters of the snow," "car-borne heroes," and misty phantoms. In Germany the admiration has not yet altogether subsided: the mania for Ossianic imagery extended even to Russia; and perhaps the only poetry which attracted the imagination of Napoleon was the wild, declamatory rhapsody which left no faint traces upon his bulletins. The vague yet monotonous imagery, the sham and theatrical sentiment, and the colossal amplifications of these works, while operating fatally upon their authenticity, will perhaps always give them a sort of charm to the taste of young and uncultivated readers. Macpherson accumulated a considerable fortune, became a political pamphleteer, sat in Parliament, and died without leaving any clew to elucidate the true secret of what is now considered an audacious imposture.

§ 9. The annals of literature hardly present a more extraordinary example of precocious genius than that of THOMAS CHATTERTON (1752–1770), nor an instance of a career more brief and melancholy. He was born in 1752, the son of a poor sexton and parish schoolmaster at Bristol, and he died, by suicide, before he had completed his eighteenth year. Within this short interval he gave evidence of powers that would in all probability have placed him at the head of the poets of his day, and he executed a series of literary forgeries which have hardly any parallel for extent and ingenuity. He produced at eleven years of age verses which will more than bear a comparison with the early poems of any author: and though he had received little education beyond that of a parish school, he conceived the project of deceiving all the learned of his age, and creating, it may almost be said, a whole literature of the past. He was passionately fond of black letter, heraldry, and old architecture, and his imagination had probably been fired by the numerous fine remains of mediæval building in which Bristol abounds. One of the most remarkable of these is the noble old church of St. Mary Redcliffe, of which Chatterton's father was sexton, and which was the place of sepulture of Canynge, a rich citizen of Bristol, and benefactor to the church in the reign of Edward IV. In the muniment-room of this edifice had been kept a chest called Canynge's coffer, in which had been preserved charters and other documents connected with Canynge's benefactions to the church. Many of these had been removed; but there remained a large mass of parchments which had been thrown aside as of no value, and had been employed by Chatterton's father for covering his scholars' copy-books. The young poet, familiarized with the sight of these antiquated writings, conceived the idea of forging a whole series of documents, which he pretended either to have found in Canynge's coffer, or to have transcribed from originals in that mysterious receptacle. These he produced gradually, generally taking advantage of some topic of public interest to bring forward and contribute either to the local newspapers or to his acquaintances in the town, the pretended originals or transcripts from the pretended originals having some relation to the matter in hand. Thus on the occasion of the opening of a new bridge over the Avon he produced an account of processions, tournaments, religious solemnities and other ceremonies which had taken place on the opening of the old bridge. To Mr. Burgum, an honest pewterer of Bristol, who happened to have a taste for heraldry, he gave a pedigree tracing his descent to Od, Earl of Blois and Lord of Holderness. Horace Walpole was then writing his Anecdotes of British Painters· Chatterton furnished him with a long list of mediæval artists who had flourished in Bristol. All these documents, which he pretended to have found in the chest of the muniment-room, he fathered upon a priest, Thomas Rowley, whom he represents to have been employed by the munificent Canynge as a sort of agent for collecting works of art, who was the author of the poems that constitute the majority of the parchments. The poems are of immense variety and unquestionable merit and though modern criticism will instantly detect in them, as did Gray and Mason when Walpole submitted some of them to their opinion, the most glaring marks of forgery, yet their brilliancy and their number were enough to deceive many learned scholars in an age when minute antiquarian knowledge of the Middle Ages was much rarer than at present. Besides, the apparent impossibility of such works being produced by an uneducated boy, without aid and without apparent motive, still further intensified the mystery. In those documents which Chatterton tried to pass off as originals he imitated as near as he could the antiquated handwriting, which his practice as an attorney's clerk assisted him to do: he also carefully discolored his parchment, and used every means to give it an air of antiquity. In those documents, far more numerous, which he brought forward as copies or transcripts of originals, he trusted to an elaborate grotesqueness of style and spelling; he carefully introduced every quaint, odd-looking word which he picked up in Chaucer and the other old authors that he greedily studied. No task is so difficult as that of successfully imitating ancient compositions, and the wonder is rather that Chatterton should have done this without immediate exposure than that he should have fallen into errors which detect him at once. Thus in his eagerness to incrust his diction with the rust, the *ærugo*, of antiquity he overlays his words with such an accumulation of consonants as belong to no orthography of any age of our language. And this *ærugo* is merely superficial: divested of their fantastic spelling, his lines have the cadence and the regularity of modern composition, and the grammatical structure in no respect differs from the English of the eighteenth century. He has also, as was inevitable, sometimes made a slip in the use of an old word, as when he borrowed the expression *mortmal*, which he found in Chaucer's description of the Cook, he employed it, having forgotten its meaning, to signify, not a disease, the gangrene, but a dish. In the same way he uses the word *drawing* in the modern sense; whereas it was unquestionably never employed with that meaning till in comparatively modern times. Of the same kind are his innumerable examples of impossible architecture and heraldry at variance with every principle of the art. Burning with pride, hope, and literary ambition, the unhappy lad betook himself to London, and unsuccessfully attempted to gain a subsistence as a political pamphleteer and satirical poet. He was a professed infidel, but his moral character is unimpeached, and he was not only frugal and industrious, but always showed himself a most affectionate son and brother. After struggling a short time with distress, and almost with starvation, in London, he shut himself up in despair in his miserable garret, left a wild and atheistical paper which he called his will, tore up all his manuscripts, and poisoned himself with a dose of arsenic on the 25th of August, 1770. Singularly enough his acknowledged poems, though indicating very great powers, are manifestly inferior to those he wrote in the assumed character of Thomas Rowley. The best of these are a Tragedy called *Alla*, the ballad of *Sir Charles Bawdin*, both connected with the ancient history of Bristol, and several pastorals, which, like that entitled *Elinour and Juga*, betray by their very nature the impossibility of their having been really produced at the time assigned for their composition.

WILLIAM HENRY IRELAND (1777–1835) deserves mention only on account of his Shakspearian forgeries, among which was a play entitled *Vortigern*, in which John Kemble acted in 1795. Ireland soon afterwards acknowledged that he was the author of these forgeries.

§ **10.** If Cowper be rightly denominated the poet of the domestic hearth, GEORGE CRABBE (1754–1832) is eminently the poet of the passions in humble life. In his long career he is the link connecting the age of Johnson and Burke with that of Walter Scott and Byron; and his admirable works, while retaining in their form much of the correctness and severity of the past age, exhibit in their subjects and treatment that intensity of human interest and that selection of real passion which constitute the distinguishing characteristic of the writers who appeared at the beginning of the present century. He was born at the little seaport-town of Aldborough, in Suffolk, where his father was an humble fisherman, and performed the duties of salt-master or receiver of the customs duties on salt; and his childhood was miserable through bodily weakness and the sight of continual dissensions between his parents. After a dreamy and studious childhood, during which his thirst for knowledge was encouraged by his father, a man of violent passions but of considerable intellectual development for one in his humble position, young Crabbe was apprenticed to a surgeon and apothecary, and first exercised his profession in his native town. Passionately fond of literature and botany his success in business was so small that he determined to seek his fortune in London, where he arrived with only about 3*l.* in his pocket, and several unfinished poems, which he published, but which were coldly received. After some stay in London he found himself reduced to despair, and even threatened with a prison for some small debts he had contracted; and after vainly applying for assistance to various persons connected with Aldborough, he addressed a manly and affecting letter to Edmund Burke, who immediately admitted him to his house and friendship. From this moment his fortune changed; he was assisted, both with money and advice, in bringing out his poem of *The Library*, was induced to enter the Church, and was promised the powerful influence of Lord Chancellor Thurlow. He became domestic chaplain to the Duke of Rutland and lived some time at the magnificent seat of Beauvoir; but this dependent position seems to have been accompanied with circumstances distasteful to Crabbe's manly character. It however enabled him to marry a young lady to whom he had been long attached, and he soon after changed the splendid restraint of Beauvoir for the humbler but more independent existence of a parish priest. From this period til his death, at the great age of seventy-eight, his life was passed in the constant exercise of his pastoral duties in various parishes, and in the cultivation of literature and his favorite science of botany.

In his first poem, *The Library*, it was evident that Crabbe had not yet hit upon the true vein of his peculiar and powerful genius. It was not till the appearance of *The Village*, in 1783, that he struck out that path in which he had neither predecessor nor rival. The manuscript of this poem was submitted to Johnson, who gave his advice and assistance in the correction and revision of the style. The success of *The Village* was very great, for it was the first attempt to paint the manners and existence of the laboring class without dressing them up in the artificial colors of fiction. Crabbe allowed about fourteen years to pass before he again appeared before the public. During the interval he was busied with his professional duties, and enjoying the happiness of domestic life, which no man was ever more capable of appreciating: he, however, does not appear to have relaxed his habit of composition. His next work was *The Parish Register*, in which the public saw the gradual ripening of his vigorous and original genius; and this was followed, at comparatively short intervals, by *The Borough*, *Tales in Verse*, and *Tales of the Hall*. These, with the striking but painful poems, written in a different measure, entitled *Sir Eustace Grey* and *The Hall of Justice*, make up Crabbe's large and valuable contribution to the poetical literature of his country. Almost all these works are constructed upon a peculiar and generally similar plan. Crabbe starts with some description, as of the Village, the Parish Church, the Bor ough, —just such a deserted seaport-town as his native Aldborough, — from which he naturally proceeds to deduce a series of separate episodes, usually of middle and humble life, appropriate to the leading idea. Thus in the *Parish Register* we have some of the most remarkable births, marriages, and deaths that are supposed to take place in a year amid a rural population; in the *Borough*, the lives and adventures of the most prominent characters that figure on the narrow stage of a small provincial town. The *Tales* are a series of stories, some pathetic and some humorous, each complete in itself; and in the *Tales of the Hall* two brothers, whose paths in life have separated them from boyhood, meet in their old age and recount their respective experiences. *Sir Eustace Grey* is the story of a madman related with terrific energy and picturesqueness by himself; and in the *Hall of Justice* a gypsy criminal narrates a still more dreadful story of crime and retribution. With the exception of the two last poems, written in a peculiar rhymed short-lined stanza, Crabbe's poems are in the classical ten-syllabled heroic verse, and the contrast is strange between the neat Pope-like regularity of the metre, and the deep passion, the intense reality, and the quaint humor of the scenes which he displays. He thoroughly knew and profoundly analyzed the hearts of men: the virtues, the vices, the weakness, and the heroism of the poor he has anatomized with a stern but not unloving hand. No poet has more subtly traced the motives which regulate human conduct; and his descriptions of nature are marked by the same unequalled power of rendering interesting, by the sheer force of truth and exactness, the most unattractive features of the external world. The village-tyrant, the poacher, the smuggler, the miserly old maid, the pauper, and the criminal, are drawn with the same gloomy but vivid force as that with which Crabbe paints the squalid streets of the fishing-town, or the fen, the quay, and the heath. The more unattractive the subject the more masterly is the painting, whether that subject be man or nature. Crabbe is generally accused of giving a gloomy and unfavorable view of human life; but his pathos, when he is pathetic, reaches the extreme limit which sensibility will bear, and in such tales as Phœbe Dawson, Edward Shore, the Parting Hour, the intensity of the effect produced by Crabbe is directly proportioned to the simplicity of the means by which the effect is attained. In painting the agonies of remorse, the wandering reason of sorrow or of crime, he is a master; and the story of *Peter Grimes* may be cited as an unequalled example of the sublime in common life. None of the great Flemish masters have surpassed Crabbe in minuteness as well as force of delineation, and like them his delineation is often most impressive when its subject is most vile, and even repulsive.

§ 11. The greatest poet, beyond all comparison, that Scotland has produced is ROBERT BURNS (1759–1796). He was born at the hamlet of Alloway in Ayrshire, and was the son of a peasant farmer of the humblest class. Popular education was at that period far more generally diffused in Scotland than in any other country in Europe; and the future glory of his nation was able to acquire, partly by the wise care of his father, and partly by his own avidity for knowledge, a degree of intellectual culture which would have been surprising in any other country. He had a good general acquaintance with the great masterpieces of English literature, and could use with perfect facility the style and diction of the great classical authors of South Britain, though by far the finest and most characteristic works are written in the provincial dialect of his native land. His passions were unusually strong, and he began, from a very early age, to express in verse the impressions made upon his fancy by the beautiful and pastoral nature which surrounded him, and the outpourings of his own feelings and heart. Nor was the tendency to song a rare or unusual accomplishment in the district he inhabited and among the class to which he belonged. The Lowland Scotch dialect, once the language of the Court and of an extensive national literature, was still cultivated with enthusiasm among the middle and lower classes; and every valley, every village, possessed its rustic poets, whose "unpremeditated strains" continued the traditions of that ancient and strongly national popular literature, which had exhibited an almost uninterrupted succession of splendid names, from David Lyndsay, Dunbar, and Gavin Douglas, to Allan Ramsay and the ill-fated Fergusson. In early life Burns labored like a peasant upon his father's farm, and afterwards endeavored, but without success, to conduct a farm with his brothers: his speculations failing he was on the eve of abandoning, in despair, his native country, and emigrating to the West Indies, where so many Scotsmen by their intelligence, their parsimony, and their industry, have acquired honorable fortunes. In order to raise funds for this voyage, he was induced to publish a collection of his poems, which had long enjoyed a great local popularity; and these were received by the highly cultivated society of Edinburgh with a tempest of enthusiasm that instantly made the "Ayrshire ploughman" the idol of the fashionable and literary world. The peasant-poet was regarded as a species of phenomenon, and plunged into the intoxicating current of gay life with an ardor that unfitted him for returning to his humble existence, but which, though it increased his natural taste for gross convivial pleasures, could neither injure the natural dignity of his character nor corrupt the benevolence of his heart. After again falling into embarrassments, rendered more inextricable by his irregularities, he obtained a humble appointment in the Excise service, the duties of which were not only arduous and very scantily paid, but were of a nature to still further engross his time and to cherish habits of intemperance that had been continually growing upon him. His strong constitution was undermined by excess and excitement of all kinds, and the poet died of fever at Dumfries, in extreme poverty, in the thirty-seventh year of his age.

In Burns the highest and most apparently incompatible qualities were united to a degree which is rarely met with, — tenderness the most exquisite, humor the broadest and the most refined, the most delicate and yet powerful perception of natural beauty, the highest finish and the easiest negligence of style. He paints with the sharp and infallible touch of Homer or of Shakspeare, and amid the wildest ebullitions of gayety he has thoughts that sound the very abysses of the heart. His writings are chiefly lyric, consisting of songs of inimitable beauty; but he has also produced works either of a narrative or satirical character, and in some of which the lyric element is combined with the descriptive. The longest and most remarkable of his poems is *Tam o'Shanter*, a tale of popular witch-superstition, in which the most brilliant descriptive power is united to a pathos the most touching, a fancy the most wild, and a humor the quaintest, slyest, and most joyous. *Tam* is a drunken ne'er-do-weel of a horse-couper, who traversing a dreary moor on All-hallow-Eve, when according to ancient tradition all demons and witches have power, passes, on his way home from a drinking-bout, near the old ruined Kirk of Alloway, which to his surprise he finds lighted up. Emboldened by John Barleycorn, he steals close to the window, looks in, and witnesses the sabbath of the witches, described by the poet with an inimitable mixture of grotesque humor and fantastic horror. Unable to conceal his delight at the agility of the dancers, he attracts their attention, and is pursued by the whole band till he can cross a running stream which defeats their power of enchantment. He is just in time to escape, and the tail of his gray mare remains as a trophy in the hands of his pursuers. Burns possesses, to a degree exceeded only by Shakspeare, the power of giving a human interest to material objects, a quality found only in poets of the highest order. Like Shakspeare, too, he brings into contact the familiar and the ideal, and combines the broadest humor with the profoundest pathos. Another inimitable poem, half-narrative, but set thick with glorious songs, is the *Jolly Beggars*: careless vagabond jollity, roaring mirth and gypsy merriment, have never been so expressed: though low in the extreme Burns is never vulgar; his ragged bacchanals swagger and drink with inimitable grace and nature. In his *Address to the De'il*, *Death and Dr. Hornbook*, *The Twa Dogs*, and the dialogue between the Old and New Bridges of Ayr, Burns combines humorous and picturesque description with reflections and thoughtful moralizing upon life and society. The first-mentioned of these poems offers that exquisite stroke of tenderness where the poet refuses to despair of the ultimate pardon of the Evil One himself, and addresses him in language of infinite softness, to ask him what pleasure he can take in tormenting poor miserable sinners. The Dialogue between the *Twa Dogs* is an elaborate comparison between the relative degree of virtue and happiness granted to the rich and the poor. Burns declares the balance to be pretty even; and there is no reason to doubt the correctness of his judgment. His description of the joys and consolations of the poor man's lot is perhaps even more beautiful in this poem than in the more generally popular *Cottar's Saturday Night*, written in stanzas, and in a language less provincial than the former. This circumstance has rendered the poem better known to such readers as are imperfectly acquainted with the Lowland dialect; but in my opinion the *Cottar's Saturday Night*, though containing many beautiful pas sages, is inferior in raciness to the *Twa Dogs*. Certainly there has never been a nobler tribute paid to the virtues of the peasant class than has been given by Burns in these two poems. In the poem descriptive of rustic fortune-telling on *Halloween*, in the *Vision of Liberty*, where Burns gives such a sublime picture of his own early aspirations, in the unequalled sorrow that breathes through the *Lament for Glencairn*, in *Scotch Drink*, the *Haggis*, the epistles to *Captain Grose* and *Matthew Henderson*, in the exquisite description of the death of the old ewe Mailie, and the poet's address to his old mare, we find the same prevailing mixture of pathos and humor, that truest pathos which finds its materials in the common every-day objects of life, and that truest humor which is allied to the deepest feeling. Examples of the same truth present themselves in every page of Burns, and quite as often in his shorter lyrics and songs. The famous lines *On Turning up a Mouse's Nest with the Plough*, and on destroying in the same way a *Mountain Daisy*, will ever remain among the chief gems of tenderness and beauty.

I may here remark the peculiar charm of that six-lined stanza of short lines which Burns has so profusely employed, and which is a form of versification exclusively Scotch. The *Songs* properly so called are exceedingly numerous, and generally of great though sometimes of unequal merit. Those written in pure English have often an artificial and somewhat pretentious air, which places them below the Doric of the Lowland Muse. Intensity of feeling, condensed force and picturesqueness of expression, and admirable melody of flow, are the qualities which distinguish them. Some were based upon older verses originally written to be sung to some ancient air: these Burns has frequently re-written, giving to them a power and a freshness altogether new. The list of subjects adapted for the purpose of the song-writer is always very limited — love, patriotism, and pleasure, constitute the whole. To give variety to this narrow repertory is a difficult task; and no poet has exhibited greater fertility than Burns. In the song *Ae fond Kiss and then we Part* is consecrated the whole essence of a thousand love-poems: the heroic outbreak of patriotism in *Scots wha hae wi' Wallace bled* is a lyric of true Tyrtæan force, and in those of a calmer and more lamenting character, as *Ye Banks and Braes*, there is the finest union of personal sentiment with the most complete assimilation of the poet's mind to the loveliness of external nature. The only defects with which this great poet can be reproached is an occasional coarseness of satire, as exemplified in the personalities of *Holy Fair*, a tone of defiant and needless opposition of one class against another, and now and then a vulgar and misplaced ornament which contrasts tawdrily with the sweet simplicity of the general style. This last is generally to be met with in such of Burns's poems as are written in English. Nor should I forget a somewhat sensual and over-ardent style of compliment which Burns has sometimes introduced into his love-verses, and which is the more reprehensible as it contrasts with the warm yet chastened spirit which generally breathes in his love strains.

§ **12.** The coarse but pungent and original humor of JOHN WOLCOT (1738–1819) gave him, during the reign of George III., a vogue which, like that of his fellow-satirist Churchill in the preceding period, was bright and brilliant. Under the pseudonyme of PETER PINDAR he ridiculed the weaknesses and oddities of the King, attacked the Royal Academy with unrelenting pasquinades, and showed no mercy to Sir Joseph Banks and the court poets. The oddity and boldness of his irregular burlesque style, the abundance of quaint images and illustrations, and the unblushing impudence of his lampoons, make his writings curious to the student, though their grossness has excluded them from general readers. His knowledge and taste in painting were considerable, but the violence of his personalities and his frequent indecency render him rather a curious literary phenomenon than a name deserving of respect in literature. Some of his humorous tales, as *The Pilgrims and the Peas*, the *Razor Seller*, and the ludicrous amœbæan strains of *Bozzy and Piozzi*, in which he laughs at the rival biographers of Johnson, exhibit the peculiar manner in which he excelled, carried to the highest pitch of absurdity.

§ **13.** In tracing the progress of the comic drama from the middle of the eighteenth century down almost to the present time, the chief names to be noted are those of Garrick, Foote, Cumberland, the two Colmans, father and son, of whom the second is by far the most considerable, and lastly Sheridan, that strange cometary genius, whose powers were so versatile and whose life was so brilliant and so disreputable. Garrick, Foote, and the Colmans were either actors or theatrical managers; DAVID GARRICK (1716–1779) was perhaps the greatest performer that the English stage had seen since the days of Burbage and Alleyn: his principal plays are the *Lying Valet* and *Miss in her Teens*, which are still acted. SAMUEL FOOTE (1721–1777) was celebrated for his convivial humor and his power of mimicry, which made him at once formidable to his victims and the idol of his associates. He produced a considerable number of farcical and amusing pieces, most of which owed their chief success to the caricatures they contained of particular persons. Only one has constantly retained possession of the theatre, the coarse but excellently humorous farce *The Mayor of Garratt*, containing in particular the two admirable types of citizen life, Major Sturgeon, the volunteer Bobadill, and Jerry Sneak, the hen-pecked husband. RICHARD CUMBERLAND (1732–1811) was a man of learning and accomplishments, who obtained some reputation in various branches of literature: his dramas, of which the *West Indian* is a favorable specimen, are neatly constructed and show vivacity of dialogue; but they are tainted with that tendency to morbid sentimentalism which was the vice of our stage during some time, being the reaction against the barefaced immorality of the school of Wycherley and Congreve. The two Colmans (GEORGE COLMAN, the elder, 1733-1794, and GEORGE COLMAN, the younger, 1762–1836), were theatrical managers and prolific writers. The best production of the younger is the *Heir at Law*, a piece in some measure belonging to the same class as Goldsmith's *She Stoops to Conquer*, relying for its interest principally on odd humors and quaint language, and in a rich abundance of absurd incidents more laughable than probable. In his piece of the *Poor Gentleman* also the farcical personages, as that of the half-militia officer, half-apothecary, Ollapod, are extremely amusing: but the sentimental scenes in this play, chiefly and most unadroitly copied from Sterne's Uncle Toby and Trim, are completely unworthy of the rest. What pleases in Colman is the air of dash and high spirits which pervades his scenes.

Richard Brinsley Sheridan (1751–1816) is certainly one of the most remarkable figures in the social, political, and intellectual life of the period. He was endowed by nature, in a degree little inferior to Burke, with the talents of an orator. His colloquial repartees and witticisms made him the darling of society, and his place in the dramatic literature of his age is inferior to that of none of his contemporaries. Byron justly said that the intellectual reputation of Sheridan was truly enviable, that he had made the best speech — that on the Begums of Oude — written the two best comedies, the *Rivals* and the *School for Scandal*, the best opera, the *Duenna*, and the best farce, the *Critic*. His whole life, both in Parliament and in the world, was a succession of extravagance and imprudence; and the ingenious shifts by which he endeavored to stave off his embarrassments, and the jokes with which he disarmed even his angriest creditors, would of themselves furnish matters for a most amusing jest-book. He died in hopeless distress, and was buried with princely pomp, and amid the applauses of an admiring country. His two great comedies belong to the two distinct types of the drama: the *Rivals* depends for its interest upon the grotesqueness of its characters and the amusing unexpectedness of its incidents, while the *School for Scandal* is essentially a piece of witty dialogue or repartee. The language of the latter was polished by the author with the most anxious care, and every passage sparkles with the cold and diamond-like splendor of Congreve. In the *Critic* we have a farce, based upon the often-employed fiction of the rehearsal of a tragedy, which gives the author the opportunity of introducing a burlesque or caricature of the imaginary piece, while at the same time he can introduce the absurdities of the author and the criticisms of his friends. The *Rehearsal* is an example of a similar plan. But on his caricature Sheridan has lavished all the treasures of his admirable wit Dangle, Sneer, and Puff, as well as the unsurpassed sketch of Sir Fretful Plagiary, an envious, irritable dramatist, intended to represent Cumberland, are as lively, as humorous, and as ever fresh as the personages in the Elizabethan drama which is being repeated before them. It is probable that not a line of these three pieces will ever cease to be popular: whether acted or read they are equally delightful — an incessant blaze of intellectual fireworks.

NOTES AND ILLUSTRATIONS.

OTHER POETS OF THE EIGHTEENTH CENTURY.

JOHN BYROM (1691-1763), born at Manchester, educated at Cambridge, inventor of a patented system of shorthand, and at last a private gentleman in his native place, is best known for a *pastoral* which first appeared in the *Spectator*, — *My time, O ye Muses, was happily spent.* He wrote several other small poems, which have lately been published by a Local Society in Manchester. His writings exhibit ease and fancy.

JOHN DYER (1698-1758) was born at Aberglasney, Carmarthenshire, educated at Westminster School, and travelled through Wales and Italy, studying painting, but afterwards became a clergyman of the Church of England. His best known poem is *Grongar Hill.* Some portions of the *Ruins of Rome* received the praise of Johnson. In 1757 he produced a poem on the unpoetic subject of *The Fleece*, and died soon afterwards, on the 24th July, 1758. Dyer is a poet who gives promise of the better school that was soon to adorn English literature. His imagination and style have received the praise of Wordsworth; and Gray, writing to Walpole, says, "Dyer has more of poetry in his imagination than almost any of our number, but rough and injudicious." The moral reflections in his poetry are introduced very naturally, whilst most pleasing pictures of nature are expressed in easy and flowing verse.

NATHANIEL COTTON (1707-1788), author of *Miscellaneous Poems.* He was a physician at St. Alban's, and deserves remembrance from having Cowper as his patient, who speaks of "his well-known humanity and sweetness of temper."

CHARLES CHURCHILL (1731-1764), the son of a clergyman, received his education at Westminster School and Cambridge, and became curate of Rainham, in Essex. In 1758 he succeeded his father as curate and lecturer of St. John's, Westminster; but his careless habits and neglect of clerical proprieties brought him into conflict with the dean, and ended in his resignation of his preferments, and retirement from the Church. He gave himself up to political and satirical writing. He was a great friend of and coadjutor with Wilkes, of the *North Briton.* His private and domestic life was embittered by quarrels with his wife and his habits of dissipation. He died at Boulogne, November 4, 1765, on a visit to his friend Wilkes. His greatest work was the *Rosciad*, published in 1761, which was placed by contemporaries on a level with the works of Pope and Dryden. It is easy in diction, and strong in language; the invective is bold, and the rhythm flowing; but it has little poetic fervor, and the author has been well called nothing but a "pamphleteer in verse." In 1762 he wrote against the Scotch the *Prophecy of Famine;* which, Lord Stanhope remarks, "may yet be read with all the admiration which the most vigorous powers of verse, and the most lively touches of wit, can earn in the cause of slander and falsehood." He also wrote a clever but savage attack in his *Epistle* to Hogarth, who in one of his pictures represented Churchill as a bear in clerical costume, with a pot of porter in his paw. Churchill sought immediate popularity and pay rather than lasting worth. He was for a time one of the most popular of English poets.

HENRY KIRKE WHITE (1785-1806) was born at Nottingham, the son of a butcher. The poet assisted his father for some time, but when about fourteen was apprenticed to a weaver. This occupation he soon abandoned, and was placed with an attorney and there made rapid progress in various studies, gaining a silver medal when about fifteen for a translation from Horace in the *Monthly Preceptor.* His poems were published in 1803, and, though scornfully noticed in the *Monthly Review*, they attracted the attention of Mr. Southey and others. Resolving to enter the Church, he was enabled through Mr. Simeon to obtain a sizarship at St. John's College, Cambridge. His course here was rapid and brilliant. He won the first place in the College examinations, but his health gave way, and he died on the 19th October, 1806. His *Remains and Memoir* were published by Southey.

The works of White must be estimated as the productions of a young writer, and rather for their high promise than intrinsic worth. He would never have taken a rank among the first class of poets, but his position would have been very high among the second. His versification is correct, his language polished. Here and there a stroke of imagination or passion bursts upon the reader: but it is generally the quiet flow of a feeling and sensitive verse that wins admiration for the poet and affection for the man.

His longest work is *Clifton Grove*, 1803, a descriptive poem. The best known of his writings are the *Song to an Early Primrose*, *Gondoline*, and some of his hymns.

SIR CHARLES HANBURY WILLIAMS (1709-1759), one of the most popular satirists of the reign of George II. Sir Robert Walpole was his chief patron and friend, and found his pen no small aid in his political course. He was a member of Parliament for some years, and afterwards was sent to the Prussian and Russian courts as an ambassador. His poems are generally fugitive pieces. They were imperfectly collected in 1822; but have now lost their interest, as they have almost entirely reference to the events of that age.

WILLIAM JULIUS MICKLE (1734-1788), a native of Dumfriesshire, at first in business in Edinburgh, and afterwards corrector of the Clarendon press, was author of *Pollio*, *The Concubine*, and a translation of the *Lusiad* of Camoens, 1775. The latter years of his life were spent near Oxford, where he died in 1788. He is said to be the author of *The Mariner's Wife*, one of the most exquisite little songs written in the Lowland Scotch. *Cumnor Hall* is perhaps the best known of the original poems of Mickle.

HANNAH MORE (1745-1833) was the daughter of Jacob More, schoolmaster at Stapleton, in Gloucestershire. The family removed to Bristol, and the future authoress was there aided by the friendship of Sir James Stonehouse. In 1762 the *Search after Happiness* was published, and was followed in a short time by *The Inflexible Captive.* When about twenty-eight Miss More removed to London, and there entered into the literary circle of Johnson, Burke, and Garrick, at the house of the last of whom she resided. Her *Percy* was put on the Drury-Lane stage by Garrick in 1777. Whilst in London she produced another tragedy, *The Fatal Falsehood*, her last dramatic composition. Some *Poems* were published in 1786, portions of which were termed by Johnson "a great performance." Hannah More now became wearied of the life of London, and retired to Bristol, where her sisters kept a large boarding-school. Her pen was most busy; prose and poetry flowed unceasingly, embracing social, political, and ethical topics. Her monthly tales in the *Repository*, 1794, written against Jacobins and Levellers, reached a million in circulation. Her best known works are — *Thoughts on the Manners of the Great*, 1788; *On Female Education*, 1799; *Cœlebs in Search of a Wife*, 1809; *Practical Piety*, 1811, &c., making in all eleven volumes. Queen Charlotte consulted Hannah More on the education of the Princess Charlotte, which was the occasion of the writing of the work *Hints towards forming the Character of a young Princess*, 1805.

Mrs. More's style is flowing, and often sparkles with the light of a pleasant humor. Her later works are of a more sombre cast, from the deeper impressions which religion seemed to be making upon her, yet she retained to the last her position as one of the greatest, if not the first, of English authoresses. Johnson considered her the best of female versifiers, but her prose is equal, if not superior, to her poetry. *Cœlebs* is perhaps the chief of her works — a fiction of much beauty in style, with a mixture of quiet irony: the plot is well evolved, but the characters are too few, and the incidents too tame, to make it in the present day a readable book. It has been well called a "dramatic sermon."

Mrs. More's dramas gave promise of much success in that form of literature, but her serious turn of mind prevented her proceeding so as to produce a masterpiece. She died on the 7th of September, 1833, at the age of 88.

ISAAC HAWKINS BROWNE (1706-1760) was Member of Parliament for Wenlock, wrote some Latin imitations of Lucretius, and a few English poems, the chief of which were a series of six parodies of contemporary writers, published in 1736, the subject of which is *A Pipe of Tobacco*. The imitations are of Cibber, Philips, Thomson. Young, Pope, and Swift.

CHRISTOPHER ANSTEY (1724-1805), author of the well-known *New Bath Guide*, which was published in 1766, and became the most popular work of the day. The impression which it produced at the time may be seen from a letter of Horace Walpole to George Montague (June 20, 1766): "What pleasure have you to come! . . . . It is called the *New Bath Guide*. It stole into the world, and for a fortnight no soul looked into it, concluding its name was its true name. No such thing. It is a set of letters in verse, in all kind of verses, describing the life at Bath, and incidentally everything else; but so much wit, so much humor, fun, and poetry, so much originality, never met together before." Other poems were written by him, but they attracted little notice.

MRS. THRALE, afterwards MRS. PIOZZI (1740-1822), whose maiden name was Esther Lynch Salusbury, a native of Bodville in Caernarvonshire, married Mr. Henry Thrale, the opulent brewer, in whose house Dr. Johnson found so frequent a home. She was the authoress of *The Three Warnings*, which is so good a piece of composition that Johnson has been supposed to have assisted in writing it. After the death of her husband, she married Piozzi, an Italian music-master, and left England. She wrote several other works, but the one by which she is best known is *Anecdotes of Dr. Johnson*, 1786. She spent the latter portion of her life at Clifton, where she died in 1822.

CHRISTOPHER SMART (1722-1770), "an unfortunate and irregular man of genius," for some time a Fellow of Pembroke Hall, Cambridge, author of a satire called the *Hilliad*, an attack on the well-known Sir John Hill, and translator of *Phædrus* and *Horace* into prose. In 1754 he was placed in a madhouse, and finally died in the King's Bench Prison. His most remarkable poem is the *Song to David*, indented on the wall of his cell with a key.

THOMAS BLACKLOCK (1721-1791), the blind poet, who lost his eyesight at the age of six months, was born in Annan; received a good education at home. and afterwards in Edinburgh; became in 1759 a preacher in the Scotch Church; wrote a treatise on Blindness in the Encyclopædia Britannica, sermons, and theological discourses, and several poems. The poetry is insipid and dull, but the correctness of description and the occasional vivid appreciation of natural beauty are most surprising in one who could not have remembered the little he himself had seen. Dr. Blacklock distinguished colors by the touch.

MICHAEL BRUCE (1746-1767), a young Scotch poet of some promise, was born at Kinnesswood, in the county of Kinross, and educated at Edinburgh, but died soon after he left college, at his father's house. In 1770 his poems were published by John Logan. Editions more complete have been brought out in later times. His chief works were *Lochleven* and *The Last Day*. The style is immature, and there are many traces of borrowing from other poets; yet the poetry gives proofs of genius, and promise of high distinction.

JOHN LOGAN (1748-1788), at first a clergyman in the Scotch Church, lecturer in Edinburgh, author of *Runnimede, a tragedy*, contributor to different magazines, and writer of several poetical pieces, some of which have been claimed for Bruce, whose literary executor Logan was. Logan's life was one of disappointment, and his ambition of excellence and literary glory was never realized. Some have said he died of a broken heart. The style of his writing is impressive, and his sermons won for him no small renown. His poetry is simple and pathetic. The *Song to the Cuckoo*, which has been ascribed to Bruce and to Logan, is one of the gems of English ballad literature.

ANNA SEWARD (1747-1809), known as the "Swan of Lichfield," daughter of a canon in the cathedral of that city, wrote *Sonnets*, and a poetical novel, called *Louisa*. Her poems were bequeathed to Walter Scott, for publication, but they are now utterly forgotten.

ANNA LETITIA BARBAULD (1743-1825), daughter of a schoolmaster in Leicestershire, named Aikin, and wife of Rochemont Barbauld, a Frenchman by extraction, and minister of a dissenting congregation at Palgrave, in Suffolk. A little before her marriage she published *Miscellaneous Poems*, and soon after *Hymns in Prose for Children*. Mr. Barbauld became minister of a church at Newington in 1802, which brought Mrs. Barbauld into greater connection with the literary circles of the day. She wrote various other poems, containing here and there some true touches of poetic genius. Her style is simple and graceful, adorned by much exquisite fancy and imagery. Her most valued contributions have been her sacred pieces. That on *The Death of the Righteous* is one of the gems of English sacred poetry.

ROBERT DODSLEY (1709-1764) deserves mention as the great publisher and patron of literature of his age. He proposed the *Annual Register*, made a *Collection of Poems by several Hands*, 1758, and was himself the author of several poetical and dramatic pieces His shop was in Pall Mall, and he commenced his business by the assistance of Pope, who lent him 100*l*.

WILLIAM HAYLEY (1745-1820), at one time a popular poet, the friend and biographer of Cowper, was educated at Trinity Hall, Cambridge. He wrote *Triumphs of Temper*, *Triumphs of Music*, poetical epistles, odes, essays, &c. His works in 1785 occupied six volumes.

ARTHUR MURPHY (1730-1805), a native of Elphin, in the county of Roscommon, Ireland, received his education at St. Omer's, gave up the trade into which he had entered for literature, published *The Gray's Inn Journal* from 1752 to 1754; went on the stage, wrote dramas, and took part in the great contest of parties; at last became a barrister, and died a commissioner of bankruptcy. He published twenty-three plays, of which the *Grecian Daughter* was the most popular. His translation of Tacitus had great repute in its day.

JOANNA BAILLIE (1762-1851), born at Bothwell, near Glasgow, the daughter of a Presbyterian clergyman, lived the greater part of her life at Hampstead. She wrote various plays, of which her tragedy of *De Montfort* is perhaps the finest.

JOHN HOME (1724-1808), author of the well-known tragedy of *Douglas*, which appeared in 1756, and was acted with great applause; but it is now almost forgotten, with the exception of the oft-repeated scene commencing with "My name is Norval." He was a minister of the Scotch Church; but his having written a tragedy gave such grave offence to the elders of the Kirk, that he was obliged to resign his parish of Athelstaneford. He retired to England, and received a pension through the influence of the Earl of Bute. Sir Walter Scott, in his Diary (April 25, 1827), thus speaks of Home's works: "They are, after all, poorer than I thought them. Good blank verse, and stately sentiment, but something lukewarmish, excepting Douglas, which is certainly a masterpiece Even that does not stand the closet. The merits are for the stage; and it is certainly one of the best acting plays going."

HENRY BROOKE (1706-1783), the son of a clergyman in Ireland, and educated at Trinity College, Cambridge, came to London, and was one of the poets patronized by Frederick Prince of Wales. His tragedy of *Gustavus Vasa* was supposed to have been directed against the prime minister Sir Robert Walpole, and the representation of it was forbidden by the Lord Chamberlain. He was also author of the *Earl of Essex*, and other plays, poems, translations, &c. He wrote *The Farmer's Letters*, which were published in Ireland at the time of the rebellion of 1745. He wrote the well-known novel, *The Fool of Quality*.

RICHARD GLOVER (1712-1785), a London merchant, and Member of Parliament for Weymouth, better known for his noble independence and worth in private and public life than for his literary efforts. He published at an early age (1737) an epic poem on the subject of the Persian wars, called *Leonidas*, which was much praised in its day, but is now deservedly forgotten. He wrote a second epic poem, or kind of continuation of the former, entitled *Athenais*, which appeared after his death (1787).

WILLIAM MASON (1725-1797), was a native of Yorkshire, received his education at Cambridge, entered the Church, became rector of Aston, in Yorkshire, and held the office of canon and precentor in the cathedral of York. His chief works were — the dramas of *Elfrida*, 1752, and *Caractacus*, 1759; *Odes on Independence*, *Memory*, &c.; *The English Garden*, 1772-1782, a poem in blank verse; and a satire of much liveliness and force, *An Heroic Epistle to Sir William Chambers, Knight*, 1773. Mason's style is wanting in simplicity. His dramas are on the model of the classic writers, the language is ornate and somewhat stilted, and at the present day his works are scarcely known. Mason was the intimate friend of Gray, superintended the publication of the poet's works, and wrote his Life. He died at Aston, April 5, 1797.

AARON HILL (1684-1749), best known through the conflict with Pope, on which he ventured after being satirized in the Dunciad. Seventeen plays are attributed to him, besides some other writings now altogether forgotten. The style is correct but cold, fashioned on the model of the French writers.

WM. WHITEHEAD (1715-1788), poet laureate on the death of Cibber, after Gray had refused the office. He wrote seven dramas, of which the most important are the *Roman Father*, 1750, and *Creusa*, 1754.

DR. JAMES GRAINGER (1721-1767) was born at Dunse, county Berwick, was a surgeon in the army, and afterwards went to the West Indies. He wrote the *Sugar Cane*, which has been severely dealt with by the critics. He calls the negroes "swains."

Among the translators of this age are to be mentioned —

GILBERT WEST (1705-1756), who translated *Pindar*, 1749, and wrote some original works. He was a friend and connection of Pitt and Lyttelton, and was appointed by Townshend one of the Clerks of the Privy Council. He is now best known by his *Observations on the Resurrection* (1730). Lord Lyttelton addressed to him his "Dissertation on the Conversion of St. Paul." (See p. 347, A.)

ELIZABETH CARTER (1717-1806), who published a translation of *Epictetus* in 1758, besides various original poems, was most highly esteemed by Johnson, and her *Ode to Wisdom* is given by Richardson in his second novel, *Clarissa Harlowe*.

The principal Scottish poet of this period is —

ROBERT FERGUSSON (1750-1774), who was born in Edinburgh, educated at St. Andrew's, and died at an early age, having ruined his health by dissipation. His style and manner exercised no small influence upon Burns, whose "poetical progenitor" he has been called His successful pieces are in the Scotch dialect.

CHAPTER XX.

WALTER SCOTT.

§ 1. **Romantic school.** Influence of BISHOP PERCY'S *Reliques of Ancient Poetry.* § 2. WALTER SCOTT. His life and writings. § 3. His poems. § 4. *Lay of the Last Minstrel, Marmion,* and the *Lady of the Lake.* § 5. *Rokeby, Lord of the Isles,* and minor poems. § 6. Classification of the *Waverley Novels.* § 7. Characteristics of the Novels. *Waverley. Guy Mannering. The Antiquary. Rob Roy.* § 8. *Tales of My Landlord: — The Black Dwarf. Old Mortality. The Heart of Mid-Lothian. The Bride of Lammermoor. The Legend of Montrose.* § 9. *Ivanhoe. The Monastery* and *The Abbot. Kenilworth. The Pirate.* § 10. *Nigel. Peveril of the Peak. Quentin Durward. St. Ronan's Well. Redgauntlet.* § 11. *Tales of the Crusaders: — The Betrothed* and *The Talisman. Woodstock.* § 12. *Chronicles of the Canongate: — The Highland Widow, The Two Drovers, The Surgeon's Daughter,* and *The Fair Maid of Perth. Anne of Geierstein. Count Robert of Paris,* and *Castle Dangerous.*

§ 1. THE great revolution in taste, substituting romantic for classical sentiment and subjects, which culminated in the poems and novels of Walter Scott, is traceable to the labors of BISHOP PERCY (1728–1811). The friend of Johnson, and one of the most accomplished members of that circle in which Johnson was supreme, Percy was strongly impressed with the vast stores of the beautiful, though rude, poetry which lay buried in obscure collections of ballads and legendary compositions, and he devoted himself to the task of explaining and popularizing the then neglected beauties of these old rhapsodists with the ardor of an antiquary and with the taste of a true poet. His publication in 1765, under the title of *Reliques of Ancient English Poetry,* of a collection of such ballads, many of which had been preserved only in manuscript, while others, having originally been printed in the rudest manner on flying sheets for circulation among the lower orders of the people, had owed their preservation only to the care of collectors, must be considered as a critical epoch in the history of our literature. Many authors before him, as for example Addison and Sir Philip Sidney, had expressed the admiration which a cultivated taste must ever feel for the rough but inimitable graces of our old ballad-poets; but Percy was the first who undertook an examination, at once systematic and popular, of those neglected treasures. His *Essay on the Ancient Minstrels,* prefixed to the pieces he selected, exhibits considerable research, and is written in a pleasing and attractive manner; and the extracts are made with great taste, and with a particular view of exciting the public sympathy in favor of a class of compositions, the merits of which were then new and unfamiliar to the general reader. It is true that he did not always adhere with scrupulous fidelity to the ancient texts, and where the poems were in a fragmentary and imperfect condition he did not hesitate, any more than Scott after him in the *Border Minstrelsy*, to fill up the rents of time with matter of his own invention. This, however, at a period when his chief object was to excite among general readers an interest in these fine old monuments of mediæval genius, was no unpardonable offence, and gave him the opportunity of exhibiting his own poetical powers, which were far from contemptible, and his skill in imitating, with more or less success, the language and manner of the ancient Border poets. Percy found, in collecting these old compositions, that the majority of those most curious from their antiquity and most interesting from their merit were distinctly traceable, both as regards their subjects and the dialect in which they were written, to the North Countree, that is, to the frontier region between England and Scotland, which, during the long wars that had raged almost without intermission between the Borderers on both sides of the Debatable Land, had necessarily been the scene of the most frequent and striking incidents of predatory warfare, such as those recorded in the noble ballads of *Chevy Chase* and the *Battle of Otterburn*. The language in the Northern marches of England and in the Scottish frontier region bordering upon them, was one and the same dialect; something between the Lowland Scotch and the speech of Cumberland or Westmoreland, and it is curious to find the ballad-singer modifying the incidents of his legend so as to suit the prejudices and flatter the national pride of his listeners according as they were inhabitants of the Northern or Southern district. In various independent copies or versions of the same legend, we find the victory given to the one side or to the other, and the English or Scottish hero alternately playing the nobler and more romantic part. Besides a very large number of these purely heroic ballads, Percy gave specimens of an immense series of songs and lyrics extending down to a comparatively late period of English history, embracing even the Civil War and the Restoration; but the chief interest of his collection, and the chief service he rendered to literature by his publication, is concentrated on the earlier portion. It is impossible to exaggerate the influence exerted by Percy's *Reliques:* this book has been devoured with the most intense interest by generation after generation of English poets, and has undoubtedly contributed to give a first direction to the youthful genius of many of our most illustrious writers. The boyish enthusiasm of Walter Scott was stirred, "as with the sound of a trumpet," by the vivid recitals of the old Border rhapsodists; and but for Percy it is possible that we should have had neither the *Lady of the Lake* nor *Waverley*. Nor was it upon the genius of Scott alone that is impressed the stamp of this ballad imitation: Wordsworth, Coleridge, even Tennyson himself have been deeply modified, in the form and coloring of their productions, by the same cause; and perhaps the influence of the *Reliques*, whether direct or indirect, near or remote, will be perceptible to distant ages in English poetry and fiction.

§ 2. Literary history presents few examples of a career so splendid as that of WALTER SCOTT (1771–1832). A genius at once so vigorous and versatile, a productiveness so magnificent and so sustained, will with difficulty be found, though we ransack the wide realms of ancient and modern letters. He occupies an immense space in the intellectual horizon of the nineteenth century; and it will be no easy task to delineate, at once clearly and rapidly, the features of this colossal figure. He was born in 1771, the son of a respectable Writer to the Signet in Edinburgh, and was connected, both by the father's and mother's side, with several of those ancient historic Border families whose warlike memories his genius was destined to make immortal. His constitution was at first weakly; and an accident he met with in childhood caused a deformity in one of his feet, and rendered it necessary that he should pass some time in country air. For this purpose he was sent to the farm of his grandfather near Kelso, where he was surrounded with legends, ruins, and localities, of which he was to make in his works so admirable a use. Though remarkable neither at the High School nor at the University of Edinburgh, where he finished his education, for anything but good nature and a love for athletic sports, he had always been a devourer of miscellaneous books — his taste and inclination naturally leading him to prefer fiction, and chiefly the picturesque fiction, whether couched in prose or verse, of mediæval chivalry. On leaving the University he was destined to the profession of the bar, and he practised during some time as an advocate before the Scottish tribunals: his real vocation was, however, that of letters; and his legal experience did little more for him than furnish him with hints of incidents and traits of human nature which he afterwards worked up with admirable effect in his romances. He was unsuccessful in obtaining the object of his first love; but he soon consoled himself, with that singular good sense which marked nearly all his conduct, and contracted an early and a happy marriage with a young lady of French extraction, named Carpenter. The first literary direction of his mind was towards the poetical and antiquarian curiosities of the Middle Ages; but just at that time there had been awakened among the intellectual circles of Edinburgh a taste for German literature, then only just beginning to become known, and Scott contributed several translations, as that of Goethe's *Erl-König*, of the *Lenore* of Bürger, and afterwards the whole drama of *Götz of the Iron Hand*. Scott was now residing with his young wife at Lasswade, and his position was probably as happy as can be conceived. He conceived the plan of rescuing from oblivion the large stores of Border ballads which were still current among the descendants of the Liddesdale and Annandale moss-troopers, and travelled into those picturesque regions, where he accumulated not only a vast treasure of unedited legends and fragments of legends, but familiarized himself with the scenery and manners of that country over which he was to cast the magic of his genius. The result of his researches he published as *Minstrelsy of the Scottish Border;* and in the skill with which he edited these poems, the immense and picturesque erudition with which he illustrated them, and the admirable manner in which he related striking and interesting facts connected with their elucidation, it was easy to see the germ of the great romantic poet, as well as of the antiquarian, then without a rival in historic and legendary lore. The learning and taste of this work gave Scott a high reputation, and in some degree contributed to induce him to abandon the profession of the law for that of literature. He was still further confirmed in his project by receiving the appointment of Sheriff of Selkirkshire, the duties of which left much leisure at his disposal. He afterwards continued his task of editor by publishing the old romance of *Sir Tristrem*, which he elucidated by a commentary; and also the very curious rhythmical poem of *Thomas of Ercyldoune*, whose prophecies had been regarded from the thirteenth century downwards with traditional awe and reverence. He now changed his residence to the pretty villa of Ashestiel on the Tweed, and in 1805 first burst upon the world in the quality of a great original romantic poet. It is difficult for us in the present day to conceive the rapture of enthusiasm with which the public received the rapid and dazzling succession of Scott's poems. They were poured forth with an unstinted freshness and uninterrupted rapidity from the above year till 1815, when he was as suddenly to burst forth with still greater splendor and still more wonderful fertility in a completely new and different line. Between 1805 and 1814 appeared the *Lay of the Last Minstrel*, *Marmion*, the *Lady of the Lake*, *Rokeby*, and the *Lord of the Isles;* not to enumerate a number of less important and less successful works, such as the *Vision of Don Roderick*, the *Bridal of Triermain*, *Harold the Dauntless*, and the *Field of Waterloo*, the first and last of which were written with the special purpose of celebrating the triumph over Napoleon, and which, as is generally the case with such productions, are unworthy of the author's genius. In about twelve years this kingly poet poured forth five works of considerable length, perfectly original in subject and construction, and which absolutely revolutionized the public taste. Though considerably varied in scenery and *dramatis personæ*, the narrative romantic fictions which so rapidly succeeded each other were found, after some repetitions, to pall to a certain degree upon the public taste; and perhaps the very frenzy of enthusiasm which had welcomed the rich, vivid, and picturesque revival of the ancient chivalric poetry in the *Lay*, the *Lady of the Lake*, and *Marmion*, made the reader more ready to find some falling-off of interest in *Rokeby* and the *Lord of the Isles*. It is certain that the popularity of Scott's poetry, though still very great, perceptibly declined with the former of these two works, which is partly to be attributed to the choice of an historical period for the action either less picturesque in itself or less favorable for the display of Scott's peculiar talent, than that remote epoch in which his immense knowledge caused him to be without a rival. Fully aware of the decline of his popularity, and with manly sense and dignified yet modest self-consciousness attributing it to its true cause just specified, and also perhaps in some degree to the startling sunrise of Byron's genius above the horizon, Scott, without a word of querulous complaint, immediately abandoned poetry to launch into a new career — a career in which he could have neither equal nor second.

In 1814 appeared *Waverley*, the commencement of which had been sketched out and thrown aside nine years before; and with *Waverley* began that inimitable series of romances which poured forth with a splendor and facility surpassing even that of the poems. During the seventeen years intervening between 1814 and 1831 were written that collection, that library, or rather that whole literature of fiction, to which is generally given, from the title of the first, the name of the Waverley Novels, and which were produced with such inconceivabl rapidity, that on comparing the number of these fictions, amounting to upwards of thirty independent works, almost all of them of considerable length, with the time during which they were composed, the result gives the surprising average of about two of such works in one year; and in reality there were years when Scott produced as many as three distinct novels. Our wonder at such fertility is still further augmented, when we learn that during this period Scott succeeded in writing, independently of the above fictions, a considerable number of works in the departments of history, criticism, and biography. I may mention only the *Life of Napoleon*, the *Tales of a Grandfather*. the amusing Letters on *Demonology and Witchcraft*, and extensive editions, with Lives, of Dryden and Swift. Such activity is rare indeed in the history of letters; still rarer, when combined with such general excellence in the products. One principal secret of this enormous productiveness is to be found in Scott's passionate and long-cherished ambition to found a territorial family, and to be able to live the life of a provincial magnate. Spurred on by this desire, and encouraged by the immense pecuniary profits which accrued from his works, Scott went on purchasing land, planting and improving, and transforming the modest cottage of Abbotsford on his beloved Tweed into a "romance in stone and lime," a baronial residence crowded with the rarest objects of mediæval antiquity. Here he exercised a truly princely hospitality, receiving every traveller of distinction, and "doing the honors of all Scotland" to those who were attracted in crowds by the splendor of his genius. The very large and continually-increasing outlay necessitated by this mode of life he supplied partly by his inexhaustible pen, and partly by engaging secretly in large commercial speculations with the printing and publishing firm of the Ballantynes, his intimate friends and schoolfellows. These latter speculations, though for a time productive, became ere long disastrous in the extreme; and the Ballantynes were involved in the fatal commercial crisis of 1825 and 1826, which also reached and ruined the still vaster speculations of Constable and Co., with whom indeed the Ballantynes' affairs were connected. Scott found himself ruined, and responsible for a gigantic amount of debt. He might easily have escaped from his liabilities by taking advantage of the bankrupt law; but his sense of honor was so high and delicate that he only asked for time, and resolutely set himself to clear off, by unremitting literary toil, the vast accumulation of nearly 120,000*l*. He all but accomplished his colossal task, nay, he did substantially accomplish it, but he died under the effort; nor does the history either of literature or commerce afford a brighter example of probity. The manifest inferiority of several of his last novels, as *Count Robert of Paris* and *Castle Dangerous*, and the somewhat gloomy and despondent tone which replaces, in those written after the crisis of his misfortunes, Scott's peculiarly healthy and joyous view of humanity, become, to those who know the history of this heroic struggle, facts and indications more touching than would have been the full continuance of Scott's wonderful powers. They tell, like the tottering step of the wounded gladiator, or the slackening pace of the noble steed, the failing of the powers so generously lavished. There is no more touching or sublime spectacle than that of this great genius, in the full plenitude of his powers, voluntarily and without a word of repining abandoning that splendor he was so well qualified to adorn, and that rural life which he so well knew how to appreciate, and shutting himself up in a small house in Edinburgh, to wipe out, by incessant literary taskwork, the liabilities which he had too much delicacy to evade.

In 1820 Scott had been raised to the dignity of the baronetcy; for the enchanting series of the *Waverley Novels*, though anonymously published, were universally ascribed to him, as to the only man in Great Britain whose peculiar acquirements and turn of genius could have given birth to them, though those who saw Scott familiarly could hardly understand how the hospitable, sport-loving country gentleman, whose time seemed always at the disposal of his friends, could have found leisure for the mere physical amount of labor implied in the mechanical composition of such voluminous works. The secret was explained by the fact that Scott had always adopted the invaluable practice of early rising; and was thus able, after devoting the first hours of morning to composition, to give the remainder of the day to pleasure and to his official duties. The mystery of the true authorship of the *Waverley Novels*, though it had been long a very transparent one, was maintained by Scott with great care; and it was not till the failure of Ballantynes' house rendered concealment any longer impossible that he formally avowed himself the author of these fictions. Towards the year 1830, his mind, exhausted by such incessant toil, began to show symptoms of hopeless weakness. A stroke of paralysis affected his memory so much that, though he still continued to labor as eagerly as before, he sometimes forgot the commencement of the phrase he was dictating; and he was sent abroad to Italy and the Mediterranean in the vain hope of re-establishing his health. He returned home to die; and after lingering in a state of almost complete unconsciousness for a short time, this great and good man terminated his earthly career on the 21st of September, 1832, at Abbotsford, on the estate which his exertions had restored to his posterity. His personal character is almost perfect. High-minded, generous, and hospitable to the extreme, he hardly had an enemy or a misunderstanding during the whole of a long and active career. He was the delight of society; for his conversation, though unpretending, kindly, and jovial, was filled with that union of old-world lore and acute and picturesque observation which renders his works so enchanting; and there never perhaps was a man so totally free from the pettinesses and affectations to which men of letters are prone. In his opinions he was a Tory of the most uncompromising stamp, which was natural enough in a man whose tastes and reading had been directed as his were; but of Toryism he exhibited only the gallant and chivalric side, and was totally free from its meaner and more narrow-minded features. He was emphatically a great and a good man, an honor to his age, to his country, and to human nature.

§ 3. The romantic narrative poems of Scott form an epoch in the history of modern literature. In their subjects, their versification, and their treatment, they were a novelty and an innovation, the success of which was as remarkable as their execution was brilliant. The materials were derived from the legends and exploits of mediæval chivalry, and the persons were borrowed partly from history and partly from imagination. Scott showed a power somewhat akin to that displayed by Shakspeare in combining into one harmonious whole actions partly borrowed from true history and partly filled up from fictitious invention; and in clothing the former with the romantic hues of imagination and picturesque fancy he showed his power no less than in giving to the latter the solidity and reality of truth. The theatre of his action was generally placed in that picturesque border region which spoke so powerfully to his heart, with whose romantic legends he was so wonderfully familiar, and which furnished, from the inexhaustible stores of his memory, such a mass of striking incident and vivid detail. The notes which he appended in illustration of his poems, like those in which he had elucidated the relics of ballad minstrelsy, show how vast was his treasury of antique lore; and these relics of antiquarian erudition are lighted up with a glow of picturesque and poetical imagination which transforms the dry bones of mediæval learning into the splendid and living body of feudal revival. The greatest of these poems are unquestionably the three first — the *Lay of the Last Minstrel*, *Marmion*, and the *Lady of the Lake*. According to Scott's own judgment, the interest of the *Lay* depends mainly upon the style, that of *Marmion* upon the descriptions, that of the *Lady of the Lake* upon the incidents. The form adopted in all these works, though it may be remotely referred to a revival of the spirit and modes of thought of the ancient French and Anglo-Norman Trouvères, was more immediately suggested, as Scott himself has confessed, by the example of Coleridge, who in his wild and irregular, but exquisitely musical and fanciful poems — as, for instance, *Christabel* — gave, so to say, the key-note upon which Scott composed his vigorous and varied harmony. The real measure of the Trouvères, the octosyllable-rhymed verse, was far too monotonous, and too liable to degenerate into tediousness to be likely to please a fastidious age. Scott, therefore, though employing this measure generally as the basis of his narrative passages, — for which purpose, from its ease and fluency, it is extremely well adapted, — had the good taste to vary and enliven it by a frequent intermixture of all other sorts of English verse, anapæstic, trochaic, or dactylic. But his principal metrical expedient was the frequent employment of two, three, or four verses of octosyllabic structure, rhyming together, and relieved at frequent intervals by a short Adonic verse of six syllables, giving at once great vigor and exquisite melody. The versification is more varied in the *Lay* than in the succeeding poems; and this work exhibits, with some traces of haste and inexperience, more of the lyric spirit, and perhaps more also of the true fire and glow of inspiration, than either of its successors. The plots or intrigues of these poems are in general neither very probable nor very logically constructed, but they allow the poet ample opportunities for striking situations and picturesque episodes. The characters are discriminated rather by broad and vigorous strokes than by any attempt at moral analysis or strong delineation of passion. They are drawn, so to say, from *without*, and not elaborated from within. The personages are rather general types of chivalric gallantry and female beauty and tenderness than individual men and women: they would interest us nearly as much were they impersonal and without names — the knight, the man-at-arms, the palmer, or the lady; and they derive their power of charming us less from their own individual feelings and experiences than from the admirable power, vivacity, and freshness of the incidents in which they move, and the details with which they are surrounded. Thus they resemble, in some degree, the figures introduced by Salvator Rosa in his landscapes, where the brigands owe their impressiveness to the magnificent background of rock and waterfall. The personages of Byron, on the contrary, like the figures of Titian, communicate their own coloring and sentiment to the landscape against which they are relieved. In his descriptions of scenery, which are exceedingly varied and intensely vivid, Scott sometimes indulges in a quaint but graceful vein of moralizing which beautifully connects inanimate nature with the sentiments of the human heart. A charming instance of this will be found in the opening description of *Rokeby*.

§ 4. The action of the *Lay of the Last Minstrel* is drawn from the legends of Border war; and necromantic agency, the tourney, the raid, and the attack on a strong castle, are successively described with unabating fire and energy. The midnight expedition of Deloraine to the wizard's tomb in Melrose Abbey, the ordeal of battle, the alarm, the feast, and the penitential procession, are painted with the force and picturesqueness of real scenes. Nothing is more wonderful than the completeness with which the poet throws himself back into past ages, and speaks and thinks like a minstrel of the fourteenth century. The various cantos of his poems Scott generally connects together by some kind of framing or setting, often very ingenious in itself, and giving him the opportunity for introducing some of his most beautiful descriptions or most attractive reflections. Thus the fiction of the old Minstrel, who is supposed to recite the *Lay* for the amusement of the Duchess of Buccleuch, the introductory prefaces of each canto of *Marmion*, giving us such an enchanting glimpse into Scott's own rural and family life, are not only beautiful in themselves, but most artfully relieve the monotony of the principal subject.

In *Marmion* the main action is of a loftier and more historical nature, and the catastrophe is made to coincide with the description of the great battle of Flodden, in which Scott gave earnest of powers in this department of painting hardly inferior to those of Homer himself. It is indeed "a fearful battle rendered you in music;" and the whole scene, from the rush and fury of the onset down to the least heraldic detail or minute trifle of armor and equipment, is delineated with the truth of an eye-witness. Much fault has been found with the awkward oversight of making the hero, a brave but unscrupulous warrior, guilty of so unknightly a crime as that of forging documents; and similar objections have been made to the whole episode of the goblin page, who plays such fantastic pranks in the *Lay;* but such blemishes are more than compensated by the scene of the opening of the tomb in the latter poem, and by those of the battle and of the immuring of Constance in *Marmion.*

In the *Lady of the Lake* Scott broke up new and fertile ground; he brought into contact the wild, half-savage mountaineers of the Highlands and the refined and chivalrous court of James V. The exquisite scenery of Loch Katrine became, when invested by the magic of the descriptions, the chief object of the traveller's pilgrimage; and it is no exaggeration to say, as Macaulay has done, that the glamour of the great poet's genius has forever hallowed not only the nature thus first shown in all its loveliness to the curiosity of the world, but even the barbarous tribes whose manners Scott has invested with all the charms of fiction. The adventures of the disguised king, whose gallant and chivalrous character is very dramatically sustained, the dark and sombre Roderick Dhu, and the graceful tenderness of Ellen Douglas, are combined and contrasted with skill; but perhaps the finest passage in this noble poem is the description by the Highland Bard of the Battle of Beal an Dhuine, and the death of the captive chieftain as he is listening to the fiery lay. Scott delighted in painting both the great warfare of the Middle Ages, and the lesser warfare, as it may be justly styled, of the chase; and the episode of the stag-hunt at the commencement of this poem is one of the most spirited of the numerous pictures of this kind. It is curious that that personality or individuality which I have asserted to be often wanting in the human characters of Walter Scott's poetry, is always to be found in his inimitable portraits of dogs and horses. This poem, as well as the others, affords striking instances of the truth and reality of his sketches of these noble animals. The sudden appearance of Roderick Dhu and his clan at Coilantogle Ford, the equally sudden vanishing of the armed men at the signal of their chief, and the combat between the royal adventurer Fitz-James with his fierce but chivalrous antagonist, are highly dramatic, and exhibit that noble and gallant spirit — the fine flower of chivalric bravery and courtesy — which so universally pervades Scott's poetry, as it animated his personal character; for not even the accomplished Sidney himself possessed to a more intense degree the mind and feelings which essentially mark what we call a *gentleman.* In his splendid and courtly scenes, of which a good example will be found in the conclusion of this tale, where the Knight of Snowdoun discloses himself in his real character to Ellen, we observe this lofty and gallant tone of sentiment; as far removed from theatrical emphasis on the one hand as it is from triviality on the other; and not excluding a kind of graceful and princely playfulness on occasion, which makes his noble personages the ideal of knightly courtesy.

§ 5. The tale of *Rokeby* contains many beautiful descriptions, and exhibits strenuous efforts to draw and contrast individual characters with force, as in the case of the ruffian buccaneer Risingham, Oswald, and Philip Northam; but the epoch — that of the Civil Wars of the Commonwealth — was one in which Scott obviously felt himself less at home than in his well-beloved feudal ages: at all events the mixture of feudal sentiment which clung to the poet's mode of feeling and treatment did not harmonize with the epoch selected for the action; and the sentimental sensitive lover who is the centre of the plot was generally found to be insipid and improbable.

The last of the greater poems, the *Lord of the Isles,* went back to Scott's favorite epoch, if not indeed somewhat farther back than was altogether advantageous for the success of the poem; for the exploits of Robert Bruce have a sort of half-mythical remoteness and vagueness which almost defied even Scott's wonderful power of realizing to make them palpable to the reader's belief. Nevertheless the voyage of the hero-king among the Isles, the scenes in the Castle of Artornish, the description of the savage and terrific desolation of the Western Highlands, show little diminution in picturesque power; and the subject gave the author the opportunity of terminating the action with one of those glorious battle-scenes in which he was unrivalled, and in which no modern poet, save Macaulay alone, and he was indeed an imitator of Scott, can be said even to have approached him. The Battle of Bannockburn reminds us of the hand that drew the field of Flodden; and Scott's ardent patriotism must have found pleasure in delineating the great victory of his country's independence, after having so gloriously described that fatal day when that independence was, for a time at least, destroyed.

Harold the Dauntless and the *Bridal of Triermain* must be regarded rather as half-serious, half-comic, poetical *jeux d'esprit* than as works on which the author wished to found his reputation. They are written in a less vigorous and muscular style than the poems I have been examining; the latter indeed was playfully intended to pass off upon the public as the production of Scott's friend Erskine. In *Triermain* we see a somewhat effeminate and theatrical treatment of a striking legend which figures in the cycle of the exploits of Arthur; and the confusion of time involved in the waking the lady from her enchanted sleep of ages is fatal to the coherency of the interest. *Harold* strives to combine the spirit of the old Berserk sagas with Christian and Chivalric manners, and the union of the two elements is too discordant to be pleasing. The *Vision of Don Roderick*, though based upon a striking and picturesque tradition, is principally a song of triumph over the recent defeat of the French arms in the Peninsula; but the moment he leaves the mediæval battle-field Scott seems to lose half his power: in this poem, as in *Waterloo*, his combats are neither those of feudal knights nor of modern soldiers, and there is throughout a struggle painfully visible to be emphatic and picturesque. Indeed it may be said that almost all poems *made to order*, and written to celebrate contemporary events, have this forced and artificial air. Many of Scott's shorter ballads, *Glenfinlas*, the *Eve of St. John*, as well as innumerable lyrics, playful or heroic, either standing alone or introduced as songs in his longer poems, are of incomparable beauty: I need only mention the intense warlike fury so gloriously embodied in the *Pibroch of Doniul Dhu*, the unsurpassable grace and gallantry of *Young Lochinvar*, which Lady Heron sings in *Marmion*, and the broad yet sly jollity of *Donald Caird*, a lyric not unworthy of Burns himself.

§ 6. If we apply to the long and splendid series of prose fictions generally known under the name of the *Waverley Novels*, the same rough analytical distribution as has been adopted in a former chapter for the purpose of giving a classification of Shakspeare's dramas, we shall obtain the following results. The novels are twenty-nine in number, of varied, though for the most part extraordinary degrees of excellence. They may be divided into the two main classes of Historical, or such as derive their principal interest and material from the delineation of some real persons or events, and those which are entirely or principally founded upon Private Life or Family Legend, and which are more remotely, if at all, connected with history. The first of these two great classes will naturally subdivide into subordinate categories, according to the epoch or country selected by the author, as Scottish, English, and Continental history. According to this rude, and merely approximative method of classification, we shall range seven works under the class of Scottish history, seven under English, also of various epochs, and three will belong to the Continental department; while the novels mainly assignable to the head of Private Life, sometimes, it is true, more or less connected, as in the cases of *Rob Roy* and *Redgauntlet*, with historical events, are twelve in number. The latter class are for the most part of purely Scottish scenery and character. I will draw up a sort of rough scheme or plan of the above arrangement, which will at least be found to assist the memory in recalling such a vast and varied cycle of works, and I will afterwards make a few rapid remarks upon these novels in the order of their composition.

I. History.

1. Scottish . *Waverley*. The period of the Pretender's attempt in 1745.

Legend of Montrose. The Civil War in the sixteenth century.

Old Mortality. The rebellion of the Covenanters.
Monastery. } The deposition and imprisonment of Mary
Abbot. } Queen of Scots.
Fair Maid of Perth. The reign of David.
Castle Dangerous. The time of the Black Douglas.

II ENGLISH . *Ivanhoe.* The return of Richard Cœur de Lion from the Holy Land.
Kenilworth. The reign of Elizabeth.
Fortunes of Nigel. Reign of James I.
Peveril of the Peak. Reign of Charles II.; period of the pretended Catholic plot.
Betrothed. The wars of the Welsh Marches.
Talisman. The first Crusade: Richard Cœur de Lion
Woodstock. The Civil War and Commonwealth.

III. CONTINENTAL . *Quentin Durward.* Louis XI. and Charles the Bold.
Anne of Geierstein. The epoch of the battle of Nancy.
Count Robert of Paris. The Crusaders at Byzantium.

II. PRIVATE LIFE AND MIXED.

Guy Mannering.	*Heart of Midlothian.*	*Redgauntlet.*
Antiquary.	*Bride of Lammermoor.*	*Surgeon's Daughter.*
Black Dwarf.	*Pirate.*	*Two Drovers.*
Rob Roy.	*St. Ronan's Well.*	*Highland Widow.*

§ 7. In this unequalled series of fictions the author's power of bringing near and making palpable to us the remote and historical, whether of persons, places, or events, is equally wonderful with the skill and certainty with which he clothes with solidity, so to say, the conceptions of his own imagination. In this respect his genius has something in common with that of Shakspeare, as shown in his historical dramas: and the two great creators have also this peculiarity in common, that their most secondary and subordinate characters stand out from the canvas with the same relief and vigor as the more prominent *dramatis personæ.* Scott was generally careless in the construction of his plots: he wrote with great rapidity, and aimed rather at picturesque effect than at logical coherency of intrigue; and his powerful imagination carried him away so vehemently, that the delight he must have felt in developing the humors and adventures of one of those inimitable persons he had invented — often by no means a chief protagonist in his action — sometimes left him no space for the elaboration of an intrigue which he in some cases had thought out beforehand. An example of this will be found, among a multitude of others, in the case of Dugald Dalgetty, or Baillie Nicol Jarvie. His style, though always easy and animated, is far from being careful or elaborate, and a curious amount of Scotticisms will be met with in almost every chapter. Description, whether of scenery, incident, or personal appearance, is very abundant in his works; and though this is sometimes carried so far as to become tedious to foreign readers, few of his countrymen, whether North or South Britons, will be found to complain of his luxuriance in this respect, for it has filled his pages with bright and vivid pictures that no lapse of time can efface from the reader's memory.

In *Waverley* this mixture of the historical with the familiar is carried out with consummate success; and the union of the stirring and romantic element with the most familiar humor gives to the story the largeness and the variety of life itself. The character of Baron Bradwardine and the description of his household are easily and yet powerfully contrasted with the Highland scenes, and they again flow naturally into the main action of the romantic campaign of Charles Edward. The innumerable personal adventures and scenes through which the hero passes, both in Scotland and England, have that combination of lively interest and fresh *out-of-door* humor which is so delightful in Fielding; and it is to the eternal honor of Scott that in spite of the immense variety of incidents and personages with which he brings us in contact, he is entirely free from every trace of that coarseness and immorality which stain the writings of the author of *Tom Jones.* Much of this superior tone of delicacy is doubtless to be attributed to the improvement in public taste which had taken place between the middle of the eighteenth and the beginning of the nineteenth century; but we must not forget that Scott, while successfully escaping, in conformity with the spirit of his age, from the coarseness of tone which marked a former epoch, is equally free from the prevailing error of his own, a morbid and sickly sentimentalism, which often veiled real immorality and more dangerous corruption under the guise of superior delicacy. His sentiments are invariably pure, manly, and elevated, and the spirit of the true gentleman is seen as clearly in his deep sympathy with the virtues of the poor and humble, as in the knightly fervor with which he paints the loftier feelings of the more educated classes.

Guy Mannering is one of the finest of those romances the interest of which is mainly derived from the incidents of private life. The character of Meg Merrilies is truly ideal, without the least overstepping the boundary of nature and probability: and the fellow-feeling of the great artist with the general sentiments of his race is visible in the redeeming qualities with which he invests even his most abandoned and flagitious personages, as Dick Hatteraick the smuggler, and even Glossin himself. The power of picturesque delineation was never more powerfully shown than in the multitude of descriptions in this powerful tale; and the mixture of the serious and humorous, the romantic and familiar, makes it one of the most truly characteristic of Scott. Dominie Sampson is a creation worthy of the greatest humorist that ever wrote.

The *Antiquary* is another admirable novel of familiar Scottish life. The character of Monkbarns, though certainly drawn from a real person, is an example of the most consummate art in idealizing matter-of-fact. It bears the same relation, for instance, to one of Galt's carefully elaborated transcripts of Scottish character, that a portrait by Reynolds does to a photograph. The scene of the danger and escape of Sir Arthur Wardour and his daughter, when nearly overwhelmed by the tide, is one of the most highly-wrought yet natural in fiction and the reader who will carefully examine this passage will be surprised at the impressive effect produced by the simplest means. The dinner at the cœnobitium of Monkbarns, and the scene of the seizure of the castle by Sir Arthur's creditors, are intensely humorous and intensely real at the same time: and the funeral of the young fisherman and the death of the conscience-haunted old crone are among the simplest and most powerful effects of fiction.

Rob Roy, among the novels, occupies a somewhat similar place to that of the *Lady of the Lake* among the poems. In this tale Scott brings into contact the wild and picturesque life of the Highlands, and the manners of the North of England and the burgess-life of Glasgow. The hero, the Robin Hood of Scotland, is a most impressive delineation; and the skill with which the humors of Baillie Jarvie are interwoven with the stirring and tragic scenes of mountaineer life exhibits Scott's extraordinary powers when following out a story which interested him, not only as an artist, but as an antiquarian in Scottish national legend. The attack on the English detachment in the defile, and the tremendous vengeance of Helen Macgregor on the cowardly spy Morris, is one of the most powerfully conceived scenes.

§ 8. Several of the novels of Scott appeared connected together in different series, and, by an expedient often adopted to give an air of authenticity to fictitious compositions, their authorship is attributed to an imaginary writer. Thus the *Black Dwarf* and *Old Mortality* form the First Series of the *Tales of My Landlord*, the manuscript of which is supposed to have been left with a country innkeeper by Peter Pattieson, a village schoolmaster, the fictitious author; the Second Series containing the *Heart of Midlothian*, and the Third the two tales of the *Bride of Lammermoor* and the *Legend of Montrose.* The fiction of Peter Pattieson is not one of the happiest, though it has given the author the opportunity for some charming descriptive passages in the introductory part. The *Black Dwarf* contains inimitable pictures of Border life and scenery; and the first appearance of the wild and terrific personage who gives a title to the tale is striking in the highest degree — not the less so when we know that the details are borrowed from a real outcast and misanthrope; but the entrance, in the last scene, of the dwarf in his real character of Sir Edward Manley, to forbid the marriage, is singularly cold and ineffective. The Timon-like recluse of Mucklestane Muir is a far more impressive personage, and as long as he is kept in the mysterious half-light of obscurity he fills the reader with terror and curiosity. The Border moss-trooper, Willie of the Westburnflat, is a sketch of consummate vigor.

Old Mortality is one of the vastest, completest, and most vivid pictures of an historical epoch that Scott has produced. The contrast between the gallant yet persecuting Cavaliers and the gloomy fanatical

Covenanters is very finely and dramatically maintained. The two skilfully opposed personages of Claverhouse and Burley exhibit the author's unrivalled power of seizing and reproducing past ages. His knowledge, both in detail and in its general character, of the epoch which he painted, was immense, and in the vast variety of subordinate characters which crowd his canvas, the wild preachers, Serjeant Bothwell, Major Morton, the old lady of Tillitudlem, we see a truly Shakspearian richness of humor and invention. The scene in the hut after the defeat of the Covenanters, when they are preparing to put to death young Morton, is one of the highest efforts of breathless dramatic interest. Scott is accused of allowing his strong Tory and Episcopalian prejudices to color his portraiture of the two parties, and of painting Claverhouse in too favorable, and the persecuted Whigs in too gloomy a tone; but we must not forget the never-failing air of general truth which pervades his pictures, nor the fact that while he certainly does full justice to the stern patriotism and fervent though mistaken piety of the victims, the qualities of the dominant party were in themselves more picturesque and engaging than those of their opponents. The portrait of a sombre Puritan may indeed be admirable as a picture, but the eye will infallibly rest with more complacency on a knight or courtier by Velasquez.

In the *Heart of Midlothian* the interest is almost exclusively of a domestic kind, and concentrated on the sufferings of a humble peasant family: for though the Porteous riot, with which the tale opens, is to a certain degree historical, and is related with Scott's unfailing animation and vividness, the reader's feelings are principally enlisted in favor of the heroism of Jeanie Deans and the fate of her unhappy sister. That heroism, as is well known, was no invention, but a real transcript from the annals of humble life: but the weary pilgrimage of Jeanie, though founded upon the self-devotion of a real Helen Walker, is none the less powerfully narrated, and no less powerfully seizes on our sympathies. Her adventures on her journey to London, and in particular the scenes with Madge Wildfire, are of a high order of fiction — at once real and intense.

The *Bride of Lammermoor* is the most tragic and gloomy in its tone of Scott's earlier romances, which are generally characterized, like all his writings, by a gay, hopeful, and cheering tone of thought. The incidents on which it is founded were drawn from the annals of an ancient Scottish family. This story is perhaps one of the most impressive of them all: there reigns throughout, from the first page to the last painful catastrophe, a sort of atmosphere of sorrow and foreboding, that weighs upon the mind like the breathless pause that presages the hurricane. The action has been compared to that of the Greek tragedy. Fate, cruel and irresistible destiny, overshadows the whole horizon, and the innocent are hurried onward to their doom by the uncontrolled force of a pitiless fatality. The personage of the Master of Ravenswood is in a high degree impressive in its melancholy grandeur; and terror and pity are powerfully combined in the concluding scenes. The death of the hero, though described with extreme simplicity, is pathetic in the extreme, and the finding of the plume of his lost master by the faithful Caleb, "who dried it and placed it in his bosom," is a touch of intense and natural pathos.

The *Legend of Montrose* is chiefly admirable for the inexhaustible humor of Dugald Dalgetty, whose selfishness, pedantry, and military quaintness render him one of the most amusing personages in fiction. This was a character after Scott's own heart, and being profoundly true not only to general nature but to particular individuality, we can easily understand the delight with which the author must have traced out its oddities and held it up in every light and attitude.

§ 9. *Ivanhoe* was the first romance in which Scott undertook the delineation of a remote historical epoch. That which he selected was the eventful period when the process of fusion was going on which ultimately united the Norman oppressors and the Saxon serfs into one nationality. The whole tale is a dazzling succession of feudal pictures: the outlaw life of the green wood, the Norman donjon, the lists, the tournament, and the stake, pass before our eyes with a splendor and animation that are truly magical, and make us forget the occasional anachronisms and errors of costume. Robin Hood, under the name of Locksley, is most felicitously introduced, and the chivalric Lion-heart is powerfully contrasted with the meanness and tyranny of John. It has always struck me as a strong proof of the inherent nobility of Scott's nature, that while faithfully representing all the base and odious features of this wretch's character, he still preserves the princely character, and makes John, though a coward, an ingrate, and a tyrant, retain the external manners of his royal blood. The personage of Rebecca is one of the most beautiful and ideal in fiction; Scott is said to have considered it as his finest female character; and the heroism is never made incompatible either with probability or with what may be called historical verisimilitude. The drinking scene between the Black Knight and the jolly Hermit is full of humor and rollicking gayety, and the whole description of the Passage of Arms at Ashby is like an illuminated MS. of the Middle Ages. The scene of the execution of the Jewess carries the reader's interest up to the highest point.

The two stories of the *Monastery* and the *Abbot* form an uninterrupted series of adventures. The life and manners of the times are painted with surprising force and variety: and the character of Mary Stuart predominates throughout the whole picture in all the grace and attractiveness of its charms and of its misfortunes. The chivalrous and noble nature of Scott shines out brilliantly in every page of these stories; and we hardly blame him for the somewhat misplaced and melodramatic introduction in the former romance of the supernatural interposition of the White Lady of Avenel. The scenes of Mary's captivity at Lochleven, and her escape, are intensely interesting: and the characters of the two brothers Glendinning, the Knight and the Priest, are very picturesquely contrasted.

Kenilworth paints, and with great vigor, the age of Elizabeth. The misfortunes of Amy Robsart ultimately culminate in a catastrophe almost too painful: but the characters of the Lion-Queen and her court stand out as in the historical dramas of Shakspeare. Perhaps there are few scenes more picturesque and telling than the forced reconciliation of Leicester and Essex in the Queen's presence; and her behavior, both there and on all the occasions when she appears, is consonant not only with abstract female nature, but is exquisitely appropriated to the particular nature of that great Princess. The episode of Wayland Smith is a melancholy example of the indiscriminate greediness with which a novelist is apt to press everything into his service: the transformation of the grand and mythical Dædalus of Scandinavian mythology into the cheat and quacksalver of the sixteenth century is extremely unfortunate: but it is more than compensated for by the touching episode of old Sir Walter Robsart's despair at the elopement of his daughter.

In the enchanting tale of the ***Pirate*** Scott gives us the fruits of a pleasure expedition which he had taken to the Northern Archipelago: the wild, simple, half-Scandinavian manners of that region furnished him with fresh and unhackneyed *dramatis personæ*, which he placed amid scenery then almost unknown, and possessing a powerful interest. The two sisters, Minna and Brenda, are among the most graceful and highly finished of his female portraits; and Norna of the Fitful Head is a creation of the same order as Meg Merrilies, though certainly inferior on the whole. The description of the wreck of the 'Revenge' is very powerfully written; and the festivities in the house of the glorious old Udaller are painted with unflagging verve. This novel offers two examples of injudicious harping upon one topic — a fault which Scott, like many other novelists, occasionally falls into. Claude Halcro, with his eternal recollections of Dryden, is singularly out of place in the Orkneys, though not more so than Jack Bunce, with his flighty manners and quotations from rhyming tragedies, among the ruffian crew of the pirate. Goffe, however, is a little sketch of consummate merit.

§ **10.** London in the reign of James I., the London of Shakspeare, was the scene of the excellent novel of *Nigel*. The character of the King is as fine and as complete as anything that Scott had hitherto done. The scenes in Alsatia, the drinking-bout at Duke Hildebrod's, and the murder of the old usurer in Whitefriars, are inimitably good. It is true that the junction between the two plots in this novel is not very artificial, and the catastrophe is both hurried and improbable; but these defects are more than counterbalanced by the astonishing force and brilliancy of particular scenes.

Peveril of the Peak is principally defective in the melodramatic and unsatisfactory parts played by Christian, the evil genius of the story, and the strange dumb dancing-girl who is made the instrument of his long-cherished revenge. These mysterious figures harmonize but ill with the gay and profligate court of Charles II. and with the somewhat prosaic details of the Popish conspiracy and the intrigues of Buckingham. The old cavalier Peveril is well contrasted with the gloomy and brooding republican Major Bridgenorth; but Scott, in this novel, has retained too much of his naturally chivalrous and mediæval tone, which is discordant when recurring amid the trivialities and Frenchified debauchery of a period which was in all essentials the very reverse of chivalric. The antithetical and epigrammatic mode in which Buckingham is described, though admirable in Dryden's satire, is quite contrary to the spirit of narrative fiction: and the dwarf, Geoffrey Hudson, is an unnatural excrescence on the story.

The striking and picturesque scenes and manners of the time of Louis XI., and the opposition of the two strongly-contrasted personages of that perfidious tyrant and Charles the Bold of Burgundy, render *Quentin Durward* a most fascinating story, in spite of the anachronisms and falsifications of historical truth; and many of the scenes, as the revelry of the Boar of Ardennes in the Bishop's palace at Liège, are executed with wonderful force and animation. The reception of the Burgundian declaration of war by Louis in the midst of his court, and the supper at which he receives Crevecœur, while the archer is secretly posted with his loaded musket behind the screen, are examples of Scott's peculiar power of delineation.

In *St. Ronan's Well* the principal plot is of so gloomy, painful, and hopeless a character that the reader follows it with reluctance. The general cloud of sorrow and suffering is perhaps not darker in this novel than in the Bride of Lammermoor; but in the latter that sorrow is elevated by dignity and picturesque association, while in this almost all the persons are as odious as they are commonplace. The Earl of Etherington, the villain of the story, is less of a nobleman than of a swindler and a blackguard, and the hopeless persecution of Clara is never relieved by a single gleam of sunshine. Nevertheless the story contains, among the twaddling and prosaic crowd which is assembled at the Spa, one of those characteristic and perfectly-drawn Scottish figures in which this great author had no rival. Meg Dods is more than enough to compensate for the coarse brutality of some of the characters, and the frivolity of the others. Scott's peculiar powers seem to have deserted him when he attempted to delineate the affectations and absurdities of contemporary fashionable or would-be fashionable society.

Redgauntlet is the only novel in which Scott has adopted the epistolary form of narration. The letters in which the narrative is couched express very agreeably the strongly-opposed character of the two young friends; and in the portions supposed to be written by Alan Fairford, the young Edinburgh advocate, we find many charming recollections of the author's early life. The old Writer, his father, is, in all probability, a portrait of Scott's own father; and his adventures, when wandering in search of his friend, bring him in contact with things and persons delineated with extraordinary force; old Summertrees, with his story of his escape, and above all Nanty Ewart, the smuggling captain, and his narrative of his own life, are masterpieces. I may also mention the admirable ghost story related by the old fiddler, than which nothing was ever more impressive. Darsie Latimer, like most of Scott's heroes, is rather too much of the walking gentleman, little more than a mere tool in the hands of more powerful plotters.

§ **11.** The two novels the *Betrothed* and the *Talisman* constitute the series entitled *Tales of the Crusaders*. In them the author returns to those feudal times of which he was so unrivalled a painter. The *Betrothed* is far inferior to its companion: perhaps the scene of the action — the Marches of the Welsh Border — and the conflict between the Wild Celts and the Norman frontier garrison — was in itself less attractive both to reader and writer: true it is, that with the exception of some vigorous and stirring scenes, as for example the desperate sally and death of Raymond Berenger amid the swarms of the Celtic savages who are beleaguering his castle, this tale is read with less pleasure and returned to with less avidity than any except the lates productions of Scott's pen. The *Talisman*, on the contrary, is one of the most dazzling and attractive of them all: the heroic splendo. of the scenery, personages, and adventures, the admirable contrast between Cœur de Lion and Saladin, and the magnificent contrast of the chivalry of Europe with the heroism and civilization of the East, — all this makes the *Talisman* a book equally delightful to the young and to the old. The introduction of familiar and even of comic details, with which Scott, like Shakspeare, knew how to relieve and set off his heroic pictures, renders this story peculiarly delightful. We seem to be brought near to the great and historic characters, and admitted as it were into their private life; we see that they are men like ourselves. The incidents in which the noble hound so picturesquely figures show how deep were Scott's sympathy with and knowledge of animal nature. There are few of his novels in which by some exquisite touch of description or some pathetic stroke of fidelity he does not interest us in the fate and character of dogs as profoundly as in the human persons. Fangs in Ivanhoe, Bevis in Woodstock, the Peppers and Mustards of Charlie's Hope, even the pointer Juno who runs away with the Antiquary's buttered toast, — every one of these animals has its distinctive physiognomy; and we cannot wonder that Scott himself was as fond of real dogs as he makes us interested in his imaginary canine personages.

The action of *Woodstock* is placed just after the fatal defeat at Worcester; and Cromwell and Charles II. both appear in the action. The interest, however, is really concentrated upon the noble figure of the chivalrous old royalist gentleman Sir Henry Lee. The lofty qualities of this cavalier patriarch are so well and so naturally tempered with weaknesses and foibles, that the character is truly living and real. Many of the subordinate scenes and characters, too, as Jocelyn the ranger, Wildrake, the plotting Dr. Rochecliffe, even Phœbe and the old woman, are ever fresh and interesting. The *euthanasia* of the old knight, amid the full triumph of the Restoration, is a scene powerfully and pathetically conceived, and may bear a comparison with that almost sublime passage, the description of the death of Mrs. Witherington in the Surgeon's Daughter. Cromwell and Charles have not been so successfully treated: the one has been unduly lowered, the other as unduly elevated, by the strong political partialities of the author.

§ 12. The *Chronicles of the Canongate* contain the short tales of the *Highland Widow*, the *Two Drovers*, and the novels of the *Surgeon's Daughter* and the *Fair Maid of Perth.* By a fiction like that of Peter Pattieson, the imaginary author of the *Tales of My Landlord*, these were supposed to be the production of Chrystal Croftangry, a retired Scottish gentleman, whose life had been full of agitation. The introductory portion, describing the life of this person, and the causes which led him to try his skill in authorship, are very agreeably written, and contain one most pathetic incident; but we see throughout in this part, as well as in the tales, a somewhat melancholy and desponding tone of thought, which may partly be ascribed to the approach of old age, but still more probably to the influence of Scott's personal calamities. The two first stories are comparatively insignificant; but the *Surgeon's Daughter* is in its general incidents and characters so sombre and gloomy that the impression it leaves is far from agreeable. The hero, Richard Middlemas, is a villain of such mean and ignoble calibre, and the innocent are throughout pursued by such hopeless and unmitigated misfortune, that the effect of the whole is unpleasing. The latter portion of the incidents takes place in India, in which country Scott does not appear at home: the descriptions read as if they had been got up out of books.

The *Fair Maid of Perth* is a romantic and half-historical picture from an interesting period of the early Scottish annals. The great defect of the story is the hazardous and unsuccessful novelty of representing the hero Conachar — or rather one of the heroes, for perhaps the Smith is the real protagonist — as a coward; an expedient that has more of novelty than felicity to recommend it. Novelists have indeed succeeded tolerably well with a plain, nay, even with an ugly heroine; but a cowardly hero — even though his poltroonery be represented as a sort of congenital disease or weakness — is what never did and never can be made interesting. And this is the more unfortunate when we think of the period of the story, the nation, the age, and the position of Conachar; the young chief of a Highland clan, in the wildest and most warlike age of Scottish history. The Smith is, however, one of Scott's happy characters, and the scene of the combat between the two clans is painted with something of the same fire that glows in Marmion and in the Lady of the Lake. Henbane Dwining, the potticarrier, though powerfully conceived, is a sort of anachronism in the story, and the assassination of the Duke of Rothsay, as a scene of horror, is not to be compared with the murder of old Trapbois in *Nigel.*

Anne of Geierstein afforded the opportunity of contrasting the wild nature and simple manners of the Swiss patriots with the feudal splendor of the Court of Burgundy. The reception of the Shepherd ambassador by Charles in his *cour plenière* is a piece of magnificent painting: the execution of de Hagenbach and the rout of Nancy are also very powerfully given : but we confess that the scene of the Vehm-tribunal, though carefully worked up, has something of an artificial and theatrical effect.

In the two last novels written by this mighty creator, ***Count Robert of Paris*** and *Castle Dangerous*, we see, with pity and respect, the last feeble runnings of this bright and abundant fountain, soon to be choked up forever. The scenes and descriptions have the air of being painfully worked up from books, the characters are conventional and without individuality, the dialogues are long and pointless, and nothing remains of the great master's manner but that free, honest, pure, and noble spirit of thought and feeling which never deserted him.

In the delineation of character, as well as in the painting of external nature, Scott proceeds objectively: his mind was a mirror that faithfully reflected the external surfaces of things. He does not show the profound analysis which penetrates into the internal mechanism of the passions and anatomizes the nature of man, nor does he communicate, like Richardson and Byron, his own personal coloring to the creations of his fancy; but he sets before you so brightly, so transparently, so vividly, all that is necessary to give a distinct idea, that his images remain indelibly in the memory.

CHAPTER XXI.

BYRON, MOORE, SHELLEY, KEATS, CAMPBELL, LEIGH HUNT, AND WALTER SAVAGE LANDOR.

§ 1. LORD BYRON. His life and writings. § 2. *Childe Harold.* § 3. Romantic Tales: The *Giaour, Siege of Corinth, Corsair,* &c. § 4. *Beppo* and the *Vision of Judgment.* The *Island* and other poems. § 5. Dramatic Works: *Manfred* and *Cain. Marino Faliero.* The *Two Foscari. Sardanapalus. Werner.* § 6. *Don Juan.* § 7. THOMAS MOORE. His life and writings. § 8. Translation of Anacreon. *Thomas Little's Works. Odes and Epistles. Irish Melodies. National Airs. Sacred Songs.* § 9. Political lampoons: the *Fudge Family in Paris.* § 10. *Lalla Rookh* and the *Loves of the Angels.* § 11. Prose works. The *Epicurean,* and *Biographies of Sheridan, Byron,* and *Lord Edward Fitzgerald.* § 12. PERCY BYSSHE SHELLEY. His life. § 13. *Queen Mab. Alastor. Revolt of Islam. Hellas.* The *Witch of Atlas. Prometheus Unbound.* The *Cenci.* § 14. *Rosalind and Helen.* The *Sensitive Plant.* § 15. JOHN KEATS. His life and writings. § 16. THOMAS CAMPBELL. His life and writings. § 17. LEIGH HUNT. His life and writings. § 18. WALTER SAVAGE LANDOR. His life and writings.

§ 1. THE immense influence exerted by Byron on the taste and sentiment of Europe has not yet passed away, and though far from being so supreme and despotic as it once was, is not likely to be ever effaced. He called himself, in one of his poems, "the grand Napoleon of the realms of rhyme;" and there is some similarity between the suddenness and splendor of his literary career and the meteoric rise and domination of the First Bonaparte. They were both, in their respective departments, the offspring of revolution; and both, after reigning with absolute power for some time, were deposed from their supremacy, though their reign will leave profound traces in the history of the nineteenth century. GEORGE GORDON, LORD BYRON (1788–1824), was born in London in 1788, and was the son of an unprincipled profligate and of a Scottish heiress of ancient and illustrious extraction, but of a temper so passionate and uncontrolled that it reached, in its capricious alternations of fondness and violence, very nearly to the limit of insanity. Her dowry was speedily dissipated by her worthless husband; and the lady, with her boy, was obliged to retire to Aberdeen, where they lived for several years in very straitened circumstances. The future poet inherited from his mother a susceptibility almost morbid, which such a kind of early training must have still further aggravated. His personal beauty was remarkable; but that fatality that seemed to poison in him all the good gifts of fortune and nature, in giving him "a head that sculptors loved to model," afflicted him with a slight malformation in one of his feet, which was ever a source of pain and mortification to his vanity. He was about eleven years old when the death of his grand-uncle, a strange, eccentric, and misanthropic recluse, mad him heir-presumptive to the baronial title of one of the most ancient aristocratic houses in England — a house which had figured in our history from the time of the Crusades, and had been for several generations notorious for the vices and even crimes of its representatives. With the title he inherited large though embarrassed estates, and the noble, picturesque residence of Newstead Abbey, near Nottingham. This sudden change in the boy's prospects of course relieved both mother and child from the pressure of almost sordid poverty; and he was sent first to Harrow School, and afterwards to Trinity College, Cambridge. At school he distinguished himself by his moody and passionate character, and by the romantic intensity of his youthful friendships. Precocious in everything, he had already felt with morbid violence the sentiment of love. At college he became notorious for the irregularities of his conduct, for his contempt for academical discipline, and for his friendship with several young men of splendid talents, but sceptical principles. He was a greedy though desultory reader, and his imagination appears to have been especially attracted to Oriental history and travels.

It was while at Cambridge that Byron made his first literary attempt, in the publication of a small volume of fugitive poems entitled *Hours of Idleness, by Lord Byron, a Minor.* This collection, though in no respect inferior to the youthful essays of ninety-nine out of every hundred young men, was seized upon and most severely critcised in the Edinburgh Review, a literary journal then just commencing that career of brilliant innovation which rendered it so formidable. The judgment of the reviewer as to the total want of value in the poems was perfectly just; but the unfairness consisted in so powerful a journal invidiously going out of its way to attack such a very humble production as a volume of feeble and pretentious commonplaces written by a young lord. The criticism, however, threw Byron into a frenzy of rage. He instantly set about taking his revenge in the satire, *English Bards and Scotch Reviewers*, in which he involved in one common storm of invective not only his enemies of the Edinburgh Review, but almost all the literary men of the day — Walter Scott, Moore, and a thousand others, from whom he had received no provocation whatever. He soon became ashamed of his unreasoning and indiscriminate violence; tried, but vainly, to suppress the poem; and became indeed, in after life, the friend and sincere admirer of many of those whom he had lampooned in this burst of youthful retaliation. Though written in the classical, declamatory, and regular style of Gifford, himself an imitator of Pope, the *English Bards* shows a fervor and power of expression which enables us to see in it, dimly, the earnest of Byron's intense and fiery genius, which was afterwards to exhibit itself under such different literary forms.

Byron now went abroad to travel, and visiting countries then little frequented, and almost unknown to English society, he filled his mind with the picturesque life and scenery of Greece, Turkey, and the East;

and accumulated those stores of character and description which he poured forth with such royal splendor in his poems. The two first cantos of *Childe Harold* absolutely took the public by storm, and carried the enthusiasm for Byron's poetry to a pitch of frenzy of which we have now no idea, and at once placed him at the summit of social and literary popularity. These were followed in rapid and splendid succession by those romantic tales, written somewhat upon the plan which Scott's poems had rendered so fashionable, the *Giaour*, *Bride of Abydos*, *Corsair*, *Lara*. As Scott had drawn his material from feudal and Scottish life, Byron broke up new ground in describing the manners, scenery, and wild passions of the East and of Greece — a region as picturesque as that of his rival, as well known to him by experience, and as new and fresh to the public he addressed. Returning to England in the full blaze of his dawning fame, the poet became the lion of the day. His life was passed in fashionable frivolities, and he drained, with feverish avidity, the intoxicating cup of fame. He at this period married Miss Milbanke, a lady of considerable expectations; but the union was an unhappy one, and domestic disagreements were embittered by improvidence and debt. In about a year Lady Byron, by the advice of her family, and of many distinguished lawyers who were consulted on the subject, suddenly quitted her husband; and the reasons for taking this step will ever remain a mystery. The scandal of the separation deeply wounded the poet, who to the end of his life asserted that he never knew the real motive of the divorce; and the society of the fashionable world, passing with its usual caprice from exaggerated idolatry to as exaggerated hostility, pursued its former darling with a furious howl of reprobation. He again left England; and from thenceforth his life was passed uninterruptedly on the Continent, in Switzerland, in Greece, and at Rome, Pisa, Ravenna, and Venice, where he solaced his embittered spirit with misanthropical attacks upon all that his countrymen held sacred, and gradually plunged deeper and deeper into a slough of sensuality and vice. While at Geneva he produced the third canto of *Childe Harold*, the *Prisoner of Chillon*, *Manfred*, and the *Lament of Tasso*. Between 1818 and 1821 he was principally residing at Venice and Ravenna; and at this period he wrote *Mazeppa*, the first five cantos of *Don Juan*, and most of his tragedies, as *Marino Faliero*, *Sardanapalus*, the *Two Foscari*, *Werner*, *Cain*, and the *Deformed Transformed*, in many of which the influence of Shelley's literary manner and philosophical tenets is more or less traceable; and here too he terminated *Don Juan*, at least as far as it ever was completed. The deep profligacy of his private life in Italy, which had undermined his constitution as well as degraded his genius, was in some measure redeemed by an illegitimate, though not ignoble connection with the young Countess Guiccioli, a beautiful and accomplished girl, united by a marriage of family interest with a man old enough to be her grandfather. In 1823, Byron, who had deeply sympathized with revolutionary efforts in Italy, and was wearied with the companionship of Leigh Hunt and others who surrounded him, determined to devote his fortune and his influence in aid of the Greeks, then struggling for their independence. He arrived at Missolonghi at the beginning of 1824; and after giving striking indications of his practical talents, as well as of his ardor and self-sacrifice, he succumbed under the marsh fever of that unhealthy region, rendered still more deleterious by the excesses which had ruined his constitution. He died, amid the lamentations of the Greek patriots, whose benefactor he had been, and amid the universal sorrow of civilized Europe, on the 19th of April, 1824, at the early age of thirty-six.

§ 2. The plan of *Childe Harold*, though well adapted for the purpose of introducing descriptive and meditative passages, and carrying the reader through widely-distant scenes, is not very probable or ingenious. It is a series of gloomy but intensely poetical monologues, put into the mouth of a jaded and misanthropic voluptuary, who takes refuge from his disenchantment of pleasure in the contemplation of the lovely or historical scenes of travel. The first canto principally describes Portugal and Spain, and contains many powerful pictures of the great battles which rendered memorable the struggle between those oppressed nationalities, aided by England, against the colossal power of Napoleon. Thus we have the tremendous combat of Talavera, and scenes of Spanish life and manners, as the bull-fight. The second canto carries the wanderer to Greece, Albania, and the Ægean Archipelago; and here Byron gave the first earnest of his unequalled genius in reproducing the scenery and the wild life of those picturesque regions. In the third canto, which is perhaps the finest and intensest in feeling of them all, Switzerland, Belgium, and the Rhine, give splendid opportunities not only for pictures of nature of consummate beauty, but of incidental reflections on Napoleon, Voltaire, Rousseau, and the great men whose glory has thrown a new magic over those enchanting scenes. This canto also contains the magnificent description of the Battle of Waterloo, and bitter and melancholy but sublime musings on the vanity of military fame. In the fourth canto the reader is borne successively over the fairest and most touching scenes of Italy, — Venice, Ferrara, Florence, Rome, and Ravenna, — and not only the immortal dead, but the great monuments of painting and sculpture, are described with an intensity of feeling that had never before been seen in poetry. The poem is written in the nine-lined or Spenserian stanza; and in the beginning of the first canto the poet makes an effort to give something of the quaint and archaic character of the Fairy Queen, by adopting old words, as Spenser had done before him; but he very speedily, and with good taste, throws off the useless and embarrassing restraint. In intensity of feeling, in richness and harmony of expression, and in an imposing tone of gloomy, sceptical, and misanthropic reflection, *Childe Harold* stands alone in our literature; and the freedom and vigor of the flow, both as regards the images and the language, make it one of the most impressive works in literature.

§ 3. The romantic tales of Byron are so numerous that it will be impossible to examine them in detail. They are all marked by similar peculiarities of thought and treatment, though they may differ in the kind and degree of their respective excellences. The *Giaour*, the *Siege of Corinth*, *Mazeppa*, *Parisina*, the *Prisoner of Chillon*, and the *Bride of Abydos* are written in that somewhat irregular and flowing versification which Scott brought into fashion, while the *Corsair*, *Lara*, and the *Island* are in the regular English-rhymed heroic measure. It is difficult to decide which of these metrical forms Byron uses with greater vigor and effect. In the *Giaour*, *Siege of Corinth*, the *Bride*, and *Corsair*, the scene is laid in Greece or the Greek Archipelago; and picturesque contrast between the Christian and Mussulman, as well as the dramatic scenery, manners, and costume of those regions, is powerfully set before the reader. These poems have in general a fragmentary character: they are made up of imposing and intensely interesting *moments* of passion and action. Neither in these nor in any of his works does Byron show the least power of delineating *variety* of character. There are but two personages in all his poems—a man in whom unbridled passions have desolated the heart, and left it hard and impenetrable as the congealed lava-stream, or only capable of launching its concealed fires at moments of strong emotion; a man contemptuous of his kind, whom he rules by the very force of that contempt, sceptical and despairing, yet feeling the softer emotions with an intensity proportioned to the rarity with which he yields to them. The woman is the woman of the East—sensual, devoted, and loving, but loving with the unreasoning attachment of the lower animals. These elements of character, meagre and unnatural as they are, are, however, set before us with such consummate force and intensity, and are framed, so to say, in such brilliant and picturesque surroundings, that the reader, and particularly the young and inexperienced reader, invariably loses sight of their contradictions; and there is a time when all of us have thought the sombre, scowling, mysterious heroes of Byron the very ideal of all that is noble and admirable. Nothing can exceed the skill with which the most picturesque light and shade is thrown upon the features of these Rembrandt-like or rather Tintoretto-like sketches. In all these poems we meet with inimitable descriptions, tender, animated, or profound, which harmonize with the tone of the *dramatis personæ:* thus the famous comparison of enslaved Greece to a corpse in the *Giaour*, the night-scene and the battle-scene in the *Corsair* and *Lara*, the eve of the storming of the city in the *Siege of Corinth*, and the fiery energy of the attack in the same poem, the exquisite opening lines in *Parisina*, besides a multitude of others, might be adduced to prove Byron's extraordinary genius in communicating to his pictures the individuality and the coloring of his own feelings and character—proceeding, in this respect, in a manner precisely opposed to Walter Scott, whose scenes are as it were reflected in a mirror, and take no coloring from the poet's own individuality. If Scott's picturesque faculty be like that of the pure surface of a lake, or the colorless plane of a mirror, that of Byron resembles those tinted glasses which convey to a landscape viewed through them the yellow gleam of a Cuyp, or the sombre gloom of a Zurbaran. *Lara* is undoubtedly the sequel of the *Corsair;* the returned Spanish noble of mysterious adventures is no other than Conrad of the preceding poem, and the disguised page is Gulnare. The *Siege of Corinth* is remarkable for the extraordinary variety and force of its descriptions — a variety greater than will generally be found in Byron's tales. *Parisina* derives its chief interest from the deep pathos with which the author has invested a painful and even repulsive story; and in the *Prisoner of Chillon* the hopeless tone of sorrow and uncomplaining suffering which runs through the whole gives it a strong hold upon the reader's feelings. *Mazeppa*, though founded upon the adventures of an historical person, is singularly and almost ludicrously at variance with the real character of the hero. The powerfully-written episode of the gallop of the wild steed, with the victim lashed on his back, makes the reader forget all incongruities.

§ 4. In *Beppo* and the *Vision of Judgment* Byron has ventured upon the gay, airy, and satirical. The former of these poems is a little episode of Venetian intrigue narrated in singularly easy verse, and exhibiting a minute knowledge of the details of Italian manners and society. It is not perhaps over moral, but it is exquisitely playful and sparkling. The *Vision* is a most severe attack upon Southey, in which Byron vigorously repels the accusations brought by his antagonist against the alleged immorality of his poems, and carries the war into the enemy's country, showing up with unmerciful bitterness the contrast between Southey's former extreme liberalism and his then rabid devotion to Court principles, and parodying the very poor and pretentious verses which Southey, as Poet Laureate, composed as a sort of apotheosis of George III. Though somewhat ferocious and truculent, this satire is brilliant, and contains many picturesque and even beautiful passages· and was certainly, under the circumstances of provocation, a fair and allowable attack. The *Island*, in four cantos, is a striking incident extracted from the narrative of the famous mutiny of the Bounty, when Captain Bligh and his officers were cast off by his rebellious crew in an open boat, and the mutineers, under the command of Christian, established themselves in half-savage life on Pitcairn's Island, where their descendants were recently living. Among the less commonly read of Byron's longer poems I may mention the *Age of Bronze*, a vehement satirical declamation; the *Curse of Minerva*, directed against the spoliation of the frieze of the Parthenon by Lord Elgin, in which the description of sunset, forming the opening of the poem, is inexpressibly beautiful; the *Lament of Tasso* and the *Prophecy of Dante*, the latter written in the difficult *terza rima*, the first attempt, I believe, of any English poet to employ that measure. The *Dream* is in some respects the most complete and touching of Byron's minor works. It is the narrative, in the form of a vision, of his early love-sorrow for Mary Chaworth. There is hardly, in the whole range of literature, so tender, so lofty, and so condensed a life-drama as that narrated in these verses. Picture after picture is softly shadowed forth, all pervaded by the same mournful glow, and "the doom of the two creatures" is set before us in all its hopeless misery.

§ 5. The dramatic works of Byron are in many respects the precise opposite of what might *à priori* have been expected from the peculiar character of his genius. In form they are cold, severe, lofty, partaking far more of the manner of Alfieri than of that of Shakspeare. Artful involution of intrigue they have not, but though singularly destitute of powerful *passion* they are full of intense sentiment. The finest of them is *Manfred*, which, however, is not so much a drama as a dramatic poem, in some degree resembling *Faust*, by which indeed it was suggested. It consists not of action represented in dialogue, but of a series of sublime soliloquies, in which the mysterious hero describes nature, and pours forth his despair and his self-pity. The scene with which it opens has a strong resemblance to the first monologue of Goethe's hero; and the invocation of the Witch of the Alps, the meditation of Manfred on the Jungfrau, the description of the ruins of the Coliseum, are singularly grand and touching as detached passages, but have no dramatic cohesion. In this work, as well as in *Cain*, we see the full expression of Byron's sceptical spirit, and the tone of half-melancholy, half-mocking misanthropy which colors so much of his writings, and which was in him partly sincere and partly put on for effect; for Byron was far from that profound conviction in his anti-religious doctrines which glows so fervently through every page written by his friend Shelley, who unquestionably exerted a very powerful influence upon Byron at one part of his career. The more exclusively historical pieces — *Marino Faliero*, the *Two Foscari* — are derived from Venetian annals; but neither in the one nor in the other has Byron clothed the events with that living and intense reality which the subjects would have received, I will not say from Shakspeare, but even from Rowe or Otway. There is in these dramas a complete failure in variety of character; and the interest is concentrated on the obstinate harping of the principal personages upon one topic — their own wrongs and humiliations. This is indeed at times impressive, and, aided by Byron's magnificent powers of expression, gives us noble occasional tirades; but it is essentially undramatic, for it is inconsistent with that play and mutual action and reaction of one character or passion upon another, in which dramatic interest essentially consists. In *Sardanapalus* the remoteness of the epoch chosen, and our total ignorance of the interior life of those times, remove the piece into the region of fiction. But the character of Myrrha, though beautiful, is an anachronism and an impossibility; and the antithetic contrast between the effeminacy and sudden heroism in Sardanapalus belongs rather to the satire or to the moral disquisition than to tragedy. *Werner*, a piece of domestic interest, is bodily borrowed, as far as regards its incidents, and even much of its dialogue, from the Hungarian's Story in Miss Lee's "Canterbury Tales." It still retains possession of the stage, because, like *Sardanapalus*, it gives a good opportunity for the display of stage decoration and declamation; but Byron's share in its composition extends little farther than the cutting up of Miss Lee's prose into tolerably regular but often very indifferent lines.

§ 6. *Don Juan* is the longest, the most singular, and in some respects the most characteristic, of Byron's poems. It is, indeed, one of the most remarkable and significant productions of the age of revolution and scepticism which almost immediately preceded its appearance It is written in octaves, a kind of versification borrowed from the Italians, and particularly from the half-serious, half-comic writers who followed in the wake of Ariosto. The outline of the story is the old Spanish legend of Don Juan de Tenorio, upon which have been founded so many dramatic works, among the rest the *Festin de Pierre* of Moliere and the immortal opera of Mozart. The fundamental idea of the atheist and voluptuary enabled Byron to carry his hero through various adventures, serious and comic, to exhibit his unrivalled power of description, and left him unfettered by any necessities of time and place. Byron's Don Juan is a young Spanish hidalgo, whose education is described with strong satiric power intermingled with frequent and bitter personal allusions to those against whom the author has a grudge, and being detected in a scandalous intrigue with a married woman, he is obliged to leave Spain. He embarks on board a ship which is wrecked in the Greek Archipelago, all hands perishing after incredible sufferings in an open boat, and is thrown, exhausted and almost dying, on one of the smaller Cyclades. Here he is cherished and sheltered by Haidee, a lovely Greek girl, the half-savage daughter of Lambro, the master of the isle, now absent on a piratical expedition. Haidee and Juan are married, and in the midst of the wedding festivities Lambro returns, Juan is overpowered, wounded, and put on board the pirate's vessel to be carried to Constantinople, and Haidee soon afterwards dies of grief and despair. Juan is exposed for sale in the slave-market at Stamboul, attracts the notice of the favorite Sultana, who buys him, and introduces him in the disguise of an odalisque into the seraglio; but Juan refuses the love of Gulbeyaz, and afterwards escapes from Constantinople in company with Smith, an Englishman whom he has encountered in slavery. The hero is then made to arrive at the siege of Izmail by the Russian army under Souvaroff; the horrible details of the storming and capture of the city are borrowed from official and historical sources, and reproduced with the same fidelity as the pictures of the shipwreck from Admiral Byron's narrative of his own calamities. Juan distinguishes himself in the assault, and is selected to carry the bulletin of victory to the Empress Catherine. The Court of St. Petersburg is then described, and Juan becomes the favorite and lover of the Northern Semiramis; but his health giving way, he is sent on a diplomatic mission to England. Here the author gives us a very minute and sarcastic account of English aristocratic society, and in the midst of what promises to turn out an amusing, though not over moral adventure, the narrative abruptly breaks off. *Don Juan*, in the imperfect state in which it was left, consists of sixteen cantos, and there is no reason why it should not have been indefinitely extended. It was the author's intention to bring his hero's adventures to a regular termination, but so desultory a series of incidents have no real coherency. The merit of this extraordinary poem is the richness of ideas, thoughts, and images, which form an absolute plethora of witty allusion and sarcastic reflection; and above all the constant passage from the loftiest and tenderest tone of poetry to the most familiar and mocking style. These transitions are incessant, and the artifice of such sudden change of sentiment which at first dazzles and enchants the reader, ultimatel wearies him. The tone of morality is throughout very low and selfish even materialistic: everything in turn is made the subject of a sneer and the brilliant but desolating lightning of Byron's sarcasm blasts alike the weeds of hypocrisy and cant, and the flowers of faith and the holiest affections. This Mephistophiles-like tone is rendered more effective by perpetual contrast with the warmest outbursts of feeling and the most admirable descriptions of nature: the air of superiority which is implied in the very nature of sarcasm renders ***Don Juan*** peculiarly dangerous, as it is peculiarly fascinating, to young readers. In spite of much superficial flippancy, this poem contains an immense mass of profound and melancholy satire, and in a very large number of serious passages Byron has shown a power, picturesqueness, and pathos which in other works may indeed be paralleled, but cannot be surpassed.

§ 7. THOMAS MOORE (1779-1852), the personal friend and biographer of Byron, is the most popular of his literary contemporaries. He was born in Dublin, of humble parentage, but through the wise affection of his parents, received as good an education as his extraordinary display of boyish ability seemed to call for. Being a Catholic, many of the avenues to public distinction were then, by the invidious laws that oppressed his country and religion, closed to him; but after distinguishing himself at the University of Dublin he passed over to London, nominally with the intention of studying law in the Temple, but in reality to commence that career as a poet, which was so long and so brilliant. He first appeared before the public as the translator of the *Odes of Anacreon*, a task for which his elegant and varied, though perhaps not very profound, scholarship, rendered him sufficiently fit, while the highly colored and voluptuous style of his version gave an attractive if not very faithful idea of the manner of the Teian bard. This work was published by subscription, and dedicated to the Prince Regent, and immediately introduced Moore into that gay and fashionable society of which he remained all his life a somewhat too assiduous frequenter. He had indeed, both in his personal and poetical character, everything calculated to make him the darling of society; great conversational talents, an agreeable voice, and a degree of musical skill which enabled him to give enchanting effect to the tender, voluptuous, or patriotic songs which he poured forth with such facile abundance. His dignity of character, perhaps, suffered from his passion for the frivolous triumphs of fashionable circles; but Moore was during his whole life the spoiled child of popularity. The only serious check he suffered in his gay career was when he obtained a small government post in the island of Bermuda (1804), which, indeed, enabled him to visit America and the Antilles, and drew from him some of the most elegant and sparkling of his early poems: but he neglected the duties for which he was totally unfit, and, by the dishonesty of a subordinate, exposed himself to serious responsibility, in consequence of the embezzlement of a considerable sum of public money. This claim of the crown, for which he was legally answerable, though no suspicion of irregularity was personally attached to Moore, he afterwards discharged by his literary labor; and nearly the whole of his long life was devoted to the production of a rapid and wonderfully varied succession of compositions, both in prose and verse, some of which obtained an immense and all a respectable success. They may, generally, be divided into lyric productions, serious and comic, the latter principally consisting of political squibs of an entirely original and most enchanting character, nothing like which had till then appeared, narrative poems, the chief of which are the *Lalla Rookh* and the *Loves of the Angels*, a novel, originally intended to be a poem in the epistolary form, entitled the *Epicurean*, and three considerable biographical works, the memoirs of *Sheridan*, of *Byron*, and of the unfortunate Irish patriot *Lord Edward Fitzgerald*. This rapid enumeration gives, of course, only the outline of Moore's very long, very successful, and very well-filled career. It will be requisite presently to enter more into detail when we come to examine his productions. As an Irishman and Catholic Moore was naturally a Whig, "and something more," and the oppression of his country, and the persecution of his faith, suggested not only the most touching and spirit-stirring passages of his patriotic lyrics, but they supplied the biting and yet pleasant sarcasm which seasons his political pasquinades. He spent the latter part of his life in a cottage near Bowood, the residence of the Marquess of Lansdowne, who had cherished his friendship.

§ 8. The poetical, which is also the larger, portion of Moore's writings, consists chiefly of lyrics, whether serious or comic, the most celebrated collection among them being the *Irish Melodies*, of which I shall speak in its proper place, after passing in rapid review his earlier efforts. The version of *Anacreon*, though tolerably faithful in the general rendering of the original, is far too brilliant and ornamental in its language to give a correct idea of the manner of the Greek poet. Moore is indeed not more voluptuous than his original, but Anacreon clothes his voluptuousness of sentiment in a garb of the most exquisite simplicity of expression. His muse is like the lovely nakedness of an undraped antique marble. Moore has adorned the statue with the dazzling but not always sterling decorations of antithesis and modern coloring. In his juvenile poems, as well as in the collection published under the pseudonyme of *Thomas Little*, in the productions suggested by his visit to America and the West Indies, and in the *Odes and Epistles*, we see that ingenious and ever-watchful invention which forms a prominent characteristic of Moore's genius; and also the strongly erotic and voluptuous tendency of sentiment, which is sometimes carried beyond the bounds of good taste and morality. But the voluptuousness of this poet is not of a very dangerous or corrupting nature: it is the result rather of a lively fancy than of a profoundly passionate temperament, and expresses itself in a perpetual sparkle of ingenious allusion and combination of ideas. If wit be properly defined as the power of perceiving relations between objects which to ordinary minds appear incapable of combination, then Moore possesses wit in a very high degree — a degree as high perhaps as Cowley himself: and like Cowley he exhibits this faculty quite as strikingly in his serious as in his comic writings. He is in particular remarkable for the felicity with which he illustrates and adorns his fancies by allusions drawn from apparently remote and unexpected sources: and though he sometimes abuses this kind of ingenuity, which is of course out of place in passages where the poet's aim is to excite deep emotion, yet it is often productive of pleasure and surprise to the reader.

The *Irish Melodies*, a collection of about one hundred and twenty-five songs, were composed in order to furnish appropriate words to a great number of beautiful national airs, some of great antiquity, which had been degraded by becoming gradually associated with lines often vulgar and sometimes even indecent. The music was arranged by Sir John Stevenson, an Irish composer of some merit, and Moore furnished the poetry, which occupied in England and Ireland a somewhat similar position as regards popularity with that of Béranger in France. The themes as well as the airs of these songs are almost entirely national; and when we think of the very narrow repertory of subjects to which the song-writer is necessarily limited, we cannot but admire the extraordinary fertility of invention he has displayed. Patriotism, love, and conviviality form the subject-matter of these charming lyrics: the past glories and sufferings and the future greatness of Ireland are indeed frequently allegorized in many of those lyrics which at first sight appear devoted to love: as the praises of wine and women in the songs of Hafiz are interpreted by orthodox Mahometan critics to signify, esoterically, the raptures of religious mysticism. The versification of these songs has never been surpassed for melody and neatness: indeed, from a simple declamation of many of them, it is easy to guess at the air to which they were intended to be sung. The language is always clear, appropriate, and concise, and sometimes reaches a high degree of majesty, vigor, or tenderness. The pathetic effect is seldom missed, except when the author is led away by his ingenuity to introduce one of those conceits or witty turns, which, by their very epigrammatic cleverness, are destructive of lofty or tender emotion. Though Moore is destitute of the intense feeling of Burns, or of that exquisite sensibility to popular feeling which makes Béranger the darling of the middle and lower classes of France, yet he appeals, as they do, to the universal sentiments of his countrymen, and his popularity is proportionally great. The *Irish Melodies* appeared in a succession of *fasciculi*, and instantly attained an immense popularity: there is not a piano in

England or Ireland upon which they are not to be seen. On a somewhat similar plan Moore composed a considerable number — about seventy — of songs intended to be accompanied by tunes peculiar to various countries. These he called *National Airs*, and they exhibit the same exquisite sensibility to the musical character of the different airs, and the same neatness of expression, as the *Irish Melodies*; but they are naturally inferior to them in intensity of patriotic feeling. In the latter as in the former collection, Moore sometimes fails in his effect by indulging in playful ingenuities of fancy and epigrammatic turns of thought. A small collection of *Sacred Songs* affords frequent examples both of the merits and defects of Moore's lyrical genius, though the latter are perhaps more prominent as destructive occasionally of the lofty religious tone which the subject required him to maintain. None of these collections, however, can be examined without the reader's meeting with many examples of consummate felicity, both in the conception and treatment of song-composition; and they all exhibit a high polish, an almost fastidious finish of style, which, though it sometimes interferes with their effect by giving a sort of artificial and drawing-room refinement, yet certainly makes them models of perfection in thei. peculiar manner.

§ 9. As a Liberal, an Irishman, and a Catholic, Moore naturally felt intense hostility to those bigoted, retrograde, and tyrannical principles which governed for so long a time the policy of England towards his country; and for many years he kept up, generally in the columns of the Opposition newspapers, a constant fire of brilliant and witty lampoons. These were directed against the Tory party in general, and were showered with peculiar vivacity and stinging effect upon the Regent, afterwards George IV., Lord Eldon, Castlereagh, and all those who were opposed to the granting of any relaxation to the Irish Catholics. Moore's political squibs form an era in the history of this class of composition. Instead of the coarse and malignant invective which generally marked, before this time, these party lampoons, the wit of which could not always obtain pardon for their grossness and personality, Moore introduced a tone of good society, an elegance, a playfulness, and an ingenuity which give them a permanent value quite independent of their momentary piquancy. The ingenious way in which out-of-the-way reading and unexpected allusion were brought to bear upon the topics of the day showed the extraordinary fertility of Moore's invention, and the brilliancy of his wit. His *Odes on Cash, Corn, and Catholics*, his *Fables for the Holy Alliance*, show an inexhaustible invention of quaint and ingenious ideas, and the power of bringing the most apparently remote allusions to bear upon the person or thing selected for attack. The sharp and highly-polished shafts of Moore's satire must have inflicted exquisitely painful wounds upon the self-love of his victims; but they were wounds which rendered complaint impossible and retaliation difficult. Some of the most celebrated of these brilliant pasquinades were combined into a sort of story, as for example the *Fudge Family in Paris*, purporting to be a series of letters written from France just at the period of the Restoration of the Bourbons. The authors of the correspondence are Mr. Fudge, a creature of Lord Castlereagh and a kind of political spy, his son Bob, a dandy and epicure of the first water, and his daughter Biddy, a delightful type of the frivolous, romance-reading Miss. The letters of the father give a bitterly ironical picture of the baseness and servility of the triumphant Royalist party, those of the son are a delicious mixture of cookery and dress, and the daughter, in high-flying romantic jargon, describes her adventures with a distinguished-looking stranger with whom she falls in love, under the idea that he is the King of Prussia, then incognito at Paris, but who afterwards turns out, to her infinite horror, to be a linen-draper's shopman. Nothing can be more animated, brilliant, and humorous than the description of the motley life and the giddy whirl of amusement in Paris at that memorable moment; and the whole is seasoned with such a multitude of personal and political allusions, that the *Fudge Family* will probably ever retain its popularity, as both a social and political sketch of a most interesting moment in modern European history.

§ **10.** The longer and more ambitious poems of Moore are *Lalla Rookh* and the *Loves of the Angels*, the former being immeasurably the best, both as regards the interest of the story and the power with which it is treated. The plan of *Lalla Rookh* is original and happy; it consists of a little prose love-tale describing the journey of a beautiful Oriental princess from Delhi to Bucharia, where she is to meet her betrothed husband, the king of the latter country. Great splendor of imagination and immense stores of Eastern reading are lavished on the description of this gorgeous *progress*, and the details of scenery, manners, and ceremonial are given with an almost overpowering luxuriance of painting, artfully relieved by a pleasant epigrammatic humor displayed in the character and criticisms of the princess's pompous and pedantic chamberlain, Fadladeen. For Lalla Rookh's amusement, when stopping for her night's repose, a young Bucharian poet, Feramoz, is introduced, who chants to the accompaniment of his national guitar four separate poems of a narrative character, which are thus, so to say, incrusted in the prose story. The princess becomes gradually enamoured of the interesting young bard, and her growing melancholy continues till her arrival at her future home, where, in the person of her betrothed husband, who comes to meet her in royal pomp, she recognizes the musician who had employed his disguise of a poor minstrel to gain that love which he deserved to enjoy as a monarch. The prose portion of the work is inimitably beautiful; the whole style is sparkling with Oriental gems, and perfumed, as it were, with Oriental musk and roses; and the very abuse of brilliancy and of a voluptuous languor, which in another kind of composition might be regarded as meretricious, only adds to the Oriental effect. The four poems to which the above story forms a setting are the *Veiled Prophet*, the *Fire-Worshippers*, *Paradise and the Peri*, and the *Light of the Harem;* all, of course, of an Eastern character, and the two first in some degree historical in their subject. The longest and most ambitious is the first, which is written in the rhymed heroic couplet, while the others are composed in that irregular animated versification which Walter Scott and Byron had brought into fashion. The *Veiled Prophet* is a story of love, fanaticism, and vengeance, founded on the career of an impostor who made his appearance in Khorassan, and after leading astray numberless dupes by a pretended miraculous mission to overthrow Mahometanism, was at last defeated by the armies of the faithful. He is, in short, a kind of Mussulman Antichrist. The betrayal of the heroine by his diabolical arts, and the voluptuous temptations by which he induces a young Circassian chieftain to join his standard, the recognition of the lovers, and the tragical death of the deceiver and his victims, form the plot of the story; but the gorgeous splendor of the descriptions, and the unvarying richness of Oriental imagery in the style. are the chief qualities of the poem. Its defects are chiefly a too uniform tone of agonized and intense feeling which becomes monotonous and strained, and the want of reality in the characters, the demoniac wickedness of Mokanna being contrasted with the superhuman exaltation of love and sorrow in the lovers. Nor did Moore possess full mastery over the grave and masculine instrument of the heroic versification; and, therefore, despite the astonishing richness of the imagery and descriptions, the poet's peculiar genius is more favorably exhibited in the beautiful songs and lyrics which are occasionally interspersed, as particularly in the scene where Azim is introduced to a kind of foretaste of the joys of Paradise. This portion of the poem is borrowed from the half-fabulous accounts given by historians of the initiation of the celebrated sect of the Assassins. The *Fire-Worshippers* is also a love-story, and is bound up with the cruel persecution by the Turks of the Guebres; but under the disguise of the tyrannical orthodoxy opposed to the patriotic defenders of their country and their faith Moore undoubtedly intended to typify the resistance of the Irish Catholics to the persecuting domination of their English and Protestant oppressors. The love-adventures of Hafed the Guebre chief, and Fatima the daughter of the Mussulman tyrant, are not very original or very new; but some of the descriptions are animated and striking, in spite of a rather over-strained and too emphatic tone. *Paradise and the Peri* is a very graceful apologue, and the scenes in which the exiled fairy seeks for the gift which is to secure her readmission to Heaven are picturesque and varied with great skill. She successively offers as her passport to the regions of bliss the last drop of blood shed by a patriot, the dying sigh of a self-devoted lover, but these are pronounced insufficient; at last she presents the tear of a repentant sinner, which is received by the guardian of the celestial portal as "the gift that is most dear to Heaven." Fanciful and tender to the highest degree, the subject of this little tale is worked out with great variety and picturesqueness of detail; many of the scenes are extremely beautiful, and the whole story has a compactness and completeness which render it very charming. The *Light of the Harem* is a little love-episode between "the magnificent son of Akbar" and his beautiful favorite Nourmahal. A momentary coldness between the lovers is terminated by the instrumentality of a mysterious and lovely enchantress, who evokes the Spirit of Music to furnish Nourmahal with a magic wreath of flowers. This has the power of giving to the voice of its wearer such a superhuman power and persuasiveness, that when she presents herself disguised, to sing before her imperial lover at the Feast of Roses, all his former passion revives, and the *amantium iræ* terminate with a reconciliation. The description of the fair flower-sorceress Namouna, the invocation, and above all the exquisitely varied and highly finished songs which are assigned to the different performers in the festival, all these afford striking examples of the rich, graceful, and deliciously musical, if somewhat fantastic and artificial genius of Moore.

The *Loves of the Angels*, the only remaining poem of any length, need not detain us long. It is manifestly inferior to *Lalla Rookh*, not only in the impracticable nature of its subject, but in the monotony of its treatment. The fundamental idea is based upon that famous and much misunderstood passage of the Book of Genesis, where it is said that in the primeval ages "the sons of God" became enamoured of "the daughters of men," the issue of which connection was the Giants. Moore introduces three of these angels, who by yielding to an earthly love have forfeited the privileges of their celestial nature, and who relate, each in his turn, the story of their passion and its punishment. Independently of the improbability which is inseparable from the idea of an amour between beings so widely dissimilar in their nature, and which is destructive of the reader's interest, the incidents themselves are so little varied that the effect is tiresome in the extreme. This poem was written during Moore's retirement to Paris, and bears some traces of the influence of Byron's somewhat similar, and not much more successful production, *Heaven and Earth*, which was in its turn generated to a certain degree by the writings of Shelley.

§ **11.** The chief prose works of Moore are the three biographies of Sheridan, Byron, and Lord Edward Fitzgerald, and the tale of the *Epicurean*, the last intended originally to appear as a poem, but re-written in prose. It is a narrative of the first ages of Christianity, and describes the conversion, under the influence of love, of a young Athenian philosopher, who travels into Egypt, and is initiated into the mysterious worship of Isis. The descriptions are sometimes animated and picturesque, but there is a languor and vagueness in the characters and in the conduct of the story, which will prevent this production from obtaining a very permanent popularity. Moore's biographies, particularly that of Byron, are of great value: indeed his memoir of his illustrious friend and fellow-poet is the best that has yet appeared. It is particularly valuable from consisting, as far as possible, of extracts from Byron's own journals and correspondence, so that the subject of the biography is delineated in his own words, Moore furnishing little more than the arrangement and the connecting matter. Byron himself furnished the materials for the biography which he desired Moore to undertake; and it is delightful to see the cordial and appreciating way in which he, though a rival poet, speaks of the genius and character of his glorious contemporary.

§ **12.** The life of Shelley presents many points of similarity with that of Byron, as well in great natural advantages, poisoned and rendered nugatory by untoward circumstances, as in unhappy domestic relations, and avowed hostility to society, forcing him to pass a great portion of his life in exile, and finally in constant revolt against religious and social opinion. PERCY BYSSHE SHELLEY (1792–1821) was of an ancient and opulent family, the eldest son of Sir Timothy Shelley, and was born at Field Place, near Horsham, in Sussex, August 4, 1792. He exhibited from his early childhood an intense and almost morbid sensibility, together with a strong inclination towards sceptical and antisocial speculation, which gradually ripened into atheism. At Eton his sensitive mind was shocked by the sight of boyish tyranny, and he went to Oxford full of abhorrence for the cruelty and bigotry which he fancied pervaded all the relations of civilized life. An eager and desultory student, he rapidly filled his mind with the sceptical arguments against Christianity; and convinced that the concealment of his opinions was unworthy of the dignity of a philosopher, he published a tract in which he boldly avowed atheistic principles. Refusing to retract these opinions, he was expelled from the University; and this scandal, together with a marriage he contracted with a beautiful girl, his inferior in rank, caused him to be renounced by his family. This runaway match was an unhappy one, and the young enthusiast resided, in great poverty, at various places in the North of England and in Wales, ardently devoting himself to metaphysical study and to the composition of his first wild but beautiful poems. He separated from his wife, who afterwards terminated her existence in a melancholy manner by suicide, and contracted during his wife's lifetime a new connection with the daughter of Godwin; and having induced his family to make him a considerable annual allowance, his life was from thenceforth relieved from pecuniary difficulties. The delicate state of his health rendered it advisable that he should leave England for a warmer climate, and the remainder of his life was passed abroad, with only one short interruption. In Switzerland he became acquainted with Byron, and the ardor of his character and the splendor of his genius undoubtedly exerted a powerful influence on his mighty contemporary. Indeed the brilliancy of Shelley's eloquence, and the boldness of his doctrines, appear to have exercised an extraordinary fascination on all who were brought within its circle. His abhorrence of what he looked upon as the social tyranny of law and custom was carried to a still higher pitch by a decision of the Court of Chancery, depriving the poet of the guardianship of his children. This has been stigmatized by Shelley's admirers as an act of odious bigotry; but it should be recollected that when he deserted his wife she took refuge with her father, and that the latter, after his daughter's death, naturally refused to surrender his grandchildren to a man who had been guilty of a great and cruel crime against his family, and who proclaimed his intention of educating his children in his own irreligious opinions. He now migrated to Italy, where he kept up an intimate companionship with Byron, still continuing to pour forth his strange and enchanting poetry in indefatigable profusion. He resided principally at Rome, and produced there many of his finest productions. His death was early and tragic. His passion had always been boating; and returning in a small yacht from Leghorn, in company with a friend and a single boatman, his vessel was caught in a squall and went down with all on board in the Gulf of Spezzia. Thus perished this great poet, at the age of thirty. His body was cast up on the coast some days after, and burned after the manner of the ancients by Byron and Leigh Hunt. His ashes were interred in the beautiful cemetery near the tomb of Cæcilia Metella at Rome.

§ 13. Shelley was all his life, both as a poet and as a man, a dreamer, a visionary: his mind was filled with glorious but unreal phantoms of the possible perfectibility of mankind. So ardent was his sympathy with his kind, and so intense his abhorrence of the corruption and suffering he saw around him, that the very intensity of that sympathy clouded his reason; and he fell into the common error of all enthusiasts, of supposing that, if the present organization of society were swept away, a millennium of virtue and happiness must ensue. He traced the misery and degradation of mankind to the institutions of religion, of government, and of marriage, and not to those passions which these institutions are intended, however imperfectly, to restrain. As a poet he was undoubtedly gifted with genius of a very high order, an immense, though somewhat vaporous richness and fertility of imagination, an intense fire and energy in the reproduction of what he conceived, and a command over all the resources of metrical harmony such as no English poet has surpassed. He began to write almost from his childhood, and his first attempts were tales in prose, which have not been preserved. His poetical career commences with *Queen Mab*, a wild phantasmagoria of beautiful description and fervent declamation, written in that irregular unrhymed versification of which Southey's Thalaba is an example. The defect of this poem, as indeed of many of Shelley's other compositions, is a vagueness of meaning which often becomes absolutely unintelligible. Lovely, ideal, but cloudy images are continually evoked; but they flit before us like the "shadow of a dream." The notes appended to *Queen Mab* exhibit the full audacity of Shelley's scepticism: his arguments, however, are little else but repetitions of the sneers of Voltaire, and the objections, many of them entirely sophistical, of preceding antagonists of Christianity.

Perhaps the finest, as it is the completest and most distinct, of Shelley's longer poems, is *Alastor, or the Spirit of Solitude*, in which he depicts the sufferings of such a character as his own, a being of the warmest sympathies, and of the loftiest aspirations, driven into solitude and despair by the ingratitude of his kind, who are incapable of understanding and sympathizing with his aims. The descriptions in this poem are inimitably beautiful: woodland and river scenery are depicted with a wealth of tropic luxuriance that places Shelley in the foremost rank among the pictorial poets; and the voyage of Alastor into his forest retreat is a passage which it would be difficult to parallel This poem is written in blank verse.

The *Revolt of Islam*, *Hellas*, and the *Witch of Atlas* are works which belong, more or less, to the category of Queen Mab — violent invectives against kingcraft, priestcraft, religion, and marriage, alternating with airy and exquisite pictures of scenes and beings of superhuman and unearthly splendor. The defect of these poems is the extreme obscurity of their general drift. Though particular objects stand out with the vividness and splendor of reality, and are lighted up with a dazzling glow of imagination, the effect of the whole is singularly vague and uncertain. Shelley's genius was of a high order; but instead of possessing it he was possessed by it, as madmen were said, in ignorant ages, to be possessed by a devil: his Muse is a Pythoness upon her tripod, torn and convulsed by the utterance of which she is the channel. This possession, if I may so style it, is the essential characteristic of Shelley's poetry — at once its strength and its weakness, the source of its charm and the origin of its defects. It is unnecessary to contrast this convulsive and morbid, though often admirable force, with the calm and godlike mastery over themselves of the true gods of poetry, of such minds as Homer, as Milton, as Shakspeare.

Two important works of Shelley are dramatic in form — the *Prometheus Unbound* and the *Cenci*. The former, however, is rather a lyric in dialogue than a drama, while the latter is a regular tragedy. The *Prometheus* is one of the wildest and most unintelligible of all this poet's works, though it contains numberless passages of the highest beauty and sublimity. The fundamental idea is based upon the gigantic drama of Æschylus, of which it is intended to be the complement; but Shelley has combined with the primeval and tremendous mythology of the Greek poet a multitude of persons and actions embodying the Titanic resistance of his philosophical creed to the abominations — as he regarded them — springing from Christianity and the present organization of society. The most incongruous personages and systems are mingled together; Paganism and Christianity, the myths of Olympus and the theology of the Bible, the systems and the beliefs of different ages and countries, are brought into bewildering contact. This piece breathes throughout that strange union of fierce hostility to social systems and intense love for humanity in the abstract which forms so singular an anomaly in the writings of Shelley. Many of the descriptive passages are sublime, and noble bursts of lyric harmony alternate with the wildest personifications and the fiercest invective. The *Cenci* is a regular tragedy on the severe and sculptural plan of Alfieri. The subject is one of the most frightful of those domestic crimes in which the black annals of mediæval Italy are so prolific. It is founded on the famous crime of Beatrice di Cenci, driven by the diabolical wickedness of her father to the crime of parricide, for which she suffered the penalty of death at Rome; but the character of the old Count is one of such monstrous and hideous depravity, that the story is in reality quite unsuited to the purpose of the dramatist. In spite of several powerful and striking scenes, this piece is of a morbid and unpleasing character, though the language is vigorous and masculine.

§ 14. The narrative poem of ***Rosalind and Helen*** is an elaborate pleading against the institution of marriage. The poet contrasts two lives, one in which the indissolubility of the marriage tie is arbitrarily made out to be productive of nothing but misery, while in the other a connection not sanctioned by law and custom is shown in a most attractive light. But the parallel, like those so often brought forward in the writings of George Sand and other advocates for what is called the emancipation of women, has the disadvantage of proving nothing at all; for it would have been just as easy to have inverted the two cases imagined; and common and universal experience shows that though married life may, in particular instances, be unhappy, the general practical tendency of the conjugal bond is unquestionably calculated to promote individual happiness as well as general morality. In the poem of *Adonais* Shelley has given us a beautiful and touching lament on the early death of Keats, whose short career gave such a noble foretaste of poetical genius that would have made him one of the greatest writers of his age. It is of the pastoral character, and is in some measure a revival of the beautiful Idyl of Moschus on the death of Bion, and reminds the reader of the eulogies of Sidney by Spenser, and the immortal *Lycidas* of Milton. One of the most imaginative and at the same time one of the obscurest of Shelley's poems is the *Sensitive Plant*, which combines the qualities of mystery and fancifulness to the highest degree, perpetually stimulating the reader with a desire to penetrate the meaning symbolized in the luxuriant description of the garden and the Plant, and filling him with the richest imagery and description. The versification of this poem is extraordinary for its melody and variety, and the reader is incessantly tantalized with the hope of unveiling the secret and abstract meaning which the poet has locked up, as the embryo is involved in the foldings of the petals of a flower. Many of Shelley's detached lyrics are of inexpressible beauty, as the *Ode to a Skylark*, which breathes the very rapture of the bird's soaring song, the wild but picturesque imagery of the *Cloud*, besides a number of minor but not less beautiful productions. By a singular anomaly or contrast, Shelley, whose mind was so filled with images of superhuman grace and beauty, exhibits occasionally a morbid tendency to dwell on ideas of a hideous and repulsive character. Like the ocean, his genius, so pure, transparent, and sublime, the parent of so many forms of strange and fairy loveliness, hides within its abysses monstrous and horrible shapes at which imagination recoils. His mode of writing is full of pictures, but the images subsidiary to or illustrative of the principal thought are often made more prominent than the thought they are intended to enforce. Nay, he very frequently goes farther, and makes the antitype and the type change places; the illustrative image becoming the principal object, and thus destroying the due subordination of the ornament to the edifice it is intended to decorate. Shakspeare's miraculous imagination, it is true, seems sometimes almost to run away with him; but when closely studied it will be found that he never fails to keep his principal idea always above and distinct from even his wildest outbursts of fancy, and ever remains master of his thought.

§ **15.** John Keats (1796–1821) was born in Moorfields, London, and was apprenticed to a surgeon in his fifteenth year. During his apprenticeship he devoted most of his time to poetry, and in 1817 he published a volume of juvenile poems. This was followed in 1818 by his long poem *Endymion*, which was severely censured by the "Quarterly Review"—an attack which has been somewhat erroneously described as the cause of his death. It is probable that it gave a rude shock to Keats's highly sensitive nature, and to a physical condition much weakened by the attention which he had bestowed upon a dying brother. But he had a constitutional tendency to consumption, which would most likely have developed itself under any circumstances. He went for the recovery of his health to Rome, where he died on the 24th of February, 1821. In the previous year he had published another volume of poems, *Lamia, Isabella, &c.*, in which was included the fragment of his remarkable poem entitled *Hyperion.*

It was the misfortune of Keats to be either extravagantly praised or unmercifully condemned. This arose on the one hand from the extreme partiality of friendship, and on the other from resentment of that friendship, connected as it was with party politics and with peculiar views of society. That which is most remarkable in his works is the wonderful profusion of figurative language, often exquisitely beautiful and luxuriant, but sometimes purely fantastical and far-fetched. The peculiarity of Shelley's style, to which we may give the name of *incatenation*, Keats carries to extravagance—one word, one image, one rhyme suggests another, till we quite lose sight of the original idea, which is smothered in its own sweet luxuriance, like a bee stifled in honey. Shakspeare and his school, upon whose manner Keats undoubtedly endeavored to form his style of writing, have, it is true, this peculiarity of language; but in them the images never run away with the thought—the guiding master-idea is ever present. These poets never throw the reins on their Pegasus, even when soaring to "the brightest heaven of invention." With them the images are produced by a force acting *ab intra;* like wild flowers springing from the very richness of the ground. In Keats the force acts *ab extra;* the flowers are forcibly fixed in the earth, as in the garden of a child, who cannot wait till they grow there of themselves. Keats deserves high praise for one very peculiar and original merit: he has treated the classical mythology in a way absolutely new, representing the Pagan deities not as mere abstractions of art, nor as mere creatures of popular belief, but giving them passions and affections like our own, highly purified and idealized, however, and in exquisite accordance with the lovely scenery of ancient Greece and Italy, and with the golden atmosphere of primeval existence. This treatment of a subject, which ordinary readers would consider hopelessly worn and threadbare, is certainly not Homeric, nor is it Miltonic, nor is it in the manner of any of the great poets who have employed the mythological imagery of antiquity; but it is productive of very exquisite pleasure, and must, therefore, be in accordance with true principles of art. In *Hyperion*, in the *Ode to Pan*, in the verses on a *Grecian Urn*, we find a noble and airy strain of beautiful classic imagery, combined with a perception of natural loveliness so luxuriant, so rich, so delicate, that the rosy dawn of Greek poetry seems combined with all that is most tenderly pensive in the calm sunset twilight of romance. Such of Keats's poems as are founded on more modern subjects — *The Eve of St. Agnes* for example, or *The Pot of Basil*, a beautiful anecdote versified from Boccaccio — are, to our taste, inferior to those of his productions in which the scenery and personages are mythological. It would seem as if the severity of ancient art, which in the last-mentioned works acted as an involuntary check upon a too luxuriant fancy, deserted him when he left the antique world; and the absence of true, deep, intense passion (his prevailing defect) becomes necessarily more painfully apparent, as well as the discordant mingling of the *prettinesses* of modern poetry with the directness and unaffected simplicity of Chaucer and Boccaccio. But Keats was a true poet. If we consider his extreme youth and delicate health, his solitary and interesting self-instruction, the severity of the attacks made upon him by hostile and powerful critics, and above all the original richness and picturesqueness of his conceptions and imagery, even when they run to waste, he appears to be one of the greatest of the young poets — resembling the Milton of *Lycidas*, or the Spenser of the *Tears of the Muses*.

§ **16.** THOMAS CAMPBELL (1777–1844), who was born on the 27th of July, 1777, at Glasgow, was educated at the University in that city, where he distinguished himself by his translations from the Greek poets. In 1799, when he was only in his twenty-second year, he published his *Pleasures of Hope*, which was received with a burst of enthusiasm as hearty as afterwards welcomed the *Lay of the Last Minstrel* and *Childe Harold*. Shortly afterwards he travelled abroad, where the warlike scenes he witnessed and the battle-fields he visited suggested some noble lyrics. To the seventh edition of the *Pleasures of Hope*, published in 1802, were added the magnificent verses on the battle of *Hohenlinden*, *Ye Mariners of England*, the most popular of his songs, and *Lochiel's Warning*. In the following year he settled in London, married, and commenced in earnest the pursuit of literature as a profession. His works were written chiefly for the booksellers, and, with the exception of his *Gertrude of Wyoming*, which appeared in 1809, do not require any notice in a history of literature. In 1843 he retired to Boulogne, where he died in the following year. His body was brought over to England and interred in Westminster Abbey.

To his lyrics, which are among the finest in any language, Campbell will owe his lasting fame. In Campbell, as in the general state of literary feeling reflected in his works, a complete and vast change had taken place. In the fluctuation of popular taste, in the setting of that current, which, flowing from the old classicism, has carried us insensibly but irresistibly first through Romanticism, and has now brought us to a species of metaphysical quietism, there have been many temporary changes of direction, nay, some apparent stoppages. Despite the effort and impulsion of the Byronian poetry — the poetry of *passion* — there were writers who not only retained many characteristics of the former school that had to appearance been exploded, but even something of the old tone of sentiment, modified, of course, by the æsthetic principles which were afterwards to be completely embodied in such a cycle of great works as constitutes a school of literature. Campbell is one of the connecting links between the two systems so opposite and apparently so incompatible; and in comparing his first work with his last we find a perfect image of the gradual transition from the one style of writing to the other.

§ 17. In the circle of poets with Byron, Shelley, and Keats, outliving by many years the latest of these, must be mentioned the names of Leigh Hunt and Walter Savage Landor.

James Henry Leigh Hunt (1784-1859) was the son of a West Indian, who, resident in the United States, had remained a firm loyalist, and after the declaration of independence found it advisable to come over to this country. The poet was born at Southgate, Middlesex, and received his education at Christ's Hospital, which he left "in the same rank, at the same age, and for the same reasons, as Lamb." He stammered, and therefore "Grecian I could not be." In 1805 he joined his brother in editing a newspaper called the *News*, and shortly afterwards established the *Examiner*, which still exists. A conviction for libel on the prince regent detained him in prison for two years, the happiest portion of his life: he was free from the worry and care which never afterwards forsook him. Soon after he left prison he published the *Story of Rimini*, an Italian tale in verse (1816), which contains some exquisite poetry, both as to conception and execution. About 1818 he started the *Indicator*, a weekly paper, in imitation of the *Spectator;* and in 1822 he went to Italy, to assist Lord Byron and Shelley in their projected paper called the *Liberal.* Shelley died soon after Hunt's arrival in Italy; and though Hunt was kindly received by Byron, and lived for a time in his house, there was no congeniality between them. The *Liberal* was discontinued, and they parted on bad terms. On his return to England, Hunt published an account of *Lord Byron and some of his Contemporaries*, which was universally condemned as both ungenerous and unjust. He continued to write for periodicals, and published various poems from time to time, of which one of the most celebrated was *Captain Sword and Captain Pen.* He died in 1859, at the age of seventy-five, having enjoyed during the latter years of his life a pension of 200*l.* a year from the Crown. Leigh Hunt's poetry is graceful, sprightly, and full of fancy. Though not possessing much soul and emotion, it has true life and genius, while here and there his verse is lit up with wit, or glows with tenderness and grace. His prose writings consist of essays, collected under the title of the *Indicator and his Companions; Sir Ralph Esher*, a novel; *The Old Court Suburb;* and his lives of *Wycherley, Congreve, Vanbrugh,* and *Farquhar*, prefixed to his edition of their dramatic writings.

§ **18.** WALTER SAVAGE LANDOR (1775–1864) was born on the 30th of January, 1775. His father was a gentleman of good family and wealthy circumstances residing in Warwickshire. The son entered Rugby at an early age, and thence proceeded to Trinity College, Oxford. Like many others who have taken important literary positions, he left the University without a degree; and though intended at first for the army, and afterwards for the bar, he declined both professions, and threw himself into literature, with the assistance of a liberal allowance from his father. In 1795 his first work — a volume of poems — appeared, followed early in the present century by a translation into Latin of *Gebir*, one of his own English poems. Landor had no small facility in classical composition, and he appeared to have the power of transporting himself into the times and sentiments of Greece and Rome. This is still more clearly seen in the *Heroic Idyls* (1820), in Latin verse; and the reproduction of Greek thought in *The Hellenics* is one of the most successful attempts of its kind. At the death of his father, the poet found himself in possession of an extensive estate; but longing for a life of greater freedom and less monotony than that of an English country-gentleman, he sold his patrimony and took up his abode on the continent, where he resided during the rest of his life, with occasional visits to his native country. The republican spirit which led him to take part as a volunteer in the Spanish rising of 1808 continued to burn fiercely to the last. He even went so far as to defend tyrannicide, and boldly offered a pension to the widow of any one who would murder a despot. Between 1820 and 1830 he was engaged upon his greatest work, *Imaginary Conversations of Literary Men and Statesmen.* This was followed in 1831 by *Poems, Letters by a Conservative, Satire on Satirists* (1836), *Pentameron and Pentalogue* (1837), and a long series in prose and poetry, of which the chief are the *Hellenics enlarged and completed, Dry Sticks Fagoted*, and *The Last Fruit off an Old Tree.* He resided towards the close of his life at Bath; but some four or five years before his death, a libel on a lady, for which he was condemned to pay heavy damages, drove him again from his country, and he retired to his Italian home near Florence, and there in serene old age "the Nestor of English poets," one of the last literary links with the age of the French Republic, passed quietly away. He died on the 17th of September, 1864, an exile from his country, misunderstood from the very individuality of his genius by the majority of his countrymen, but highly appreciated by those who could rightly estimate the works he has left behind him.

It has been well said of the author of *Imaginary Conversations* that no writer presents "as remarkable an instance of the strength and weakness of the human understanding." Landor was a man of refined tastes and cultured mind. A gentleman by birth, every line of his writings gives proofs of the learned and polished intellect. But unhappily his great powers were marred by the heedlessness and rashness of his disposition, strong passions, and an unrestrained will. There is no regard for the thoughts and feelings of others. He therefore is too fond of paradox and unfounded assertion. His opinion must be received, because it is his; he runs against every one else, and believe what no one else believes, and scouts those ideas which have received universal assent. Thus Napoleon Bonaparte was a man of no genius; Alfieri the greatest man that Europe has seen; Pitt was a poor creature, and Fox a charlatan. It was this unhappy inconsistency, paradox, and wilfulness, which prevented his writings obtaining that position which was their due. His style is nervous and graceful. In the *Imaginary Conversations* the tones and manners of the age or individual are well rendered, and the whole work is evidently that of a man deeply in earnest, yet wanting in that gentleness, considerateness, and prudence which are required in a really valuable production.

CHAPTER XXII.

WORDSWORTH, COLERIDGE, AND SOUTHEY.

1. WILLIAM WORDSWORTH: his life and works. § 2. Criticism of his poetry § 3. SAMUEL TAYLOR COLERIDGE: his life. § 4. His literary character and poems. § 5. His prose works and conversation. § 6. ROBERT SOUTHEY: his life. § 7. His poems. *Joan of Arc. Madoc. Thalaba. Kehama. Roderick* § 8. His prose works.

§ 1. WILLIAM WORDSWORTH (1770–1850), the founder of the so-called Lake School of poetry, was born at Cockermouth, in Cumberland, April 7, 1770. In his ninth year he was sent to a school at Hawkshead, in the most picturesque district of Lancashire, where the scholars, instead of living under the same roof with a master, were boarded among the villagers. They were at liberty to roam over the surrounding country by day and by night, and Wordsworth largely availed himself of this privilege. The relish for the beauties of creation, to which he mainly owes his place among poets, was early manifested and rapidly developed. In his fourteenth year his father died, and the care of the orphans devolved on their uncles. The poet was sent to St. John's College, Cambridge, in 1787, where he spent his time chiefly in the study of the English poets, and in the ordinary amusements of the University. After taking his degree in 1791, he went over to France, where he eagerly embraced the ideas of the wildest champions of liberty in that country. Wordsworth's eye, much more practised to scan landscapes than men, nowhere penetrated beneath the surface; and he concluded that a king and his courtiers were the only Frenchmen by whom power could be abused. His political sentiments, however, became gradually modified, till in later life they settled down into steady Conservatism in Church and State. To vindicate his talents, which his Cambridge career had brought into question, he, in 1793, produced to the world — hurriedly, he says, though reluctantly — two little poems, *An Evening Walk* and *Descriptive Sketches*. If the *Evening Walk* was hastily corrected it had not been hastily composed, for it was begun in 1787, and continued through the two succeeding years. The metre and language are in the school of Pope, but they are the work of a promising scholar, and not of a master. The *Descriptive Sketches* had been penned at Orleans and Blois, in 1791 and 1792. The execution is of the same school as the *Evening Walk*, but the language is simpler, and so far superior.

In 1793 Wordsworth commenced, and in 1794 completed, the story of *Salisbury Plain, or, Guilt and Sorrow*, which did not appear entire till 1842, but of which he published an extract in 1798, under the title of *The Female Vagrant*. In regard to time it is separated from the

Descriptive Sketches by a span, but in respect of merit they are parted by a gulf. He had ceased to write in the train of Pope, and composed in the stanza of his later favorite Spenser. There is an exquisite simplicity and polish in the language, equally removed from the bald prattle of many of the Lyrical Ballads and the turgid verbosity of many pages in *The Excursion*. It was about this time that the poet received a legacy of 900*l.*, which enabled him to indulge the great wish of his heart — to live with his sister Dorothy, and to devote himself entirely to poetry. The autumn of 1795 found them settled in a house at Racedown, in Dorsetshire. It is a remarkable feature of his history that, during all the time he was a hotheaded, intractable rover, he had lived a life of Spartan virtue. His Hawkshead training had inured him to cottage board and lodging, and the temptations of London and Paris had failed to allure him to extravagance or vice. His temperance and economy enabled him to derive more benefit from the above-mentioned small bequest than would have accrued to poets in general from five times the sum.

Wordsworth now entered upon his poetical profession by paraphrasing several of the satires of Juvenal, and applying them to the abuses which he conceived to reign in high places. These, however, he never published. His second experiment was the tragedy of *The Borderers*, which was considered, when it appeared, an unqualified failure. I was in June, 1797, when this tragedy was on the verge of completion, that its first critic arrived at Racedown. Coleridge formed a close friendship with Wordsworth and his sister, and the following year they started upon a tour together in Germany. To furnish funds for this journey the two friends published their *Lyrical Ballads*, the first piece in which was Coleridge's *Ancient Mariner*, but the remaining poems were all by Wordsworth. Of these, three or four were in Wordsworth's finest manner — about the same number partly good, partly puerile; and the remainder belonged to a class all but universally condemned.

On their return to England in 1798 Wordsworth and his sister settled at Grasmere, from whence they afterwards went to Allan Bank, and finally in 1813 to Rydal Mount. It was from his residence in this district that he and his friends Coleridge, Southey, De Quincey, and Wilson, received the name of the *Lake School*. He now set himself to work, both by precept and practice, to inculcate those peculiar views of poetry which are mentioned more particularly below, and which encountered for a long time the fierce hostility of the critics. In 1799 he commenced *The Prelude*, which was not published in full till after his death. This metrical autobiography is valuable because it preserves many facts and opinions which might otherwise have gone unrecorded; but, upon the whole, it is bald and cumbrous as a poem. In 1800 he published an enlarged edition of the *Ballads*. Thirty-seven pieces were added to the original collection, and the supplement materially increased the proportion of good to bad.

The year 1802 was an eventful one to the poet. He received a considerable accession of fortune, which had been due to his father at the time of his death, but which the children had not recovered till now The poet's share enabled him to marry a lady to whom he had been long attached, Mary Hutchinson, his sister's friend. In 1807 he gave to the world two new volumes of *Poems*, which contained the *Song at the Feast of Brougham Castle*, and many more of his choicest pieces. Here appeared his first sonnets, and several of them are still ranked among his happiest efforts in that department. Wordsworth's next publication was in prose. His indignation rose at the grasping tyranny of Napoleon; and in 1809 he put forth a pamphlet against the Convention of Cintra. The sentiments were spirit-stirring, but the manner of conveying them was the reverse, and his protest passed unheeded. His great work, *The Excursion*, appeared in 1814. This is a fragment of a projected great moral epic, discussing and solving the mightiest questions concerning God, nature, and man, our moral constitution, our duties, and our hopes. Its dramatic interest is exceedingly small; its structure is very inartificial; and the characters represented in it are devoid of life and probability. That an old Scottish pedler, a country clergyman, and a disappointed visionary, should reason so continuously and so sublimely on the destinies of man, is in itself a gross want of verisimilitude; and the purely speculative nature of their interminable arguments,

"On knowledge, will, and fate,"

are not relieved from their monotony even by the abundant and beautiful descriptions and the pathetic episodes so thickly interspersed. It is Wordsworth, too, who is speaking always and alone; there is no variety of language, none of the shock and vivacity of intellectual wrestling; but, on the other hand, so sublime are the subjects on which they reason, so lofty and seraphic is their tone, and so deep a glow of humanity is perceptible throughout, that no reader, but such as seek in poetry for mere food for the curiosity and imagination, can study this grand composition without ever-increasing reverence and delight.

In 1815 appeared *The White Doe of Rylstone*, the only narrative poem of any length which Wordsworth ever wrote. The incidents are of a simple and exceedingly mournful kind; turning chiefly on the complete ruin of a north-country family in the civil wars: but the atmosphere of mystical and supernatural influences in which the personages move, the superhuman purity and unearthliness of the characters, and above all the part played in the action by the white doe, which gives name to the work, — all these things contribute to communicate to the production a fantastic, unreal, and somewhat affected air. *Peter Bell* was published in 1819, and was received with a shout of ridicule. The hierophant had neglected no precaution to provoke the sneers of the profane. He stated in the dedication that the work had been completed twenty years, and that he had continued correcting it in the interval to render it worthy of a permanent place in our national literature. An announcement so well calculated to awaken the highest expectation was followed by a prologue more puerile than anything which ever proceeded from a man with a fiftieth part of his powers. The work is meant to be serious, and is certainly not facetious, but there is so much farcical absurdity of detail and language that the mind is revolted. This poem was followed by *The Wagoner*, which was not more successful. Wordsworth's whole returns from his literary labors up to 1819 had not amounted to 140*l.*; but through the influence of Lord Lonsdale, he had been appointed in 1813 distributor of stamps for the County of Westmoreland, which brought him about 500*l.* a year; and it was between 1830 and 1840 that the flood which floated *him* into favor rose to its height. Scott and Byron had in succession entranced the world. They had now withdrawn, and no third king arose to demand homage. It was in the lull which ensued that the less thrilling notes of the Lake bard obtained a hearing. It was during this time that he published his *Ecclesiastical Sonnets* and *Yarrow revisited*, and in 1842 he brought forth a complete collection of his poems. His fame was now firmly established. On the death of Southey in 1843 he was made Poet-Laureate. He died on April 23, 1850, when he had just completed his eightieth year.

§ 2. The poetry of Wordsworth has passed through two phases of criticism, in the first of which his defects were chiefly noted, and in the second his merits. Already we have arrived at the third era, when the majority of readers are just to both. An acute critic, to whom we have been much indebted in the preceding sketch of the poet's life and works, gives the fairest estimate that has appeared of Wordsworth's poetry "It is constantly asserted that he effected a reform in the language of poetry, that he found the public bigoted to a vicious and flowery diction, which seemed to mean a great deal and really meant nothing, and that he led them back to sense and simplicity. The claim appears to us to be a fanciful assumption, refuted by the facts of literary history. Feebler poetasters were no doubt read when Wordsworth began to write than would now command an audience, however small: but they had no real hold upon the public, and Cowper was the only *popular* bard of the day. His masculine and unadorned English was relished in every cultivated circle in the land, and Wordsworth was the child, and not the father, of a reaction, which, after all, has been greatly exaggerated. Goldsmith was the most celebrated of Cowper's immediate predecessors, and it will not be pretended that *The Deserted Village* and *The Traveller* are among the specimens of inane phraseology. Burns had died before Wordsworth had attracted notice. The wonderful Peasant's performances were admired by none more than by Wordsworth himself: were they not already far more popular than the Lake-poet's have ever been — or ever will be? and were they, in any respect or degree, tinged with the absurdities of the Hayley school? When we come forward we find that the men of the generation were Scott, Byron, Moore, Campbell, Crabbe, and one or two others. Wordsworth himself was little read in comparison, and if he had anything to do with weaning the public from their vitiated predilections, it must have been through his influence on these more popular poets, whose works represented the reigning taste of the time. But nothing is more certain than that not a single one of them had formed his style upon that of the *Lyrical Ballads* or *The Excursion*. . . . Whatever influence Wordsworth may have exercised on poetic style, be it great or small, was by deviating in practice from the principles of composition for which he contended. Both his theory, and the poems which illustrate it, continue to this hour to be all but universally condemned. He resolved to write as the lower orders talked; and though where the poor are the speakers it would be in accordance with strict dramatic propriety, the system would not be tolerated in serious poetry. Wordsworth's rule did not stop at the wording of dialogues. He maintained that the colloquial language of rustics was the most philosophical and enduring which the dictionary affords, and the fittest for verse of every description. Any one who mixes with the common people can decide for himself whether their conversation is wont to exhibit more propriety of language than the sayings of a Johnson or the speeches of a Burke. If it were really the case, it would follow that literary cultivation is an evil, and that we ought to learn English of our ploughboys, and not of our Shakspeares and Miltons. But there can be no risk in asserting that the vocabulary of rustics is rude and meagre, and their discourse negligent, diffuse, and weak. The vulgarisms, which are the most racy, vigorous, and characteristic part of their speech, Wordsworth admitted must be dropped, and either he must have substituted equivalent expressions, when the language ceases to be that of the poor, or he must have put up with a stock of words which, after all these deductions, would have been scarcely more copious than that of a South-Sea savage. When his finest verse is brought to the test of his principle, they agree no better than light and darkness. Here is his way of describing the effects of the pealing organ in King's College Chapel, with its 'self-poised roof, scooped into ten thousand cells:'—

> 'But from the arms of silence — list! O list! —
> The music bursteth into second life;
> The notes luxuriate, every stone is kissed
> With sound, or ghost of sound, in mazy strife!'

"This is to write like a splendid poet, but it is not to write as rustics talk. A second canon laid down by Wordsworth was, that poetic diction is, or ought to be, in all respects the same with the language of prose; and as prose has a wide range, and numbers among its triumphs such luxuriant eloquence as that of Jeremy Taylor, the principle, if just, would be no less available for the advocates of ornamental verse than for the defence of the homely style of the *Lyrical Ballads*. But the proposition is certainly too broadly stated, and, though the argument holds good for the adversary, because the phraseology which is not too rich for prose can never be considered too tawdry for poetry, yet it will not warrant the conclusions of Wordsworth, that poetry should never rise above prose, or disdain to descend to its lowest level.' *

* *Quarterly Review*, vol. xcii. p. 233 seq.

§ **3.** Samuel Taylor Coleridge (1772–1834) was born at Ottery St.-Mary, in Devonshire, October 21, 1772. He was left an orphan at an early age, and was educated at Christ's Hospital; from whence he proceeded to Jesus College, Cambridge. He never took his degree, leaving the University in his second year in a fit of despondency, occasioned, it is said, by unrequited love, and enlisting in the 15th Dragoons, under the assumed name of Comberbatch. One of the officers, learning his real history, communicated with his friends, by whom his discharge was at once effected. After this adventure he formed a scheme for emigrating to the banks of the Susquehanna in North America, and there founding a model republic, with a community of goods, from which all selfishness was to be banished. He found in Southey and some other young men, as ardent and inexperienced as himself, warm support; but the "Pantisocracy," as Coleridge called it, could not be carried into effect from want of funds. Coleridge then turned his attention to literature. He had been introduced to Joseph Cottle, a benevolent bookseller at Bristol, who gave him thirty guineas for a small volume of poems, which were published in 1794. In the following year the poet married Miss Sarah Fricker of Bristol, a sister of Southey's wife. At this time he contributed verses to one of the London papers. Another volume of poems appeared in 1796. During the three first years after his marriage he lived in Wordsworth's neighborhood, and his share in the celebrated *Lyrical Ballads*, published in 1797, has been already mentioned. At this period also his tragedy, *Remorse*, was written. In 1798 Coleridge visited Germany, where he studied the language and literature. After his return he again took up his abode in the Lake District, near Wordsworth and Southey. He now contributed to some periodicals, and wrote both on politics and literature. In 1810 he quitted the Lakes, leaving his wife and children wholly dependent upon Southey, — a striking illustration of his well-known indifference to personal and pecuniary obligations. He then took up his residence in London, finding a home in the house of Mr. Gillman at Highgate, where he died, July 25, 1834.

§ **4.** The literary character of Coleridge resembles some vast but unfinished palace; all is gigantic, beautiful, and rich, but nothing is complete, nothing compact. He was all his days, from his youth to his death, laboring, meditating, projecting; and yet all that he has left us bears a painful character of imperfection. His mind was eminently dreamy, tinged with that incapacity for *acting* which forms the characteristic of the German intellect; his genius was multiform, many-sided; and for this reason, perhaps, could not at once seize upon the right point of view. No man, probably, ever existed who thought more, and more intensely, than Coleridge; few ever possessed a vaster treasury of learning and knowledge; and yet how little has he given us, or rather how few of his works are in any way worthy of the undoubted majesty of his genius! *Materials*, indeed, he has left us in enormous quantity — a store of thoughts and principles, particularly in the department of æsthetics cience — golden masses of reason, either painfully sifted from the rubbish of obscure and forgotten authors, or dug up from the rich depths of his own mind; but these are still in the state of raw materials, or only partially worked.

He began life as a Unitarian and republican; his intellectual powers were chiefly formed in the transcendental schools of Germany, but he ultimately became from conviction a most sincere adherent to the doctrines of the Anglican church, and an enthusiastic defender of our monarchical constitution. Though the lyrics to which we have alluded (the finest of which are the odes *On the Departing Year*, and that supposed to be written *At Sunrise in the Valley of Chamouni*) are somewhat injured by their air of effort, they are indubitably works of singular richness and exquisitely melodized language. In his translation of Schiller's *Wallenstein* Coleridge was most successful. With almost all readers it will forever have the charm of an original work. Indeed, many beautiful parts of the translation are exclusively the property of the English poet, who used a manuscript copy of the German text before its publication by the author. Although he has not scrupled in some instances to open out the hint of the original, and even to graft new thoughts upon it, his translation is, in the best and highest sense of that term, pre-eminently faithful. That Coleridge had no power of true dramatic creation is strongly proved by his tragedy of *The Remorse*, in which, in spite of very striking features of character (as in Ordonio), and a multitude of incidents of the most violent kind, he has not produced a drama which either excites curiosity or moves any strong degree of pity. What is most beautiful in the work is all pure description, and in no sense advances the action or exhibits human passions. It is strange, perhaps, but yet by no means unintelligible, that a man who was so unsuccessful in creating emotions of a theatrical kind should have been a most consummate critic of the dramatic productions of others. Till he wrote, deep and universal as had been the admiring love — almost the adoration — of the English for Shakspeare, there still remained, in their judgment, something of that *de haut en bas* tone which characterizes all the criticisms anterior to Coleridge's *Lectures on Shakspeare*. Coleridge first showed that the creator of *Hamlet* and *Othello* was not only the greatest genius, but also the most consummate artist, that ever existed. Nothing can give us a higher opinion of the nobility of Coleridge's mind than the fact that he was the first to make some approach to the discovery of those laws which, expressly or intuitively, governed the evolutions of the Shakspearian drama — that he possessed a soul vast enough, deep enough, multiform enough, to give us some faint idea of the dimensions, the length, and breadth, and depth, of that huge sea of truth and beauty.

Of the poems by which Coleridge is best known, both in England and abroad, the most universally read is undoubtedly *The Ancient Mariner*, a wild, mystical, phantasmagoric narrative, most picturesquely related in the old English ballad measure, and in language to which an air of antiquity is skilfully given in admirable harmony with the spec tral character of the events. The whole poem is a splendid dream, filling the ear with the strange and floating melodies of sleep, and the eye with a shifting, vaporous succession of fantastic images, gloomy or radiant.

The poem of *Christabel*, and the fragment called *Kubla Khan*, are of the same mystic, unreal character: indeed, Coleridge asserted that the latter was actually composed in a dream — an affirmation which may well be believed, for it is a thousand times more unintelligible than the general run of dreams. It is a dream, perhaps; but it is an *opium dream* — " ægri somnium " — without so much as that faint coherency which even a dream must have to give pleasure in a picture or in a poem. Like everything that Coleridge ever wrote, the versification is exquisite. His language puts on every form, it expresses every sound; he almost writes to the eye and to the ear. But in *Christabel*, which has some slight pretension to be an intelligible narrative, or, at least, part of an intelligible narrative, the mixture of two realities is not harmoniously subordinated; and the effect is, of course, fatal to the poem as a work of art. In point of completeness, exquisite harmony of feeling, and unsurpassable grace of imagery and language, Coleridge has left nothing superior to the charming little poem entitled *Love, or Genevieve.*

§ **5.** Coleridge takes rank also as a psychologist, moralist, and general philosopher. The *Friend*, the *Lay Sermon*, the *Aids to Reflection*, and the *Church and State*, are works which have exercised a great influence upon the intellectual character of his generation. But his chief reputation through life was founded less upon his writings than upon his conversation, or rather what may be called his conversational oratory, which must have resembled those disquisitions of the Greek philosophers, of which the dialogues of Plato give some idea. It is in his innumerable fragments, in his rich but desultory remains (published posthumously under the title of *Table Talk*), in casual remarks scribbled like Sibylline leaves, often on the margin of borrowed books, and in imperfectly-reported conversations, that we must look for proofs of Coleridge's immense but incompletely recorded powers. From a careful study of these we shall conceive a high admiration of his genius, and a deep regret at the fragmentary and desultory manifestations of his powers. We shall also appreciate the vastness and multiform character of a mind to which nothing was too difficult, or too obscure; a noble tone of moral dignity "softened into beauty" by the largest sympathy, and, above all, an admirable catholicity of taste, which could unerringly pitch upon what was beautiful and true, and find its *pabulum* in all schools, all writers; perceiving, as it were intuitively, the value and the charm of the most unpromising books and systems.

§ **6.** ROBERT SOUTHEY (1774–1843) was born on August 12, 1774, at Bristol, where his father carried on the business of a draper, but most of his early childhood was spent with his mother's family. While living with his aunt, Miss Tyler, he made the acquaintance of every actor of merit who came to Bristol or Bath, and he became fixed in his aunt's persuasion that there was only one thing grander than being a great tragic actor — and that was, to be a great author of tragedies. He was sent to Westminster at the age of fourteen, but he had had no proper classical training previously, and the defect was never repaired. After spending four years at Westminster he was expelled for writing an article against flogging in public schools, which appeared in the *Flagellant*, a periodical commenced by Southey and his friend and schoolfellow, Grosvenor Bedford. The following year he went to Oxford, and was entered at Balliol. At the University he made one or two fitful efforts to read Tacitus and Homer, but speedily relinquished the attempt. His hope of being able to assist his family chiefly depended upon his taking Orders, but his religious opinions prevented him from entering the Church. He lingered at Oxford, undecided what to do, until Coleridge appeared with his scheme of "Pantisocracy,' already related. Quitting Oxford, Southey attempted to raise by authorship funds for the American scheme, and in 1794 published at Bath, in conjunction with Robert Lovell, a small volume of poems, which brought neither fame nor profit. His chief reliance, however, was on his epic poem *Joan of Arc*, which had been composed in six weeks in 1793. He had the good fortune to meet with a bookseller as inexperienced and as ardent as himself. This was Joseph Cottle of Bristol, the patron of Coleridge, who offered fifty guineas for the copyright. The work required much correction, and in the mean time, in order to defray the immediate expenses of subsistence, Southey gave lectures on History at Bristol. At this time he was often unable to pay for a dinner, and in 1795 he was compelled by want to return to his mother's house. In November of the same year Southey accompanied his uncle to Lisbon. On the morning of his departure he secretly united himself to Miss Fricker, a young lady to whom he had for some time been engaged, thus frustrating one portion of his uncle's intentions in taking him out, which had been to break off an apparently hopeless engagement. After an absence of six months Southey returned, and immediately commenced that life of patient literary toil from which he never swerved again while health and intellect remained. He had from the outset an allowance of 160*l.* a year, from his friend Mr. Wynn, till he had obtained for him a pension of equal value from the Government. Yet, with his talents and industry, he was constantly on the verge of poverty, and not even his philosophy and hopefulness were always proof against the difficulties of his position. In 1804 he took up his residence at Greta Hall, near Keswick, in Cumberland, where he continued to reside for the remainder of his life. From being a sceptic and a republican, he became a firm believer in Christianity, and a stanch supporter of the English Church and Constitution; and many of his works and essays in the *Quarterly Review* were written in defence of the doctrines and discipline of the Church. In 1813 he was appointed Poet-Laureate, and in 1835 received a pension of 300*l.* a year from the Government of Sir Robert Peel. During the last four years of his life, he had sunk into a state of hopeless imbecility. He died March 21, 1843.

§ 7. Southey's literary activity was prodigious. The list of his writings, published under his own name, amounts to *one hundred and nine* volumes. In addition to these he contributed to the *Annual Review* fifty-two articles, to the *Foreign Quarterly* three, to the *Quarterly* ninety-four. The composition of these works was a small part of the labor they involved: they are all, even to his poems, books of research, which obliged him to turn over numerous volumes for the production of one.

Joan of Arc, the earliest of his long poems, was a juvenile production published in 1795. It was received with favor by most of the critical journals on account of the republican doctrines which it espoused. The critics praised the poetry for the sake of the principles, and the public, who rejected the principles, accepted the verdict. *Madoc*, which was completed in 1799, was not given to the world till 1805. Upon this poem he was contented to rest his fame. It is founded on one of the most absurd legends connected with the early history of America. Madoc is a Welsh prince of the twelfth century, who is represented as making the discovery of the Western world; and his contests with the Mexicans, and ultimate conversion of that people from their cruel idolatry, form the main action of the poem, which, like *Joan of Arc*, is written in blank verse. The poet thus had at his disposal the rich store of picturesque scenery, manners, and wonderful adventure to be found in the Spanish narratives of the exploits of Columbus, Pizarro, Cortes, and the Conquestadors. But the victories which are so wonderful, when related as gained over the Mexicans by the comparatively well-armed Spaniards of the fifteenth and sixteenth centuries, are perfectly incredible when attributed to a band of savages little superior in civilization and the art of war to the people they invaded. Though the poem is crowded with scenes of more than possible splendor — of more than human cruelty, courage, and superstition — the effect is singularly languid; and the exaggeration of prowess and suffering produces the same effect upon the mind as the extravagance of fiction in the two Oriental poems which we shall next notice.

Thalaba was published in 1801, and the *Curse of Kehama* in 1810. Both these poems are, in their subjects, wild, extravagant, unearthly, full of supernatural machinery, but of a kind as difficult to manage with effect as at first sight splendid and attractive. *Thalaba* is a tale of Arabian enchantment, full of magicians, dragons, hippogriffs, and monsters. In *Kehama* the poet has selected for his groundwork the still more unmanageable mythology of the Hindoos — a vast, incoherent, and clumsy structure of superstition, more hopelessly unadapted to the purposes of poetry than even the Fetishism of the savages of Africa. The poems are written in an irregular and wandering species of rhythm — the *Thalaba* altogether without rhyme; and the language abounds in an affected simplicity and perpetual obtrusion of vulgar and puerile phraseology. The works have a most painful air of laxity, and a want of intellectual bone and muscle. There are many passages of gorgeous description, and many proofs of powerful fancy and imagination; but the persons and adventures are so supernatural, so completely out of the circle of human sympathies, both in their triumphs and sufferings, and they are so scrupulously divested of all the passions and circumstances of humanity, that these gorgeous and ambitious works produce on us the impression of a splendid but unsubstantial nightmare: they are the vast disjointed visions of fever and delirium. In *Thalaba* we have a series of adventures, encountered by an Arabian hero who fights with demons and enchanters, and finally overthrows the dominion of the powers of evil in the Domdaniel caverns, "under the roots of the ocean." It is more extravagant than anything in the "Thousand and One Nights:" indeed it is nothing but a quintessence of all the puerile and monstrous fictions of Arabian fancy. In the Oriental legends these extravagances are pardonable, and even characteristic; for in them we take into account the childish and wonder-loving character of the audience to which such fantastic inventions were addressed, and we remember that they are scattered, in the books of the East, over a much greater surface, so to speak, whereas here we have them all consolidated into one mass of incoherent monstrosity. We miss, too, the exquisite glimpses afforded us by those tales of the common and domestic life of the East. These poems, like everything of Southey's, exhibit an incredible amount of multifarious learning; but it is learning generally rather curious than valuable, and it is not vivified by any truly genial, harmonizing power of originality.

In the volume of metrical tales, which appeared in the interval between the publication of these poems, as in general in his minor poems, Southey exhibits a degree of vigor and originality of thought for which we look in vain in his longer works. Some of his legends, translated from the Spanish and Portuguese (in which languages Southey was a proficient), or from the obscurer stores of the Latin chronicles of the Middle Ages, or the monkish legends of the saints, are very vigorous and characteristically written. The author's spirit was strongly legendary; and he has caught the true accent, not of heroic and chivalric tradition, but of the religious enthusiasm of monastic times. Some of his minor original poems have great tenderness and simple dignity of thought, though often injured by a studied meanness and creepingness of expression; for the fatal error of the school to which he belonged was, as we have already shown, a theory that the real every-day phraseology of the common people was better adapted to the purposes of poetry than the language of cultivated and educated men.

Kehama was followed, at an interval of four years, by ***Roderick**, the Last of the Goths*, a poem in blank verse, and of a much more modest and credible character than its predecessors. The subject is the punishment and repentance of the last Gothic King of Spain, whose vices, oppressions, and in particular an insult offered to the virtue of Florinda, daughter of Count Julian, incited that noble to betray his country to the Moors. The general insurrection of the Spaniards against their Moslem oppressors, the exploits of the illustrious Pelayo, and the reappearance of Roderick at the great battle which put an end to the infidel dominion, form the materials of the action. The King, in the disguise of a hermit, figures in most of the scenes; and his agonizing repentance for his past crimes, and humble trust in the mercy of God, are the key-note or prevailing tone of the work. Though free from the injudicious employment of supernatural machinery, and though containing some descriptions of undeniable merit, and several scenes of powerful tenderness and pathos, there is the same want of reality and human interest which characterizes his other poems.

The tone of Southey's poems in general is too uniformly ecstatic and agonizing. His personages, like his scenes, have something unreal, phantom-like, dreamy: they are often beautiful, but it is the beauty not of the earth, or even of the clouds, but of the *mirage* and the Fata Morgana. His robe of inspiration sits gracefully and majestically upon him, but it is too voluminous in its folds, and too heavy in its gorgeous texture, for the motion of real existence: he is never "succinct for speed," and his flowing drapery obstructs and embarrasses his steps. He has *power*, but not *force*: his genius is rather passive than active.

On being appointed poet-laureate, Southey paid his tribute of Court adulation with an eagerness and regularity which showed how complete was his conversion from the political faith of his youthful days. A convert is generally a fanatic; and Southey's laureate odes exhibit a fierce, passionate, controversial hatred of his former liberal opinions which gives interest even to the ambitious monotony, the convulsive mediocrity, of his official lyrics. In one of them, the *Vision of Judgment*, he has essayed to revive the hexameter in English verse. This experiment, tried in so many languages, and with such indifferent success, had been attempted by Gabriel Harvey in the reign of Elizabeth; and the universal ridicule which hailed Southey's attempt was excited quite as much by the absurdity of the metre as by the extravagant flattery of the poem itself. The deification, or rather beatification, of George III. drew from Byron some of the severest strokes of his irresistible ridicule, and gave him the opportunity of severely revenging upon Southey some of the attacks of the laureate upon his principles and poetry.

§ **8.** Southey's prose works are very numerous, and valuable on account of their learning; but the little *Life of Nelson*, written to furnish young seamen with a simple narrative of the exploits of England's greatest naval hero, has perhaps never been equalled for the perfection of its style. In his other works — the principal of which are *The Book of the Church*, *The Lives of the British Admirals*, *The Life of Wesley*, a *History of Brazil*, and of the *Peninsular War* — we find the same admirable art of clear, vigorous English, and no less that strong prejudice, violent political and literary partiality, and a tone of haughty, acrimonious, arrogant self-confidence, which so much detract from his many excellent qualities as a writer and as a man, his sincerity, his learning, his conscientiousness, and his natural benevolence of character.

NOTES AND ILLUSTRATIONS.

OTHER POETS OF THE NINETEENTH CENTURY.

SAMUEL ROGERS (1763-1855) was born at Newington Green, a suburb of London. After a careful private education he was placed, while yet a lad, in his father's banking-house to learn the business, in which he afterwards became a nominal partner. In the enjoyment of large wealth and ample leisure, he devoted himself to literature and to the cultivation of the society of men distinguished in politics, literature, and art. His chief works are the *Pleasures of Memory*, published in 1792; *Human Life*, in 1819; and *Italy*, in 1822. His poetry is highly finished, but not characterized by much power or imagination.

REV. WILLIAM LISLE BOWLES (1762-1850) was born at King's Sutton, on the borders of Northamptonshire. He was educated at Westminster School and Trinity College, Oxford. In 1805 he obtained the valuable living of Bremhill, in Wiltshire. He occupies an important place in the history of English literature, from the great influence which his poetry appears to have exercised over the productions of Coleridge, Wordsworth, and Southey. His *Sonnets*, his *Missionary of the Andes*, and his *Village Verse Book*, are among the best of his works.

REV. CHARLES WOLFE (1791-1823) was born in Ireland. He is chiefly known as the author of the celebrated lines on the death of Sir John Moore, published in 1817. His literary compositions were collected and published in 1825.

BERNARD BARTON (1784-1849) was a member of the Society of Friends, and the amount of attention which he attracted is perhaps mainly owing to the then unusual phenomenon which he presented of a Quaker poet — the title, indeed, by which he came to be commonly known. He published a volume of *Metrical Effusions* in 1812; *Napoleon and other Poems*, 1822; *Poetic Vigils*, 1824; *Devotional Verses*, 1826. Numerous other pieces appeared separately and in magazines.

JAMES MONTGOMERY (1771-1854), educated by the Moravians at Fulneck, near Leeds, wrote many poems while yet a boy, but first attracted public attention by *The Wanderer in Switzerland*, published in 1806, which, though not exhibiting much power, is written in very melodious verse. His subsequent poems were *The West Indies* (1809), *The World before the Flood* (1812), *Greenland* (1810), and *The Pelican Island and other Poems* (1827).

JAMES SMITH (1775-1839), known best in connection with his brother Horace, wrote clever parodies and criticisms in the *Picnic*, the *London Review*, and the *Monthly Mirror*. In the last appeared those imitations, from his own and brother's hand, which were published in 1813 as *The Rejected Addresses;* one of the most successful and popular works that has ever appeared. James wrote the imitations of Wordsworth, Cobbett, Southey, Coleridge, and Crabbe; Horace, those of Scott, Moore, Monk Lewis, Fitzgerald, and Dr. Johnson.

James did little more in the way of literature, except an occasional piece in some of the monthlies. Lady Blessington said, "If James Smith had not been a wealthy man, he would have been a great man." He died on Christmas Eve, 1839, in his 65th year.

HORACE SMITH (1779-1849) was a more voluminous writer than his brother. He was the author of several novels and verses. *Brambletye House*, 1826, was in imitation of Scott's historical novels. Besides this he wrote *Tor Hill*, *Walter Colyton*, *The Moneyed Man*, *The Merchant*, and several others. His best performance is the *Address to the Mummy*, some parts of which exhibit the finest sensibility and an exquisite poetic taste.

FELICIA DOROTHEA HEMANS (1793-1835), whose maiden name was Browne, was a native of Liverpool, and spent the early part of her life in North Wales, not far from Abergele. She was not more than fifteen years of age when her first work was published. In 1812 appeared the *Domestic Affections* and other poems; and in the same year Miss Browne was married to Captain Hemans. She was fortunate in her competition for prizes, gaining that for the best poem on *Wallace* in 1819; and two years afterwards she won a prize for a poem on *Dartmoor*. Her dramatic attempt, the *Vespers of Palermo*, 1823, was not successful. Other works quickly followed: *The Forest Sanctuary*, 1826; *Records of Women*, 1828; *Lays, Lyrics*, &c., *Songs of the Affections*, 1830. Mrs. Hemans for the latter portion of her life resided at Dublin with her brother, and whilst there published in 1834 her *Hymns for Childhood*, and *Scenes and Hymns of Life*, with a few sonnets entitled *Thoughts during Sickness*. Mrs. Hemans's writings are extensively read. Her subjects are those which find a ready admission to the hearts of all classes. The style is graceful, but presenting, as Scott said, "too many flowers for the fruit." There is little intellectual or emotional force about her poetry, and the majority of it will soon be forgotten. A few of the smaller pieces will perhaps remain as English gems, such as *The Graves of a Household*, and the *Homes of England*.

REV. WILLIAM HERBERT (1778-1847), at first a lawyer, then Member of Parliament, finally entered the Church, and died Dean of Manchester. He is the author of several translations from the Norse, Italian, Spanish, and Portuguese — the original poems, *Helga*, 1815, and *Attila*, 1838 — besides tales, sermons, and scientific treatises.

THOMAS HAYNES BAYLY (1797-1839), a celebrated song-writer. The best known are *The Soldier's Tear*, *She wore a Wreath of Roses*, *I'd be a Butterfly*, *O, no, we never mention her*, and *We met — 'twas in a Crowd.*

FRANCIS WRANGHAM (1769-1843), Archdeacon

of Chester, was author of translations from the classical poets, and other poetic and prose writings.

HENRY FRANCIS CARY (1772-1844), published in 1804 a translation of Dante's *Inferno*, and ten years later a translation of the *Divina Commedia*, in blank verse, &c.

WILLIAM STEWART ROSE (1775-1843) was also celebrated as a translator. His chief works were *Amadis de Gaul*, 1803, and the well-known translation of the *Orlando Furioso* of Ariosto, published in 1831.

WILLIAM TAYLOR (1765-1836), of Norwich, translated some of the works of Goethe, Schiller, and Lessing, and gave a great impulse to the study of German literature in England.

JAMES GRAHAME (1765-1811), a native of Glasgow, at first a barrister, then entered the English Church, where he became a well-known preacher. In 1801 he published *Mary Queen of Scotland*, a dramatic poem. This was followed by the *Sabbath*, *Sabbath Walks*, and other poems of a religious character. Grahame is not an easy, graceful poet; and though his verse is full of tender and devout feeling, it has little vigor or imagination. He has been compared to Cowper, but wants that poet's humor, force, and depth of poetic passion.

WILLIAM SOTHEBY (1757-1833), born in London and educated at Harrow, was for some time in the army; but retired about 1780, and devoted himself to literature. He was a man of great learning, and translated some classical works with much elegance and skill. His chief works were, *Poetical Description of Wales*, 1789; *Translation of Virgil's Georgics*, 1800; *Constance de Castille*, 1810, written after the style of Scott's romantic poems; translations of *The Iliad*, 1831; and *The Odyssey*, 1832. His translation from Wieland's *Oberon* has received great commendation.

JOHN HOOKHAM FRERE (1769-1846), a friend of Canning, whom he assisted in the paper called *The Anti-Jacobin;* was Charge d'Affaires in Spain with General Moore, and afterwards Resident at Malta, where he died, aged seventy-seven. He was the author of the once celebrated satiric poem, published in 1817, entitled *Prospectus and Specimen of an intended National Work by William and Robert Whistlecraft*, &c. It was written in *ottava rima*, and was a clever burlesque of romantic writings, with here and there a touch of real poetry. It was the model on which Byron wrote his *Beppo*. He was also the author of the *War Song of Brunnenburg*, published by Ellis as a fourteenth century production, but really written by the author when at school at Eton during the great discussion on the Rowley poems by Chatterton. Frere also made an admirable translation into English verse of the *Acharnians*, *Knights*, *Birds*, and *Frogs* of Aristophanes, which was printed at Malta.

DR. REGINALD HEBER (1783-1826) was born at Malpas, Cheshire, educated at Brasenose College, Oxford, and successively Vicar of Hodnet and Bishop of Calcutta. He died at Trichinopoly, April, 3, 1826. He was author of the *Bampton Lectures*, 1815; *Life of Jeremy Taylor*, 1822; miscellaneous prose writings; and many poems, chiefly religious, of great beauty and feeling.

ROBERT POLLOK (1799-1827), the author of a long poem in blank verse, called the *Course of Time;* a work of real value. A few passages have quite a Miltonic ring. The poem is a sketch of the life and end of man. The sentiments are Calvinistic. The tone and coloring are often too sombre. Sometimes the style becomes rather inflated. Robert Pollok was a native of Muirhouse, Renfrewshire, studied at Glasgow, and became a minister in the United Secession Church. He also wrote *Tales of the Covenanters*, in prose.

ROBERT BLOOMFIELD (1766-1823), the son of a tailor at Honington, near Bury St. Edmund's, worked as a shoemaker in London, where he composed his poetry, which was rejected by London booksellers, but published at Bury, at the expense of Capel Lofft, Esq. He was patronized by the Duke of Grafton, and obtained a situation in the Seal Office. He died on the 19th of August, 1823, at Shefford, Bedfordshire. The chief poems are *The Farmer's Boy* (1798), *Rural Tales* (1810), *Wild Flowers*, &c. His style is descriptive. The rhythm is correct, and the language choice, but the gentle flow seldom bursts into the rush of passion. He never sinks, and never soars.

JOHN LEYDEN (1775-1811), a native of Scotland, wrote a few poems and miscellaneous prose articles in the *Edinburgh Magazine*, entered the Church (1798), but afterwards became a surgeon in the East India Company's service (1802). In India he devoted himself to the study of the Oriental languages. He accompanied Lord Minto in the expedition against Java, where he died in 1811. His *Poetical Remains* were published in 1819, by Rev. James Morton. Sir Walter Scott has spoken in high terms of his poetry.

THOMAS NOON TALFOURD (1795-1854) was born at Reading, rose to distinction at the bar, and was made a judge in 1849. He died on the bench whilst addressing the Grand Jury at Stafford in 1854. He wrote the tragedies of *Ion*, *The Athenian Captive*, *The Massacre of Glencoe*, and *The Castilian;* and in prose, *Vacation Rambles* (1851), *Life of Charles Lamb*, and an *Essay on the Greek Drama*. He is best known by the tragedy of *Ion*, perhaps one of the most striking additions to tragic literature in modern times.

WINTHROP MACKWORTH PRAED (1802-1839), son of Mr. Serjeant Praed, entered the House of Commons, and became Secretary of the Board of Control. His early life and writings gave promise of future eminence. While at Eton he started *The Etonian*, and was one of the chief contributors to *Knight's Quarterly Magazine*. His poems, which have been recently published in a collected form, are some of the most remarkable which have appeared in modern times.

HARTLEY COLERIDGE (1796-1849) and SARA COLERIDGE (1803-1852) were the children of the great Samuel Taylor Coleridge, and themselves well known in the world of letters. The brother was author of *Poems*, *Essays*, *Lives of the Northern Worthies*, and other miscellaneous works. His poems were published, with a Memoir of his life, in 1851. The sister married in 1829 her cousin Henry Nelson Coleridge. The dissertations which she appended to many of her father's works, published after his death, are remarkable both for power of thought and of expression.

MRS. SOUTHEY [CAROLINE ANNE BOWLES]

(1787-1854) was born at Lymington, Hants. Her early life was spent in retirement and literary pursuits. Several poems were published by her of much taste and sentiment. She was married to Southey on the 5th June, 1839. She completed the poem *Robin Hood*, commenced by Southey. Her best known piece is the little lyric called *The Pauper's Death-bed.*

EBENEZER ELLIOTT (1781-1849), the son of an ironfounder of Masborough, Yorkshire, worked himself at his father's business. In 1823 he published some poems; but is best known for the *Corn Law Rhymes*, which appeared between 1830-36. His affection and advocacy of the working classes endeared his name to them; whilst his genius and pure poetic fervor, though sometimes leading him beyond the limits of good taste, claimed the recognition of Southey, Bulwer, and Wilson.

ROBERT MONTGOMERY (1808-1855), a popular preacher at Percy Chapel, Charlotte Street, Bedford Square. His poems passed through numerous editions; but they are stilted and unnatural in expression. Their religious subjects, and the clever puffing which they received, contributed to their success. The chief of them were the *Omnipresence of the Deity*, *Satan*, *Luther*, *Messiah*, and *Oxford*. He is perhaps best known by the scathing criticism which he received in the celebrated essay by Macaulay.

LETITIA ELIZABETH LANDON (1802-1838), best known by her initials L. E. L., under which her poems appeared in various periodicals, which have been collected and published separately. She was the daughter of an army agent, born at Chelsea, and married in 1838 Mr. Maclean, governor of the Gold Coast Colony, West Africa, where she died, October 15, 1839.

REV. GEORGE CROLY (1780-1863), a native of Dublin, and rector of St. Stephen's, Walbrook, London. His style was gorgeous and his imagination fertile. He was the author of several works in poetry and prose. *Paris in* 1815, *Angel of the World* (1820), *Pride shall have a Fall*, *Catiline*, *The Modern Orlando* (1846), are his chief poems. In fiction he produced *Salathiel*, *Tales of the Great St. Bernard*, and *Marston;* the first of which is a romance of great power and eloquence.

MRS. MARY TIGHE (1773-1810), a native of Wicklow County, Ireland, the authoress of *Psyche*, a poem founded on the story of Cupid and Psyche in Apuleius, and exhibiting much imagination and graceful fancy.

JAMES SHERIDAN KNOWLES (1794-1862), one of the principal modern tragic writers, was born at Cork in 1794. He went on the stage, and there distinguished himself as an actor and writer of plays. He afterwards retired from the stage, and occupied himself with teaching elocution, and sometimes preaching in the chapels of the Christian body to which he belonged. *Caius Gracchus* was performed in 1815; and was followed by *Virginius*, one of the most popular dramas that has appeared in recent times upon the English stage. *The Hunchback* and *William Tell* are perhaps his two best works. Two novels were written by him, *George Lovell* and *Henry Fortescue*. His plots are natural, and the characters well sustained.

JAMES HOGG (1770-1835), known better as the "Ettrick Shepherd," a native of Ettrick Vale, Selkirkshire. His school was the mountain's side, where he kept the cattle and sheep. His education was scanty; but a quick and retentive memory, great natural gifts, and a fine appreciation of the wondrous scenes around him, called up the slumbering muse, and in 1801 he published a small volume of songs. *The Mountain Bard* followed in 1807. Soon afterwards he left his occupation and resided at Edinburgh, supporting himself entirely by his pen. The *Queen's Wake* (1813) brought him into very favorable notice. It was followed by *Mador of the Moor*, *Winter Evening Tales*, &c. Hogg's chief delight was in legendary tales and folk lore. Fancy rather than the description of life and manners is the prevailing character of the poet's writings. A modern critic says, "He wanted art to construct a fable, and taste to give due effect to his imagery and conceptions. But there are few poets who impress us so much with the idea of direct inspiration, and that poetry is indeed an art 'unteachable and untaught.'"

MORE MODERN POETS.

The poets of the latter part of the nineteenth century have been very numerous; but there are only four who stand out in any prominence worthy of comparison with that illustrious band which adorned the early years of the century. These are ALFRED TENNYSON, ROBERT BROWNING, MRS. BROWNING, and THOMAS HOOD. The two former are excluded from the scope of this work. The other two must not be passed by without a short notice.

THOMAS HOOD (1799-1845) has, unfortunately, been regarded only as a humorist; and as the English reader would accept from him nothing but wit and humor, the most valuable of his writings are in danger of being forgotten. He was born on the 23d of May, 1799; and in 1821 he became sub-editor of the *London Magazine*, where his poem on *Hope* appeared. He was associated with the brilliant circle who then contributed to the Magazine; among whom were Lamb, Hazlitt, the Smiths, De Quincey, and Reynolds. The latter of these was united with Hood in the publication of the *Odes and Addresses*, which appeared anonymously, and were ascribed by Coleridge to Lamb. These were followed by *Whims and Oddities*. Hood became at once a popular writer; but in the midst of his success a firm failed which involved him in its losses. The poet, disdaining to seek the aid of bankruptcy, emulated the example of Scott, and determined by the economy of a life in Germany to pay off the debt which he had thus involuntarily contracted. In 1835 the family took up their residence in Coblenz; from thence removed to Ostend (1837); and returned to London in 1840. He subsequently became editor of the *New Monthly* in 1841, and held it until 1843, when the first number of his own Magazine was issued. A pension was obtained for him, with reversion to his wife and daughter, in 1844; and he died upon the 3d of May in the following year.

Hood stands very high among the poets of the second order. He was not a creative genius. He has given little indication of the highest imaginative faculty; but his fancy was most delicate and full of graceful play. His appreciation of the beau ties of nature was very vivid; and some of his descriptions are models of their class. His most distinctive mark was the thorough *humanity* of his thoughts and expressions. His poems are amongst the most valuable contributions to English literature of sympathy with, and insight into, human life and character. Every reader is struck by the sadness and melancholy always present in his works. The author of the Comic Annuals can scarcely be conceived of as writing such a poem as the *Bridge of Sighs*. Yet it is true that humor is generally united with sadness. It has been well said by Hood himself, that

"There's not a string attuned to mirth,
But has its chord in melancholy."

Hood was without a doubt the greatest humorist and wit of his age. He possessed in a most remarkable degree the power of perceiving the ridiculous and the odd. Words seemed to break up into the most queer and droll syllables. His wit was caustic, and yet it bore with itself its remedy. It was never coarse. An impurity even in suggestion cannot be found in Hood's pages. With the humor was associated a most tender pathos. The *Death-bed* is one of the most affecting little poems in our language, and is equalled only by another of his ballads entitled *Love's Eclipse*. The deep melancholy that colors "I remember" is carried almost too far. The last verse of that little poem seems to contain the sorrows of a whole life. Amongst his larger works, the *Plea of the Midsummer Fairies*, and *Hero and Leander*, are the most sustained and elaborate. The descriptive pieces in both are full of the most careful observation of nature, and most musical expression of her beauties. The best known of his poems are *The Bridge of Sighs*, *Eugene Aram*, and the *Song of the Shirt*.

ELIZABETH BARRETT BROWNING (d. 1861), wife of Robert Browning, himself an eminent poet, was a native of London, and contributed in very early life to some of the leading periodicals. Her first acknowledged work was *Prometheus Bound*, a translation from the great Greek dramatist, 1833. In 1844 her poems were published in two volumes. After her marriage with Robert Browning, her failing health compelled them to reside in Italy, and they took up their residence first in Pisa, and afterwards in Florence. Here she sympathized warmly with the cause of her adopted and suffering nation. Her poem of *Casa Guidi Windows* appeared in 1851, where the Italian revolutions of 1848 and 1849 kindled her indignation at foreign oppression, and her longings for Italian liberty. Her greatest poem, *Aurora Leigh*, was published in 1856; and her *Poems before Congress* and *Later Poems* were not given to the public till shortly before her death, which took place at the Casa Guidi, Florence, June 29, 1861.

Mrs. Browning stands very high in the rank of English poets. The creative or imaginative faculty she possessed in the highest degree. Her Satan in the *Drama of Exile* is one of the finest creations in the whole range of our literature. So intense, however, was the subjective in this poetess, that all her writings are tinged by herself. We can see the woman of deep emotion, of high-toned thought, of devout spirit, with soul strong enough to have filled the body of a Joan of Arc, shut in her darkened chamber, reading "almost every book worth reading in almost every language," mingling with a few friends, the smallness of which circle prevented a loss of emotional force by too great expanse, her heart going forth in sympathy with the wretched and down-trodden, and at last finding a man and poet worthy of her best affection; and then, gathering up her strength, she seems to fling her own soul into her verse, now with all the passion which gleams through "Aurora Leigh," and now in the tenderer sonnets so full of pathos and love. It is not to be wondered at therefore that some of her writing has been called *spasmodic*. Mrs. Browning has not the calm, unfailing flow of thought and feeling which we find in her only modern superior, the Laureate. But the woman rises to heights on which the man has never stood, and finds deeps which he has never fathomed. Her style is therefore often rugged, unfinished, and at times utterly without rhythm. Some portions of *Aurora Leigh* might be written as prose as well as poetry.

The sadness which pervades all the writing of Mrs. Browning is what might be well expected from such a life as hers. Her ill health, the sudden loss of her younger brother, the long-continued confinement in that chamber where no sunbeam ever cheered, must all have deepened the sorrow in which she ever dwelt. Her verse is therefore but rarely sportive. She deals sometimes in satire, but satire is always sad. Her own idea of the poet's work seems to bear this view. "Poetry has been as serious a thing to me as life itself; and life has been a very serious thing. I never mistook pleasure for the final cause of poetry, nor leisure for the hour of the poet." From such a view of poetry and life, we cannot wonder at the moral purpose, the soul which is found in all her writing.

CHAPTER XXIII.

THE MODERN NOVELISTS.

§ 1. Classification of Romances and Novels. § 2. I. *Romances*. HORACE WALPOLE. § 3. MRS. RADCLIFFE. § 4. LEWIS, MATURIN, and MRS. SHELLEY. § 5. JAMES. § 6. II. *Novels of real life and society*. MISS BURNEY. § 7 MRS. CHARLOTTE SMITH, MRS. INCHBALD, and MRS. OPIE. § 8. GODWIN. § 9. WILLIAM MAKEPEACE THACKERAY. His life and writings. § 10. Criticism of his works. § 11. MISS EDGEWORTH. § 12. *Local Novels*. GALT, PROFESSOR WILSON, LADY MORGAN, &c. § 13. *Fashionable Novels*. LISTER, WARD, and LADY BLESSINGTON. § 14. MISS AUSTEN. THEODORE HOOK. MRS. TROLLOPE. MISS MITFORD. § 15. III. *Oriental Novels*. BECKFORD, HOPE, and MORIER. § 16. IV. *Naval and Military Novels*. CAPTAIN MARRYAT, &c.

§ 1. THE department of English literature which has been cultivated during the later half of the last and the commenement of the present century with the greatest assiduity and success is undoubtedly that of prose fiction — the romance and the novel.

This branch of our subject is so extensive, and it embraces such a multitude of works and names, that the only feasible method of treating it so as to give an idea of its immense riches and fertility will be to classify the authors and their productions into a few great general species: and though there are some names which may appear to belong to several of these subdivisions, our plan will be found, we trust, to secure clearness and aid the memory. The divisions which we propose are as follows: I. Romances properly so called; *i. e.* works of narrative fiction, embodying periods of ancient or middle-age history, the adventures of which are generally of a picturesque and romantic character, and the personages (whether taken from history, or invented so as to accord with the time and character of the action) of a lofty and imposing kind. II. The vast class of pictures of society, whether invented or not. These are generally novels, *i. e.* tales of private life, though some, as those of Godwin, may be highly imaginative, and even tragic. This class contains a great treasury of what may be called pictures of local manners, as of Scottish and Irish life. III. Oriental novels — a branch almost peculiar to English fiction; and originating partly in the acquaintance with the East derived by Great Britain from her gigantic Oriental empire, and partly from the Englishman's restless, inappeasable passion for travelling. IV. Naval and military novels; giving pictures of striking adventure, and containing records of England's innumerable triumphs, by sea and land, together with sketches of the manners, habits, and feelings of our soldiers and sailors.

§ 2. I. ROMANCES. — The history of modern prose fiction in England will be found to accord pretty closely with the classification we have just adopted. We have spoken in another place of the three patriarchs of the English novel — Richardson, Fielding, and Smollett; and the immense class of works we are about to consider may be looked upon as totally distinct from the immortal productions of these great men, though the first impulse given to prose fiction will be found to have been in no sense communicated by *Clarissa*, *Tom Jones*, or *Roderick Random*. This impulse was given by HORACE WALPOLE (1717–1797), the fastidious *dilettante* and brilliant chronicler of the court scandal of his day a man of singularly acute penetration, of sparkling epigrammatic style. but of a mind devoid of enthusiasm and elevation. Rather a French courtier in taste and habits than an English nobleman, he retired early from political life, veiling a certain consciousness of political incapacity under an effeminate and affected contempt for a parliamentary career, and shut himself up in his little fantastic Gothic castle of Strawberry Hill, to collect armor, medals, manuscripts, and painted glass, and to chronicle with malicious assiduity, in his vast and brilliant correspondence, the absurdities, follies, and weaknesses of his day. *The Castle of Otranto* is a short tale, written with great rapidity and without preparation, in which the first successful attempt was made to take the Feudal Age as the period, and the passion of mysterious, superstitious terror as the prime mover, of an interesting fiction. The supernatural machinery consists of a gigantic armed figure dimly seen at midnight in the gloomy halls and huge staircases of this feudal abode — of a colossal helmet which finds its way into the court-yard, filling everybody with dread and consternation — of a picture which descends from its frame to upbraid a wicked oppressor — of a vast apparition at the end — and a liberal allowance of secret panels, subterranean passages, breathless pursuit and escape. The manners are totally absurd and unnatural the heroine being one of those inconsistent portraits in which the sentimental languor of the eighteenth century is superadded to the female character of the Middle Ages — in short, one of those incongruous contradictions which we meet in all the romantic fictions before Scott.

§ 3. The immense success of Walpole's original and cleverly-written tale encouraged other and more accomplished artists to follow in the same track. After mentioning CLARA REEVE (1725–1803), whose *Old English Baron* contains the same defects without the beauties of Walpole's haunted castle, we come to the great name of this class, ANN RADCLIFFE (1764–1823), whose numerous romances exhibit a surprising power (perhaps never equalled) over the emotions of fear and undefined mysterious suspense. Her two greatest works are, *The Romance of the Forest*, and *The Mysteries of Udolpho*. The scenery of her predilection is that of Italy and the South of France; and though she does not place the reader among the fierce and picturesque life of the Middle Ages, she has, perhaps, rather gained than lost by choosing the ruined castles of the Pyrenees and Apennines for the theatre, and the dark passions of profligate Italian counts for the principal moving power, of her wonderful fictions. The substance of them all is pretty nearly the same; and the author's total incapacity to paint individual character only makes us the more admire the power by which she interests us through the never-failing medium of suspense. Mystery is the whole spell. Nothing can be poorer and more conventional than the personages: they are not human beings, nor even the types of classes; they have no more individuality than the pieces of a chess-board; they are merely counters; but the skill with which the author juggles with them gives them a kind of awful necromantic interest. The characters are mere abstract algebraical expressions, but they are made the exponents of such terrible and intense fear, suffering, and suspense, that we sympathize with their fate as if they were real. Her repertory is very limited: a persecuted sentimental young lady, a wicked and mysterious count, a haggard monk, a tattling but faithful waiting-maid, — such is the poor *human* element out of which these wonderful structures are created. Balzac, in one of his tales, speaks with great admiration of an artist who, by a few touches of his pencil, could give to a most commonplace scene an air of overpowering horror, and throw over the most ordinary and prosaic objects a spectral air of crime and blood. Through a half-opened door you see a bed with the clothes confusedly heaped, as in some death-struggle, over an undefined object which fancy whispers must be a bleeding corpse; on the floor you see a slipper, an upset candlestick, and a knife, perhaps; and these hints tell the story of blood more significantly and more powerfully than the most tremendous detail, because the imagination of man is more powerful that art itself: —

> "Over all there hung a cloud of fear,
> A sense of mystery the spirit daunted,
> And said, as plain as whisper to the ear,
> The place is haunted."

The great defect of Ann Radcliffe's fictions is not their tediousness of description, nor even the somewhat mawkish sentimentality with which they may be reproached, nor the feebly-elegant verses which the heroines are represented as writing on all occasions (indeed all these things indirectly conduce to the effect by contrast and preparation); but the unfortunate principle she had imposed upon herself, of clearing up at the end of the story all the circumstances that appeared supernatural — of carrying us, as it were, behind the scenes at the end of the play, and showing us the dirty ropes and trap-doors, the daubed canvas, the Bengal fire by which these wonderful impressions had been produced. If we had supped after the play with the "blood-boltered Banquo," or the "majesty of buried Denmark," we should not probably be able to feel a due amount of terror the next time we saw them on the stage; but in Mrs. Radcliffe, where the feeling of terror is the principal thing aimed at, this discovery of the mechanism deprives us of all future interest in the story; for, after all, pure fear — *sensual*, not moral, fear — is by no means a legitimate object of high art.

§ 4. A class of writing *apparently* so easy, and likely to produce so powerful and universal an effect, — an effect even more powerful on the least critical minds, — was, of course, followed by a crowd of writers

Most of these have descended to oblivion and a deserved neglect. We may, however, say a few words upon Lewis, Maturin, and Mrs. Shelley. MATTHEW GREGORY LEWIS (1775–1818), a good-natured, effeminate man of fashion, the friend of Byron, and one of the early literary advisers of Scott, was the first to introduce into England a taste for the infant German literature of that day, with its spectral ballads and diablerie of all kinds. He was a man of lively and childish imagination; and besides his metrical translations of the ballads of Bürger, and others of the same class, he published in his twentieth year a prose romance called *The Monk*, full of horrible crimes and diabolic agency. It contains several passages of considerable power, particularly the episode of *The Bleeding Nun*, in which the wandering Jew — that god-send for all writers, good, bad, and indifferent, of the "intense" or demoniac school — is introduced with picturesque effect; but the book owes its continued popularity (though, we are happy to say, only among half-educated young men and ecstatic milliners) chiefly to the licentious warmth of many of its scenes. CHARLES ROBERT MATURIN (d. 1824) was an Irish clergyman of great promise and still greater vanity, who carried the intellectual merits and defects of his countrymen to an extreme little short of caricature: his imagination was vivid, and he possessed a kind of extravagant and convulsive eloquence, but his works are full of the most outrageous absurdities. He perpetually mistakes monstrosity for power, and lasciviousness for warmth. His life was short and unhappy. He wrote several romances, the chief of which is *Melmoth*, a farrago of impossible and inconceivable adventures, without plan or coherence, in which the Devil (who is represented as an Irish gentleman of good family in the eighteenth century) is the chief agent. He was likewise the author of a tragedy named *Bertram*, which was acted with success at Drury Lane in 1816.

MRS. SHELLEY (1798–1851), the wife of the poet, and the daughter of W. Godwin, wrote in Italy, in 1816, the powerful tale of *Frankenstein*, in which a young student of physiology succeeds in constructing, out of the horrid remnants of the churchyard and dissecting-room, a kind of monster, to which he afterwards gives, apparently by the agency of galvanism, a kind of spectral and convulsive life. This existence, rendered insupportable to the monster by his vain cravings after human sympathy, and by his consciousness of his own deformity, is employed in inflicting (in some cases involuntarily) the most dreadful retribution on the guilty philosopher; and some of the chief appearances of the monster, particularly the moment when he begins to mov for the first time, and, towards the end of the book, among the eterna snows of the arctic circle, are managed with a striking and breathless effect, that makes us for a moment forget the childish improbability and melodramatic extravagance of the tale.

§ 5. To this subdivision belong the works of that most easy and prolific writer, G. P. R. JAMES (1801–1862) — the most industrious, if not always most successful, imitator of Scott, in revival of chivalric and Middle-Age scenes. The number of James's works is immense, but they bear among themselves a family likeness so strong, and ever oppressive, that it is impossible to consider this author otherwise than as an ingenious imitator and copyist — first of Scott, and secondly of himself. The spirit of repetition is, indeed, carried so far, that it is possible to guess beforehand, and with perfect certainty, the principal contents, and even the chief persons, of one of James's historical novels. His heroes and heroines, whose features are almost always gracefully and elegantly sketched in, have more of the English than continental character. We are sure to have a nondescript grotesque as a secondary personage — a half-crazy jester, ever hovering between the hare-brained villain and the faithful retainer: we may count upon abundance of woodland scenery (often described with singular delicacy and tenderness of language) and moonlight rendezvous of robbers and conspirators. But whereas Scott has all these things, it must be remembered how much more he has *beside*. He looks through all things "with a learned spirit:" James stops short here, unless we notice his innumerable pictures of battles, tournaments, hunting-scenes, and old castles, where we find much more of the forced and artificial accuracy of the antiquary, than of the poet's all-embracing, all-imagining eye. James is particularly versed in the history of France, and some of his most successful novels have reference to that country, among which we may mention *Richelieu*. His great deficiency is want of real, direct, powerful human passion, and consequently of life and movement in his intrigues. There is thrown over his fictions a general air of good-natured, frank, and well-bred refinement, which, however laudable. cannot fail to be found rather tiresome and monotonous.

§ 6. II. Our second subdivision — the *Novels of real life and society* — is so extensive that we can but throw a rapid glance on its principal productions. To do this consistently with clearness, we must begin rather far back, with the novels of Miss Burney. FRANCES BURNEY (1752–1840) was the daughter of Dr. Burney, author of the *History of Music*. While yet residing at her father's house, she composed, in her stolen moments of leisure, the novel of *Evelina*, published in 1778, and is related not to have communicated to her father the secret of her having written it, until the astonishing success of the fiction rendered her avowal triumphant and almost necessary. *Evelina* was followed in 1782 by *Cecilia*, a novel of the same character. In 1786 Miss Burney received an appointment in the household of Queen Charlotte, where she remained till her marriage in 1793 with Count d'Arblay, a French refugee officer. She published, after her marriage, a novel entitled *Camilla;* and her name has more recently come before the public by her *Diary and Letters*, which appeared in 1842, after her death. The chief defect of her novels is vulgarity of feeling; not that falsely-called vulgarity which describes with congenial animation low scenes and humble personages, but the affectation of delicacy and refinement. The heroines are perpetually trembling at the thought of *impropriety*, and exhibit a nervous, restless dread of appearing indelicate, that absolutely renders them the very essence of vulgarity. All the difficulties and misfortunes in these plots arise from the want, on the part of the principal personages, of a little candor and straightforwardness, and would be set right by a few words of simple explanation: in this respect the authoress drew from herself; for her *Diary* exhibits her as existing in a perpetual fever of vanity and petty expedients; and in her gross affectation of more than feminine modesty and bashfulness — literary as well as personal — we see the painful, incessant flutter of her "darling sin" — "the pride that apes humility." Women are endowed by nature with a peculiar delicacy of tact and sensibility; and being excluded, by the existing laws of society, from taking an active part in the rougher struggles of life, they acquire much more than the other sex a singular penetration in judging of character from slight and external peculiarities. In acquiring this power they are manifestly aided by their really subordinate, though apparently supreme, position in society, by the seductions to which they are exposed, and by the tone of artificial deference in which they are always addressed: men who appear to each other in comparatively natural colors never approach women (particularly unmarried women) but with a mask of chivalry and politeness on their faces; and women, in their turn, soon learn to divine the real character under all these smooth disguisements.

The prevailing literary form or type of the present age is undoubtedly the novel — the narrative picture of manners; just as the epic is the natural literary form of the heroic or traditionary period: and the above remarks will, we think, sufficiently explain the phenomenon of so many women now appearing in France, Germany, and England, as novel-writers. Our society is highly artificial: the broad distinctions and demarcations which anciently separated one class of men and one profession from another, have been polished away, or filled up by increasing refinement and the extension of personal liberty: the artisan and the courtier, the lawyer and the divine, are no longer distinguished either by professional costume, or by any of those outward and visible signs which formerly stamped their manners and language, and furnished the old comic writer with strongly-marked characters ready made to his hand. We must now go deeper: the coat is the same everywhere; consequently, we must strip the man — nay, we must anatomize him — to show how he differs from his neighbors. To do this well, fineness of penetration is, above all, necessary — a quality which women possess in a higher degree than men.

§ **7.** Miss Burney was followed by a number of writers, chiefly women, among whom the names of Mrs. Charlotte Smith, Mrs. Inchbald, and Mrs. Opie are prominent. Their fictions, like those of Miss Edgeworth in more recent times, have a high and never-failing moral aim; and these ladies have exhibited a power over the feelings, and an intensity of pathos, not much inferior to Richardson's in *Clarissa Harlowe*. But their works are very unequal, and the pathos of which we speak is not diffused, but concentrated into particular *moments* of the action, and is also obtained at the expense of great preparation and involution of circumstances; so that to compare their genius to that of Richard son, on the strength of a few powerful pictures of intense moral pathos, would be a gross injustice to the admirable and consummate artist in whose works the pathos, inimitable as it is, forms but one item in a long list of his excellences.

MRS. CHARLOTTE SMITH'S (1749-1806) novels, though now forgotten, are praised by Sir Walter Scott, who included her in his British Novelists. Her best novel is the *Old English Manor House*, published in 1793. She also wrote several pathetic poems. MRS. ELIZABETH INCHBALD'S (1753-1821) *Simple Story* (1791) and *Nature and Art* (1796) obtained much celebrity in their time. She also wrote several popular plays. MRS. AMELIA OPIE (1769-1853) was the widow of the celebrated painter, and her first novel, *The Father and Daughter*, published in 1801, may still be read with interest.

§ 8. At the head of the second division of our fictions is undoubtedly WILLIAM GODWIN (1756-1836), a man of truly powerful and original genius, who devoted his whole life to the propagation of certain social and political theories — visionary, indeed, and totally impracticable, but marked with the impress of benevolence and philanthropy. With these ideas Godwin's mind was perfectly saturated and possessed, and this intensity of conviction, this ardent *propagandism*, not only gives to his writings a peculiar character of earnestness and thought, — earnestness, the rarest and most impressive of literary qualities, — but may be considered to have made him, in spite of all the tendencies of his intellectual character — a novelist. Godwin was born in 1756, and appears to have sucked with his mother's milk those principles of resistance to authority and attachment to free opinions in church and state which had been handed down from one sturdy Dissenter to another from the days of the civil war and the republic. He was in reality one of those hard-headed enthusiasts — at once wild visionaries and severe logicians — who abounded in the age of Marvell, Milton, and Harrington; and his true epoch would have been the first period of Cromwell's public life. His own career, extending down to his death in 1836, was incessantly occupied with literary activity: he produced an immense number of works, some immortal for the genius and originality they display, and all for an intensity and gravity of thought, for reading and erudition. The first work which brought him into notice was the *Inquiry concerning Political Justice* (1793), a Utopian theory of morals and government, by which virtue and benevolence were to be the *primum mobile* of all human actions, and a philosophical republic — that favorite dream of visionaries — was to take the place of all our imperfect modes of polity. Animated during his whole life by these opinions, he has embodied them under a variety of forms, among the rest in his immortal romances. The first and finest of these is *Caleb Williams* (1794). Its chief didactic aim is to show the misery and injustice arising from our present imperfect constitution of society, and the oppression of our imperfect laws, both written and unwritten — the *jus scriptum* of the statute-book, and the *jus non scriptum* of social feeling and public opinion. Caleb Williams is an intelligent peasant-lad, taken into the service of Falkland, the true hero, an incarnation of honor, intellect, benevolence, and a passionate love of fame. This model of all the chivalrous and elevated qualities has previously, under the provocation of the cruelest, most persevering, and tyrannic insult, in a moment of ungovernable passion, committed a murder: his fanatic love of reputation urges him to conceal this crime; and, in order to do this more effectually, he allows an innocent man to be executed, and his family ruined. Williams obtains, by an accident, a clew to the guilt of Falkland, when the latter, extorting from him an oath that he will keep his secret, communicates to his dependant the whole story of his double crime, of his remorse and misery. The youth, finding his life insupportable from the perpetual suspicion to which he is exposed, and the restless surveillance of his master, escapes, and is pursued through the greater part of the tale by the unrelenting persecution of Falkland, who, after having committed one crime under unsupportable provocation, and a second to conceal the first, is now led, by his frantic and unnatural devotion to fame, to annihilate, in Williams, the evidence of his guilt. The adventures of the unfortunate fugitive, his dreadful vicissitudes of poverty and distress, the steady, bloodhound, unrelaxing pursuit, the escapes and disguises of the victim, like the agonized turnings and doublings of the hunted hare — all this is depicted with an incessant and never-surpassed power of breathless interest. At last Caleb is formally accused by Falkland of robbery, and naturally discloses before the tribunal the dreadful secret which had caused his long persecution, and Falkland dies of shame and a broken heart. The interest of this wonderful tale is indescribable; the various scenes are set before us with something of the minute reality, the dry, grave simplicity of Defoe. But in Godwin, the faculty of the picturesque, so prominent in the mind of Defoe, is almost absent; everything seems to be ***thought out***, elaborated by an effort of the will. Defoe seems simply to describe things as they really were, and we feel it impossible to conceive that they were otherwise; Godwin describes them (and with a wondrous power of coherency) as we feel they would be in such and such circumstances. His descriptions and characters are masterly pieces of construction; or, like mathematical problems, they are deduced step by step, infallibly from certain *data*. This author possesses no humor, no powers of description, at least of nature — none of that magic which communicates to inanimate objects the light and glow of sentiment — very little pathos; but, on the other hand, few have possessed a more penetrating eye for that recondite causation which links together motive and action, a more watchful and determined consistency in tracing the manifestations of such characters as he has once conceived, or a more prevailing spirit of self-persuasion as to the reality of what he relates. The romance of *Caleb Williams* is indeed ideal; but it is an ideal totally destitute of all the trappings and ornaments of the ideal: it is like some grand picture painted in dead-color.

In 1799 appeared *St. Leon;* in 1804, *Fleetwood;* in 1817, ***Maundeville***; and in 1830, shortly before his death, ***Cloudesley***. These four works are romances in the same manner as *Caleb Williams*, but there is perceptible in them a gradual diminution in vigor and originality: we do not mean of *positive*, but of *relative* originality. *St. Leon* is, however, a powerful conception, executed in parts with a gloomy energy peculiar to this author. The story is of a man who has acquired possession of the great arcanum — the secret of boundless wealth and immortal life; and the drift of the book is to give a terrible picture of the misery which would result from the possession of such an immortality and such riches, when deprived (as such a being must be) of the sympathies of human affection, and the joys and woes of human nature. This novel contains several powerfully delineated scenes, generally of a gloomy tone, and a female character, Marguerite, of singular beauty and interest.

§ 9. Of more modern novelists WILLIAM MAKEPEACE THACKERAY (1811–1863) is unquestionably one of the greatest. He was born at Calcutta in 1811, and was educated at the Charter-house, to which he makes loving reference in his *Vanity Fair* and *The Newcomes*, under the name of "Gray Friars." He afterwards went to Cambridge, which he left without taking his degree. His great desire at this time was to become an artist; and with a considerable fortune he started for the continent, where he studied for four or five years, in France, Italy, and Germany. But though a master of the pencil, Thackeray was not destined to become a great artist. By his life abroad, mingling with different societies, catching the features of this and that city and its people, he was, however, laying in stores of knowledge of the highest value for his after life. At Weimar he was one "of at least a score of young English lads" who were there "for study, or sport, or society." He was introduced to Goethe, and no small pride he felt when some of his sketches were examined by the old poet. On returning to London Thackeray continued his art studies, but the loss of his fortune compelled him to throw himself with all his powers into the field of literature. He entered himself at the Middle Temple, and in 1848 was called to the bar, but he never followed the profession of the law. He was first known by his articles in *Fraser*, to which he contributed under the names of Michael Angelo Titmarsh and George Fitzboodle, Esq. Tales, criticism, and poetry appeared in great profusion. They have a dash, a brilliancy, and fun, which were in after times toned down, and which in the present day are rarely seen in the magazines. As Titmarsh he published *The Paris Sketch Book* (1840), *The Second Funeral of Napoleon*, *The Chronicle of the Drum* (1841), and *The Irish Sketch Book* (1843). These works were illustrated by the author's pencil. The chief of his contributions to *Fraser* as Fitzboodle was the tale of *Barry Lyndon, The Adventures of an Irish Fortune Hunter*. This was full of humor and incident, but the reading public was not yet expecting a greater future from this unknown writer. In 1841 *Punch* was commenced, and Thackeray became at once one of its most diligent supporters. The *Snob Papers* and *Jeames's Diary* appeared from "The Fat Contributor," besides many other pieces in prose and verse. M. A. Titmarsh in 1846 gave to the world *The Notes of a Journey from Corn hill to Grand Cairo*, and a Christmas book followed in the next year. These works had brought Thackeray into more notice, but he was still regarded as nothing but a clever magazine writer. The sly humor, the wise philosophy, the earnest morality, had not yet been recognized. *The Hoggarty Diamond* obtained from John Stirling a prophecy of future fame, but he was not far from forty before his name became illustrious. In 1846 and the two following years appeared *Vanity Fair*, by many supposed to be the best of his works — certainly the most original. The novel was not complete before its author took his place among the great writers of English fiction. It seized all circles with astonishment. The author of satirical sketches and mirthful poems had shown himself to be a consummate satirist and a great novelist.

Mr. Thackeray's fame was now complete. He had only to write and his writings were at once read. A Christmas volume was published in 1848, *Our Street*, and was followed in 1849 by *Dr. Birch and his Young Friends*. His next great work was also in course of publication. In 1849 and 1850 *Pendennis* appeared, inferior in plot, but quite equal to *Vanity Fair* in humor, character, and incident. Another Christmas story appeared in 1851, *The Kickleburys on the Rhine*, which brought down the indignation of the *Times* in the oft-repeated charge of cynicism, to which Mr. Titmarsh replied in the clever little preface to the second edition, *An Essay on Thunder and Small Beer*. In 1851 the lectures on *The English Humorists of the Eighteenth Century* were delivered at Willis's Rooms, where the best men of London society crowded to hear some of the most interesting, brilliant, and yet profound criticism on the greatest prose writers of our nation. These were repeated with similar success in Scotland and America; and in the latter country, in 1855-6, he delivered, on a second visit, his course on *The Georges*, which were received with the greatest enthusiasm on his return to England. In 1852 Thackeray wrote his *Esmond*, in our estimation his most perfect work of art. *The Newcomes* followed in 1855, perhaps the most popular of Thackeray's works. The heartiness and earnestness of the author are not so much concealed as in his other novels. Whilst the charges of severity against him were unfounded, he seemed to have profited by them, and this work evinces more of the tenderness which marked his generous nature.

In 1857 Thackeray made his first and only attempt to enter public life. He stood for Oxford, but was defeated by Mr. Cardwell by a majority of sixty-seven. He returned with more vigor than ever to literature, and before the end of that year commenced *The Virginians*, which was a sort of sequel to *Esmond*. There was still the master hand visible, but it was too much of a repetition of his older stories. On the establishment of the *Cornhill Magazine* in 1860, Thackeray became editor, and whilst connected with it he contributed his later stories, *The Adventures of Philip*, *Lovell the Widower*, and a little monthly sketch *de omnibus rebus et quibusdam aliis*, though oftener *de nihilo*, called the *Roundabout Papers*. He died suddenly in the house which he had built at Kensington on December 23, 1863.

§ **10.** In presenting some sketch of the works of this great novelist we must exclude from our notice his smaller and earlier writings. Of them as a whole it may be said that they are full of humor and irony, the moral purpose of the writer not so clearly evident, but yet present in them all. Social foibles, individual weaknesses, the lesser sins of society, are all shown up and treated with quiet satire. Most of his smaller writings are collected in the four volumes of *Miscellanies* published in 1857. Here appears the poetry of Thackeray. It has been well said, "Thackeray was not *essentially* poetic;" that is, he did not look at everything through the medium of the poetic faculty; his thoughts and imaginings were not always governed by a poetic law. He concealed what was poetic in his nature. He is half ashamed of the sentiment which must have expression. The characters he loves best are the characters where emotion and affection hold their sway, and he cannot keep telling you so as he writes, but he does it with a sort of bashful reticence. He was thoroughly English in the structure of his mind. He could have wept as well as a native of Southern Europe, and sometimes the eye is moist, but the old Gothic spirit despises a man in tears; and so he stands proudly up in self-reliance and a generous manliness. The poetry of his nature was something he ever kept in the recess of his soul. It gave a tenderness to his rebuke, it shed a beauty on his conceptions; and as his countenance was lit with an expression of almost womanly tenderness, so his writing is pervaded with a gentle and loving pathos. But he was able to express himself in a poetic form with much beauty and grace. What finer little poem can be mentioned than his *Bouillabaisse?* and how grand are some of the strains in his poem on the opening of the Great Exhibition of 1851! One of his best humorous poems was that on the *Battle of Limerick*, and we scarcely know which most to admire, the inimitable catching of the spirit and tones of Irish agitators, or the quiet humor, which laughs at the folly of the people, and yet in which laughter they themselves could scarcely help joining. Surely the charge against him of cynicism was unfounded. His humor is almost as trenchant as Jerrold's, while it causes as little pain as that of Sydney Smith.

Vanity Fair, the first of Thackeray's chief works, is called a "Novel without a Hero." It is possessed, however, of two heroines — Rebecca Sharp, the impersonation of intellect without heart, and Amelia Sedley, who has heart without intellect. "Becky Sharp" is without doubt the ablest creation of modern fiction. The selfish, prudent, brave little woman, who without friend or helper wins her way, claims the reader's interest, and very artistic is the set-off which the silly, yet most lovable Amelia presents to the character of Rebecca. As a whole the book is full of quiet sarcasm and severe rebuke. It is replete with humor and morality, and rivets attention to the end by the vivid reality of all the persons and scenes. This work alone might bear out the charge of cynicism against Thackeray; but a careful reading will perceive the kindly heart that is beating under the bitterest sentence and the most caustic irony.

Pendennis was the immediate successor of *Vanity Fair*, and is the life of a Tom Jones of the present age. Literary life presents scope for description, and is well used in the history of Pen, who is a hero of no very great worth. His somewhat silly love adventures and introduction to fashionable life through Major Pendennis form the groundwork of the story. The Major is a most truthful picture of a modern tuft hunter. He and his patrons afford room for the satire and the wisdom the scorn and the counsel, with which the book abounds. As *Vanity Fair* gives us Thackeray's knowledge of life in the present day, so *Esmond* exhibits his intimate acquaintance with the society of the reign of the later Stuarts and earlier Georges. Like *Vanity Fair* it is without plot, and gives in an autobiographical form the life of Colonel Henry Esmond. The style of some hundred and fifty years ago is reproduced with marvellous fidelity. The *Lady Beatrice* is really another Becky Sharp; not equal to the modern woman of the world in tact and power, she is superior in beauty, grace, and other womanly perfections. The story of Esmond is probably the best of Thackeray's writings. Though Esmond is too much of the Sir Charles Grandison type, he is a noble character, and the delicacy of delineation under the guise of autobiography is one of the most sustained dramatic efforts in the whole range of English fiction. The fall of 'Trix is a mistake, for it is both unnatural and unneeded. Lady Castlewood has all the gentleness of Amelia, with much more intellect. We love her so much that we can almost forgive the author marrying her to Esmond.

Of the other works of Thackeray a passing mention must suffice The *Virginians* is the history of the grandsons of Esmond, and though not published till 1857, we mention it next as related to *Esmond* in history. It consists of a series of well-described scenes and incidents in the reign of George II. In 1853 was ended the most popular and best liked of Thackeray's novels, *The Newcomes.* "The leading theme or moral of the story is the misery occasioned by forced and ill-assorted marriages." The noble courtesy, the Christian gentlemanliness, of *Colonel Newcome* is perhaps a complete reflection of the author himself. *Ethel Newcome* is Thackeray's favorite female character. The minor personages are most life-like, while over the whole there is a clear exhibition of the real kindliness of heart which Thackeray possessed. *Philip* and *Lovel the Widower* appeared in the *Cornhill*, and here too was published the fragment left by him at his death. These are reproductions of the old stories. The chief characteristics of his later writings are increased mellowness of tone, maturity of thought and more expressed kindliness and generosity of sentiment.

The two courses of lectures *On the English Humorists* and *The four Georges* are models of style and criticism. The latter is a clever sketch of the home and court life of the first Hanoverians. The lectures are full of thoughts sternly abhorrent of the falsity and rottenness which these courts presented, while admiration for the goodness and kindness of the third George almost makes the lecturer forget his weaknesses. As in his novels, so in his history, Thackeray always elevates the heart above the head, the emotions above the intellect. The *Humorists* is a more valuable work, containing some of the most complete criticism on those writers which is to be found in our language. The principle on which some of the writers, such as Pope, have been included, has been questioned. The treatment of Sterne is too severe, while before Swift it has been well said that "Thackeray seemed to quail," and the sketch of the Dean of St. Patrick is perhaps the feeblest. That of Addison must receive the first place. None could better estimate the essayist than Thackeray. The wit, the man of literary fashion, the kindly gentleman of the reign of Anne could not be better described and judged than by the wit, the essayist, and novelist of the reign of Victoria. In both there were the same graceful humor and gentle piety.

§ **11.** At the head of the very large class of female novelists who have adorned the more recent literature of England, we must place MARIA EDGEWORTH (about 1765–1849). This place she deserves, not only for the immense number, variety, and originality of her works of fiction, but also, and perhaps in a superior degree, for their admirable good sense and utility. Her power of delineating character, and particularly Irish character, renders, however, her tales exceedingly attractive; and by a complete series of stories, graduated so as to interest and describe almost every age from early childhood to maturity, and adapted to the moral requirements of various classes in society, she has certainly rendered immense services to the cause of prudence and practical virtue. Her long and useful life was chiefly passed in Ireland, and many of her earlier works were produced in partnership with her father, Richard Lovell Edgeworth, a man of eccentric character and great intellectual activity, who devoted himself to experiments in education and social ameliorations. The most valuable series of Miss Edgeworth's educational stories were the charming tales entitled *Frank*. *Harry and Lucy*, *Rosamond*, and others, combined under the general heading of *Early Lessons*. These are written in the simplest style and language, and are intelligible and intensely interesting even to very young readers, while the knowledge of character they display, the naturalness of their incidents, and the sound practical principles they inculcate, make them delightful even to the adult reader. In the *Parents' Assistant* the same qualities are applied to the moral and intellectual improvement of a more advanced age; and the common errors, weaknesses, and prejudices of boys and girls are combated in a series of stories which in the good sense and observation they display, are as admirable as in their artistic construction. Some of these — as, for example, *Simple Susan* — are little masterpieces of style and execution. Miss Edgeworth constantly opposes not only the meaner vices and errors, but that tendency to enthusiasm which in the young is so often, though generous in its origin, the source of much misfortune and disappointment; and she strenuously inculcates the happiness and the duty of industry, moderation, and contentment. Her writings for the young form a striking contrast with those of almost all the other authors who have undertaken the same difficult task. They generally, as Berquin for example, fall into the gross error of representing virtue as uniformly triumphant, and vice as uniformly punished, — a false picture of life, which the experience of the youngest reader shows to be fallacious, — while at the same time they adopt a didactic and preaching tone, from which, whether young or old, we instinctively revolt. The tales of the *Parents' Assistant* are completed by the excellent three collections respectively called *Moral Tales*, *Popular Tales*, and *Fashionable Tales;* in which the errors and temptations of middle and aristocratic life are most ably exhibited. Some of these, as the stories of *Ennui*, *Leonora*, *Belinda*, &c., approach, in extent and importance, to regular novels, though they all have some specific moral aim. But perhaps the most truly original of Miss Edgeworth's stories is the inimitable *Castle Rackrent*, giving the biographies, equally humorous and pathetic, of a series of Irish landlords. The follies and vices which have caused no small proportion of the social miseries that have afflicted Ireland are here shown up with a truly dramatic effect. In the novels of *Patronage* and the *Absentee* other social errors, either peculiar to that country or common to it with others, are powerfully delineated. Almost all these works show a delicate appreciation of the merits and the weaknesses of the Irish character, and especially of the Irish peasantry; and Miss Edgeworth has in some sense done for her humbler countrymen what Scott did with such loving genius for the Scottish people. In her writings we see the Irish peasant as he is; and it is impossible to conceive a greater contrast than that of her animated sketches and the conventional Irishman of the stage or of fiction. The services rendered by Maria Edgeworth to the cause of common sense are incalculable; and the singular absence of enthusiasm in her writings, whether religious, political, or social, only makes us more wonder at the force, vivacity, and consistency with which she has drawn a large and varied gallery of characters.

§ **12.** Miss Edgeworth's never-failing success in the delineation of Irish character will warrant us in placing her at the head of a class of novelists almost peculiar to English literature, and which ought to form a subdivision in this part of our subject: we mean writers whose works are devoted to the delineation of *local* manners and character. Thus there are many excellent writers of fiction who have devoted themselves to the painting of the peculiar manners, oddities, and domestic life of Scotland and Ireland exclusively. JOHN GALT (1779–1839), in a long series of novels, has confined himself to the minute delineation — as rich, as original, and as careful as the workmanship of Douw, Mieris, or Teniers — of the interior life of the Scottish peasantry and provincial tradespeople. The *Annals of the Parish*, the supposed journal of a quaint, simple-minded Presbyterian pastor, give us a singularly amusing insight into the microscopic details of Scottish life in the lower classes. Galt's primary characteristic is a dry, subdued, quaint humor a quality very perceptible in the lower orders of Scotland, and which in his works, as in the national character of his countrymen, is often accompanied by a very profound and true sense of the pathetic. The more romantic and tragical side of the national idiosyncrasy has been exquisitely portrayed in the touching tales of PROFESSOR JOHN WILSON (1785–1854), also celebrated as a poet and the author of *Noctes Ambrosianæ*, of whom we shall speak more fully in the subsequent chapter. In his *Lights and Shadows of Scottish Life*, published in 1822, and in *The Trials of Margaret Lyndsay*, which appeared in 1823, he exhibits a deep feeling for the virtues and trials of humble life. In this department of *local* manners the Irish have peculiarly distinguished themselves, as might indeed be expected, when we remember the intense vivacity of the Hibernian character, and the abundance of materials for the novelist afforded by the incessant social, religious, and political discord which for three centuries has never ceased to convulse that country. A long list of names presents itself to our notice, of which it is only possible to mention — LADY MORGAN (about 1786–1859), JOHN BANIM (d. 1842), CROFTON CROKER (1798–1854), and WILLIAM CARLETON. All these persons have devoted themselves, with more or less success, to the depicting the humors or the passions, the bright or dark, the light and shadow, of Irish life. Some — as, for example, Banim — have attached themselves more exclusively to the tragic, or rather melodramatic, scenes of Irish society, generally in the peasant class; and though it is impossible not to appreciate in their works a very marked degree of power, picturesqueness, imagination, and eloquence, yet these high qualities are often eclipsed by an exaggerated and ferocious energy which defeats its own object, and renders the work ridiculous instead of sublime. In the Irish character there is no repose, and where there is no repose there can be no contrast — the only element of strong impressions. Other authors, again, as Crofton Croker, have attached themselves more particularly, and with more effect, to the merely romantic and imaginative features of the national legends and superstitions; and the latter has produced a little collection of fairy tales worthy to be placed beside the delicious *Haus und Kindermärchen* of the brothers Grimm.

§ **13.** Of those who have devoted themselves to the delineation of purely English manners in all ranks of society, the number is so immense that it would be as useless as tedious to give even a catalogue of their names and works. We shall content ourselves with selecting a few of the most prominent, or rather such as appear *typical*, and as consequently will give, in each instance, the general idea of the class at whose head we place them; and first, of the writers of what are called "fashionable novels" — *i. e.* such as pretend to depict the manners, habits, and sentiments of aristocratic life. There is no country in the world, assuredly, in which the middle and lower classes possess so much personal liberty, and consequently so much enlightenment and independence, as England; but at the same time there is hardly any nation in which, generally speaking, there is such a tendency in each class to admire and ape the manners of the class immediately above it. Our present business is with the *literary* effect of this peculiar admiration of aristocracy. Its tendency has been to flood our literature with a preposterous amount of trashy writings, proposing to give a faithful reflection of the manners and habits of high life. Frequently composed, and as a mere speculation, by persons totally unacquainted with the scenes they essayed to describe, and relying for their interest either on grotesque exaggerations of what they supposed to exist in those favored regions, — the Empyrean of fashion, — or on coarse scandal and misrepresentation, these egregious books were either signpost caricatures of what the authors had never seen, or were clumsy réchauffés of forgotten scandal, without wit, sense, probability, or nature. The more extravagant, however, were these pictures, and the less they resembled the ordinary life of the reader, the more eagerly were they admired; and it is not to be wondered at that the time should come when persons, either themselves members of aristocratic society, or men capable of forming true ideas on the subject, should have taken in hand to give something like a true picture of the life of these envied circles. Among the best of these fashionable novels are those of T. H. LISTER (d. 1842), R. PLUMER WARD (d. 1846), and LADY BLESSINGTON (1790-1849). The novels of Ward are distinguished by the author's attempt to unite with an interesting story a good deal of elevated philosophical and literary speculation, so that many of his works — as, for instance, *Tremaine, De Vere, De Clifford,* &c. — are something which is neither a good narrative nor a collection of good essays. Either the philosophy impedes the narrative, or the narrative destroys the interest and coherency of the philosophy. But the writings of Ward, as well as of Lister, whose *Granby* may be read with pleasure, are valuable for the simple and unaffected tone of their language, for the moral truth and elevation of their sentiment, and for the charm that can only be expressed by that most untranslatable of English words — "gentlemanliness."

§ **14.** Descending the social scale, we come to a very large and characteristic department of works — the department which undoubtedly possesses not only the greatest degree of value for the English reader, but will have the most powerful attraction for foreign students of our literature. This is that class of fictions which depicts the manners of the middle and lower classes; and here again we shall encounter a singular amount of female names. The first in point of time, and the first in point of merit, in this class, is MISS AUSTEN (1775-1817), whose novels may be considered as models of perfection in a new and very difficult species of writing. She depends for her effect upon no surprising adventures, upon no artfully-involved plot, upon no scenes deeply-pathetic or extravagantly humorous. She paints a society which, though virtuous, intelligent, and enviable above all others, presents the fewest salient points of interest and singularity to the novelist: we mean the society of English country-gentlemen. Whoever desires to know the interior life of that vast and admirable body, the rural gentry of England, — a body which absolutely exists in no other country on earth, and to which the nation owes many of its most valuable characteristics, — must read Miss Austen's novels, *Sense and*

Sensibility, Pride and Prejudice, Mansfield Park, and ***Emma.*** In these works the reader will find very little variety and no picturesqueness of persons, little to inspire strong emotion, nothing to excite wonder or laughter; but he will find admirable good sense, exquisite discrimination, and an unrivalled power of easy and natural dialogue. MISS FERRIER (d. 1854) has also written a number of novels, generally depicting, with great vivacity and truth, the oddities and affectations of semi-vulgar life; but her works are far inferior, as artistic productions, to the elegant sketches of Miss Austen.

Of the purely comic manner of fiction there are few better examples than the novels of THEODORE HOOK (1788–1842). He is greatest in the description of London life, and particularly in the rich drollery with which he paints the vulgar efforts of suburban gentility to ape the manners of the great. There is not one of his numerous novels and shorter tales in which some scene could not be cited carrying this kind of drollery almost to the brink of farce. Many of his works — as *Sayings and Doings* — consist of short tales, each destined to develop the folly or evil consequences of some particular inconsistency or affectation: thus the work just cited consists of a set of detached stories, each written on the text, as it were, of some common well-known proverb: and though the narratives are of very slight construction, and do not contain very profound views of *character*, they none of them are devoid of some incredibly droll caricatures of *manners*. What, for example, can be more irresistible than the Bloomsbury evening party in *Maxwell*, or the dinner at Mr. Abberley's in the *Man of Many Friends*? Hook's more exclusively serious novels are generally considered as inferior to those in which there is a mixture of the ludicrous; and for one of the last works produced by this clever writer before his death, he selected a subject admirably adapted to the peculiar strength of his talent. This was *Jack Brag*, a most spirited embodiment of the arts employed by a vulgar pretender to creep into aristocratic society, and the ultimate discomfiture of the absurd hero. Hook was a man of great but superficial powers, one of the most amusing conversationists of the day, an inimitable relater of anecdotes, a singer, and an *improvvisatore;* but he was himself afflicted with the same passion for the society of the great as he has so wittily caricatured in Mr. Brag, and his life was passed in incessant but desultory literary labor as a novelist and journalist, in frequent disappointments, in debt, and in the empty applauses of the circle he amused. He died in 1842, leaving a large number of works, all of them exhibiting strong proofs of humor, but mostly deprived of permanent value by the haste perceptible in their execution. The best of them are, perhaps, *Gilbert Gurney*, and its continuation, *Gurney Married.*

Very similar to Theodore Hook in the subject and treatment of her novels, and not unlike him in the general tone of her talent, is MRS. TROLLOPE, whose happiest efforts are the exhibition of the gross arts and impudent stratagems employed by the pretenders to fashion. Mrs. Trollope's chief defect is coarseness and violence of contrast: she does not know where to stop, and is too apt to render her characters not ridiculous only, but odious, in which she offends against the primary laws of comic writing. Moreover she neglects light and shade in her pictures: her personages are either mere embodiments of all that is contemptible, or cold abstractions of everything refined and excellent. Her best work is, perhaps, *The Widow Barnaby*, in which she has reached the ideal of a character of gross, full-blown, palpable, complete pretension and vulgar assurance. The widow, with her coarse handsome face, and her imperturbable unconquerable self-possession, is a truly rich comic conception. Mrs. Trollope's plots are exceedingly slight and ill-constructed, but her narrative is lively, and she particularly excels in her characters of good-natured, shrewd old maids.

It would be a great injustice were we not to devote a few words of admiration to the charming sketches of Miss Mitford (1789–1855), a lady who has described the village life and scenery of England with the grace and delicacy of Goldsmith himself. *Our Village* is one of the most delightful books in the language: it is full of those *home scenes* which form the most exquisite peculiarity, not only of the external nature, but also of the social life of the country. In nothing is our nation so happily distinguished from all others as in the enlightenment, the true refinement, the virtue, and the dignity of her middle and lower classes, and in no position are those classes so worthy of admiration as in the quiet, tranquil existence of the country. She describes with the truth and fidelity of Crabbe and Cowper, but without the moral gloom of the one, and the morbid sadness of the other. Whether it is her pet greyhound Lily, or the sunburnt, curly, ragged village child, the object glows before us with something of that daylight sunshine which we find in its highest perfection in the rural and familiar images of Shakspeare.

§ 15. III. Oriental Novels. — The immense colonial possessions of Great Britain, and particularly her colossal empire in the East, combined with the passion for travelling so strongly manifested in the nation, have created in our literature a class of works which may be considered as forming almost a separate department of fiction. These are novels which have for their aim the delineation of the manners and scenery of distant countries; and as among these works the Oriental are naturally the most splendid and prominent, we shall take three which seem the most favorable specimens of this subdivision. They are different from each other in form, in tone, and in scope, but are equally distinguished for their cleverness and individuality. Of these Oriental novels, then, we select, as the most striking examples, *The History of the Caliph Vathek*, by William Beckford (1759–1844); the romance of *Anastasius*, by Thomas Hope (about 1770–1831); and the inimitable *Hajji Baba* of James Morier (d. 1849). The first of these fictions was as wild, strange, and dreamily magnificent as the character and biography of its author — a man almost as rich, as splendidly luxurious, and as coldly meditative as the Comte de Monte-Christo, in Dumas's popular story. *Vathek* is an Arabian tale, and was originally published in 1784, *in French*, being one of the rare instances of an Englishman being able to write that difficult language with the grace and purity of a native. Being afterwards translated by the author into his mother tongue, it forms one of the most extraordinary monuments of splendid imagery and caustic wit which literature can afford. It is very short, and in some respects resembles (at least in its cold sarcasm of tone and exquisite refinement of style) the *Zadig* of Voltaire. But *Vathek* is immeasurably superior in point of imagination, and in its singular fidelity to the Oriental coloring and costume. Indeed, if we set aside its contemptuous and sneering tone, it might pass for a translation of one of *The Thousand and One Nights*. It narrates the adventures of a haughty and effeminate monarch, led on by the temptations of a malignant genie and the sophistries of a cruel and ambitious mother, to commit all sorts of crimes, to abjure his faith, and to offer allegiance to Eblis, the Mahometan Satan, in the hope of seating himself on the throne of the Preadamite sultans. The gradual development in his mind of sensuality, cruelty, atheism, and insane and Titanic ambition, is very finely traced: the imagery throughout is truly splendid, its Eastern gorgeousness tempered and relieved by the sneering, sarcastic irony of a French Encyclopédiste; and the concluding scene soars into the highest atmosphere of grand descriptive poetry. Here he descends into the subterranean palace of Eblis, where he does homage to the Evil One, and wanders for a while among the superhuman splendors of those regions of punishment. The fancy of genius has seldom conceived anything more terrible than "the vast multitude, incessantly passing, who severally kept their right hands on their heart, without once regarding anything around them. They all avoided each other, and, though surrounded by a multitude that no one could number, each wandered at random, unheedful of the rest, as if alone on a desert where no foot had trodden."

Hope, like Beckford, was a man of refined taste, luxurious habits, and possessed of a colossal fortune accumulated in commerce. His work, though very different in form from that of Beckford, was not unlike it in some points. *Anastasius*, published in 1819, purports to be the autobiography of a Greek, who, to escape the consequences of his own crimes and villanies of every kind, becomes a renegade, and passes through a long series of the most extraordinary and romantic vicissitudes. The hero is a compound of almost all the vices of his unfortunate and degraded nation; and in his vicissitudes of fortune we see passing before us, as in a diorama, the whole social, political, and religious life of Turkey and the Morea. The style is elaborate and passionate: and this, as well as the character of the principal personage, —

"Linked with one virtue, and a thousand crimes" —

reminds us, in reading *Anastasius*, very strongly of the manner of Lord Byron. Indeed this romance is very much what Byron would have written in prose — the same splendid, vivid, and ever-fresh pictures of the external nature of the most beautiful and interesting region of the world, the same intensity of passion, the same gloomy coloring of unrepenting crime.

But if the darker side of Oriental nature be presented to us in *Vathek* and *Anastasius*, in the former combined with the caustic irony of Voltaire, in the second with the mournful grandeur of Byron, the *Hajji Baba* of Morier will make us ample amends in drollery and a truly comic *verve*. This is the *Gil Blas* of Oriental life. Hajji Baba is a barber of Ispahan, who passes through a long but delightfully varied series of adventures, such as happen in the despotic and simple governments of the East, where the pipe-bearer of one day may become the vizier of the next. The hero is an easy, merry good-for-nothing, whose dexterity and gayety it is impossible not to admire, even while we rejoice in the punishment which his manifold rascalities draw down upon him; and perhaps there is no work in the world which gives so vast, so lively, and so accurate a picture of every grade, every phase of Oriental existence. Mr. Morier, who resided nearly all his life in various parts of the East, and whose long sojourn as British minister in Persia made him profoundly acquainted with the character of the people of that country, has most inimitably sustained his imaginary personage. The Hajji is not only a thorough Oriental, but intensely Persian, and a Persian of the lower class into the bargain; a perfect specimen of his nation, — the French of the East, — gay, talkative, dexterous, vain, enterprising, acute, not over scrupulous, but always amusing. The worthy Hajji, in the continuation of the story, comes to England in the suite of an embassy from "the asylum of the universe;" and perhaps nothing was ever more truly natural and comic than the way in which he relates his impressions and adventures in this country, his surprise at the condition of women among us, his admiration of the "moonfaces," and, above all, his astonished wonder at the "Coompany," the great enigma to all Orientals.

§ 16. IV. Naval and Military Novels. — It now remains only to speak of one species of prose fiction — that which has for its subject the manners and personages of marine or military life. It may easily be conceived that, the former service being most entwined with all the sympathies of the national heart, the subdivision of marine novels should be the richest. The contrary might be naturally expected in France; and in France we accordingly find that though, particularly in modern times, numerous novelists have endeavored to put in a picturesque and attractive light the manners and scenes of a sea-life, yet that it is the army which has supplied popular literature — the novel the chanson, and the vaudeville — with the types of character most identified with the national feeling and predilection. What the *militaire* is to the French public, the sailor is to the English: in the songs of the people, on their stage, in their favorite books, the "Jack Tar," the "old Agamemnon" who followed Nelson to the Nile, is as perpetually recurring and indispensable a personage as the "vieux moustache," the "grogneur de la vieille garde," to the French. And this is natural enough. Each country is peculiarly proud of that class to which it owes its brightest and least disputable glory: as the Frenchman naturally hugs himself in the idea that France is incontestably the first military nation in the world, so the Englishman, no less naturally, is peculiarly vain of his country's naval achievements; not that in either case the former at all forgets or undervalues the naval triumphs of his flag, or the latter the military exploits of his; but simply because France is not essentially maritime, and England is, and therefore the natives of each attach themselves to that species of glory which they consider the peculiar property of their nation.

At the head of our marine novelists stands CAPTAIN MARRYAT (1792–1848), one of the most easy, lively, and truly humorous story-tellers we possess. One of the chief elements of his talent is undoubtedly the tone of high, effervescent, irrepressible animal spirits which characterizes everything he has written. He seems as if he sat down to compose without having formed the least idea of what he is going to say, and sentence after sentence seems to flow from his pen without thought, without labor, and without hesitation. He seems half tipsy with the very gayety of his heart, and never scruples to introduce the most grotesque extravagances of character, language, and event, provided they are likely to excite a laugh. This would produce absurdity and failure as often as laughter were it not that he has a natural *tact* and judgment in the ludicrous; and this happy audacity — this hit-or-miss boldness — serves him admirably well. Nothing can surpass the liveliness and drollery of his *Peter Simple*, *Jacob Faithful*, or *Mr. Midshipman Easy*. What an inexhaustible gallery of originals has he paraded before us! The English national temperament has a peculiar tendency to produce eccentricity of manner, and a sea-life in particular seems calculated to foster these oddities till they burst into full blow and luxuriance. Marryat's narratives are exceedingly inartificial, and often grossly improbable; but we read on with gay delight, never thinking of the story, but only solicitous to follow the droll adventures, and laugh at the still droller characters. Smollett himself has nothing richer than Captain Kearney, with his lies and innocent ostentation; Captain To, with his passion for pig, his lean wife and her piano; or than Mr. Easy fighting his ship under a green petticoat for want of an ensign. This author has also a peculiar talent for the delineation of boyish characters: his Faithful and Peter Simple (the "fool of the family") not only amuse but interest us; and in many passages he has shown no mean mastery over the pathetic emotions. Though superficial in his view of character, he is generally faithful to reality, and shows an extensive if not very deep knowledge of what his old waterman calls "human natur." There are few authors more amusing than Marryat; his books have the effervescence of champagne.

CAPTAINS GLASSCOCK and CHAMIER, MR. HOWARD and MR. TRELAWNEY, have also produced naval fictions of merit: the two last authors have followed a more tragic path than the others mentioned above, and have written passages of great power and impressiveness;

but their works are injured by a too frequent occurrence of exaggerated pictures of blood and horror — a fatal fault, from which they might have been warned by the example of Eugene Sue.

The tales called *Tom Cringle's Log* and *The Cruise of the Midge* are also works in this kind (although not exclusively naval) of striking brilliancy and imaginative power. In these we have a most gorgeously colored and faithful delineation of the luxuriant scenery of the West Indian Archipelago, and the manners of the creole and colonist population are reproduced with consummate drollery and inexhaustible splendor of language. They were the production of MR. MICHAEL SCOTT (d. 1835), a gentleman engaged in commerce and personally familiar with the scenes he described; and the admiration they excited at their first appearance (anonymously) in *Blackwood's Magazine* cause them to be ascribed to the pen of some of the most distinguished of living writers, particularly to that of PROFESSOR WILSON.

The military novels are mostly by living authors, and are therefore excluded from our work. MR. GLEIG has recorded in a narrative form many striking episodes of that "war of giants" whose most glorious and terrific scenes were the lines of Torres Vedras, the storm of Badajoz, and the field of Waterloo; and a number of younger authors, chiefly Irishmen, as MESSRS. LEVER and LOVER, have detailed with their national vivacity the grotesque oddities and gay bravery of their countrymen, who never appear to so much advantage as on the field of battle.

NOTES AND ILLUSTRATIONS.

OTHER NOVELISTS.

A few other Novelists, omitted in the preceding chapter, deserve a few words:—

HENRY MACKENZIE (1745-1831), a Scotchman and a resident in Edinburgh, where he enjoyed great literary celebrity. He is best known by *The Man of Feeling*, published in 1771, in which he imitated with considerable success the style of Sterne. He also wrote *The Man of the World*, which is inferior to the former novel.

THOMAS HOLCROFT (1745-1809), an ardent admirer of the French revolutionary doctrines, which he introduced into his novel, *Anna St. Ives*, published in 1792. He is better known by his comedy, *The Road to Ruin*.

SOPHIA LEE (1750-1824) and HARRIET LEE (1766-1851), the authoresses of the *Canterbury Tales*, of which the greater part was written by the younger sister. The first volume appeared in 1797. These Tales are of real merit, and will well repay perusal. "*Kruitzner, or the German's Tale*," says Lord Byron, "made a deep impression upon me, and may indeed be said to contain the germ of much that I have since written." He produced in 1821 a dramatic version of this tale, under the title of *Werner, or the Inheritance*.

DR. JOHN MOORE (1729-1802), a native of Stirling, and a medical man, wrote numerous works, of which his novel called *Zeluco*, published in 1785, is the best known. Dr. Moore had lived abroad for some years, and the scene of the novel is laid chiefly in Italy.

ANNA MARIA PORTER (1781-1832) and JANE PORTER (1776-1850), two sisters whose works were very popular in their day. The *Thaddeus of Warsaw* (1803) and the *Scottish Chiefs* (1809) of the latter are the best known. The style is animated, and some of the scenes striking; but they exhibit little knowledge of real life or character.

MRS. MARY BRUNTON (1778-1818), a native of the Orkneys, and the authoress of *Self-Control* (1811) and *Discipline* (1814), two novels of considerable power.

MRS. ELIZABETH HAMILTON (1758-1816), a native of Belfast, but brought up in Scotland, the authoress of the popular moral tale, *The Cottagers of Glenburnie*, published in 1808.

JOHN GIBSON LOCKHART (1794-1854), who will claim a fuller notice in the following chapter, must be mentioned here on account of his four remarkable novels: *Valerius, a Roman Story* (1821), a tale of the times of Trajan; *Adam Blair* (1822), *Reginald Dalton* (1823), and *Matthew Wald* (1824).

JAMES BAILLIE FRASER (d. 1856), the author of two Oriental romances, *The Kuzzilbash, a Tale of Khorasan* (1828), and *The Persian Adventurer*, of the same character as Mr. Morier's novels.

CHARLOTTE BRONTE (1824-1855), better known by her pseudonyme CURRER BELL, the daughter of a Yorkshire clergyman, published in 1847 a novel, entitled *Jane Eyre*. This was followed by *Shirley* in 1849, and *Villette* in 1853. These novels are remarkable works, exhibiting great knowledge of human nature and striking power.

ALBERT SMITH (1816-1860), a native of Chertsey, was educated for the medical profession, which he abandoned for literature. His *Adventures of Mr. Ledbury*, *Christopher Tadpole*, *The Poppleton Legacy*, and smaller works, are amusing, and have had an extensive circulation.

DOUGLAS JERROLD (1803-1757) was a native of London, but spent his early life at Sheerness, where his father was manager of the theatre. His education was scanty. He went to sea at an early age, sailing with Captain Austen, as a midshipman. When peace came he left the navy, and was apprenticed to a printer. It was at this time that his first literary production appeared — a criticism upon the opera "Der Freischutz." This was followed by a number of dramatic pieces, among which *Black-Eyed Susan* was the most celebrated. He now became a most industrious writer of plays. *Rent Day* was his crowning success, performed at the leading theatres, and obtaining the kindly notice of the artist Wilkie, from whose picture it had been elaborated. This was followed by *The Prisoner of War*, *Time works Wonders*, *The Heart of Gold*.

Contemporaneously with these dramatic writings, his prose works were claiming the ear of the public. *A Man made of Money*, *The Chronicles of Clovernook*, *St. Giles's and St. James's*, were contributed to different magazines of the day. *Punch* found him one of its most successful supporters. In this paper appeared his *Story of a Father*, *Punch's Letters to his Son*, and the *Caudle Lectures*.

He took a leading part also in political writings. He contributed to the *Ballot* and the *Examiner*, started the weekly newspaper called after his own name, and at last undertook the editorship of the popular and largely circulated *Lloyd's Newspaper*. Douglas Jerrold was best known in the social circle. His wit and repartee, his trenchant and mirthful sayings, are still remembered and repeated. He died on the 8th of June, 1857.

CHAPTER XXIV.

PROSE LITERATURE OF THE NINETEENTH CENTURY.

§ 1. Characteristics of the period. § 2. Progress of Historical Literature. The influence of Niebuhr. § 3. Writers upon Ancient History. DR. ARNOLD. SIR GEORGE CORNEWALL LEWIS. § 4. Writers upon Modern History. LORD MACAULAY. § 5. HENRY HALLAM. § 6. Theological Literature. ROBERT HALL. JOHN FOSTER. THOMAS CHALMERS. § 7. Philosophical Literature. SIR WILLIAM HAMILTON. ARCHBISHOP WHATELY. § 8. Physical Science. HUGH MILLER. § 9. Periodical Literature. *The Edinburgh Review.* FRANCIS JEFFREY. SYDNEY SMITH. § 10. *The Quarterly Review.* WILLIAM GIFFORD. JOHN GIBSON LOCKHART. § 11. *Blackwood's Magazine.* JOHN WILSON. § 12. CHARLES LAMB. § 13. THOMAS DE QUINCEY. § 14. Political Economy and Jurisprudence. JEREMY BENTHAM.

§ **1.** IN presenting a brief sketch of the prose literature of the present century, it will be useful in the first place to obtain some general veiw of the period, and to point out the features by which it has been marked. Some critics have divided the age into two periods, and on a careful consideration of the literature of the century a marked distinction will be perceived between the writings of the first generation and those of the generation which has just ended. The close of the reign of the fourth George will present as near a line of division as can be chronologically obtained, and the distinctive features of the first thirty years are well marked from those which belong to the period succeeding. The early years of this century were years of conflict and excitement. The public mind was wrought to the highest pitch, now of fear, and now of triumph. England fought for the liberties of Europe; at times the struggle seemed to be for her own existence. The literature of a people always reflects something of the prevalent tone of its age, and we may therefore expect that the chief compositions of the first part of the period will be marked by intense feeling, passion, and emotion. Such is the case. A larger amount of the highest poetry is to be referred to the first period. There is no age in English history which can exhibit such an array of masters of song. The most passionate states of the human mind demand an expression in song. In the "Victorian age," on the other hand, the prose element has predominated. The calmer inquiries into politics, philosophy, art, and physical science, have been prosecuted in the more tranquil period, and the first noticeable feature in the writers of the present century is the growing prevalence of our prose literature. Another distinguishing characteristic of the prose of this age is the increasing sphere occupied by works of a fictitious character. The present day is, without doubt, the day of novels. The works of fiction of past generations have been few. Richardson was the father of the modern novel, and till recently there have been comparatively few names in fictitious literature that deserve remembrance.

A third feature of the present age is the growth of periodical literature. The rise of our leading reviews will be noticed presently, and together with these have sprung up the countless magazines and newspapers which form the chief part of most men's reading. The *Book* has become too laborious, too tedious a thing for the study of this overworked age. We have come to require stimulants in our reading. Everybody reads something, and few read much. The result of this wide-spread craving for brief and striking compositions must be a weakening of thought, an impoverishing of ideas, and a supply of what is superficial and often crude.

The chief external influence affecting the literature of the age has come from Germany. The study of the language, and the increased facilities of communication, have brought us into close union with that country. The thoughts and even style of this philosophical literature have done much to shape and regulate English thoughts and language. Coleridge introduced it largely, and he has been followed in the work by Thomas Carlyle. The place once held by the French has been almost usurped by the German.

Having thus given a general view of the age, we shall proceed to sketch more in detail the different portions of our prose literature, with brief notices of the most eminent writers.

§ 2. In no department of literature has Europe made greater progress during the present century than in that of History. A new impulse was given to the study of Ancient History by the publication of the first volume of Niebuhr's *Roman History* in Germany in 1811. This remarkable work taught scholars not only to estimate more accurately the value of the original authorities, but to enter more fully into the spirit of antiquity, and to think and feel as the Romans felt and thought. Previous writers of Ancient History, with the exception of Gibbon, had seldom apprehended the ancient world as a living reality; while in the use of their authorities they had shown no critical sagacity and no appreciation of the value of evidence, quoting equally as of the same importance the fabulous tales of a late mythographer and the sober statements of a contemporary writer. In the treatment of Modern History the advance has been equally striking. An *historical sense*, so to speak, has grown up. A writer of any period of modern history is now expected to produce in support of his facts the testimony of credible contemporary witnesses; while the public records of most of the great European nations, now rendered accessible to students, have imposed upon historians a labor, and opened sources of information, quite unknown to Hume, Robertson, and the historical writers of the preceding century.

§ 3. The most eminent English writers upon Ancient History are BISHOP THIRLWALL and GEORGE GROTE, both of whom have produced *Histories of Greece* far superior to any existing in other European languages, but who, as living writers, are excluded from the present work.

DR. THOMAS ARNOLD (1795-1842), Head-Master of Rugby School, wrote a *History of Rome* in three volumes (1838-40-42), which was broken off, by his death, at the end of the Second Punic War. This work is chiefly valuable as a popular exhibition of Neibuhr's views, and is written in clear and masculine English. Dr. Arnold also published some *Introductory Lectures on Modern History* (1842), which display more independence of thought. He was also the author of several theological works, which exercised great influence upon his generation. The most formidable opponent of Neibuhr's views was SIR GEORGE CORNEWALL LEWIS (1806-1863), equally remarkable as a statesman and a scholar, and whose untimely death the country still mourns. He was educated at Eton and Christ Church, Oxford, and, after holding the office of Poor-Law Commissioner and other public appointments, he became Chancellor of the Exchequer in 1855. Subsequently he was Secretary of State for the Home Department, and finally Secretary of State for War, which latter office he held at the time of his death (April 13, 1863). Sir George Lewis's most important historical work is *An Inquiry into the Credibility of the early Roman History*, published in 1855. While rejecting with Niebuhr the received narrative of early Roman history, Sir George Lewis attacks the defective method adopted by the German historian in attempting to reconstruct this portion of Roman history. He observes that Niebuhr, "instead of employing those tests of credibility which are consistently applied to modern history, attempts to guide his judgment by the indications of internal evidence, and assumes that the truth can be discovered by an occult faculty of historical divination." It would not be within the province of the present work to discuss this question; but it cannot admit of doubt that Sir George has rendered an important service to historical investigations, and that the principles which he has laid down are in the main correct. Sir George Lewis was also the author of many valuable political works, of which the most important are *A Treatise on the Method of Observation and Reasoning in Politics*, the *Influence of Authority in Matters of Opinion*, and the *Use and Abuse of Political Terms*.

§ 4. The most illustrious recent writer upon modern history is THOMAS BABINGTON MACAULAY (1800-1859), born October 25, 1800. He was the son of Zachary Macaulay, an ardent philanthropist, and one of the earliest opponents of the slave trade. Educated at Trinity College, Cambridge, of which College he became a Fellow, and called to the bar at Lincoln's Inn, he suddenly achieved a literary reputation by an article on Milton in the *Edinburgh Review* in 1825. This was the first of a long series of brilliant literary and historical essays which he contributed to the same periodical. He entered Parliament in 1830, and was almost immediately acknowledged to be one of the first orators in the House. He went to India in 1834 as a Member of the Council in Calcutta and as President of the Law Commission. Soon after his return he was elected by the city of Edinburgh as their representative in Parliament (1840), and became successively Secretary at War and

Paymaster of the Forces. He lost his election in 1847, in consequence of opposing the religious prejudices of his constituents, and from this time he devoted all his powers to the undivided cultivation of letters. Although he sat in Parliament again from 1852 to 1856, he took little part in the debates of the House. He was raised to the peerage in 1857, and died on December 28, 1859.

Macaulay is distinguished as a Poet, an Essayist, and an Historian. His *Lays of Ancient Rome* are the best known of his poems; but the lines which he wrote upon his defeat at Edinburgh in 1847, and in which he turns for consolation to literature, are, in our judgment, the finest of all his poetical pieces. His Essays and his History will, in virtue of their inimitable style, always give Macaulay a high place among English classics. His style has been well characterized by a friendly but discerning critic: "It was eminently his own, but his own not by strange words, or strange collocation of words, by phrases of perpetual occurrence, or the straining after original and striking terms of expression. Its characteristics were vigor and animation, copiousness, clearness, above all sound English, now a rare excellence. The vigor and life were unabating; perhaps in that conscious strength which cost no exertion he did not always gauge and measure the force of his own words. Those who studied the progress of his writing might perhaps see that the full stream, though it never stagnated, might at first overflow its banks; in later days it ran with a more direct, undivided torrent. His copiousness had nothing tumid, diffuse, Asiatic; no ornament for the sake of ornament. As to its clearness, one may read a sentence of Macaulay twice to judge of its full force, never to comprehend its meaning. His English was pure, both in idiom and in words, pure to fastidiousness; not that he discarded, or did not make free use of the plainest and most homely terms (he had a sovereign contempt for what is called the dignity of history, which would keep itself above the vulgar tongue), but every word must be genuine English, nothing that approached real vulgarity, nothing that had not the stamp of popular use, or the authority of sound English writers, nothing unfamiliar to the common ear." *

Macaulay's Essays are philosophical and historical disquisitions, embracing a vast range of subjects; but the larger number and the most important relate to English History. These Essays, however, were only preparatory to his great work on the *History of England*, which he had intended to write from the accession of James II. to the time immediately preceding the French Revolution. But of this subject he lived to complete only a portion. The two first volumes, published in 1849, contain the reign of James II. and the Revolution of 1688; two more, which appeared in 1855, bring down the reign of William III. to the peace of Ryswick in 1697; while a fifth, published in 1861, after the author's death, nearly completes the history of that reign. Macaulay in a Review of Sir James Mackintosh's *History of the Revolution*, observed that "a History of England, written throughout in this man

* Dean Milman's *Memoir of Lord Macaulay*, p. 22.

ner, would be the most fascinating book in the language. It would be more in request at the circulating libraries than the last novel." The unexampled popularity of Macaulay's own History verified the prediction. In a still earlier Essay he had remarked that we had good historical romances and good historical essays, but no good histories; and it cannot be denied that he has, to a great extent, attained his ideal of a perfect history, which he defines to be "a compound of poetry and philosophy, impressing general rules on the mind by a vivid representation of particular characters and incidents."

§ 5. The other great writer on modern history in the present century, superior in judgment to Macaulay, though inferior in graces of style, is HENRY HALLAM (1777-1859). He was born at Windsor, July 9, 1777, the only son of a Canon of Windsor and Dean of Wells. He was educated at Eton and Christ Church, Oxford, and practised at the bar for a few years; but having an ample income, which was augmented by his being appointed one of the Commissioners of Audit, he withdrew from the profession of the law, and devoted himself entirely to literature. He was one of the early contributors to the *Edinburgh Review*, and his criticism in that Journal in 1808 of Sir Walter Scott's edition of Dryden's works was marked by that power of discrimination and impartial judgment which characterized all his subsequent writings. As one of the Edinburgh Reviewers, he was pilloried by Lord Byron —

"And classic Hallam, much renowned for Greek."

Mr. Hallam was an excellent classical scholar; and to his knowledge of antiquity he added an accurate and profound acquaintance with the language, literature, history, and institutions of the chief nations of modern Europe. The result of his long-continued studies first appeared fully in his *View of the State of Europe during the Middle Ages*, published in 1818, and exhibiting, in a series of historical dissertations, a comprehensive survey of the chief circumstances that can interest a philosophical inquirer during the period usually denominated the Middle Ages. Mr. Hallam's next work was *The Constitutional History of England from the Accession of Henry VII. to the Death of George II.*, published in 1827; and his third great production was *An Introduction to the Literature of Europe in the Fifteenth, Sixteenth, and Seventeenth Centuries*, which appeared in 1837-9. Mr. Hallam's latter years were saddened by the loss of his two sons, the eldest of whom formed the subject of Tennyson's *In Memoriam*. The historian himself died January 21, 1859.

An estimate of Hallam's literary merits has been given by Macaulay, his illustrious contemporary, in a review of the Constitutional History: "Mr. Hallam is, on the whole, far better qualified than any other writer of our time for the office which he has undertaken. He has great industry and great acuteness. His knowledge is extensive, various, and profound. His mind is equally distinguished by the amplitude of its grasp and by the delicacy of its tact. His speculations have none of that vagueness which is the common fault of political philosophy. On the contrary, they are strikingly practical, and teach us not only the general rule, but the mode of applying it to solve particular cases. In this respect they often remind us of the Discourses of Machiavelli. The manner of the book is, on the whole, not unworthy of the matter. The language, even when most faulty, is weighty and massive, and indicates strong sense in every line. It often rises to an eloquence, not florid or impassioned, but high, grave, and sober; such as would become a State paper, or a judgment delivered by a great magistrate, a Somers or a D'Aguesseau. In this respect the character of Mr. Hallam's mind corresponds strikingly with that of his style. His work is eminently judicial. The whole spirit is that of the bench, not that of the bar. He sums up with a calm, steady impartiality, turning neither to the right nor to the left, glossing over nothing, exaggerating nothing, while the advocates on both sides are alternately biting their lips to hear their conflicting misstatements and sophisms exposed. On a general survey, we do not scruple to pronounce the *Constitutional History* the most impartial book that we have ever read."

§ 6. The theological and religious literature of this age is marked by a less metaphysical character than that of former times. Works of a controversial kind have been fewer, while greater attention has been paid to exegetical studies. The practical and homiletical works have been very numerous. The array of Sermons which the last sixty years have seen published is appalling, and if the good accomplished has been proportioned to the number of tracts and sermons issued, there must certainly have been an effect which should cheer the believer in human progress. Space forbids even a mention of the Societies whose special work is the publication of religious literature, of which many were founded in the present century, and all have received their greatest success in the present age. Many of the best known religious writers have won their chief literary honors in the other fields of criticism, history, or philosophy, and will receive notice there. The three most distinguished theological writers are perhaps Hall, Foster, and Chalmers.

ROBERT HALL (1764-1831) was born at Arnsby, near Leicester, the son of a Baptist minister of that place. After studying first at a dissenting academy at Bristol, and afterwards at Aberdeen, he became a minister successively of the Baptist Churches at Bristol, Cambridge, and Leicester, and finally at Bristol for a second time, where he died, February 21, 1831. Mr. Hall was without doubt the "prince of modern preachers." With his eloquence and fervor were united a scholarship and intellectual vigor not often found in the pulpit. His style was chaste, polished, and refined. His great sermons were on *Modern Infidelity* (1799), *Reflections on War* (1802), and *The Sentiments proper to the present Crisis* (1803).

JOHN FOSTER (1770-1843), like his friend Robert Hall, was a minister among the Baptists, but was never celebrated as a preacher, though his writings, in the form of literary and religious essays, are among the most valuable additions to English literature. In his Essays the energy and force of the thought are only equalled by the beauty of the expression. There is a manly tone about everything he wrote. With less impassioned eloquence than Hall, he has more intellectual vigor.

THOMAS CHALMERS (1780–1847) was born at Anstruther, Fifeshire, and educated for the Scotch Church at the University of St. Andrew's. In 1803 he became minister at Kilmany, whence in 1815 he removed to St. John's, Glasgow. In 1823 he was appointed Professor of Moral Philosophy at St. Andrew's, and in 1828 Professor of Divinity at Edinburgh. In 1843 he headed the secession from the Scotch Church, and remained the most eminent of the Free Church ministers until his death in 1847. In the pulpit Chalmers reigned supreme. Though his manner was rough, and his accent broadly Scotch, the impassioned earnestness, the thorough *abandon*, of the preacher overcame these drawbacks, and enabled him to thrill his audience with something of the emotion which possessed himself. His writings embrace a great variety of subjects, and all are treated ably by his capacious intellect; but he is not the leader of a school. He established no great principle. He added nothing to divinity, science, or philosophy. He shone not with the blaze of the meteor, or the self-radiance of a sun, but he was the brightest star amongst the other constellations that shone around him. His style was incorrect and often awkward, but there is at times a grandeur of language that bears away the most fastidious critic. The hold he took of a subject was like the grip of a bulldog He never let it go. He turned it this side and that, holding it up in every light, adorning it with every fancy and illustration. It stood forth before the hearer or reader as clearly as before the preacher or writer.

§ 7. In philosophy a large number of contributions to our literature has been made during the period under our consideration. Though perhaps there has been but little original speculation, and no great discovery in mental science, the investigation of metaphysical phenomena has been profound and accurate. Philosophy has not passed through a crisis, but it has made a brilliant and yet secure advance. The scope of this work forbids a notice of living writers; otherwise we might refer to some names, such as WHEWELL and MILL, whose analysis and investigations, more especially in the systems of inductive science, have had none to compare with them since the great work of Bacon, while in the more direct examination of mental phenomena the Scotch school has had some of its ablest members in the present era, and the materialist schools of different color have found their strongest advocates and expounders in writers, many of whom are still living. The influence of Germany has been felt in no department of our literature so greatly as here. The followers of Reid owe no little to the writings of Kant, while the idealists of England have borrowed no little of the truth they hold from the profound though the very obscure speculations of Hegel. The study of logic in England proper has been revived almost within our own memory, and the once-neglected studies have emerged from their misapprehension and obloquy, and are rapidly gaining in the universities their proper position abreast of classics and mathematics.

SIR WILLIAM HAMILTON (1788-1856), the son of Dr. Hamilton of Glasgow, was educated at Oxford, and called to the bar in 1813. He became Professor of Universal History at Edinburgh in 1821, and in 1836 obtained the Chair of Logic and Metaphysics, which he occupied until his death. His chief works were essays in the *Edinburgh Review*, collected as *Discussions on Philosophy*, &c. (1852), and *An Edition of Reid, with Dissertations.* His *Lectures* have been published since his death, under the editorship of Mr. Mansel and Mr. Veitch. Sir William Hamilton was without doubt the greatest philosopher of his age. He founded his system on consciousness, following Reid more than any other master, and guiding his speculations by Aristotle and Kant This is not the place for a discussion of his philosophical views; but he has done much, perhaps more than any other English writer, to raise philosophical studies in this country. His style is a model of philosophical writing. It is clear, capacious, and appropriate. It neither perplexes by technicalities nor misleads by figure and illustration. It has been well said of his diction that it fills others with the "desire and despair of writing like a philosopher."

ARCHBISHOP WHATELY (1787-1863), the son of Dr. Whately of Nonsuch Park, Surrey, was born in London, and educated at Oriel College, Oxford. Having entered the Church, he became Rector of Halesworth in 1822, Principal of St. Alban's Hall in 1825, then Professor of Political Economy, and in 1831 was raised to the archiepiscopal see of Dublin. His first publications were, in 1821, three sermons on the *Christian's Duty with respect to the Government*, followed by his *Bampton Lectures;* and, in 1826 and 1828, by his *Logic* and *Rhetoric.* To enumerate all the publications of this diligent writer would not be possible in this sketch. The chief were his essays on *New Testament Difficulties* (1828), the *Sabbath*, and *Romanism*, which were produced together two years later. His lectures on *Political Economy* appeared in 1831; and later he published other works on social and economical questions.

Whately had a mind of great logical power, with little imagination or fancy. His clear, unanswerable arguments produce conviction in his readers. He says of himself that he was personally of no influence among men; but he was able so conclusively to exhibit his processes of reasoning and arguments, that he produced a great impression upon the circles which they affected. His views of questions are often shallow, but always practical. His style is luminous, easy, and well adorned with every-day illustrations. A moralist of much higher tone than Paley,—which fact arose from the general spirit of his time,—he is the best representative of Paley in the present age. He is, as Paley was, clear rather than profound, vigorous rather than subtle; with little speculation he unites much practical sense.

§ 8. A very important portion of modern literature embraces those subjects which have reference to physical science. Our forefathers were more satisfied with reasons than with facts. The aim of modern investigators is to discover what is hidden in nature, rather than, by a course of deductive reasoning from pre-established principles, to display what ought to be found in nature. The inductive method of Bacon has never been so carefully applied and diligently followed as in the scientific researches of the nineteenth century; and the advance of physical science has therefore been more rapid than that of any other branch of human knowledge. The greatest writers on physical science are still alive; and many of them will deserve a place in English literature on account of the style of their writings, such as HERSCHEL, LYELL, FARADAY, OWEN, and HUXLEY. One of the most popular, who has died within the last few years, was HUGH MILLER (1802–1856), the eminent geologist. He spent the early portion of his life in the quarries of his native town of Cromarty in the north of Scotland, but by self-study and diligent application he rose from manual to mental labor; and after a few publications — *Poems*, &c. (1829), *Letters on the Herring Fishery*, &c. — he became editor of the *Witness*, a bi-weekly newspaper. He had meantime devoted himself to geology; and in 1841 appeared his *Old Red Sandstone*, and in 1850 another geological work, entitled *Footprints of the Creator*. He published an autobiography, in 1854, *My Schools and Schoolmasters;* and since his death there have appeared *The Cruise of the Betsy, a Summer Ramble among the Fossiliferous Deposits of the Hebrides* (1858), and *Lectures on Geology*, delivered before the Philosophical Institution at Edinburgh. There is no writer who has done more for the spread of geological knowledge than Hugh Miller. His earnest, manly spirit, his lively style, and his religious character, won him a hearing in his native land among every rank and condition in society. His *Testimony of the Rocks*, completed but not published during his life, is full of some of the most poetic and eloquent passages in the English language.

§ 9. No review is here required of the fictitious literature of the age, as that has already been treated at length in the preceding chapter. We therefore now pass on to the most important and most extensive of the prose writings of the nineteenth century, — namely, those which are for the most part found scattered in magazines and serials, and which embrace the critical essays and other compositions on social, political, and moral subjects. The increased facilities of printing and a larger class of readers have combined to render the "periodicals" the great feature of the age. These range from the valuable quarterlies, through the various forms of magazine and review, down to the daily paper, the peculiar feature of the literature of the times. Some of the most valuable of our essays have been contributed to these magazines. Every shade of politics, every school of philosophy, every sect of religion, has its paper or its magazine. The events of the day, the deliberations and acts of the government, the condition of society, the progress of commerce, the works of art, and the discoveries of science, are thus placed under constant and Argus-eyed surveillance. Perhaps the cheap daily paper is the wonder of the age. What a marvel of literary skill is the *Times!* and very little inferior are the other chief newspapers. No feature is so striking in this class of writings as the real worth and ability displayed in many of the articles of the periodicals. The criticism of the day shows a great improvement in conception and views upon those of past generations. To give a history of all these periodicals is of course impossible, but the establishment of the *Edinburgh* and *Quarterly Reviews* imparted such an impulse to literature as to demand a few words.

The Edinburgh Review was established in 1802 by a small party of young men, obscure at that time, but ambitious and enterprising, who were all destined to attain a high degree of distinction. It founded its claim to success upon the boldness and vivacity of its tone, its total rejection of all precedent and authority, and the audacity with which it discussed questions previously held to be "hedged in" with the "divinity" of prescription. *The Edinburgh* was an absolute literary Fronde; and its founders — Brougham, Jeffrey, Sydney Smith, Francis Horner — were soon convinced that they had not erred in calculating upon an extraordinary degree of success. The criticisms (many of which were *retrospective*, that is, discussing the merits of past eras in the history and literature of England and other countries) were marked by a singular boldness and pungency; and in contemporary and local subjects the *Review* exhibited a power and extent of vision which made its appearance an era in journalism. It was conducted from 1802 to 1829 by FRANCIS JEFFREY (1773-1850), a Scotch advocate, who was subsequently raised to the bench. He wrote a large number of critical articles, marked by good taste and discrimination, the most important of which were republished by him in a collected form in 1844. Another of the most important of the early contributors to the *Review*, and who indeed edited the first number, was SYDNEY SMITH (1771-1845), an English clergyman, and in the later period of his life Canon of St. Paul's. He wrote chiefly upon political and practical questions with a richness of comic humor, and an irresistible dry sarcasm, employed generally in *exhaustive* reasoning — in the *reductio ad absurdum* — which is not only exquisitely amusing, but is full of solid truth as well as pleasantry.

§ 10. The influence which the *Edinburgh Review* soon acquired was exercised in favor of political principles opposed to those of the existing administration; and its authority in matters of literature and taste became almost paramount. Under these circumstances the late Mr. Murray, after consulting Mr. Canning and other distinguished politicians and men of letters, determined in 1809 to start a new review to counteract the danger of those liberal opinions which seemed to be menacing the very integrity of the Constitution. This new periodical, which was called *The Quarterly Review*, was warmly welcomed by the friends of the government, and immediately obtained a literary reputation at least equal to that of the *Edinburgh*. The editorship of it was intrusted to WILLIAM GIFFORD (1757-1826), the translator of Juvenal (1802), and the author of the *Baviad* (1794) and *Mæviad* (1795), two of the most bitter, powerful, and resistless literary satires which modern days have produced. Gifford was a self-taught man, who had raised himself, by dint of almost superhuman exertions and admirable integrity, to a high place among the literary men of his age. Distinguished as a satirist, as a translator of satires, and as the editor of several of the illustrious but somewhat neglected dramatists of the Elizabethan age, his writings, admirable for sincerity, good sense, and learning, were also strongly tinged with bitterness and personality.

Gifford was succeeded in the editorship of the *Quarterly*, after a short interregnum, by JOHN GIBSON LOCKHART (1794–1854), a man of undoubted genius, the author of several novels which have been already mentioned, and one of the earliest and ablest contributors to *Blackwood's Magazine*. He was born in 1794, in Lanarkshire, and was educated at Oxford, where he took a first class in classics. He possessed a clear, penetrating intellect, and under his editorship, which continued from 1826 to 1853, the reputation of the *Quarterly* was not only maintained, but augmented. Many of the ablest articles were written by himself; and those which combine the biography and criticism of distinguished authors are unsurpassed by anything of the kind in the English language. In 1820 he married the eldest daughter of Sir Walter Scott, and in 1837–39 he published the charming life of his father-in-law. In biography he was unrivalled; and his *Life of Napoleon*, which appeared without his name, is far superior to many more ambitious performances.

§ **11.** The same reasons which led to the establishment of the *Quarterly Review* in London, induced another enterprising publisher to start, in the city in which the *Edinburgh Review* exercised undivided sway, a periodical which might serve as an organ of Toryism in Scotland. *Blackwood's Magazine* first appeared in 1817, and was distinguished by the ability of its purely literary articles, as well as by the violence of its political sentiments. Among the many able men who wrote for it, two stood pre-eminent, John Wilson and John Gibson Lockhart. Of the latter we have already spoken in connection with the *Quarterly Review;* the former, upon whom fell the chief burden of the magazine after Lockhart's removal to London, must not be dismissed without a short notice. JOHN WILSON (1785-1854) was born in Paisley, May 18, 1785, the son of a wealthy merchant. After studying at Oxford, he took up his abode on the banks of the Windermere, attracted thither by the society of Worsdworth, Southey, Coleridge, and other eminent men. Wilson was an ardent admirer of Wordsworth, whose style he adopted, to some extent, in his own poems, the *Isle of Palms* (1812), and *The City after the Plague* (1816). The year before the publication of the latter poem, Wilson had been compelled, by the loss of his fortune, to remove to Edinburgh, and to adopt literature as a profession. Though Mr. Blackwood was the editor of his own magazine, Wilson was the presiding spirit, and under the name of Christopher North and other pseudonymes, he poured forth article after article with exuberant fertility. His *Noctes Ambrosianæ*, in which politics, literary criticism, and fun, were intermingled, enjoyed extraordinary popularity. His novels likewise were eagerly read (see p. 450). In 1820 he was elected Professor of Moral Philosophy at Edinburgh. He died April 2, 1854. "With respect to Wilson's merits as a writer, a variety of judgments will be formed. His poetry can never, in our opinion, take a foremost place among English classics. His prose tales, *Lights and Shadows of Scottish Life*, *The Trials of Margaret Lindsay*, *The Foresters*, &c., had their day. Probably no man, living or dead, could have written them except himself, yet we doubt whether they will find many readers a dozen years hence. Of his criticism, likewise, we are constrained to observe that it is at all times the decision of an impulsive rather than of a judicial mind. But far above all his contemporaries, and, indeed, above writers of the same class in any age, he soars as a rhapsodist. As Christopher North, by the loch, or on the moors, or at Ambrose's, he is the most gifted and extraordinary being that ever wielded pen. We can compare him, when such fits are on, to nothing more aptly than to a huge Newfoundland dog, the most perfect of its kind; or, better still, to the 'Beautiful leopard from the valley of the palm-trees,' which, in sheer wantonness and without any settled purpose, throws itself into a thousand attitudes, always astonishing and often singularly graceful." *

§ 12. It would be impossible in our limits to give an account of the many other writers who distinguished themselves by their contributions to the Reviews and Magazines; but in addition to those already mentioned two essayists stand forth pre-eminent — Charles Lamb and Thomas de Quincey.

CHARLES LAMB (1775–1834) is one of the most admirable of those *humorists* who form the peculiar feature of the literature, as the ideas they express are the peculiar distinction of the character, of the English people. He was born February 18, 1775, in the Temple, where his father was clerk to one of the Benchers, and was educated at Christ's Hospital. He was essentially a *Londoner:* London life supplied him with his richest materials; and yet his mind was so imbued, so saturated with our older writers, that he is original by the mere force of self-transformation into the spirit of the older literature: he was, in short, an old writer, who lived by accident a century or two after his real time. Wordsworth is peculiarly the poet of solitary rural nature; Lamb drew an inspiration as true, as delicate, as profound, from the city life in which he lived; and from which he never was for a moment removed but with pain and a yearning to come back. In him the organ of *locality* must have been enormously developed: "his household gods planted a terribly fixed foot, and were not to be rooted up without blood." During the early and greater part of his life, Lamb, poor and unfriended, was drudging as a clerk in the India House; and it was not till late in life that he was unchained from the desk. Yet in this, the most monotonous and unideal of all employments, he found

* *Quarterly Review*, No. 225, p. 240.

means to fill his mind with the finest aroma of our older authors; particularly of the prose writers and dramatists of the sixteenth and seventeenth centuries: and in his earliest compositions, such as the drama of *John Woodvil*, and subsequently in the *Essays of Elia*, although the world at first perceived a mere imitation of their quaintness of expression, there was, in reality, a revival of their very spirit. The *Essays of Elia*, contributed by him at different times to the *London Magazine*, are the finest things, for humor, taste, penetration, and vivacity, which have appeared since the days of Montaigne. Where shall we find such intense delicacy of feeling, such unimaginable happiness of expression, such a searching into the very body of truth, as in these unpretending compositions? A chance word, dropped half by accident, a parenthesis. an exclamation, often let us into the very mechanism of the sentiment — admit us, as it were, behind the scenes The style has a peculiar and most subtle charm; not the result of labor for it is found in as great perfection in his familiar letters — a certain quaintness and antiquity, not affected in Lamb, but the natural garb of his thoughts. This arises partly from the saturation of his mind with the rich and solid reading in which he delighted; and partly, but in a much higher degree, from the sensibility of his mind. The manure was abundant, but the soil was also of a "Sicilian fruitfulness." As in all the true humorists, his pleasantry was inseparably allied with the finest pathos: the merry quip on the tongue was but the commentary on the tear which tembled in the eye. He possessed the power, which is seen in Shakspeare's Fools, of conveying a deep philosophical verity in a jest — of uniting the wildest merriment with the truest pathos and the deepest wisdom. It is not only the easy laugh of Touchstone in the forest of Arden, but the heart-rending pleasantry of Lear's Fool in the storm. The inspiration that other poets find in the mountains, in the forest, in the sea, Lamb could draw from the crowd of Fleet Street, from the remembrances of an old actor, from the benchers of the Temple. In his poems, also, so few in number and so admirable in originality, we have the quintessence of familiar sentiment, expressed in the diction of Herbert, Wither, and the great dramatists.

Lamb was the schoolfellow, the devoted admirer and friend, of Coleridge; and perhaps there never was an individual so *loved* by all his contemporaries, by men of every opinion, of every shade of literary, political, and religious sentiment, as this great wit and amiable man The passionate enemy of everything like cant, commonplace, or conventionality, his writings derive a singular charm, a kind of fresh and wild flavor, from his delight in paradox. The man himself was full of paradox: and his punning repartees, delivered with all the pangs of stuttering, often contained a decisive and unanswerable settlement of the question. In his drama of *John Woodvil* he endeavored to revive the forms of the Elizabethan drama; and the work might be mistaken for some woodland play of Heywood or Shirley. But it was his *Specimens of the Old English Dramatists* which showed what treasures of the richest poetry lay concealed in the unpublished, and in modern times unknown, writers of that wonderful age, whose fame had been eclipsed by the glory of some two or three names of the same period. In the few lines, often only the few words, of criticism in which Lamb sketched the characters of the dramatists (with whose writings, from the greatest to the least, from Shakspeare down to Broome or Tourneur, no man was ever more familiar), we see perpetual examples of the delicacy and penetration of his critical faculty.

Lamb's mind, in its sensitiveness, in its mixture of wit and pathos, was eminently Shakspearian; and his intense and reverent study of the works of Shakspeare doubtless gave a tendency to this: the glow of his humor was too pure and steady not to have been reflected from the sun. In his poems, as for instance the *Farewell to Tobacco*, the *Old Familiar Faces*, and his few but beautiful sonnets, we find the very essence and spirit of this quaint tenderness of fancy, the simplicity of the child mingled with the learning of the scholar.

Among the *Essays of Elia* are several little narratives, generally visions and parables, inexpressibly simple and beautiful. The one named *Dream-Children*, and another entitled *The Child-Angel*, are worthy of Jean Paul himself: while the little tale *Rosamond Gray* is perhaps one of the most inimitable gems ever produced in that difficult style.

§ **13.** Perhaps the greatest master of English prose in the present century, not excepting even Macaulay, is THOMAS DE QUINCEY (1785-1859). He was born of wealthy parents near Manchester, August 15, 1785, and in his *Confessions of an English Opium-Eater* he has left us an extraordinary account of his early life, in which, however, there is clearly a mixture of *Dichtung and Wahrheit*. As an undergraduate at Oxford, he was remarkable for his extraordinary stock of knowledge upon every subject that was started in conversation; but even at that period he had commenced taking large doses of opium. After leaving Oxford he settled at Grasmere, but resided during the latter part of his life at Glasgow and Edinburgh. He died December 8, 1859. Upon De Quincey's position in the literature of the present day an able critic observes, "De Quincey's mind never wholly recovered from the effects of his eighteen years' indulgence in opium. He himself says, half jocularly, but apparently quite truly, that it is characteristic of the opium-eater never to finish anything. He himself never finished anything, except his sentences, which are models of elaborate workmanship. But many of his essays are literally fragments, while those which are not generally convey the impression of being mere prolegomena to some far greater work of which he had formed the conception only. Throughout his volumes, moreover, we find allusions to writings which have never seen the daylight. And finally, there is *The Great Unfinished*, the *De Emendatione Humani Intellectus*, to which he had at one time devoted the labor of his whole life. It is, in fact, the one half melancholy reflection which his career suggests, that a man so capable as he was of exercising a powerful influence for good upon the political and religious thought of the present age, should have comparatively wasted his opportunities, and left us his most precious ideas in the condition of the Sibyl's leaves after they had been scattered by the wind. Hence those who approach him with any serious purpose are only too likely to come away disappointed. It is, therefore, rather on his style, at once complex and harmonious, at once powerful and polished, than on the substance of his works, that his posthumous fame will be dependent. The extraordinary compass and unique beauty of his diction, accommodating itself without an effort to the highest flights of imagination, to the minutest subtleties of reasoning, and to the gayest vagaries of humor, are by themselves indeed a sure pledge of a long if not undying reputation."*

De Quincey's writings have been collected in fourteen volumes. The best known is the *Confessions of an English Opium-Eater*, published in 1821, in which the language frequently soars to astonishing heights of eloquence. Of his historical essays and narratives, the finest is his *Flight of the Kalmuck Tartars*, which is equal, in many passages, to the English *Opium-Eater*. His literary criticisms, both upon English and German writers, are very numerous, but cannot be further noticed here. Some of his essays are almost exclusively humorous, among which *Murder considered as one of the Fine Arts* is the best known. The critic whom we have already quoted, thus sums up De Quincey's literary merits: "A great master of English composition a critic of uncommon delicacy; an honest and unflinching investigato of received opinions; a philosophic inquirer, second only to his first and sole hero (Coleridge), — De Quincey has left no successor to his rank. The exquisite finish of his style, with the scholastic rigor of his logic, forms a combination which centuries may never reproduce, but which every generation should study as one of the marvels of English literature."

§ **14.** One of the studies peculiar to the present century has been that of political economy. Adam Smith has been well called the creator of the science, and his followers in the present age have exercised no small influence in moulding the character of public opinion and in controlling the course of public events. RICARDO, SENIOR, MACULLOCH, and MILL are writers whose place in a history of literature would perhaps be small, but whose influence on politics and commerce have been so great, that it would be a serious omission not to call the attention of the student to their works. The most important writer upon ethics, jurisprudence, and political economy is undoubtedly JEREMY BENTHAM (1748–1832). He was the son of a solicitor in London, was educated at Oxford, and called to the bar, but did not pursue it as a profession. For half a century Bentham was the centre of a small but influential circle of philosophical writers, and was the founder of what

* *Quarterly Review*, No. 219, pp. 15, 16.

is called the utilitarian school. In one of his earliest works he laid down the principle that "utility was the measure and test of all virtue;" and the fundamental principle of his philosophy was, that happiness is the end and test of all morality. It is, however, as a writer on jurisprudence that his fame rests; and almost all the improvements in English law that have since been carried into effect may be traced, either directly or indirectly, to his exertions.

NOTES AND ILLUSTRATIONS.

OTHER PROSE WRITERS OF THE NINETEENTH CENTURY.

WILLIAM WILBERFORCE (1759-1833) was born at Hull, and educated at Cambridge. He took a leading part in Parliament for the abolition of the Slave-trade, and deserves a notice in English literature on account of his *Practical View of Christianity*, published in 1797, which had an immense sale, and exercised throughout the earlier part of the nineteenth century a great influence upon religious literature.

SIR JAMES MACKINTOSH (1765-1832) was born at Aldourie, on Loch Ness, Inverness-shire, October 24, 1765, and was educated at the Universities of Aberdeen and Edinburgh, for the medical profession; but he soon abandoned medicine, and maintained himself by literature in London. In 1791 he published his *Vindiciæ Gallicæ*, a reply to Burke on the French Revolution, a work which at once gained him a great reputation. In 1795 he was called to the bar, and four years afterwards he delivered, with great applause, in the hall of Lincoln's Inn, his lectures *On the Law of Nature and Nations.* He rose rapidly at the bar; and his speech in defence of Peltier (February 21, 1803), who had been prosecuted for a libel on Bonaparte, then First Consul, placed him among the great orators of the age. In 1804 he was appointed Recorder of Bombay; and after spending seven years in India he returned to England, was made a Privy Councillor, and in 1830 Commissioner for the Affairs of India. He died May 22, 1832. His principal works are, a *Dissertation on Ethical Philosophy*, prefixed to the seventh edition of the *Encyclopædia Britannica;* three volumes of a *History of England;* a *Life of Sir Thomas More*, in Lardner's Cyclopædia; and a fragment of a *History of the Revolution of* 1688, which was published in 1834. Everything which Sir James Mackintosh has written is pleasing, but nothing striking; and in a few years more his writings will probably be forgotten.

WILLIAM HAZLITT (1778-1830), son of a Unitarian minister, was born at Maidstone, April 10, 1778, was educated as an artist, but lived by literature. He was one of the best critics in the earlier part of this century. His paradoxes are a little startling, and sometimes lead him astray; but there is a delicacy of taste, a richness of imagination, and a perceptive power, that make him a worthy second to De Quincey. His style is vivid and picturesque, and his evolutions of character are clear. His chief works are *Principles of Human Action*, *Characters of Shakspeare's Plays*, *Table Talk*, *Lectures* on various authors, *Essays* on English novelists in the *Edinburgh*, and a *Life of Napoleon* in four volumes.

WILLIAM COBBETT (1762-1835) was a native of Farnham in Suffolk. From an agricultural laborer he became a soldier, then a writer on political questions, and finally member of Parliament for Oldham. In his paper, called *The Weekly Register*, he attacked all sides with rancor and bitterness. His English is forcible and idiomatic. He published several other works, of which his English Grammar most deserves mention.

JOHN WILSON CROKER (1780-1857), born in Galway, December 20, 1780, and educated at Trinity College, Dublin. He entered Parliament, and held the office of Secretary to the Admiralty from 1809 to 1830. He was one of the chief writers in the *Quarterly Review*. His *Essays on the French Revolution*, which originally appeared in that Review, have been republished in a separate form, and exhibit a remarkable knowledge of that period of history. His principal work is an edition of *Boswell's Life of Johnson*, which was criticised most severely, but most unfairly, by Macaulay in the *Edinburgh Review*. Croker also edited the *Suffolk Papers*, *Lady Hervey's Letters*, *Lord Hervey's Memoirs of the Reign of George II.*, and *Walpole's Letters to Lord Hertford.*

The following historians deserve a brief notice: —

JAMES MILL (1773-1836), a native of Montrose, rose to eminence as a writer in the leading periodicals of his time. His *History of British India* (1817 1818) is written with great impartiality, and procured for the author a place in the India House. The *Analysis of the Mind* is a useful contribution to mental science, and has done much to illustrate the principle of association as one of the first general laws of mind.

DR. JOHN GILLIES (1747-1836) was born at Brechin in the county of Forfar, Scotland, and succeeded Dr. Robertson as Historiographer Royal for Scotland. He published several historical works, of which his *History of Greece* is the best known.

WILLIAM MITFORD (1744-1827), born in London February 10, 1744, was the eldest son of a country gentleman in Hampshire. He became captain in the same regiment of militia in which Gibbon was then major; and the conversation of the latter probably strengthened in him the determination to become himself an historian. His *History of Greece*, though grossly unjust to the great leaders of the Athenian democracy, had no small merits, and was far superior to that of Gillies, though it is now entirely superseded by the works of Thirlwall and Grote.

REV. WILLIAM COXE (1747-1828), Archdeacon of Wilts, wrote several works on various periods of modern history, such as the *History of the House of Austria*, *History of the Kings of Spain of the House of Bourbon*, *Memoirs of the Duke of Marlborough*, *Sir Robert Walpole*, &c. These works may still be consulted with advantage.

SHARON TURNER (1768-1847), a solicitor in London, wrote the *History of the Anglo-Saxons*, upon which his reputation chiefly rests. He continued the history of England down to the death of Elizabeth. He also published a *Sacred History of the World*.

DR. JOHN LINGARD (1771-1859) was born at Winchester, and entered the Roman Catholic Church. His principal work is a *History of England* from the earliest times to 1688. He also wrote *Antiquities of the Anglo-Saxon Church* (1809). Though his History is a valuable addition to our historical literature, he has allowed his religious views to color his conclusions as an historian and slightly warp his judgment.

PATRICK FRASER TYTLER (1791-1849), born at Edinburgh, August 30, 1791, was the son of ALEXANDER FRASER TYTLER (1747-1813), the author of *Elements of General History*, a work which has gone through several editions. The son has written the best *History of Scotland* in the English language.

SIR WILLIAM NAPIER (1785-1860), born at Celbridge, in the county of Kildare, Ireland, was a distinguished officer in the Peninsular war, but deserves mention here on account of his *History of the War in the Peninsula and the South of France from the year* 1807 *to the year* 1814, which is unquestionably the best military history in the English language. He had a thorough knowledge of the art of war, had been present in many of the scenes which he describes, and, possessing a lively imagination and great command of language, he brings the events vividly before the mind of the reader. This is his great work; but he also wrote a *History of Sir Charles Napier's Administration of Scinde*, a *Life of Sir Charles Napier*, &c.

A
SKETCH OF AMERICAN LITERATURE.

CHAPTER I.

Literature in the Colonies imitative. Relation of American to English Literature. Gradual Advancement of the United States in Letters. Their first Development theological. Writers in this Department. JONATHAN EDWARDS. Religious Controversy. WILLIAM E. CHANNING. Writings of the Clergy. Newspapers and School Books. Domestic Literature. Female Writers. Oratory. Revolutionary Eloquence. American Orators. ALEXANDER HAMILTON. DANIEL WEBSTER and others. EDWARD EVERETT. American History and Historians. JARED SPARKS. DAVID RAMSAY. GEORGE BANCROFT. HILDRETH. ELLIOT. LOSSING. WILLIAM H. PRESCOTT. IRVING. WHEATON. COOPER. PARKMAN.

LITERATURE is a positive element of civilized life; but in different countries and epochs it exists sometimes as a passive taste or means of culture, and at others as a development of productive tendencies. The first is the usual form in colonial societies, where the habit of looking to the fatherland for intellectual nutriment as well as political authority is the natural result even of patriotic feeling. The circumstances, too, of young communities, like those of the individual, are unfavorable to original literary production. Life is too absorbing to be recorded otherwise than in statistics. The wants of the hour and the exigencies of practical responsibility wholly engage the mind. Half a century ago, it was usual to sneer in England at the literary pretensions of America; but the ridicule was quite as unphilosophical as unjust, for it was to be expected that the new settlements would find their chief mental subsistence in the rich heritage of British literature, endeared to them by a community of language, political sentiment, and historical association. And when a few of the busy denizens of a new republic ventured to give expression to their thoughts, it was equally natural that the spirit and the principles of their ancestral literature should reappear. Scenery, border-life, the vicinity of the aborigines, and a great political experiment were the only novel features in the new world upon which to found anticipations of originality; in academic culture, habitual reading, moral and domestic tastes, and cast of mind, the Americans were identified with the mother country, and, in all essential particulars, would naturally follow the style thus inherent in their natures and confirmed by habit and study. At first, therefore, the literary development of the United States was imitative; but with the progress of the country, and her increased leisure and means of education, the writings of the people became more and more characteristic; theological and political occasions gradually ceased to be the exclusive moulds of thought; and didactic, romantic, and picturesque compositions appeared from time to time. Irving peopled "Sleepy Hollow" with fanciful creations; Bryant described not only with truth and grace, but with devotional sentiment, the characteristic scenes of his native land; Cooper introduced Europeans to the wonders of her forest and sea-coast; Bancroft made her story eloquent; and Webster proved that the race of orators who once roused her children to freedom was not extinct. The names of Edwards and Franklin were echoed abroad; the bonds of mental dependence were gradually loosened; the inherited tastes remained, but they were freshened with a more native zest; and although Brockden Brown is still compared to Godwin, Irving to Addison, Cooper to Scott, Hoffman to Moore, Emerson to Carlyle, and Holmes to Pope, a characteristic vein, an individuality of thought, and a local significance is now generally recognized in the emanations of the American mind; and the best of them rank favorably and harmoniously with similar exemplars in British literature; while, in a few instances, the nationality is so marked, and so sanctioned by true genius, as to challenge the recognition of all impartial and able critics. The majority, however, of our authors are men of talent rather than of genius; the greater part of the literature of the country has sprung from New England, and is therefore, as a general rule, too unimpassioned and coldly elegant for popular effect. There have been a lamentable want of self-reliance, and an obstinate blindness to the worth of native material, both scenic, historical, and social. The great defect of our literature has been a lack of independence, and too exclusive a deference to hackneyed models; there has been, and is, no deficiency of intellectual life; it has thus far, however, often proved too diffusive and conventional for great results.

The intellect of the country first developed in a theological form. This was a natural consequence of emigration, induced by difference of religious opinion, the free scope which the new colonies afforded for discussion, and the variety of creeds represented by the different races who thus met on a common soil, including every diversity of sentiment, from Puritanism to Episcopacy, each extreme modified by shades of doctrine and individual speculation. The clergy, also, were the best educated and most influential class: in political and social as well as religious affairs, their voice had a controlling power; and, for a considerable period, they alone enjoyed that frequent immunity from physical labor which is requisite to mental productiveness. The colonial era, therefore, boasted only a theological literature, for the most part fugitive and controversial, yet sometimes taking a more permanent shape, as in the Biblical Concordance of Newman, and some of the writings of Roger Williams, Increase and Cotton Mather, Mayhew, Cooper, Stiles, Dwight, Elliot, Johnson, Chauncey, Witherspoon, and Hopkins. There is no want of learning or reasoning power in many of the tracts of those once formidable disputants; and such reading accorded with the stern tastes of our ancestors; but, as a general rule, the specimens which yet remain in print are now only referred to by the curious student of divinity or the antiquarian. One enduring relic, however, of this epoch survives, and is held in great estimation by metaphysicians for its subtlety of argument, its originality and vigor and masterly treatment of a profound subject. I allude to the celebrated *Treatise on the Will*, by Dr. Edwards, a work originally undertaken to furnish a philosophical basis for the Calvinistic dogmas, and, in its sagacious hardihood of thought, forming a characteristic introduction to the literary history of New England.

Jonathan Edwards was the only son of a Connecticut minister of good acquirements and sincere piety. He was born in 1703, in the town of Windsor; he entered Yale College at the age of thirteen, and at nineteen became a settled preacher in New York. In 1723 he was elected a tutor in the college at New Haven; and after discharging its duties with eminent success for two years, he became the colleague of his grandfather, in the ministry, at the beautiful village of Northampton, in Massachusetts. Relieved from all material cares by the affection of his wife, his time was entirely given to professional occupations and study. An ancient elm is yet designated in the town where he passed so many years, in the crotch of which was his favorite seat, where he was accustomed to read and think for hours together. His sermons began to attract attention, and several were republished in England. As a writer, he first gained celebrity by a treatise on *Original Sin*. He was inaugurated President of Princeton College, N. J., on the 16th of February, 1785; and on the 22d of the ensuing March died of small-pox, which then ravaged the vicinity.

"This remarkable man," says Sir James Mackintosh, "the metaphysician of America, was formed among the Calvinists of New England, when their stern doctrine retained its vigorous authority. His power of subtle argument, perhaps unmatched, certainly unsurpassed among men, was joined, as in some of the ancient mystics, with a character which raised his piety to fervor. He embraced their doctrine, probably without knowing it to be theirs. Had he suffered this noble principle to take the right road to all its fair consequences, he would have entirely concurred with Plato, with Shaftesbury and Malebranche, in devotion to 'the first good, first perfect, and first fair.' But he thought it necessary afterwards to limit his doctrine to his own persuasion, by denying that such moral excellence could be discovered in divine things by those Christians who did not take the same view with him of their religion." *

Although so meagre a result, as far as regards permanent literature, sprang from the early theological writings in America, they had a cer

* Progress of Ethical Philosophy.

tain strength and earnestness which tended to invigorate and exercise the minds of the people; sometimes, indeed, conducive to bigotry, but often inciting reflective habits. The mental life of the colonists seemed, for a long time, identical with religious discussion; and the names of Anne Hutchinson, Roger Williams, George Fox, Whitefield, the early field-preacher, and subsequently those of Dr. Hopkins, and Murray, the father of Universalism in America, were rallying words for logical warfare: the struggle between the advocates of Quakerism, baptism by immersion, and other of the minority against those of the old Presbyterian and Church of England doctrine, gave birth to a multitude of tracts, sermons, and oral debates which elicited no little acumen, rhetoric, and learning. The originality and productiveness of the American mind in this department have, indeed, always been characteristic features in its development. Scholars and orators of distinguished ability have never been wanting to the clerical profession among us; and every sect in the land has its illustrious interpreters, who have bequeathed, or still contribute, written memorials of their ability. Davies, Bellamy, Robinson, Stuart, Tappan, Williams, Bishop White, Dr. Jarvis, Dr. Hawks, Hooker, Cheever, and others, have materially adorned the literature of the church; the diversity of sects is one of the most curious and striking facts in our social history, and is fully illustrated by the literary organs of each denomination, from the spiritual commentaries of Bush to the ardent Catholicism of Brownson.* About the commencement of the present century, a memorable conflict took place between the liberal and orthodox party; and among the writings of the former may be found more finished specimens of composition than had previously appeared on ethics and religion. Independent of their opinions, the high morality and beautiful sentiment, as well as chaste and graceful diction, of the leaders of that school, gave a literary value and interest to pulpit eloquence which soon exercised a marked influence on the literary taste of the community. Religious and moral writings now derived from style a new interest. At the head of this class, who achieved a world-wide reputation for genius in ethical literature, is William Ellery Channing.

"Half a century ago, there might have been seen, threading the streets of Richmond, a diminutive figure, with a pale, attenuated face, eyes of spiritual brightness, an expansive and calm brow, and movements of nervous alacrity. An abstraction of manner and intentness of expression denoted the scholar, while the scrupulously neat yet worn attire as clearly evidenced restricted means and habits of self-denial. The youth

* The clergy have been among the prominent laborers in the field of useful literature. The names of Dehon, Payson, Potter, Abbott, Bedell, Knox, Todd, Woods, Sprague, Baird, Barnes, Alexander, Tyng, Bacon, Stuart, Bushnell, Beecher, Coxe, Croswell, Hudson, Shelton, Spencer, of the Orthodox and the Episcopal denomination, and of Buckminster, William and Henry Ware, Dewey, Whitman, Osgood, Greenwood, Frothingham, Brooks, Furness, Hedge, Clarke, Hale, W. H. Channing, Peabody, Stetson, and many others of the Unitarian, are identified with current educational and religious literature.

was one of those children of New England, braced by her discipline, and early sent forth to earn a position in the world by force of character and activity of intellect. He was baptized into the fraternity of Nature by the grandeur and beauty of the sea as it breaks along the craggy shore of Rhode Island; the domestic influences of a Puritan household had initiated him into the moral convictions; and the teachings of Harvard yielded him the requisite attainments to discharge the office of private tutor in a wealthy Virginian family. Then and there, far from the companions of his studies and the home of his childhood, through secret conflicts, devoted application to books, and meditation, amid privations, comparative isolation, and premature responsibility, he resolved to consecrate himself to the Christian ministry. Illness had subdued his elasticity, care shadowed his dreams, and retirement solemnized his desires. Thence he went to Boston, and for more than forty years pursued the consistent tenor of his way as an eloquent divine and powerful writer, achieving a wide renown, bequeathing a venerated memory, and a series of discourses, reviews, and essays, which, with remarkable perspicuity and earnestness, vindicate the cause of freedom, the original endowments and eternal destiny of human nature, the sanctions of religion, and 'the ways of God to man.' Sectarian controversy, the duties of the pastoral office, journeys abroad and at home, intercourse with superior minds and the seclusion made necessary by disease, — the quiet of home, the refining influence of literary taste, and the vocations of citizen, father, and philanthropist, occupied those intervening years. He died, one beautiful October evening, at Bennington, Vermont, while on a summer excursion, and was buried at Mount Auburn. A monument commemorates the gratitude of his parishioners and the exalted estimation he had acquired in the world. A biography prepared by his nephew recounts the few incidents of his career, and gracefully unfolds the process of his growth and mental history.

"It is seldom that ethical writings interest the multitude. The abstract nature of the topics they discuss, and the formal style in which they are usually embodied, are equally destitute of that popular charm that wins the common heart. A remarkable exception is presented in the literary remains of Channing. The simple yet comprehensive ideas upon which he dwells, the tranquil gravity of his utterance, and the winning clearness of his style, render many of his productions universally attractive as examples of quiet and persuasive eloquence. And this result is entirely independent of any sympathy with his theological opinions, or experience of his pulpit oratory. Indeed, the genuine interest of Dr. Channing's writings is ethical. As the champion of a sect, his labors have but a temporary value; as the exponent of a doctrinal system, he will not long be remembered with gratitude, because the world is daily better appreciating the religious sentiment as of infinitely more value than any dogma; but as a moral essayist, some of the more finished writings of Channing will have a permanent hold upon reflective and tasteful minds. His nephew has compiled his biography with singular judgment. He has followed the method of Lockhart in the *Life of Scott*. As far as possible, the narrative is woven from letters and diaries, — the subject speaks for himself, and only such intermediate observations of the editor are given as are necessary to form a connected whole. Uneventful as these memoirs are, they are interesting as revelations of the process of culture, the means and purposes of one whose words have winged their way, bearing emphatic messages, over both hemispheres, — who, for many years, successfully advocated important truths, and whose memory is one of the most honored of New England's gifted divines.

"To Dr. Channing's style is, in a great degree, ascribable the popularity of his writings; and we are struck with its remarkable identity from the earliest to the latest period of his career. A petition to Congress, penned while a student at the University, which appears in these volumes, has all its prominent characteristics — its brief sentences, occasionally lengthened where the idea requires it — its emphasis, its simplicity, directness, and transparent diction. This is a curious evidence of the purely meditative existence he must have passed; for it is by attrition with other minds and subjection to varied influences, that the style of writing as well as the tone of manners undergoes those striking modifications which we perceive in men less intent upon a few thoughts. His character is, therefore, justly described as more indebted to 'the influences of solitary thought than of companionship.' Such is the process by which all truth becomes clearly impressed and richly developed to consciousness; on the same principle that, according to Mary Wollstonecraft, reflection is necessary to the realization even of a great passion. 'I derive my sentiments from the nature of man,' says one of Channing's letters. Perhaps it would have been more strictly true if he had said one man; for an inference we long ago derived from his writings, we find amply confirmed in his memoirs — that he was a very inadequate observer. Some of his attempts to portray character are as complete fancy sketches as we ever perused. They show an utter blindness to the real traits even of familiar persons. Beautiful in themselves, it is usually from the graceful drapery of his imagination that the charm is derived. Indeed, Dr. Channing hardly came near enough to see the features in their literal significance. He drew almost exclusively from within. His subjects were what the lay-figure is to the artist — frames for his thoughts to deck with effective costume. When he reasoned of a truth or an idea, he was more at home; for in the abstract he was at liberty to expatiate, without keeping in view the actual relations of things — the stern facts and bare realities of life and character. Indeed nothing can be more delightful to a refined and thoughtful mind, than to follow Channing in his exposition of a striking idea or truth — so clearly and dispassionately stated, then gradually unfolded to its ultimate significance, with, here and there, a striking illustration; and then wound up, like a fine strain of music, which seems to raise us more and more into light and tranquillity on invisible pinions!" *

* Characteristics of Literature. First Series.

Of all the foreign commentators on our political institutions and national character, De Tocqueville is the most distinguished for philosophical insight; and although many of his speculations are visionary, not a few are pregnant with reflective wisdom. He says in regard to the literary development of such a republic as our own, that its early fruits "will bear marks of an untutored and rude vigor of thought, frequently of great variety and singular fecundity." What may be termed the casual writing and speaking of the country, confirms this prophecy. The two most prolific branches of literature in America are journalism and educational works. The aim in both is to supply that immediate demand which, according to the French philosopher, is more imperative and prevailing than in monarchical lands. Newspapers and school-books are, therefore, the characteristic form of literature in the United States. The greatest scholars of the country have not deemed the production of the latter an unworthy labor, nor the most active, enterprising, and ambitious failed to exercise their best powers in the former sphere. An intelligent foreigner, therefore, who observed the predominance of these two departments, would arrive at the just conclusion, that the great mental distinction of the nation is twofold — the universality of education and a general, though superficial intellectual activity in the mass of the people. There is, however, still another phase of our literary condition equally significant and that is the popularity of what may be termed domestic reading — a species of books intended for the family, and designed to teach science. religion, morality, the love of nature, and other desirable acquisitions. These works range from a juvenile to a mature scope and interest, both in form and spirit, but are equally free of all extravagance, — except it be purely imaginative, — and are unexceptionable, often elevated, in moral tone. They constitute the literature of the fireside, and give to the young their primary ideas of the world and of life. Hence their moral importance can scarcely be overrated. Accordingly, children's books have not been thought unworthy the care of the best minds: philosophers like Guizot, poets like Hans Andersen, popular novelists like Scott and Dickens, have not scorned this apparently humble but most influential service. The reform in books for the young was commenced in England by Maria Edgeworth and Mrs. Barbauld, when the *Parents' Assistant* and *Original Poems for Infant Minds* superseded *Mother Goose* and *Jack the Giant-Killer;* and with the instinct of domestic utility so prevalent on this side of the water, this impulse was caught up and prolonged here, and resulted in a class of books and writers not marked by high genius or striking originality, yet honorable to the good sense and moral feeling of the country. These have supplied the countless homes scattered over the western continent with innocent, instructive and often refined reading, sometimes instinct not only with a domestic but a national spirit; often abounding with the most fresh and true pictures of scenery, customs, and local traits, and usually conceived in a tone of gentleness and purity fitted to chasten and improve the taste. These writers have usually adapted them selves equally to the youngest and to the most advanced of the family circle — extended their labor of love from the child's story-book to the domestic novel.*

Oratory is eminently the literature of republics. Political freedom gives both occasion and impulse to thought on public interests; and its expression is a requisite accomplishment to every intelligent and patriotic citizen. American eloquence, although not unknown in the professional spheres of colonial life, developed with originality and richness at the epoch of the revolution. Indeed, the questions that agitated the country naturally induced popular discussions, and as a sense of wrong and a resolve to maintain the rights of freemen, took the place of remonstrance and argument, a race of orators seems to have sprung to life, whose chief traits continue evident in a long and illustrious roll of names, identified with our statesmen, legislators, and divines. From the stripling Hamilton, who, in July, 1774, held a vast concourse in breathless excitement, in the fields near New York, while he demonstrated the right and necessity of resistance to British oppression, to the mature Webster, who, in December, 1829, defended the union of the states with an argumentative and rhetorical power ever memorable in the annals of legislation, there has been a series of remarkable public speakers who have nobly illustrated this branch of literature in the United States. The fame of American eloquence is in part traditionary. Warren, Adams, and Otis in Boston, and Patrick Henry in Virginia, by their spirit-stirring appeals, roused the land to the assertion and defence of its just rights; and Alexander Hamilton, Gouverneur Morris, Pinckney, Jay, Rutledge, and other firm and gifted men gave wise and effective direction to the power thus evoked, by their logical and earnest appeals.

"At the time the contest began," says Guizot, "there were in each colony some men already honored by their fellow-citizens, already well known in the defence of public liberty, influential by their property, talent, or character; faithful to ancient virtues, yet friendly to modern improvement; sensible to the splendid advantages of civilization, and yet attached to simplicity of manners; high-toned in their feelings, but of modest minds, at the same time ambitious and prudent in their patriotic impulses." Foremost among these remarkable men was Alexander Hamilton; by birth a West Indian, by descent uniting the

* It is creditable to the sex that this sphere has been filled, in our country, chiefly by female writers, the list of whom includes a long array of endeared and honored names, at the head of which stands Hannah Adams, with her once popular histories, Catharine M. Sedgwick, with her moral and graphic illustrations of New England life, and Lydia M. Child, with her poetic and generous suggestiveness. Among others may be mentioned Mrs. Lydia H. Sigourney, Miss Leslie, sister of the artist, Eliza Robbins, Mrs. Gilman, of Charleston, S. C., Mrs. Lee, of Boston, Mrs. E. Oakes Smith, Miss Beecher, Mrs. Kirkland, Mrs. Ellett, Mrs. Stowe, Miss Prescott, Miss Coles, Julia Ward Howe, Mrs. S. J. Hale, and such *noms de plume* as Fanny Forrester, Grace Greenwood, and Gail Hamilton; also Mrs. Embury, of Brooklyn, L. I., Miss McIntosh, Mrs Neal, Alice Carey, Mrs. Farrar, Mrs. Willard, Mrs. Hall, and Miss Wetherell.

Scottish vigor and sagacity of character with the accomplishment of the French. While a collegian in New York, his talents, at once versatile and brilliant, were apparent in the insight and poetry of his debates, the solemn beauty of his devotion, the serious argument of his ambitious labors, and the readiness of his humorous sallies; with genuine religious sentiment, born perhaps of his Huguenot blood, he united a zest for pleasure, a mercurial temperament, and grave aspirations. In his first youth the gentleman, the pietist, the hero, and the statesman alternately exhibited, sometimes dazzled, at others impressed, and always won the hearts of his comrades. His first public demonstration was as an orator, when but seventeen; and notwithstanding his slender figure and extreme youth, he took captive both the reason and feeling of a popular assembly. Shortly after he became involved in the controversy then raging between Whigs and Tories; and his pamphlets and newspaper essays were read with mingled admiration and incredulity at the rare powers of expression and mature judgment thus displayed by the juvenile antagonist of bishops and statesmen. But his arm not less than his tongue was dedicated to the cause he thus espoused with equal ardor and intelligence. He studied the military art, gained Washington's notice in the retreat of the American forces through New Jersey, and from that moment became his intimate coadjutor. His next intellectual labor was devoted to explaining and enforcing the principles of finance — a subject of which his countrymen were practically ignorant. To his zeal and sagacity in this department, combined with the noble efforts of Robert Morris, the country was indebted for the pecuniary means of carrying on the war of the revolution, and finally for a regulated currency and established credit.

As first secretary of the treasury, Hamilton may be said to have laid the foundation of our national prosperity. His mind, even at a period most burdened with official cares, was given to the successful advocacy of a neutral course in regard to France; after honorable service attaining the rank of lieutenant-general, when the army disbanded, Hamilton resumed the legal profession. The idol of the Federal party, and a candidate for the chief magistracy, he became entangled in a duel planned by political animosity, and fell at Weehawken, opposite the city of New York, by the hand of Aaron Burr, on the eleventh of July, 1804. The impression caused by his untimely death was unprecedented in this country; for no public man ever stood forth "so clear in his great office," more essentially useful in affairs, courageous in battle, loyal in attachment, gifted in mind, or graceful in manner. During a life of such varied and absorbing occupation, he found time to put on record his principles as a statesman: not always highly finished, his writings are full of sense and energy; their tone is noble, their insight often deep, and the wisdom they display remarkable. His letters are finely characteristic, his state papers valuable, and the *Federalist* a significant illustration both of his genius and the age.*

* No small part of the political writing of the United States is fugitive in its character; but the state papers, including the correspondence of the chief actors

The historical and literary anniversaries of such frequent occurrence in this country, and the exigencies of political life, give occasion for the exercise of oratory to educated citizens of all professions — from the statesman who fills the gaze of the world, to the village pastor and country advocate. Accordingly, a large and, on the whole, remarkably creditable body of discourses, emanating from the best minds of the country, have been published in collected editions, to such an extent as to constitute a decided feature of American literature. They are characteristic also as indicating the popular shape into which intellectual labors naturally run in a young and free country, and the fugitive and occasional literary efforts which alone are practicable for the majority even of scholars. The most solid of this class of writings are the productions of statesmen; and of these, three are conspicuous, although singularly diverse both in style and cast of thought — Webster, Calhoun, and Clay. The former's oration at Plymouth in 1820; his address at the laying of the corner-stone of the Bunker Hill Monument, half a century after the battle; his discourse on the deaths of Adams and Jefferson, the following year; and his reply to Hayne, in the U. S. Senate, in 1829, are memorable specimens of oratory, and recognized everywhere as among the greatest instances of genius in this branch of letters in modern times. These are, however, but a very small part of his speeches and forensic arguments, which constitute a permanent and characteristic, as well as intrinsically valuable and interesting portion of our native literarure.

Daniel Webster was the son of a New Hampshire farmer. He was born in 1782, graduated at Dartmouth College, and began the practice of law at a village near Salisbury, his birthplace, but removed to Portsmouth in 1807. He soon distinguished himself at the bar, and as a member of the House of Representatives; retired from Congress and removed to Boston in 1817; and by his able arguments in the Supreme Court, as well as his unrivalled eloquence on special occasions, was very soon acknowledged to be one of the greatest men America had produced. His career as a senator, a foreign minister, and secretary of state, has been no less illustrious than his professional triumphs; but, as far as literature is concerned, he will be remembered by his state papers and speeches. His style is remarkable for great clearness of statement. It is singularly emphatic. It is impressive rather than brilliant, and occasionally rises to absolute grandeur. It is evidently formed on the highest English models; and the reader conjectures his love of Milton from the noble simplicity of his language, and fondness

in the revolutionary war, and the adoption of the Constitution, form a mine of political ideas and principles. After these, the speeches of the leading statesmen contain, in themselves, a history of the political opinions and crises of the nation; and an armory of logical weapons, of more or less value, may easily be drawn from the works of Franklin, Hamilton, Morris, Jay, Quincy, Dickinson, Paine, John and Samuel Adams, Jefferson, Madison, Livingston, Ames, Freneau, Noah Webster, Rawle, William Sullivan, Leggett, and other political essayists. The *Federalist*, the joint production of Hamilton, Madison, and Jay, is a standard book of this class.

for sublime rather than apt figures. Clearness of statement, vigor of reasoning, and a faculty of making a question plain to the understanding by the mere terms in which it is presented, are the traits which uniformly distinguish his writings, evident alike in a diplomatic note, a legislative debate, and an historical discourse. His dignity of expression, breadth of view, and force of thought, realize the ideal of a republican statesman, in regard, at least, to natural endowments; and his presence and manner, in the prime of his life, were analogous. Independent of their logical and rhetorical merit, these writings may be deemed invaluable from the nationality of their tone and spirit. They awaken patriotic reflection and sentiment, and are better adapted to warn, to enlighten, and to cheer the consciousness of the citizen, than any American works, of a didactic kind, yet produced.

In the speeches of Clay there is a chivalric freshness which readily explains his great popularity as a man: not so profound as Webster, he is far more rhetorical, and equally patriotic. Calhoun was eminently sophistical, but his mind had that precise energy which is so effectual in debate; his style of argument is concise; and in personal aspect he was quite as remarkable — the incarnation of intense purpose and keen perception. These and many other eminent men have admirably illustrated that department of oratory which belongs to statesmen.

Fisher Ames, William Wirt, John Quincy Adams, Hugh S. Legare, and others, famed as debaters, have united to this distinction the renown of able rhetoricians on literary and historical occasions; and to these we may add the names of Verplanck, Chief Justice Story, Chancellor Kent, Rufus Choate, Randolph, Winthrop, Burgess, Preston, Benton, Prentiss, Bethune, Bushnell, Dewey, Birney, Hillhouse, Sprague, Wayland, A. H. Everett, Horace Binney, Dr. Francis, Sumner, Whipple, Hillard, and other authors of occasional addresses, having, by their scope of thought or beauty of style, a permanent literary value. The most voluminous writer in this department, however, is Edward Everett. His two large and elegant volumes not only exhibit the finest specimens of rhetorical writing, but they more truly represent the cultivated American mind in literature than any single work with which we are acquainted. Oratory has always flourished in republics: it is a form of intellectual development to which free political institutions give both scope and inspiration; and we hesitate not to declare that Edward Everett's *Orations* are as pure in style, as able in statement, and as authentic as expressions of popular history, feeling, and opinion in a finished and elegant shape, as were those of Demosthenes and Cicero in their day. Let not the frequency of public addresses, and the ephemeral character they so often possess, blind our countrymen to the permanent and intrinsic merits of these *Orations*. They embody the results of long and faithful research into the most important facts of our history; they give "a local habitation and a name" to the most patriotic associations; their subjects, not less than their sentiments, are thoroughly national; not a page but glows with the most intelligent love of country, nor a figure, description, or appeal but what bears evidence of scholarship, taste, and just sentiment. If a highly-cultivated foreigner were to ask us to point him to any single work which would justly inform him of the spirit of our institutions and history, and, at the same time, afford an adequate idea of our present degree of culture, we should confidently designate these *Orations.* The great battles of the revolution, the sufferings and principles of the early colonists, the characters of our leading statesmen, the progress of arts, sciences, and education among us — all those great interests which are characteristic to the philosopher, of a nation's life — are here expounded, now by important facts, now by eloquent illustrations, and again in the form of impressive and graceful comments. History, essays, descriptive sketches, biographical data, picturesque detail, and general principles, are all blent together with a tact, a distinctness, a felicity of expression, and a unity of style unexampled in this species of writing. Mr. Everett has made the art of oratory his peculiar study: again and again his beautiful elocution has charmed audiences composed of the most intelligent and fairest of our citizens. Many of these occasions have a traditional renown. Indeed, whoever has heard one of these addresses delivered has enjoyed a memorable gratification; not one of them but has to every true American heart and mind a sterling value, as well as an enduring fascination. They include the most salient points in our annals; they consecrate the memories of some of the noblest spirits who have blessed our country; they celebrate events hallowed by results which, at this hour, are agitating the world; and all these attractions are independent of the rare and invaluable literary merit which distinguishes them. No public or private library should be without them; the old should grow familiar with their pages to keep alive the glow of enlightened patriotism; and the young to learn a wise love of country and the graces of refined scholarship.

There is no branch of literature that can be cultivated in a republic with more advantage to the reader, and satisfaction to the author, than History. Untrammelled by proscription, and unawed by political authority, the annalist may trace the events of the past, and connect them, by philosophical analogy, with the tendencies of the present, free to impart the glow of honest conviction to his record, to analyze the conduct of leaders, the theory of parties, and the significance of events. The facts, too, of our history are comparatively recent. It is not requisite to conjure up fabulous traditions or explore the dim regions of antiquity. From her origin the nation was civilized. A backward glance at the state of Europe, the causes of emigration, and the standard of political and social advancement at the epoch of the first colonies in North America, is all that we need to start intelligently upon the track of our country's marvellous growth, and brief, though eventful career. There are relations, however, both to the past and future, which render American history the most suggestive episode in the annals of the world, and give it a universal as well as special dignity. To those who chiefly value facts as illustrative of principles, and see in the course of events the grand problem of humanity, the occurrences in the New World, from its discovery to the present hour, offer a comprehensive interest unrecognized by those who only regard details. Justly interpreted, the liberty and progress of mankind, illustrated by the history of the United States, are but the practical demonstration of principles which the noblest spirits of England advocated with their pens, and often sealed with their blood. It is as lineal descendants, in the love of freedom and humanity, of Milton, Locke, and Sidney, that the intelligent votaries of American liberty should be considered. It is easy to trace in the municipal regulations the tone of society, and in the press of the colonists a recognition of and familiarity with the responsibilities and progressive tendency of liberal institutions. Their minds were fed upon the manly nutriment of English letters; they knew by heart the bold sentiments of those intellectual benefactors who adorned the age of Elizabeth and the times of Cromwell; they gloried in the best triumphs of the Commonwealth; and to the earnest reflection and generous knowledge thus derived from their ancestral country they united the adventurous spirit of the pioneer, and the enthusiasm of the colonist, having a new and open field for experiment both of thought and action: accustomed to the elective franchise, imbued with attachment to freedom, and enlightened by sympathy with those who had nobly pleaded and bravely suffered in her cause at home, we cannot but perceive that the colonists achieved a revolution in the manner, rather than in the spirit, of their institutions; they carried out what had long existed in idea; and, as it were, actualized the views of Algernon Sidney and his illustrious compeers. It is through this intimate and direct relation with the past of the Old World, and as initiative to her ultimate self-enfranchisement, that our history daily grows in value and interest, unfolds new meaning, and becomes endeared to all thinking men. It is a link between two great cycles of human progress; the ark that, floating safely on the ocean-tide of humanity, preserves those elements of national freedom which are the vital hope of the world.

Glorious, however, as is the theme, it is only within the last quarter of a century that it has found any adequate illustration. The labors of American historians have been, for the most part, confined to the acquisition of materials, the unadorned record of facts; their subjects have been chiefly local; and in very few cases have their labors derived any charm from the graces of style, or the resources of philosophy: they are usually crude memoranda of events, not always reliable, though often curious. In a few instances care and scholarship render such contributions to American history intrinsically valuable. but, taken together, they are rather materials for the annalist than complete works, and as such will prove of considerable value. It is to collect and preserve these and other records that historical societies have been formed in so many of the states. A storehouse of data is thus formed, to which the future historian can resort; and probably the greater part of the local narratives is destined either to be re-written with all the amenities of literary tact and refinement, or, cast in the mould of genius, become identified with the future triumphs of the American novelist and poet. In the mean time, all honor is due to those who have assiduously labored to record the great events which have here occurred, and to preserve the memories of our patriots. Jared Sparks, late president of Harvard University, has labored most effectually in this sphere. In a series of well-written biographies, and in the collected Letters of Washington and Franklin, which he has edited, we have a rich fund of national material. Nor should the "Archives" of the venerable Peter Force be forgotten.*

* Among the local and special histories, all more or less valuable as books of reference, and some having both literary and authentic merit, are Belknap's *New Hampshire*, Sullivan's *Maine*, Morton's *New England Memorial*, Trumbull's *Connecticut*, Smith's *New York*, Watson's *Annals of Pennsylvania*, Williams's *Vermont*, Stephens's *Georgia*, Minot's *Massachusetts*, Stith's *Virginia*, Winthrop's *Journal*, Thatcher's *Journal*, Flint's *Western States*, Gayarre's *Louisiana*, O'Callahan's *New York*, Proud's *Pennsylvania*, Moultrie's *Revolution in North and South Carolina and Georgia*, Bishop White's *History of the Episcopal Church*, Jefferson's *Notes on Virginia*, Barton's *Florida*, Young's *Chronicles of the First Planters of Massachusetts Bay* and *Chronicles of the Pilgrim Fathers of New Plymouth*, in N. E. Cheever's *Journal of the Pilgrims*, Frothingham's *History of the Siege of Boston*, Hammond's *Political History of New York*, Holmes's *Annals*, Kip's *Early Jesuit Missions in North America*, Upham's *History of the Salem Witchcraft*, Mayer's *History of the Mexican War*, Miner's *History of Wyoming*, Monette's *History of the Valley of the Mississippi*, Newell's *History of the Revolution in Texas*, Smith's *Virginia*, Sprague's *History of the Florida War*, J. T. Irving's *Conquest of Florida*, Thomas's *Historical Account of Pennsylvania*, Thompson's *Long Island*, Buckingham's *Reminiscences*, Whittier's *Supernaturalism in New England*, Pickett's *Alabama*, Thomas's *History of Printing*, Martin's *Louisiana*, Macy's *Nantucket*, Sewell's *Quakers*, Drake's *Indians*, Carruther's *Cavaliers of Virginia*, Alden's *Collections*, Francis Baylies's *Colony of Plymouth*, Bradford's *History*, and Green's *Historical Studies*.

There are also many interesting volumes of American biography. Those of revolutionary and colonial times are embodied in the series edited by Sparks and among other pleasing and valuable works in this department are the following: Marshall's *Life of Washington*, Tudor's *Otis*, Austin's *Gerry*, Wirt's *Patrick Henry*, Wheaton's *Pinckney*, the *Life of Josiah Quincy* by his son, Colden's *Fulton*, the *Life of John Adams* by his grandson, Tucker's *Jefferson*, Knapp's *American Biographies*, Biddle's *Cabot*, the *Life of Alexander Hamilton* by his son, the *Life of Washington, Franklin, John Jay, Gouverneur Morris*, by Sparks, Gibbs's *Life of Wolcott*, Kennedy's *Life of Wirt*, *Life of Judge Story* by his son, *Life of William E. Channing* by his nephew, *Life of Samuel Adams, of General Greene, of Joseph Warren, of Chief Justice Parsons* by his son, *of Governor Winthrop, of Theodore Parker, of Washington Irving*, &c., Parton's *Lives of Franklin, Burr*, and *Jackson*, and the *Life and Letters of Washington Irving* by his nephew, P. M. Irving, *Life of Margaret Fuller Ossoli*, Dunlap's *American Theatre* and *History of the Arts of Design*, *Lives of Generals Putnam, Greene, Marion, and Captain Smith*, by W. Gilmore Simms, Colonel Stone's *Life of Brant and Red-Jacket*, Davis's *Life of Aaron Burr*, *Life of Reed*, *Life of Stirling* Sabine's *American Loyalists*, Wynne's *Lives of Eminent Americans*, Osgood's *Studies in Christian Biography*, Mrs. Lee's *Huguenots*, Mrs. Ellett's *Women of the Revolution*, Sherburne's *Paul Jones*, and Mackenzie's *Decatur* and *Perry*.

Among the earliest and most indefatigable laborers in the field of history was Ramsay. His *Historical View of the World, from the earliest Record to the Nineteenth Century, with a particular Reference to the State of Society, Literature, Religion, and Form of Government of the United States of America*, was published in 1819; a previous work early in 1817; and more than forty years, during intervals of leisure in an active life, were thus occupied by a man not more remarkable for mental assiduity than for all the social graces and solid excellences of human character.

Dr. David Ramsay, a native of Lancaster county, Pennsylvania, was the son of an Irish emigrant. After graduating at Princeton College, and, according to the custom of the period, devoting two years to private tuition, he studied medicine, and removed to Charleston, South Carolina, where he soon became a distinguished patriotic writer. He was a surgeon in the American army, and active in the councils of the land, suffering, with other votaries of independence, the penalty of several months' banishment to St. Augustine. He earnestly opposed, in the legislature of the state, the confiscation of loyalist property. In 1782 he became a member of the Continental Congress; he three years after represented the Charleston district, and for a year was president of that body, in the absence of Hancock. He died in 1815, in consequence of wounds received from the pistol of a maniac. Remarkable for a conciliatory disposition and ardent patriotism, he was a fluent speaker, and a man of great literary industry. Besides a *History of the Revolution in South Carolina*, which was translated and published in France, a *History of the American Revolution*, which reached a second edition, a *Life of Washington*, and a *History of South Carolina*, he left a *History of the United States*, from their first settlement to the year 1808, — afterwards continued, by other hands, to the treaty of Ghent, and published in three octavo volumes, — a monument of his unwearied and zealous research, and patient labor for the good of the public and the honor of his country.

The most successful attempt yet made to reduce the chaotic but rich materials of American history to order, beauty, and moral significance, is the work of George Bancroft.* The inadequate history of Judge Marshall, and the careful one relating to the colonial period by Grahame, were previously the only works devoted to the subject. Our

* George Bancroft was born in Worcester, Massachusetts, in the year 1800: he is the son of Rev. Aaron Bancroft, D. D., for more than half a century minister of that town, a man highly venerated, and devoted to historical research, particularly as regards his native country. Thus under the paternal roof, and from his earliest age, the sympathies and taste of the son were awakened to the subject of American history. He graduated in the first rank of Harvard College in 1817. In 1834 appeared the first volume of his *History of the Colonization of the United States*, in 1837 the second, in 1840 the third, and in 1852 the fourth, being the introductory *History of the Revolution*, in 1866 the ninth.

revolution, in its most interesting details, was known in Europe chiefly through the attractive pages of Carlo Botta. With the ground thus unoccupied, Mr. Bancroft commenced his labors. He was prepared for them not only by culture and talent, but by an earnest sympathy with the spirit of the age he was to illustrate. Having passed through the discipline of a brilliant scholastic career at the best university in the country, studied theology, and engaged in the classical education of youth, he had also visited Europe, and become imbued with the love of German literature; he was for two years a pupil of Heeren, at Gottingen, and mingled freely with the learned coteries of Berlin and Heidelberg. His two first published works, after his return to the United States, are remarkably suggestive of his traits of mind, and indicate that versatility which is so desirable in an historian. These were a small volume of metrical pieces, mainly expressive of his individual feelings and experience; and a translation of Professor Heeren's *Reflections on the Politics of Ancient Greece:* thus early both the poetic and the philosophic elements were developed; and although, soon after, Mr. Bancroft entered actively into political life, and held several high offices under the general government, including that of minister to Great Britain, he continued to prosecute his historical researches, under the most favorable auspices, both at home and abroad, and from time to time put forth the successive volumes of his *History of the United States.* To this noble task he brought great and patient industry, an eloquent style, and a capacity to array the theme in the garb of philosophy. Throughout he is the advocate of democratic institutions; and in the early volumes, where, by the nature of the subject, there is little scope for attractive detail, by infusing a reflective tone, he rescues the narrative from dryness and monotony. Instead of a series of facts arranged without any unity of sentiment, we have the idea and principle of civic advancement towards freedom, as a thread of gold upon which the incidents are strung. He is remarkably assiduous in unfolding the experience of the first dicoverers, and the political creeds of the early settlers; many curious and authentic details of aboriginal habits are also given; there are everywhere signs of careful research and genuine enthusiasm. Owing, perhaps, to the unequal interest of the subject, the same glow and finish are not uniformly perceptible in the style, in which we occasionally discern an obvious strain after rhetorical effect; and sometimes the influence of the author's political opinions is too apparent; but these are incidental defects; the general spirit, execution, and effect of the work are elevated, genial, and highly instructive. Mr. Bancroft has, at least, vindicated his right to compose the annals of his country, by giving to the record that vitality, both of description and of thought, which distinguishes a genius for history from the mere ability to collate facts. His manner and reflection rise, too, with his subject; the outline becomes firmer, and the inferences clearer, as he emerges from the colonial and enters the revolutionary era. Combining, apparently, in his own mind, the traits of his twofold culture, we have the speculative tendency of the German, and the graphic delineation of the English writers; in a word, he gives us pictures, like the one, and arguments and suggestions, like the other, carefully stating the fact, and earnestly deducing from it the idea; he is more comprehensive as a philosopher than a limner; and yet no tyro in the latter's art, for here and there we encounter a character as tersely drawn, and a scene as vividly painted, as any of those which have rendered the best modern historians popular. But it is the under-current of thought, rather than the brilliant surface of description, which gives intellectual value to Bancroft's *History*, and has secured for it so high and extensive a reputation. In sentiment and principles, it is thoroughly American; but in its style and philosophy it has that broad and eclectic spirit appropriate both to the general interest of the subject and the enlightened sympathies of the age. Perhaps the best way to appreciate the literary merits of Bancroft's *History* is to compare it with the cold and formal annals familiar to our childhood. Unwearied and patient in research, discriminating in the choice of authorities, and judicious in estimating testimony, Bancroft has the art and the ardor, the intelligence and the tact, required to fuse into a vital unity the narrative thus carefully gleaned. He knows how to condense language, evolve thought from fact, and make incident and characterization illustrate the progress of events. This bold, active, concentrated manner is what is needed to give permanent and living interest to history. Portraits of individuals, scenes pregnant with momentous results and philosophic inferences, alternate in his pages. The character of Pitt, the death of Montcalm, and the *rationale* of Puritanism, are very diverse subjects; yet they are each related to the development of the principle of freedom on this continent, and accordingly received both the artistic and analytical treatment of the American historian.

Hildreth's *History of the United States* will probably become a standard book of reference. Rhetorical grace and effect, picturesqueness and the impress of individual opinion, are traits which the author either rejects or keeps in abeyance. His narrative is plain and straightforward, confined to facts which he seems to have gleaned with great care and conscientiousness. The special merit of his work consists in the absence of whatever can possibly be deemed either irrelevant or ostentatious. A *History of Liberty*, by Samuel Eliot, is the work of scholarship and taste, but not of poetic inspiration or philosophy; it is, however, an elegant addition to our native writings in this sphere. In a popular form, the most creditable performance is the *Field-Book of the Revolution*, by Benson J. Lossing, a wood-engraver by profession who has visited all the scenes of that memorable war, and, with pen and pencil, delineated each incident of importance, and every object of local interest. His work is one which is destined to find its way to every farmer's heart, and to all the school libraries of our country.

The freshness of his subjects, the beauty of his style, and the vast difficulties he bravely surmounted, gained for William H. Prescott* not only an extensive but a remarkably speedy reputation, after the appearance of his first history. Many years of study, travel, and occasional practice in writing, preceded the long-cherished design of achieving an historical fame. Although greatly impeded, at the outset, by a vision so imperfect as to threaten absolute blindness, in other respects he was singularly fortunate. Unlike the majority of intellectual aspirants, he had at his command the means to procure the needful but expensive materials for illustrating a subject more prolific, at once, of romantic charms and great elements of human destiny, than any unappropriated theme offered by the whole range of history. It included the momentous voyage of Columbus, the fall of the Moorish empire in Spain, and the many and eventful consequences thence resulting. Aided by the researches of our minister at Madrid,† himself an enthusiast in letters, Mr. Prescott soon possessed himself of ample documents and printed authorities. These he caused to be read to him, and during the process dictated notes, which were afterwards so frequently repeated orally that his mind gradually possessed itself of all the important details; and these he clothed in his own language, arranged them with discrimination, and made out a consecutive and harmonious narrative. Tedious as such a course must be, and laborious in the highest degree as it proved, I am disposed to attribute to it, in a measure at least, some of Mr. Prescott's greatest charms as an historian — the remarkable evenness and sustained harmony, the unity of conception and ease of manner, as rare as it is delightful. The *History of Ferdinand and Isabella* is a work that unites the fascination of romantic fiction with the grave interest of authentic events. Its author makes no pretension to analytical power, except in the arrangement of his materials; he is content to describe, and his talents are more artistic than philosophical; neither is any cherished theory or principle obvious; his ambition is apparently limited to skilful narration. Indefatigable in research, sagacious in the choice and comparison of authorities, serene in temper, graceful in style, and pleasing in sentiment, he possesses all the requisites for an agreeable writer; while his subjects have yielded so much of picturesque material and romantic interest, as to atone for the lack of any more original or brilliant qualities in the author. *Ferdinand and Isabella* was followed by *The Conquest of*

* William H. Prescott was the grandson of Colonel William Prescott, who commanded the Americans at the battle of Bunker Hill. He was born in Salem, Massachusetts, on the 4th of May 1796. Educated in boyhood by Dr. Gardiner, a fine classical teacher, he entered Harvard College in 1814. He studied law, and passed two years in Europe. In 1838 was published his *History of Ferdinand and Isabella*, which met with almost immediate and unprecedented success. It was soon translated into all the modern European languages. He died in Boston, January 23, 1859.

† Alexander H. Everett.

Mexico, and *The Conquest of Peru*. The scenic descriptions and the portraits of the Spanish leaders, and of Montezuma and Guatimozin, in the former work, give to it all the charm of an effective romance Few works of imagination have more power to win the fancy and touch the heart. The insight afforded into Aztec civilization is another source of interest. The moral qualities of considerate reflection and frankness are memorable characteristics of Prescott. He has added to the standard literature of the age, and to the literary fame of his country, by his graceful, judicious, and attractive labors in a field comparatively new, and abounding in artistic material.

Prescott at the time of his death was engaged on a history of *Philip II. of Spain*. In his previous efforts, he had the advantage of subjects not identified with the prejudices and passions of the present age, and not demanding for their just display any great reach of thought. His well-balanced periods, quiet and sustained tone, and agreeable manner, therefore, had their full effect. Perhaps, had he thus discussed historical themes nearer the sympathies of the hour, this absence of earnestness and reflection would have been more consciously felt by his many delighted readers.

Another of the few standard works in this department, of native origin, is the *Life and Voyages of Columbus*, by Washington Irving. Ostensibly a biography, it partakes largely of the historical character. As in the case of Prescott, the friendly suggestions of our minister at Madrid greatly promoted the enterprise. The work is based on the researches of Navarette; and it is a highly fortunate circumstance that the crude though invaluable data thus gathered was first put in shape and adorned with the elegances of a polished diction, by an American writer at once so popular and so capable as Irving. The result is a Life of Columbus, authentic, clear, and animated in narration, graphic in its descriptive episodes, and sustained and finished in style. It is a permanent contribution to English as well as American literature,—one which was greatly needed, and most appropriately supplied.

Henry Wheaton, long our minister at Berlin, is chiefly known to literary fame by his able *Treatise on International Law;* but, while chargé d'affaires in Denmark, he engaged with zeal in historical studies, and published in London, in 1831, a *History of the Northmen*, a most curious, valuable, and suggestive, though limited work.

James Fenimore Cooper's *Naval History of the United States*, although not so complete as is desirable, is a most interesting work, abounding in scenes of generous valor and rare excitement, recounted with the tact and spirit which the author's taste and practice so admirably fitted him to exhibit on such a theme. Some of the descriptions of naval warfare are picturesque and thrilling in the highest degree The work, too, is an eloquent appeal to patriotic sentiment and national pride. It is one of the most characteristic histories, both in regard to subject and style, yet produced in America.

One of the most satisfactory of recent historical works is *The Con spiracy of Pontiac*, by Francis Parkman, of Boston. During a tour in the Far West, where he hunted the buffalo and fraternized with the Indians, the author gained that practical knowledge of aboriginal habits and character which enabled him to delineate the subject chosen with singular truth and effect. Having faithfully explored the annals of the French and Indian war, he applied to its elucidation the vivid impressions derived from his sojourn in forest and prairie, his observation of Indian life, and his thorough knowledge of the history of the Red Men. The result is not only a reliable and admirably planned narrative, but one of the most picturesque and romantic yet produced in America. Few subjects are more dramatic and rich in local associations; and the previous discipline and excellent style of the author have imparted to it a permanent attraction. *Pioneers of France in the New World*, is a charming historical narrative from the same pen.

CHAPTER II.

Belles Lettres. Influence of British Essayists. FRANKLIN. DENNIE. Signs of Literary Improvement. JONATHAN OLDSTYLE. WASHINGTON IRVING. His Knickerbocker. Sketch-Book. His other WORKS. Popularity. Tour on the Prairies. Character as an Author. DANA. WILDE. HUDSON. GRISWOLD. LOWELL. WHIPPLE. TICKNOR. WALKER. WAYLAND. JAMES EMERSON. Transcendentalists. MADAME OSSOLI. Emerson's Essays. ORVILLE DEWEY. Humorous Writers. Belles Lettres. TUDOR. WIRT. SANDS. FAY. WALSH. MITCHELL. KIMBALL. American Travellers. Causes of their Success as Writers. Fiction. CHARLES BROCKDEN BROWN. His Novels. JAMES FENIMORE COOPER. His Novels — their Popularity and Characteristics. NATHANIEL HAWTHORNE. His Works and Genius. Other American Writers of Fiction.

THE colloquial and observant character given to English literature by the wits, politicians, and essayists of Queen Anne's time — the social and agreeable phase which the art of writing exhibited in the form of the *Spectator*, *Guardian*, *Tatler*, and other popular works of the kind, naturally found imitators in the American colonies. The earliest indication of a taste for belles lettres is the republication, in the newspapers of New England, of some of the fresh lucubrations of Steele and Addison. *The Lay Preacher*, by Dennie, was the first successful imitation of this fashionable species of literature: more characteristic, however, of the sound common sense and utilitarian instincts of the people, were the essays of Franklin, commenced in his brother's journal, then newly established at Boston. Taste for the amenities of intellectual life, however, at this period, was chiefly gratified by recourse to the emanations of the British press; and it is some years after that we perceive signs of that native impulse in this sphere which proved the germ of American literature. "If we are not mistaken in the signs of the times," says Buckminster (in an oration delivered at Cambridge, and published in the *Anthology*, a Boston magazine, which, with the *Port Folio*, issued at Philadelphia, were the first literary journals of high aims in America) — "the genius of our literature begins to show symptoms of vigor, and to meditate a bolder flight. The spirit of criticism begins to plume itself, and education, as it assumes a more learned form, will take a higher aim. If we are not misled by our hopes, the dream of ignorance is at least broken, and there are signs that the period is approaching when we may say of our country, *Tuus jam regnat Apollo*." This prophecy had received some confirmation in the grace and local observation manifest in a series of letters which appeared in the *New York Chronicle*, signed Jonathan Oldstyle, Gent. — the first productions of Washington Irving, the Goldsmith of America, who was born in New York, April 6, 1783. Symptoms of alarming disease soon after induced a voyage to Europe; and he returned to the Island of Manhattan, the scene of his boyish rambles and youthful reveries, with a mind expanded by new scenes, and his natural love of travel and elegant literature deepened. Although ostensibly a law student in the office of Judge Hoffman, his time was devoted to social intercourse with his kindred, who were established in business in New York, and a few genial companions, to meditative loiterings in the vicinity of the picturesque river so dear to his heart, and to writing magazine papers. The happy idea of a humorous description of his native town, under the old Dutch governors, was no sooner conceived than executed with inimitable wit and originality. Not then contemplating the profession of letters, he did not take advantage of the remarkable success that attended this work, of which Sir Walter Scott thus speaks in one of his letters to an American friend: "I beg you to accept my best thanks for the uncommon degree of entertainment which I have received from the most excellently jocose history of New York. I am sensible that as a stranger to American parties and politics, I must lose much of the concealed satire of the piece; but I must own that, looking at the simple and obvious meaning only, I have never read anything so closely resembling the style of Dean Swift as the annals of Diedrich Knickerbocker. I have been employed these few evenings in reading them aloud to Mrs. S. and two ladies who are our guests, and our sides have been absolutely sore with laughing. I think, too, there are passages which indicate that the author possesses power of a different kind, and has some touches which remind me much of Sterne." *Salmagundi*, which Mr. Irving had previously undertaken, in conjunction with Paulding, proved a hit, and established the fame of its authors; it was in form and method of publication imitated from the *Spectator*, but in details, spirit, and aim, so exquisitely adapted to the latitude of New York, that its appearance was hailed with a delight hitherto unknown; it was, in fact, a complete triumph of local genius. From these pursuits, the author turned to commercial toil, in connection with which he embarked for England in 1815; and while there, a reverse of fortune led to his resuming the pen as a means of subsistence. In his next work, the *Sketch-Book*, Sir Walter's opinion of his pathetic vein was fully realized; *The Wife*, *The Pride of the Village*, and *The Broken Heart*, at once took their places as gems of English sentiment and description. Nor were the associations of home inoperative; and the *Legend of Sleepy Hollow* first gave a "local habitation," in our fresh land, to native fancy. His impressions of domestic life in Great Britain were soon after given to the public in *Bracebridge Hall*, and some of his continental experiences embodied in the *Tales of a Traveller*. Soon after, Mr. Irving visited Spain to write the *Life of Columbus*, to which we have before alluded. His sojourn at the Alhambra, and at Abbotsford and Newstead Abbey, are the subjects of other graceful and charming volumes; while *Astoria, or Anecdotes of an Enterprise beyond the Rocky Mountains*, and the *Life of Mohammed*, proved solid as well as elegant contributions to our standard literature; and the *Life of Washington*, a standard national biography.

There are writers who have so ministered to our enjoyment as to become associated with our happiest literary recollections. The companionship of their works has been to us as that of an entertaining and cherished friend, whose converse cheers the hours of languor, and brightens the period of recreative pleasure. We are wont to think and to speak of them with quite a different sentiment from that which prompts us to speculate upon less familiar and less endeared productions. There is ever within us a sense of obligation, an identification of our individual partiality with the author, when the fruits of his labor are alluded to, his merits discussed, or his very name mentioned. The sensitiveness appropriate to the writer's self seems, in a manner, transferred to our own bosoms; his faults are scarcely recognized, and we guard his laurels as if our own efforts had aided in their winning, and our own happiness was involved in their preservation. Such feelings obtain, indeed, to a greater or less extent, with reference to all the master spirits in literature, whose labors have been devoted, with signal success, to the gratification and elevation of humanity. But the degree of permanency for such tributary sentiment in the general mind depends very much upon the field of effort selected by the favorite author, and his own peculiar circumstances and character. Subjects of temporary interest, however admirably treated, and with whatever applause received, are obviously ill calculated to retain, for any considerable length of time, a strong hold upon human regard; and, notwithstanding the alleged inconsistency between an author's personal character and history and the influence of his works, the motives adduced by Addison for prefacing the Spectator with an account of himself are deeply founded in human nature. Not merely contemporary sentiment, but after opinion in relation to literary productions, will be materially affected by what is known of the author. The present prevailing tendency to inquire, often with a truly reprehensible minuteness, into whatever in the most distant manner relates to the leading literary men of the age, affords ample evidence of this truth. Indeed, we may justly anticipate that literary, if not general biography, will, ere long, from the very interest manifested in regard to it, attain an importance, and ultimately a philosophical dignity, such as shall engage in its behalf the sedulous labors of the best endowed and most accomplished minds.

The occasion which first induced Geoffrey Crayon to delineate, and those which have suggested his subsequent pencillings, were singularly happy; and the circumstances under which these masterly sketches were produced, nay, the whole history of the man, are signally fitted to deepen the interest which his literary merits necessarily excited. In saying this, we are not unmindful of the prejudices so ungenerously forced upon the attention of the absentee, and so affectingly alluded to in the opening of his first work after returning from Europe; but do we err in deeming those prejudices as unchargeable upon the mass of his countrymen as they were essentially unjust and partial? Nay, are we not, in this volume, with our author's characteristic genuineness of feeling and simplicity, assured of his own settled and happy sense of the high place he occupies in the estimation and love of Americans?

The *Tour on the Prairies* appeared in 1836. It is an unpretending account, comprehending a period of about four weeks, of travelling and hunting excursions upon the vast western plains. The local features of this interesting region have been displayed to us in several works of fiction, of which it has formed the scene; and more formal illustrations of the extensive domain denominated The West, and its denizens, have been repeatedly presented to the public. But in this volume one of the most extraordinary and attractive portions of the great subject is discussed, not as the subsidiary part of a romantic story, nor yet in the desultory style of epistolary composition, but in the deliberate, connected form of a retrospective narration. When we say that the *Tour on the Prairies* is rife with the characteristics of its author, no ordinary eulogium is bestowed. His graphic power is manifest throughout. The boundless prairies stretch out illimitably to the fancy, as the eye scans his descriptions. The athletic figures of the riflemen, the gayly arrayed Indians, the heavy buffalo, and the graceful deer, pass in strong relief and startling contrast before us. We are stirred by the bustle of the camp at dawn, and soothed by its quiet or delighted with its picturesque aspect under the shadow of night. The imagination revels amid the green oak clumps and verdant pea vines, the expanded plains and the glancing river, the forest aisles and the silent stars. Nor is this all. Our hearts thrill at the vivid representations of a primitive and excursive existence; we involuntarily yearn, as we read, for the genial activity and the perfect exposure to the influences of Nature in all her free magnificence, of a woodland and adventurous life; the morning strain of the bugle, the excitement of the chase, the delicious repast, the forest gossiping, the sweet repose beneath the canopy of heaven — how inviting, as depicted by such a pencil!

Nor has the author failed to invigorate and render doubly attractive these descriptive drawings, with the peculiar light and shade of his own rich humor, and the mellow softness of his ready sympathy. A less skilful draughtsman would, perhaps, in the account of the preparations for departure (Chapter III.), have spoken of the hunters, the fires, and the steeds — but who, except Geoffrey Crayon, would have been so quaintly mindful of the little dog, and the manner in which he regarded the operations of the farrier? How inimitably the Bee Hunt is portrayed! and what have we of the kind so racy as the account of the Republic of Prairie Dogs, unless it be that of the Rookery in Bracebridge Hall? What expressive portraits are the delineations of our rover's companions! How consistently drawn throughout, and in what fine contrast, are the reserved and saturnine Beatte, and the vain-glorious, sprightly, and versatile Tonish! A golden vein of vivacious, yet chaste comparison — that beautiful, yet rarely well-managed species of wit, and a wholesome and pleasing sprinkling of moral comment — that delicate and often most efficacious medium of useful impressions — intertwine and vivify the main narrative. Something, too, of that fine pathos which enriches his earlier productions, enhances the value of the present. He tells us, indeed, with commendable honesty, of his new appetite for destruction, which the game of the prairie excited; but we cannot fear for the tenderness of a heart that sympathizes so readily with suffering, and yields so gracefully to kindly impulses. He gazes upon the noble courser of the wilds, and wishes that his freedom may be perpetuated; he recognizes the touching instinct which leads the wounded elk to turn aside and die in retiracy; he reciprocates the attachment of the beast which sustains him, and, more than all, can minister even to the foibles of a fellow-being, rather than mar the transient reign of human pleasure.

Washington Irving's last days were passed at his congenial home, "Sunnyside," on the banks of his favorite river, the Hudson. The revised edition of his works had a large sale, and to these he added many Spanish legends, home sketches, and his elaborate biography of Washington. After so many years passed abroad, and his residence as American minister at the Court of Spain, and after so long and prosperous a literary, and so genial and endeared a social, career, he died — surrounded by his kindred, to whom he was the life-long benefactor, crowned with honorable fame and the affection of his countrymen — on the 29th of November, 1859, at the age of seventy-six. His publisher, George P. Putnam, has issued, and continues to issue, three different editions of his writings, of which the following is a list: ***Alhambra, Astoria, Bonneville, Bracebridge, Columbus, Crayon, Goldsmith, Granada, Knickerbocker, Mahomet, Salmagundi, Sketch-Book, Spanish Papers, Traveller, Wolfert's Roost, Life of Washington.***

It has been said that Mr. Irving, at one period of his life, seriously proposed to himself the profession of an artist. The idea was a legitimate result of his intellectual constitution; and although he denied its development in one form, in another it has fully vindicated itself. Many of his volumes are a collection of sketches, embodied happily in language, since thereby their more general enjoyment is insured, but susceptible of immediate transfer to the canvas of the painter. These are like a fine gallery of pictures, wherein all his countrymen delight in many a morning lounge and evening reverie.

Until within the last half century, not only the standard literature, but the critical opinions, of America were almost exclusively of transatlantic origin. But within that period a number of writers, endowed with acute perceptions and eloquent expression, as well as the requisite knowledge, have arisen to elucidate the tendencies, define the traits, and advocate the merits of modern writers. By faithful translations, able reviews, lectures and essays, the best characteristics of men of literary genius, schools of philosophy, poetry, and science have been rendered familiar to the cultivated minds of the nation. Thus Richard H. Dana has explored and interpreted, with a rare sympathetic intelligence, the old English drama; Andrews Norton, the authenticity of the Gospels; Richard H. Wilde, the love and madness of Tasso; Alexander H. Everett, the range of contemporary French and German literature; Professor Reed, the poetry of Wordsworth; Henry N. Hudson, the plays of Shakspeare; John S. Hart, the Faery Queen; Russell Lowell, the older British poets; and Edwin P. Whipple, the best authors of Great Britain and America. W. A. Jones, Hoffman, Duyckinck, and others, have also illustrated our critical literature.

For the chief critical and biographical history of literature in the United States, we are indebted to E. A. and George Duyckinck's *Cyclopedia of American Literature*, two copious and interesting volumes, popular at home and useful abroad, giving an elaborate account of what has been done by American writers from the foundation of the country to the present hour. These works are the fruit of great research, and an enthusiasm for native literature as rare as it is patriotic. Our numerous "*Female Prose Writers*" have also found an intelligent and genial historian and critic in Professor Hart.

The philosophic acuteness, animated and fluent diction, and thorough knowledge of the subjects discussed, render Mr. Whipple's critical essays among the most agreeable reading of the kind. His reputation as an eloquent and sagacious critic is now firmly established. Both in style and thought these critical essays are worthy of the times; bold without extravagance, refined, yet free of dilettanteism, manly and philosophic in sentiment, and attractive in manner.* The most elaborate single work, however, in the history of literature, is George Ticknor's *History of Spanish Literature*, the result of many years' research, and so complete and satisfactory, that the best European critics have recognized it a permanent authority; it is both authentic and tasteful; the translations are excellent, the arrangement judicious, and the whole performance a work of genuine scholarship. It supplies a desideratum, and is an interesting and thorough exposition of a subject at once curious, attractive, and of general literary utility. James Walker and Francis Wayland, although of widely diverse theological opinions, are both expositors of moral philosophy, to which they have made valuable contributions. Henry James, of Albany, is the most argumentative and eloquent advocate of new social principles in the country; and Waldo Emerson, by a certain quaintness of diction and boldly speculative turn of mind, has achieved a wide popularity. It is, however, to a peculiar verbal facility and aphoristic emphasis, rather than to any constructive genius, that he owes the impression he creates. He is regarded as the leader of a sect, who, some years since, from the reaction of minds oppressed and narrowed by New England conventionalism and bigotry, and, in some instances, kindled by the speculations of German literature, broke away from the conventional and sought freedom in the transcendental school. In the *Memoirs of Margaret Fuller Ossoli*, the movement is described and the principles of its disciples hinted rather than explained. "The rise of this enthusiasm," says her biographer, "was as mysterious as that of any form of revival; and only they who were of the faith could comprehend how bright was this morning-time of a new hope. Transcendentalism was an assertion of the inalienable integrity of man, of the ordinances of Divinity in instinct. In part it was a reaction against Puritan orthodoxy; in part an effect of renewed study of the ancients, of Oriental Pantheists, of Plato, and the Alexan-

* **Essays and Reviews**; Literature and Life; **Character and Characteristic Men.**

drians, of Plutarch's Morals, Seneca, and Epictetus; in part the natural product of the place and time. On the somewhat stunted stock of Unitarianism — whose characteristic dogma was trust in individual reason as correlative to Supreme Wisdom — had been grafted German idealism as taught by masters of most various schools."

Whoever turns to Emerson's *Essays*, or to the writings of this transcendental sibyl (whose remarkable acquirements, moral courage, and tragic fate, render her name prominent among our female authors) for a system, a code, or even a set of definite principles, will be disappointed. The chief good thus far achieved by this class of thinkers has been negative; they have emancipated many minds from the thraldom of local prejudices and prescriptive opinion, but have failed to reveal any positive and satisfactory truth unknown before. Emerson has an inventive fancy; he knows how to clothe truisms in startling costume; he evolves beautiful or apt figures and apothegms that strike at first, but when contemplated, prove, as has been said, usually either true and not new, or new and not true. His volumes, however, are suggestive, tersely and often gracefully written; they are thoughtful, observant, and speculative, and indicate a philosophic taste rather than power. As contributions to American literature, they have the merit of a spirit, beauty, and reflective tone previously almost undiscoverable in the didactic writings of the country. A writer of more consistency in ethics, and a sympathy with man more human, is Orville Dewey, whose discourses abound in earnest appeals to consciousness, in a noble vindication of human nature, and a faith in progressive ideas, often arrayed in touching and impressive rhetoric.

We have not been wanting in excellent translators, especially of German literature; our scholars and poets have admirably used their knowledge of the language in this regard. The first experiment was Bancroft's translation of Heeren, already referred to; and since then, some of the choicest lyrics and best philosophy of Germany have been given to the American public by Professor Longfellow, George Ripley, R. W. Emerson, John S. Dwight, S. M. Fuller, George H. Calvert, Rev. C. T. Brooks, W. H. Channing, F. H. Hedge, Samuel Osgood, and others. Dr. Mitchell, of New York, translated Sannazario's Italian poems, Mrs. Nichols the *Promessi Sposi* of Manzoni, and Dr. Parsons, of Boston, has made the best metrical translations into English of Dante's great poem.

The most elaborate piece of humor in our literature has been already mentioned — as Irving's facetious history of his native town. The sketch entitled *The Stout Gentleman*, by the same genial author, is another inimitable attempt in miniature, as well as some of the papers in *Salmagundi*. The *Letters of Jack Downing* may be considered an indigenous specimen in this department; and also the *Charcoal Sketches* of Joseph C. Neal, the *Ollapodiana* of Willis G. Clarke, the *Puffer Hopkins* of Cornelius Matthews, and many scenes by Thorpe, in Mrs. Kirkland's *New Home*, and the *Biglow Papers* of J. R. Lowell. The original aspects of life in the West and South, as well as those of Yankee Land have also found several apt and graphic delineators, although the coarseness of the subjects, or the carelessness of the style, will seldom allow them a literary rank.

That delightful species of literature which is neither criticism nor fiction — neither oratory nor history — but partakes somewhat of all these, and owes its charm to a felicitous blending of fact and fancy, of sentiment and thought — the belles lettres writing of our country, has gradually increased as the ornamental has encroached on the once arbitrary domain of the useful. Among the earliest specimens were the *Letters of a British Spy*, and the *Old Bachelor* of William Wirt, and Tudor's *Letters on New England:* in New York this sphere was gracefully illustrated by Robert C. Sands and Theodore S. Fay, by tale, novelette, and essay; in Philadelphia, by Robert Walsh, who gleaned two volumes from his newspaper articles; and at present, by the *Reveries of a Bachelor* of Mitchell, and the contributions of N. P. Willis, and in a more vigorous manner in the *St. Leger Papers* of Kimball. Professors Frisbie, Caldwell, Henry, and others have contributed to the taste and culture of the belles lettres in America.*

The literature of no country is more rich in books of travel. From Carter's *Letters from Europe*, Dwight's *Travels in New England*, and Lewis and Clark's *Expedition to the Rocky Mountains*, to the *Yucatan* of Stephens, and the *Two Years before the Mast* of Dana, American writers have put forth a succession of animated, intelligent, and most agreeable records of their explorations in every part of the globe. In many instances, their researches have been directed to a special object, and resulted in positive contributions to natural science; thus Audubon's travels are associated with his discoveries in ornithology, and those of Schoolcraft with his Indian lore. Stephens revealed to our gaze the singular and magnificent ruins of Central America; Sanderson unfolded the hygiene of life in Paris; Flint guided our steps through the fertile valleys of the West, and Irving and Hoffman brought its scenic wonders home to the coldest fancy †

* There are a few American books which cannot be strictly classified under either of these divisions, which not only have a sterling value, but a wide and established reputation, such as the *Legal Commentaries* of Chancellor Kent, the *Dictionary* of Noah Webster; Dr. Rush's *Treatise on the Philosophy of the Human Voice; Lectures on Art*, by Washington Allston; the *Classical Manuals* of Professor Anthon, and Rev. P. Bullions, D. D.; Dr. Bowditch's translation of the *Mécanique Céleste* of La Place; the *Ornithology* of Wilson and Audubon, Catlin's and Schoolcraft's works on the Indians; — the ethnological contributions of Squier, Pickering's philological researches, and the essays on political economy by Albert Gallatin, Raguet, Dr. Cooper, Tucker, Colton, Wayland, Middleton, Raymond, A. H. Everett, and Henry C. Carey. Francis Bowen has published able lectures on metaphysical subjects. James D. Nourse, of Kentucky, has published a clever little treatise, the *Philosophy of History;* Dr. Palfrey, of Massachusetts, a series of erudite lectures on Jewish antiquities; J. Q. Adams a course on rhetoric; Judge Buell and Henry Colman valuable works on agriculture, and A. J. Downing on rural architecture and horticulture.

† It is difficult to enumerate the works in this department; but among them may be justly commended, either for graces of style, effective description, or interesting narrative, — and, in some instances, for all these qualities combined,

"Americans are thought by foreign critics to excel as writers of travels; and the opinion is confirmed by the remarkable success which has so often attended their works. Indeed, in scarcely any other field of literature has the talent of this country been so generally recognized abroad; and this superiority appears to be a natural result of American life and character. With few time-honored customs or strong local associations to bind him to the soil, with little hereditary dignity of name or position to sustain, and accustomed, from infancy, to witness frequent changes of position and fortune, the inhabitant of no civilized land has so little restraint upon his vagrant humor as a native of the United States. The American is by nature locomotive; he believes in change of air for health, change of residence for success, change of society for improvement. Pioneer enterprise is a staple of our history. Not only do the economy of life and the extent of territory in the New World train her citizens, as it were, to travel, — their temperament and taste also combine to make them tourists. Their existence favors quickness of perception, however inimical it may be to contemplative energy. Self-reliance leads to adventure. The freedom from prejudice incident to a new country gives more ample scope to observation; and the very freshness of life renders impressions from new scenes more vivid. Thus free and inspired, it is not surprising that things often wear a more clear and impressive aspect to his mind, than they do to the jaded senses and the conventional views of more learned and reserved, but less flexible and genial travellers. The sympathetic grace of Irving, the impersonal fidelity of Stephens, the Flemish details of Slidell Mackenzie, the picturesque and spirited description of Hoffman, and the De Foe-like narratives of Melville and Dana, are qualities that have gained them more readers than fall to the lot of the nerd of travellers, who have lavished on pictures of the same scenes more learning and finish, perhaps, but less of integrity of statement and naturalness of feeling." *

Romantic fiction, in the United States, took its rise with the publication of *Wieland* by Charles Brockden Brown, in 1798; attained its most complete and characteristic development in the long and brilliant career, as a novelist, of James Fenimore Cooper; and is now represented, in its artistic excellence, by Nathaniel Hawthorne. The parents of Brown were Philadelphia Quakers, and he was born in that

— the *Year in Spain* of Mackenzie, the *Winter in the West* of C. F. Hoffman, the *Oregon Trail* of Francis Parkman, the *Pencillings by the Way* of Willis, the *Scenes and Thoughts in Europe* of George H. Calvert, Longfellow's *Outre mer*, the *Typee* of Melville, the *Views afoot* of Taylor, *Fresh Gleanings* by Mitchell, *Nile Notes* by Geo. W. Curtis, Squier's *Nicaragua*, and the writings of this kind by Robinson, Long, Melville, Jewett, Spencer, Gregg, Townsend, Fremont, Lanman, Bryant, Thorpe, Kendall, Wilson, Webber, Colton, Gillespie, Headley, Dewey, Kip, Silliman, Bigelow, Cushing, Wise, Warren, Mitchell, Cheever, Catlin, Norman, Wallis, Shaler, Ruschenberger, King, Breckenridge, Kidder, Brown, Fisk, Lyman, the Exploring Expedition by Wilkes, the Dead Sea Expedition by Lynch, and the voyages of Delano, Cleveland, Coggeshall, and others.

* Characteristics of Literature. Second Series.

city on the 17th of January, 1771. An invalid from infancy, he had the dreamy moods and roaming propensity incident to poetical sympathies; after vainly attempting to interest his mind in the law, except in a speculative manner, he became an author, at a period and under circumstances which afford the best evidence that the vocation was ordained by his idiosyncrasy. With chiefly the encouragement of a few cultivated friends in New York to sustain him, with narrow means and feeble health, he earnestly pursued his lonely career, inspired by the enthusiasm of genius. His literary toil was varied, erudite, and indefatigable. He edited magazines and annual registers, wrote political essays, a geography, and a treatise on architecture, translated Volney's *Travels in the United States*, debated at clubs, journalized, corresponded, made excursions, and entered ardently into the quiet duties of the fireside and the family. His character was singularly gentle and pure; and he was beloved, even when not appreciated. It is by his novels, however, that Brown achieved renown. They are remarkable for intensity and supernaturalism. His genius was eminently psychological; Godwin is his English prototype. To the reader of the present day, these writings appear somewhat limited and sketch-like; but when we consider the period of their composition, and the disadvantages under which they appeared, they certainly deserve to be ranked among the wonderful productions of the human mind. Brown delighted to analyze the phenomena of consciousness, to bring human nature under mystic or extraordinary influences, and mark the consequences. In *Ormond*, *Arthur Mervyn*, *Jane Talbot*, *Edgar Huntley*, and *Wieland*, we have such agencies as pestilence, somnambulism, rare coincidence, and ventriloquism, brought to act upon individuals of excitable or introspective character, and the result is often thrilling. The descriptions are terse and suggestive, the analysis thorough, and the feeling high-strung and reflective. The pioneer of American fiction was endowed with rare energy of conception, and a style attractive from its restrained earnestness and minute delineation. He died at the close of his thirty-ninth year. Had his works been as artistically constructed as they were profoundly conceived and ingeniously executed, they would have become standard. As it is, we recognize the rare insight and keen sensibility of the man, acknowledge his power to "awaken terror and pity," and lament the want of high finish and effective shape visible in these early and remarkable fruits of native genius.

The first successful novel by an American author was the *Spy*. A previous work by the same author, entitled *Precaution*, had made comparatively little impression. It was strongly tinctured with an English flavor, in many respects imitative, and, as it afterwards appeared, written and printed under circumstances which gave little range to Cooper's real genius. In 1823, he published the *Pioneers*. In this and the novel immediately preceding it, a vein of national association was opened, an original source of romantic and picturesque interest revealed, and an epoch in our literature created. What Cooper had the bold invention to undertake, he had the firmness of purpose and the elasticity of spirit to pursue with unflinching zeal Indeed, his most characteristic trait was self-reliance. He commenced the arduous career of an author in a new country, and with fresh materials: at first, the tone of criticism was somewhat discouraging; but his appeal had been to the popular mind, and not to a literary clique, and the response was universal and sincere. From this time, he gave to the press a series of prose romances conceived with so much spirit and truth, and executed with such fidelity and vital power, that they instantly took captive the reader. His faculty of description, and his sense of the adventurous, were the great sources of his triumph. Refinement of style, poetic sensibility, and melodramatic intensity, were elements that he ignored; but when he pictured the scenes of the forest and prairie, the incidents of Indian warfare, the vicissitudes of border life, and the phenomena of the ocean and nautical experience, he displayed a familiarity with the subjects, a keen sympathy with the characters, and a thorough reality in the delineation, which at once stamped him as a writer of original and great capacity. It is true that in some of the requisites of the novelist he was inferior to many subsequent authors in the same department. His female characters want individuality and interest, and his dialogue is sometimes forced and ineffective; but, on the other hand, he seized with a bold grasp the tangible and characteristic in his own land, and not only stirred the hearts of his countrymen with vivid pictures of colonial, revolutionary, and emigrant life, with the vast ocean and forest for its scenes, but opened to the gaze of Europe phases of human existence at once novel and exciting. The fisherman of Norway, the merchant of Bordeaux, the scholar at Frankfort, and the countess of Florence, in a brief period, all hung with delight over Cooper's daguerreotypes of the New World, transferred to their respective languages. This was no ordinary triumph. It was a rich and legitimate fruit of American genius in letters. To appreciate it we must look back upon the period when the *Spy*, the *Pioneers*, the *Last of the Mohicans*, the *Pilot*, the *Red Rover*, the *Wept of the Wish-ton-Wish*, the *Water Witch*, and the *Prairie*, were new creations, and remember that they first revealed America to Europe through a literary medium. In the opinion of some critics, the unity and completeness of Cooper's fame have been marred by those novels drawn from foreign subjects and induced by a long residence in Europe; by his honest but injudicious attempts to reform his countrymen in some of their particular habits and modes of thought or action; and also by his persistency in issuing volume after volume of fiction, less directly inspired by observation, and comparatively devoid of interest. Whatever truth may exist in such a view of his course, it is to be considered that all temporary defects are soon forgotten in those memorials of individual genius which have the stamp of the author's best powers, and the recognition of the world. Leather-Stocking and Long Tom Coffin are standard characters; the woodland landscapes, the sailing matches of men-of-war, the sea-fights, wrecks, and aboriginal heroes, depicted, as they are, by Cooper to the very life, and in enduring colors, will be identified both with his name and country, and ever vindicate his claims to remembrance. His youth was passed in a manner admirably fitted to develop his special talent, and provide the resources of his subsequent labors. Born in Burlington, N. J., on the 15th of September, 1789, he was early removed to the borders of Otsego Lake, where his father, Judge Cooper, erected a homestead, afterwards inhabited and long occupied by the novelist. He was prepared for college by the Rector of St. Peter's Church, in Albany, and entered Yale in 1802. Three years after, having proved an excellent classical student, and enjoyed the intimacy of several youth afterwards eminent in the land, he left New Haven, and joined the United States navy as a midshipman. After passing six years in the service, he resigned, married, and soon after established himself on his paternal domain, situated amid some of the finest scenery and rural attraction of his native state. Thus Cooper was early initiated into the scenes of a newly-settled country and a maritime life, with the benefit of academical training and the best social privileges. All these means of culture and development his active mind fully appreciated; his observation never slumbered, and its fruits were industriously garnered.

His nautical and Indian tales form, perhaps, the most characteristic portion of our literature. The *Bravo* is the best of his European novels, and his *Naval History* is valuable and interesting. He was one of the most industrious of authors; his books of travel and biographical sketches are numerous, and possess great fidelity of detail, although not free from prejudice. Cooper represents the American mind in its adventurous character; he glories in delineating the "monarch of the deck;" paints the movements of a ship at sea as if she were, indeed, "a thing of life;" follows an Indian trail with the sagacity of a forest-king; and leads us through storms, conflagration, and war with the firm, clear-sighted, and all-observant guidance of a master-spirit. His best scenes and characters are indelibly engraven on the memory. His best creations are instinct with nature and truth. His tone is uniformly manly, fresh, and vigorous. He is always thoroughly American. His style is national; and when he died in the autumn of 1851, a voice of praise and regret seemed to rise all over the land, and a large and distinguished assembly convened soon after, in New York, to listen to his eulogy — pronounced by the poet Bryant.

Hawthorne is distinguished for the finish of his style, and the delicacy of his psychological insight. He combines the metaphysical talent of Brown with the refined diction of Irving. For a period of more than twenty years he contributed, at intervals, to annuals and magazines, the most exquisite fancy sketches and historical narratives, the merit of which was scarcely recognized by the public at large, although cordially praised by the discriminating few. These papers have been recently collected under the title of *Twice-told Tales*, and *Mosses from an Old Manse;* and, seen by the light of the author's present reputation, their grace, wisdom, and originality are now generally acknowledged. But it is through the two romances entitled the *Scarlet Letter*, and the *House of the Seven Gables*, that Hawthorne's eminence has been reached. They are remarkable at once for a highly finished and beautiful style, the most charming artistic skill, and intense characterization. To these intrinsic and universal claims they add that of native scenes and subjects. Imagine such an anatomizer of the human heart as Balzac, transported to a provincial town of New England, and giving to its houses, streets, and history the analytical power of his genius, and we realize the triumph of Hawthorne. Bravely adopting familiar materials, he has thrown over them the light and shadow of his thoughtful mind, eliciting a deep significance and a prolific beauty: if we may use the expression, he is ideally true to the real. His invention is felicitous, his tone magnetic; his sphere borders on the supernatural, and yet a chaste expression and a refined sentiment underlie his most earnest utterance; he is more suggestive than dramatic. The early history of New England has found no such genial and vivid illustration as his pages afford. At all points his genius touches the interests of human life, now overflowing with a love of external nature as gentle as that of Thomson, now intent upon the quaint or characteristic in life with a humor as zestful as that of Lamb, now developing the horrible or pathetic with something of John Webster's dramatic terror, and again buoyant with a fantasy as aerial as Shelley's conceptions. And, in each instance, the staple of charming invention is adorned with the purest graces of style. Hawthorne was born in Salem, Massachusetts, educated at Bowdoin College, and after having filled an office in the Salem custom-house, and the post-office of his native town, lived a year on a community farm, and acted as United States consul at Liverpool for several years, was settled in the pleasant country town of Concord, Mass. He died with the pure and permanent fame of genius, having embalmed the experience he enjoyed in Italy and England in the romances of the *Marble Faun* and *Our Old Home.*

"What we admire in this writer's genius is his felicity in the use of common materials. It is very difficult to give an imaginative scope to a scene or a topic which familiarity has robbed of illusion. It is by the association of ideas, by the halo of remembrance and the magic of love, that an object usually presents itself to the mind under fanciful relations. From a foreign country our native spot becomes picturesque; and from the hill of manhood the valley of youth appears romantic; but that is a peculiar and rare mental alchemy which can transmute the dross of the common and the immediate into gold. Yet so doth Hawthorne. His *Old Apple Dealer* yet sits by the Old South Church, and the *Willey House* is inscribed every summer-day by the penknives of ambitious cits. He is able to illustrate, by his rich invention, places and themes that are before our very eyes and in our daily speech. His fancy is as free of wing at the north end of Boston, or on Salem turnpike, as that of other poets in the Vale of Cashmere or amid the Isles of Greece. He does not seem to feel the necessity of distance, either of time or space, to realize his enchantments. He has succeeded in attaching an ethereal interest to home subjects, which is no small triumph. Somewhat of that poetic charm which Wilson has thrown over Scottish life in his *Lights and Shadows*, and Irving over English in his *Sketch-Book*, and Lamb over metropolitan in his *Elia*, has Hawthorne cast around New England, and his tales here and there blend, as it were, the traits which endear these authors. His best efforts are those in which the human predominates. Ingenuity and moral significancy are finely displayed, it is true, in his allegories; but sometimes they are coldly fanciful, and do not win the sympathies as in those instances where the play of the heart relieves the dim workings of the abstract and supernatural. Hawthorne, like all individualities, must be read in the appropriate mood. This secret of appreciation is now understood as regards Wordsworth. It is due to all genuine authors. To many, whose mental aliment has been exciting and coarse, the delicacy, meek beauties, and calm spirit of these writings will but gradually unfold themselves; but those capable of placing themselves in relation with Hawthorne will discover a native genius for which to be grateful and proud, and a brother whom to know is to love. He certainly has done much to obviate the reproach which a philosophical writer, not without reason, has cast upon our authors, when he asserts their object to be to astonish rather than please." *

There is a host of intermediate authors between the three already described in this sphere of literature, of various and high degrees, both of merit and reputation, but whose traits are chiefly analogous to those of the prominent writers we have surveyed. Some of them have ably illustrated local themes, others excelled in scenic limning, and a few evinced genius for characterization. Paulding, for instance, in *Westward Ho*, and the *Dutchman's Fireside*, has given admirable pictures of colonial life; Richard H. Dana, in the *Idle Man*, has two or three remarkable psychological tales; Timothy Flint, James Hall, Thomas, and more recently M'Connell, of Illinois, have written very graphic and spirited novels of western life; John P. Kennedy, of Baltimore, has embalmed Virginia life in the olden time in *Swallow Barn*, and Fay that of modern New York; Gilmore Simms, a prolific and vigorous novelist, in a similar form has embodied the traits of southern character and scenery; Hoffman, the early history of his native state; Dr. Robert Bird, of Philadelphia, those of Mexico; William Ware has rivalled Lockhart's classical romance in his *Letters from Palmyra*, and *Probus;* Allston's artist-genius is luminous in *Monaldi;* Judd in *Margaret* has related a tragic story arrayed in the very best hues and outlines of New England life; and Edgar A. Poe, in his *Tales of the Grotesque and Arabesque*, evinces a genius in which a love of the marvellous and an intensity of conception are united with the wildest sympathies, as if the endowments of Mrs. Radcliffe and Coleridge were partially united in one mind. In adventurous and descriptive narration we have Melville and Mayo. John Neal struck off at a heat some half score of novels that, at least, illustrate a facility quite remarkable; and, indeed, from the days of the *Algerine Captive* and the *Foresters*—the first attempts at such writing in this country—to the present day, there has been no lack of native fictions. The minor specimens which possess the highest literary excellence are by Irving, Willis, and Longfellow; but their claims rest entirely on style and sentiment; they are brief and polished, but more graceful than impressive.

* Leaves from the Diary of a Dreamer.

CHAPTER III.

POETRY.

Its essential Conditions. FRENEAU **and the early Metrical Writers.** MUMFORD, CLIFFTON, ALLSTON, **and others.** PIERPONT. DANA. HILLHOUSE SPRAGUE. PERCIVAL. HALLECK. DRAKE. HOFFMAN. WILLIS. LONGFELLOW. HOLMES. LOWELL. BOKER. **Favorite Single Poems. Descriptive Poetry.** STREET, WHITTIER, **and others.** BRAINARD. **Song-Writers. Other Poets. Female Poets.** BRYANT.

"IT has been well observed by an English critic, that poetry is not a branch of authorship. The vain endeavor to pervert its divine and spontaneous agency into a literary craft is the great secret of its decline. Poetry is the overflowing of the soul. It is the record of what is best in the world. No product of the human mind is more disinterested. Hence comparatively few keep the poetic element alive beyond the period of youth. All that is genuine in the art springs from vivid experience, and life seldom retains any novel aspect to those who have long mingled in its scenes, and staked upon its chances. A celebrated artist of our day, when asked the process by which his delineations were rendered so effective, replied that he drew them altogether from memory. Natural objects were portrayed, not as they impressed him at the moment, but according to the lively and feeling phases in which they struck his senses in boyhood. For this reason it has been truly observed, that remembrance makes the poet; and, according to Wordsworth, 'emotions recollected in tranquillity' form the true source of inspiration. A species of literature depending upon conditions so delicate is obviously not to be successfully cultivated by those who hold it in no reverence. The great distinction between verse-writers and poets is, that the former seek and the latter receive; the one attempt to command, the other meekly obey the higher impulses of their being." *

The first metrical compositions in this country, recognized by popular sympathy, were the effusions of Philip Freneau, a political writer befriended by Jefferson. He wrote many songs and ballads in a patriotic and historical vein, which attracted and somewhat reflected the feelings of his contemporaries, and were not destitute of merit. Their success was owing, in part, to the immediate interest of the subjects, and in part to musical versification and pathetic sentiment. One of his Indian ballads has survived the general neglect to which more artistic skill and deeper significance in poetry have banished the mass of his verses: to the curious in metrical writings, however, they yet afford a characteristic illustration of the taste and spirit of the times. Freneau was born in 1752, and died in 1832. The antecedent speci-

* Thoughts on the Poets.

mens of verse in America were, for the most part, the occasional work of the clergy, and are remarkable chiefly for a quaint and monotonous strain, grotesque rhymed versions of the Psalms, and tolerable attempts at descriptive poems. The writings of Mrs. Bradstreet, Governor Bradford, Roger Williams, Cotton Mather, and the witty Dr. Byles, in this department, are now only familiar to the antiquarian. Franklin's friend Ralph, and Thomas Godfrey, of Philadelphia, indicate the dawn of a more liberal era, illustrated by Trumbull, Dwight, Humphreys, Alsop, and Honeywood; passages from whose poems show a marked improvement in diction, a more refined scholarship, and genuine sympathy with nature; but, although in a literary point of view they are respectable performances, and, for the period and locality of their composition, suggestive of a rare degree of taste, there are too few salient points, and too little of an original spirit, to justify any claim to high poetical genius. One of the most remarkable efforts in this branch of letters, at the epoch in question, was doubtless William Mumford's translation of the *Iliad* — a work that, when published, elicited some authentic critical praise. He was a native of Virginia, and his great undertaking was only finished a short period before his death, which occurred in 1825. The verses which have the earliest touch of true sensibility and that melody of rhythm which seems intuitive, are the few bequeathed by William Cliffton, of Philadelphia, born in 1772. After him we trace the American muse in the patriotic songs of R. T. Paine, and the scenic descriptions of Paulding, until sh began a loftier though brief flight in the fanciful poems of Allston.

"In the moral economy of life, sensibility to the beautiful must have a great purpose. If the Platonic doctrine of pre-existence be true, perhaps ideality is the surviving element of our primal life. Some individuals seem born to minister to this influence, which, under the name of beauty, sentiment, or poetry, is the source of what is most exalting in our inmost experience and redeeming in our outward life. Does not a benign Providence watch over these priests of nature? They are not necessarily renowned. Their agency may be wholly social and private, yet none the less efficient. We confess that, to us, few arguments for the benevolent and infinite design of existence are more impressive than the fact that such beings actually live, and, wholly unfitted as they are to excel in or even conform to the Practical, bear evidence, not to be disputed, of the sanctity, the tranquil progress, and the serene faith, that dwell in the Ideal. Washington Allston was such a man. He was born in South Carolina in 1779, and died at Cambridge, Mass., in 1843. By profession he was a painter, and his works overflow with genius; still it would be difficult to say whether his pen, his pencil, or his tongue chiefly made known that he was a prophet of the true and beautiful. He believed not in any exclusive development. It was the spirit of a man, and not his dexterity or success, by which he tested character. In painting, reading, or writing, his mornings were occupied, and at night he was at the service of his friends. Beneath his humble roof, in his latter years, there were often a flow of wit, a community of mind, and a generous exercise of sympathy which kings might envy. To the eye of the multitude his life glided away in secluded contentment, yet a prevailing idea was the star of his being—the idea of beauty. For the high, the lovely, the perfect, he strove all his days. He sought them in the scenes of nature, in the masterpieces of literature and art, in habits of life, in social relations, and in love. Without pretence, without elation, in all meekness, his youthful enthusiasm chastened by suffering, he lived above the world. Gentleness he deemed true wisdom, renunciation of all the trappings of life a duty. He was calm, patient, occasionally sad, but for the most part happy in the free exercise and guardianship of his varied powers. His sonnets are interesting as records of personal feeling. They eloquently breathe sentiments of intelligent admiration or sincere friendship, while the *Sylphs of the Season* and other longer poems show a great command of language and an exuberant fancy.

"On his return to America, the life of our illustrious painter was one of comparative seclusion. The state of his health, devotion to his art, and a distaste for promiscuous society and the bustle of the world, rendered this course the most judicious he could have pursued. His humble retirement was occasionally invaded by foreigners of distinction, to whom his name had become precious; and sometimes a votary of letters or art entered his dwelling, to gratify admiration or seek counsel and encouragement. To such, an unaffected and sincere welcome was always given, and they left his presence refreshed and happy. The instances of timely sympathy which he afforded young and baffled aspirants are innumerable.

"Allston's appearance and manners accorded perfectly with his character. His form was slight, and his movements quietly active. The lines of his countenance, the breadth of the brow, the large and speaking eye, and the long, white hair, made him an immediate object of interest. If not engaged in conversation, there was a serene abstraction in his air. When death so tranquilly overtook him, for many hours it was difficult to believe that he was not sleeping, so perfectly did the usual expression remain. His torchlight burial harmonized, in its beautiful solemnity, with the bright and thoughtful tenor of his life." *

John Pierpont, a Unitarian clergyman of Massachusetts, has written numerous hymns and odes for religious and national occasions, remarkable for their variety of difficult metres, and for the felicity both of the rhythm, sentiment, and expression. His *Airs of Palestine*, a long poem in heroic verse, has many eloquent passages; and several of his minor pieces, especially those entitled *Passing Away* and *My Child*, are striking examples of effective versification. The most popular of his occasional poems is *The Pilgrim Fathers*, an ode written for the anniversary of the landing at Plymouth, and embodying in truly musical verse the sentiment of the memorable day.

* Artist-Life, or Sketches of American Painters.

Richard H. Dana is the most psychological of American poets. His *Buccaneer* has several descriptive passages of singular terseness and beauty, although there is a certain abruptness in the metre chosen. The scenery and phenomena of the ocean are evidently familiar to his observation; the tragic and remorseful elements in humanity exert a powerful influence over his imagination; while the mysteries and aspirations of the human soul fill and elevate his mind. The result is an introspective tone, a solemnity of mood lightened occasionally by touches of pathos or beautiful pictures. There is a compactness, a pointed truth to the actual, in many of his rhymed pieces, and a high music in some of his blank verse, which suggest greater poetical genius than is actually exhibited. His taste evidently inclines to Shakspeare, Milton, and the old English dramatists, his deep appreciation of whom he has manifested in the most subtle and profound criticisms. Of his minor pieces, the *Intimations of Immortality* and *The Little Beach-Bird* are perhaps the most characteristic of his two phases of expression.

James A. Hillhouse excelled in a species of poetic literature, which, within a few years, has attained eminence from the fine illustrations of Taylor, Browning, Horne, Talfourd, and other men of genius in England. It may be called the written drama, and, however unfit for representation, is unsurpassed for bold, noble, and exquisite sentiment and imagery. The name of Hillhouse is associated with the beautiful elms of New Haven, beneath whose majestic boughs he so often walked. His home in the neighborhood of this rural city was consecrated by elevated tastes and domestic virtue. He there, in the intervals of business, led the life of a true scholar; and the memorials of this existence are his poems *Hadad*, *The Judgment*, *Percy's Masque*, *Demetria*, and others. In the two former, his scriptural erudition and deep perceptions of the Jewish character, and his sense of religious truth, are evinced in the most carefully finished and nobly-conceived writings. Their tone is lofty, often sublime; the language is finely chosen, and there is about them evidence of gradual and patient labor rare in American literature. On every page we recognize the Christian scholar and gentleman, the secluded bard, and the chivalric student of the past. *Percy's Masque* reproduces the features of an era more impressed with knightly character than any in the annals of England. Hillhouse moves in that atmosphere quite as gracefully as among the solemn and venerable traditions of the Hebrew faith. His dramatic and other pieces are the first instances, in this country, of artistic skill in the higher and more elaborate spheres of poetic writing. He possessed the scholarship, the leisure, the dignity of taste, and the noble sympathy requisite thus to "build the lofty rhyme;" and his volumes, though unattractive to the mass of readers, have a permanent interest and value to the refined, the aspiring, and the disciplined mind.

Charles Sprague has been called the Rogers of America; and there is an analogy between them in two respects — the careful finish of their verses, and their financial occupation. The American poet first attracted notice by two or three theatrical prize addresses; and his success, in this regard, attained its climax in a *Shakspeare Ode* which grouped the characters of the great poet with an effect so striking and happy, and in a rhythm so appropriate and impressive, as to recall the best efforts of Collins and Dryden united. A similar composition, more elaborate, is his ode delivered on the second centennial anniversary of the settlement of Boston, his native city. A few domestic pieces, remarkable for their simplicity of expression and truth of feeling, soon became endeared to a large circle; but the performance which has rendered Sprague best known to the country as a poet is his metrical essay on *Curiosity*, delivered in 1829 before the literary societies of Harvard University. It is written in heroic measure, and recalls the couplets of Pope. The choice of a theme was singularly fortunate. He traces the passion which "tempted Eve to sin" through its loftiest and most vulgar manifestations; at one moment rivalling Crabbe in the lowliness of his details, and at another Campbell in the aspiration of his song. The serious and the comic alternate on every page. Good sense is the basis of the work; fancy, wit, and feeling warm and vivify it; and a nervous tone and finished versification, as well as excellent choice of words, impart a glow, polish, and grace that at once gratify the ear and captivate the mind.

James G. Percival has been a copious writer of verses, some of which, from their even and sweet flow, their aptness of epithet and natural sentiment, have become household and school treasures; such as *The Coral Grove*, *New England*, and *Seneca Lake*. His command both of language and metre is remarkable; his acquirements were very extensive and various, and his life eccentric. Perhaps a facile power of expression has tended to limit his poetic fame, by inducing a diffuse, careless, and unindividual method; although choice pieces enough can easily be gleaned from his voluminous writings to constitute a just and rare claim to renown and sympathy.

The poems of Fitz-Greene Halleck, although limited in quantity, are, perhaps, the best known and most cherished, especially in the latitude of New York, of all American verses. This is owing, in no small degree, to their spirited, direct, and intelligible character, the absence of all vagueness and mysticism, and the heartfelt or humorous glow of real inspiration; and in a measure, perhaps, it can be traced to the *prestige* of his youthful fame, when, associated with his friend Drake, he used to charm the town with the admirable local verses that appeared in the journals of the day, under the signature of Croaker and Co. His theory of poetic expression is that of the most popular masters of English verse — manly, clear, vivid, warm with genuine emotion, or sparkling with true wit. The more recent style of metrical writing, suggestive rather than emphatic, undefined and involved, and borrowed mainly from German idealism, he utterly repudiates. All his verses have a vital meaning, and the clear ring of pure metal. They are few, but memorable. The school-boy and the old Knickerbocker both know them by heart. In his serious poems he belongs to the same school as Campbell, and in his lighter pieces reminds us of *Beppo* and the best parts of *Don Juan*. *Fanny*, conceived in the latter vein, has the point of a fine local satire gracefully executed. *Burns*, and the lines on the death of Drake, have the beautiful impressiveness of the highest elegiac verse. *Marco Bozzaris* is perhaps the best martial lyric in the language, *Red Jacket* the most effective Indian portrait, and *Twilight* an apt piece of contemplative verse; while *Alnwick Castle* combines his grave and gay style with inimitable art and admirable effect. As a versifier, he is an adept in that relation of sound to sense which embalms thought in deathless melody. An unusual blending of the animal and intellectual with that full proportion essential to manhood, enables him to utter appeals that wake responses in the universal heart. An almost provoking mixture of irony and sentiment is characteristic of his genius. Born in Connecticut, his life has been chiefly passed in the city of New York, and occupied in mercantile affairs. He is a conservative in taste and opinions, but his feelings are chivalric, and his sympathies ardent and loyal; and these, alternating with humor, glow and sparkle in the most spirited and harmonious lyrical compositions of the American muse.

"Centuries hence, perchance, some lover of 'The Old American Writers' will speculate as ardently as Monkbarns himself about the site of Sleepy Hollow. Then the Hudson will possess a classic interest, and the associations of genius and patriotism may furnish themes to illustrate its matchless scenery. *The Culprit Fay* will then be quoted with enthusiasm. Imagination is a perverse faculty. Why should the ruins of a feudal castle add enchantment to a knoll of the Catskills? Are not the Palisades more ancient than the aqueducts of the Roman Campagna? Can bloody tradition or superstitious legends really enhance the picturesque impression derived from West Point? The heart forever asserts its claim. Primeval nature is often coldly grand in the view of one who loves and honors his race; and the outward world is only brought near to his spirit when linked with human love and suffering, or consecrated by heroism and faith. Yet, if there ever was a stream romantic in itself, superior, from its own wild beauty, to all extraneous charms, it is the Hudson. Who ever sailed between its banks and scanned its jutting headlands — the perpendicular cliffs — the meadows over which alternate sunshine and cloud — umbrageous woods, masses of gray rock, dark cedar groves, bright grain-fields, tasteful cottages, and fairy-like sails; who, after thus feasting both sense and soul through a summer day, has, from a secluded nook of those beautiful shores, watched the moon rise and tip the crystal ripples with light, and not echoed the appeal of the bard? —

Tell me — where'er thy silver bark be steering,
  By bright Italian or soft Persian lands,
Or o'er those island-studded seas careering,
  Whose pearl-charged waves dissolve on coral strands;

Tell, if thou visitest, thou heavenly rover,
A lovelier scene than this the wide world over'*

"It was where

'The moon looks down on old Cro'nest,
And mellows the shade on his shaggy breast,'

that Drake laid the scene of his poem. The story is of simple construction. The fairies are called together, at this chosen hour, not to join in dance or revel, but to sit in judgment on one of their number who has broken his vestal vow. Evil sprites, both of the air and water, oppose the Fay in his mission of penance. He is sadly baffled and tempted, but at length conquers all difficulties, and his triumphant return is hailed with 'dance and song, and lute and lyre.'

"It is in the imagery of the poem that Drake's genius is preëminent. What, for instance, can be more ingenious than the ordeals prescribed, had any 'spot or taint' in his ladye-love deepened the Fay's sacrilege? Most appropriate tortures, these, for a fairy inquisition! Even without the metrical accompaniment, how daintily conceived are all the appointments of the fairies! Their lanterns were owlet's eyes. Some of them repose in cobweb hammocks, swinging, perhaps, on tufted spears of grass, and rocked by the zephyrs of a midsummer night. Others make their beds of lichen-green, pillowed by the breast-plumes of the humming-bird. A few, whose taste for upholstery is quite magnificent, find a couch in the purple shade of the four-o'clock, or the little niches of rock lined with dazzling mica. The table of these minikin epicureans is a mushroom, whose velvet surface and Quaker hue make it a very respectable festal board at which to drink dew from buttercups. The king's throne is of sassafras and spice-wood, with tortoise-shell pillars, and crimson tulip-leaves for drapery. But the quaint shifts and beautiful outfit of the Culprit himself comprise the most delectable imagery of the poem. He is worn out with fatigue and chagrin at the very commencement of his journey, and therefore makes captive of a spotted toad, by way of a steed. Having bridled her with silk-weed twist, his progress is rapid by dint of lashing her sides with an osier thong. Arrived at the beach, he launches fearlessly upon the tide, for among his other accomplishments, the Fay is a graceful swimmer; but his tender limbs are so bruised by leeches, star-fish, and other watery enemies, that he is soon driven back.

"The *materia medica* of Fairy-land is always accessible; and cobweb lint, and balsam dew of sorrel and henbane, speedily relieve the little penitent's wounds. Having refreshed himself with the juice of the calamus root, he returns to the shore, and selects a neatly-shaped muscle shell, brightly painted without, and tinged with pearl within. Nature seemed to have formed it expressly for a fairy-boat. Having notched the stern, and gathered a colen bell to bale with, he sculls into the midst of the river, laughing at his old foes as they grin and chatter around his way. There, in the sweet moonlight, he sits until a sturgeon

* Hoffman's Moonlight on the Hudson.

comes by, and leaps, all glistening, into the silvery atmosphere; then balancing his delicate frame upon one foot, like a Lilliputian Mercury, he lifts the flowery cup, and catches the one sparkling drop that is to wash the stain from his wing. Gay is his return voyage. Sweet nymphs clasp the boat's side with their tiny hands, and cheerily urge it onward. His next enterprise is of a more knightly species; and he proceeds to array himself accordingly, as becomes a fairy cavalier. His acorn helmet is plumed with thistle-down, a bee's nest forms his corselet, and his cloak is of butterflies' wings. With a lady-bug's shell for a shield, and wasp-sting lance, spurs of cockle-seed, a bow made of vine-twig strung with maize-silk, and well supplied with nettle-shafts, he mounts his firefly Bucephalus, and waving his blade of blue grass, speeds upward to catch a 'glimmering spark' from some flying meteor. Again the spirits of evil are let loose upon him, and the upper elements are not more friendly than those below. Fays are as hardly beset, it seems, as we of coarser clay, by temptations in a feminine shape. A sylphid queen of the skies, 'the loveliest of the forms of light,' enchants the wanderer by her beauty and kindness. But though she played very archly with the butterfly cloak, and handled the tassel of his blade while he revealed to her pitying ear the 'dangers he had passed,' the memory of his first love and the object of pilgrimage kept his heart free. Escorted with great honor by the sylph's lovely train, his career is resumed, and his flame-wood lamp at length rekindled, and before the 'sentry elf' proclaims 'a streak in the eastern sky,' the Culprit has been welcomed to all his original glory.

"It will be observed that the materials — the costume, as it were — of this fairy tale are of native and familiar origin. The effect is certainly quite as felicitous as that of many similar productions where the countless flowers and rich legends of the East furnish the poet with an exhaustless mine of pleasing images. It has been remarked that the dolphin and flying-fish are the only poetical members of the finny tribes; but who, after reading the *Culprit Fay*, will ever hear the plash of a sturgeon in the moon-lit water without recalling the genius of Drake? Indeed, the poem which we have thus cursorily examined is one of those happy inventions of fancy, superinduced upon fact, which afford unalloyed delight. There are various tastes as regards the style and spirit of different bards; but no one, having the slightest perception, will fail to realize at once that the *Culprit Fay* is a genuine poem. This is, perhaps, the highest of praise. The mass of versified compositions are *not* strictly poems. Here and there only the purely ideal is apparent. A series of poetical fragments are linked by rhymes to other and larger portions of commonplace and prosaic ideas. It is with the former as with moonbeams falling through dense foliage — they only checker our path with light. 'Poetry,' says Campbell, 'should come to us in masses of ore, that require little sifting.' The poem before us obeys this important rule. It is 'of imagination all compact.' It takes us completely away from the dull level of ordinary associations. As the portico of some beautiful temple, through it we are introduced into a scene of calm delight, where fancy asserts her joyous supremacy, and wooes us to forgetfulness of all outward evil, and to fresh recognition of the lovely in nature, and the graceful and gifted in humanity." *

For some of the best convivial, amatory, and descriptive poetry of native origin, we are indebted to Charles Fenno Hoffman. The woods and streams, the feast and the vigil, are reflected in his verse with a graphic truth and sentiment that evidence an eye for the picturesque, a sense of the adventurous, and a zest for pleasure. He has written many admirable scenic pieces that evince not only a careful, but a loving observation of nature: some touches of this kind in the *Vigil of Faith* are worthy of the most celebrated poets. Many of his songs, from their graceful flow and tender feeling, are highly popular, although some of the metres are so like those of Moore as to provoke a comparison. They are, however, less tinctured with artifice; and many of them have a spontaneous and natural vitality.

The Scripture pieces of N. P. Willis, although the productions of his youth, have an individual beauty that renders them choice and valuable exemplars of American genius. In his other poems there is apparent a sense of the beautiful and a grace of utterance, often an exquisite imagery, and rich tone of feeling, that emphatically announce the poet; but in the chastened and sweet, as well as picturesque elaboration of the miracles of Christ, and some of the incidents recorded in the Bible, Willis succeeded in an experiment at once bold, delicate, and profoundly interesting. *Melanie* is a narrative in verse, full of imaginative beauty and expressive music. The high finish, rare metaphors, verbal felicity, and graceful sentiment of his poems are sometimes marred by a doubtful taste that seems affectation; but where he obeys the inspiration of nature and religious sentiment, the result is truly beautiful. A native of Maine, he has been an extensive traveller, and has gathered his illustrations from a wide range of observation and experience.

Henry W. Longfellow has achieved an extended reputation as a poet, for which he is chiefly indebted to his philological aptitudes and his refined taste. Trained as a verbal artist by the discipline of a poetical translator, he acquired a tact and facility in the use of words, which great natural fluency and extreme fastidiousness enabled him to use to the utmost advantage. His poems are chiefly meditative, and have that legendary significance peculiar to the German ballad. They also often embody and illustrate a moral truth. There is little or no evidence of inspiration in his verse, as that term is used to suggest the power of an overmastering passion; but there is a thoughtful, subdued feeling that seems to overflow in quiet beauty. It is, however, the manner in which this sentiment is expressed, the appositeness of the figures, the harmony of the numbers, and the inimitable choice of words that give effect to the composition. He often reminds us of an excellent mosaic worker, with his smooth table of polished marble indented to receive

* **Thoughts on the Poets.**

the precious stones that are lying at hand, which he calmly, patiently, and with exquisite art, inserts in the shape of flowers and fruit. Almost all Longfellow's poems are gems set with consummate taste His *Evangeline* is a beautiful reflex of rural life and love, which, from the charm of its pictures and the gentle harmony of its sentiment, became popular, although written in hexameters. His *Skeleton in Armor* is the most novel and characteristic of his shorter poems; and his *Psalms of Life* and *Excelsior* are the most familiar and endeared. He is the artistic, as Halleck is the lyrical and Bryant the picturesque and philosophical, of American poets.

The most concise, apt, and effective poet of the school of Pope, this country has produced, is Oliver Wendell Holmes, a Boston physician, and son of the excellent author of the *Annals*, long a minister of the parish of Cambridge, at which venerable seat of learning this accomplished writer was born. His best lines are a series of rhymed pictures, witticisms, or sentiments, let off with the precision and brilliancy of the scintillations that sometimes illumine the northern horizon. The significant terms, the perfect construction, and acute choice of syllables and emphasis, render some passages of Holmes absolute models of versification, especially in the heroic measure. Besides these artistic merits, his poetry abounds with fine satire, beautiful delineations of nature, and amusing caricatures of manners. The long poems are metrical essays, more pointed, musical, and judicious, as well as witty, than any that have appeared, of the same species, since the *Essay on Man* and *The Dunciad*. His description of the art in which he excels is inimitable, and illustrates all that it defines. His *Old Ironsides* — an indignant protest against the destruction of the frigate Constitution — created a public sentiment that prevented the fulfilment of that ungracious design. His verses on *Lending an old Punch Bowl* are in the happiest vein of that form of writing. About his occasional pieces, there is an easy and vigorous tone like that of Praed; and some of them are the liveliest specimens of finished verse yet written among us. His command of language, his ready wit, his concise and pointed style, the nervous, bright, and wise scope of his muse, now and then softened by a pathetic touch, or animated by a living picture, are qualities that have firmly established the reputation of Dr. Holmes as a poet, while in professional character and success he has been equally recognized.

James R. Lowell, also the son of a clergyman and a native of Cambridge, unites, in his most effective poems, the dreamy, suggestive character of the transcendental bards with the philosophic simplicity of Wordsworth. He has written clever satires, good sonnets, and some long poems with fine descriptive passages. He reminds us often of Tennyson, in the sentiment and the construction of his verse. Imagination and philanthropy are the dominant elements in his writings, some of which are marked by a graceful flow and earnest tone, and many unite with these attractions that of high finish.

George H. Boker, the author of *Calaynos*, *Anne Boleyn*, and other dramatic pieces, is a native and resident of Philadelphia. "The glow of his images is chastened by a noble simplicity, keeping them within the line of human sympathy and natural expression. He has followed the masters of dramatic writing with rare judgment. He also excels many gifted poets of his class in a quality essential to an acted play — spirit. To the tragic ability he unites aptitude for easy, colloquial, and jocose dialogue, such as must intervene in the genuine Shakspearian drama, to give relief and additional effect to high emotion. His language, also, rises often to the highest point of energy, pathos, and beauty."*

A casual dalliance with the Muses is characteristic of our busy citizens, in all professions; some of these poetical estrays have a permanent hold upon the popular taste and sympathy. Among them may be mentioned Frisbie's *Castle in the Air*, Norton's *Scene after a Summer Shower*, Henry Ware's *Address to the Ursa Major*, Pinkney's verses entitled *A Health*, Palmer's ode to *Light*, Poe's *Raven* and *The Bells*, Cooke's *Florence Vane*, Parsons's *Lines to a Bust of Dante*, Wilde's *My Life is like a Summer Rose*, Albert G. Greene's *Old Grimes*, Butler's *Nothing to Wear*, and Woodworth's *Old Oaken Bucket*.

Extensive circulation is seldom to be hoped for works which appeal so faintly to the practical spirit of our times and people as the class we have thus cursorily examined. Yet, did space allow, we should be tempted into a somewhat elaborate argument, to prove that the cordia reception of such books agrees perfectly with genuine utilitarianism. As a people, it is generally conceded that we lack nationality of feeling. Narrow reasoners may think that this spirit is best promoted by absurd sensitiveness to foreign comments or testy alertness in regard to what is called national honor. We incline to the opinion, founded on well-established facts, both of history and human nature, that the best way to make an individual true to his political obligations is to promote his love of country; and experience shows that this is mainly induced by cherishing high and interesting associations in relation to his native land. Every well-recorded act honorable to the state, every noble deed consecrated by the effective pen of the historian, or illustrated in the glowing page of the novelist, tends wonderfully to such a result. Have not the hearts of the Scotch nurtured a deeper patriotism since Sir Walter cast into the furrows of time his peerless romances? No light part in this elevated mission is accorded to the poet. Dante and Petrarch have done much to render Italy beloved. Beranger has given no inadequate expression to those feelings which bind soldier, artisan, and peasant to the soil of France. Here the bard can draw only upon brief chronicles, but God has arrayed this continent with a sublime and characteristic beauty, that should endear its mountains and streams to the American heart; and whoever ably depicts the natural glory of the country touches a chord which should yield responses of admiration and loyalty. In this point of view alone, then, we deem the minstrel who ardently sings of forest and sky, river and highland, as eminently

* Characteristics of Literature. Second Series.

worthy of recognition. This merit may be claimed for Aalfred B. Street, of Albany, who was born and reared amid the most picturesque scenery of the State of New York. That he is deficient occasionally in high finish — that there is repetition and monotony in his strain — that there are redundant epithets and a lack of variety in his effusions, is undeniable; and having frankly granted all this to the critics, we feel at liberty to utter his just praise with equal sincerity. Street has an eye for Nature in all her moods. He has not roamed the woodlands in vain, nor have the changeful seasons passed him by without leaving vivid and lasting impressions. These his verse records with unusual fidelity and genuine emotion. I have wandered with him on a summer's afternoon, in the neighborhood of his present residence, and, stretched upon the greensward, listened to his woodland talk, and can therefore testify that he observes *con amore* the play of shadows, the twinkle of swaying herbage in the sunshine, and all the phenomena that makes the outward world so rich in meaning to the attentive gaze. He is a true Flemish painter, seizing upon objects in all their verisimilitude. As we read him, wild flowers peer up from among the brown leaves; the drum of the partridge, the ripple of waters, the flickering of autumn light, the sting of sleety snow, the cry of the panther, the roar of the winds, the melody of birds, and the odor of crushed pine boughs, are present to our senses. In a foreign land his poems would transport us at once to home. He is no second-hand limner, content to furnish insipid copies, but draws from reality. His pictures have the freshness of originals. They are graphic, detailed, never untrue, and often vigorous. He is essentially an American poet. His range is limited, and he has had the good sense not to wander from his sphere, candidly acknowledging that the heart of man has not furnished him the food for meditation which inspires a higher class of poets. He is emphatically an observer. In England we notice that these qualities have been recognized. His *Lost Hunter* has been finely illustrated there, thus affording the best evidence of the picturesque fertility of his muse. Many of his pieces also glow with patriotism. His *Gray Forest Eagle* is a noble lyric, full of spirit; his *Forest Scenes* are minutely, and at the same time elaborately, true. His Indian legends and descriptions of the seasons have a native zest we have rarely encountered. Without the classic refinement of Thomson, he excels him in graphic power. There is nothing metaphysical in his tone of mind, or highly artistic in his style. But there is an honest directness and cordial faithfulness about him that strikes us as remarkably appropriate and manly. Delicacy, sentiment, ideal enthusiasm, are not his by nature; but clear, bold, genial insight and feeling he possesses in a rare degree, and his poems worthily depict the phases of Nature, as she displays herself in this land, in all her picturesque wildness, solemn magnificence, and serene beauty.

To the descriptive talent as related to natural scenery, which we have noted as the gift of our best poets, John G. Whittier unites the enthusiasm of the reformer and the sympathies of the patriot. There is a prophetic anathema and a bard-like invocation in some of his pieces He is a true son of New England, and, beneath the calm, fraternal bearing of the Quaker, nurses the imaginative ardor of a devotee both of nature and humanity. The early promise of Brainard, his fine poetic observation and sensibility, enshrined in several pleasing lyrics, and his premature death, are analogous to the career of Henry Kirke White. John Neal has written some odes, carelessly put together, but having memorable passages. Emerson has published a small volume of quaint rhymes; Croswell wrote several short but impressive church poems, in which he has been ably followed by Cleveland Cox: Bayard Taylor's California ballads are full of truth, spirit, and melody, and his "Picture of St. John," a melodious and graphic metrical tale; Albert Pike, of Arkansas, is the author of a series of hymns to the gods, after the manner of Keats, which have justly commanded favorable notice; Willis G. Clarke is remembered for his few but touching and finished elegiac pieces. Epes Sargent's *Poems of the Sea* are worthy of the subject, both in sentiment and style. F. S. Key, of Baltimore, was the author of the *Star-Spangled Banner*, and Judge Hopkinson, of Philadelphia, wrote *Hail, Columbia.* George P. Morris, among the honored contributors to American poetry,* whose pieces are more or less familiar, is recognized as the song-writer of America.

A large number of graceful versifiers, and a few writers of poetical genius, have arisen among the women of America. Southey has recorded, in no measured terms, his estimation of Mrs. Brooks, the author of *Zophiel.* The sentiment and melody of Mrs. Welby have made the name of *Amelia* precious in the west. Mrs. Sigourney's metrical writings are cherished by a large portion of the New England religious public. The *Sinless Child* of Mrs. Oakes Smith is a melodious and imaginative poem, with many verses of graphic and metaphysical significance. The occasional pieces of Mrs. Embury, Mrs. Whitman, Mrs. Hewitt, and Miss Lynch are thoughtful, earnest, and artistic. The facility, playfulness, and ingenious conception of Mrs. Osgood rendered her a truly gifted *improvvisatrice.* Miss Gould has written several pretty fanciful little, poems, and Miss Sara Clark's *Ariadne* is worthy of Mrs. Norton. The Davidsons are instances of rare, though melancholy precocity in the art. The moral purity, love of nature, domestic affection, and graceful expression which characterize the writings of our female poets, are remarkable. Many of them enjoy

* Among them are Hill, Godwin, Mellen, Griffin, Ware, Doane, Colton, Rockwell, Sanford, Ward, Gallagher, Aldrich, J. F. Clarke, Hosmer, Burleigh, Noble, Hirst, Read, Matthews, Lord, Wallace, Legaré, Miller, Walter, Eastburn, Barker, Schoolcraft, Tappan, Jackson, Meek, Seba Smith, Thacher, Peabody, Ellery, Channing, Snelling, Murray, Fay, C. C. Moore, J. G. Brooks, A. G. Greene, Bethune, Carlos Wilcox, Frisbie, Goodrich, Clason, Leggett, Fairfield, Dawes, Bright, Conrad, Prentice, Simms, John H. Bryant, Lawrence, Benjamin, Very, Cutter, Cranch, Peabody, Steadman, Huntington, Saxe, Dewey, Fields, Hoyt, Stoddard. For biographical notices and a critical estimate of these metrical writers, with specimens of their verse, the reader is referred to Griswold's *Poets and Poetry of America*, last edition.

a high local reputation, and their effusions are quoted with zeal at the fireside. Taste rather than profound sympathies, sentiment rather than passion, and fancy more than imagination, are evident in these spontaneous, gentle, and often picturesque poems. They usually are more creditable to the refinement and pure feelings, than to the creative power or original style of the authors. Among a reading people, however, like our own, these beautiful native flowers, scattered by loving hands, are sweet mementos and tokens of ideal culture and gentle enthusiasm, in delightful contrast to the prevailing hardihood and materialism of character.*

In the felicitous use of native materials, as well as in the religious sentiment and love of freedom, united with skill as an artist, William Cullen Bryant is recognized as the best representative of American poetry; and we cannot better close this brief survey of native literature than by an examination of his poems; in which the traits of our scenery, the spirit of our institutions, and the devotional faith that proved the conservative element in our history, are all consecrated by poetic art.

The first thought which suggests itself in regard to Bryant is his respect for the art which he has so nobly illustrated. This is not less commendable than rare. Such an impatient spirit of utility prevails in our country, that even men of ideal pursuits are often infected by it. It is a leading article in the Yankee creed to turn every endowment to account; and although a poet is generally left "to chew the cud of sweet and bitter fancies" as he lists, occasions are not infrequent when even his services are available. Caliban's lowly toil will not supply al needs. The more "gentle spiriting" of Ariel is sometimes desired. To subserve the objects of party, to acquire a reputation upon which office may be sought, and to gratify personal ambition, the American poet is often tempted to sacrifice his true fame and the dignity of Art to the demands of Occasion. To this weakness Bryant has been almos

* For a very complete and interesting survey of this class of writings, the reader is referred to Griswold's *Female Poets of America.* His list comprises nearly a hundred names; the biographical sketches afford a good insight into the domestic culture of the nation; and the specimens are various, and often beautiful, including, besides the writers of colonial and revolutionary times, and those already mentioned, the names of Miss Townsend, Mrs. Gilman, Mrs. Hale, Mrs. Wells, Miss James, Mrs. Ward, Mrs. Ware, Mrs. Gray, Mrs. Little, Mrs. Child, Mrs. Hall, Mrs. Follen, Mrs. Green, Miss Taggart, Mrs. Canfield, Miss Bogart, Mrs. Mary E. Brooks, Mrs. Loud, Mrs. Chandler, Mrs. Barnes, Mrs. Kinney Mrs. Ellett, Mrs. Scott, Mrs. Dinnies, Mrs. Stephens, Mrs. St. John, Mrs. L. P Smith, Mrs. Oliver, Miss Mary E. Lee, Mrs. Esling, Mrs. Sawyer Mrs. Bailey, Mrs. Thurston, Miss Day, Mrs. Dodd, Mrs. Judson, Mrs. Eames, Mrs. Emeline Smith, Miss Fuller, Mrs. Pierson, Mrs. Worthington, Mrs. Lewis, Mrs. Mowatt, Mrs. M'Donald, Lucy Hooper, Mrs. Mayo, Miss Jacobs, Mrs. Case, Mrs. Bolton, Miss Woodman, Mrs. Nichols, Mrs. Wakefield, Miss E. Lee, Miss Susan Pindar, Caroline May, Mrs. Neal, Mrs. Sproat, Mrs. Winslow, Miss Campbell, Miss Bayard, Mrs. Lascom, Edith May, Alice and Phœbe Carey, Miss Dawson, Mr Lowell, and Miss Phillips.

invariably superior. He has preserved the elevation which he so early acquired. He has been loyal to the Muses. At their shrine his ministry seems ever free and sacred, wholly apart from the ordinary associations of life. With a pure heart and a lofty purpose has he hymned the glory of Nature and the praise of Freedom. To this we cannot but, in a great degree, ascribe the serene beauty of his verse. The mists of worldly motives dim the clearest vision, and the sweetest voice falters amid the strife of passion. As the patriarch went forth alone to muse at eventide, the reveries of genius have been to Bryant holy and private seasons. They are as unstained by the passing clouds of this troubled existence as the skies of his own 'Prairies' by village smoke.

Thus it should be, indeed, with all poets; but we deem it singularly happy when it is so with our own. The tendency of all action and feeling with us is so much the reverse of poetical, that only the high, sustained, and consistent development of the imagination would command attention or exert influence. The poet, in this republic, does not address ignorance. In truth, the great obstacle with which he has to deal, so to speak, is intelligence. It is not the love of gain and physical comfort alone that deadens the finer perceptions of our people. Among the highly educated there is less real enjoyment of poetry than is discovered by those to whom reading is almost a solitary luxury. No conformity to fashion or affectation of taste influences the latter. They seek the world of imagination and sentiment, with the greater delight from the limited satisfaction realized in their actual lot. To them Poetry is a great teacher of self-respect. It unfolds to them emotions familiar to their own bosoms. It celebrates scenes of beauty amid which they also are free to wander. It vindicates capacities and a destiny of which they partake. Intimations like these are seldom found in their experience, and for this reason: cherished and hallowed associations endear an art which consoles while it brings innocent pleasure to their hearts. It is, therefore, in what is termed society, that the greatest barriers to poetic sympathy exist, and it is precisely here that it is most desirable the bard should be heard. But the idea of culture with this class lies almost exclusively in knowledge. They aim at understanding every question, are pertinacious on the score of opinion, and would blush to be thought unacquainted with a hundred subjects with which they have not a particle of sympathy. The wisdom of loving, even without comprehending; the revelations obtained only through feeling; the veneration that awes curiosity by exalted sentiment, — all this is to them unknown. Life never seems miraculous to their minds; Nature wears a monotonous aspect, and routine gradually congeals their sensibilities. To invade this vegetative existence is the poet's vocation. Hazlitt says all that is worth remembering in life is the poetry of it. If so, habits wholly prosaic are as alien to wisdom as to enjoyment; and the elevated manner in which Bryant has uniformly presented the claims of poetry, the tranquil eloquence with which his chaste and serious muse appeals to the heart, deserves the most grateful recognition. There is something accordant with the genius of our country in the mingled clearness and depth of his poetry. The glow of unbridled passion seems peculiarly to belong to southern lands, where despotism blights personal effort, and makes the ardent pursuit of pleasure almost a necessity. The ancient communities of northern latitudes have rich literatures from whence to draw materials for their verse. But here, where Nature is so magnificent, and civil institutions so fresh, where the experiment of republicanism is going on, and each individual must think, if he do not work, Poetry, to illustrate the age and reach its sympathies, should be thoughtful and vigorous. It should minister to no weak sentiment, but foster high, manly, and serious views. It should identify itself with the domestic affections, and tend to solemnize rather than merely adorn, existence. Such are the natural echoes of American life, and they characterize the poetry of Bryant.

Bryant's love of Nature gives the prevailing spirit to his poetry. The feeling with him seems quite instinctive. It is not sustained by a metaphysical theory, as in the case of Wordsworth, while it is imbued with more depth of pathos than is often discernible in Thomson. The feeling with which he looks upon the wonders of Creation is remarkably appropriate to the scenery of the New World. His poems convey, to an extraordinary degree, the actual impression which is awakened by our lakes, mountains, and forests. There is in the landscape of every country something characteristic and peculiar. The individual objects may be the same, but their combination is widely different. The lucent atmosphere of Switzerland, the grouping of her mountains, the effect of glacier and waterfall, of peaks clad in eternal snow, impending over valleys whose emerald herbage and peaceful flocks realize our sweetest dreams of primeval life — all strike the eye and affect the mind in a manner somewhat different from similar scenes in other lands. The long, pencilled clouds of an Italian sunset, glowing above plains covered with brightly-tinted vegetation, seem altogether more placid and luxuriant than the gorgeous masses of golden vapor towering in our western sky at the close of an autumnal day. These and innumerable other minute features are not only perceived, but intimately felt, by the genuine poet. We esteem it one of Bryant's great merits that he has not only faithfully pictured the beauties, but caught the very spirit, of our scenery. His best poems have an anthem-like cadence, which accords with the vast scenes they celebrate. He approaches the mighty forests, whose shadowy haunts only the footstep of the Indian has penetrated, deeply conscious of its virgin grandeur. His harp is strung in harmony with the wild moan of the ancient boughs. Every moss-covered trunk breathes to him of the mysteries of Time, and each wild flower which lifts its pale buds above the brown and withered leaves, whispers some thought of gentleness. We feel, when musing with him amid the solitary woods, as if blessed with a companion peculiarly fitted to interpret their teachings; and while intent, in our retirement, upon his page, we are sensible, as it were, of the presence of those sylvan monarchs that crown the hill-tops and grace the valleys of our native land. No English park formalized by the hand of Art, no legendary spot like the pine grove of Ravenna, surrounds us. It is not the gloomy German forest, with its phantoms and banditti, but one of those primal, dense woodlands of America, where the oak spreads its enormous branches, and the frost-kindled leaves of the maple glow like flame in the sunshine; where the tap of the woodpecker and the whirring of the partridge alone break the silence that broods, like the spirit of prayer, amid the interminable aisles of the verdant sanctuary. Any reader of Bryant, on the other side of the ocean, gifted with a small degree of sensibility and imagination, may derive from his poems the very awe and delight with which the first view of one of our majestic forests would strike his mind.

The kind of interest with which Bryant regards Nature is common to the majority of minds in which a love of beauty is blended with reverence. This in some measure accounts for his popularity. Many readers, even of poetical taste, are repelled by the very vehemence and intensity of Byron. They cannot abandon themselves so utterly to the influences of the outward world as to feel the waves bound beneath them "like a steed that knows his rider;" nor will their enthusiasm so far annihilate consciousness as to make them "a portion of the tempest." Another order of imaginative spirits do not greatly affect the author of the Excursion, from the frequent baldness of his conceptions and not a few are unable to see the Universe through the spectacles of his philosophy. To such individuals, the tranquil delight with which the American poet expatiates upon the beauties of Creation is perfectly genial. There is no mystical lore in the tributes of his muse. All is clear, earnest, and thoughtful. Indeed, the same difference that exists between true-hearted, natural affection and the metaphysical love of the Platonists may be traced between the manly and sincere lays of Bryant and the vague and artificial effusions of transcendental bards. The former realize the definition of a poet which describes him as superior to the multitude only in degree, not in kind. He is the priest of a universal religion, and clothes in appropriate and harmonious language sentiments warmly felt and cherished. He requires no interpreter. There is nothing eccentric in his vision. Like all human beings, the burden of daily toil sometimes weighs heavily on his soul; the noisy activity of common life becomes hopeless; scenes of inhumanity, error, and suffering grow oppressive, or more personal causes of despondency make "the grasshopper a burden." Then he turns to the quietude and beauty of Nature for refreshment. There he loves to read the fresh tokens of creative beneficence. The scented air of the meadows cools his fevered brow. The umbrageous foilage sways benignly around him. Vast prospects expand his thoughts beyond the narrow circle of worldly anxieties. The limpid stream, upon whose banks he wandered in childhood, reflects each fleecy cloud and soothes his heart as the emblem of eternal peace. Thus faith is revived; the soul acquires renewed vitality, and the spirit of love is kindled again at the altar of God. Such views of Nature are perfectly accordant with the better impulses of the heart. There is nothing in them strained, unintelligible, or morbid. They are more or less familiar to all, and are as healthful overflowings of our nature as the prayer of repentance or the song of thanksgiving. They distinguish the poetry of Bryant, and form one of its dominant charms.

Nothing quickens the perceptions like genuine love. From the humblest professional attachment to the most chivalric devotion, what keenness of observation is born under the influence of that feeling which drives away the obscuring clouds of selfishness, as the sun consumes the vapor of the morning! I never knew what varied associations could environ a shell-fish until I heard an old oyster-merchant discourse of its qualities; and a landsman can have no conception of the fondness a ship may inspire before he listens, on a moonlight night, amid the lonely sea, to the details of her build and workings, unfolded by a complacent tar. Mere instinct or habit will thus make the rude and illiterate see with better eyes than their fellows. When a human object commands such interest, how quickly does affection detect every change of mood and incipient want — reading the countenance as if it were the very chart of destiny! And it is so with the lover of Nature. By virtue of his love comes the vision, if not "the faculty divine." Objects and similitudes seen heedlessly by others, or passed unnoticed, are stamped upon his memory. Bryant is a graphic poet, in the best sense of the word. He has little of the excessive detail of Street, or the homely exactitude of Crabbe. His touches, like his themes, are usually on a grander scale, yet the minute is by no means neglected. It is his peculiar merit to deal with it wisely. Enough is suggested to convey a strong impression, and often by the introduction of a single circumstance, the mind is instantly enabled to complete the picture. It is difficult to select examples of his power in this regard. The opening scene from *A Winter Piece* is as picturesque as it is true to fact.

Bryant is eminently a contemplative poet. His thoughts are not less impressive than his imagery. Sentiment, except that which springs from benevolence and veneration, seldom lends a glow to his pages. Indeed, there is a remarkable absence of those spontaneous bursts of tenderness and passion which constitute the very essence of a large portion of modern verse. He has none of the spirit of Campbell, or the narrative sprightliness of Scott. The few humorous attempts he has published are unworthy of his genius. Love is merely recognized in his poems; it rarely forms the staple of any composition. His strength obviously consists in description and philosophy. It is one advantage of this species of poetry that it survives youth, and is, by nature, progressive. Bryant's recent poems are fully equal, if not superior, to any he has written. With his inimitable pictures there is ever blended high speculation, or a reflective strain of moral command. Some elevating inference or cheering truth is elicited from every scene consecrated by his muse. A noble simplicity of language, combined with these traits, often leads to the most genuine sublimity of expression. Some of his lines are unsurpassed in this respect. They so quietly unfold a great thought or magnificent image, that we are often taken by surprise. What a striking sense of mortality is afforded by the idea, —

"The oak
Shall send his roots abroad and pierce thy mould"!

How grand the figure which represents the evening air, as

"God's blessing breathed upon the fainting earth"!

In the same poem he compares

"The gentle souls that passed away"

to the twilight breezes sweeping over a churchyard, —

"Sent forth from heaven among the sons of men,
And gone into the boundless heaven again."

And what can be more suggestive of the power of the winds than the figure by which they are said to

"Scoop the ocean to its briny springs"?

He would make us feel the hoary age of the mossy and gigantic forest-trees, and not only alludes to their annual decay and renewal, but significantly adds, —

"The century-living crow,
Whose birth was in their tops, grew old and died."

To those who have never seen a prairie, how vividly does one spread before the imagination, in the very opening of the poem devoted to those "verdant wastes"!

The progress of Science is admirably hinted in a line of *The Ages*, when man is said to

"Unwind the eternal dances of the sky."

Instances like these might be multiplied at pleasure, to illustrate the efficacy of simple diction, and to prove that the elements of real poetry consist in truly grand ideas, uttered without affectation, and in a reverent and earnest spirit.

A beautiful calm, like that which rests on the noble works of the sculptor, breathes from the harp of Bryant. He traces a natural phenomenon, or writes, in melodious numbers, the history of some familiar scene, and then, with almost prophetic emphasis, utters to the charmed ear a high lesson or sublime truth. In that pensive hymn in which he contrasts Man's transitory being with Nature's perennial life, solemn and affecting as are the images, they but serve to deepen the simple monition at the close.

In *The Fountain*, after a descriptive sketch that brings its limpid flow and flowery banks almost palpably before us, how exquisite is the chronicle that follows! Guided by the poet, we behold that gushing stream, ages past, in the solitude of the old woods, when canopied by the hickory and plane, the humming-bird playing amid its spray, and visited only by the wolf, who comes to "lap its waters," the deer who leaves her "delicate footprint" on its marge, and the "slow-paced beat that stopped and drank, and leaped across." Then the savage war-cry drowns its murmur, and the wounded foeman creeps slowly to its brink to "slake his death-thirst." Ere long a hunter's lodge is built, "with poles and boughs, beside the crystal well," and at length the lonely place is surrounded with the tokens of civilization.

Thus the minstrel, even

"From the gushing of a simple fount,
Has reasoned to the mighty universe."

The very rhythm of the stanzas *To a Waterfowl*, gives the impression of its flight. Like the bird's sweeping wing, they float with a calm and majestic cadence to the ear. We see that solitary wanderer of the "cold thin atmosphere;" we watch, almost with awe, its serene course, until "the abyss of heaven has swallowed up its form," and then gratefully echo the bard's consoling inference.

But it is unnecessary to cite from pages so familiar; or we might allude to the grand description of Freedom, and the beautiful *Hymn to Death* as among the noblest specimens of modern verse. The great principle of Bryant's faith is that

"Eternal Love doth keep
In his complacent arms the earth, the air, the deep."

To set forth, in strains the most attractive and lofty, this glorious sentiment, is the constant aim of his poetry. Gifted must be the man who is loyal to so high a vocation. From the din of outward activity, the vain turmoil of mechanical life, it is delightful and ennobling to turn to a true poet, — one who scatters flowers along our path, and lifts our gaze to the stars, — breaking, by a word, the spell of blind custom, so that we recognize once more the original glory of the universe, and hear again the latent music of our own souls. This high service has Bryant fulfilled. It will identify his memory with the loveliest scenes of his native land, and endear it to her children forever.*

* Thoughts on the Poets

NOTE TO SKETCH OF AMERICAN LITERATURE.

To the works of American authors above enumerated, the fifteen years which have since elapsed have added characteristic and valuable materials. Bancroft's *History of the United States* has now reached its ninth volume, which brings the record far into the epoch of the Revolution. Emerson has added *English Traits*, and *The Conduct of Life*, to his series of essays; Longfellow, *Hiawatha*, *Miles Standish*, *The Wayside Inn*, *Flower de Luce*, and a translation of Dante's *Divina Commedia* to his poetical writings. Holmes has written a new volume of essays and a novel. Donald G. Mitchell has given to the public two pleasant volumes of rural essays—*My Farm at Edgewood*, and *Wet Days at Edgewood*, a book of *Traveller's Tales*, and a novel of New England life—*Dr. Johns*. Bayard Taylor has published two American stories, *Hannah Thurston*, and the *Story of Kenneth*, and two poems, *The Poet's Story*, and *The Picture of St. John*. Sabine and Lossing have continued their popular historical labors; Bushnell added to his philosophical exposition of religious and social subjects; Higginson and Parkman in prose, and Bryant, Whittier, and Halleck in poetry, contributed new writings to the nation's stock; while to the previous excellent translations of the masterpieces of German literature by Charles T. Brooks, are to be added the *Titan* and *Hesperus* of Richter, the humorous *Jobsiad*, and Goethe's *Faust*.

Henry James has published a religious and metaphysical treatise called *Substance and Shadow;* George H. Calvert, a new volume of foreign travel and sojourn, entitled *First Years in Europe*, and an interesting essay, *The Gentleman*. William W. Story has embodied in a work with the title *Roba di Roma*, the results of long and patient observation of the habits, customs, and normal aspects of the Eternal City; and William D. Howell gives us a charming record of *Venetian Life*. James Jackson Jarves, in two substantial volumes, *Art Studies*, and the *Art Idea*, has imparted much general historical information and æsthetic philosophy in regard to the fine arts. Saxe, Aldrich, Street, Stoddard, Mrs. Howe, Mrs. Aken, Alice Carey, and other poetical writers have added fresh volumes to the library of American verse; while in the departments of educational literature, political disquisition, theology, science, popular and juvenile books, adapted to wants of a vast and wide-spread population, the supply of new and desirable works has been constant, and, for the most part, creditable to the average taste, love of knowledge, and prevalent intelligence and rectitude.

Since the preceding Sketch was written, the obituary record of our authors has withdrawn some of the earliest and most endeared. Washington Irving died on the 28th of November, 1859, in the ripeness of his age and fame, having, but a few months previous, finished the *Life of Washington*—his last and appropriate labor of love in the field of native literature. To the complete edition of his writings, revised by his own hand in the pleasant autumn of his life, and received by his countrymen with renewed evidences of sympathy and respect, have been added, since his decease, two volumes of uncollected papers consisting of Spanish legends, early contributions to the newspaper press, and a few personal memoirs and reminiscences. William Hickling Prescott closed his brief but brilliant literary career on the 28th of January, 1859. His last historical work, *Philip II.*, was left unfinished. James Paulding did not long survive the old friend and literary comrade with whom he wrote *Salmagundi;* and the best of this pioneer author's writings will soon be published in a revised and uniform series.

Theodore Parker died in Florence, Italy, May 10, 1860. His latest work is entitled *Theodore Parker's Experience as a Minister, with some Account of his Early Life and Education for the Ministry*—an autobiographical narrative which throws much light on the early influences and original endowments whose combination led eventually to his peculiar opinions and original course as a reformer and theologian. For a complete understanding of his career and character, however, which in many respects were exceptional, a perusal of his life and correspondence is requisite.*

Edward Everett, after the issue of three substantial volumes of orations, which, in view of both topics and treatment, may be justly regarded as of national value and significance, at the age of sixty traversed the United States to deliver his oration on the character of Washington, for the twofold patriotic purpose of allaying the sectional animosity which afterwards culminated in civil war, and to raise the funds requisite for the purchase of Mount Vernon—the home and tomb of Washington. During the civil conflict the eloquent voice and pen of Everett were constantly pleading and protesting for the Union, and, crowned with this final work of honor and patriotism, he died on the 15th of January, 1865.

Nathaniel Hawthorne, since the previous mention of his writings, passed a year in Italy, and gave to the public the graceful fruit of that sojourn in one of his most beautiful and characteristic romances—the *Marble Faun*. After relinquishing the consulship at Liverpool, and returning to Concord, Massachusetts, the results of his observation and reflection during several years' residence in England appeared in a delightful volume of local sketches entitled *Our Old Home*—in style, insight, descriptive skill and quiet humor, worthy of his artistic pen and genial yet subtle observation. Hawthorne died at Plymouth, New Hampshire, May 19, 1864, while on a journey for his health, which had gradually failed. He left a story of English life unfinished, and the passages from his note-books which have appeared

* *The Life and Correspondence of Theodore Parker, by John Weiss.* New York, 1864.

in the Atlantic Monthly since his death, indicate the thoughtfulness with which he contemplated even the most familiar phenomena of life and nature, and the elaborate study whereby he prepared himself to interpret and illustrate them. The wayward yet studious career of Percival terminated in Illinois, soon after his geological survey of Wisconsin, May 2, 1856. Many of his poems have obtained a merited popularity; and the eccentricities growing out of his sensitive organization, independent spirit, and scientific zeal, are well set forth in the recently published *Life and Letters* of the gifted but perverse poet.*

To this list of the eminent departed must be added the names of many of our clergy who enjoyed and exerted a literary as well as religious influence — such as Dr. Edward Hitchcock, Dr. Robinson, Francis Wayland, George Bush, Clement C. Moore, Dr. Alexander, Pise, C. W. Upham, George W. Bethune, Dr. Baird, Starr King, John Pierpont, and others, as well as several useful and respected female authors: — among them, Mrs. Caroline Kirkland, Mrs. Sigourney, Mrs. Farnham, Hannah F. Gould, Alice B. Haven, Mrs. Emma C. Embury, Mrs. Farrar, Miss Leslie, and Miss Maria Cummins; with a number of miscellaneous writers, whose labors illustrated special subjects, as Schoolcraft, in aboriginal history and ethnology. Goodrich in popular education, and Walsh and Buckingham in editorial essays; Theodore Sedgwick, Horace Mann, Hildreth, Benjamin, Choate, Kettell, Dr. Francis, Josiah Quincy, and G. L. Duyckink.

During the interval which has elapsed, and notwithstanding a civil conflict of four years, unparalleled in history for patriotic self-devotion and the lavish sacrifice of life and treasure to reassert and vindicate forever the integrity of the nation, several new and important additions have been made to our catalogue of able and honored authors and of standard works in native literature. John Lothrop Motley has gained a European reputation by his *History of the Dutch Republic and of the Netherlands* — works of elaborate research and artistic finish, written with an earnest sympathy in the struggles of those who laid the foundations of civil and religious freedom, and with a force and grace of style both appropriate and attractive. A valuable addition to this department also is the *History of New England*, by John Gorham Palfrey, wherein is evident much original research and a more comprehensive and vivid treatment than had before been given to the subject. In the sphere of philology and economical science, George P. Marsh has written with erudition and efficiency: his *History and Origin of the English Language*, his *Lectures on the English Language*, and his treatise entitled *Man and Nature* have been recognized as singularly able and suggestive works on both sides of the ocean. In popular biography James Parton has won deserved distinction by the thoroughness of his investigation, and the dramatic form of his delineation; his lives of *Burr*, *Jackson*, and *Franklin* are read and relished by thousands. William R. Alger's *History of the Doctrine of a Future Life*, is the most complete, curious, and interesting work of its kind which has appeared in our country.

* *The Life and Letters of James Gates Percival, by Julius H. Ward. Boston.* Ticknor & Fields, 1866.

Robert S. Lowell has published a local romance of freshness and picturesque attraction, and several expressive poems; Edward S. Rand, Jr., a pleasant and useful series of horticultural works; John Milton Mackie, two or three sprightly and graceful books of travel; and the lamented Dr. Kane, a most successful narrative of his arctic adventures. One of the most individual of the American authors who have become known to fame since the preceding record was written, is Henry D. Thoreau, intimately known and highly esteemed by a few near neighbors and friends during his life, including Emerson and Hawthorne. It is only since his death, which occurred May 7, 1862, that his peculiar traits have been generally recognized through his writings. He aspired to a life of frugal independence and moral isolation, and carried out the desire with singular heroism and patience. His experience as a hermit on the Concord River, his observant excursions to the woods of Maine, the sands of Cape Cod, and other native scenes, rarely explored by such curious and loving eyes, have a remarkable freshness of tone and fulness of detail; while on themes of a social and political nature his comments are those of a bold and ardent reformer. Few books possess a more genuine American scope and flavor than Thoreau's.

Gail Hamilton has become a household word in New England as the *nom de plume* of a trenchant and graphic female essayist; and Trowbridge has gained popularity as an American story-teller. J. G. Holland has proved one of the most successful of American authors, if pecuniary results and popularity may be regarded as the test. Long engaged in the editorial charge of a New England daily newspaper, and brought into intimate contact with the people, their tastes and wants seem to have been remarkably appreciated by this prolific literary purveyor thereto. He has written novels, poems, lectures, and essays, founded on or directed to the wants and tendencies of life and nature in New England, and reflecting, with great authenticity, the local peculiarities, natural phases, and characteristic qualities of the region and the people.

Although the war for the Union elicited many memorable utterances in the form of logical discussion, eloquent appeal and invective, graphic narration, and lyric pathos or power, perhaps it revealed no more interesting literary phenomena than the advent of a young writer of romance previously quite unappreciated. A vivid sketch which Theodore Winthrop wrote of the march of the Seventh Regiment from New York to Baltimore on the outbreak of the rebellion, first awakened public attention to his spirit and skill as a *raconteur;* and when, a few months later, he gallantly laid down his young life for his country, the writings which had vainly sought a publisher while he lived were hailed by a host of sympathetic readers as the literary legacy of a youthful martyr. This natural reaction from indifference to eulogy was not, however, a mere tribute to valor and fealty. The chivalrous nature and artistic sympathies of Major Winthrop, his love of adventure, his narrative skill, and a certain dramatic fire, are embodied and embalmed in these volumes of travel and romance in a manner full of high literary promise and genuine personal interest.

TO ENGLISH LITERATURE.

T.

U.

V.

W.

Y.

TO SKETCH OF AMERICAN LITERATURE.

N.

O.

P.

Q.

R.

S.

T.

U.

V.

W.

Y.

www.ingramcontent.com/pod-product-compliance
Lightning Source LLC
LaVergne TN
LVHW021259110826
845150LV00003B/434